County Borough Elections in England and Wales, 1919–1938: A Comparative Analysis

Volume 2

County Borough Elections in England and Wales, 1919–1938: A Comparative Analysis

Volume 2
Bradford – Carlisle

SAM DAVIES and BOB MORLEY

Ashgate

Aldershot • Burlington USA • Singapore • Sydney

Published by

Ashgate Publishing Limited
Gower House, Croft Road,
Aldershot, Hampshire GU11 3HR
Great Britain

Ashgate Publishing Company
131 Main Street
Burlington, , Vermont 05401–5600
USA

ISBN 1–84014–247–2

British Library CIP Data
Davies, Sam
    County Borough Elections in England and Wales, 1919–1938:
    A Comparative Analysis.
    Volume 2: Bradford to Carlisle.
    1. Local Elections – England – History. 2. Local Elections – England –
    Statistics. I. Title. II. Morley, Bob.
    324.9'42'083

US Library of Congress CIP Data
The Library of Congress Control Number has been preassigned as:
    00–108277

This volume is printed on acid free paper.

Printed and bound by Athenaeum Press, Ltd.,
Gateshead, Tyne & Wear.

Contents

List of tables

Conclusion (continued)

List of appendices

List of figures

Abbreviations

The following abbreviations for parties or candidates have been used in the tables. Due to limitations of space, some party names have been abbreviated more in some tables than in others. Both forms are given here. Names of organisations abbreviated in the essays have been given in full on the first occasion they occur in each essay.

Al	Allotments (candidate)
A-S	Anti-socialist (candidate)
A-W	Anti-Waste Party
BMC	Brighton Municipal Committee
C	Conservative and Unionist Party
Ch T	Chamber of Trade
Cit	Citizens (candidate, or party)
Co C	Coalition Conservative
Co L	Coalition Liberal
Coa	Coalition
Com	Communist Party of Great Britain
Const	Constitutionalist (candidate, or party)
Coop	Co-operative Party
Ex-S	Ex-services
Fr S	Friendly Societies
IDL	Irish Democratic League
ILG	Independent Labour Group
ILP	Independent Labour Party

Ind or I	Independent (candidate, or party)
Ind C	Independent Conservative (candidate)
Ind L	Independent Liberal (candidate)
I Lab	Independent Labour (candidate)
L	Liberal Party
Lab	Labour Party
MCU	Middle Classes Union
NCU	National Citizens Union
NCW	National Council of Women
NDP	National Democratic and Labour Party
NFDDSS or Nfds	National Federation of Discharged and Demobilised Sailors and Soldiers
NUWM or Nuwm	National Unemployed Workers Movement
O	Other (candidate, or party)
PC	Plaid Cymru
Peop	People's
Prog	Progressive (candidate, or party)
R	Ratepayers (candidate, or party)
WCA	Women's Citizens Association
Wkrs	Workers (candidate, or party)
U	Unionist
UEA	Unemployed Electoral Association
UIL	United Irish League

Acknowledgements

As with Volume One, our main acknowledgement is again to the staff of the various libraries we have visited in the process of collecting the material for this volume. These include the local history sections of the central libraries of Bradford, Brighton, Bristol, Burnley, Burton, Bury, Canterbury, Cardiff and Carlisle. In addition, the British Library newspaper section at Colindale in London provided some material, and the staff of the libraries of Liverpool John Moores University and Liverpool University were extremely helpful.

Various individuals have also helped us. We are again indebted to Phil Cubbin for his help on maps. Jo Morley provided great help in collecting material for Brighton, Burton and Canterbury, as did Julie Des Forges for Carlisle. Dave McEvoy collected material for Bradford on several occasions, and provided the maps for that borough. Our thanks go to all of these.

We would also like to acknowledge those who have given us constructive comments on the work so far. Chris Wrigley was kind enough to let us present a paper to the November 1999 conference of the Labour History Society in Nottingham. Tony Adams likewise enabled Sam Davies to give a paper to the conference held at Manchester Metropolitan University in March 2000 on the 100th anniversary of the Labour Party. We received much valuable feedback on our work from the audiences at both events. We owe a special debt of thanks to Duncan Tanner and Chris Williams, who were kind enough to lend us advance copies of their forthcoming work on Welsh politics. Duncan also made incisive and constructive comments on some aspects of our project. In addition, Professor J.D. Stewart of Birmingham University has been generous in his praise of our efforts, and has encouraged us to keep on with the project.

We have benefited from financial support from the Higher Education Funding Council for England and Wales, which has enabled both of us to have some time off from teaching in order to write this volume. Our head of school, Vince Gardiner, has also been supportive of our efforts in completing this volume before the dreaded 'RAE' deadline expired. John Herson and other colleagues in the History section of Liverpool John Moores University have also been encouraging.

At Ashgate Alec McAulay, now departed from the company, was instrumental in setting up the whole project. His achievement in building up an impressive catalogue in the field of labour history should be acknowledged. Rachel Lynch, Ruth Peters, Kirsten Weissenberg and Elizabeth Wickens have continued to give us excellent advice and support. Tom Norton provided the excellent index.

Finally, and as we forgot to say in Volume One, we alone are of course entirely responsible for the facts and views expressed here, including any errors.

Sam Davies and Bob Morley
Liverpool

July 2000

Introduction

This second volume of *County Borough Elections in England and Wales* carries on the task of developing a comparative analysis of the electoral politics of all eighty-three county boroughs in England and Wales between the wars. Having taken the decision at the outset to analyse the boroughs in alphabetical order, ten boroughs were examined in volume one. The next nine in alphabetic terms are included in this volume. This means that almost a quarter of the task has now been completed, leaving another sixty-four boroughs to be covered in the six remaining volumes over the coming years. The aims, methods, assumptions and historiographical background of this series of volumes were set out in the introduction to volume one. The points made there apply equally to this second volume, and an abridged version follows here for new readers, along with some further points relating to the comparative nature of these volumes.

The volumes are intended as a contribution to the task of putting a local perspective into the history of twentieth-century British politics and society. There has been a peculiar hostility to the importance of the local dimension in British political history, especially in relation to the study of the twentieth century. This is perhaps unsurprising in a country where political power has long been concentrated at the centre. Whatever the economic and social weight British regions or cities may have possessed historically, London was where national politics was conducted. The contrast with, say, Germany makes the point. City-states like Hamburg or *länder* (local states) like Bavaria retained political significance and power to a much greater extent than Birmingham or Lancashire. The balance within historical study began to be redressed somewhat by the growth of social history in the second half of this century, and of more specialised fields such as labour history and women's history. From these new perspectives, the distinctive economic functions and varied social and cultural features of localities were much more obvious and more important. At least to some extent this greater concern with the local has spilled over into political history. To a degree as well, recent political trends have encouraged this development. For instance, the results of British elections since the 1980s have begun to contradict long-held beliefs amongst political scientists in the immutable connections between social class and political allegiance. Thus other factors such as gender, age and locality have begun to assume greater importance in political analysis. The concept of the 'north–south divide', much discussed after the 1983 and 1987 general elections, is the best example of how the political significance of locality has become of greater interest. The great potential, and also the pitfalls, of local studies have by now been much discussed, and there is not the space here to repeat the debate.[1] It is sufficient to say that a degree of consensus exists that local histories should play some part in the wider understanding of British politics and society. However,

---

[1]   See especially the thought-provoking comments on local studies in Savage, M., 'The rise of the Labour party in local perspective', *Journal of Regional and Local Studies*, vol. 10, no. 1, (1990), pp. 1–16.

there is one important qualification to the claims of local history that should not be ignored. The 'national and local pictures' should be 'put together', and 'there still will be a "national" level to consider, not merely as an aggregate of local cases but also in its own right'.[2] Local studies taken on their own become a collection of empirical data, and they must still be put into a national or even wider context to have an historical meaning.

These volumes then must be seen as part of a wider historical project. They are focused on local elections, which were an important part of the political system. By 1918 local government had become a significant arena of party politics. The scope and scale of municipal governance had been extended progressively over the previous century to a point where it was no longer of purely local interest, culminating in the absorption of the Poor Law Guardians into municipalities in 1929.[3] Concurrently the local government franchise had been extended beyond the ranks of wealthy property-owners to include most local inhabitants, culminating in the enfranchisement of women in the legislation of 1918 and 1928.[4] So the control of municipal power mattered politically in this period, and the elections to decide that control were a real test of the popular will. National political parties therefore played a full role in municipal politics. National issues were reflected in council politics, and the results of local elections were of national significance.

The recording and analysis of British municipal election results between the wars was limited, though. There was, and still is, no official centralized system of collecting local election data. Each council was responsible for recording its own results. In most cases these were simply stored within the council's own internal records, and it was only the local press that published them in varying detail. As a result there was little substantive analysis of local elections as they happened. Subsequently the records have remained scattered in local libraries in the pages of the press and obscure council committee minutes. Historians and political scientists have barely touched this data since, aside from a handful of local studies.[5] Least of all has the data been pulled together to analyse aggregate trends, or to carry out comparative studies. Useful attempts at the former task have been made, but they have all been based on a limited range of available evidence.[6]

[2] Thompson, E.P., 'Homage to Tom Maguire', in Briggs, A. and Saville, J., *Essays in Labour History*, (London, 1967), p. 277; Breuilly, J., *Labour and Liberalism in Nineteenth-Century Europe: Essays in Comparative History*, (Manchester, 1992), p. 22.
[3] On the development of local government see Keith-Lucas, B. and Richards, P.G., *A History of Local Government in the Twentieth Century*, (London, 1978); Redlich, J. and Hirst, F.W., *Local Government in England*, (abridged version, London, 1958); Waller, *Town, City and Nation*, chs 6 and 7.
[4] Although the municipal franchise between 1919 and 1938 was not as comprehensive as the parliamentary franchise; see notes at the end of this volume, p. 671.
[5] For instance, Bealey, F., Blondel, J. and McCann, W.P., *Constituency Politics: A Study of Newcastle-under-Lyme*, (London, 1965); Savage, M., *The Dynamics of Working-Class Politics: The Labour Movement in Preston, 1880–1940*, (Cambridge, 1987); Marriot, J., *The Culture of Labourism: The East End between the Wars*, (Edinburgh, 1991); Davies, S., *Liverpool Labour: Social and Political Influences on the Development of the Labour Party in Liverpool, 1900–1939*, (Keele, 1996).
[6] For example, Rhodes, E.C., 'Voting at municipal elections', *Political* Quarterly, vol. 9, pt. 2, (1938), pp. 271–280; Cook, C., *The Age of Alignment: Electoral Politics in Britain*,

Genuine comparative studies for the inter-war period have not been attempted at all. This is very much in contrast with other European states such as Germany or the Netherlands, where state systems of collection of results were well developed by the 1920s. Extensive analysis of the data collected was possible in these countries, both at the time and in subsequent historical study.

The volumes of this book will fulfil two main purposes. First, they will constitute a comprehensive work of reference for all county borough election results in England and Wales between the wars. Second, they will provide a multi-layered analysis of municipal politics in the same period. This will include the investigation of politics in the individual boroughs concerned, as well as the comparative study of political issues and movements in different boroughs, and also the identification of aggregate patterns of political behaviour across the country as a whole. In doing so, these volumes will fill an important gap in the historical record. They will take in the crucial period of the rise of Labour, the decline of Liberalism, and the consolidation of Toryism. They will span critical years of international political turmoil, as well as economic depression and mass unemployment. Being annual, the local elections will give an idea of how political opinion varied between general elections, especially in the longer gaps such as 1924–29 or 1935–45, or in crisis periods such as 1929–31. The volumes will provide new and detailed evidence for issues such as the role of women in politics, the significance of ethnic and religious differentiation, the connection between occupational and class divisions and party allegiance, the local impact of the decline of staple industries, and the political significance of housing change and movement of population. The volumes will also illuminate the impact of fringe parties such as the Communist Party and the British Union of Fascists, and pressure groups such as the National Unemployed Workers' Movement and the Middle Classes' Union.

The scope of the volumes is limited to the county boroughs of England and Wales. There were a number of different units of local government which had evolved over the previous century. The boroughs of England and Wales in their modern form had originated in the reform of 1835, representing the main urban centres. The larger boroughs were given county status, as opposed to the generally smaller municipal boroughs. There were eighty-three county boroughs by 1931. Other local government units included the predominantly rural county councils, and the later-developed urban district councils and rural district councils. London had its own structure of local government after the 1899 Act, with twenty-eight metropolitan boroughs and the over-arching London county council. Scotland, with its burghs, and Ireland also had their own separate systems. Collating the election results for all these different units of local government would be a massive task, and for logistical reasons alone it would be necessary to narrow the limits to make it feasible. There are a number of other compelling arguments for concentrating on the county boroughs.

1922–1929, (London, 1975), ch. 3; Stevenson, J. and Cook, C., *The Slump: Society and Politics during the Depression*, (London, 1977), ch. 13; Rowett, J.S., 'The Labour Party and Local Government: Theory and Practice in the Inter-War Years', (D.Phil. thesis, University of Oxford, 1979), pp. 4–28; 368–389.

First, the elections for the county boroughs took place annually on the same day (normally the first day in November, except when this was a Sunday, in which case they were held a day later). Thus they were directly comparable. By contrast, the annual rural and urban district council elections were held in the spring, while the elections for the London boroughs took place in November, but only in every third year. Second, the parameters of the elections for the county boroughs were clearly defined and unvarying. One-third of the councillors were elected each year, and for every three councillors there was an additional alderman. This pattern was not necessarily applicable to other tiers of local government. In the London boroughs, for instance, all the councillors came up for election every three years, and there was only one alderman for every six councillors. In the urban districts there were no aldermen at all. Third, party politics in local government was developed to the greatest extent in the larger, urban authorities. Only three out of the eighty-three county boroughs had a population below 50,000 by 1931, and in most cases their elections were fought out on party lines by this period. In the smaller municipal boroughs and district councils, and in the more rural county councils, this was much less the case, making their elections much less interesting and significant politically. London was a special case. Party politics was well defined there, but many of the boroughs were dominated overwhelmingly by one party, and many seats were therefore regularly uncontested. Detailed changes in political support were thus hard to glean from such scattered and spasmodic evidence.

Concentrating solely on the county boroughs then, these volumes will cumulatively build up the complete tabulated record of local elections between 1919 and 1938 (the first and last years between the wars when a full round of contests was held). Included in the coverage are: summary tables of statistical data relating to the population and employment structure of the borough; maps showing ward boundaries (including any changes during the period); summary tables of the municipal election record, showing results by ward and by year, turnout and Labour party share of the vote by ward and by year, party gains and losses in each year, and the overall party composition of the council in each year (including aldermen); full lists of the results of the elections held each year in November, arranged by ward, including the names and sex of candidates, party labels, the votes cast for each candidate and the total number of votes, the percentages of the vote for each candidate, the total electorate, the turnout, and any party gains or losses. More detailed explanation of the scope of the material, and the conventions and assumptions used in the tabulated data, will be found in the explanatory notes at the end of each volume.

For each of the boroughs there will also be included an essay. These essays will aim to outline the socio-economic context of the locality and its historical development, to examine significant or interesting aspects of its political traditions and culture, and to draw attention to prominent features of the electoral record. They will also provide a guide to further reading. It should be noted that the length and form of these essays will vary, depending on the available secondary historical sources for each borough, and the nature of the particular issues or events that were important in each borough. While each essay will constitute an original and self-contained piece of analysis which can be read on its own, readers at times will be referred to other essays for detailed analysis of particular topics. This is to avoid excessive repetition of points that apply to more than one borough. The essays included in this second volume are mostly longer than those in the first volume, averaging around 10,000 words in length. This is primarily because it is increasingly possible to make comparative statements regarding the different boroughs as the evidence for them builds up in these volumes.

In each volume there will also be a concluding chapter giving the aggregate and comparative analysis for all the boroughs contained in the volume. From this volume onwards, there will also be a cumulative analysis for all the volumes completed so far, and later in the series some regional and other comparative investigation will also be provided. In this way it is envisaged that a comprehensive picture of voting behaviour and political life in all the county boroughs will be built up. As a further aid to comparison, there will also be a series of appendices at the end of each volume, in which all eighty-three county boroughs will be ranked in relation to various aspects of their population and employment structure. Unless otherwise indicated in the notes, these tables have been constructed from data contained in the 1931 census.

It is necessary to stress the strengths, and also the limitations, of the material contained in these volumes. For the first time, detailed and comprehensive data on local elections will be available in one single, consolidated source. This will be an important contribution to future historical research, which others will be able to use and develop as they see fit. At the same time, the analysis of the individual boroughs, the comparative studies, and the aggregated data, which will be included in these volumes, will in themselves provide new insights into the politics of inter-war England and Wales. Two cautionary notes need to be sounded though. First, historical evidence on its own does not, in some empiricist fashion, provide the historical answers. Theories and concepts have to be applied to the evidence in order to make sense of it. The authors will strive to achieve this especially in the essays that accompany the results for each borough, and in the aggregate and comparative analysis for each volume. However, given the large scale of the task it has not been possible to do the in-depth historical research that is still needed for most of the boroughs included here. That is a task for other researchers in future years, who will find these volumes of use.

Second, the other caveat is on the nature of electoral data as an historical source. Recent writing has criticised the often unsophisticated interpretation of such data employed by historians, derived mainly from the assumptions of the political sociology of the 1950s and 1960s.[7] It is plain that a more subtle approach is called for, which for instance sees voting itself as a multi-faceted activity determined by a range of factors, and the relationship between party and voter as more complex than has previously been assumed. No simplistic conclusions should be drawn from the data contained in these volumes, as the essays on each borough will show. Instead what is clear is the diversity of political experience revealed in each borough. In demonstrating this, these volumes accurately reflect 'the attention

---

[7]   See the important essay, Lawrence, J. and Taylor, M., 'Introduction: electoral sociology and the historians', in *Party, State and Society: Electoral Behaviour in Britain since 1820*, (Aldershot, 1997), pp. 1–26; also, Lawrence, J., *Speaking for the People: Party, Language and Popular Politics in England, 1867–1914*, (Cambridge, 1998), pp. 21–25.

given in recent work to the importance of locality, or the "politics of place" in influencing electoral behaviour well into the twentieth century'.[8]

Finally, it is necessary to stress that ultimately these volumes are intended to be a fully comparative analysis. There are a number of points that need to be considered in writing comparative history.[9] First, the comparative historian should not start with one case as the norm, and then assessing other examples by seeing how much they correspond to, or differ from, the norm. All instances to be considered should be of equal interest to the comparative historian from the beginning. Unless this principle is adhered to, pre-conceived ideas based on the analysis of the 'normal' case may be imposed on the others.[10] In these volumes, therefore, there should be no presupposition from the outset that any one of the county boroughs represents the 'typical' case. All the county boroughs, with their widely differing historical evolution, varied socio-economic and cultural contexts, and distinctive inter-war experiences, are equally worthy of consideration in this series.

A further principle of comparative history is that the instances under consideration must be capable of being analysed using the same methods. It is essential to start with general questions that are not based on one particular case, and to construct a general framework for the analysis within which the different examples can be described and examined. In these volumes that framework is defined very precisely by the electoral evidence itself, which of course lies at the heart of the analysis, around which a number of questions relating to the formative influences on the electoral process have been asked for each and every county borough dealt with so far. What has been accomplished in these first two volumes is an accumulation of systematic descriptions, which will be added to in the succeeding volumes. These descriptions provide of course the basis for developing comparative observations. Comparative history, however, is not simply a cumulative process, but is also a reflexive and iterative method. It is necessary to return and reflect on the evidence in order to produce further comparative analysis. This process has begun in these two volumes, but it is by no means complete as yet. It is also the case that comparative history involves the identification of similarities and differences. The comparative historian must begin by treating all instances as of equal interest, but this does not imply that all historical cases can only be understood on their own terms. This would by definition exclude the possibility of comparison. What the comparative historian should do is to identify important aspects and recurring themes in the cases under examination, and to seek to explain how and why particular cases diverge from the rest. This is the most important outcome of comparative history, and one which these volumes will seek to develop. The comparative approach does much to bring into relief the interconnections between locale, socio-economic structure, cultural differences and historical contingency. In applying it to the inter-war electoral politics of the

---

[8]   Lawrence and Taylor, 'Introduction', p. 17.
[9]   For discussion of the comparative method, see Breuilly, *Labour and Liberalism in Nineteenth-Century Europe*, pp. 1–25, 273–295.
[10] Breuilly, *Labour and Liberalism in Nineteenth-Century Europe*, pp. 1–2, 14.

county boroughs, it will deepen the historical understanding of twentieth-century British politics and society.

ONE
Bradford

BRADFORD

Bradford was at various times dubbed 'the largest village of Britain' or 'Worstedopolis', both of which terms conveyed important aspects of the development of the city. It lay at the heart of the woollen textile district of the West Riding of Yorkshire. Bradford became the mercantile centre of the wool textile industry and the manufacturing centre of worsteds. A worsted was a smooth type of woollen cloth, which was later combined with cotton warp from the 1830s to give a cheaper and lighter cloth. Bradford was also from the 1830s the centre of the wool-dyeing industry. The mechanisation of the wool textile industry east of the Pennines came later than that of its cotton counterpart in Lancashire, but the expansion of the industry was as rapid, and Bradford shared in this meteoric growth. A number of factors account for Bradford's rise to dominance in the industry. These included connection to the canal system from the 1770s, easy access to the iron and coal supplies necessary to build and drive textile machinery, the concentration of the marketing of the product within the locality, the serviceable and cheap type of cloth produced, and the heavy capitalisation and centralisation of the West Riding industry. The significance of the religious faith of many of the leading entrepreneurs in the industry should not be discounted, either, their attitudes to work and investment being shaped by their Quaker and Nonconformist sensibilities. The export trade in particular was increasingly dominated by the West Riding, leaving the Norfolk and the West of England woollen industries far behind and having to concentrate on specialised fabrics for the home market. Mechanisation of the industry was complete by the 1850s, by which time Bradford had 32 per cent of the spindles, 40 per cent of the power looms and 32 per cent of the labour force of the worsted industry.[1] By 1885 it was estimated that 92 per cent of the British worsted industry was based in the Bradford area. At that date women made up two-thirds of the adult workforce.[2] The worsted industry was at its peak in the third quarter of the nineteenth century, beginning its long decline in the face of increasing foreign competition in the Great Depression after 1874. Alongside textiles, the associated industries of coal, iron and engineering made up much smaller subsidiary sectors of the local economy, and were important in the surrounding region.

The mid 1870s downturn in the dominant worsted industry had various effects. The main markets for exports of woollen goods had previously been the USA and Europe, but in the wake of foreign tariffs the British Empire became more important. Mergers and combinations of firms took place. There was also a shift down the production cycle away from the weaving of finished goods, towards the export of spun yarn for weaving in developing overseas mills, and down again to the export of tops and noils (the prepared raw material for spinning). Between 1880 and 1904 exports of piece goods grew by only 4 per cent, but exports of yarns increased by 40 per cent, and tops and noils by 53 per cent. These changes tended to increase the employment of lower-paid unskilled and semi-skilled labour

---

[1]   James, D., *Bradford*, (Halifax, 1990), pp. 25–32.

[2]   James, *Bradford*, p. 61.

in the industry. Employers also responded to falling profits by attempting to cut the cost of labour. From the 1880s more part-time workers were taken on, the pace of work was increased, piece-rates became more common and trade unions came under attack. The social and political consequences of this were profound, as will be shown below. Overall the decline of the industry down to 1914 was unchecked.[3] Inter-war depression and the fall in world trade compounded the earlier signs of decline, and Bradford's reliance on one main industry proved problematic. The sharp slump of 1920–21 saw the value of woollen and worsted exports fall from £140 million to £60 million, and in the even greater crash of 1929–31 to £30 million. Four hundred Bradford textile firms ceased business between 1928 and 1932, and over 35,000 men and women were unemployed in the borough in July 1931. Recovery was slow, with the value of woollen goods restored to £44 million by 1937. Subsidiary industries like coal and iron also suffered, with the Low Moor ironworks closing in 1928 with 3,000 redundancies. There was some compensatory growth of employment in other areas, notably in the production of artificial silk, white-collar work, electrical engineering, printing and motor-car production, but far from enough to fully restore the local economy before the Second World War.[4]

The trajectory of economic growth and decline was reflected in population change. What was to become the borough of Bradford in 1847 was barely more than a village at the beginning of the nineteenth century. More accurately it consisted of a cluster of weaving villages in Bradford Dale including Bradford itself and others surrounding it including Bowling, Horton and Manningham, and further out Allerton, Clayton, Eccleshill and Heaton. As industrial and population growth accelerated, so these various villages were drawn together within the ambit of the borough of Bradford. This gave the borough a distinctive spatial structure, with no clearly defined and concentrated industrial and residential zones, but rather an intermixture of both, with the various scattered industrial villages each retaining their identity to a degree. Even though this structure had changed considerably by the inter-war period, it still had social and political implications that will be raised later.[5] The combined population of the four central townships was 13,000 in 1801, but by 1821 Bradford's population had increased to 26,000, subsequently rising to 66,000 in 1841 and over 100,000 in 1851. Growth continued in the second half of the nineteenth century, Bradford's population reaching 280,000 by 1901, but it slowed dramatically thereafter, being 290,000 in 1921 and just under 300,000 in 1931. At that date Bradford was the eighth largest county borough in England and Wales.[6]

The pattern of employment in 1931 as revealed by the industry tables of the census confirms the central position that the worsted and dyeing industries still occupied in Bradford. Over 60,000 were in textiles, 38.8 per cent of the total workforce. Of those, over 33,000 were women (55 per cent of female workers),

---

[3] James, *Bradford*, pp. 47–52.
[4] James, *Bradford*, pp. 135–141.
[5] Pelling, H., *Social Geography of British Elections 1885–1910*, (Aldershot, 1994), p. 298.
[6] Briggs, A., *Victorian Cities*, (Harmondsworth, 1968), p. 140; James, *Bradford*, pp. 25–32.

and nearly 29,000 were men (29 per cent of male workers). Other significant areas of manual employment for men included metals and engineering (over 9 per cent) and transport (nearly 8 per cent). The second-largest sector of male employment, though, was in commerce and finance (20.5 per cent), of which over a quarter were employed in the trading and retailing of drapery, hosiery and millinery, emphasising again the importance of textiles to the local economy. The growth of white-collar work was partly reflected in this group, as well as in the 6.6 per cent employed in local government. For women, the main areas of employment other than textiles were in personal service (12.6 per cent of female employment), commerce and finance (12.4 per cent), and clothing manufacture (4.5 per cent). 12.3 per cent of the total workforce was classified in the own account and managerial categories, and only 2 per cent as professionals, placing Bradford twenty-ninth and fifty-fifth respectively amongst the eighty-three county boroughs in these terms. This suggests a predominantly working-class borough with only a moderately-sized middle class, further confirmed by the fact that female domestic servants as a proportion of the total population amounted to only 2.5 per cent (sixty-fifth amongst the county boroughs).

The significance of Nonconformity, traditionally strong in the West riding of Yorkshire as a whole and noted already amongst the employers of Bradford, applied to the wider population of the borough. Early Nonconformist manufacturers like the Hustlers, Garnetts and Fawcetts were succeeded later on by prominent local figures such as Titus Salt, Robert Milligan, the Kell brothers and Alfred Illingworth. In the 1851 religious census 64.5 per cent of church attenders in Bradford were Dissenters, 22.9 per cent were Anglicans and 9.1 per cent were Catholics. Bradford was 'one of the most militantly non-conformist towns in England'.[7] The Methodists were the most numerous, but the Congregationalists and Baptists were the most active. The tradition of radical Dissent was an important influence on the Liberalism that dominated Bradford's politics for much of the nineteenth century, and also contributed to the later rise of Labour. It is also necessary to stress the importance of employer paternalism in shaping the society and politics of Bradford in its Victorian heyday. This was a more austere, remote and self-improving version of the populist Tory paternalism that dominated many of the cotton towns on the Lancashire side of the Pennines. Firmly based on the relative prosperity and job security of the years between Chartism and the Great Depression, and strongly underpinned by shared religious and moral values, this paternalism was felt in the factory and in wider society. It was reciprocated by working-class deference and a political commitment to Liberalism. As one employer observed, 'business and religion are not two antagonistic forces ... they both mingle together forming one stream of service to God and man'.[8] The breakdown of this Liberal paternalist tradition from the 1870s and the early and strong development of Labour were inter-connected features of the local political landscape before 1914. A number of factors can be adduced to explain these crucial changes.

[7]   James, *Bradford*, p. 69.
[8]   Quoted in James, *Bradford*, p. 56,

First, the economic prosperity upon which Liberal paternalism was based faded away after the 1870s. As indicated above, labour and labour organisation in the worsted industry bore the brunt of this decline as employers attempted to reduce labour costs, and a polarisation of class feeling was the result. This was crystallised in the bitter and protracted struggle of the Manningham Mills strike from December 1890 to April 1891. The dispute was sparked off by the attempt of the owner of the largest mill in Bradford, Samuel Lister, to impose wage cuts on his employees. The hitherto non-unionised workforce struck in response, and drew support from the Weavers' Union and the local Trades Council. Better-paid velvet and plush weavers initiated the action, but thousands of semi and unskilled workers, including many women, were drawn into the dispute. On the employers' side most of the Liberal mill-owners supported the Tory Lister, and the Liberal-dominated municipality was harsh in its treatment of the strikers, banning meetings and suppressing demonstrations. The whole community of Bradford was forced to take sides in the dispute, with profound political consequences. As the *Yorkshire Factory Times* commented, 'the operatives have from the first been fought not only by their own employers at Manningham but by the whole of the monied classes of Bradford', and 'in future capitalists will have to reckon with whole communities of labour rather than sections'.[9] The strikers were eventually defeated, but out of the defeat came the formation of the Bradford Labour Union, whose objects were 'to advance the interests of working men in whatever way it might ... be thought advisable ... irrespective of the convenience of any political party'.[10] This was a 'pragmatic, yet firm' statement of the principle of Independent Labour, and out of the Union came the formation of the ILP in 1893.

Second, trends in Bradford Liberalism from the 1880s gave its working-class supporters reason to turn to Independent Labour. Anger over Liberal attitudes in the Manningham Mills strike was only a symptom of a wider disillusionment. Free trade and the free market remained the rallying cry of Bradford Liberalism. Proponents of ideas such as social reform and state intervention, later to be defined as 'New Liberalism', were frozen out of the Bradford Liberal party. The most prominent local figure of this type was W.P. Byles, editor of the *Bradford Observer*. Byles, significantly, was one of the few Liberals who did not support Lister in the Manningham Mills strike. He eventually left local politics in disgust at the attitudes of Bradford Liberalism, and later stood as a Lib–Lab candidate for parliament in the more conducive surroundings of Shipley, Salford and Leeds. Bradford Liberalism was instead dominated by leaders who 'combined wealth, adherence to "laissez faire" and disregard for Labour demands.'[11] Most notable was Alfred Illingworth, the 'embodiment of "Old" Liberalism', 'opposed to many social and economic reforms', 'an uncompromising opponent of organised Labour', who held 'rooted objections to any amendments to a laissez-faire

[9] Quoted in Thompson, E.P., 'Homage to Tom Maguire', in Briggs, A. and Saville, J., *Essays in Labour History*, (London, 1967), p. 307.
[10] Quoted in Howell, D., *British Workers and the Independent Labour Party 1888–1906*, (Manchester, 1983), p. 179.
[11] Howell, *British Workers and the Independent Labour Party*, p. 176.

system'.[12] The Liberal party in Bradford refused to countenance working-class candidates standing under its banner. David Howell makes the perceptive point that this was partly to do with the unusual socio-spatial geography of Bradford. As alluded to earlier, the conglomeration of industrial villages that became Bradford borough meant there were few distinct and consolidated working-class and middle-class areas in the town. As Howell explains,

> until around 1900, Bradford was distinctive in that socially segregated housing had developed only a little compared with other cities; a corollary of this was that there were few municipal wards that could be regarded as solidly working class. Indeed, West Bradford ... contained both Manningham Mills and the city's most select residential area ... If such social heterogeneity reduced the scope for working-class solidarity, it also reduced the incentive for Liberal flexibility. In most wards, Liberal organisations could be controlled by middle-class residents and therefore both the willingness and the need to make concessions were absent.[13]

Third, concerning the working-class side of Bradford's politics, the rise of Independent Labour was not pre-ordained by socio-economic circumstances and did not appear overnight in the aftermath of the Manningham Mills strike. As E.P. Thompson insists characteristically, the formation of the ILP was not 'spontaneous', but rather 'the result of the work, over many years, of a group of exceptionally gifted propagandists and trade unionists', the product of 'conscious action in a conscious historical role.'[14] Borrowing from strong traditions of Nonconformism and radicalism, local activists like Fred Jowett created a powerful new political movement. The ILP was, in Thompson's words, a 'sturdy cross-bred', of the old radicalism and new socialism. One of the first manifestations of this cross-breeding was the founding of a Labour Church in Bradford. As the Nonconformist Jowett warned the clergy,

> If you persist in opposing the labour movement there will soon be more reason than ever to complain of the absence of working men from your chapels ... The labourers would establish a Labour Church (cheers and 'Bravo Jowett') and there they would cheer for Jesus Christ, the working man of Nazareth (cheers).[15]

It was also the case that paradoxically the relative weakness of trade unionism in Bradford encouraged the rise of Independent Labour. As David Howell points out, industrial weakness was an 'incentive to political action'. As he explains, 'the absence of strong trade unions in the woollen industry deprived working-class

[12] Laybourn, K., "'One of the little breezes blowing across Bradford": The Bradford Independent Labour Party and trade unionism c. 1890–1914', in Laybourn, K. and James, D., (eds), *'The Rising Sun of Socialism': The Independent Labour Party in the Textile District of the West Riding of Yorkshire between 1890 and 1914*, (Bradford, 1991), p. 16; Howell, *British Workers and the Independent Labour Party*, p. 182.
[13] Howell, *British Workers and the Independent Labour Party*, pp. 180–181.
[14] Thompson, 'Homage to Tom Maguire', p. 279.
[15] Quoted in Thompson, 'Homage to Tom Maguire', p. 291.

electors of one channel through which demands could have been ventilated and pressure imposed.' In addition, Liberal rejection of the representational and policy claims of Labour was reinforced by the 'lack of strong trade unions, whereby bargains could have been obtained.'[16] Unionism only took off in Bradford in the wake of the Manningham Mills strike, and the impact of socialism, especially associated with the leaders of the 'new unionism' of the period, was also significant. As Thompson says, 'it took a new generation, and the new militant unionism, to twist "self-help" into socialist campaigning.'[17] In summary, Howell states,

> Basically, there existed political space in the woollen district to the left of official Liberalism. A combination of economic pressures and trade union weakness, Liberal conservatism and complacency, a vital radical tradition and socialist creativity produced a crucial breakthrough of broadly based Labour organisations, to which socialists added a distinctive ingredient. As a consequence the nineties were marked by bitter hostilities between Liberal and Labour.[18]

The ramifications of the complex political changes affecting Bradford can be seen in the pre-1918 electoral record. As far as parliamentary politics were concerned, the strength of Liberalism up to the 1890s was pronounced. Between 1847 and 1885, when Bradford sent two members to parliament from a single division, Liberal candidates almost completed a clean sweep, with only one Tory ever being returned. Between 1885 and 1910 the single division was split into three, each returning one member. Bradford Central remained strongly Liberal, although a Liberal Unionist won the seat from the Liberals in 1895 and 1900. In the 1906 and two 1910 elections, however, Sir G.S. Robertson held it for the Liberals comfortably against Tory or Unionist opposition. Bradford East became more marginal, with Tories taking the seat off the Liberals in 1886, 1895 and 1900, but again Liberal control was returned in the last three general elections before the First World War. In this division as well the rise of Labour was manifested, Keir Hardie winning 17 per cent of the vote for the ILP in a by-election in 1896, and E.R. Hartley, an ex-ILPer standing for the SDF, winning 23 per cent and 12 per cent respectively in the elections of 1906 and January 1910. Bradford West marked the biggest political changes, with the Liberals being deposed by the Tories in 1895 and 1900, who were in turn overthrown by Labour from 1906 onwards. Ben Tillett had first stood for Labour in 1892, winning 30 per cent of the vote, and in 1895 he had stood again for the ILP, winning 23 per cent of the vote. From 1900 the leading local ILP figure Fred Jowett was the Labour candidate, losing only narrowly in that year, and being the MP from 1906. In both 1910 elections, however, Jowett was unopposed by the Liberals, a significant point that will be returned to later in this chapter.

[16] Howell, *British Workers and the Independent Labour Party*, pp. 176, 180, 200.
[17] Thompson, 'Homage to Tom Maguire', p. 281.
[18] Howell, *British Workers and the Independent Labour Party*, p. 180.

Liberal decline was also seen in municipal elections before the First World War. In 1890 Liberals held forty-two of the sixty council seats, yet three years later they held only twenty-nine to the Tories twenty-six seats. By 1913 in a council now enlarged to eighty-four members, Conservatives outnumbered Liberals by thirty-four to twenty-nine. By contrast the advance of the Labour party over the same period was impressive. Labour won its first representatives in 1892, and by 1901 the ILP held eight out of the eighty-four seats on the council. There was little distinction between the ILP and the Labour party locally, and the ILP operated in close alliance with the Workers' Municipal Federation, founded with the aims of securing 'the return of Labour representatives on the City Council, Board of Guardians and the now defunct School Board'.[19] By 1913 Labour had twenty seats, and would have held the balance of power had it not been for the operation of a Liberal–Tory pact.[20] Labour's influence on the council was already notable, with pioneering efforts over such issues as the provision of school meals and slum clearance indelibly associated with ILPers like Fred Jowett and Margaret McMillan.[21] Labour in Bradford before 1914 was in a much stronger position than in most other county boroughs, and the city's reputation as the birthplace of the ILP and the home of progressive municipal reform gave it a special resonance in the labour movement.

To assess how much Labour capitalised on its position in Bradford between the wars, it is necessary first to give an overview of the electoral trends over the twenty-year period. In the general election of 1918 Labour lost its one Bradford MP, Fred Jowett's division of Bradford West having been abolished in the war-time boundary redistribution, and Jowett himself losing in the newly-created Bradford East. In the first municipal elections after the First World War, however, Labour in Bradford gained ten seats, four from the Liberals and six from the Tories, while there was one Liberal gain from the Conservatives. The *Bradford Daily Argus* declared 'it was an open question which side were taken most by surprise when the results were made known'.[22] Labour became the largest party in the council, with thirty seats to the Conservatives' twenty-eight and the Liberals' twenty-six, and the pre-war strength of the party seemed to be coming to fruition. Labour won 51.7 per cent of all the votes cast in the 1919 municipal elections, a figure exceeded only once in subsequent years between the wars. However, after this initial municipal triumph, as elsewhere the early 1920s saw a rapid reversal of fortunes. Having won in fourteen of the twenty-one contests in 1919, Labour won not a single contest in 1920, and lost six seats overall. Its share of the poll fell dramatically to 36.8 per cent, while turnout jumped from 55.3 per cent to 67.5 per cent, the highest level between the wars in Bradford. 'Ringing cheers' and 'scenes of great enthusiasm' were reported at the Bradford and County Conservative Club, 'volleys of heart cheering' at the Liberal club, but at the Trades Hall there was 'great disappointment among the gathering of Socialist supporters'.[23] In

[19] Laybourn, ' "One of the little breezes blowing across Bradford" ' p. 11.
[20] Laybourn, ' "One of the little breezes blowing across Bradford" ' p. 19.
[21] See Brockway, F., *Socialism Over Sixty Years: The Life of Jowett of Bradford (1864–1944)*, (London, 1946), pp. 44–63.
[22] *Bradford Daily Argus*, 3 Nov. 1919.
[23] *Bradford Daily Argus*, 2 Nov. 1920.

subsequent years down to 1925 Labour made little headway, except in 1923 when it made six net gains, recouping some of its disastrous losses of 1920. In 1925 Labour held twenty-seven seats, three fewer than it had had in 1919. While Labour was roughly on a par with the other two main parties in this period, Liberal–Tory alliance on the council ensured their overall control. Over the same period in parliamentary elections, Labour fared much better in the Bradford divisions, Jowett and Willie Leach winning the East and Central divisions respectively in 1922 and 1923, and W. Hirst the South division in 1924. It was significant, though, that all these victories were achieved in three-way contests, and when Jowett faced a lone Liberal and Leach a lone Tory in 1924, they were both defeated. By contrast, in municipal elections three-way contests were the exception, rather than the rule, as will be shown in detail later in this essay.

Between 1926 and 1929 the municipal trend was strongly towards Labour again, with Labour's share of the vote rising to the high-40s level and peaking at 52.1 per cent in 1929, and Labour making twelve net gains in the three years 1926–28. Having also increased its share of the twenty-one aldermen on the council from six to eight, the Labour party in 1928 was poised to take overall control, with forty-one seats to its opponents' forty-three. The results of the May 1929 general election only reinforced this expectation, Labour winning all four Bradford divisions. Jowett and Leach both regained their seats, their wins being achieved this time in straight contests with their successful 1924 opponents. The pre-war strength of the Labour party in Bradford seemed to be coming to fruition at this point, and its future political domination of the borough seemed assured. Subsequent events, however, were to result in a rather different outcome.

Labour did take power after the 1929 municipal elections, but the celebrations were muted. Despite gaining the highest share of the vote between the wars in this year, Labour actually suffered a net loss of one seat, and 'a sigh of regret went round the hall' at this news when the Labour post-election meeting was held.[24] Two Labour gains were offset by three Labour losses in Heaton, Idle and North Bierley (West). The reasons for this paradoxical result were relatively simple. None of the wards where the Labour losses occurred were strong Labour territory, but in both Heaton and Idle Liberal–Tory co-operation in the 1920s had been difficult to maintain, and in 1926 Labour had made fortunate gains there (with 37.7 and 35.1 per cent of the vote respectively) in three-way contests. Three years later with Liberal–Tory agreement restored, Labour lost both seats in straight fights with a Conservative in Heaton and a Liberal in Idle, despite the Labour candidates winning over 40 per cent of the poll on this occasion. North Bierley West had also been gained fortuitously by Labour previously in a by-election on a low poll, only for it to be regained by the Liberals in the regular November elections. Significantly, one of the two Labour gains in 1929, in Eccleshill, was also the result of a three-way contest, to be lost three years later in a straight fight with the Liberals. Labour took power in Bradford in 1929 only because it was 'entitled to three additional aldermen' under an agreement between the parties to maintain proportionality on the aldermanic bench.[25]   There were a number of significant

---

[24] *Bradford Telegraph and Argus*, 2 Nov. 1929.
[25] *Bradford Telegraph and Argus*, 2 Nov. 1929.

implications of the curious outcome in 1929. One was that Liberal–Conservative electoral pacts were vital factors affecting Labour's strength on the council. The second was that the agreement over proportionality of aldermen, which was operative for the whole of the inter-war period in Bradford, was an important advantage to Labour in Bradford, and one which the party did not enjoy in many other county boroughs at this time.[26] The third was that Labour's maximum strength in municipal politics in Bradford had effectively been reached at this time, with the party only being able to make substantial further gains if three-way contests were restored. This was to be proved in the 1930s, with Labour never again having as many representatives on the council as in 1929–30.

The electoral situation in 1930 and 1931 was again complicated, however. These were bad years for Labour across the country, as the impact of mass unemployment and the failures of the second Labour government hit home municipally. The position in Bradford had also been altered by the fact that the new ward of Clayton had been added to the borough, with three additional councillors and an aldermen having been elected in by-elections. As all these new members were Liberals or Tories, the net effect was that prior to the 1930 elections control of the council was on a knife-edge, with Labour holding forty-four of the eighty-eight seats. Labour's share of the vote in Bradford fell sharply from 52.1 to 44.2 per cent in 1930, and to its lowest point between the wars of 34.9 per cent in 1931. Remarkably though, Labour suffered no net losses in 1930, but a shattering twelve losses in 1931. The contrast between the two years in terms of losses can only be explained as a quirk of the electoral arithmetic of the borough. Despite the Labour vote falling in all but one of the wards in the 1930s, the decline was only sufficient to cause one sitting Labour member to lose in 1930. Moreover, this loss was compensated by one astonishing gain in North Bierley West ward, the only one where the Labour vote went up. Labour had never won a seat in this ward before, but a new candidate, T. Helliwell, appears to have forged a strong personal vote in the area. He claimed to have held no public meetings in the campaign, but instead he and his wife had personally canvassed 3,000 voters in the ward.[27] Helliwell was a singular figure, very much in the moderate wing of the local Labour party, so much so that in the late 1930s he converted to an Independent Labour position. While his personal standing allowed him to retain his seat in subsequent elections in 1933, 1936 and 1937, no other Labour candidate was able to win a seat in the ward. In 1936 indeed Helliwell was given a free run by Labour's opponents, showing both how strong his personal vote was, and how moderate his Labour politics were.

In Bradford in 1931 there was no moratorium on contesting municipal elections in the atmosphere of national emergency and calls for cost-cutting. In some other boroughs all-party agreements to suspend elections spared Labour widespread losses, but every seat in Bradford was contested in 1931, and Labour felt the full effects of its national unpopularity. The results of the November elections were described as a 'cold bath for Labour' by Foster Sunderland, president of the party,

---

[26] See for instance the chapters on Birkenhead, Blackburn and Bootle in volume one of this series, and on Burnley, Cardiff and Carlisle in this volume.
[27] *Bradford Telegraph and Argus*, 3 Nov. 1930.

while a Conservative leader hailed them as 'a magnificent victory', and a victorious Liberal stated that he had 'got in on a wave of discontent against the Socialists.'[28] A further fall in the Labour share of the vote meant that the party failed to win a single contest in this year, as it had before in 1920. With thirty-one of the eighty-eight seats on the council, Labour was still the largest party, but power was firmly back in the hands of the Tory–Liberal alliance of fifty-four members. Even normally solid Labour seats were lost in 1931. Its two strongest inter-war wards (before they were both abolished in the boundary revisions of 1936–7), North and West, illustrate the full scale of the disaster very well. Labour had not lost in either of these wards since 1920, and in 1929 had won with 74.3 and 61.5 per cent of the votes respectively. In 1930 Labour's share of the vote fell to 56.1 per cent in North and 55.2 per cent in West, so the sitting candidates were returned. In 1931 Labour's vote fell to a catastrophic 39.3 per cent in North, almost halved from its 1929 level and resulting in a Conservative gain, and to 44.7 per cent in West, giving the Liberals a gain.

The municipal disaster for Labour in 1931 only compounded the gloom felt by its supporters at the results of the general election held five days earlier, in which all four Bradford divisions had been lost. Labour was as badly hit in Bradford in 1931 as in any county borough. The depths of the recession that had damaged the local economy may have been one reason for this, but there were political reasons as well. Most notably, the earlier advantages of the strong ILP base to the local party may well have counted against it now. Sections of the ILP had been vociferous in its criticism of the Labour government's performance, especially over its handling of unemployment, and this had had a divisive effect in Bradford, culminating in a bitter debate at the ILP's annual conference in April 1930. To an extent the personal prestige of the nearby Keighley-born ILPer and Labour Chancellor of the Exchequer helped to defuse local criticism for a time, 'but local attitudes towards Snowden and the Labour Government became more critical from the end of 1930.'[29] The ILP's very position as an affiliate to the Labour party was beginning to be debated, leading eventually to its secession from the party in 1932. All this could only have caused great disillusionment amongst Labour's supporters in Bradford, with severe electoral effects in the short term at least.

Support for the Labour party was, though, restored to somewhere near its former levels in the following few years. The Labour share of the vote rose back to the 45–50 per cent range between 1932 and 1936, but nevertheless the huge losses of 1931 in terms of seats were only partially recovered. Although Willie Leach declared that 'the tide has begun to turn', one seat was lost in the 1932 elections, and subsequently two Labour aldermen were deposed to bring the party back to its proportionate representation.[30] Labour made one gain in 1933, and seven of the 1931 losses were restored in 1934, but 1935 and 1936 were years of stasis. From 1934 there were also two ILP councillors, now standing on a separate ticket, but even if they could have been relied upon to always vote with their Labour

[28]   *Bradford Telegraph and Argus*, 3 Nov. 1931.
[29]   Reynolds, J. and Laybourn, K., *Labour Heartland: The History of the Labour Party in West Yorkshire During the Inter-War Years, 1918–1939*, (Bradford, 1987), p.92.
[30]   *Bradford Telegraph and Argus*, 2 Nov. 1932.

colleagues, Tory–Liberal rule was secure. The general election of 1935 saw only a partial Labour recovery as well, with Bradford Central being regained narrowly, but the North and South divisions being retained with large majorities by a Tory and Liberal respectively. The result in Jowett's old seat of Bradford East was the most dispiriting for Labour, however, with Jowett standing for the ILP against a Labour candidate, allowing a Tory to come through in a four-way split to win with only 33 per cent of the poll. The electoral impact of the ILP defection was plainly important at both the municipal and parliamentary levels in Bradford by the mid 1930s, and it will be dealt with in greater detail later in this essay.

The political situation in Bradford was strongly affected by the municipal boundary revision that took place in 1937, and the full implications of this change will also be analysed later. The net effect was disastrous for Labour, with the Labour share of the poll falling to 36 per cent. After the aldermanic elections had been completed Labour held only 20 of the eighty seats in the reformed council. There were also seven assorted Labour defectors on the council, including both left and right-wing Independent Labour members as well as the familiar ILP presence. Tory–Liberal control of the new council was assured, however, and while Labour's vote share recovered to 44.7 per cent in 1938, this resulted in only one net gain. Even if Labour's defectors could have been returned to the fold, the party would still have been some way off realising the pre-1914 promise of 'the rising sun of socialism' in Bradford, before the intervention of the Second World War postponed such a possibility for seven years in any case. When next Bradford voters went to the polls, in the huge Labour general election victory of July 1945, all four parliamentary divisions were won by Labour. In the subsequent municipal elections in November 1945 a Labour majority was elected. Neither eventuality could have been predicted confidently from the pre-1939 trends. The remarkable fact is that in 1938 the Labour party had twenty representatives on the council and one Bradford MP, exactly the same number that it had had in 1913. Almost as surprising is that there were still as many as twenty-three Liberals on Bradford council, compared to the twenty-nine in 1913. The central question to be asked about inter-war politics in Bradford, therefore, is this: why did Labour fail to build on its earlier strength and go on to dominate local politics between the wars?

A complex series of interconnected developments need to be uncovered to throw light on this, some of which have been mentioned in passing already. First, Labour's main opponents need to be considered. In Fenner Brockway's biography of Fred Jowett, there is a description of the Liberal and Tory leaders facing the socialist Jowett when he entered Bradford council. The Liberal leader, Alderman John Hill, was 'typical of the wealthier elements' in his party. He was

> a sixty-year-old textile manufacturer, a strong Nonconformist, self-righteous, and an extreme individualist. He had done well by hard work and moral living: why could not everyone else do so? He considered that nothing beyond charity was necessary to assist the 'failures' in life.

By contrast the Tory leader, Alderman H.B. Ratcliffe, was

of a different type, a butcher, bulky in build, big-boned and big-featured, a man of the world, not claiming high principles, openly the defender of the property owners.[31]

This was a beautiful encapsulation of the subtle differences between nineteenth-century Liberalism and Conservatism, of course, although Brockway went on to assert that 'on most social issues there was no difference in attitude between the two men'. Implicit in the description was the fact that counterposed to these defenders of property were principled, high-minded socialist pioneers like Jowett himself. Brockway was an early exponent of a school of thought that has tended to reduce Bradford politics to a simple polarity. Keith Laybourn has expressed this well. He writes:

> Bradford politics was undergoing fundamental changes between the 1880s and 1914 ... many working-class voters were identifying with the ILP as the Liberal Party failed to go far enough in meeting their expectations ... The Bradford Liberal Association palpably failed to offer 'New' Liberal policies to the electorate and sought to staunch Labour's growth by allying with the Conservatives in municipal elections. This ploy did not work.[32]

In other words, an unreconstructed Gladstonian Liberalism, its true nature revealed in the Manningham Mills dispute, abandoned its loyal working-class supporters and became allied with Toryism. The Bradford working class, in turn, recognised its true class interest and united behind a powerful ILP. There was an element of truth in this polarity, but if it was the whole truth then it would be difficult to explain why Labour failed to fulfil its promise between the wars. The relationship between Liberalism and Labour, however, and also between the Liberals and Tories, was more complicated than this in twentieth-century Bradford politics.

For a start, David Howell, the pre-eminent historian of the early ILP, shows how after the initial Liberal–Labour conflict of the 1890s, a 'progressive understanding' between Labour and Liberalism was the dominant element in Bradford politics in the Edwardian period, especially at the level of parliamentary elections.[33] Much has been made of the 1906 contest in Bradford West, when Jowett was faced with a three-way contest with a Liberal and a Tory, as evidence of continuing Liberal–Labour conflict. Laybourn, for example, identifies this contest as proof for him of the 'failure of local Liberal attempts to work with the ILP.'[34] As Howell points out, though, '1906 was an exception'. Liberals stood down against Jowett in 1900 and in the two 1910 general elections, while Labour gave Liberals a free run in the other Bradford seats. The existence of a 'progressive unity in Bradford was obscured to some extent by the 1906 contest', Howell asserts, but nevertheless such unity was a 'key development'.[35] Duncan

[31]   Brockway, F., *Socialism Over Sixty Years: The Life of Jowett of Bradford (1864–1944)*, (London, 1946), p. 46.
[32]   Laybourn, ' "One of the little breezes blowing across Bradford" ' p. 21.
[33]   Howell, *British Workers and the Independent Labour Party*, pp. 193–203.
[34]   Laybourn, ' "One of the little breezes blowing across Bradford" ' p. 20.
[35]   Howell, *British Workers and the Independent Labour Party*, p. 197.

Tanner, in his important work on political change and the rise of Labour down to 1918, echoes Howell's argument, and goes on to argue that Labour made most progress in Bradford before 1906, when the Liberals were 'extremely conservative'. It was much less successful once the Liberals 'put up a fight by modifying their image'. Moreover, Labour's success was 'not necessarily the result of Labour's radical approach. Labour had paid considerable attention to conventional issues; it had also operated in a Progressive framework.' [36] Tanner asserts:

> A Liberal political culture so penetrated people's outlooks that challenges to the status quo inevitably came from within that tradition ... The ILPs ethical socialism drew its approach from a Nonconformist revivalism, its content from a radical Liberal/working-class sense of a moral entitlement to a degree of security ... the similarity between ethical socialism and radical Liberalism helped place a ceiling on the level of support which the ILP could attract.[37]

Two important points to stress in this debate are that there were limits to Labour's pre-1914 appeal, and Labour's strength in Bradford was at least in part dependent on a 'Progressive alliance' with Liberalism, rather than simply a confirmation of its sturdy independence. This gives a more realistic assessment of how strong Labour was before 1914, and makes its subsequent development between the wars more explicable.

Also significant is Tanner's assertion of the changing nature of Liberalism. Whatever was happening locally, the national image of Liberalism was different after 1906. Tanner states, 'once the national Liberal party reaffirmed its belief in social reform, the one electoral space which Socialists might exploit narrowed very considerably'.[38] Laybourn on the other hand emphasises the intransigence of Bradford Liberalism, and points to its pre-1914 municipal pact with the Conservatives as proof of its resistance to working-class demands. Yet the Liberal actions in the 1910 general elections present a rather different picture. The strength of the Liberal–Tory alliance in Bradford is also debatable. The figures given by Laybourn for straight fights between Labour and either Tories or Liberals as a result of the pact suggest that it was only partial. At most only eight of the twenty-one wards were straight fights in any one year between 1906 and 1913.[39] Even after 1918, when the pact was more solid, at least down to 1929 Liberal–Tory co-operation was not perfect. In four wards, Eccleshill, Heaton, Idle and Thornton, three-way contests were numerous, and in six other wards occurred occasionally.

It is also the case that in the pre-1914 years, and even more so after 1918, there is evidence that Bradford Liberalism did move away from the stern 'Illingworthism' that had driven out W.P. Byles in the 1890s. A telling example can be found in Jowett's biography. Most of the Liberals on the council opposed

[36] Tanner, D., *Political Change and the Labour Party 1900–1918*, (Cambridge, 1990), pp. 259–260.
[37] Tanner, *Political Change and the Labour Party*, pp. 261–262.
[38] Tanner, *Political Change and the Labour Party*, p. 262.
[39] Laybourn, ' "One of the little breezes blowing across Bradford" ' p. 20.

Jowett's proposal of free school meals in 1904, while most of the Conservatives supported it, stern self-help Liberalism and Tory paternalism personified. The leading Liberal opponent, also a fierce antagonist over the provision of municipal housing, was E.J. Smith. Yet Alderman E.J. Smith in the inter-war period became famous locally for his contributions to civic social improvement, especially in the field of child welfare and housing.[40] The fact is that under almost unbroken Liberal–Tory rule between the wars, Bradford maintained its reputation as a progressive municipality. 'Education in Bradford between the wars was arguably more progressive than in most places', in medical provision 'improvement continued after 1918', 'the council made a number of contributions towards improving environmental health', and in housing and transport 'Bradford made considerable advances'.[41]

There were individual Liberals and Tories who opposed these measures, of course, and low rates were always promised along with careful and efficient use of public funds. Labour might also have advanced this programme of 'municipal socialism' faster and further if it had been in power for longer, and Labour pressure on the council committees no doubt encouraged bolder schemes. The key point, however, is that the Liberal–Tory alliance stole many of Labour's clothes in the inter-war years. At the same time, as will be discussed below, Labour's policies became more moderate, and the party moved nearer to its opponents in political terms. There was a degree of political convergence, and Liberals and Tories benefited electorally from this process. While electoral pacts between the two parties were imperfect in the 1920s, they were solid in the 1930s. Liberals and Conservatives never opposed each other in any municipal contest after 1930, and this helped to consolidate their strength after the brief spell of Labour rule. In the examples quoted earlier in both parliamentary and municipal elections, Labour had on occasions been able to steal seats in three-way contests that it would normally lose in straight fights. This possibility was closed down in the 1930s, and in part this explains why Labour's relatively high level of support in terms of votes cast in the 1932–36 period did not translate itself into large numbers of seats gained.

Labour itself also changed, as has already been indicated. Most significant was the changing relationship between the strong ILP base in Bradford and the Labour party itself. In the pre-1914 situation where there was no formal Labour party organisation as such, but only a loose alliance of affiliated trade unions and socialist organisations, the energy and enthusiasm of the Bradford ILP had been a real benefit to Labour in the borough. In conjunction with the Workers' Municipal Federation, which channelled trade union support, it provided a high level of organisation and a permanent campaigning body of support. Even before the new 1918 party constitution set up individual membership and a formal ward and constituency party structure, Bradford had already reorganised itself along these lines in 1917–18.[42] Yet the new arrangements contained an inherent tension between the ILP branches and the four constituency and twenty-one ward parties. Differences between the ILP and the rest of the labour movement had already been

[40] Brockway, *Socialism Over Sixty Years*, pp. 56–58.
[41] James, *Bradford*, pp. 155–165.
[42] Reynolds and Laybourn, *Labour Heartland*, p. 38.

manifested during the First World War, when the anti-war sentiments of Jowett and other ILPers had alienated much rank and file support. The Bradford ILP recovered its membership losses after the armistice, having 2,377 members by 1926,[43] but its political weight was relatively less important as Labour party branches increasingly developed their own independent activity. Moreover, within the national organisation of the ILP, Bradford became less important as the Scottish and London branches became the dominant force. It also became politically isolated, the ethical socialism personified by Jowett appearing increasingly old-fashioned by comparison with the more militant and revolutionary tone of the Clydesiders.

By the mid 1920s the ILP's relationship nationally with the Labour Party was also coming under increasing strain. The dispute in 1926 over the ILP's 'Socialism in our Time' policy, Snowden's resignation from the ILP in 1927, followed by Ramsay MacDonald's in 1929, and conflict over the 'Cook–Maxton' Manifesto in 1928, were all forewarnings of the major disagreements between the ILP and the second Labour government of 1929–31, especially over unemployment policy. The ultimate secession of the ILP from the Labour party in 1932 was the culmination of these developing differences. The impact in Bradford was disastrous for Labour. Within the local ILP itself there was disagreement, as there was also between ILP branches and ward and divisional Labour parties.[44] The ILP's prestige locally was gradually undermined, while at the same time Labour's morale and activity was weakened by internal division. One indicator of the ILP's decline in Bradford was Fred Jowett's attempt to get back on to the council while he was out of parliament between 1924 and 1929. In 1927 he stood for Tong ward, which Labour had won comfortably in the two previous years. This was a good year for Labour, the party making four gains, yet the best-known politician in the borough was unable to take the seat, Jowett winning only 45.5 per cent of the vote against his Liberal opponent. The following year he stood in Heaton ward, admittedly a tougher nut to crack as Labour had only won there recently when there had been a three-way contest in 1926. Again this was a good year for Labour, three gains being made in 1928, but Jowett lost again, winning 43.3 per cent of the vote against a Tory opponent. Moreover, Jowett's performance was considerably worse than the Labour candidate's in the previous year in this ward, who had come very close to winning with 48.9 per cent of the poll.

After the 1932 disaffiliation, the ILP 'collapsed rapidly in its Yorkshire heartland.'[45] Of the 32 Labour members on Bradford council, only one left the Labour party and stayed with the ILP. Before the split the Bradford ILP had already dwindled to only 750 members, and half of these were lost after disaffiliation.[46] This hit Labour party morale in general, and in some wards where the ILP had been particularly strong it also caused organisational problems at least in the short term. When the ILP began to stand its own candidates, this had a more direct adverse effect on Labour's electoral performance. In the 1935 general

[43] Reynolds and Laybourn, *Labour Heartland*, p. 66.
[44] Reynolds and Laybourn, *Labour Heartland*, pp. 65–74.
[45] Reynolds and Laybourn, *Labour Heartland*, p. 107.
[46] Reynolds and Laybourn, *Labour Heartland*, p. 108.

election, Jowett for the ILP and W.L. Heywood for Labour split the socialist vote, allowing the Tory through with only 33 per cent of the vote.

In municipal elections, the ILP stood candidates only occasionally at first. In 1933 there were two, one in Tong ward where Labour avoided a clash, and one in West Bowling where splitting the vote gave the seat to a Liberal. In the following three years the main problems were in East Bowling ward, where the ILP candidate J. Cariss won in 1934, gaining 46.6 per cent of the vote compared to 17.7 per cent for Labour. Labour was given a free run the following year, and Cariss was similarly treated when he came up for re-election in 1937, but in 1936 the Labour candidate beat off the ILP challenge. In the 1937 'municipal general election' the ILP stood three candidates in East Bowling, as well as one in Tong. The year 1938, however, saw open warfare break out between Labour and the ILP. The Labour party announced it was to challenge the ILP candidate in Tong ward, and in retaliation the ILP fielded candidates in eight wards,[47] in three of which the splitting of the socialist vote was decisive in handing the seat to the opposition. In North East, Tong and West Bowling wards, the combined Labour and ILP vote came to more than 50 per cent of the poll, but in each case a Conservative came through to win.

Labour's position was also worsened by the intervention of other breakaway 'Independent Labour' candidates in 1937. A moderate group picked up four seats in Little Horton, Manningham (two seats) and North Bierley West wards, all but one of their successful candidates being Labour councillors previously. There was also an ex-ILP councillor who stood and won as a 'Workers' and Socialist' candidate in Tong ward. The net effect of all the splits in Labour in Bradford was plainly deleterious in electoral terms, and without them Labour's position on the council in 1938 would undoubtedly have been stronger. It should also be noted that the departure of the ILP changed the political tone of the Bradford Labour party. The influence of trade unionism in the party was increased, and there was a shift to more pragmatic municipal policies. The 'broad church' of Labour became significantly narrower. There were advantages to this in one sense, as there was less space for the division and disagreement that had sapped party morale for some time. Labour was internally more cohesive, albeit at the cost of losing the more expansive vision of the ILP pioneers. A local activist, Frank Betts, (the father of the future Barbara Castle), expressed the new Labour outlook well in 1935, when he stated

> The one thing above all others we can do is to settle down to win the municipalities and show ... that our aims are constructive, that we are neither extravagant nor perverse, that our programme brings direct amelioration to simple people ... blazing hearths, busy playing fields, short hours and peace of mind.[48]

As noted already, the gap between this rhetoric and that of Conservatism and Liberalism was not as great as it had been in earlier decades.

---

[47] *Bradford Telegraph and Argus*, 2 Nov. 1938.
[48] Quoted in James, *Bradford*, pp. 166-167.

It was remarked earlier that the 1936–37 ward boundary revision hurt Labour electorally, and it is appropriate to consider this in some detail now. To do this, it is first necessary to establish the socio-spatial pattern of political support in the borough before 1936. From the electoral data it can be seen that Labour strength was concentrated mainly in the older districts surrounding the city centre, spreading further out towards the east and south where much of the industrial production was concentrated. The main city centre ward was Exchange, where retail and distribution activity was predominant, and plural business voters ensured Liberal–Tory dominance. Surrounding this was a swathe of wards where Labour was generally, if variably, strong, running clockwise from Manningham through West, North, South, East Bowling, West Bowling, Little Horton and Listerhills wards. Of these, West Bowling and Listerhills were the most marginal. Then to the east Labour had good support in Bradford Moor, and to the south and east more marginal strength in Tong and North Bierley (East) wards. Most of the Labour wards were included in the parliamentary divisions of Bradford Central and Bradford East, unsurprisingly where Labour was most successful in general elections.

Apart from Exchange, the only central ward that was predominantly non-Labour was East ward, containing better-quality and larger residential properties. The marked difference between this ward and the other Labour-leaning central wards was clearly shown by the persons per room figures in the 1931 census. While the North, South and West wards were well above the borough-average of 0.88 persons per room, ranging from 1.03 to 1.17 persons per room, East was slightly below the average at 0.85 persons per room. The northern and eastern suburbs were the most affluent at this time, and these were where the predominantly anti-Labour wards were situated. To the north Heaton and Bolton were Tory strongholds, while Eccleshill was shared with the Liberals, and Idle was mainly Liberal. To the west, Great Horton, Allerton and Thornton were mainly Liberal, while Clayton and North Bierley (West) were again shared by Liberals and Conservatives. The persons per room figures were again indicative, these wards tending to have the lowest levels in the borough, mostly in the 0.70 to 0.85 range.

There were two important implications of this pattern of political support. First, the nineteenth-century lack of social segregation that was noted earlier plainly no longer applied to inter-war Bradford. The central areas had become predominantly working-class, including Manningham where previously the rich and the poor had lived in close proximity. The industrial districts to the south-east were also mainly working-class, if slightly more affluent. The western and northern suburbs were overwhelmingly middle-class. This was a much more typical twentieth-century British city. Second, the political arithmetic showed that Labour support was concentrated in eleven wards, with the other eleven wards being anti-Labour. It would have been difficult for Labour to build a solid majority in the council-chamber without making substantial inroads into hostile territory, something that was not achieved in the inter-war years. It was also the case that housing developments between the wars had little effect on patterns of political support in Bradford. Approximately 8,500 council houses were constructed, not an extraordinarily large number given the size of the borough. There were also roughly 14,500 houses built by private developers.[49] Most of the private housing was situated in the western and northern suburbs, while the council housing was mostly built in Labour-supporting wards. A considerable amount of rehousing took place in the central districts, including the Longlands scheme, White Abbey, Wapping, Whetley Lane, Leeds Road. There were also estates at Canterbury Avenue in Little Horton ward, and in Eccleshill ward, but the latter was not large enough to have any significant effect on the politics of the ward. This was the situation, then, leading up to the boundary changes of 1936–37.

The boundaries of the county borough had last been fully revised in 1898–99, and subsequent population change had created inequality in the size of wards. While the mean size of electorate in the 1936 wards was 7,080, there were a number of significantly smaller central wards which had lost population due to housing clearance, including Exchange (electorate of 2,045 in 1936, many of them business voters), West (3,088) and North (4,211). There were also a number of smaller suburban wards, mainly consisting of middle-class private housing estates and/or semi-rural areas, including Clayton (2,993), Thornton (3,332) and Tong (3,504). Conversely, there were some larger than average wards, again of two types. First, there were predominantly middle-class suburban wards which were large in area, and within which considerable private housing development had taken place since 1899, including Allerton (10,750) and Great Horton (13,582). Second, there were densely-populated mainly working-class wards with reasonably good-quality housing where population growth had not been offset by house clearance, such as Bradford Moor (13,274), Manningham (10,334) and West Bowling (10, 242). Equalisation of ward size was desirable, but it is unlikely that any perceived party political advantage was a strong motivation for change, as the inequalities of the old boundaries favoured neither side to any great extent. Of the over-represented smaller wards, West and North were Labour wards, but Exchange, Clayton, Thornton and Tong were predominantly non-Labour. Of the under-represented larger wards, Allerton and Great Horton were non-Labour, but Bradford Moor and Manningham were Labour territory, and West Bowling was best described as a marginal Labour ward.

Moreover, the net political effects of the new boundaries were on the whole relatively insignificant. Bradford was not a case of obvious gerrymandering of boundaries, such as was found in the examples of Birkenhead and Bury in these volumes. While all the wards boundaries were altered in 1936–37, most of the changes were politically neutral. The only major changes were the abolition of East, North and West wards, and their absorption into a new ward, North East, and a much-enlarged Exchange ward. The old East and Exchange had been predominantly non-Labour wards, North and West strongly Labour. The enlarged Exchange, having taken in West, became a mainly Labour ward after the revision, while North East became a mainly non-Labour ward. Neither side appeared to have been particularly advantaged by the changes in any permanent and long-term way, therefore.

There was another decision taken at the time of the revision, however, that in the short term had unintended but nevertheless significant political effects. All the

---

[49] James, *Bradford*, pp. 161–162.

seats on the new council were contested together in what was described as 'Bradford's "municipal" general election' in 1937.[50] In many of the boundary revisions that took place in other boroughs in this period, usually all the seats were contested at once only in those wards that had been radically altered. This was the case, for instance, in Birkenhead and Bristol, as shown elsewhere in these volumes. In Bradford, with all the seats decided on the same day, much extra public interest was generated in the November elections of 1937. Turnout in municipal elections in the 1930s had declined considerably in the borough, falling from well above the 60 per cent level in the 1920s, to only 40.9 per cent in 1936. In 1937, however, turnout leapt up sharply to 58.4 per cent, only to fall back even more dramatically to 38 per cent in 1938. It has already been noted in a number of chapters in these volumes that in the inter-war period high turnout was usually associated with poor Labour performance. This applied almost across the board, for instance, in both 1920 and 1931. Conversely, when turnout was low, Labour usually did well, as in 1919 and 1929.[51] Thus Labour predictably did badly in the high-turnout election of 1937 in Bradford, its share of the vote falling from 48.7 per cent in 1936 to 36.0 in 1937, before recovering again to 44.7 per cent in 1938. Nationally Labour was in any case doing badly in most boroughs in the late 1930s, but nevertheless the very sharp drop in Labour support in one year in Bradford suggests a connection with the very pronounced rise in the level of turnout.

For Labour to have done so badly in one year would have been bad enough in the normal cycle of municipal elections, when one-third of the councillors would have been up for election. With all the seats on the council up for election, however, the effects were tripled. This accounts for the sudden transformation of Labour's position in Bradford in 1937. From being the largest party, with thirty-five of the eighty-eight seats on the council, it became overnight the smallest of the main parties, with only twenty out of eighty seats. Thus the revision of boundaries in Bradford, despite being conducted in an even-handed manner as far as long-term party advantage was concerned, did have an adverse effect on the Labour party in the short-term. The opposite effect could be observed elsewhere, depending on the particular circumstances. In Coventry in 1928, for instance, at a time when Labour was doing very well electorally, all the seats were contested after boundary revision. Labour made eleven gains, never before having made any more than two in any one year in the previous decade. From being a minor presence on Coventry council, the Labour party became a contender, eventually taking power in 1937.[52] In Bradford, though, the effect was plainly to contribute to Labour's poor standing on the council in 1938.

There was one other intriguing feature of the 'municipal general election' of 1937 that is worth mentioning. So far in these volumes the question of the

[50] *Bradford Telegraph and Argus*, 3 Nov. 1937.

[51] For aggregate figures on turnout for the nineteen boroughs of the first two volumes of this series, see table 10.1 in this volume, p. 656.

[52] Carr, F., 'Municipal socialism: Labour's rise to power', in Lancaster, B. and Mason, T., (eds), *Life and Labour in a Twentieth Century City: The Experience of Coventry*, (Coventry, 1986), p. 197. For further discussion of the significance of ward boundaries in inter-war municipal politics, see Davies, S., *Liverpool Labour: Social and Political Influences on the Development of the Labour Party in Liverpool, 1900–1939*, pp. 97–109.

efficiency and probity of the process of collecting and counting the votes in municipal elections has never been raised. The count in Exchange ward in 1937 proved spectacularly flawed, however. In the first declaration on the morning after the poll it was announced that 3,975 voters had cast their votes out of a total electorate of 7,415. Each of these voters could cast a maximum of three votes, so the total number of votes cast could not have been higher than 11,925. The three Labour candidates topped the poll, each receiving between 4,845 and 5,156 votes, and were duly declared elected. The other three defeated candidates, a Liberal, a Tory and an Independent, were credited with between 4,432 and 4,447 votes. The total number of votes cast were supposedly 28,292, plainly an impossibility. Some time later in the day the defeated candidates realised something was amiss. As the Independent candidate stated, 'really we ought to have spotted it much sooner than we did'. Legal action to render the declaration invalid was contemplated, but in the end the Town Clerk and all the candidates agreed to a recount. On the new figures, 10,979 votes had been cast. The three Labour candidates received between 2,016 and 1,705 votes, while three other candidates received between 1,816 and 1,799 votes. Two of the Labour candidates were again at the top of the poll and declared elected, but the third now came last, and the Independent candidate took the third seat. It is not clear from the press coverage how this gross error had occurred, but it appears that some but not all of the votes had been wrongly trebled. The Town Clerk was reported as stating that 'apart from the mishap over the Exchange ward the counting of the votes was, in his opinion, expeditiously carried out and he would like to compliment the staff on their achievement.'[53] How much this reassured the electors of Bradford is open to question.

In conclusion, the inter-war politics of Bradford provide an interesting case of a county borough where the Labour party failed to take advantage of its pre-1914 strength. In this respect Bradford was very different to most of the boroughs covered in these volumes so far, where post-1918 Labour growth far outstripped earlier development. It contrasts starkly with Bristol, for instance, where Labour was very weak before 1918, but supplanted Liberalism rapidly thereafter, and by 1938 was in control of the council. There were some short-term and contingent reasons for Labour's relative failure in Bradford. The fact that all council seats were contested in the one year of 1937 proved disastrous for Labour, raising turnout and sweeping away many Labour hopefuls. The damaging contests with the ILP and other rebel Labour defectors in 1937–38 could also be seen as an unfortunate and possibly temporary contingency. On the other hand, there were more fundamental causes of Labour's relative lack of success. For a start, the rupture of working-class support for Liberalism and the shift to independent labour after the Manningham Mills strike of 1891 was not as complete as sometimes has been argued. Labour did not quite pose the clear alternative to Liberalism in Bradford that some accounts have claimed, but to an extent shared with the Liberals a Nonconformist, Progressive heritage. Liberalism rallied after 1918 in Bradford, and in alliance with Conservatism remained surprisingly resilient. The strength of the ILP in Bradford, a boon to Labour before 1914, was also a more problematic legacy after 1918. As the ILP became more critical of Labour in

---

[53] *Bradford Telegraph and Argus*, 3 Nov. 1937.

power, so in Bradford disunity and disagreement was fostered in Labour ranks. When the ILP finally disaffiliated, the electoral effects were damaging, the impact on Labour party morale probably even more deleterious. By 1938 the Bradford Labour party was the purveyor of a pragmatic municipal socialism, elements of which its Tory and Liberal opponents could live with. Labour cautiously looked forward to steady municipal and parliamentary gains in order to advance piecemeal elements of socialism. It was barely recognisable as the same party of idealistic pioneers who had confidently heralded the 'rising sun of socialism' before 1914. In 1938 Jowett, the embodiment of Bradford socialism since the 1890s, was in the political wilderness, an ageing figure from another generation. It was to be a new generation after 1945 that was to take Labour forward again in Bradford. Perhaps the reinvention of the party in the inter-war period was the necessary, albeit painful, prelude to the later success.

A guide to further reading

Newspapers

Bradford Daily Argus
Bradford Telegraph and Argus
Yorkshire Evening Argus
Yorkshire Post

Other secondary sources

Briggs, A., *Victorian Cities*, (Harmondsworth, 1968), pp. 139–157.
Brockway, F., *Socialism Over Sixty Years: The Life of Jowett of Bradford (1864–1944)*, (London, 1946).
Howell, D., *British Workers and the Independent Labour Party 1888–1906*, (Manchester, 1983), ch. 8, pp. 174–203.
Hudson, P., *The Genesis of Industrial Capital: A Study of the West Riding Textile Industry*, (Cambridge, 1986).
James, D., *Bradford*, (Halifax, 1990).
Laybourn, K., '"One of the little breezes blowing across Bradford": The Bradford Independent Labour Party and trade unionism c. 1890–1914', in Laybourn, K. and James, D., (eds), *'The Rising Sun of Socialism': The Independent Labour Party in the Textile District of the West Riding of Yorkshire between 1890 and 1914*, (Bradford, 1991).
Le Lohe, M.J., 'Local Elections in Bradford County Borough, 1937–1967', (Ph.D. thesis, University of Leeds, 1972).
Priestley, J.B., *English Journey*, (London, 1934).
Reynolds, J. and Laybourn, K., *Labour Heartland: The History of the Labour Party in West Yorkshire during the Inter-War Years, 1918–1939*, (Bradford, 1987).
Thompson, E.P., 'Homage to Tom Maguire', in Briggs, A. and Saville, J., *Essays in Labour History*, (London, 1967), pp. 276–316.

Bradford wards 1919–1936

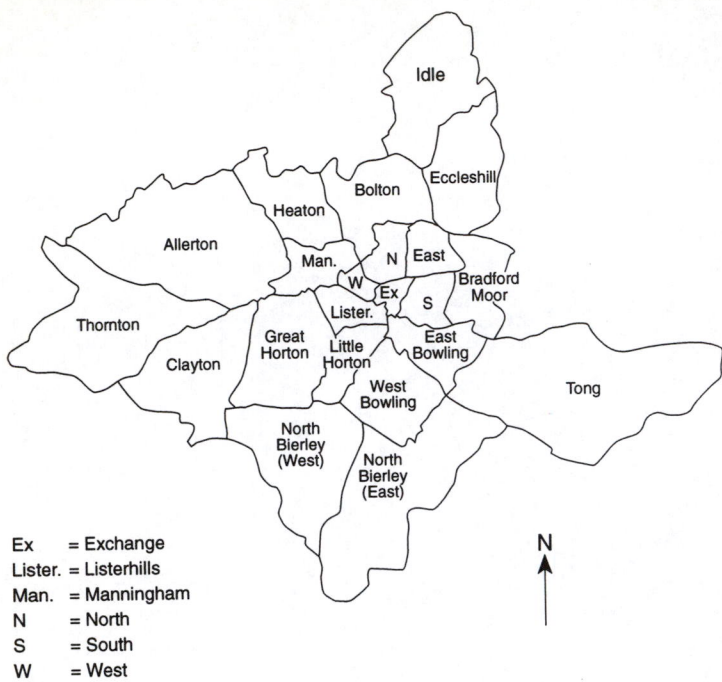

Ex   = Exchange
Lister. = Listerhills
Man.   = Manningham
N   = North
S   = South
W   = West

Bradford wards 1937–1938

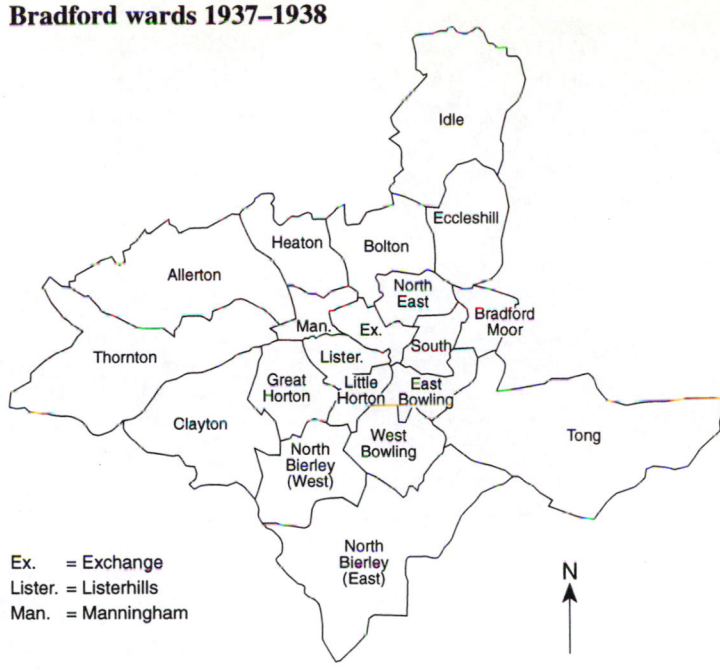

Ex. = Exchange
Lister. = Listerhills
Man. = Manningham

N

Persons aged fourteen and over classified by industry 1931

	Male	%	Female	%	Total	%
Metal and engineering	9,336	9.4	896	1.5	10,232	6.4
Textiles	28,678	29.0	33,085	55.0	61,763	38.8
- Wool and worsted	*19,864*	*20.1*	*28,112*	*46.8*	*47,976*	*30.2*
- Silk	*2,279*	*2.3*	*2,757*	*4.6*	*5,036*	*3.2*
- Dyeing and bleaching	*5,773*	*5.8*	*1,510*	*2.5*	*7,283*	*4.6*
Clothing	1,467	1.5	2,733	4.5	4,200	2.6
Paper and printing	1,901	1.9	1,524	2.5	3,425	2.2
Building	5,510	5.6	70	0.1	5,580	3.5
Transport	7,764	7.9	195	0.3	7,959	5.0
Commerce and finance	20,250	20.5	7,438	12.4	27,688	17.4
- Drapery, hosiery, millinery	*5,572*	*5.6*	*1,000*	*1.7*	*6,572*	*4.1*
Public admin. and defence	7,720	7.8	2,527	4.2	10,247	6.4
- Local government	*6,537*	*6.6*	*2,172*	*3.6*	*8,709*	*5.5*
Personal service	3,056	3.1	7,566	12.6	10,622	6.7
Others	13,200	13.3	4,074	6.8	17,274	10.9
Total (a)	**98,882**		**60,108**		**158,990**	
Total population (b)	136,532		161,509		298,041	
(a) as % of (b)	72.4		37.2		53.3	
Total out of work (c)	13,834		6,999		20,833	
(c) as % of (a)	14.0		11.6		13.1	
Managerial and own account	13,560	15.9	3,419	6.4	16,979	12.3
Operative	71,488	84.1	49,690	93.6	121,178	87.7
Total (excluding out of work)	85,048		53,109		138,157	

Population statistics 1931

Ward	Acres	Population	Persons/acre	Persons/room
Allerton	2,871	16,239	5.66	0.76
Bolton	1,003	11,379	11.34	0.76
Bradford Moor	676	24,261	35.89	0.89
Clayton	1,462	5,491	3.76	0.80
East	385	15,176	39.42	0.85
East Bowling	562	15,894	28.28	0.99
Eccleshill	1,221	14,722	12.06	0.81
Exchange	119	2,717	22.83	1.31
Great Horton	1,288	23,652	18.36	0.81
Heaton	885	16,356	18.48	0.70
Idle	1,693	9,518	5.62	0.84
Listerhills	320	14,583	45.57	0.88
Little Horton	425	14,632	34.43	0.94
Manningham	449	20,907	46.56	0.89
North	353	10,465	29.65	1.07
North Bierley(E)	2,419	15,443	6.38	0.99
North Bierley(W)	1,837	12,694	6.91	0.91
South	304	13,501	44.41	1.03
Thornton	2,252	6,226	2.76	0.95
Tong	2,659	6,568	2.47	0.99
West	162	7,623	47.06	1.17
West Bowling	998	19,994	20.03	0.89
Total	**24,343**	**298,041**	**12.24**	**0.88**

Overall position on the council 1919–38

	Position						Gains					Losses				
	C	Lab	L	Ind	ILP	I Lab	C	Lab	L	Ind	ILP	C	Lab	L	Ind	ILP
1919	28	30	26	–	–	–	0	10	1	–	–	7	0	4	–	–
1920	30	25	29	–	–	–	3	0	4	–	–	0	6	1	–	–
1921	30	24	30	–	–	–	1	3	2	–	–	1	3	2	–	–
1922	33	21	30	–	–	–	3	0	1	–	–	0	4	0	–	–
1923	28	28	28	–	–	–	0	7	3	–	–	5	1	4	–	–
1924	28	28	28	–	–	–	0	0	0	–	–	0	0	0	–	–
1925	27	27	30	–	–	–	0	0	2	–	–	1	1	0	–	–
1926	24	32	28	–	–	–	0	5	1	–	–	4	0	2	–	–
1927	21	38	25	–	–	–	0	4	0	–	–	2	0	2	–	–
1928	21	41	22	–	–	–	1	3	0	–	–	1	0	3	–	–
1929[a]	19	41	23	–	–	–	1	2	2	–	–	1	3	1	–	–
1930	19	44	25	–	–	–	0	1	1	–	–	0	1	1	–	–
1931[b]	27	31	27	2	–	–	8	0	2	2	–	0	12	0	0	–
1932[b]	27	31	27	2	–	–	0	0	1	0	–	0	1	0	0	–
1933	29	30	26	3	–	–	0	1	0	1	–	1	0	1	0	–
1934	23	36	25	2	2	–	0	7	0	0	1	6	0	1	1	0
1935	23	36	25	2	2	–	0	0	0	0	0	0	0	0	0	0
1936	24	35	25	2	2	–	1	1	1	0	0	0	1	2	0	0
1937[c]	17	15	16	2	2	5	–	–	–	–	–	–	–	–	–	–
1938[d]	27	20	23	1	4	4	1	2	0	0	0	0	1	1	1	0

Aldermen 1919–38

1919	Lab–6, Others–15		1929[a]	Lab–8, Others–12
1920	Lab–6, Others–15		1930	Lab–11, Others–11
1921	Lab–6, Others–15		1931	Lab–11, Others–11
1922	Lab–6, Others–15		1932	Lab–11, Others–11
1923	Lab–6, Others–15		1933	Lab–9, Others–13
1924	Lab–7, Others–14		1934	Lab–9, Others–13
1925	Lab–7, Others–14		1935	Lab–9, Others–13
1926	Lab–7, Others–14		1936	Lab–9, Others–13
1927	Lab–8, Others–13		1937[c]	–
1928	Lab–8, Others–13		1938	Lab–5, Others–15

[a] 1929 – 1 aldermanic seat vacant.

[b] 1931, 1932 –1 seat vacant.

[c] 1937 – 3 seats vacant, and 20 aldermanic posts to be filled.

[d] 1938 – 1 seat vacant.

Municipal elections: winning party 1919–28

Ward	1919	1920	1921	1922	1923	1924	1925	1926	1927	1928
Allerton	C	L	L	C	L	L	C	L	L	C
Bolton	L	C	C	L	C	C	L	C	C	L
Bradford Moor	Lab	L	C	Lab	Lab	C	Lab	Lab	Lab	Lab
Clayton	-	-	-	-	-	-	-	-	-	-
East	Lab	C	L	C	C	L	C	C	L	C
East Bowling	Lab	L	Lab	Lab	Lab	Lab	Lab	Lab	Lab	Lab
Eccleshill	L	C	L	L	C	L	L	L	C	C
Exchange	C	L	C	C	L	C	C	L	C	C
Great Horton	Lab	L	C	L	L	C	L	L	C	L
Heaton	C	C	C	C	C	C	C	Lab	C	C
Idle	Lab	C	L	C	L	L	L	Lab	L	L
Listerhills	Lab	C	C	L	C	C	L	C	Lab	Lab
Little Horton	Lab	C	L	Lab	Lab	L	Lab	Lab	Lab	Lab
Manningham	Lab	L	Lab	**Lab**	Lab	Lab	Lab	Lab	Lab	Lab
North	Lab	L	Lab	Lab	Lab	Lab	Lab	Lab	Lab	Lab
North Bierley (E)	Lab	L	L	C	L	L	C	Lab	Lab	Lab
North Bierley (W)	C	L	L	C	L	L	C	L	L	C
South	Lab	C	Lab	Lab	Lab	Lab	Lab	Lab	Lab	Lab
Thornton	L	C	<u>C</u>	L	L	C	L	L	C	L
Tong	Lab	C	L	Lab	C	L	Lab	Lab	L	Lab
West	Lab	L	Lab	Lab	Lab	Lab	Lab	Lab	Lab	Lab
West Bowling	Lab	C	L	Lab	Lab	L	L	Lab	L	Lab

Municipal elections: party wins per year 1919–28

	1919	1920	1921	1922	1923	1924	1925	1926	1927	1928
C	4	11	7	7	6	7	6	3	6	6
Lab	14	0	5	9	8	5	8	12	9	11
L	3	10	9	5	7	9	7	6	6	4
Other	0	0	0	0	0	0	0	0	0	0
Total	21	21	21	21	21	21	21	21	21	21
Turnout %	55.3	67.5	64.6	65.6	63.9	62.9	62.6	63.9	65.8	63.8
Labour %	51.7	36.8	42.7	43.8	38.3	42.2	46.7	48.9	47.9	48.7

Municipal elections: winning party 1929–36

Ward	1929	1930	1931	1932	1933	1934	1935	1936
Allerton	L	L	C	L	L	C	L	**L**
Bolton	C	C	L	**C**	**C**	**L**	C	C
Bradford Moor	Lab	Lab	C	Lab	Lab	Lab	Lab	Lab
Clayton	-	-	L	L	**C**	L	**L**	**C**
East	C	L	C	C	L	C	**C**	L
East Bowling	Lab	Lab	C	Lab	Lab	ILP	**Lab**	Lab
Eccleshill	Lab	C	C	L	C	C	L	C
Exchange	L	C	C	L	Ind	**C**	**L**	**Ind**
Great Horton	L	C	L	**L**	C	L	L	C
Heaton	C	C	C	C	C	**C**	**C**	**C**
Idle	L	L	L	L	L	L	L	C
Listerhills	Lab	C	C	Lab	Lab	Lab	Lab	L
Little Horton	Lab	Lab	C	Lab	Lab	Lab	**Lab**	Lab
Manningham	Lab	Lab	Ind	Lab	Lab	Ind	**Lab**	**Lab**
North	Lab	Lab	C	Lab	Lab	Lab	**Lab**	**Lab**
North Bierley (E)	Lab	Lab	C	Lab	Lab	C	**Lab**	**Lab**
North Bierley (W)	L	Lab	C	L	Lab	C	L	**Lab**
South	Lab	L	Ind	Lab	Lab	Lab	**Lab**	Lab
Thornton	L	C	L	L	**C**	**L**	**L**	C
Tong	Lab	L	L	Lab	L	L	**ILP**	**L**
West	Lab	Lab	L	Lab	Lab	Lab	Lab	Lab
West Bowling	Lab	L	C	Lab	L	Lab	**Lab**	Lab

Municipal elections: party wins per year 1929–36

	1929	1930	1931	1932	1933	1934	1935	1936
C	3	7	13	3	6	7	3	7
Lab	12	8	0	11	10	7	10	10
L	6	6	7	8	5	6	8	4
Other	0	0	2	0	1	2	1	1
Total	21	21	22	22	22	22	22	22
Turnout %	55.0	52.5	62.9	54.1	50.5	50.7	43.7	40.9
Labour %	52.1	44.2	34.9	48.0	50.8	45.1	44.3	46.5

Municipal elections: winning party 1937–38

Ward	1937 (1)	1937 (2)	1937 (3)	1938
Allerton	L	C	L	L
Bolton	C	L	C	C
Bradford Moor	Lab	Lab	Lab	Lab
Clayton	**L**	**L**	**C**	**L**
East Bowling	ILP	Lab	Lab	Lab
Eccleshill	C	L	C	C
Exchange	Lab	Lab	Ind	Lab
Great Horton	L	L	C	**C**
Heaton	C	C	Ind	**Ind**
Idle	**L**	**C**	**L**	**L**
Listerhills	-	-	-	L
Little Horton	I Lab	C	Lab	Lab
Manningham	I Lab	I Lab	Lab	Lab
North East	C	Lab	L	C
North Bierley (E)	C	C	L	Lab
North Bierley (W)	I Lab	C	L	**L**
South	Lab	Lab	Lab	Lab
Thornton	L	L	C	C
Tong	Wkrs	ILP	C	C
West Bowling	Lab	L	Lab	C

Municipal elections: party wins per year 1937–38

	1937	1938
C	17	7
Lab	15	7
L	16	5
Other	9	1
Total	57	20
Turnout %	**58.4**	**38.0**
Labour %	**36.0**	**44.7**

Municipal elections: party wins per ward 1919–36

	C	Lab	L	Other	Total	Turnout %	Labour % of all votes
Allerton	6	0	12	0	18	58.1	38.4
Bolton	12	0	6	0	18	53.1	32.4
Bradford Moor	3	14	1	0	18	54.7	54.6
Clayton	2	0	4	0	6	60.7	34.1
East	11	1	6	0	18	60.1	41.5
East Bowling	1	15	1	1	18	57.7	54.0
Eccleshill	9	1	8	0	18	58.9	34.3
Exchange	10	0	6	2	18	45.9	32.2
Great Horton	6	1	11	0	18	57.2	37.5
Heaton	17	1	0	0	18	64.3	37.5
Idle	3	2	13	0	18	61.1	28.8
Listerhills	7	8	3	0	18	56.5	44.5
Little Horton	2	14	2	0	18	60.6	52.9
Manningham	0	15	1	2	18	56.4	55.9
North	1	16	1	0	18	59.1	56.7
North Bierley (E)	4	10	2	0	18	63.2	47.7
North Bierley (W)	6	3	9	0	18	60.1	40.7
South	1	15	1	1	18	55.4	55.2
Thornton	7	0	11	0	18	65.5	25.6
Tong	2	7	8	1	18	70.7	43.4
West	0	16	2	0	18	58.6	53.9
West Bowling	2	10	6	0	18	59.7	49.3
Total	**112**	**149**	**114**	**7**	**384**	**58.6**	**45.0**

Seats won by Labour as a percentage of all wins 1919–36　　　　　　　**38.8**

Municipal elections: party wins per ward 1937–38

	C	Lab	L	Other	Total	Turnout %	Labour % of all votes
Allerton	1	0	3	0	4	49.7	26.8
Bolton	3	0	1	0	4	44.7	33.1
Bradford Moor	0	4	0	0	4	52.9	53.4
Clayton	1	0	3	0	4	-	-
East Bowling	0	3	0	1	4	37.9	45.5
Eccleshill	3	0	1	0	4	46.4	24.9
Exchange	0	3	0	1	4	50.4	48.0
Great Horton	2	0	2	0	4	60.3	35.0
Heaton	2	0	0	2	4	49.2	0
Idle	1	0	3	0	4	-	-
Listerhills	0	0	1	0	1	38.5	41.9
Little Horton	1	2	0	1	4	49.8	42.7
Manningham	0	2	0	2	4	45.6	50.4
North East	2	1	1	0	4	51.4	47.2
North Bierley (E)	2	1	1	0	4	55.5	46.7
North Bierley (W)	1	0	2	1	4	58.4	0
South	0	4	0	0	4	44.9	66.5
Thornton	2	0	2	0	4	45.4	43.5
Tong	2	0	0	2	4	53.5	8.8
West Bowling	1	2	1	0	4	49.6	47.9
Total	**24**	**22**	**21**	**10**	**77**	**49.0**	**38.4**

Seats won by Labour as a percentage of all wins 1937–38　　　　　**28.6**

Seats won by Labour as a percentage of all wins 1919–38　　　　　**37.1**

Parliamentary election results

Central constituency
(the following wards [1918 boundaries] were included in Central:
East, Exchange,Manningham, North, South, West)

General election	Winner	Conservative %	Labour %	Liberal %
14 Dec. 1918	Co C	51.0	31.3	17.7
15 Nov. 1922	Lab	36.1	42.4	21.5
6 Dec. 1923	Lab	30.4	44.6	25.0
29 Oct. 1924	C	51.7	48.3	-
30 May 1929	Lab	41.0	59.0	-
27 Oct. 1931	C	61.4	38.6	-
14 Nov. 1935	Lab	48.2	51.8	-

East constituency
(the following wards [1918 boundaries] were included in East:
Bradford Moor, East Bowling, Tong, West Bowling)

General election	Winner	Conservative %	Labour %	Liberal %
14 Dec. 1918[a]	Co NDP	-	37.9	21.0
15 Nov. 1922[b]	Lab	-	45.4	21.4
6 Dec. 1923	Lab	23.5	48.1	28.4
29 Oct. 1924	L	-	49.9	50.1
30 May 1929	Lab	-	54.7	45.3
27 Oct. 1931[c]	C	58.8	41.2 (ILP)	-
14 Nov. 1935[d]	C	33.0	21.7	18.7

[a] 1918 – Coalition NDP candidate gained 41.1% of poll.
[b] 1922 – National Liberal gained 33.2% of poll.
[c] 1931 – ILP candidate did not have official endorsement of Labour Party.
[d] 1935 – ILP candidate gained 26.6 % of poll.

Parliamentary election results *(continued)*

North constituency
(the following wards [1918 boundaries] were included in North:
Allerton, Bolton, Eccleshill, Heaton, Idle, Thornton)

General election	Winner	Conservative %	Labour %	Liberal %
14 Dec. 1918	Co C	49.7	29.2	21.1
15 Nov. 1922	C	36.5	31.5	32.0
6 Dec. 1923	L	33.3	32.7	34.0
29 Oct. 1924	C	39.6	32.7	27.7
30 May 1929	Lab	35.4	41.0	23.6
27 Oct. 1931	C	71.8	28.2	-
14 Nov. 1935[a]	C	53.1	35.2	-

[a] 1935 – Independent candidate gained 11.7% of the poll.

South constituency
(the following wards [1918 boundaries] were included in South:
Great Horton, Listerhills, Little Horton, North Bierley [East],
North Bierley [West])

General election	Winner	Conservative %	Labour %	Liberal %
14 Dec. 1918[a]	Co C	44.5	-	24.6
15 Nov. 1922	**L**	26.7	35.3	38.0
6 Dec. 1923	L	28.1	34.9	37.0
29 Oct. 1924	Lab	32.4	39.0	28.6
30 May 1929	Lab	25.3	48.9	25.8
27 Oct. 1931	L	-	33.7	66.3
14 Nov. 1935	L	-	41.6	58.4

[a] 1918 – Cooperative candidate gained 30.9% of poll.

Allerton ward

Candidate	Party	Votes	%	Electors	Turnout	Gains
1919						
J.W. Longley*	C	1,526	52.2	5,322	55.0	-
W. Mackinder	Lab	1,400	47.8			
Total votes		2,926				
1920						
T.E. Precious*	L	2,347	67.5	5,238	66.4	-
W.J. Riley	Lab	1,130	32.5			
Total votes		3,477				
1921						
W. Sutcliffe*	L	2,122	63.4	5,282	63.4	-
W. Mackinder	Lab	1,226	36.6			
Total votes		3,348				
1922						
J.W Longley*	C	2,022	61.5	5,277	62.3	-
H. Milward	Lab	1,268	38.5			
Total votes		3,290				
1923						
A. Hill	L	2,326	64.5	5,332	67.7	-
Mrs J. Clayton	Coop	1,282	35.5			
Total votes		3,608				
1924						
W. Sutcliffe*	L	2,095	61.0	5,398	63.6	-
T. Battersby	Lab	1,337	39.0			
Total votes		3,432				
1925						
J.W Longley*	C	2,066	59.2	5,528	63.1	-
T. Battersby	Lab	1,421	40.8			
Total votes		3,487				
1926						
A. Hill*	L	2,232	56.8	5,812	67.7	-
T. Battersby	Lab	1,701	43.2			
Total votes		3,933				

Allerton ward *(continued)*

Candidate	Party	Votes	%	Electors	Turnout	Gains
1927						
C. Raper	L	2,707	58.0	6,789	68.7	-
T. Battersby	Lab	1,958	42.0			
Total votes		4,665				
1928						
F.J. Cowie*	C	2,536	52.1	7,283	66.9	-
T. Battersby	Lab	2,333	47.9			
Total votes		4,869				
1929						
S. Packett	L	2,473	54.2	8,264	55.3	-
Mrs N. Flenburgh	Lab	2,093	45.8			
Total votes		4,566				
1930						
C. Raper*	L	2,868	65.6	8,584	51.0	-
H.G. Green	Lab	1,507	34.4			
Total votes		4,375				
1931						
F.J. Cowie*	C	3,886	68.7	8,641	65.4	-
F. Sunderland	Lab	1,767	31.3			
Total votes		5,653				
1932						
S. Packett*	L	2,711	55.2	9,263	53.0	-
F. Sunderland	Lab	2,201	44.8			
Total votes		4,912				
1933						
D. Hellewell	L	3,190	61.1	9,992	52.3	-
C. Bloor	Lab	2,034	38.9			
Total votes		5,224				
1934						
W. Watmuff*	C	2,707	56.1	10,138	47.6	-
C. Bloor	Lab	2,117	43.9			
Total votes		4,824				

Allerton ward *(continued)*

Candidate	Party	Votes	%	Electors	Turnout	Gains
1935						
S. Packett*	L	2,818	60.3	10,444	44.7	-
Mrs E. Brett	Lab	1,853	39.7			
Total votes		4,671				
1936						
D. Hellewell*	L	Unopp.	-		-	-
1937						
D. Hellewell*	L	3,023	22.2	8,228	65.5	-
F.J. Cowie*	C	2,841	20.9			
S. Packett*	L	2,696	19.8			
J.A. Sullivan	Ind	2,008	14.7			
Mrs A. Barber	Lab	1,578	11.6			
E.A. Windle	Lab	1,479	10.9			
Total votes		13,625				
Total voters		5,393				
(3 elected)						
1938						
S. Packett*	L	1,829	64.8	8,298	34.0	-
Mrs A. Barber	Lab	993	35.2			
Total votes		2,822				

Overall Labour vote:		**Overall turnout:**	
1919–36	**38.4%**	**1919–36**	**58.1%**
1937–38	**26.8%**	**1937–38**	**49.7%**

Bolton ward

Candidate	Party	Votes	%	Electors	Turnout	Gains
1919						
P.L. Craven*	L	1,023	60.0	3,646	46.8	-
G. Withey	Lab	682	40.0			
Total votes		1,705				
1920						
R.S. Dawson	C	1,862	72.6	3,700	69.3	-
A.R. Ellis	Lab	702	27.4			
Total votes.		2,564				
1921						
W.H. Brocklehurst*	C	1,724	74.5	3,748	61.7	-
A.R. Ellis	Lab	589	25.5			
Total votes		2,313				
1922						
T.I. Clough*	L	1,484	64.9	3,692	61.9	-
T. Ashworth	Lab	803	35.1			
Total votes		2,287				
1923						
H. Sugden	C	1,577	67.6	3,743	62.3	-
A.M. Emsley	Lab	755	32.4			
Total votes		2,332				
1924						
T.J. Robinson	C	1,830	72.0	3,820	66.5	-
A.M. Emsley	Lab	710	28.0			
Total votes		2,540				
1925						
T.I. Clough*	L	1,650	70.5	3,877	60.3	-
A.M. Emsley	Lab	689	29.5			
Total votes		2,339				
1926						
H. Sugden*	C	1,593	66.2	4,006	60.0	-
W. Radford	Lab	812	33.8			
Total votes		2,405				

Bolton ward (*continued*)

Candidate	Party	Votes	%	Electors	Turnout	Gains
1927						
T.J. Robinson*	C	1,816	67.4	4,119	65.4	-
Mrs G.T. Meggison	Lab	877	32.6			
Total votes		2,693				
1928						
T.I. Clough*	L	1,683	63.3	4,898	54.2	-
J.M. Halliday	Lab	974	36.7			
Total votes		2,657				
1929						
F.W. Hutchinson	C	1,560	57.5	5,677	47.8	-
A.M. Emsley	Lab	1,152	42.5			
Total votes		2,712				
1930						
T.J. Robinson*	C	1,870	68.0	5,642	48.8	-
A.M. Emsley	Lab	881	32.0			
Total votes		2,751				
1931						
T.I. Clough*	L	2,265	73.7	5,662	54.3	-
W. Ainsworth	Lab	810	26.3			
Total votes		3,075				
1932						
Mrs H. Drake*	C	Unopp.	-		-	-
1933						
G.R. Rose	C	Unopp.	-		-	-
1934						
T.I. Clough*	L	Unopp.	-		-	-
1935						
Mrs H. Drake*	C	1,198	61.9	5,931	32.6	-
J.M. Halliday	Lab	738	38.1			
Total votes		1,936				

Bolton ward *(continued)*

Candidate	Party	Votes	%	Electors	Turnout	Gains
1936						
J.R. Rose*	C	1,370	71.2	6,017	32.0	-
A.E. Setchfield	Lab	554	28.8			
Total votes		1,924				
1937						
T.J. Robinson*	C	1,914	19.9	6,519	52.5	-
T.I. Clough*	L	1,813	18.8			
Mrs H. Drake*	C	1,707	17.7			
Miss F.J. Dale	Ind	1,200	12.4			
R. Thorpe	Lab	1,038	10.8			
A.E. Setchfield	Lab	1,022	10.6			
J. Foster	Lab	947	9.8			
Total votes		9,641				
Total voters		3,422				
(3 elected)						
1938						
E.V. Heaton	C	1,579	64.2	6,649	37.0	-
C. Finlay	Lab	882	35.8			
Total votes		2,461				

Overall Labour vote:			**Overall turnout:**		
1919–36	**32.4%**		**1919–36**	**58.1%**
1937–38	**33.1%**		**1937–38**	**44.7%**

Bradford Moor ward

Candidate	Party	Votes	%	Electors	Turnout	Gains
1919						
W. Leach	Lab	2,898	63.8	9,908	45.8	Lab from C
J. Conchar	Ind	1,641	36.2			
Total votes		4,539				
1920						
D. Astley	L	3,336	55.3	9,974	60.5	L from Lab
J.H. Palin*	Lab	2,702	44.7			
Total votes		6,038				
1921						
A. Collinson	C	3,180	52.6	10,072	60.1	C from Lab
Mrs J. Clayton*	Lab	2,871	47.4			
Total votes		6,051				
1922						
J.H. Palin	Lab	3,567	51.7	10,325	66.9	Lab from L
W. Whittingham*	L	3,336	48.3			
Total votes		6,903				
1923						
A. Conway	Lab	3,449	56.5	10,563	57.8	Lab from L
R.C. Denby	L	2,652	43.5			
Total votes		6,101				
1924						
G. Langley	C	3,282	51.2	10,601	60.5	-
C. Fitzgerald	Lab	3,131	48.8			
Total votes		6,413				
1925						
J.H. Palin MP*	Lab	3,151	90.0	11,085	31.6	-
J. Bottomley	Ind	351	10.0			
Total votes		3,502				
1926						
A.W. Goodison	Lab	3,690	54.2	11,368	59.9	Lab from L
F. Pattison	L	3,124	45.8			
Total votes		6,814				

Bradford Moor ward *(continued)*

Candidate	Party	Votes	%	Electors	Turnout	Gains
1927						
C.H. Tarbuck	Lab	3,924	54.7	11,696	61.4	Lab from C
G.A. Langley*	C	3,253	45.3			
Total votes		7,177				
1928						
J.H. Palin MP*	Lab	3,901	52.7	11,734	63.1	-
F. Pattison	L	3,506	47.3			
Total votes		7,407				
1929						
A.W. Goodison*	Lab	3,665	60.9	12,558	47.9	-
R. Sharp	C	2,350	39.1			
Total votes		6,015				
1930						
J. Shee*	Lab	3,305	52.0	12,459	51.0	-
R. Sharp	C	3,051	48.0			
Total votes		6,356				
1931						
R. Sharp	C	4,802	59.4	12,537	64.4	C from Lab
J.H. Palin*	Lab	3,278	40.6			
Total votes		8,080				
1932						
J.H. Palin	Lab	3,798	53.0	12,452	57.6	-
P. Pattison	L	3,371	47.0			
Total votes		7,169				
1933						
J. Shee*	Lab	4,448	59.9	12,458	59.6	-
Ms N. Hughes	C	2,972	40.1			
Total votes		7,420				
1934						
W. Brooke	Lab	3,815	59.0	12,924	50.0	Lab from C
R. Sharp*	C	2,650	41.0			
Total votes		6,465				

Bradford Moor ward *(continued)*

Candidate	Party	Votes	%	Electors	Turnout	Gains
1935						
S. Rennard*	Lab	3,407	59.4	13,195	43.5	-
R. Sharp	C	2,331	40.6			
Total votes		5,738				
1936						
J. Shee*	Lab	3,480	55.7	13,274	47.1	-
R. Sharp	C	2,772	44.3			
Total votes		6,252				
1937						
S. Rennard*	Lab	3,062	18.3	9,342	64.6	-
J. Shee*	Lab	3,028	18.1			
J. Harrison*	Lab	2,883	17.3			
R. Sharp	C	2,775	16.6			
W.H. Dean	L	2,511	15.0			
H.T. Manknell	C	2,445	14.6			
Total votes		16,704				
Total voters		6,038				
(3 elected)						
1938						
J. Harrison*	Lab	2,007	52.8	9,270	41.0	-
Rev J.B. Allen	C	1,794	47.2			
Total votes		3,801				

Overall Labour vote: **Overall turnout:**
1919–36   54.6%   1919–36   54.7%
1937–38   53.4%   1937–38   52.9%

Clayton ward
(created by extension of the borough in 1931)

Candidate	Party	Votes	%	Electors	Turnout	Gains
1931						
H. Boyes*	L	1,201	65.7	2,719	67.2	-
L. Jagger	Lab	626	34.3			
Total votes		1,827				
1932						
A. Ward*	L	1,150	75.6	2,768	55.0	-
T. Stott	Lab	372	24.4			
Total votes		1,522				
1933						
W.A. Leach	C	Unopp.	-		-	-
1934						
H. Boyes*	L	982	57.5	2,843	60.1	-
H. Wardman	Lab	726	42.5			
Total votes		1,708				
1935						
A. Ward*	L	Unopp.	-		-	-
1936						
W.A. Leach*	C	Unopp.	-		-	-
1937						
W. Hindle	L	Unopp.	-		-	-
H. Boyes*	L	Unopp.				
W.A. Leach*	C	Unopp.				
(3 elected)						
1938						
B. Galloway	L	Unopp.	-		-	-

Overall Labour vote:			**Overall turnout:**	
1919–36	**34.1%**		**1919–36**	**60.7%**
1937–38	**-**		**1937–38**	**-**

East ward
(merged with North ward to form North East ward in 1937 reorganisation)

Candidate	Party	Votes	%	Electors	Turnout	Gains
1919						
E. O'Neill	Lab	1,807	44.8	6,923	58.2	Lab from C
J. Haley*	C	1,400	34.7			
J. Speight	L	824	20.4			
Total votes		4,031				
1920						
H. Hammond	C	3,151	67.9	7,011	66.2	-
J. Smith	Lab	1,487	32.1			
Total votes		4,638				
1921						
G. Walker*	L	2,960	64.3	7,045	65.4	-
J.H. Palin	Lab	1,646	35.7			
Total votes		4,606				
1922						
T. Thornton	C	2,953	60.4	7,027	69.6	C from Lab
F. Egan	Lab	1,939	39.6			
Total votes		4,892				
1923						
F.S. Bottomley	C	2,527	60.5	7,068	59.1	-
F. Egan	Lab	1,647	39.5			
Total votes		4,174				
1924						
G. Walker*	L	2,887	66.2	7,032	62.0	-
A.R. Ellis	Lab	1,475	33.8			
Total votes		4,362				
1925						
T. Thornton*	C	2,538	54.7	7,179	64.6	-
H. Millward	Lab	2,099	45.3			
Total votes		4,637				

East ward *(continued)*

Candidate	Party	Votes	%	Electors	Turnout	Gains
1926						
E. Brooks*	C	2,312	51.6	7,072	63.4	-
J. Shee	Lab	2,171	48.4			
Total votes		4,483				
1927						
J.W. Turner*	L	2,707	54.5	7,165	69.3	-
J. Shee	Lab	2,256	45.5			
Total votes		4,963				
1928						
T. Thornton*	C	2,424	51.5	7,065	66.6	-
J. Shee	Lab	2,282	48.5			
Total votes		4,706				
1929						
E. Brooks*	C	2,132	50.2	7,566	56.1	-
J. Hey	Lab	2,112	49.8			
Total votes		4,244				
1930						
J.W. Turner*	L	2,298	58.9	7,458	52.3	-
J. Hey	Lab	1,603	41.1			
Total votes		3,901				
1931						
G.A. Hirst	C	3,518	71.9	7,544	64.9	C from Lab
W.H. Semper	Lab	1,375	28.1			
Total votes		4,893				
1932						
E. Brooks*	C	2,297	56.7	7,436	54.5	-
W.H. Semper	Lab	1,755	43.3			
Total votes		4,052				
1933						
J.W. Turner*	L	2,044	54.8	7,307	51.1	-
W.H. Semper	Lab	1,689	45.2			
Total votes		3,733				

East ward *(continued)*

Candidate	Party	Votes	%	Electors	Turnout	Gains
1934						
G.A. Hirst*	C	2,279	56.1	7,376	55.1	-
F. Ratcliffe	Lab	1,782	43.9			
Total votes		4,061				
1935						
H.J. White*	C	Unopp.	-		-	-
1936						
J.W. Turner*	L	1,880	55.6	7,512	45.0	-
J. Emmott	Lab	1,504	44.4			
Total votes		3,384				

Overall Labour vote:			**Overall turnout:**	
1919–36	**34.1%**		**1919–36**	**60.7%**
1937–38	**-**		**1937–38**	**-**

East Bowling ward

Candidate	Party	Votes	%	Electors	Turnout	Gains
1919						
M.F. Titterington	Lab	2,725	67.0	7,376	55.2	Lab from C
A. Booth*	C	825	20.3			
W. Cook	L	518	12.7			
Total votes		4,068				
1920						
R. Peel	L	2,535	52.3	7,412	65.4	L from Lab
R. Hill*	Lab	2,309	47.7			
Total votes		4,844				
1921						
R. Hill	Lab	2,703	58.7	7,539	61.1	Lab from L
L.J. Parker*	L	1,905	41.3			
Total votes		4,608				
1922						
M.F. Titterington*	Lab	2,679	53.4	7,561	66.4	-
F.W. Hutchinson	C	1,313	26.2			
L.J. Parker	L	1,027	20.5			
Total votes		5,019				
1923						
R.C. Ruth	Lab	2,399	51.1	7,594	61.9	Lab from L
R. Peel*	L	2,298	48.9			
Total votes		4,697				
1924						
H.V. Tewson*	Lab	2,819	54.5	7,611	68.0	-
R. Peel	L	2,355	45.5			
Total votes		5,174				
1925						
M.F. Titterington*	Lab	2,888	60.6	7,757	61.5	-
Mrs E. Mitchell	C	1,880	39.4			
Total votes		4,768				

East Bowling ward (continued)

Candidate	Party	Votes	%	Electors	Turnout	Gains
1926						
R.C. Ruth*	Lab	2,845	56.6	7,779	64.6	-
W.M. Morrison	L	2,179	43.4			
Total votes		5,024				
1927						
W. Leach*	Lab	2,917	60.7	7,660	62.7	-
T. McEvoy	C	1,886	39.3			
Total votes		4,803				
1928						
M.F. Titterington*	Lab	2,843	61.7	7,755	59.4	-
T. McEvoy	C	1,765	38.3			
Total votes		4,608				
1929						
R.C. Ruth*	Lab	2,814	61.2	8,190	56.1	-
J. Hepworth	C	1,781	38.8			
Total votes		4,595				
1930						
T.K. Wilkinson	Lab	1,947	51.4	8,011	47.3	-
A. Gissing	C	1,843	48.6			
Total votes		3,790				
1931						
J. Clough	C	2,568	51.0	7,942	63.4	C from Lab
J. Cariss*	Lab	2,464	49.0			
Total votes		5,032				
1932						
R.C. Ruth*	Lab	2,380	53.5	7,930	56.1	-
L.J. Parker	L	2,065	46.5			
Total votes		4,445				
1933						
T.K. Wilkinson*	Lab	2,383	56.9	7,915	52.9	-
B.G. Whitaker	L	1,807	43.1			
Total votes		4,190				

East Bowling ward *(continued)*

Candidate	Party	Votes	%	Electors	Turnout	Gains
1934						
J. Cariss	ILP	1,962	46.6	7,726	54.5	ILP from C
J. Clough*	C	1,501	35.7			
Mrs N. Feinburgh	Lab	746	17.7			
Total votes		4,209				
1935						
R.C. Ruth*	Lab	Unopp.	-		-	-
1936						
T.K. Wilkinson*	Lab	969	54.7	7,458	23.8	-
J.W. Jowett	ILP	803	45.3			
Total votes		1,772				
1937						
J. Cariss*	ILP	1,777	13.5	8,708	51.8	-
M.F. Titterington	Lab	1,729	13.2			
R.C. Ruth*	Lab	1,572	12.0			
T.K. Wilkinson*	Lab	1,535	11.7			
J. Clough	C	1,487	11.3			
Miss G. Land	C	1,320	10.1			
D. Greenwood	C	1,317	10.0			
Mrs E. Garside	ILP	1,304	9.9			
G.E. Wilson	ILP	1,080	8.2			
Total votes		13,121				
Total voters		4,512				
(3 elected)						
1938						
R.C. Ruth*	Lab	1,199	67.5	7,897	22.5	-
Mrs E. Garside	ILP	576	32.5			
Total votes		1,775				

Overall Labour vote: **Overall turnout:**

1919–36	**54.0%**	**1919–36**	**57.7%**
1937–38	**45.5%**	**1937–38**	**37.9%**

Eccleshill ward

Candidate	Party	Votes	%	Electors	Turnout	Gains
1919						
J.A. Guy*	L	1,510	59.2	4,812	53.0	-
Mrs I. Carling	Lab	1,041	40.8			
Total votes		2,551				
1920						
J.W. Mason	C	2,822	73.1	4,833	79.8	C from Lab
J. Cox	Lab	1,037	26.9			
Total votes		3,859				
1921						
H.T. Pullan*	L	2,246	69.4	4,954	65.4	-
J.H. Watson	Lab	992	30.6			
Total votes		3,238				
1922						
J.H. Heap*	L	1,311	35.4	5,013	74.0	-
C. Barnett	C	1,301	35.1			
H. Child	Lab	1,096	29.6			
Total votes		3,708				
1923						
J.W. Mason*	C	2,522	66.8	5,069	74.5	-
H. Child	Lab	1,255	33.2			
Total votes		3,777				
1924						
H.T. Pullan*	L	2,241	67.8	5,164	64.0	-
H. Child	Lab	1,062	32.2			
Total votes		3,303				
1925						
J.H. Heap*	L	1,523	36.7	5,273	78.8	-
C. Barnett	C	1,429	34.4			
H. Child	Lab	1,203	29.0			
Total votes		4,155				

Eccleshill ward *(continued)*

Candidate	Party	Votes	%	Electors	Turnout	Gains
1926						
J.A. Guy	L	2,067	64.5	5,471	58.6	L from C
G. Malton	Lab	1,137	35.5			
Total votes		3,204				
1927						
C. Barnett*	C	1,666	40.6	5,672	72.4	-
J.A. Thistlethwaite	L	1,477	36.0			
G. Malton	Lab	964	23.5			
Total votes		4,107				
1928						
H. Smith	C	1,970	43.1	6,393	71.5	C from L
J. Cox	Lab	1,382	30.2			
J.H. Heap*	L	1,219	26.7			
Total votes		4,571				
1929						
J. Cox	Lab	1,752	40.6	7,589	56.9	Lab from L
A. Brook	L	1,477	34.2			
W. Hudson	C	1,086	25.2			
Total votes		4,315				
1930						
C. Barnett*	C	2,682	60.9	7,877	55.9	-
F. Sunderland	Lab	1,723	39.1			
Total votes		4,405				
1931						
H. Smith*	C	3,443	72.5	7,922	59.9	-
R. Barber	Lab	1,304	27.5			
Total votes		4,747				
1932						
J. Clayton	L	2,018	52.0	7,932	48.9	L from Lab
J. Cox*	Lab	1,862	48.0			
Total votes		3,880				

Eccleshill ward (continued)

Candidate	Party	Votes	%	Electors	Turnout	Gains
1933						
C. Barnett*	C	2,405	61.7	8,020	48.6	-
S. Rennard	Lab	1,492	38.3			
Total votes		3,897				
1934						
H. Smith*	C	2,290	61.6	7,999	46.5	-
J. Cockcroft	Lab	1,430	38.4			
Total votes		3,720				
1935						
J. Clayton*	L	1,828	56.0	7,997	40.8	-
J. Cockcroft	Lab	1,436	44.0			
Total votes		3,264				
1936						
C. Barnett*	C	2,331	65.0	8,037	44.6	-
E.A. Busby	Lab	1,255	35.0			
Total votes		3,586				
1937						
C. Barnett*	C	2,716	25.4	7,908	58.5	-
W. Illingworth*	L	2,523	23.6			
H. Smith*	C	2,432	22.8			
M.R. Barber	Lab	1,624	15.2			
R. Bakes	Ind	1,391	13.0			
Total votes		10,686				
Total voters		4,628				
(3 elected)						
1938						
H. Smith*	C	1,676	59.3	8,162	34.6	-
K. Atkinson	Lab	1,152	40.7			
Total votes		2,828				

Overall Labour vote: **Overall turnout:**

1919–36	**34.3%**	**1919–36**		**58.9%**
1937–38	**24.9%**	**1937–38**		**46.4%**

Exchange ward
(West ward incorporated in it in 1937 reorganisation)

Candidate	Party	Votes	%	Electors	Turnout	Gains
1919						
A.H. Rhodes*	C	472	55.2	2,625	32.6	-
J.H. Heap	L	383	44.8			
Total votes		855				
1920						
T. Pratt*	L	782	69.3	2,826	40.0	-
L. Senior	Lab	347	30.7			
Total votes		1,129				
1921						
J.D. Law	C	915	69.4	2,842	46.4	-
T. Ashworth	Lab	404	30.6			
Total votes		1,319				
1922						
A.H. Rhodes*	C	923	68.3	2,818	47.9	-
N. Gallacher	Lab	428	31.7			
Total votes		1,351				
1923						
W. Illingworth	L	783	64.7	2,778	43.6	L from Lab
J. Harrison*	Lab	428	35.3			
Total votes		1,211				
1924						
J.D. Law*	C	822	64.4	2,777	46.0	-
J.F. McHugh	Lab	455	35.6			
Total votes		1,277				
1925						
A.H. Rhodes*	C	914	67.4	2,712	50.0	-
J.F. McHugh	Lab	442	32.6			
Total votes		1,356				
1926						
W. Illingworth*	L	689	59.8	2,632	43.8	-
Mrs E. Naylor	Lab	463	40.2			
Total votes		1,152				

Exchange ward *(continued)*

Candidate	Party	Votes	%	Electors	Turnout	Gains
1927						
A. Highley	C	797	59.4	2,603	51.5	-
J. Mullarkey	Lab	544	40.6			
Total votes		1,341				
1928						
F. Greenwood*	C	815	62.5	2,495	52.2	-
J. Mullarkey	Lab	488	37.5			
Total votes		1,303				
1929						
D.H. Waterhouse*	L	661	59.8	2,565	43.1	-
L.E. Godfrey	Lab	444	40.2			
Total votes		1,105				
1930						
G.H. Eady*	C	701	63.2	2,356	47.1	-
H. Young	Lab	409	36.8			
Total votes		1,110				
1931						
F. Greenwood*	C	800	72.9	2,256	48.7	-
Miss E. Wilson	Lab	298	27.1			
Total votes		1,098				
1932						
D.H. Waterhouse*	L	685	68.8	2,201	45.2	-
Miss E. Wilson	Lab	197	19.8			
C. Fieldhouse	Nuwm	113	11.4			
Total votes		995				
1933						
G. Hamilton	Ind	483	42.9	2,162	52.1	Ind from C
G. Muff	Lab	358	31.8			
G.H. Eady MP*	C	285	25.3			
Total votes		1,126				
1934						
F. Greenwood*	C	Unopp.	-		-	-

Exchange ward *(continued)*

Candidate	Party	Votes	%	Electors	Turnout	Gains
1935						
D.H. Waterhouse*	L	Unopp.	-		-	-
1936						
D. Hamilton*	Ind	Unopp.	-		-	-
1937						
J.W. Flanagan	Lab	2,016	18.4	7,415	53.6	-
W. Donoghue	Lab	1,840	16.8			
D. Hamilton*	Ind	1,816	16.5			
A.H. Rhodes	C	1,803	16.4			
D.H. Waterhouse*	L	1,799	16.4			
J.F. McHugh	Lab	1,705	15.5			
Total votes		10,979				
Total voters		3,975				
(3 elected)						
1938						
E. Allen	Lab	1,327	44.6	6,384	46.6	Lab from Ind
A. Shaw	C	945	31.7			
J.A. Sullivan	Ind	619	20.8			
C. Pickles	ILP	86	2.9			
Total votes		2,977				

Overall Labour vote: **Overall turnout:**

1919–36	**32.2%**	**1919–36**	**45.9%**
1937–38	**48.0%**	**1937–38**	**50.4%**

Great Horton ward

Candidate	Party	Votes	%	Electors	Turnout	Gains
1919						
T.W. Stamford*	Lab	2,967	42.4	10,735	65.2	-
H. Hudson	L	2,090	29.9			
E.E. Thackery	C	1,941	27.7			
Total votes		6,998				
1920						
W. Turner*	L	5,505	71.0	10,872	71.3	-
Mrs T. Pomeroy	Lab	2,252	29.0			
Total votes		7,757				
1921						
J. Pearson	C	4,551	63.3	11,019	65.3	-
G. Muff	Lab	2,643	36.7			
Total votes		7,194				
1922						
J.W. Sutcliffe	L	4,966	64.0	11,219	69.2	L from Lab
T.W. Stamford*	Lab	2,796	36.0			
Total votes		7,762				
1923						
H. Hudson*	L	4,762	61.5	11,530	67.2	-
H.V. Tewson	Lab	2,985	38.5			
Total votes		7,747				
1924						
J. Pearson*	C	4,184	62.3	11,784	57.0	-
E. Jenkins	Lab	2,537	37.7			
Total votes		6,721				
1925						
L. Jessop	L	4,779	61.3	12,053	64.7	-
A. Haigh	Lab	3,019	38.7			
Total votes		7,798				
1926						
H. Hudson*	L	4,872	61.4	12,108	65.5	-
A. Haigh	Lab	3,064	38.6			
Total votes		7,936				

Great Horton ward (*continued*)

Candidate	Party	Votes	%	Electors	Turnout	Gains
1927						
J. Pearson*	C	4,381	59.8	12,104	60.5	-
A. Haigh	Lab	2,944	40.2			
Total votes		7,325				
1928						
L. Jessop*	L	4,352	60.8	12,387	57.8	-
F. Palframan	Lab	2,803	39.2			
Total votes		7,155				
1929						
H. Hudson*	L	4,313	59.5	13,130	55.2	-
Miss E. Stead	Lab	2,933	40.5			
Total votes		7,246				
1930						
J. Pearson*	C	3,834	60.8	13,107	48.1	-
G. Heighton	Lab	2,470	39.2			
Total votes		6,304				
1931						
L. Jessop*	L	5,784	72.2	13,068	61.3	-
G. Heighton	Lab	2,224	27.8			
Total votes		8,008				
1932						
H. Hudson*	L	Unopp.	-	13,114	-	-
1933						
W.A. Ross*	C	3,303	57.7	13,098	43.7	-
P. Thornton	Lab	2,421	42.3			
Total votes		5,724				
1934						
L. Jessop*	L	3,586	60.4	13,294	44.6	-
G. Green	Lab	2,349	39.6			
Total votes		5,935				

Great Horton ward (*continued*)

Candidate	Party	Votes	%	Electors	Turnout	Gains
1935						
H. Hudson*	L	4,186	65.5	13,466	47.4	-
G. Green	Lab	2,201	34.5			
Total votes		6,387				
1936						
W.A. Ross*	C	3,220	60.6	13,582	39.1	-
F. Whittaker	Lab	2,095	39.4			
Total votes		5,315				
1937						
H. Hudson*	L	3,564	23.4	9,005	60.3	-
L. Jessop*	L	3,187	20.9			
J. Pearson	C	3,147	20.7			
I. Cockcroft	Lab	1,861	12.2			
Mrs I.F. England	Lab	1,742	11.4			
Mrs M. King	Lab	1,737	11.4			
Total votes		15,238				
Total voters		5,430				
(3 elected)						
1938						
W.A. Ross*	C	Unopp.	-		-	-

Overall Labour vote:			Overall turnout:	
1919–36	**37.5%**		1919–36	**57.2%**
1937–38	**35.0%**		1937–38	**60.3%**

Heaton ward

Candidate	Party	Votes	%	Electors	Turnout	Gains
1919						
J.A. Hill*	C	1,902	43.0	7,491	59.1	-
J. Smith	Lab	1,845	41.7			
Mrs M.H. Duff	L	681	15.4			
Total votes		4,428				
1920						
F.V. Gill	C	3,707	65.0	7,649	74.6	-
A. Shaw	Lab	1,998	35.0			
Total votes		5,705				
1921						
A.T. Parkinson*	C	3,331	62.0	7,770	69.1	-
A. Shaw	Lab	2,041	38.0			
Total votes		5,372				
1922						
L. Smith	C	2,585	46.1	7,789	71.9	-
Mrs A. Sykes	Lab	2,047	36.5			
C. Wade	L	971	17.3			
Total votes		5,603				
1923						
F.V. Gill*	C	3,200	60.4	7,898	67.1	-
Mrs A.A. Sykes	Lab	2,096	39.6			
Total votes		5,296				
1924						
A.T. Parkinson*	C	3,202	62.8	7,998	63.8	-
F.C. Woollett	Lab	1,900	37.2			
Total votes		5,102				
1925						
L.W.F.S. Smith*	C	3,220	60.6	8,059	65.9	-
F.C. Woollett	Lab	2,092	39.4			
Total votes		5,312				

Heaton ward *(continued)*

Candidate	Party	Votes	%	Electors	Turnout	Gains
1926						
F.C. Woollett	Lab	2,122	37.7	8,111	69.4	Lab from C
F.V. Gill*	C	2,117	37.6			
E.H. Illingworth	L	1,391	24.7			
Total votes		5,630				
1927						
J.W. Gidley	C	2,247	51.1	8,067	54.5	-
C. Edmondson	Lab	2,150	48.9			
Total votes		4,397				
1928						
L.W.F.S. Smith*	C	3,324	56.7	8,074	72.6	-
F.W. Jowett	Lab	2,540	43.3			
Total votes		5,864				
1929						
J.R. Singleton	C	3,097	58.6	8,459	62.5	C from Lab
Mrs L. Aspinall	Lab	2,186	41.4			
Total votes		5,283				
1930						
A. Smith	C	3,257	67.1	8,350	58.2	-
C. Hewson	Lab	1,599	32.9			
Total votes		4,856				
1931						
L.W.F.S. Smith*	C	4,273	73.3	8,401	69.4	-
C.F. Tumber	Lab	1,556	26.7			
Total votes		5,829				
1932						
J.R. Singleton*	C	3,191	66.6	8,246	58.1	-
C.F. Tumber	Lab	1,600	33.4			
Total votes		4,791				
1933						
A. Smith*	C	2,726	67.1	8,297	48.9	-
C.F. Tumber	Lab	1,334	32.9			
Total votes		4,060				

Heaton ward *(continued)*

Candidate	Party	Votes	%	Electors	Turnout	Gains
1934						
Dr J.J. Bell*	C	Unopp.	-		-	-
1935						
J.R. Singleton*	C	Unopp.	-		-	-
1936						
A. Smith*	C	Unopp.	-		-	-
1937						
J.R. Singleton*	C	2,484	26.5	8,191	49.2	-
L.F.W.S. Smith	C	2,346	25.0			
A.F. Mombert	Ind	2,299	24.5			
A. Smith*	C	2,260	24.1			
Total votes		9,389				
Total voters		4,030				
(3 elected)						
1938						
A.F. Mombert*	Ind	Unopp.	-		-	-

Overall Labour vote: **Overall turnout:**

1919–36	**37.5%**	**1919–36**		**64.3%**
1937–38	**–**	**1937–38**		**49.2%**

Idle ward

Candidate	Party	Votes	%	Electors	Turnout	Gains
1919						
J. Hainsworth	Lab	941	38.3	3,353	73.2	Lab from L
J. Bland	C	777	31.6			
J. Lennon	L	737	30.0			
Total votes		2,455				
1920						
J. Bland	C	1,002	38.0	3,436	76.8	-
H. Stansfield	L	979	37.1			
J.H. Bottomley	Lab	657	24.9			
Total votes		2,638				
1921						
H. Stansfield*	L	1,544	69.0	3,564	62.8	-
T. Watson	Lab	693	31.0			
Total votes		2,237				
1922						
E. Waddilove	C	843	29.5	3,748	76.1	C from Lab
F. Duce	Lab	756	26.5			
F. Oddy	L	733	25.7			
A. Dickinson	Coa	522	18.3			
Total votes		2,854				
1923						
J. Stringer	L	1,150	42.9	3,749	71.5	L from C
A. Crowther*	C	816	30.4			
F. Morton	Coop	715	26.7			
Total votes		2,681				
1924						
H. Stansfield*	L	1,305	43.4	3,811	78.9	-
H. Garnett	C	1,049	34.9			
W.J. Cubitt	Lab	653	21.7			
Total votes		3,007				

Idle ward *(continued)*

Candidate	Party	Votes	%	Electors	Turnout	Gains
1925						
J. Lennon	L	1,279	39.3	4,076	79.9	L from C
E. Waddilove*	C	1,034	31.7			
A.W. Brown	Lab	945	29.0			
Total votes		3,258				
1926						
A.W. Brown	Lab	1,165	35.1	4,310	76.9	Lab from C
E. Whitfield	L	1,131	34.1			
H.L. Nutton*	C	1,020	30.8			
Total votes		3,316				
1927						
H. Stansfield*	L	2,118	67.1	4,575	69.0	-
Mrs L. Carling	Lab	1,039	32.9			
Total votes		3,157				
1928						
J. Lennon*	L	1,542	43.7	4,742	74.4	-
Mrs L. Carling	Lab	1,064	30.2			
W. Mitchell	C	923	26.2			
Total votes		3,529				
1929						
J. Stringer	L	2,024	59.5	5,136	66.3	L from Lab
A.W. Brown*	Lab	1,379	40.5			
Total votes		3,403				
1930						
H. Stansfield*	L	1,662	69.4	5,133	46.7	-
T.V. Child	Lab	734	30.6			
Total votes		2,396				
1931						
J. Lennon*	L	2,474	76.8	5,185	62.2	-
A.M. Emsley	Lab	749	23.2			
Total votes		3,223				

Idle ward *(continued)*

Candidate	Party	Votes	%	Electors	Turnout	Gains
1932						
T. Keighley	L	1,739	68.9	5,152	49.0	-
J.M. Halliday	Lab	786	31.1			
Total votes		2,525				
1933						
H. Stansfield*	L	1,179	57.5	5,171	39.6	-
J.M. Halliday	Lab	871	42.5			
Total votes		2,050				
1934						
J. Lennon*	L	1,701	69.7	5,188	47.1	-
J. Foster	Lab	741	30.3			
Total votes		2,442				
1935						
T. Keighley*	L	1,457	73.3	5,211	38.2	-
J. Foster	Lab	531	26.7			
Total votes		1,988				
1936						
J. Garnett	C	1,667	76.2	5,246	41.7	C from L
Mrs A.H. Feather	Lab	522	23.8			
Total votes		2,189				
1937						
J. Lennon*	L	Unopp.	-		-	-
J. Garnett*	C	Unopp.	-		-	
T. Keighley*	L	Unopp.	-		-	
(3 elected)						
1938						
T. Keighley*	L	Unopp.				-

Overall Labour vote:		Overall turnout:	
1919–36	28.8%	1919–36	61.1%
1937–38	-	1937–38	-

Listerhills ward

Candidate	Party	Votes	%	Electors	Turnout	Gains
1919						
R.F. Smith	Lab	1,750	52.5	6,765	49.3	Lab from C
H.H. Tetley*	C	1,584	47.5			
Total votes		3,334				
1920						
H.H. Tetley*	C	2,319	50.0	6,905	67.1	-
H. Child	Lab	1,588	34.3			
T.R. Hill	L	727	15.7			
Total votes		4,634				
1921						
G.H. Eady	C	2,577	60.9	6,958	60.8	-
H. Child	Lab	1,653	39.1			
Total votes		4,230				
1922						
Mrs M. Law	L	1,976	51.6	6,990	54.8	L from Lab
R.F. Smith*	Lab	1,856	48.4			
Total votes		3,832				
1923						
Dr H. Shackleton*	C	2,496	57.5	7,038	61.7	-
W. Hirst	Coop	1,848	42.5			
Total votes		4,344				
1924						
G.H. Eady*	C	2,335	57.5	7,032	57.8	-
R.F. Smith	Lab	1,728	42.5			
Total votes		4,063				
1925						
Miss M. Law*	L	2,165	53.7	7,063	57.1	-
F. Duce	Lab	1,865	46.3			
Total votes		4,030				
1926						
Dr H. Shackleton*	C	2,231	52.4	7,093	60.0	-
F. Duce	Lab	2,025	47.6			
Total votes		4,256				

Listerhills ward (*continued*)

Candidate	Party	Votes	%	Electors	Turnout	Gains
1927						
F. Duce	Lab	2,323	51.3	6,794	66.6	Lab from C
G.H. Eady*	C	2,205	48.7			
Total votes		4,528				
1928						
J. Bailey	Lab	2,237	53.0	7,064	59.8	Lab from L
Miss M. Law*	L	1,985	47.0			
Total votes		4,222				
1929						
H.J. Wilson	Lab	2,114	51.0	7,345	56.4	Lab from C
Dr H. Shackleton*	C	2,030	49.0			
Total votes		4,144				
1930						
F. Duce*	Lab	1,840	50.7	7,183	50.5	-
A.W. Heap	L	1,788	49.3			
Total votes		3,628				
1931						
F. Wilkinson	C	2,752	61.2	7,168	62.8	C from Lab
J. Bailey*	Lab	1,746	38.8			
Total votes		4,498				
1932						
H.J. Wilson*	Lab	1,880	50.2	7,025	53.3	-
D. Hellewell	L	1,867	49.8			
Total votes		3,747				
1933						
F. Duce*	Lab	1,952	53.1	6,979	52.7	-
A.W. Heap	L	1,725	46.9			
Total votes		3,677				
1934						
P. Thornton	Lab	1,848	52.9	6,840	51.0	Lab from C
H.G. Manknell	C	1,643	47.1			
Total votes		3,491				

Listerhills ward *(continued)*

Candidate	Party	Votes	%	Electors	Turnout	Gains
1935						
H.J. Wilson*	Lab	1,618	53.3	6,729	45.1	-
H.T. Manknell	C	1,415	46.7			
Total votes		3,033				
1936						
J.J. McIntyre	L	1,556	52.2	6,121	48.7	L from Lab
F. Duce*	Lab	1,422	47.8			
Total votes		2,978				
1937						
(no elections held)	-	-	-		-	-
1938						
R.A. Mortimer*	L	1,685	53.6	8,160	38.5	-
F. Duce	Lab	1,317	41.9			
Ms L.M. Fortune	ILP	143	4.5			
Total votes		3,145				

Overall Labour vote:		**Overall turnout:**	
1919–36	**44.5%**	**1919–36**	**56.5%**
1937–38	**41.9%**	**1937–38**	**38.5%**

Little Horton ward

Candidate	Party	Votes	%	Electors	Turnout	Gains
1919						
G.R. Carter	Lab	2,012	63.0	6,329	50.5	Lab from L
M. Wilson	L	1,184	37.0			
Total votes		3,196				
1920						
H.F. Kirby	C	2,467	54.5	6,385	70.9	-
W. Rushworth	Lab	2,060	45.5			
Total votes		4,527				
1921						
J. Hoyle*	L	2,756	56.1	6,474	75.9	-
W. Rushworth	Lab	2,157	43.9			
Total votes		4,913				
1922						
G.R. Carter*	Lab	2,241	50.9	6,478	67.9	-
F. Greenwood	C	2,160	49.1			
Total votes		4,401				
1923						
W. Rushworth	Lab	2,301	51.8	6,522	68.2	Lab from C
H.F. Kirby*	C	2,144	48.2			
Total votes		4,445				
1924						
J. Hoyle*	L	2,666	57.5	6,737	68.8	-
H. Millward	Lab	1,968	42.5			
Total votes		4,634				
1925						
G.R. Carter*	Lab	2,546	53.5	6,841	69.6	-
J. Wright	C	2,213	46.5			
Total votes		4,759				
1926						
W. Bateson	Lab	2,503	57.3	6,855	63.7	-
W.E. Collins	L	1,863	42.7			
Total votes		4,366				

Little Horton ward *(continued)*

Candidate	Party	Votes	%	Electors	Turnout	Gains
1927						
E. Jenkins	Lab	2,660	58.2	6,739	67.8	Lab from L
G. Drake	C	1,910	41.8			
Total votes		4,570				
1928						
G.R. Carter*	Lab	2,458	56.2	6,787	64.4	-
H. Mitchell	C	1,915	43.8			
Total votes		4,373				
1929						
W. Bateson*	Lab	2,325	64.6	7,203	50.0	-
J.S. Cowling	L	1,273	35.4			
Total votes		3,598				
1930						
E. Jenkins*	Lab	1,894	55.6	7,103	48.0	-
D. Pearson	C	1,513	44.4			
Total votes		3,407				
1931						
D. Pearson	C	2,554	59.4	7,078	60.8	C from Lab
J. Hey	Lab	1,749	40.6			
Total votes		4,303				
1932						
G.R. Carter	Lab	2,326	58.5	7,091	56.0	-
H.T. Manknell	C	1,648	41.5			
Total votes		3,974				
1933						
J. Bailey	Lab	2,199	58.1	7,054	53.7	-
H.T. Manknell	C	1,586	41.9			
Total votes		3,785				
1934						
G. Muff	Lab	2,110	57.3	6,961	52.9	Lab from C
D. Pearson*	C	1,571	42.7			
Total votes		3,681				

Little Horton ward *(continued)*

Candidate	Party	Votes	%	Electors	Turnout	Gains
1935						
G.R. Carter*	Lab	Unopp.	-		-	-
1936						
J. Bailey*	Lab	1,634	50.6	7,128	45.3	-
A.E. Warren	C	1,594	49.4			
Total votes		3,228				
1937						
G.R. Carter*	I Lab	1,960	22.5	6,496	57.3	-
A.E. Warren	C	1,602	18.4			
E. Jenkins	Lab	1,379	15.9			
Mrs L. Aspinall	I Lab	1,305	15.0			
G.T. Meggison	Lab	1,294	14.9			
M. Cooney	Lab	1,154	13.3			
Total votes		8,694				
Total voters		3,722				
(3 elected)						
1938						
H.J. Wilson	Lab	1,234	41.1	7,012	42.8	-
P. Singleton	L	1,137	37.9			
Mrs L. Aspinall	I Lab	628	20.9			
Total votes		2,999				

Overall Labour vote:		**Overall turnout:**	
1919–36	**52.9%**	**1919–36**	**60.6%**
1937–38	**42.7%**	**1937–38**	**49.8%**

Manningham ward

Candidate	Party	Votes	%	Electors	Turnout	Gains
1919						
T. Blythe*	Lab	3,094	60.5	9,611	53.2	-
G. Smith	C	2,018	39.5			
Total votes		5,112				
1920						
A.C+A99. Day	L	3,378	54.8	9,823	62.8	L from Lab
L.W. Mackinder	Lab	2,786	45.2			
Total votes		6,164				
1921						
E. Siddle*	Lab	3,372	55.2	9,839	62.1	-
W. Walker	C	2,737	44.8			
Total votes		6,109				
1922						
T. Blythe*	Lab	Unopp.	-	9,933	-	-
1923						
A. Pickles	Lab	3,422	53.7	9,977	63.9	Lab from L
A.C. Day*	L	2,954	46.3			
Total votes		6,376				
1924						
E. Siddle*	Lab	3,303	53.1	9,941	62.6	-
W. Walker	C	2,917	46.9			
Total votes		6,220				
1925						
T. Blythe*	Lab	3,873	56.1	9,964	69.3	-
E.H. Illingworth	L	1,885	27.3			
Mrs Paulson	C	1,146	16.6			
Total votes		6,904				
1926						
G. Muff*	Lab	3,682	58.8	9,943	63.0	-
A.C. Day	L	2,584	41.2			
Total votes		6,266				

Manningham ward *(continued)*

Candidate	Party	Votes	%	Electors	Turnout	Gains
1927						
E. Siddle*	Lab	3,640	58.5	9,732	63.9	-
L.P. Ratcliffe	C	2,578	41.5			
Total votes		6,218				
1928						
A.R. Ellis*	Lab	3,456	59.9	9,822	58.8	-
J.S. Cowling	L	2,315	40.1			
Total votes		5,771				
1929						
R. Hiles	Lab	3,398	64.7	10,327	50.9	-
Mrs E. Paulson	C	1,855	35.3			
Total votes		5,253				
1930						
A.W. Brown*	Lab	2,642	58.2	10,441	43.4	-
A. House	Ind	1,894	41.8			
Total votes		4,536				
1931						
J.E. Haygarth	Ind	3,863	60.2	10,556	60.8	Ind from Lab
A.R. Ellis*	Lab	2,559	39.8			
Total votes		6,422				
1932						
W. Leach	Lab	2,790	52.0	10,262	52.3	-
A. Mombert	Ind	2,452	45.7			
T.F. Tynan	Com	124	2.3			
Total votes		5,366				
1933						
A.W. Brown*	Lab	3,136	92.6	10,313	32.8	-
T.F. Tynan	Com	249	7.4			
Total votes		3,385				

Manningham ward (continued)

Candidate	Party	Votes	%	Electors	Turnout	Gains
1934						
J.G. Haygarth*	Ind	2,530	50.1	10,292	49.0	-
Mrs L. Aspinall	Lab	2,408	47.7			
T.F. Tynan	Com	107	2.1			
Total votes		5,045				
1935						
W. Leach*	Lab	Unopp.	-		-	-
1936						
A.W. Brown*	Lab	Unopp.	-		-	-
1937						
A.W. Brown*	I Lab	2,270	19.3	8,459	56.5	-
Mrs K. Chambers	I Lab	2,029	17.3			
E.A. Busby	Lab	1,627	13.8			
A.R.B. Pridden	C	1,544	13.1			
J. Mullarkey	Lab	1,476	12.5			
L.E. Godfrey	Lab	1,421	12.1			
Mrs M. Dewhirst	Ind	1,395	11.9			
Total votes		11,762				
Total voters		4,779				
(3 elected)						
1938						
E.A. Busby*	Lab	1,761	61.6	8,283	34.5	-
A.R.B. Priddin	C	1,096	38.4			
Total votes		2,857				

Overall Labour vote: **Overall turnout:**
1919–36   **55.9%**   **1919–36**   **56.4%**
1937–38   **50.4%**   **1937–38**   **45.6%**

North ward
(merged with East ward to form North East ward in 1937 reorganisation)

Candidate	Party	Votes	%	Electors	Turnout	Gains
1919						
W. Crossley	Lab	1,495	63.6	4,646	50.6	Lab from C
S.W. Hymans	C	856	36.4			
Total votes		2,351				
1920						
S. Horsfall	L	1,869	60.9	4,763	64.4	L from Lab
J. Dunn	Lab	1,200	39.1			
Total votes		3,069				
1921						
A.T. Sutton*	Lab	1,740	60.5	4,851	59.3	-
T. Johnson	C	1,136	39.5			
Total votes		2,876				
1922						
W.H. Crossley*	Lab	1,659	56.8	4,857	60.2	-
T. Nelson	C	1,263	43.2			
Total votes		2,922				
1923						
F.V. Butler*	Lab	1,776	53.4	4,845	68.6	-
T. Nelson	C	1,548	46.6			
Total votes		3,324				
1924						
J. Harrison*	Lab	1,638	51.5	4,965	64.0	-
T. Nelson	C	1,541	48.5			
Total votes		3,179				
1925						
W.H. Crossley*	Lab	1,798	55.2	4,938	66.0	-
T. Nelson	C	1,459	44.8			
Total votes		3,257				
1926						
F.V. Butler*	Lab	2,067	68.7	4,932	61.0	-
H. Foster	C	941	31.3			
Total votes		3,008				

North ward *(continued)*

Candidate	Party	Votes	%	Electors	Turnout	Gains
1927						
J. Harrison*	Lab	1,953	56.5	4,793	72.2	-
T. Nelson	C	1,506	43.5			
Total votes		3,459				
1928						
W.H. Crossley*	Lab	1,841	64.5	4,894	58.3	-
W. Ackrel	L	1,014	35.5			
Total votes .		2,855				
1929						
F.V. Butler*	Lab	1,912	74.3	5,154	50.0	-
Mrs M.A. Marr	C	663	25.7			
Total votes		2,575				
1930						
J. Harrison*	Lab	1,404	56.1	4,952	50.5	-
H. Jowett	C	1,097	43.9			
Total votes		2,501				
1931						
T. Nelson	C	1,894	60.7	4,928	63.3	C from Lab
T.M. Halliday*	Lab	1,226	39.3			
Total votes		3,120				
1932						
F.V. Butler*	Lab	1,614	59.1	4,858	56.2	-
H.A. Sissling	C	1,012	37.0			
J.E. Durkin	Nuwm	106	3.9			
Total votes		2,732				
1933						
J. Harrison*	Lab	1,442	64.0	4,694	48.0	-
H.A. Sissling	C	812	36.0			
Total votes		2,254				

North ward (*continued*)

Candidate	Party	Votes	%	Electors	Turnout	Gains
1934						
Mrs M.J. Sutton	Lab	1,276	52.9	4,533	53.2	Lab from C
T. Nelson*	C	1,086	45.0			
J. Durkin	Wkrs	50	2.1			
Total votes		2,412				
1935						
F.V. Butler*	Lab	Unopp.	-		-	-
1936						
J. Harrison*	Lab	Unopp.	-		-	-

Overall Labour vote: **Overall turnout:**

1919–36	**56.7%**	**1919–36** **59.1%**
1937–38	**-**	**1937–38** **-**

North East ward
(created from merger of East and North wards in 1937 reorganisation)

Candidate	Party	Votes	%	Electors	Turnout	Gains
1937						
G.A. Hirst	C	2,609	18.1	8,056	61.6	-
F.V. Butler	Lab	2,472	17.2			
J.W. Turner	L	2,443	17.0			
H.J. White	C	2,389	16.6			
A.T. Sutton	Lab	2,279	15.8			
Mrs M.J. Sutton	Lab	2,219	15.4			
Total votes		14,411				
Total voters		4,963				
(3 elected)						
1938						
J.E. Albrow*	C	1,598	49.9	7,829	40.9	-
A.T. Sutton	Lab	1,452	45.4			
C.A. Stainthorpe	ILP	151	4.7			
Total votes		3,201				

Overall Labour vote: **Overall turnout:**
1919–36   -   **1919–36**   -
1937–38   47.2%   **1937–38**   51.4%

North Bierley (East) ward

Candidate	Party	Votes	%	Electors	Turnout	Gains
1919						
W. Hirst*	Lab	1,787	56.9	4,957	63.3	-
F. Schofield	L	1,351	43.1			
Total votes		3,138				
1920						
J.H.Lincoln*	L	2,561	68.6	5,041	74.0	-
E. Jenkins	Lab	1,170	31.4			
Total votes		3,731				
1921						
W.S.Worsman	L	2,150	61.3	5,129	68.3	L from Lab
H. Mitchell*	Lab	1,355	38.7			
Total votes		3,505				
1922						
F. Womersley	C	2,187	59.0	5,123	72.3	C from Lab
W. Hirst*	Lab	1,517	41.0			
Total votes		3,704				
1923						
G. Wilkinson	L	1,895	58.0	5,170	63.2	
H. Mitchell	Lab	1,370	42.0			
Total votes		3,265				
1924						
W.S.Worsman*	L	2,010	61.3	5,226	62.7	
M. Pennock	Lab	1,268	38.7			
Total votes		3,278				
1925						
F.W.Hutchinson	C	1,861	54.1	5,488	62.7	
A. Stott	Lab	1,578	45.9			
Total votes		3,439				
1926						
A. Stott	Lab	2,031	53.2	6,003	63.6	Lab from L
G. Wilkinson*	L	1,789	46.8			
Total votes		3,820				

North Bierley (East) ward *(continued)*

Candidate	Party	Votes	%	Electors	Turnout	Gains
1927						
H. Mitchell	Lab	2,394	51.9	6,534	70.6	Lab from L
W.S.Worsman*	L	2,221	48.1			
Total votes		4,615				
1928						
Mrs A. Meggison	Lab	2,484	55.9	6,775	65.6	Lab from C
S.Y.Dixon	C	1,961	44.1			
Total votes ·		4,445				
1929						
A. Stott*	Lab	2,227	52.3	7,662	55.5	
T. Rawling	L	2,028	47.7			
Total votes		4,255				
1930						
H. Mitchell*	Lab	2,213	46.4	7,838	60.9	
T. Rawling	L	1,407	29.5			
J.K.Hodgson	C	1,151	24.1			
Total votes		4,771				
1931						
W. Smith	C	3,205	58.7	7,813	69.8	C from Lab
Mrs A.Meggison*	Lab	2,252	41.3			
Total votes		5,457				
1932						
A. Stott*	Lab	2,409	55.4	7,852	55.3	
N. Broxholme	L	1,936	44.6			
Total votes		4,345				
1933						
Mrs A.Meggison	Lab	2,489	58.8	7,820	54.2	
C.M.Turner	C	1,746	41.2			
Total votes		4,235				
1934						
W. Smith*	C	2,377	51.1	7,831	59.4	
J. Kennie	Lab	2,277	48.9			
Total votes		4,654				

North Bierley (East) ward *(continued)*

Candidate	Party	Votes	%	Electors	Turnout	Gains
1935						
A. Stott*	Lab	Unopp.				
1936						
Mrs A.Meggison*	Lab	Unopp.				
1937						
W. Smith*	C	3,210	19.9	9,203	62.5	
S. Armitage	C	2,910	18.0			
A. Hudson	L	2,859	17.7			
Mrs A.Meggison*	Lab	2,595	16.1			
A. Stott*	Lab	2,294	14.2			
W.C.Lacey	Lab	2,282	14.1			
Total votes		16,150				
Total voters		5,752				
(3 elected)						
1938						
A. Winterburn	Lab	2,210	49.7	9,177	48.5	Lab from L
A. Hudson*	L	2,058	46.3			
T. Stott	ILP	179	4.0			
Total votes		4,447				

Overall Labour vote: **Overall turnout:**

1919–36	**47.7%**	**1919–36**	**63.2%**
1937–38	**46.7%**	**1937–38**	**55.5%**

North Bierley (West) ward

Candidate	Party	Votes	%	Electors	Turnout	Gains
1919						
O. Holden*	C	1,572	52.3	4,811	62.4	-
E. Fox	Lab	1,432	47.7			
Total votes		3,004				
1920						
W.H. Barraclough*	L	2,405	65.4	4,938	74.5	-
C. Lightowler	Lab	1,275	34.6			
Total votes		3,680				
1921						
I. Smith*	L	2,248	65.4	4,995	68.8	-
I. Holmes	Lab	1,191	34.6			
Total votes		3,439				
1922						
J.W. Lightowler*	C	1,943	63.0	5,158	59.8	-
G. Muff	Lab	1,139	37.0			
Total votes		3,082				
1923						
W.H. Barraclough*	L	2,076	63.8	5,263	61.8	-
F. Duce	Coop	1,177	36.2			
Total votes		3,253				
1924						
I. Smith*	L	1,824	62.0	5,391	54.5	-
J. Stansfield	Lab	1,116	38.0			
Total votes		2,940				
1925						
S. Wilkinson	C	1,893	62.1	5,656	53.9	-
J. Stansfield	Lab	1,154	37.9			
Total votes		3,047				
1926						
W.H. Barraclough*	L	2,231	60.0	6,002	61.9	-
J.W. Blanchfield	Lab	1,487	40.0			
Total votes		3,718				

North Bierley (West) ward *(continued)*

Candidate	Party	Votes	%	Electors	Turnout	Gains
1927						
I. Smith*	L	2,236	54.7	6,304	64.8	-
Mrs W. Nichol	Lab	1,850	45.3			
Total votes		4,086				
1928						
S. Wilkinson*	C	2,229	52.1	6,452	66.4	-
Mrs M.E. Nichol	Lab	2,053	47.9			
Total votes		4,282				
1929						
J. Wilson	L	2,361	55.2	6,944	61.6	L from Lab
A. Haigh	Lab	1,914	44.8			
Total votes		4,275				
1930						
T. Helliwell	Lab	2,485	53.7	7,079	65.4	Lab from L
N.F. Broxholme	L	2,146	46.3			
Total votes		4,631				
1931						
S. Wilkinson*	C	3,118	68.2	7,194	63.5	-
Mrs Woodcock	Lab	1,452	31.8			
Total votes		4,570				
1932						
J. Wilson*	L	2,470	58.1	7,236	58.7	-
J. Bailey	Lab	1,779	41.9			
Total votes		4,249				
1933						
T. Helliwell*	Lab	2,228	54.2	7,370	55.7	-
N. Broxholme	L	1,880	45.8			
Total votes		4,108				
1934						
S. Wilkinson*	C	2,070	51.6	8,245	48.7	-
W.C. Lacey	Lab	1,945	48.4			
Total votes		4,015				

North Bierley (West) ward *(continued)*

Candidate	Party	Votes	%	Electors	Turnout	Gains
1935						
J. Wilson*	L	2,442	57.2	8,613	49.6	-
W.C. Lacey	Lab	1,830	42.8			
Total votes		4,272				
1936						
T. Helliwell*	Lab	Unopp.	-		-	-
1937						
T. Helliwell*	I Lab	3,388	30.3	9,087	58.4	-
S. Wilkinson*	C	2,802	25.0			
W.H. Barraclough	L	2,753	24.6			
W.E. Collins	L	2,247	20.1			
Total votes		11,190				
Total voters		5,305				
(3 elected)						
1938						
W.H. Barraclough*	L	Unopp.	-		-	-

Overall Labour vote:		**Overall turnout:**	
1919–36	**40.7%**	**1919–36**	**60.1%**
1937–38	–	**1937–38**	**58.4%**

South ward

Candidate	Party	Votes	%	Electors	Turnout	Gains
1919						
G.T. Megginson	Lab	1,813	57.1	5,986	53.0	Lab from L
E. Mitchell*	L	700	22.0			
T. Thornton	C	662	20.9			
Total votes		3,175				
1920						
J. Harrison*	C	2,133	59.6	6,110	58.6	-
F. Edmondson	Lab	1,448	40.4			
Total votes		3,581				
1921						
Mrs K. Sykes	Lab	1,953	52.0	6,204	60.6	Lab from L
J.W. Turner*	L	1,804	48.0			
Total votes		3,757				
1922						
G.T. Megginson*	Lab	2,047	53.2	6,200	62.0	-
J.W. Turner	L	1,800	46.8			
Total votes		3,847				
1923						
T. Ashworth	Lab	1,871	54.6	6,249	54.8	Lab from C
A. Paley	C	1,553	45.4			
Total votes		3,424				
1924						
Mrs A.A. Sykes	Lab	1,951	53.6	6,285	57.9	-
J.W. Turner	L	1,690	46.4			
Total votes		3,641				
1925						
F. Egan*	Lab	1,900	50.9	6,309	59.2	-
L.J. Parker	L	1,835	49.1			
Total votes		3,735				
1926						
T. Ashworth*	Lab	2,375	60.4	6,278	62.6	-
L.J. Parker	L	1,555	39.6			
Total votes		3,930				

South ward (*continued*)

Candidate	Party	Votes	%	Electors	Turnout	Gains
1927						
Mrs A. Sykes*	Lab	2,121	56.5	5,971	62.9	-
A.C. Day	L	1,633	43.5			
Total votes		3,754				
1928						
F. Egan*	Lab	1,944	53.2	6,238	58.6	-
L.J. Parker	L	1,709	46.8			
Total votes		3,653				
1929						
T. Ashworth*	Lab	2,295	58.0	6,589	60.0	-
Sir B. Dawson	C	1,660	42.0			
Total votes		3,955				
1930						
E. Webster	L	1,768	51.5	6,494	52.9	L from Lab
H.W. Semper	Lab	1,601	46.6			
J. Bottomley	Ind	67	1.9			
Total votes		3,436				
1931						
E. Fox	Ind	2,254	58.2	6,492	59.7	Ind from Lab
F. Egan*	Lab	1,563	40.3			
J. Bottomley	Ind	58	1.5			
Total votes		3,875				
1932						
T. Ashworth*	Lab	1,993	64.1	6,428	48.4	-
H.J. Bilsborough	Ind	928	29.8			
J.W. Boyle	Nuwm	142	4.6			
J. Bottomley	Ind	46	1.5			
Total votes		3,109				
1933						
Dr D. Black	Lab	2,425	72.7	6,257	53.3	Lab from L
B. Galloway	L	911	27.3			
Total votes		3,336				

South ward (*continued*)

Candidate	Party	Votes	%	Electors	Turnout	Gains
1934						
H.W. Semper	Lab	1,696	60.7	6,045	46.2	Lab from Ind
B. Johnson	Ind	981	35.1			
H. Robinson	I Lab	117	4.2			
Total votes		2,794				
1935						
T. Ashworth*	Lab	Unopp.	-		-	-
1936						
Dr D. Black*	Lab	1,317	85.8	5,601	27.4	-
J. Bottomley	Ind	218	14.2			
Total votes		1,535				
1937						
Dr D. Black*	Lab	2,708	27.3	7,969	55.5	-
T. Ashworth*	Lab	2,519	25.4			
H.W. Semper*	Lab	2,412	24.3			
T. Lund	C	1,847	18.6			
J. Bottomley	Ind	442	4.5			
Total votes		9,928				
Total voters		4,422				
(*3 elected*)						
1938						
A. Walker*	Lab	1,248	48.6	7,601	33.8	-
F. Baxter	C	1,026	40.0			
Ms A.A. Sykes	ILP	292	11.4			
Total votes		2,566				

Overall Labour vote:		**Overall turnout:**	
1919–36	**55.2%**	1919–36	**55.4%**
1937–38	**66.5%**	1937–38	**44.9%**

Thornton ward

Candidate	Party	Votes	%	Electors	Turnout	Gains
1919						
W. Hodgson	L	567	36.6	2,361	65.7	L from C
J. Briggs*	C	542	34.9			
J.W. Ormanroyd	Lab	442	28.5			
Total votes		1,551				
1920						
J. Briggs	C	880	43.2	2,444	83.3	C from L
J. Clegg	L	779	38.3			
J.W. Ormanroyd	Lab	377	18.5			
Total votes		2,036				
1921						
F. Spencer*	C	Unopp.	-	2,497	-	-
1922						
W. Hodgson*	L	978	68.1	2,524	56.9	-
A.R. Ellis	Lab	459	31.9			
Total votes		1,437				
1923						
C. Watkin	L	814	41.1	2,547	77.8	L from C
J. Briggs*	C	713	36.0			
A.R. Ellis	Lab	455	23.0			
Total votes		1,982				
1924						
F. Spencer*	C	1,198	78.3	2,522	60.7	-
Mrs M. Tarbuck	Lab	332	21.7			
Total votes		1,530				
1925						
W. Hodgson*	L	921	44.8	2,571	80.0	-
J. Briggs	C	810	39.4			
Mrs M. Tarbuck	Lab	327	15.9			
Total votes		2,058				

Thornton ward (*continued*)

Candidate	Party	Votes	%	Electors	Turnout	Gains
1926						
C. Watkin*	L	891	43.0	2,703	76.6	-
G. Drake	C	640	30.9			
S. Andrews	Lab	540	26.1			
Total votes		2,071				
1927						
F. Spencer*	C	960	42.1	2,920	78.1	-
T. Prest	L	661	29.0			
S. Andrews	Lab	659	28.9			
Total votes		2,280				
1928						
W. Hodgson*	L	947	39.7	3,058	78.0	-
J. Briggs	C	752	31.5			
S. Andrews	Lab	686	28.8			
Total votes		2,385				
1929						
C. Watkin*	L	1,134	61.7	3,333	55.1	-
C. Hewson	Lab	703	38.3			
Total votes		1,837				
1930						
J. Briggs	C	988	42.3	3,285	71.2	-
Mrs Emmett	Ind	851	36.4			
Mrs L. Aspinall	Lab	499	21.3			
Total votes		2,338				
1931						
W. Hodgson*	L	1,483	78.5	3,304	57.2	-
L.E. Godfrey	Lab	406	21.5			
Total votes		1,889				
1932						
C. Watkin*	L	1,239	76.4	3,291	49.3	-
Mrs N. Fineburgh	Lab	382	23.6			
Total votes		1,621				

Thornton ward *(continued)*

Candidate	Party	Votes	%	Electors	Turnout	Gains
1933						
G. Drake	C	Unopp.	-		-	-
1934						
W. Hodgson*	L	Unopp.	-		-	-
1935						
C. Watkin*	L	Unopp.	-		-	-
1936						
G. Drake*	C	828	63.6	3,332	39.0	-
H. Howard	Lab	473	36.4			
Total votes		1,301				
1937						
C. Watkin*	L	2,100	20.4	6,389	57.2	-
W. Hodgson*	L	2,070	20.1			
G. Drake*	C	1,950	18.9			
H. Howard	Lab	1,531	14.9			
F. Rigby	Lab	1,342	13.0			
Mrs M. Brook	Lab	1,299	12.6			
Total votes		10,292				
Total voters		3,654				
(3 elected)						
1938						
G. Drake*	C	1,125	51.6	6,461	33.7	-
O.H. Jackson	Lab	1,054	48.4			
Total votes		2,179				

Overall Labour vote:		**Overall turnout:**	
1919–36	25.6%	1919–36	65.5%
1937–38	43.5%	1937–38	45.4%

Tong ward

Candidate	Party	Votes	%	Electors	Turnout	Gains
1919						
F. Ratcliffe	Lab	1,223	58.0	3,217	65.6	Lab from C
J.F. Waugh*	C	886	42.0			
Total votes		2,109				
1920						
F. Wilkinson	C	1,297	55.3	3,258	71.9	C from Lab
T.K. Wilkinson	Lab	1,047	44.7			
Total votes		2,344				
1921						
E.T. Bolland*	L	1,397	56.4	3,291	75.3	-
T.K. Wilkinson	Lab	1,082	43.6			
Total votes		2,479				
1922						
F. Ratcliffe*	Lab	1,242	50.6	3,314	74.0	-
E. Brooksbank	C	1,212	49.4			
Total votes		2,454				
1923						
F. Wilkinson*	C	1,306	52.6	3,275	75.9	-
W. Brook	Lab	1,179	47.4			
Total votes		2,485				
1924						
E.T. Bolland*	L	1,382	52.0	3,372	78.8	-
W. Brook	Lab	1,275	48.0			
Total votes		2,657				
1925						
W. Brook	Lab	1,564	55.3	3,434	82.4	-
W.E. Tetley	C	1,264	44.7			
Total votes		2,828				
1926						
A. Tetley	Lab	1,489	57.0	3,441	75.9	Lab from C
F. Wilkinson*	C	1,122	43.0			
Total votes		2,611				

Tong ward *(continued)*

Candidate	Party	Votes	%	Electors	Turnout	Gains
1927						
E.T. Bolland*	L	1,484	54.5	3,428	79.5	-
F.W. Jowett	Lab	1,241	45.5			
Total votes		2,725				
1928						
W. Brook*	Lab	1,355	55.5	3,431	71.1	-
J. Taylor	C	1,059	43.4			
F. Walsh	Com	27	1.1			
Total votes		2,441				
1929						
A. Tetley*	Lab	1,311	55.5	3,612	65.4	-
W.S. Worsman	L	1,052	44.5			
Total votes		2,363				
1930						
E.T. Bolland*	L	1,608	69.2	3,537	65.7	-
H. Siddle	Lab	716	30.8			
Total votes		2,324				
1931						
W. Hutchinson	L	1,651	67.7	3,506	69.5	L from Lab
Mrs N. Feinburgh	Lab	786	32.3			
Total votes		2,437				
1932						
A. Tetley*	Lab	1,219	57.3	3,482	61.1	-
T. Law	C	910	42.7			
Total votes		2,129				
1933						
E.T. Bolland*	L	1,294	62.2	3,486	59.6	-
J.S. Lyness	ILP	785	37.8			
Total votes		2,079				
1934						
W. Hutchinson*	L	1,231	58.4	3,492	60.4	-
G.E. Wilson	ILP	878	41.6			
Total votes		2,109				

Tong ward *(continued)*

Candidate	Party	Votes	%	Electors	Turnout	Gains
1935						
A. Tetley*	ILP	Unopp.	-		-	-
1936						
E.T. Bolland*	L	Unopp.	-		-	-
1937						
A. Tetley*	Wkrs	2,933	28.4	7,900	64.3	-
A. Brown	ILP	2,615	25.3			
Rev J. Savage	C	2,418	23.4			
E.T. Bolland*	L	2,375	23.0			
Total votes		10,341				
Total voters		5,078				
(3 elected)						
1938						
Rev J. Savage*	C	1,518	44.7	7,927	42.8	-
G.E. Wilson	ILP	1,129	33.3			
J.C. Stephenson	Lab	748	22.0			
Total votes		3,395				

Overall Labour vote:
1919–36 43.4%
1937–38 8.8%

Overall turnout:
1919–36 70.7%
1937–38 53.5%

West ward
(merged into Exchange ward in 1937 reorganisation)

Candidate	Party	Votes	%	Electors	Turnout	Gains
1919						
W. Donoghue	Lab	1,262	66.0	4,007	47.7	Lab from L
E. Hoyle*	L	650	34.0			
Total votes		1,912				
1920						
T. Taylor*	L	1,096	46.7	4,095	57.3	
J.W. Flanagan	Lab	934	39.8			
J.J. Roscoe	Ind	316	13.5			
Total votes		2,346				
1921						
J.W. Flanagan	Lab	1,392	51.3	4,144	65.5	Lab from C
G. Smith*	C	1,321	48.7			
Total votes		2,713				
1922						
W. Donoghue*	Lab	1,473	53.9	4,197	65.2	-
G. Smith	C	1,262	46.1			
Total votes		2,735				
1923						
P. Walsh	Lab and UIL	1,331	55.3	4,201	57.3	Lab from L
T. Taylor*	L	1,078	44.7			
Total votes		2,409				
1924						
J.W. Flanagan*	Lab	1,495	54.8	4,232	64.5	-
G. Smith	C	1,233	45.2			
Total votes		2,728				
1925						
J. Coe*	Lab	1,473	51.2	4,309	66.8	-
A.A. McDermott	C	1,404	48.8			
Total votes		2,877				

West ward (*continued*)

Candidate	Party	Votes	%	Electors	Turnout	Gains
1926						
Ms E.K. Chambers*	Lab	1,611	58.1	4,264	65.0	-
J. Briggs	C	1,095	39.5			
J.J. Roscoe	Ind	67	2.4			
Total votes		2,773				
1927						
J.W. Flanagan*	Lab	1,582	58.4	3,812	71.1	-
J.L. Llanwarne	C	1,128	41.6			
Total votes		2,710				
1928						
C. Edmondson	Lab	1,411	55.6	4,178	60.7	-
H.J. White	C	1,127	44.4			
Total votes		2,538				
1929						
J. McHugh*	Lab	1,362	61.5	4,454	49.7	-
G.E. Schoon	C	851	38.5			
Total votes		2,213				
1930						
J.W. Flanagan*	Lab	1,171	55.2	4,077	52.1	-
J. Shaw	C	952	44.8			
Total votes		2,123				
1931						
A. Smith	L	1,383	55.3	4,029	62.1	L from Lab
C. Edmondson*	Lab	1,118	44.7			
Total votes		2,501				
1932						
J.F. McHugh*	Lab	1,081	48.5	3,969	56.2	-
F. Baxter	C	1,042	46.7			
S. Ogden	Nuwm	107	4.8			
Total votes		2,230				

West ward *(continued)*

Candidate	Party	Votes	%	Electors	Turnout	Gains
1933						
J.W. Flanagan*	Lab	1,409	59.9	3,878	60.6	-
F. Baxter	C	942	40.1			
Total votes		2,351				
1934						
M. Cooney	Lab	854	43.1	3,763	52.6	Lab from L
A. Smith*	L	750	37.9			
C. Edmundson	I Lab	377	19.0			
Total votes		1,981				
1935						
J.F. McHugh*	Lab	973	59.6	3,682	44.3	-
F. Baxter	C	659	40.4			
Total votes		1,632				
1936						
E. Allen	Lab	927	57.1	3,088	52.6	-
J.A. Sullivan	Ind	697	42.9			
Total votes		1,624				

Overall Labour vote:		**Overall turnout:**	
1919–36	**53.9%**	**1919–36**	**58.6%**
1937–38	-	**1937–38**	-

West Bowling ward

Candidate	Party	Votes	%	Electors	Turnout	Gains
1919						
W. Bateson*	Lab	2,872	55.6	9,149	56.4	-
W.H. Sykes	L	1,912	37.0			
R. Thorn	NDP	378	7.3			
Total votes		5,162				
1920						
E. Cummings	C	3,441	55.7	9,192	67.2	-
F. Thornton	Lab	2,737	44.3			
Total votes		6,178				
1921						
W.H. Sykes	L	3,651	57.1	9,251	69.1	L from Lab
F. Morton	Lab	2,743	42.9			
Total votes		6,394				
1922						
W. Bateson*	Lab	3,080	53.7	9,271	61.9	-
J. Parkinson	C	2,660	46.3			
Total votes		5,740				
1923						
T. Grundy	Lab	3,030	50.8	9,279	64.3	Lab from C
E. Cummins*	C	2,934	49.2			
Total votes		5,964				
1924						
W.H. Sykes*	L	3,547	57.3	9,349	66.2	-
W. Barber	Lab	2,638	42.7			
Total votes		6,185				
1925						
J.W. Waterhouse	L	3,120	50.1	9,578	65.0	L from Lab
W. Bateson*	Lab	3,107	49.9			
Total votes		6,227				
1926						
Mrs H.A. Grundy*	Lab	3,451	56.7	9,567	63.6	-
W.E. Tetley	C	2,633	43.3			
Total votes		6,084				

West Bowling ward *(continued)*

Candidate	Party	Votes	%	Electors	Turnout	Gains
1927						
W.H. Sykes*	L	3,394	51.5	9,543	69.1	-
H. Wood	Lab	3,198	48.5			
Total votes		6,592				
1928						
H. Wood	Lab	3,330	51.9	9,657	66.5	Lab from L
J.T. Waterhouse*	L	3,090	48.1			
Total votes		6,420				
1929						
Mrs H.A. Grundy*	Lab	3,471	61.0	10,222	55.7	-
L.A. Sellers	C	2,219	39.0			
Total votes		5,690				
1930						
J.T. Waterhouse	L	2,870	52.6	10,160	53.7	-
W. Westman	Lab	2,450	44.9			
J. Gledhill	Com	133	2.4			
Total votes		5,453				
1931						
J.W. Mawson	C	3,735	58.2	10,196	63.0	C from Lab
H. Wood*	Lab	2,568	40.0			
J. Gledhill	Com	119	1.9			
Total votes		6,422				
1932						
Mrs H.A. Grundy*	Lab	2,643	50.2	10,169	51.7	-
E. Mortimer	C	2,404	45.7			
H. Goldthorpe	Nuwm	215	4.1			
Total votes		5,262				
1933						
J.T. Waterhouse*	L	2,283	43.8	10,137	51.5	-
F. Sunderland	Lab	2,209	42.3			
T. Stott	ILP	726	13.9			
Total votes		5,218				

West Bowling ward *(continued)*

Candidate	Party	Votes	%	Electors	Turnout	Gains
1934						
F. Sunderland	Lab	2,883	55.2	10,175	51.3	Lab from C
J.W. Mawson*	C	2,341	44.8			
Total votes		5,224				
1935						
Mrs H.A. Grundy*	Lab	Unopp.	-		-	-
1936						
F. Ratcliffe	Lab	2,225	50.1	10,242	43.4	Lab from L
J.T. Waterhouse*	L	2,217	49.9			
Total votes		4,442				
1937						
Mrs H.A. Grundy*	Lab	2,684	18.0	9,032	60.8	-
J.T. Waterhouse	L	2,476	16.6			
G. Green	Lab	2,271	15.2			
J.W. Mawson	C	2,157	14.4			
J. Hardy	L	1,993	13.3			
A. Walker	Lab	1,957	13.1			
Mrs Holmes	C	1,398	9.4			
Total votes		14,936				
Total voters		5,488				
(3 elected)						
1938						
H. Hornby	C	1,732	48.5	9,248	38.6	C from Lab
G. Green*	Lab	1,538	43.0			
Ms E.L. Worrall	ILP	304	8.5			
Total votes		3,574				

Overall Labour vote: **Overall turnout:**

1919–36	**49.3%**	**1919–36**	**59.7%**
1937–38	**47.9%**	**1937–38**	**49.6%**

TWO
Brighton

BRIGHTON

Brighton only became a centre of some importance in the eighteenth century. Initially a small fishing port and a point of departure for France, it was to develop in the Regency period as a playground for the gentry. From that beginning and given the alleged healthy properties of its seaside location and climate, Brighton became an early tourist and leisure resort. The *Gentleman's Magazine* reported as early as 1776:

> Brighton is a small ill-built town, situated on the sea coast, at present greatly resorted to in the summer season by persons labouring under various diseases, for the benefit of sea bathing and drinking sea water; and by the gay and polite on account of the company which frequent it at this season ...[1]

Brighton made its name in the eighteenth century as a resort for the upper classes. Made fashionable by the Prince Regent, the future George IV, its clientele began to have more of a social mix after the Napoleonic Wars. Regency architecture aided Brighton's development in the nineteenth century. In 1832 Cobbett had described the town 'as certainly surpassing in beauty all other towns in the world'.[2] This was no doubt a slight exaggeration but the splendour of the borough's architectural heritage provided, by way of the *season*, another economic resource that could be exploited. Such a heritage, intimately connected to the elites of society, perhaps contributed to the conservative nature of the town's local politics.

It was the advent of the railway age however, in the thirty years after 1841, that made Brighton a mass holiday resort.[3] This subsequently led to the development of cheap excursions for working-class day-trippers from London. The first excursion trains were recorded as early as Easter 1844. In one week in 1850, 73,000 passengers were brought to Brighton. This had risen to 132,000 in the peak week of 1862.[4] By 1876 a ballad could describe Brighton as 'London by the Sea'.[5] Mass tourism had become an economic resource that the city leaders exploited fully in the second half of the nineteenth century. Initially Brighton's hoteliers and local elite had viewed the rise of day-tripping as a mixed blessing. Some locals held that these new visitors, as opposed to the 'quality', brought little economic benefit to the town. Thus the *Brighton Gazette* could argue that 'it is to yield to false sentiment to sacrifice the interests of the town to the rabble who are here today and gone tomorrow and leave nothing behind them but the injured feelings of friends and patrons'.[6] Happily for the economic future of the county borough in the inter-war years, such snobbery and condescension towards its 'Cockney' visitors did not

---

[1] Quoted in Beevers, D. and Roles, J., *A Pictorial History of Brighton*, (Derby, 1993), introduction.
[2] Quoted in Beevers and Roles, *A Pictorial History of Brighton*, introduction.
[3] Freeman, T.W., *The Conurbations of Great Britain*, (Manchester, 1959), p. 269.
[4] Gilbert, E.M., *Brighton: Old Ocean's Bauble*, (Hassocks, 1975), p. 152.
[5] Gilbert, *Brighton*, p. 183.
[6] Quoted in Beevers and Roles, *A Pictorial History of Brighton*, introduction.

prevail as the dominant sentiment. Tourism and the associated leisure and entertainment industries became the most important enterprises of the town, which were to provide the economic bedrock of Brighton between the two World Wars. On the other hand, the construction and preservation of Regency Brighton meant that the town was not entirely 'sacrificed' to mass taste. Indeed until the 1920s the *season* continued largely in the autumn months. Here was a fortuitous harmony of interests, for by then the day-trippers and working-class holiday-makers were safely back working in their factories.

The physical and economic growth of Brighton in the nineteenth century was as dramatic as that of the mill towns of northern England. A population of 2,000 in 1730 had risen above 65,000 on incorporation as a municipal borough in 1854, reaching 115,873 when county borough status was achieved in 1888.[7] By 1921 the population was 134,739 rising to 147,427 by the 1931 Census. From the mid-nineteenth century onwards, there were openings for mass employment in the construction industry, transport (especially the railways), personal service and the retail trades. The great influx of working-class people, mostly Londoners, provided opportunities for male and female employment. The town developed a distinctive demographic structure with significantly more women than men. Brighton provided economic opportunities for 'respectable single women of all levels of society to earn a living, something that was rare in the nineteenth century.'[8] Working-class women were employed as laundresses and in other domestic activity while middle-class widows and unmarried women owned boarding and lodging houses or even small private schools. Of special importance for working class women was the domestic sector with large quantities of labour required for the lodging and boarding houses, as well as for the up-market hotels patronised by the middle class. Reflecting this demographic structure, women were in the majority on the municipal roll of inter-war electors. The implications of this gender imbalance will be examined further below.

Fogarty's comment on the Sussex towns, including Brighton, brings into clear relief the nature of the borough's success in the period of this study. He argued that 'tourists, pensioners, rentiers and dormitory dwellers' all boosted Brighton.[9] Freeman on the other hand stresses that the town 'owes much to the fact that it is the nearest and most accessible place on the south coast from London'.[10] With the electrification of the rail link to London in 1931–32, Brighton had the added advantage of speedy communications over its rivals. Increasingly then, in the 1930s, Brighton became a dormitory town of London. Commuting grew throughout that decade, and in 1938 season tickets reached 2,436 for daily use.[11] Given the cost of the rail fare, these were used mainly by people in middle-class occupations. In addition, there was an increasing proportion of wealthy elderly

[7] See Baxter, R.G. and Howe, D.G., 'Municipal activities in Brighton during the past twelve years', *Proceedings of the Institute of Municipal and County Engineers*, vol. LXIII, (1936–37) p. 33; also Gilbert, *Brighton*, p. 56.

[8] Beevers and Roles, *A Pictorial History of Brighton*, introduction.

[9] Fogarty, M.P., *Prospects of the Industrial Areas of Great Britain*, (London, 1945), p. 400.

[10] Freeman, *The Conurbations of Great Britain*, p. 269.

[11] Gilbert, *Brighton*, p. 269.

retiring to Sussex as a whole and to Brighton in particular.[12] Brighton's residential advantages attracted retired incomers predominantly in middle and higher income brackets. Given differential rates of longevity, the female retired outnumbered their male counterparts. There was much residential development for the retired as well as short term visitors. Brighton (including Hove, which then lay outside the boundaries of the county borough) was fourth in Gilbert's comparative table of numbers of retired males for this period. Gilbert also pointed out that one characteristic in common to the fourteen largest resorts (inland and seaside) is that they were all predominantly Conservative in their politics.[13] Fogarty argued that the pensioners in Brighton and along the east Sussex coast were 'an inert mass, the vast majority of whom neither could nor would participate in any developments of a social or industrial nature'. Apart from this wealthy section of the local population there were 'many more with small independent incomes'.[14]

Brighton was the economic centre of Sussex rather than the county capital of Lewes. The importance of the tourist and leisure industries in the borough resulted in a prevalence of employment in the personal service sector, high levels of female employment and much seasonal work. This in turn meant large numbers of 'people living and working locally on a range of service occupations in which earnings and conditions of employment were in many ways unsatisfactory'.[15] Seasonal unemployment was lowest in the summer months, the main holiday period being for the four weeks around the August Bank holiday. The winter months were the worst, though in some years public works provided some relief. Many of the seasonally unemployed would not have qualified for the municipal franchise, either because they lived in cheap furnished lodgings and were therefore not ratepayers, or because they were transients looking for seasonal work and thus could not meet the residential qualification.[16]

The First World War gave Brighton a fair degree of prosperity. Hotels and lodging houses did well because wealthier visitors could not visit continental Europe and Brighton was out of reach of German air-raids.[17] The town became a centre for convalescent and wounded soldiers and further income from high rents resulted. There was a boom in property during and after the First World War with lodgings at a premium. Such favourable circumstances did not last and post-war dislocation brought a downturn by the early 1920s. The resort was seen to be losing its position as a haven for the wealthy at this time and there were general economic difficulties resulting from the performance of the British economy. A good deal of poverty and unemployment resulted in the first half of the 1920s, though by 1925 Brighton was emerging from the depression.[18] Overall Brighton appears to have escaped relatively lightly in terms of rates of unemployment

[12] Fogarty, *Prospects of the Industrial Areas*, p. 399.

[13] Gilbert, *Brighton*, p. 238.

[14] Fogarty, *Prospects of the Industrial Areas*, p. 405.

[15] Fogarty, *Prospects of the industrial Areas*, p. 405, who was also discussing the Sussex towns.

[16] On the municipal franchise, see the notes at the end of this volume, p. 677.

[17] Gilbert, *Brighton*, p. 219.

[18] Musgrave, C., *Life in Brighton: From the Earliest Times to the Present*, (London, 1970), pp. 377–380.

between the wars. In terms of the percentage of all workers recorded as 'out of work' in the 1931 census industry tables, at just over 8 per cent, Brighton was a lowly seventy-second in the ranking table. The reasons why Brighton escaped the worst effects of the depression were various. The growth of light industry detailed below was one off-setting factor, and the effects of the slump were also staved off by the impact of the electrification of the railway to London in 1932–33. No serious decline in the holiday industry in the 1930s was noted. One publication on Brighton has even claimed that the 1930s were 'one of the most prosperous and successful periods of its history, not only as a holiday resort, but as a residential town'.[19] There was some hyperbole in this claim, but nevertheless Brighton, like another south coast borough Bournemouth, did relatively well in the 1930s.[20]

The 1930s development of light industry and light engineering was partly situated in the Hollingbury valley. Brushes, cardboard boxes, electrical elements and spirals, pressing and stamping of metals, decorative glass and heaters were all manufactured. The main growth of light engineering in Brighton took place after 1945, but even by 1939 the nature of Brighton was changing. In that year Brighton had 2,100 recognised lodging and apartment houses, 205 hotels in the centre of the town and 100 public houses within half a mile of Palace Pier. Twice as many people, however, were engaged in the manufacture of metal goods, vehicles and in general or electrical engineering.[21] The economic functions of Brighton could be accurately summed up by then as a health and pleasure resort, a residential centre, a dormitory for London, and lastly, as an area of light manufacturing.[22] Thus if the residential and retired helped produce a conservative ethos to Brighton, the tourist and growing manufacturing industries could, at least in theory, have moderated this somewhat. The balance of population however, still lay with tourism and the retired rather than manufacturing in the inter-war period. This ensured, as it did in other resorts such as Bournemouth and Blackpool, that the Labour party was electorally weak.

The main features of the social and economic structure can be seen in the industrial tables of the 1931 census. Tourism and care for the wealthier residents of Brighton made personal service by far the most important sector numerically with nearly 17,000 women (51 per cent of the female workforce) and over 12,000 men (10 per cent). This accounted overall for 24 per cent of Brighton's labour force. Brighton was also described 'as the most important banking and insurance centre east of Portsmouth and south of London'.[23] Thus over a fifth of the working population was found in the commerce and finance category, amounting to just under 11,000 men and 5,000 women. Over 11 per cent of men (5,119) were found in the metal and engineering sector, many engaged in electrical engineering (4 per cent) and vehicle construction (just under 4 per cent). Brighton stood eleventh in the borough rankings for male workers in vehicle construction. Worthy of note was the location of the Thomas Harrington works, which made motor vehicle bodies in

[19] Musgrave, *Life in Brighton*, p. 383.
[20] On Bournemouth, see volume one in this series, pp. 589–640.
[21] Freeman, *The Conurbations of Great Britain*, p. 271.
[22] Gilbert, *Brighton*, p. 237.
[23] Freeman, *The Conurbations of Great Britain*, p. 271.

King Street (Pavilion ward) until its removal to the Old Shoreham Road in 1930.[24] It seems certain that many of these skilled and semi-skilled workers lived outside this solidly anti-Labour ward where only independents were returned. The railway works of the London, Brighton and South Coast Railway employed over 2,500 workers at the end of the nineteenth century. Railway locomotive construction was run down before the First World War, the last steam engine being built in 1922, and the workshops partly closed in 1928. Nevertheless nearly 1,000 workers were engaged in repair and maintenance between the World Wars, with 850 workers left in employment as late as 1947.[25] The main railway works was situated in Montpelier ward, but the evidence points to the railway workers living in nearby St. Peter's ward. This was reflected in Labour doing well there, it being the party's third strongest ward overall. Railwaymen were also noted as an important group in the organisation and activities of the Labour party, confirmed by the analysis of occupations below, which shows railwaymen were the largest single occupational group amongst Labour's candidates for the council.

Public administration and defence was another important category of employment with 10 per cent of men (over 4,500) and over 5 per cent of women (1,343) so employed. Local government was the most important element of this category, accounting for over 2,700 men and just under 1,000 women. A significant proportion of these workers was employed in a quasi-industrial area of six acres which fronted Lewes Road. Here nearly 1,500 persons were employed at the corporation transport depot and electrical engineering works. Again, such a density of working-class inhabitants probably accounts for Labour's strong performance in the Lewes Road ward. The indicators of social class derived from the 1931 census and referred to throughout these volumes, however, confirm the dominance of the middle class in Brighton. The managerial and own account categories accounted for nearly 20 per cent of the male workforce (over 8,000) and 14 per cent of the female (over 3,000). With almost 18 per cent of the total work force in these categories, Brighton was placed eighth amongst the county boroughs. Brighton was also eleventh in terms of the proportions of professionals (almost 5 per cent), and sixth in terms of the ratio of female domestic servants to the total population (almost 9 per cent), all indicators of the borough's high social class. Finally, the population tables of the 1931 census show that Brighton, with an average of 0.79 persons per room, was fifty-seventh amongst the eighty-three county boroughs in terms of this indicator. This relatively low degree of overcrowding again suggests a relatively affluent population overall, but Brighton had a significantly higher density of room-occupation than Blackpool (0.67 persons per room, eighty-first of the county boroughs) and Bournemouth (0.64, eighty-third). Although all these boroughs were tourist resorts, Brighton's more varied economic functions and greater degree of manufacturing differentiated it somewhat from the other two.

[24] Gilbert, *Brighton*, p. 246.
[25] Gilbert, *Brighton*, p. 245.

Brighton was made a municipal borough in 1854, and a county borough in 1889.[26] The fourteen ward structure was devised in 1894 and remained in place until the borough extension of 1928. Although a small part of Patcham was added in 1923, the 56-person council was left unaltered until the creation of 'Greater Brighton' in 1928. From 1929 the borough had nineteen wards with a council of 57 councillors and 19 aldermen. By the 1928 extension, rural districts were added to the established urban areas of the borough: 'the boundary between Brighton and Hove was adjusted, and the parishes of Patcham (part) and West Blatchington (part) in the Rural District of Steyning East and the parishes of Falmer (part), Ovingdean, and Rottingdean in the rural district of Newhaven were added to the borough'.[27] These new districts formed, in the view of two contemporary borough engineers 'an almost separate section'.[28] Almost 12,000 acres of downland were bought very cheaply bringing about the ending of low-quality development on the suburban ring. This helped to preserve the Downs and also allowed planned development of the suburbs by the corporation by both public and private enterprise.[29] Four new wards, Patcham, Hollingbury, Moulsecoomb (variously spelt as Moulescoomb or Moulscombe) and Rottingdean resulted. These new wards formed an outer suburban ring from Rottingdean in the east to Patcham in the west. Most of the extension was downland, though Patcham had been partly developed already. Brighton increased its acreage from 2,714 to 12,565.[30] One other change occurred in 1928, Lewes Road ward being roughly divided into two, with the eastern part becoming Elm Grove ward. It should be noted that for municipal purposes Hove remained outside the boundaries of the county borough. Hove formed the western extension along the coast of the conurbation as a whole, and contained many of the most affluent districts. Its exclusion from the borough shifted the balance of politics to an extent, making it less strongly anti-Labour than it otherwise might have been.

At Westminster level, the residential and sea-side resorts were, in the main, strongly Conservative between the two world wars. Brighton acquired two seats in 1832 which were predominantly Liberal in the early years, but the borough became a strong Conservative haven. The 1851 Census showed that twelve of the borough's thirty-eight churches were Anglican and the Church of England had a large expansion programme in the high and late Victorian age. As early as 1866 'another nine or ten' Anglican churches had been built.[31] This Anglicanism almost certainly had political implications. Religious affiliation to the Church of England invariably strengthened both the conservative ethos of the borough and the Conservative party as well. Pelling noted that Brighton 'was heavily Anglican and safely Conservative' in late Victorian and Edwardian times. He went on to suggest that 'the growth of "Papism" in the Church appeared more of a threat to the orthodox Conservative representation of the town than the rivalry of the Liberal

[26] *Encyclopaedia of Brighton*, (Brighton, undated), Section 48, unpaginated, located in Brighton Central Reference Library.

[27] Baxter and Howe, 'Municipal activities in Brighton', p. 33.

[28] Baxter and Howe, 'Municipal activities in Brighton', p. 34.

[29] Gilbert, *Brighton*, p. 223.

[30] Gilbert, *Brighton*, p. 222.

[31] Gilbert, *Brighton*, p. 201.

Party.'[32] After the First World War, the Conservatives swept the board in Brighton, winning both the parliamentary seats on all occasions in the seven elections between 1918 and 1935. Apart from 1918, when two Coalition Conservatives were returned, the Conservative share of the vote did not fall below 62 per cent and peaked above 70 per cent in 1922. Labour's best performances were in the general elections of 1929 and 1935, when the party's share of the vote was over 23 per cent on both occasions.[33] It should be noted again that Hove *was* included in the parliamentary constituency of Brighton, making it even more safely Tory than the borough. This parliamentary situation provides the background to a non-existent Liberalism and a weak Labour party in Brighton's municipal politics. The high Anglicanism Pelling noted, together with a weak Nonconformity both mitigated against a popular Liberalism or a strong Labour party.

In municipal politics in Brighton independents made up the most powerful group on the council. It is best to use the term independent in the lower case, for this was a description of a broad political position and an ideological orientation to local politics rather than a more formal political organisation. The views of these independents were similar to those of independents in many other boroughs in the period. Thus an independent in 1935 stood for 'sane progress combined with efficiency and economy'.[34] This stance was reinforced by a rugged desire to be 'independent men' (and almost all were men) who allegedly acted in the interest of all without fear or favour. The independents shunned party organisation and labels and governed 'in the interests of the ratepayers'. Such an Olympian standpoint invariably covered a multitude of political positions, generally of a conservative persuasion. Independents continually purported to view municipal politics as not being about 'party politics', and the local press went along with this in its election coverage by refraining from using party labels apart from the Labour candidates. In the 1920 elections the *Argus* went even further, referring to prospective Labour councillors as the 'Red candidates'.[35] Labour usually saw such tactics as underhand and undemocratic. It was their belief that local politicians, like those at Westminster, should fly under their true colours.[36] Independents, although avoiding party labels and assuming an apolitical position, in reality usually followed an anti-Labour policy.[37] By the 1930s there were increasing press reports of many independents being backed by the Conservative party machine. Few openly 'came out' as Conservatives at the hustings, but Conservatives in the council chamber were seen as formally lining up against Labour. Thus a candidate in 1935 referred to 'the balance between the two sides' on the council.[38] Unusually in the new ward of Rottingdean in 1929, referred to in the Press as 'a stronghold of

[32] Pelling, H. *Social Geography of British Elections 1885–1910*, (Aldershot, 1994), p. 77.

[33] Craig, F.W.S., *British Parliamentary Election Results 1918–1949*, Third Edition, (Chichester, 1983), p. 103.

[34] *Evening Argus*, 2 Nov. 1935.

[35] *Argus*, 2 Nov. 1920.

[36] *Argus*, 2 Nov. 1925 and *Evening Argus*, 2 Nov. 1935.

[37] Davies, S. and Morley, B., *County Borough Elections in England and Wales, 1919–1938: A Comparative Analysis*, vol. 1, (Aldershot, 1999), p. 560.

[38] *Evening Argus*, 2 Nov. 1935.

Toryism', the Conservatives were quite open. Thus the successful independent candidate, A.E. Neild, declared 'I am a Conservative by birth and conviction'.[39]

There were genuine 'independents' who stood for the council, however. One such was Andrew Melville, who stood five times in St Nicholas's ward from 1926 to 1930, sometimes against other 'independents' as well as Labour. In 1927 he stated 'he had the support of no political party, preferring to be independent, as he believed he could do more good as a man unfettered by party labels'. In his defeat at the hands of J. Holmes, another fellow independent the next year, Melville could say in conceding:

> May I add ... that I can get there [the council] without joining any party (hear, hear, and applause). I don't think that politics should have anything to do with municipal affairs.(Hear, hear). His opponent had had the help of the Citizens' Union and the Conservative Association ... His election literature showed it'.[40]

Others were less believable. In bemoaning his fate in 1933 on losing Hanover ward, Charles Cashman restated the typical Independent position: 'Thanking his supporters, Mr. Cashman said he still maintained that party politics should not govern municipal matters (loud cries of protest and a voice Where's your colours?)'.[41]

Sometimes when independent fought independent bitterness and uproar could result, especially when a sitting councillor was defeated. It seems that the anti-drink lobby brought Michael Marten low in 1933. Marten had held St. Nicholas ward for twelve years, winning four elections. He had been a powerful man on the council, commonly believed to be a leader of a clique within the corporation.[42] He was bitter in defeat, saying it was 'the dirtiest, rottenest election I have ever had. I never believed my people would believe what those rotten teetotallers said. If I had plenty of money like these people have I should have got somewhere else. That rotten man there – (pointing to his opponent)'. From then uproar followed, his opponent left and 'with the protest showing no sign of subsiding Mr. Marten abandoned the attempt to speak'.[43] On another occasion, in 1934 in Pavilion ward, the defeated independent, William Loader, was accused of being a fascist. His reply was revealing: 'I fought this ward as an independent. My imperial politics is that of a Fascist because that stands for King and Country. I served my country for 15 years and there is an element in this country who want Moscow to rule it'.[44]

There were also organised pressure groups of an apparently non-party nature which appeared occasionally in Brighton. Many of the independents in 1920 and 1921 stood as candidates representing the Middle Classes Union (MCU). Local branches of this organisation were formed in many boroughs at this time, representing something of a political revolt by sections of the middle-class

[39] *Argus*, 2 Nov. 1929.
[40] *Argus*, 2 Nov. 1928.
[41] *Argus*, 2 Nov. 1933.
[42] *Evening Argus*, 2 Nov. 1935.
[43] *Argus*, 2 Nov. 1933.
[44] *Evening Argus*, 2 Nov. 1934.

electorate fearful of the rise of organised labour and rising levels of taxation.[45] Seven stood for the MCU in Brighton in 1920, of whom five won, and six stood the following year, three successfully. Significantly those councillors who stood again three years later had dropped the MCU label and become independents, signalling the end of this short-lived political diversion. Later in 1938 there also appeared candidates representing either one or both of two bodies, the Brighton Municipal Committee, (BMC) and the Associated Ratepayers' Protection League (ARPL). Eleven of these appeared under the slogan of 'economy', eight of whom won seats on the council. Several had stood before as independents. As the *Argus* commented, the polls were heavy in 1938 with 'more interest taken in the election than for many years. The campaign for economy had at last roused the ratepayers to play their part'.[46] The precise nature of this intervention is unclear, however. There had occasionally been others who had stood as 'ratepayers', and in Pavilion ward in 1938 an ARPL candidate ran against, and beat, the BMC challenger. He stated what he believed to be the essence of their stance, saying that the 'League would stand for Brighton, clean play and fair rates'.[47]

Turning to the Labour side in Brighton, up to 1911 there appeared to be no Labour party or Labour Representation Committee in the borough. Trevor Hopper has, however, emphasised that parts of southern England like Brighton, without the usual association of Labour development with the heavy industrialisation of the factory system, nonetheless possessed an early labour movement. It is his argument that Edwardian Brighton had an identifiable working class which recognised itself as a separate class. Hopper further contends that this class was influenced by socialist and Labour activities, 'with a variety of socialist groups and parties grappling for the working-class vote in Brighton.'[48] He points out that on the borough council between the 1890s and 1914 there was always at least one councillor from the Fabians, Independent Labour Party or Social Democratic Federation. Hopper also stresses the depth of religious Nonconformity amongst the Brighton working class, especially of the Congregational variety.[49]

Despite these pre-1914 socialist stirrings, membership of the Brighton Labour party appears to have been small throughout the period 1918 to 1929, with a total membership of less than 200 in those years. Throughout the 1930s the party in Brighton and Hove together had an average of 500 members, and in 1938 it had a membership of 762. This figure included members of the Trades Council (or the Council of Industries, as it was sometimes referred to) as well. One study concluded that 'a thriving and active Labour party' did not exist in Brighton during the inter-war period.[50] There were some signs of greater activity in local Labour

[45] For further details on the MCU, see the comments in chapter seven of this volume, (Canterbury), pp. 484–485.

[46] *Evening Argus*, 2 Nov. 1938.

[47] *Evening Argus*, 2 Nov. 1938.

[48] Hopper, T., 'Transformation of Political Consciousness in South East England, 1880–1914', (Ph.D. thesis, University of Brighton, 1998), p. 4.

[49] Hopper, 'Transformation', p. 5; see also Hopper, T., 'The beginnings of the labour movement in south east England, 1880–1914', *Journal of Regional and Local Studies*, vol. 17, (1997), pp. 23–32.

[50] Forester, T., *The Labour Party and the Working Class*, (London, 1976), pp. 110–111.

circles, such as the establishment of an Unemployed Men's Club in Tichborne Street. The General Strike in 1926 also provoked some unrest, most notably when strikers and supporters attempted to prevent the trams leaving the Lewes Road depot. It was reported that

> about 300 mounted and foot police in cars came down to Tram Depot, charged the crowd, hitting them with sticks, two feet long with knobs on the end. Object – to get the trams out (none were running); 22 arrests were made. Trial next day, sentences from 1 to 6 months.[51]

The Council of Action that ran the strike locally included delegates from the Trades Council, the railways and transport sectors, the printing trades, the local Labour party itself, and the Working Women's Council. Most of the delegates were apparently of the 'moderate' type.[52] One local history stated that Brighton workers 'achieved almost complete unity in bringing local industries and services to a standstill'.[53] The longer-term impact on industrial and political organisation seemed negligible, however, as the analysis of election results below seems to confirm.

Labour in Brighton also suffered from the split in its ranks nationally in 1931, not only in terms of its electoral support, but also directly by defections from the party. Thus Tommy Morris, first elected for the strong Labour ward of Lewes Road in 1927, defected with Ramsay MacDonald in 1931. Morris held onto the ward in 1933, defeating the official Labour candidate Felix Steel comfortably by 445 votes. Morris struck a pose that any Independents would have been proud of, saying that 'in the Lewes-road Ward we are not going to have political influence'. Steel was generous in defeat, saying he would have 'preferred Tommy Morris to have stuck to his guns and been returned a Labour man'.[54] Other Labour defeats were put down to different factors. In 1933 in St. Peter's ward Herbert Cole was defeated after nine years service on the council. He attributed his defeat to the power of the local church and 'the one-sidedness of the Press'. Replying to a charge of not going to church enough, Cole retorted:

> My religion is and always has been, as a working man, to try to serve my fellow workmen (hear, hear) and I have given twenty years service to the working men of this town. I have no regrets as far as my defeat is concerned, and I congratulate Miss Stringer upon beating me, but I must say this, it is the friends of St. Bartholomew's who have beaten me. If I had been a strong member of the Church, in all probability I should have been returned by a very large majority.[55]

---

[51] Burns, E., *The General Strike, May 1926: Trades Councils in Action*, (London, 1975), pp. 107–108.
[52] Burns, *The General Strike*, p. 107.
[53] Musgrave, *Life in Brighton*, p. 313–314.
[54] *Evening Argus*, 2 Nov. 1933.
[55] *Evening Argus*, 2 Nov. 1933.

It is clear from the accusations of Labour candidates that by the 1930s they began to see the full weight of Conservative party organisation behind their independent opponents. In Hollingbury in 1932 for instance, the defeated Labour candidate, who was 'greeted with tremendous cheers', said the time would come 'when independents would have to fight in their true colour (cries of "Like you did! They ain't got none!"). The three present representatives of the Ward all gave their votes for the representatives of big business in the town'.[56] Again in Elm Grove in 1935, the Labour candidate stated of his opponent:

> I am disappointed and disgusted, however, that the Conservative
> Party ran him as an Independent. That is dishonest politics, and
> they ought to be ashamed of themselves. I would rather be beaten
> by one who honestly says what his political opinions are.[57]

In reply the winning independent stated that 'the Conservative party did not run him; he ran himself as an Independent because he believed that party politics should not be introduced into municipal life'.[58] A similar charge was made by the Labour victor in Lewes Road ward in that year, who said 'he would sooner fight a man who was an honest Tory'.[59]

It is also interesting that unemployment, despite being relatively low in Brighton, nevertheless prompted the intervention of the National Unemployed Worker's Movement (NUWM). Following the national formation of the NUWM in 1921, eight candidates stood in Brighton, all coming bottom of the poll. In Montpelier ward the NUWM gained only ten votes, and in St Nicholas's only six out of a total of 1,378. Later in 1931, when the NUWM was influenced strongly by the 'third period' policies of the British Communist Party and sought to take on what that party described as the 'social fascists' of Labour, two further candidates appeared, and fared little better. In Pier ward the NUWM contender, after thanking the eighteen electors who had voted for him, said that 'he had not put up with any idea of getting a seat on the Council, but with the intention of protesting against the injustice which was being done to the unemployed'.[60]

Turning to the analysis of the municipal election results now, it should be stated first that control of Brighton council rested firmly in the hands of the independents throughout the inter-war period. Between 1919 and 1928 they never held fewer than forty-three of the fifty-six seats in the council chamber, while Labour fluctuated between nine and thirteen seats. The borough extension operational from 1929 produced an enlarged seventy-six member council. The independents held fifty-eight seats, while Labour achieved a high point of eighteen members of the chamber in that year, before falling back in the early 1930s. By 1932 Labour held only eight seats, its lowest point between the wars. Labour's recovery in the mid and late 1930s meant that it was restored to its position of eighteen seats in 1937–38. Nevertheless the anti-Labour majority of independents and Conservatives in the 1930s never fell below its 1929 level of fifty-eight

[56] *Evening Argus*, 2 Nov. 1932.
[57] *Evening Argus*, 2 Nov. 1935.
[58] *Evening Argus*, 2 Nov. 1935.
[59] *Evening Argus*, 2 Nov. 1935.
[60] *Evening Argus*, 3 Nov. 1931.

members of the council. The Labour party achieved no real breakthrough in Brighton, and never threatened to take control of the council.

On the other hand, it ought to be pointed out that Labour had a far greater presence on the council here than it did in other resorts such as Blackpool or Bournemouth. There was a working-class of some size in Brighton, even if it was numerically in a minority, which provided Labour with some bed-rock of support. The exclusion of the affluent suburbs of Hove from the borough, as mentioned above, also worked to Labour's advantage. Tracing Labour's electoral performance over time in more detail, Labour contested eight wards in 1919 and were successful in four of them, one being uncontested, reflecting the strong national performance of Labour in that year. This represented one gain for Labour, and a further net gain of one was made in 1920. The years from 1921 to 1926 were generally difficult years for Labour in Brighton, reaching a nadir in 1926 when Labour lost a seat despite the strong performance of the party nationally. Jimmy Clynes stated on the national picture:

> Although municipal elections results are not always a barometer of national opinion, the sweeping Labour victory affords unmistakable proof of revolt against local conditions and growing confidence in the Labour Party. In spite of heavy municipal burdens and the Tory cry of so-called economy, that cry has failed and in all these contests, the coal lock-out was made a leading topic of discussion. The results have an intimate bearing upon the rising protest against the Government's policy.[61]

The fact that Brighton went against the national picture was noted by the *Argus*.[62] The reported militancy and class solidarity noted above in the General Strike plainly was not converted into political support for Labour in the borough. Labour did, however, make gains in the following three years, only to be hit severely by the effects of the onset of the depression and MacDonald's National coalition in 1931. There was only one Labour loss in 1930, partly because the party was fortunate to have two of its candidates win unopposed, but 1931 was a disaster with six seats being lost. Even in its most solid wards – Elm Grove, Hanover, Lewes Road, St. John's and St. Peter's – Labour could not hold on to one seat. There were cries of anguish from its candidates. One in St. John's blamed the electorate, saying 'you see how you have let me down', while another in Lewes Road thought 'the Labour party had found its utmost depth'. The defeated candidate in Hollingbury said 'the result ...is due to the national wave. It has got hold of you, but the time is coming when you will wish you had never seen the national wave'.[63] There was no respite in 1932, however, with another three losses, but Labour slowly recovered in the mid 1930s, making six gains in 1934–35. Thereafter Labour did not fall away again in the late 1930s quite as badly as it did in some other boroughs. Labour actually made two gains in 1937, but suffered a net loss of one in 1938. Nevertheless there was little sign overall in Labour's

---

[61] *Argus*, 2 Nov. 1926.
[62] *Argus*, 2 Nov. 1926.
[63] *Evening Argus*, 3 Nov. 1931.

performance in Brighton in the years immediately before 1939 of the post-war Atlee landslide.

Turning to the spatial distribution of political support, a clear pattern can be seen. The strongest independent wards, where Conservatives also began to appear in the 1930s, were situated mainly in the north-west and west of the borough, and also along the seafront. These included Preston, Hollingbury and Patcham to the north, Preston Park, Montpellier and West along the boundary with Hove to the west, and Regency, Pavilion, Pier, Queen's Park and King's Cliff along the seafront. In all of these wards Labour won no seats between the wars, with the exception of Preston Park which it took narrowly in 1919 and retained unopposed in 1922. These were the most affluent of the suburban wards, and also the most pleasant seafront areas. It was noted by two of Brighton's borough engineers that 'better class developments' went out east and west along the coast towards Hove and Kemp Town (King's Cliff Ward after 1908).[64] The closer to Hove, the more the tone was one of 'middle-class affluence', as Pelling noted.[65] The old nucleus of Brighton, Pavilion, became 'the city ward' of offices and shops, sometimes referred to as 'the businessman's ward'.[66] This applied also to Pier and Queen's Park wards to an extent, and at night a fair proportion of their population commuted back to their homes.[67] These were the business voters, entitled to two votes by reason of paying rates both on their business premises and their residences. The persons per room figures in the 1931 census confirm the general picture of the strongly anti-Labour wards. Apart from the business wards they all averaged between 0.62 and 0.74 person per room, a low rate of occupancy and all below the borough average of 0.79.

Labour found most of its support in a cluster of six wards of denser and lower-class housing set back from the coastal belt, situated to the north and east of the town centre. These were St John's, St Nicholas's, St Peter's, Hanover, Lewes Road and Elm Grove. Both St John's and St Peter's were referred to as 'working class districts' in 1925 press coverage, while Hanover and Lewes Road were referred to as 'working class' wards later in 1938.[68] Labour also won seats in two of the suburban wards added in 1928, Moulsecoomb on the northern boundary and Rottingdean on the east, where council-house development took place. All told Brighton built nearly 4,000 council houses in the inter-war years, a ratio of one council house for every thirty-seven people.[69] This was a relatively modest achievement compared with more urban boroughs, but it still had some political effect. By 1936, 478 council houses and 48 flats had been built in the South Moulsecoomb estate, a further 390 in North Moulsecoomb, while some 800 houses were projected for East Moulsecoomb.[70] It is significant that Rottingdean was referred to 'as a stronghold of Toryism' in 1929, yet by 1937 was solidly Labour.[71]

[64] Baxter and Howe, 'Municipal activities in Brighton', p. 32.
[65] Pelling, *Social Geography*, p. 77.
[66] *Argus*, 30 Oct. 1919.
[67] Gilbert, *Brighton*, p. 214.
[68] *Evening Argus*, 2 Nov. 1938 and 2 Nov. 1925.
[69] See appendix 16 of this volume, p. 692.
[70] Baxter and Howe, 'Municipal activities in Brighton', pp. 52–53.
[71] *Argus*, 2 Nov. 1929.

It originally had a rural and dispersed structure, consisting 'of five little townships scattered over an area of eight or nine square miles' to the east of the borough.[72] The Whitehawk estate (1,171 houses), however, was built in its south-western corner, changing its nature considerably. The Manor Farm estate (422 houses) was also constructed in King's Cliff ward.[73] Labour did not contest this seat for some time before 1937, but it is noticeable that when it did it picked up almost 40 per cent of the votes, compared to nearer 20 per cent in the early 1920s. The persons per room figures again show a degree of correspondence with the strength of Labour support. In the group of six central wards and the two outlying wards where Labour was strongest, persons per room ranged between 0.82 and 0.98, all above the borough average.

In terms of the occupations of prospective councillors, data is available for the years 1920, 1921, 1923, 1925 and 1931.[74] Out of a total of seventy-nine independent candidates in these five elections, the main identifiable groups were thirty small businessmen, ten professionals (including teachers and a bank manager), ten 'gentlemen', seven retired officials and businessmen and six company directors. The tourist trade was represented by four hotel and theatre managers and there were seven women classified simply as 'married' or 'unmarried'. For Labour out of thirty-two candidates the main groups were nine railwaymen of various descriptions, five insurance workers, five small businessmen, four skilled workers, three professionals and two trade union officials. A clear-cut demarcation of the two main political groups is apparent. A far more prosperous middle class background – a professional and business orientation – was the hallmark of the independents. Labour, on the other hand, has more candidates from working class occupations together with insurance agents and trade union officials. An additional nine candidates for the unemployed for the same elections presented themselves as either unemployed or general labourers.

The role of women in politics was raised briefly in the municipal elections in Brighton. There were more females than males on the municipal electoral roll, typical of a borough in which a significant number of wealthy pensioners resided (amongst whom female longevity was greater than male), and employment in domestic service was important. There were, however, very few women who stood for the council between 1919 and 1938. In total women were candidates on twenty-seven occasions, five times for Labour and twenty-two times under all other labels. This represented only five per cent of all candidatures, and only 3 per cent of Labour's, some of the lowest figures encountered so far in these volumes. This did not include two women who won as independents in by-elections in 1918, the first women on the council being Mrs Blatch and Mrs Ryle. In all only seven women became councillors in the twenty-year period of this study, of whom only one stood for Labour, Mrs E.J. Smith. The issue of the need for more women on the council was raised by Mrs. Blatch in the election of 1919. Mrs Blatch said 'that she would like to see enough women on the Council to allow of two sitting on each

[72] *Evening Argus*, 2 Nov. 1935.

[73] Baxter and Howe, 'Municipal activities in Brighton', pp. 52–53.

[74] Collated from the declaration of candidates in the *Brighton Herald* or the *Argus* in those years.

Committee'. In the same edition of the *Argus* there was an announcement from the Women's Local Government Association (Brighton) calling for the ratepayers to vote for Councillor Mrs. Ryle in Pavilion and for Mrs. Hutton in Pier.[75] Again in 1920, 'Women's Questions', as the editor of the *Brighton Herald and Hove Gazette* put it, were raised directly in a letter from the Brighton and Hove Union for Women's Local Government and Equal Citizenship. The letter listed a series of questions put to prospective candidates for the council, including the following:

> 1. Will you support equal pay for equal work for all men and women employed by your Council?
> 2. Will you support the application of the principle of the Sex Disqualification (Removal) Act, 1919, so that a woman shall not be disqualified on account of her sex from any post or office in your Council?
> 3. Will you oppose the compulsory retirement on marriage of the women employees of your Council?
> 4. Will you oppose any systematic dismissal of women in favour of men other than men returning from active service?[76]

After this concentration on the issue in the elections held soon after the partial enfranchisement of women in 1918, though, there was little further discussion. On the whole therefore women's involvement in the politics of Brighton appeared to be limited.

More attention was focused on the public expenditure of the borough in the discourse of municipal politics. Like many local authorities, Brighton owned and ran a range of public utilities from the tramways to electricity generation and sewage plants. This was the heritage from the high Victorian age of 'gas and water socialism' (although in Brighton the gas supply remained in private hands). In the inter-war years there were two different but not always totally contradictory views on the purposes of expenditure by the council. On the one hand interest groups connected to the leisure and entertainment industries, such as builders and developers, favoured municipal expenditure on capital projects. Two of the borough engineers, writing in 1936, made an important though obvious point, that a seaside town 'is dependent for its continued prosperity upon the maintenance of its attraction for visitors'. Despite having the advantages of pleasant scenery and proximity to London, Brighton 'was compelled to spend large sums of money upon more spectacular appeals to the public'.[77] Capital expenditure in Brighton therefore, as in other resorts, was closely related to the needs of the hotel and tourist trade, rather than being intended for the improvement of social conditions to the advantage of the majority of the population. On the other hand, in the face of economic depression, public works were often put forward as a panacea to the problems of unemployment and poverty by Labour and NUWM candidates for the council.

[75] *Argus*, 30 Oct. 1919.
[76] *Brighton Herald and Hove Gazette*, 6 Nov. 1920.
[77] Baxter and Howe, 'Municipal activities in Brighton', p. 34.

The issue of public works does not however, appear to have been as divisive in Brighton as it was in other resorts.[78] There was some consensus that money should be spent to enhance Brighton's attractiveness as a resort. The atmosphere of bitterness on these issues, noted in both Bournemouth and Blackpool, seemed more muted in Brighton. The use of direct labour, partly as a tool to mitigate the worst effects of unemployment rather than simply in pursuit of an economic goal, was more in evidence in Brighton than elsewhere. The borough was seen as a relatively high-spending authority of its type, to the extent that it was claimed that some wealthier residents migrated to Bournemouth 'in order to escape the increasing burden of the rates occasioned by Brighton's heavy municipal expenditure'.[79] There were also few charges that the ruling majority voted for public expenditure on tourism and the leisure industries in a way that went beyond legitimate public interest. It was implied in other resorts that private builders and property developers directly represented on the council corruptly feathered their own nests at the expense of the ratepayers. There seems no parallel in Brighton to the overt machinations of economic interest groups that were seen in inter-war Blackpool's council chamber.

Thus outdoor relief schemes were in operation in 1919 and referred to in pre-election debates,[80] and road widening and the renovation of buildings, especially in the shopping centre, ensured that extensive works were carried out by the council in both decades of this study. Public works in Carden Avenue in 1920 and 1921, finally completed between 1928–31, were carried out 'to provide some form of unemployed relief work'.[81] Grants from the Ministry of Transport and a £1,000 contribution from the Local Distress Committee aided this construction. Again, during another highpoint of social distress in 1929–30, there were substantial promenade improvements and structural alterations to the entrance to Palace Pier at a total cost of £51,400.[82] There was further sea-wall, groyne and beach construction both before and after 1932. At Rottingdean, the Black Rock beach construction led to further work for the unemployed as 'the labour of loading the lorries is regarded as a useful unemployment relief work during the winter months'.[83] The three mile long sea-wall and Undercliffe Walk was built too by direct labour at a total cost of £374,000 in the early 1930s. A large proportion of the costs of the coastal road schemes were met by the Government Unemployed Grant Committee. Five hundred men, mainly the locally unemployed, found work in those schemes.[84] The Rottingdean bathing pool built on Undercliffe Wall between 1934–35 at a cost of £8,648 was constructed entirely by direct labour. Lastly a recreation ground was created on the site of the old Brapool barn. This again was done as unemployment relief work in the winter months of 1934–35 and 1935–36 at an estimated cost of £312,000.[85]

[78] Davies and Morley, *County Borough Elections*, vol. 1, pp. 405–418, 589–599.
[79] Gilbert, *Brighton*, p. 277.
[80] *Argus*, 30 Oct. 1919.
[81] Baxter and Howe, 'Municipal activities in Brighton', p. 43.
[82] Baxter and Howe, 'Municipal activities in Brighton', p. 38.
[83] Baxter and Howe, 'Municipal activities in Brighton', p. 58.
[84] Musgrave, *Life in Brighton*, p. 391.
[85] Baxter and Howe, 'Municipal activities in Brighton', pp. 57, 62 and 72.

The question of expenditure on the provision of council houses was also relatively uncontroversial. As mentioned above, roughly 4,000 council houses were constructed between the wars, a ratio of one house for every thirty-seven persons in the borough. This makes an interesting contrast with other resorts like Blackpool, with only 1,500 houses constructed (one for every sixty-nine persons), or Bournemouth with 750 (one for every 152 persons). In part this was a reflection of the fact that there was a larger working-class presence in Brighton, whose housing needs had to be met. The Labour party made housing and over-crowding an election issue in the first post-war election, and continued to do so in the succeeding years, but independents also raised the issue at times.[86] One independent in 1934 in the predominantly business ward of Regency made a cheap point at the expense of the council's housing policies, saying 'he thought the housing question in Brighton should really be looked into when they were pulling down places and sending the people away from where they had been living all their lives (hear, hear)'.[87] But this was an isolated event, and overall it seems that there was a degree of consensus over housing issues which kept them off the political agenda, while the corporation's efforts in this area were enough to have kept most of the electorate satisfied.

In conclusion, the first point to emphasise is that Brighton was a seaside resort, but one whose local economy made it distinct from other resorts. Despite the numbers of affluent pensioners who retired to the borough and the importance of the holiday, leisure and tourist industries, there was also an element of light manufacturing industry which was growing during the inter-war period. Thus while the political rule of independents was unchallenged between the wars, as might have been expected, there was a significant Labour opposition. The borough escaped the worst effects of inter-war depression, and the ruling independent group spent public money on capital projects to support the leisure industries which helped to sustain the basis of the local economy. At the same time the use of direct labour in some of these projects helped to minimise unemployment and mollify working-class voters. There were also relatively generous amounts spent on the construction of council houses.

Second, the Labour party was weak in Brighton but certainly not as weak as in other coastal resorts. This was due to the presence of a significant working class based on the local manufacturing industries, which provided a bed-rock of Labour support. They supplemented workers in the service sector who were traditionally seen as less well organised industrially and less active in Labour politics, although it should be pointed out that Brighton's shopworkers provided a prominent national Labour politician in Margaret Bondfield.[88] Labour's support was concentrated in the mainly working-class districts to the east and north of the town centre, and later in the outlying wards where council-house building took place also to the east and north. The wards in the coastal belt and the western suburbs

---

[86] *Argus*, 30 Oct. 1919 and 2 Nov. 1929.

[87] *Evening Argus*, 2 Nov. 1934.

[88] Margaret Bondfield, Minister of Labour in the Labour government of 1929–31, began her working life in a draper's shop in the Western Road, Brighton in 1887.

were by contrast independent strongholds, although the exclusion of Hove from the borough reduced their number to an extent.

Third, there was not so much a strange death of Liberalism in Brighton but rather its well-nigh total absence. In parliamentary terms Brighton even before 1919 was strongly Conservative while Liberalism was extremely weak. High Anglicanism together with a low degree of Nonconformity both mitigated against a popular Liberalism. The independents, of a growing Conservative hue in the 1930s, provided a safe refuge for the propertied and middle-class electorate, and their control of the council remained secure between the wars.

Last, although the majority of councillors came from a business and professional background, including some from the leisure and tourist industries, there did not appear to be the interest group manipulation of the council that was noted elsewhere. The cliques of builders and property developers seen in Blackpool and the rings of landlords in Bournemouth did not have their equivalent in Brighton's municipal politics. Either Brighton's local politicians were especially disinterested, or they managed to keep any involvement in direct money-making at the ratepayers' expense out of the public eye. More likely, the indirect profits of their enterprises from the economic success of Brighton as a holiday and residential resort were enough to keep the members of the corporation content.

A guide to further reading

Newspapers

Argus
Brighton Herald and Hove Gazette
Evening Argus

Works of reference

Encyclopaedia of Brighton, (Brighton, n.d.), located in Brighton Central Reference Library

Secondary sources

Baxter, R.G. and Howe, D.G., 'Municipal activities in Brighton during the past twelve years', *Proceedings of the Institute of Municipal and County Engineers*, vol. LXIII, (1936–37).
Beevers, D. and Roles, J., *A Pictorial History of Brighton*, (Derby, 1993).
Fogarty, M.P., *Prospects of the Industrial Areas of Great Britain*, (London, 1945).
Forester, T., *The Labour Party and the Working Class*, (London, 1976).
Freeman, T.W., *The Conurbations of Great Britain*, (Manchester, 1959).
Gilbert, E.M., *Brighton: Old Ocean's Bauble*, (Hassocks, 1975).
Hopper, T., 'Transformation of Political Consciousness in South East England, 1880–1914', (Ph.D. thesis, University of Brighton, 1998).

Hopper, T., 'The beginnings of the labour movement in south east England, 1880–1914', *Journal of Regional and Local Studies*, vol. 17, (1997), pp. 23–32.

Musgrave, C., *Life in Brighton: From the Earliest Times to the Present*, (London, 1970).

Pelling, H., *Social Geography of British Elections 1885–1910*, (Aldershot, 1994).

Walton, J., *Blackpool*, (Edinburgh, 1998).

Brighton wards 1919–1928

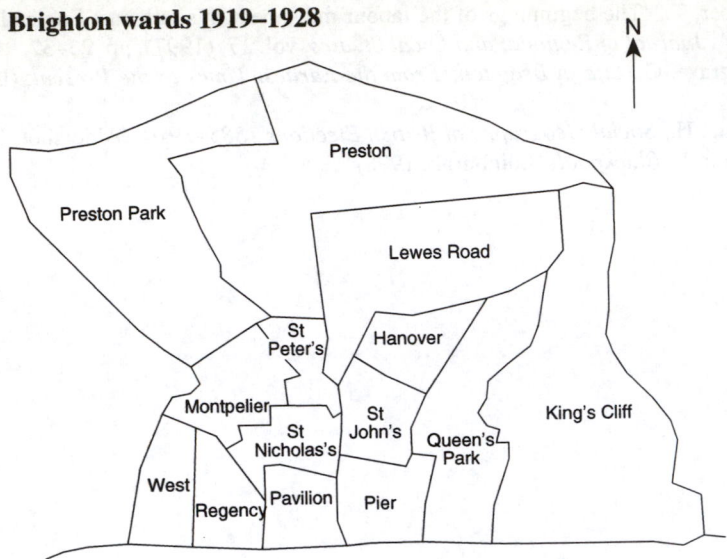

N

Preston

Preston Park

Lewes Road

St Peter's

Hanover

Montpelier

St John's

King's Cliff

St Nicholas's

Queen's Park

West

Regency

Pavilion

Pier

English Channel

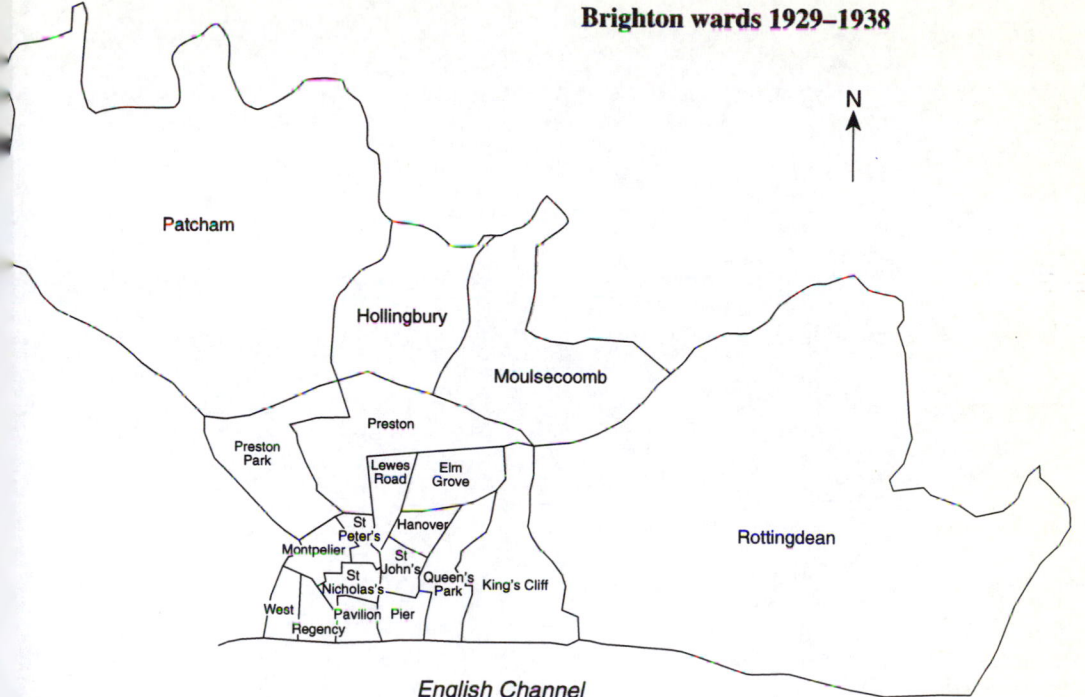

Brighton wards 1929–1938

N

Patcham

Hollingbury

Moulsecoomb

Preston

Preston
Park

Lewes
Road

Elm
Grove

Rottingdean

St
Peter's

Hanover

Montpelier

St
John's

Queen's
Park

King's Cliff

St
Nicholas's

West

Pavilion

Pier

Regency

English Channel

Persons aged fourteen and over classified by industry 1931

	Male	%	Female	%	Total	%
Metal and engineering	5,119	11.3	479	2.0	5,598	8.0
- *Engineering*	*1,016*	*2.2*	*32*	*0.1*	*1,048*	*1.5*
- *Electrical engineering*	*1,793*	*4.0*	*354*	*1.4*	*2,147*	*3.1*
- *Vehicle construction*	*1,717*	*3.8*	*36*	*0.1*	*1,753*	*2.5*
Clothing	799	1.8	1,075	4.4	1,874	2.7
Building	5,325	11.8	69	0.3	5,394	7.7
Transport	4,612	10.2	139	0.6	4,751	6.8
- *Rail*	*2,004*	*4.4*	*28*	*0.1*	*2,032*	*2.9*
- *Road*	*2,353*	*5.2*	*92*	*0.4*	*2,445*	*3.5*
Commerce and finance	10,883	24.1	4,865	19.9	15,748	22.6
Public admin. and defence	4,540	10.0	1,343	5.5	5,883	8.4
- *Local government*	*2,722*	*6.0*	*998*	*4.1*	*3,720*	*5.3*
Professions	1,712	3.8	1,732	7.1	3,444	4.9
Personal service	4,473	9.9	12,445	51.0	16,918	24.3
Other	7,767	17.2	2,270	9.3	10,037	14.4
Total (a)	**45,230**		**24,417**		**69,647**	
Total population (b)	65,677		81,750		147,427	
(a) as % of (b)	68.9		29.9		47.2	
Total out of work (c)	4,026		1,637		5,663	
(c) as % of (a)	8.9		6.7		8.1	
Managerial and own account	8,219	19.9	3,190	14.0	11,409	17.8
Operative	32,985	80.1	19,590	86.0	52,575	82.2
Total (excluding out of work)	41,204		22,780		63,984	

Population statistics 1931

Ward	Acres	Population	Persons/acre	Persons/room
Elm Grove	176	9,343	53.09	0.88
Hanover	70	9,266	132.37	0.95
Hollingbury	258	10,395	40.29	0.68
King's Cliff	472	10,719	22.71	0.74
Lewes Road	106	6,340	59.81	0.82
Montpelier	113	6,305	55.80	0.70
Moulsecoomb	249	9,096	36.53	0.90
Patcham	4,310	2,757	0.64	0.63
Pavilion	77	3,294	42.78	0.77
Pier	81	9,291	114.70	0.86
Preston	187	8,417	45.01	0.62
Preston Park	305	8,687	28.48	0.63
Queen's Park	195	11,432	58.63	0.86
Regency	77	6,319	82.06	0.72
Rottingdean	5,550	6,586	1.19	0.81
St John's	78	10,585	135.71	0.98
St Nicholas	77	7,695	99.94	0.91
St Peter's	54	5,271	97.61	0.89
West	68	5,629	82.78	0.67
Total	**12,503**	**147,427**	**11.79**	**0.79**

Overall position on the council 1919–38

	Position			Gains			Losses	
	Other	Lab		Other	Lab		Other	Lab
1919	45	11		0	1		1	0
1920	44	12		1	2		2	1
1921	44	12		0	0		0	0
1922	45	11		1	0		0	1
1923	43	13		0	1		1	0
1924	45	11		2	0		0	2
1925	46	10		0	0		0	0
1926	47	9		1	0		0	1
1927	44	12		0	2		2	0
1928	43	13		0	1		1	0
1929	58	18		-	-		-	-
1930	59	17		1	0		0	1
1931	65	11		6	0		0	6
1932	68	8		3	0		0	3
1933	68	8		1	1		1	1
1934	63	13		0	4		4	0
1935	60	16		0	2		2	0
1936	60	16		1	1		1	1
1937	58	18		0	2		2	0
1938	58	18		2	1		1	2

Aldermen 1919–38

1919	Others – 14		1929	Others – 18, Lab – 1
1920	Others – 14		1930	Others – 18, Lab – 1
1921	Others – 14		1931	Others – 18, Lab – 1
1922	Others – 14		1932	Others – 18, Lab – 1
1923	Others – 13, Lab – 1		1933	Others – 18, Lab – 1
1924	Others – 13, Lab – 1		1934	Others – 18, Lab – 1
1925	Others – 13, Lab – 1		1935	Others – 17, Lab – 2
1926	Others – 13, Lab – 1		1936	Others – 17, Lab – 2
1927	Others – 13, Lab – 1		1937	Others – 17, Lab – 2
1928	Others – 13, Lab – 1		1938	Others – 16, Lab – 3

Municipal elections: winning party 1919–28

Ward	1919	1920	1921	1922	1923	1924	1925	1926	1927	1928
Elm Grove	-	-	-	-	-	-	-	-	-	-
Hanover	**Lab**	Lab	Lab	Lab	Lab	**Lab**	**Lab**	Lab	**Lab**	**Lab**
Hollingbury	-	-	-	-	-	-	-	-	-	-
King's Cliff	O	O	**O**	**O**	O	**O**	**O**	O	**O**	**O**
Lewes Road	Lab	Lab	Lab	**Lab**	Lab	O	**Lab**	Lab	Lab	Lab
Montpelier	O	**O**	O	**O**	**O**	**O**	O	**O**	**O**	**O**
Moulsecoomb	-	-	-	-	-	-	-	-	-	-
Patcham	-	-	-	-	-	-	-	-	-	-
Pavilion	O	O	**O**	**O**	O	**O**	**O**	O	**O**	**O**
Pier	O	O	O	O	O	O	**O**	O	O	O
Preston	O	**O**	O	O	**O**	O	**O**	**O**	**O**	**O**
Preston Park	Lab	**O**	**O**	**Lab**	**O**	**O**	**O**	**O**	**O**	**O**
Queen's Park	**O**	O	O	**O**	**O**	**O**	**O**	O	O	**O**
Regency	**O**	**O**	O	O	**O**	**O**	**O**	O	O	**O**
Rottingdean	-	-	-	-	-	-	-	-	-	-
St John's	Lab	Lab	Lab	O	Lab	Lab	O	Lab	Lab	Lab
St Nicholas's	O	O	O	O	Lab	O	O	O	O	O
St Peter's	O	Lab	Lab	O	Lab	O	O	Lab	Lab	Lab
West	**O**	**O**	**O**	O	**O**	**O**	**O**	O	**O**	**O**

Municipal elections: party wins per year 1919–28

	1919	1920	1921	1922	1923	1924	1925	1926	1927	1928
Other	10	10	10	11	9	12	12	10	10	10
Lab	4	4	4	3	5	2	2	4	4	4
Total	14	14	14	14	14	14	14	14	14	14
Turnout (%)	41.2	43.8	34.4	32.5	36.1	34.0	43.6	38.6	38.8	37.2
Lab (%)	36.6	37.0	30.0	25.4	53.2	36.0	32.1	38.6	32.7	37.4

Municipal elections: winning party 1929–38

Ward	1929	1930	1931	1932	1933	1934	1935	1936	1937	1938
Elm Grove	Lab	Lab	O	Lab	Lab	Lab	Lab	O	Lab	O
Hanover	Lab	O	O	Lab	Lab	Lab	Lab	O	Lab	Lab
Hollingbury	O	O	O	O	O	O	O	O	O	O
King's Cliff	O	O	O	O	O	O	O	O	O	O
Lewes Road	Lab	Lab	O	O	O	O	O	O	O	Lab
Montpelier	O	O	O	O	O	O	O	O	O	O
Moulsecoomb	Lab	O	O	Lab	O	O	Lab	O	O	Lab
Patcham	O	O	O	O	O	O	O	O	O	O
Pavilion	O	O	O	O	O	O	O	O	O	O
Pier	O	O	O	O	O	O	O	O	O	O
Preston	O	O	O	O	O	O	O	O	O	O
Preston Park	O	O	O	O	O	O	O	O	O	O
Queen's Park	O	O	O	O	O	O	O	O	O	O
Regency	O	O	O	O	O	O	O	O	O	O
Rottingdean	O	O	O	O	O	O	Lab	Lab	Lab	Lab
St John's	Lab	Lab	O	O	Lab	Lab	Lab	Lab	Lab	Lab
St Nicholas's	O	O	O	O	O	O	O	O	Lab	O
St Peter's	Lab	Lab	O	O	O	Lab	Lab	O	Lab	O
West	O	O	O	O	O	O	O	O	O	O

Municipal elections: party wins per year 1929–38

	1929	1930	1931	1932	1933	1934	1935	1936	1937	1938
Other	13	15	19	16	16	15	13	17	13	14
Lab	6	4	0	3	3	4	6	2	6	5
Total	19	19	19	19	19	19	19	19	19	19
Turnout (%)	33.0	35.3	46.8	36.9	38.1	39.1	40.1	40.5	40.8	38.5
Lab (%)	33.7	22.6	25.1	30.0	31.2	31.5	45.7	28.4	34.4	34.3

Municipal elections: party wins per ward 1919–38

	Other	Lab	Total	Turnout %	Labour % of all votes
Elm Grove	3	7	10	37.5	52.2
Hanover	3	17	20	32.8	57.1
Hollingbury	10	0	10	36.0	28.0
King's Cliff	20	0	20	41.3	27.2
Lewes Road	8	12	20	39.7	55.6
Montpelier	20	0	20	37.6	3.2
Moulsecoomb	6	4	10	39.4	54.2
Patcham	10	0	10	49.2	14.4
Pavilion	20	0	20	44.7	5.1
Pier	20	0	20	30.7	7.4
Preston	20	0	20	36.2	14.9
Preston Park	18	2	20	43.2	19.6
Queen's Park	20	0	20	40.0	22.1
Regency	20	0	20	44.6	-
Rottingdean	6	4	10	34.6	39.4
St John's	4	16	20	33.7	48.8
St Nicholas's	18	2	20	39.2	17.3
St Peter's	9	11	20	49.9	49.9
West	20	0	20	39.7	-
Total	**255**	**75**	**330**	**38.3**	**33.3**

Seats won by Labour as a percentage of all wins 1919–38   **22.7**

Parliamentary election results

Brighton constituency *(double-member seat)*
(all wards within the borough [1918 boundaries] were included in the constituency, along with municipal borough of Hove)

General election	Winner	Conservative %	Labour %	Liberal %
14 Dec. 1918	Co C(1)	39.7	10.8	-
	Co C(2)	39.2	10.3	-
15 Nov. 1922[a]	C(1)	32.0	-	24.7
	C(2)	30.0	-	-
6 Dec. 1923	C(1)	26.8	8.5	15.5
	C(2)	26.5	8.0	14.7
29 Oct. 1924	C(1)	42.5	15.2	-
	C(2)	42.3	-	-
30 May 1929	C(1)	29.1	12.2	9.3
	C(2)	29.0	11.7	8.7
27 Oct. 1931	C(1)	42.7	7.4	-
	C(2)	42.6	7.3	-
14 Nov. 1935	C(1)	38.2	12.1	-
	C(2)	38.0	11.7	-

[a] 1922 – Independent Conservative candidate received 13.3% of the poll.

Elm Grove ward
(created in 1928, previously comprised eastern part of Lewes Road ward)

Candidate	Party	Votes	%	Electors	Turnout	Gains
1929						
S.D. Deason*	Lab	907	59.6	4,654	32.7	-
Mrs E.M. Beven		357	23.5			
Mrs H. Burden		258	17.0			
Total votes		1,522				
1930						
F. Howell	Lab	769	47.4	4,695	34.6	-
W.J. Milton		658	40.5			
Mrs H. Burden		197	12.1			
Total votes		1,624				
1931						
A.S. Tilley		1,044	53.5	*4,693*	41.6	Other from
F.W. Larkin*	Lab	840	43.1			Lab
Mrs H. Burden		67	3.4			
Total votes		1,951				
1932						
L.C. Cohen	Lab	1,013	57.9	*4,691*	37.3	-
A.E. Dyson		736	42.1			
Total votes		1,749				
1933						
T. Cochrane	Lab	918	65.5	*4,689*	29.9	-
J. Enves		483	34.5			
Total votes		1,401				
1934						
F.W. Larkin	Lab	903	55.4	*4,687*	34.8	Lab from
H.H. Hartnell		728	44.6			Other
Total votes		1,631				
1935						
L.C. Cohen*	Lab	1,072	54.6	4,682	42.0	-
H. Taylor	Ind	893	45.4			
Total votes		1,965				

Elm Grove ward *(continued)*

Candidate	Party	Votes	%	Electors	Turnout	Gains
1936						
A.A. Illman	Lab	Unopp.	-		-	-
1937						
F.W. Larkin*	Lab	Unopp.	-		-	-
1938						
J.V. Reeves	BMC and R	1,277	58.5	4,589	47.6	Other from Lab
L.C. Cohen*	Lab	907	41.5			
Total votes		2,184				

Overall Labour vote **52.2%**   **Overall turnout** **37.5%**

Hanover ward

Candidate	Party	Votes	%	Electors	Turnout	Gains
1919						
A.E. Horn*	Lab	Unopp.	-		-	-
1920						
M.W. Huggett*	Lab	985	46.8	3,984	52.8	-
E.S. Hardiman	MCU	624	29.6			
G. Calcutt		496	23.6			
Total votes		2,105				
1921						
T. Cochrane	Lab	836	64.9	4,094	31.5	-
J. Ireland	Ind	385	29.9			
A.E. Richardson	Nuwm	68	5.3			
Total votes		1,289				
1922						
Mrs E.J. Smith	Lab	827	66.6	4,286	29.0	-
H. Peters		414	33.4			
Total votes		1,241				
1923						
M.W. Huggett*	Lab	991	81.2	4,287	28.5	-
H. Peters		230	18.8			
Total votes		1,221				
1924						
T. Cochrane*	Lab	Unopp.	-		-	-
1925						
Mrs E.J. Smith*	Lab	Unopp.	-		-	-
1926						
M.W. Huggett*	Lab	991	92.5	*4,419*	24.2	-
W.E. English		80	7.5			
Total votes		1,071				
1927						
T. Cochrane	Lab	Unopp.	-		-	-

Hanover ward (continued)

Candidate	Party	Votes	%	Electors	Turnout	Gains
1928						
Mrs E.J. Smith*	Lab	Unopp.	-		-	-
1929						
M.W. Huggett*	Lab	764	74.3	4,550	22.6	-
A. Somerville		264	25.7			
Total votes		1,028				
1930						
C. Cashman		568	50.2	4,177	27.1	Other from
T. Cochrane*	Lab	564	49.8			Lab
Total votes		1,132				
1931						
C.F. Marner		1,053	53.2	4,184	47.3	Other from
L.C. Cohen*	Lab	855	43.2			Lab
H. Cowley	Nuwm	72	3.6			
Total votes		1,980				
1932						
M.W. Huggett*	Lab	Unopp.	-		-	-
1933						
H. Harris	Lab	714	54.3	4,198	31.3	Lab from
C. Cashman*		602	45.7			Other
Total votes		1,316				
1934						
H.J. Robbins	Lab	725	51.6	4,205	33.4	Lab from
E.A. Lambert		679	48.4			Other
Total votes		1,404				
1935						
M.W. Huggett*	Lab	Unopp.	-		-	-
1936						
F.D. Ingham		1,096	69.6	4,217	37.3	Other from
F.G. Chadwick	Lab	478	30.4			Lab
Total votes		1,574				

Hanover ward *(continued)*

Candidate	Party	Votes	%	Electors	Turnout	Gains
1937						
H.J. Robbins*	Lab	Unopp.	-		-	-
1938						
W.C. Chinchen	Lab	747	60.4	4,025	30.7	-
E. Goulding	BMC and R	490	39.6			
Total votes		1,237				

Overall Labour vote   **57.1%**   **Overall turnout**   **32.8%**

Hollingbury ward
(added by extension of the borough in 1928)

Candidate	Party	Votes	%	Electors	Turnout	Gains
1929						
J. Routley*		1,142	62.5	5,433	33.6	-
J.A. Smith	Lab	686	37.5			
Total votes		1,828				
1930						
H. Hone*		1,315	70.9	5,711	32.5	-
J.A. Smith	Lab	539	29.1			
Total votes		1,854				
1931						
Miss M.J. Hardy*		1,845	68.2	5,761	47.0	-
G. Gander	Lab	862	31.8			
Total votes		2,707				
1932						
J. Routley*		1,363	62.6	5,812	37.4	-
G. Gander	Lab	813	37.4			
Total votes		2,176				
1933						
H. Hone*		Unopp.	-		-	-
1934						
Miss M.J. Hardy*		Unopp.	-		-	-
1935						
J. Routley*		Unopp.	-		-	-
1936						
H. Hone*		Unopp.	-		-	-
1937						
A. Jones*		Unopp.	-		-	-

Hollingbury ward *(continued)*

Candidate	Party	Votes	%	Electors	Turnout	Gains
1938						
T.W. Gardner*		969	53.7	6,115	29.5	-
P.E. Gwyer	BMC	836	46.3			
Total votes		1,805				

Overall Labour vote   **28.0%**   **Overall turnout**   **36.0%**

King's Cliff ward

Candidate	Party	Votes	%	Electors	Turnout	Gains
1919						
J. Carter		995	72.2	2,522	54.7	-
H.H. Perry	Ind	384	27.8			
Total votes		1,379				
1920						
E.D. Stafford	MCU	1,040	80.7	3,469	37.2	-
H. Weller	Lab	249	19.3			
Total votes		1,289				
1921						
C.J. Teasdale*		Unopp.	-		-	-
1922						
J. Carter*		Unopp.	-		-	-
1923						
E.D. Stafford*		550	39.3	2,877	48.7	-
T.E. Morris	Lab	518	37.0			
P.R. Jacklin		332	23.7			
Total votes		1,400				
1924						
C.J. Teasdale*		Unopp.	-		-	-
1925						
J. Carter*		Unopp.	-		-	-
1926						
W.E. Radford		1,090	79.7	3,195	42.8	-
T.E. Morris	Lab	277	20.3			
Total votes		1,367				
1927						
H.G. Winterton*		Unopp.	-		-	-
1928						
J. Carter*		Unopp.	-		-	-

King's Cliff ward *(continued)*

Candidate	Party	Votes	%	Electors	Turnout	Gains
1929						
W.E. Radford*		Unopp.	-		-	-
1930						
H.G. Winterton*		Unopp.	-		-	-
1931						
J.B. Reiner*		Unopp.	-		-	-
1932						
W.E. Radford*		Unopp.	-		-	-
1933						
H.G. Winterton*		Unopp.	-		-	-
1934						
W. Marsh*		Unopp.	-		-	
1935						
W.E. Radford*		Unopp.	-		-	-
1936						
G.C. Wallington*		Unopp.	-		-	-
1937						
H.B. Hartnell		1,269	62.1	*5,347*	38.2	-
R.P.M. Polling	Lab	773	37.9			
Total votes		2,042				
1938						
W.E. Radford*	BMC	1,240	62.1	5,543	36.0	-
R.P.M. Polling	Lab	758	37.9			
Total votes		1,998				

Overall Labour vote   **27.2%**   **Overall turnout**   **41.3%**

Lewes Road ward
(eastern part of the ward removed to form Elm Grove ward in 1928)

Candidate	Party	Votes	%	Electors	Turnout	Gains
1919						
H.B. Elliott	Lab	1,923	65.0	6,726	44.0	-
G. Privett	Ind	638	21.6			
E.S. Hardiman		399	13.5			
Total votes		2,960				
1920						
A.J. Grinstead	Lab	1,496	51.5	6,913	42.0	Lab from
A. Martin*	MCU	1,409	48.5			MCU
Total votes		2,905				
1921						
H.M. Black*	Lab	1,639	95.7	7,118	24.1	-
F.G. Blackman	Nuwm	73	4.3			
Total votes		1,712				
1922						
H.B. Elliott*	Lab	Unopp.	-		-	-
1923						
A.J. Grinstead*	Lab	1,424	88.6	7,311	22.0	-
H. Glass		183	11.4			
Total votes		1,607				
1924						
Mrs J.M. Buckwell		1,246	53.0	*7,359*	32.0	Other from
W. Smith*	Lab	1,106	47.0			Lab
Total votes		2,352				
1925						
H.B. Elliott*	Lab	Unopp.	-		-	-
1926						
A.J. Grinstead*	Lab	1,702	57.4	7,455	39.7	-
F.J. Matthews		1,261	42.6			
Total votes		2,963				

Lewes Road ward (continued)

Candidate	Party	Votes	%	Electors	Turnout	Gains
1927						
T.E. Morris	Lab	1,579	58.5	7,457	36.2	Lab from
Mrs J.M. Buckwell*		1,122	41.5			Other
Total votes		2,701				
1928						
H.B.Elliott*	Lab	843	52.6	3,132	51.2	
W.J. Milton	NCU	631	39.4			
Mrs H. Burden	NCU	129	8.0			
Total votes		1,603				
1929						
A.J. Grinstead*	Lab	746	60.2	3,376	36.7	-
W. Clout		494	39.8			
Total votes		1,240				
1930						
T.E. Morris*	Lab	777	59.9	2,365	54.8	-
C. Smart		520	40.1			
Total votes		1,297				
1931						
W. Clout		1,055	62.4	*2,541*	66.5	Other from
T. Cochrane	Lab	636	37.6			Lab
Total votes		1,691				
1932						
F.C. Schofield		824	61.8	*2,717*	49.1	Other from
W.H. Baker	Lab	510	38.2			Lab
Total votes		1,334				
1933						
T.E. Morris*		968	64.9	*2,903*	51.4	-
F.A. Steel	Lab	523	35.1			
Total votes		1,491				
1934						
W. Clout*		Unopp.	-		-	-

Lewes Road ward *(continued)*

Candidate	Party	Votes	%	Electors	Turnout	Gains
1935						
F.C. Schofield*	Ind	913	60.6	3,245	46.4	-
A.A. Illman	Lab	593	39.4			
Total votes		1,506				
1936						
T.E. Morris*		858	55.5	3,245	47.6	-
R.H. Thompson	Lab	688	44.5			
Total votes		1,546				
1937						
W. Clout*		Unopp.	-		-	-
1938						
R.H. Thompson	Lab	820	51.3	3,175	50.4	Lab from
F.C. Schofield*		780	48.8			Other
Total votes		1,600				

Overall Labour vote   **55.7%**   **Overall turnout**   **39.6%**

Montpelier ward

Candidate	Party	Votes	%	Electors	Turnout	Gains
1919						
J. Mansfield*		684	77.9	2,200	39.9	-
Mrs J. Canter	Lab	194	22.1			
Total votes		878				
1920						
S.C. Thompson*		Unopp.	-		-	-
1921						
S.G. Gibson	MCU	814	62.7	2,565	50.6	-
Lady R. Pelham	Ind	474	36.5			
H.M. Steer	Nuwm	10	0.8			
Total votes		1,298				
1922						
J. Mansfield*		Unopp.	-		-	-
1923						
S.C. Thompson*		Unopp.	-		-	-
1924						
S.G. Gibson*		Unopp.	-		-	-
1925						
J. Mansfield*		717	89.2	2,768	29.0	-
F. Howells	Lab	87	10.8			
Total votes		804				
1926						
S.C. Thompson*		Unopp.	-		-	-
1927						
S.G. Gibson*		Unopp.	-		-	-
1928						
T. Read		Unopp.	-		-	-

Montpelier ward (continued)

Candidate	Party	Votes	%	Electors	Turnout	Gains
1929						
G.W. Fabian*		497	41.8	3,176	37.5	-
J.D. Green		413	34.7			
E.D. Stafford		280	23.5			
Total votes		1,190				
1930						
S.G. Gibson*		508	61.4	3,161	26.2	-
E.C. Jones		320	38.6			
Total votes		828				
1931						
T. Read*		1,005	79.8	3,161	39.8	-
E.C. Jones		254	20.2			
Total votes		1,259				
1932						
G.W. Fabian*		Unopp.	-		-	-
1933						
S.G. Gibson*		Unopp.	-		-	-
1934						
S. Davey		796	58.0	3,162	43.4	-
J.W. Green		576	42.0			
Total votes		1,372				
1935						
G.W. Fabian*		Unopp.	-		-	-
1936						
A. Rostance*		Unopp.	-		-	-
1937						
S. Davey*		Unopp.	-		-	-

Montpelier ward *(continued)*

Candidate	Party	Votes	%	Electors	Turnout	Gains
1938						
H. Ford*	BMC and R	594	51.6	3,164	36.4	-
F.J. Wellman		557	48.4			
Total votes		1,151				

Overall Labour vote   **3.2%**   **Overall turnout**   **37.6%**

Moulsecoomb ward
(added by extension of the borough in 1928)

Candidate	Party	Votes	%	Electors	Turnout	Gains
1929						
G. Simcock*	Lab	830	75.0	3,825	28.9	-
H.G. Katte		276	25.0			
Total votes		1,106				
1930						
C.J. Manton*		Unopp.	-		-	-
1931						
A.V. Nicholls		907	53.9	*3,921*	42.9	Other from
Miss E.L. Pickworth*	Lab	777	46.1			Lab
Total votes		1,684				
1932						
G. Simcock*	Lab	993	55.3	*3,969*	45.2	-
E. Heaps	Ind	676	37.7			
H. Weller		126	7.0			
Total votes		1,795				
1933						
C.G. Manton*		Unopp.	-		-	-
1934						
A.V. Nicholls*		916	51.0	*4,065*	44.2	-
J.M. Galyer	Lab	880	49.0			
Total votes		1,796				
1935						
G. Simcock*	Lab	Unopp.	-		-	-
1936						
C.G.Manton*		Unopp.	-		-	-
1937						
Ms E.R. Richards		Unopp.	-		-	-

Moulsecoomb ward *(continued)*

Candidate	Party	Votes	%	Electors	Turnout	Gains
1938						
W. Whiting	Lab	798	52.9	4,260	35.4	-
E. Richardson	BMC and R	710	47.1			
Total votes		1,508				

Overall Labour vote   **54.2%**   **Overall turnout**   **39.4%**

Patcham ward
(added by extension of the borough in 1928)

Candidate	Party	Votes	%	Electors	Turnout	Gains
1929						
E.E. Lyons		Unopp.	-		-	-
1930						
H.J. Morriss*		Unopp.	-		-	-
1931						
J.B. Pollitt*		Unopp.	-		-	-
1932						
E.E. Lyons		469	64.7	*1,500*	48.3	
W. Dillistone		256	35.3			
Total votes		725				
1933						
B. Dutton Briant*		Unopp.	-		-	-
1934						
E.G. Ross	R	Unopp.	-		-	-
1935						
E. Idle		Unopp.	-		-	-
1936						
B. Dutton Briant*		1,051	53.6	3,666	53.5	-
H. Ogden		910	46.4			
Total votes		1,961				
1937						
F.H. Woods		1,457	60.6	*4,696*	51.2	-
E.G. Ross*	R	946	39.4			
Total votes		2,403				

Patcham ward *(continued)*

Candidate	Party	Votes	%	Electors	Turnout	Gains
1938						
E.A. Idle*	BMC and R	1,482	57.3	5,725	45.2	-
E.G. Ross	Lab	1,104	42.7			
Total votes		2,586				

Overall Labour vote   **14.4%**   **Overall turnout**   **49.2%**

Pavilion ward

Candidate	Party	Votes	%	Electors	Turnout	Gains
1919						
J.L. Thompson		356	58.0	1,480	41.5	-
Mrs C. Ryle*		258	42.0			
Total votes		614				
1920						
E.C. Baldwin	MCU	374	55.6	1,463	46.0	-
H.T. Ashly		195	29.0			
Mrs E. Hutton		104	15.5			
Total votes		673				
1921						
A.L.B. Tindall*		Unopp.	-		-	-
1922						
J.L. Thompson*		Unopp.	-		-	-
1923						
E.C. Baldwin*		381	55.7	1,593	42.9	-
F.A. Rice		303	44.3			
Total votes		684				
1924						
A.L.B. Tyndall*		Unopp.	-		-	-
1925						
J.L. Thompson*		Unopp.	-		-	-
1926						
H.J. Preston		708	91.8	1,660	46.4	-
J.W. Norris		63	8.2			
Total votes		771				
1927						
A.L.B. Tyndall*		Unopp.	-		-	-
1928						
W.E. Trory*		Unopp.	-		-	-

Pavilion ward (*continued*)

Candidate	Party	Votes	%	Electors	Turnout	Gains
1929						
H.G.W. Bishop		478	66.5	1,780	40.4	-
L.C. Cohen	Lab	241	33.5			
Total votes		719				
1930						
A.L.B. Tyndall*		Unopp.	-		-	-
1931						
R.W. Bristow		632	71.2	*1,706*	52.1	-
W.E. Trory*		256	28.8			
Total votes		888				
1932						
H.G.W. Bishop*		Unopp.	-		-	-
1933						
C.H. Tyson		394	61.0	*1,632*	39.6	-
W.E. Trory*		252	39.0			
Total votes		646				
1934						
R.W. Bristow*		429	70.2	*1,595*	38.3	-
W.R. Loader		182	29.8			
Total votes		611				
1935						
H.G.W. Bishop*		Unopp.	-		-	-
1936						
C.H. Tyson*		453	63.2	1,524	47.0	-
H.L.V. Pearn		264	36.8			
Total votes		717				
1937						
R.W. Bristow*		Unopp.	-		-	-

Pavilion ward *(continued)*

Candidate	Party	Votes	%	Electors	Turnout	Gains
1938						
G. Fitzgerald	R	340	47.2	1,319	54.6	-
H.G.W. Bishop*	BMC	261	36.3			
A. Trigg	Lab	119	16.5			
Total votes		720				

Overall Labour vote		**5.1%**		**Overall turnout**		**44.7%**

Pier ward

Candidate	Party	Votes	%	Electors	Turnout	Gains
1919						
A.E. Mellor*		711	59.0	3,073	39.2	-
Mrs Hutton		494	41.0			
Total votes		1,205				
1920						
W.W. Savage*	MCU	792	77.3	3,160	32.4	-
T. Harper	Lab	233	22.7			
Total votes		1,025				
1921						
C.J. Galliers*	MCU	746	86.6	2,294	37.5	-
P. Gallagher	Nuwm	115	13.4			
Total votes		861				
1922						
A.E. Mellor*		676	57.4	4,012	29.4	-
T. Harper	Lab	404	34.3			
A.E. Richardson		98	8.3			
Total votes		1,178				
1923						
S.B. Titcomb		799	79.8	3,454	29.0	-
T. Harper	Lab	192	19.2			
P. Gallagher		10	1.0			
Total votes		1,001				
1924						
H.J. Galliers*		950	83.0	*3,496*	32.8	-
F. Howell	Lab	195	17.0			
Total votes		1,145				
1925						
R.W. Herriott		Unopp.	-		-	-
1926						
S.B. Titcomb*		707	85.8	3,581	23.0	-
A.E. Richardson		117	14.2			
Total votes		824				

Pier ward *(continued)*

Candidate	Party	Votes	%	Electors	Turnout	Gains
1927						
H.J. Galliers*		925	69.7	3,632	36.6	-
P.J. Brady		403	30.3			
Total votes		1,328				
1928						
R.W. Herriott*		607	59.5	3,631	28.1	-
P.J. Brady		414	40.5			
Total votes		1,021				
1929						
S.B. Titcombe*		493	63.9	3,813	20.2	-
C.A. Colwell		279	36.1			
Total votes		772				
1930						
O. Dalton	Unopp.	-			-	-
1931						
J.H. Bassett		756	44.0	*3,737*	45.9	-
R.W. Herriott*		585	34.1			
F.O. Hilson		358	20.9			
A.E. Richardson	Nuwm	18	1.0			
Total votes		1,717				
1932						
S.B. Titcomb*		485	70.2	*3,699*	18.7	-
E.A. West		206	29.8			
Total votes		691				
1933						
O. Dalton*	Unopp.	-			-	-
1934						
J.H. Bassett*	Unopp.	-			-	-
1935						
W.G. Dudeney*	Unopp.	-			-	-

Pier ward *continued)*

Candidate	Party	Votes	%	Electors	Turnout	Gains
1936						
G.A. Moore-Lynch		735	66.8	3,544	31.1	-
E.D. Stafford		366	33.2			
Total votes		1,101				
1937						
J.H. Bassett*		Unopp.	-		-	-
1938						
W.G. Dudeney*		Unopp.	-		-	-

Overall Labour vote   **7.4%**   **Overall turnout**   **30.7%**

Preston ward

Candidate	Party	Votes	%	Electors	Turnout	Gains
1919						
J.N. Ward		2,416	64.4	7,280	51.5	-
A.F. Gasston	Lab	1,334	35.6			
Total votes		3,750				
1920						
H. Cane*		Unopp.	-		-	-
1921						
B.N. Southall*		2,152	96.7	7,809	28.5	-
W.H. Dawson		73	3.3			
Total votes		2,225				
1922						
J.N. Ward*		1,969	95.2	8,848	23.4	-
T.G. Swain		100	4.8			
Total votes		2,069				
1923						
H. Cane*		Unopp.	-		-	-
1924						
W.E. Cox		1,825	67.1	7,698	35.3	Other from
A. Robertson*	Lab	896	32.9			Lab
Total votes		2,721				
1925						
J.N. Ward*		Unopp.	-		-	-
1926						
H. Cane*		Unopp.	-		-	-
1927						
F.J. Beal*		Unopp.	-		-	-
1928						
H.W. Aldrich*		Unopp.	-		-	-

Preston ward *(continued)*

Candidate	Party	Votes	%	Electors	Turnout	Gains
1929						
A.G. Beckett*		1,547	72.3	4,821	44.4	-
C.P. Pearson		592	27.7			
Total votes		2,139				
1930						
F.G. Beal*		Unopp.	-		-	-
1931						
J.N. Ward*		Unopp.	-		-	-
1932						
A.G. Beckett*		Unopp.	-		-	-
1933						
F.G. Beal*		Unopp.	-		-	-
1934						
E.J. Neale*		Unopp.	-		-	-
1935						
A.G. Beckett*		Unopp.	-		-	-
1936						
Sir C.G. Grey*		Unopp.	-		-	-
1937						
E.J. Neale*		Unopp.	-		-	-
1938						
H.L. Harvey	BMC and R	1,167	57.8	4,805	42.0	-
A.G. Beckett*		852	42.2			
Total votes		2,019				

Overall Labour vote   **14.9%**   **Overall turnout**   **36.2%**

Preston Park ward

Candidate	Party	Votes	%	Electors	Turnout	Gains
1919						
H. Aldrich	Lab	865	47.5	5,853	31.1	Lab from Ind
C.G. Yates*		845	46.4			
J. Jeffs		110	6.0			
Total votes		1,820				
1920						
W.L. Campbell*		Unopp.	-		-	-
1921						
C.G. Yates		Unopp.	-		-	-
1922						
H. Aldrich*	Lab	Unopp.	-		-	-
1923						
W.L. Campbell*		Unopp.	-		-	-
1924						
C.J. Yates*		Unopp.	-		-	-
1925						
H.W. Aldrich*		Unopp.	-		-	-

(this Independent candidate had succeeded a Labour councillor of the same surname — it is not known if the two were related)

Candidate	Party	Votes	%	Electors	Turnout	Gains
1926						
E. Denne		Unopp.	-		-	-
1927						
C.J. Yates		Unopp.	-		-	-
1928						
J.N. Ward*		Unopp.	-		-	-
1929						
E. Denne*		Unopp.	-	4,596	-	-
1930						
C.J. Yates*		Unopp.	-		-	-

Preston Park ward *(continued)*

Candidate	Party	Votes	%	Electors	Turnout	Gains
1931						
W.H. Humphreys		1,821	70.3	*4,344*	59.6	-
M. Milner		499	19.3			
G. Privett		269	10.4			
Total votes		2,589				
1932						
E. Denne*		Unopp.	-		-	-
1933						
H.W. Mursell*		Unopp.	-		-	-
1934						
W.H. Humphreys*		Unopp.	-		-	-
1935						
E. Denne*		Unopp.	-		-	-
1936						
H.W. Mursell*		Unopp.	-		-	-
1937						
W.H. Humphreys*		Unopp.	-		-	-
1938						
J. Horton-Stephens*		Unopp.	-		-	-

Overall Labour vote   **19.6%**   **Overall turnout**   **43.2%**

Queen's Park ward

Candidate	Party	Votes	%	Electors	Turnout	Gains
1919						
G.N. Jacklin*		Unopp.	-		-	-
1920						
G. Bridle	MCU	1,159	77.7	2,748	54.3	-
T.E. Morris	Lab	332	22.3			
Total votes		1,491				
1921						
T.J. Braybon*	Ind	1,001	93.3	3,049	35.2	-
G. Kipling	Nuwm	72	6.7			
Total votes		1,073				
1922						
G.N. Jacklin*		Unopp.	-		-	-
1923						
G. Bridle*		Unopp.	-		-	-
1924						
T.J. Braybon*		Unopp.	-		-	-
1925						
G.N. Jacklin*		Unopp.	-		-	-
1926						
G. Bridle*		1,125	63.7	3,839	46.0	-
W. Smith	Lab	641	36.3			
Total votes		1,766				
1927						
T.J. Braybon*	NCU	1,124	74.7	4,063	37.0	-
H.G. Briault	Lab	380	25.3			
Total votes		1,504				
1928						
G.N. Jacklin*		Unopp.	-		-	-

Queen's Park ward (continued)

Candidate	Party	Votes	%	Electors	Turnout	Gains
1929						
G. Bridle*		744	45.8	4,391	37.0	-
M. Milner		445	27.4			
W.C. Lewery		437	26.9			
Total votes		1,626				
1930						
W.J. Steers*		913	69.7	4,352	30.1	-
W.C. Lewery		396	30.3			
Total votes		1,309				
1931						
G.N. Jacklin*		1,427	77.5	4,338	42.5	-
J.A. Andrews	Lab	415	22.5			
Total votes		1,842				
1932						
S.G. White		977	49.1	4,324	46.0	-
G. Bridle*		625	31.4			
H.J. Robbins	Lab	388	19.5			
Total votes		1,990				
1933						
W.J. Steers*		Unopp.	-		-	-
1934						
G.N. Jacklin*		1,084	66.9	4,296	37.7	-
R.P.M. Polling	Lab	536	33.1			
Total votes		1,620				
1935						
S.G. White*		981	59.8	4,281	38.3	-
R.P.M. Polling	Lab	660	40.2			
Total votes		1,641				
1936						
A.J. Lux*		1,079	62.5	4,281	40.3	-
R.P.M. Polling	Lab	648	37.5			
Total votes		1,727				

Queen's Park ward (*continued*)

Candidate	Party	Votes	%	Electors	Turnout	Gains
1937						
G.N. Jacklin*	Unopp.		-		-	-
1938						
S.G.White*	BMC	924	53.3	*4,281*	40.5	-
W.R.J. Ford	Lab	808	46.7			
Total votes		1,732				

Overall Labour vote   **22.1%**   **Overall turnout**   **40.0%**

Regency ward

Candidate	Party	Votes	%	Electors	Turnout	Gains
1919						
H.B. Lewis*		Unopp.	-		-	-
1920						
W.E. Parry*		Unopp.	-		-	-
1921						
A. Peter*	MCU and A-W	545	65.0	2,154	39.0	-
A.W. Blessley	Ind	294	35.0			
Total votes		839				
1922						
H.B. Lewis*		646	93.1	2,521	27.5	-
A.E. Grover		48	6.9			
Total votes		694				
1923						
W.E. Parry*		Unopp.	-		-	-
1924						
A.E. Peter*		Unopp.	-		-	-
1925						
H.B. Lewis*		Unopp.	-		-	-
1926						
A.W. Wardell		431	65.0	2,425	27.3	-
W.E. Parry*		232	35.0			
Total votes		663				
1927						
A.E. Peter*		404	38.7	2,409	43.3	-
W.F. Lees		385	36.9			
H.C. Burchett		255	24.4			
Total votes		1,044				
1928						
J. Ireland*		Unopp.	-		-	-

Regency ward *(continued)*

Candidate	Party	Votes	%	Electors	Turnout	Gains
1929						
H. Ford		460	56.6	2,585	31.5	-
A.W. Wardell*		353	43.4			
Total votes		813				
1930						
W.F. Lees		491	41.9	2,444	48.0	-
J.E. Hay		425	36.3			
A.E. Peter*		256	21.8			
Total votes		1,172				
1931						
J.E. Hay		967	66.0	2,303	63.6	-
J. Ireland*		498	34.0			
Total votes		1,465				
1932						
H. Ford*		582	58.3	2,162	46.2	-
A.W. Wardell		417	41.7			
Total votes		999				
1933						
G.H. Walpole		607	50.8	2,021	59.2	-
W.F. Lees*		589	49.2			
Total votes		1,196				
1934						
J.E. Hay*		917	69.3	1,880	70.4	-
C. Foster-Marner		406	30.7			
Total votes		1,323				
1935						
H. Ford*	Unopp.	-		-		-
1936						
G.H. Walpole*	Unopp.	-		-		-
1937						
J.E. Hay*	Unopp.	-		-		-

Regency ward *(continued)*

Candidate	Party	Votes	%	Electors	Turnout	Gains
1938						
J.K. Butler*	Unopp.	-			-	-

Overall Labour vote   -   **Overall turnout**   **44.6%**

Rottingdean ward
(added by extension of the borough in 1928)

Candidate	Party	Votes	%	Electors	Turnout	Gains
1929						
A.E. Nield*		641	66.8	2,487	38.6	-
H.E. Price	Lab	319	33.2			
Total votes		960				
1930						
Miss M. Crookenden		649	48.3	2,784	48.3	-
W.H. Howell		351	26.1			
H.J. Robbins		344	25.6			
Total votes		1,344				
1931						
C. Foster-Marner	Unopp.	-		-		-
1932						
A.E. Nield*		644	89.3	4,164	17.3	-
C. Luker		77	10.7			
Total votes		721				
1933						
Miss M. Crookenden*		1,168	94.0	4,854	25.6	-
C. Luker		75	6.0			
Total votes		1,243				
1934						
H.E. Price		1,029	50.4	5,544	36.8	-
J.H. Downs	Lab	1,011	49.6			
Total votes		2,040				
1935						
F.A. Steel	Lab	1,324	56.4	6,235	37.7	Lab from
I. Goodman		1,024	43.6			Other
Total votes		2,348				
1936						
A.W. Briggs	Lab	1,259	55.1	6,235	36.7	Lab from
R.D. Swann		1,027	44.9			Other
Total votes		2,286				

Rottingdean ward *(continued)*

Candidate	Party	Votes	%	Electors	Turnout	Gains
1937						
J.H. Downs	Lab	1,339	55.9	*6,235*	38.4	Lab from
H.E. Price*		1,058	44.1			Other
Total votes		2,397				
1938						
F.A. Steel*	Lab	Unopp.	-		-	-

Overall Labour vote   **39.4%**   **Overall turnout**   **34.6%**

St John's ward

Candidate	Party	Votes	%	Electors	Turnout	Gains
1919						
H.D. Long	Lab	544	48.8	4,227	26.4	-
Mrs Hewett		331	29.7			
W. Smith		239	21.5			
Total votes		1,114				
1920						
G.W. Canter	Lab	858	39.7	4,461	48.4	-
F.D. Ingham	I Lab	772	35.7			
H.C. Burchett	MCU	530	24.5			
Total votes		2,160				
1921						
E. Marsh*	Lab	870	49.7	4,627	37.9	-
W.J. Steers	MCU and A-W	843	48.1			
H. Cowley	Nuwm	39	2.2			
Total votes		1,752				
1922						
W.J. Steers		1,221	62.4	4,555	42.9	Other from
H.D. Long*	Lab	573	29.3			Lab
H. Cowley		162	8.3			
Total votes		1,956				
1923						
G.W. Canter*	Lab	1,217	58.1	4,747	44.1	-
H.E.H. Smedley		570	27.2			
H. Cowley		306	14.6			
Total votes		2,093				
1924						
E. Marsh*	Lab	695	63.6	4,779	22.9	-
H. Cowley		398	36.4			
Total votes		1,093				

St John's ward *(continued)*

Candidate	Party	Votes	%	Electors	Turnout	Gains
1925						
W.J. Steers*		1,010	50.4	4,811	41.7	-
G. Monk	Lab	623	31.1			
H. Cowley		371	18.5			
Total votes		2,004				
1926						
J. Brewer	Lab	809	51.1	4,721	33.5	-
H.C. Burchett		478	30.2			
H. Cowley		225	14.2			
W. Lewington		71	4.5			
Total votes		1,583				
1927						
E. Marsh*	Lab	881	51.5	4,706	36.3	-
W.H. Howell		829	48.5			
Total votes		1,710				
1928						
G. Monk	Lab	800	52.9	4,677	32.3	Lab from
W.J. Steers*		712	47.1			Other
Total votes		1,512				
1929						
J. Brewer*	Lab	864	67.9	4,991	25.5	-
R.H. Filtness		409	32.1			
Total votes		1,273				
1930						
E. Marsh	Lab	Unopp.	-		-	-
1931						
J.C. Sherrott		685	46.9	*4,823*	30.3	Other from
G. Monk*	Lab	680	46.5			Lab
R.W. Light		97	6.6			
Total votes		1,462				

St John's ward (continued)

Candidate	Party	Votes	%	Electors	Turnout	Gains
1932						
E.H. Puttock		769	50.4	4,739	32.2	Other from
F.A. Steel*	Lab	614	40.2			Lab
S.J. Rooke		143	9.4			
Total votes		1,526				
1933						
E. Marsh*	Lab	880	56.2	4,655	33.6	-
D. Rolf		686	43.8			
Total votes		1,566				
1934						
G. Monk	Lab	751	47.4	4,571	34.7	Lab from
D. Rolf		451	28.5			Other
J.C. Sherrott*		369	23.3			
T.J. Regan		13	0.8			
Total votes		1,584				
1935						
J. White	Lab	695	51.5	4,485	30.1	Lab from
E.H. Puttock*		655	48.5			Other
Total votes		1,350				
1936						
F.G. Field*	Lab	683	51.7	4,485	29.5	-
Mrs A.C. Steers		639	48.3			
Total votes		1,322				
1937						
G. Monk*	Lab	Unopp.	-		-	-
1938						
J. White*	Lab	620	66.0	4,047	23.2	-
B. Breeds	BMC and R	320	34.0			
Total votes		940				

Overall Labour vote	**48.8%**			**Overall turnout**	**33.7%**

St Nicholas's ward

Candidate	Party	Votes	%	Electors	Turnout	Gains
1919						
H.B. Matthews		671	60.2	3,061	36.4	-
T.E. Morris	Lab	444	39.8			
Total votes		1,115				
1920						
W.T. Ashby	MCU	762	63.6	3,168	37.8	MCU from
T. Hussey*	Lab	436	36.4			Lab
Total votes		1,198				
1921						
M. Marten	Ind	712	51.7	3,289	41.9	Ind from
T. Reeves*	MCU	534	38.8			MCU
T. Hussey	Lab	126	9.1			
H. Stone	Nuwm	6	0.4			
Total votes		1,378				
1922						
H.B. Matthews*		776	57.7	3,897	34.5	-
W.A. Stringer		358	26.6			
A. Robertson	Lab	212	15.8			
Total votes		1,346				
1923						
A. Gordon	Lab	731	50.0	3,373	43.3	Lab from
W.T. Ashby*		626	42.8			MCU
W.E. English		104	7.1			
Total votes		1,461				
1924						
M. Marten*		847	77.4	_3,386_	32.3	-
W. Evans		187	17.1			
W.E. English		60	5.5			
Total votes		1,094				
1925						
J. Holmes*A54		1,154	73.6	3,399	46.1	-
L.C. Cohen	Lab	414	26.4			
Total votes		1,568				

St Nicholas's ward (continued)

Candidate	Party	Votes	%	Electors	Turnout	Gains
1926						
G.W. Fabian		758	45.6	3,413	48.7	Ind from
A.G. Gordon*	Lab	596	35.9			Lab
A.E. Melville		307	18.5			
Total votes		1,661				
1927						
M. Marten*		851	63.8	3,406	39.1	-
A. Melville		482	36.2			
Total votes		1,333				
1928						
J. Holmes*		721	61.4	3,412	34.4	-
A. Melville		454	38.6			
Total votes		1,175				
1929						
W.A. Stringer		482	36.4	3,711	35.7	-
A. Melville		428	32.4			
T. Hussey	Lab	230	17.4			
D. Lettres		183	13.8			
Total votes		1,323				
1930						
M. Marten*		613	51.7	3,567	33.2	-
A. Melville		572	48.3			
Total votes		1,185				
1931						
J. Holmes*		Unopp.	-		-	-
1932						
W. Palmer		647	46.8	*3,483*	39.7	-
W.H. Stringer*		544	39.3			
E.A. West		192	13.9			
Total votes		1,383				

St Nicholas's ward *(continued)*

Candidate	Party	Votes	%	Electors	Turnout	Gains
1933						
W.A. Stringer		854	53.0	*3,441*	46.8	-
M. Marten*		757	47.0			
Total votes		1,611				
1934						
W.P. Wyatt		618	54.7	*3,399*	33.2	-
J. Holmes*		512	45.3			
Total votes		1,130				
1935						
M. Marten	Ind	523	34.6	3,358	45.0	-
G. Woods		336	22.3			
J.C. Sherrott		329	21.8			
A.H. Douglas	Lab	322	21.3			
Total votes		1,510				
1936						
J.C. Sherrott		651	44.9	3,358	43.2	-
W.A. Stringer*		523	36.1			
J.H. Downs	Lab	250	17.3			
W.E. English		20	1.4			
H. Cowley		5	0.3			
Total votes		1,449				
1937						
A.H. Douglas	Lab	644	55.5	*3,358*	34.5	Lab from
W.A. Stringer		516	44.5			Ind
Total votes		1,160				
1938						
J.F.L. Terry*		Unopp.	-		-	-

Overall Labour vote	**17.3%**		**Overall turnout**	**39.2%**

St Peter's ward

Candidate	Party	Votes	%	Electors	Turnout	Gains
1919						
R. Major*		631	52.5	2,541	47.3	-
T. Lewis	Lab	571	47.5			
Total votes		1,202				
1920						
T. Lewis	Lab	578	51.4	2,532	44.4	Lab from
A. Pelkinhorn		546	48.6			MCU
Total votes		1,124				
1921						
H.J. Cole	Lab	607	51.1	2,592	45.8	-
J.W. Green	MCU	538	45.3			
J.F. Stevenson	Nuwm	42	3.5			
Total votes		1,187				
1922						
R. Major*		778	53.4	2,615	55.8	-
H. Weller	Lab	680	46.6			
Total votes		1,458				
1923						
H. Weller	Lab	753	50.6	2,672	55.7	-
H.A. Stringer		734	49.4			
Total votes		1,487				
1924						
S.F. Ashdown		872	55.5	2,669	58.9	Ind from
H.J. Cole*	Lab	700	44.5			Lab
Total votes		1,572				
1925						
R. Major*		793	50.3	2,665	59.2	-
H.J. Cole	Lab	784	49.7			
Total votes		1,577				
1926						
H. Weller*	Lab	839	51.7	2,637	61.6	-
J.A. Ballard		785	48.3			
Total votes		1,624				

St Peter's ward (continued)

Candidate	Party	Votes	%	Electors	Turnout	Gains
1927						
H.J. Cole	Lab	757	55.1	2,665	51.6	Lab from
J.T. Nanson		618	44.9			Ind
Total votes		1,375				
1928						
J. Lintott, jun*	Lab	784	66.4	2,597	45.4	-
G. Privett		396	33.6			
Total votes ·		1,180				

(Lintott's father was an alderman, but apparently not for Labour)

Candidate	Party	Votes	%	Electors	Turnout	Gains
1929						
H. Weller*	Lab	677	63.2	2,760	38.8	-
Sir J. Wallinger		394	36.8			
Total votes		1,071				
1930						
H.J. Cole*	Lab	Unopp.	-		-	-
1931						
G.C. Wallington		725	54.8	2,674	49.5	Ind from
J. Lintott, jun*	Lab	598	45.2			Lab
Total votes		1,323				
1932						
T.H. Knowling	Ind	580	51.9	2,631	42.5	Ind from
J. Lintott, jun	Lab	537	48.1			Lab
Total votes		1,117				
1933						
Miss D.E. Stringer		682	51.5	2,588	51.1	Ind from
H.J. Cole*	Lab	641	48.5			Lab
Total votes		1,323				
1934						
H.J. Cole	Lab	653	58.8	2,545	43.6	Lab from
G.C. Wallington*		457	41.2			Ind
Total votes		1,110				

St Peter's ward *(continued)*

Candidate	Party	Votes	%	Electors	Turnout	Gains
1935						
T. Hussey*	Lab	612	50.2	2,504	48.6	-
J.W. Green		606	49.8			
Total votes		1,218				
1936						
Miss D.E. Stringer*		818	62.2	2,504	52.5	-
H.O. Steer	Lab	497	37.8			
Total votes		1,315				
1937						
H.J. Cole*	Lab	Unopp.	-		-	-
1938						
W.H.G. Button	BMC and R	688	66.3	2,273	45.7	Other from Lab
T. Hussey*	Lab	350	33.7			
Total votes		1,038				

Overall Labour vote   **49.9%**   **Overall turnout**   **49.9%**

West ward

Candidate	Party	Votes	%	Electors	Turnout	Gains
1919						
G. Roach	Unopp.	-		-		-
1920						
C. Wilkinson*	Unopp.	-			-	-
1921						
Mrs J. Blatch*	Unopp.	-		1,644	-	-
1922						
C. Kingston*		479	72.6	1,925	34.3	-
Miss J. Mannall		181	27.4			
Total votes		660				
1923						
C. Wilkinson*	Unopp.	-			-	-
1924						
H.S. Davis	Unopp.	-			-	-
1925						
C. Kingston*	Unopp.	-			-	-
1926						
C. Wilkinson*		554	63.7	1,925	45.2	-
W.P. Trory		316	36.3			
Total votes		870				
1927						
H.S. Davis*	Unopp.	-			-	-
1928						
Captain Hills*	Unopp.	-			-	-
1929						
C. Wilkinson*	Unopp.	-			-	-
1930						
E. Simms*	Unopp.	-			-	-

West ward *(continued)*

Candidate	Party	Votes	%	Electors	Turnout	Gains
1931						
J.T. Nanson*		Unopp.	-		-	-
1932						
W.J. Cook*		Unopp.	-		-	-
1933						
E. Simms*		Unopp.	-		-	-
1934						
J.T. Nanson*		Unopp.	-		-	-
1935						
W.J. Cook*		Unopp.	-		-	-
1936						
E. Simms*		Unopp.	-		-	-
1937						
J.T. Nanson*		Unopp.	-		-	-
1938						
W.J. Cook*		Unopp.	-		-	-

Overall Labour vote   -   **Overall turnout**   **39.7%**

THREE
Bristol

BRISTOL

Situated on the border between Gloucestershire and Somerset, Bristol was the sixth-largest county borough in 1931, with a population of just under 400,000. It was still by far the most important town of south-west England, but it had earlier been one of the largest provincial urban centres of the country. In the 1730s it was the second city in the land, but it was rapidly to be overtaken by the growing industrial towns of the Midlands and the North. By 1828 a local publication lamented: 'Bristol for centuries ranked as the second city in England in respect of riches, trade and population; but the present extent of its foreign commerce will bear no comparison with that of the port of Liverpool; and it appears to be exceeded in population by the manufacturing town of Manchester.'[1]

The city's earlier importance was based on the fact that it became the main port serving the rich area of woollen-cloth production of Somerset, Wiltshire and Gloucestershire. In the medieval period the port had established itself on the basis of trade mainly with France, primarily the exporting of wool cloth and the importing of wine. The city also established an industrial base in its cloth-finishing workshops. The French wine-cloth trade went into decline by the end of the fifteenth century, but Bristol's merchants diversified into other areas such as the Iberian peninsula and the wider Atlantic economy. The import of luxury goods like port-wine was supplemented by others such as tobacco and sugar, and Bristol became one of the earliest ports to profit from the growing trans-Atlantic slave trade. Local industry was also diversified, with the declining cloth-finishing being supplemented and eventually eclipsed by the processing of imported raw materials and semi-finished goods. The city developed a broadly-based industrial structure, encompassing shipbuilding, engineering and metalworking, leather and ropemaking, glassmaking, soap boiling, sugar refining, chocolate production and tobacco processing amongst others.

Bristol's nineteenth-century decline was relative. While other centres of the industrial revolution mushroomed, Bristol grew at a more sedate pace. The physical limitations of the port and a failure to modernise it rapidly enough meant that other ports, most notably Liverpool and also Glasgow, overtook it. Liverpool's merchants assumed the unsavoury mantle of the main profiteers from slavery, for instance, while Liverpool and Glasgow took over much of the sugar and tobacco trade. Moreover Bristol's hinterland experienced only moderate industrial growth, whereas other ports such as Cardiff, Liverpool, Hull and Glasgow benefited from their location near the centres of the nineteenth-century staples of the British economy – cotton, coal, metals and engineering. So Bristol's importance receded in relative terms, but it would be wrong to overstate its decline. In the late nineteenth century the shift of the port down the Avon and the construction of deepwater docks at Avonmouth and Portishead helped to retain some trade through Bristol. The broad base of the city's industrial structure was also maintained, and

---

[1] Quoted in Morgan, K, 'The economic development of Bristol, 1700–1850', in Dresser, M. and Ollerenshaw, P., (eds), *The Making of Modern Bristol*, (Tiverton, 1996), p. 49.

its pre-eminence as 'a regional capital for a large part of the southwest'[2] ensured that its economy remained on a sound footing into the twentieth century.

It is also the case that the varied industrial structure of Bristol meant that it avoided the worst effects of inter-war industrial depression. Regions and towns that specialised in the staple industries of the British economy were worst-hit, whereas Bristol's earlier failure to capitalise fully on the massive industrial growth of the nineteenth century was a blessing in disguise by the 1930s. The figures in Appendix Six confirm this view. Bristol lay fifty-eighth amongst the county boroughs in terms of unemployment, with 10.9 per cent of its workforce in 1931 defined as out of work. An important new industrial development also helped to boost the inter-war local economy. The Bristol Tramways and Carriage Company was manufacturing its own trams at its works in Brislington in south-east Bristol by the turn of the century, and in 1910 diversified into the production of aeroplane bodies at Filton to the north of the city. War production between 1914 and 1918 helped to stimulate the nascent industry, and the British and Colonial Aeroplane Company employed 8,000 workers at the peak of the war effort in 1918. Peace saw a retrenchment, but from 1920 the newly-named BAC also moved into production of its own aeroplane engines with workshops in Patchway. After some precarious years in the late 1920s and early 1930s, rearmament saw BAC grow rapidly. By 1935 it again employed 8,000, and by the early months of the war it was the biggest single employer in Bristol with over 20,000 workers.[3]

The broadly-based nature of Bristol's economy was accurately reflected in the industrial structure of the workforce in 1931. The industrial tables show that no one group of workers predominated in Bristol, both amongst men and women. The biggest single group overall was in commerce and finance, amounting to 19 per cent of all workers. Apart from that, amongst men there were 14 per cent in transport, almost 12 per cent in metal and engineering, and around 9 per cent in both the building and the food, drink and tobacco categories. Two further points on male employment should be noted. First, within the transport category, there were only 3,500 workers on the docks out of a total figure of over 18,000, signifying the reduced importance of the docks by this time. Second, much of the growth of employment in aircraft production came after 1931, and is therefore poorly reflected in these figures. Even so, within the metal and engineering category there were almost 5,000 men in the production of vehicles, mostly aircraft. Amongst women, the largest group was the 27 per cent in personal service, and other notable sectors included 18 per cent in food, drink and tobacco, almost 10 per cent in clothing manufacture, 7.5 per cent in paper and printing, and 6 per cent in the professions. Overall there was a mix of skilled workers, semi-skilled and unskilled factory operatives, casually employed dockers and building workers, and domestic servants, making up a large but variegated working class. As befits such a large regionally-important city, Bristol was also mixed in terms of social class. There was a substantial middle-class, ranging from wealthy business, commercial, managerial and professional groups down to moderately well-off administrative

[2]   Freeman, T.W., *The Conurbations of Great Britain*, (Manchester, 1959), p. 282.
[3]   Little, B.D.G., *The City and County of Bristol: A Study in Atlantic Civilisation*, (London, 1954), pp. 296–298.

and supervisory workers. Appendices Three, Four and Five in this volume, which can be read as useful indicators of social class, support this claim. Bristol was thirtieth amongst the county boroughs in terms of female domestic servants as a proportion of the total population in 1931, twenty-eighth in terms of the proportion of the workforce in the own account and managerial categories, and sixteenth in terms of the professional category.

One other feature of Bristol's population stands out. The significance of religion, and especially Nonconformity, should not be underestimated. The city was noted for its late medieval Lollardy, and its heretical traditions were continued when it became a leading centre of Protestant reformation, and later again of Old Dissent.[4] The eighteenth-century upsurge of Methodism was also important in Bristol, with many groups such as the miners of Kingswood to the east of the city being evangelised *en masse*. The pattern by the nineteenth century was well-established: 'upper and professional-class Anglicanism, middle and lower-class nonconformity'.[5] The 1851 religious census showed that 44 per cent of attenders were Anglican, most of the rest Nonconformists, with an additional small number of Catholics.[6] In the 1880s it was noted that church attendance in Bristol was high compared to other large industrial towns, showing the continuing influence of religion in the city.[7] The political significance of Nonconformity to both the Liberal tradition and the developing labour movement in Bristol was important.

Turning to the politics of Bristol, of the four pre-war parliamentary constituencies, only one, the predominantly affluent Bristol West, could be described as a Tory stronghold. Strongly working-class Bristol East was overwhelmingly Liberal, the seat never being lost between 1885 and 1910, while the North and South constituencies were marginal. The only challenge to the two main parties from the rising labour movement was in the East constituency, but it was only occasional and ultimately ineffectual. In 1886 the Trades Council was unable to raise a candidate due to lack of funds and the 'still firm commitment of the majority of working men to the Liberal cause'.[8] By the mid–1890s the local labour movement 'still retained many links with Liberalism'.[9] In 1895 an 'Independent Labour' candidate, H.H. Gore, did manage to gain almost 49 per cent of the poll against the Liberal tobacco magnate, Sir W.H. Wills, in a by-election in Bristol East. This apparently straightforward and successful socialist intervention, however, appears more complex on further analysis. As David Howell has shown, Gore was an 'acknowledged Tory socialist', an Anglican and an opponent of tee-totalism. Local ILPers alleged that he was supported financially by the 'High

[4] Fleming, P., 'The emergence of modern Bristol', in Dresser and Ollerenshaw, *The Making of Modern Bristol*, pp. 6–13.
[5] Brace, K., *Portrait of Bristol*, (Second edition, London ,1976), p.131.
[6] Dresser, M., 'Protestants, Catholics and Jews: religious difference and political status in Bristol, 1750–1850', in Dresser and Ollerenshaw, *The Making of Modern Bristol*, p. 116.
[7] Pelling, H., *Social Geography of British Elections 1885–1910*, (Aldershot, 1994), p. 145.
[8] Large, D. and Whitfield, R., *The Bristol Trades Council 1873–1973*, (Bristol, 1973), p. 6.
[9] Howell, D., *British Workers and the Independent Labour Party 1888–1906*, (Manchester, 1983), p. 385.

Church Party', and were aghast at his 'Unionist leanings'. Gore himself confided that he would be supported by the Unionist party in Bristol, and with the support of what he described as the 'illiterate' he might oust the Liberal. It was the ILP leadership nationally that supported his campaign, rather than local sympathisers. Gore's candidacy was a manifestation of the feasibility of what Howell describes as a Tory–socialist position, one which ultimately of course was sidelined in the development of the ILP. Gore 'played the Tory game almost to a win', but his intervention actually retarded the development of the ILP in Bristol by arousing local suspicions. Despite winning a substantial number of working-class votes, he 'alienated office holders in labour organisations', without whose support the ILP could not advance. The whole episode in the end demonstrated the strength of the Liberal and Nonconformist traditions of the organised Labour movement in Bristol.[10] A local ILP branch was established during the campaign, but foundered soon after. In the general election later the same year an ILP candidate gained 31 per cent of the vote, but no further labour challenges to Liberalism were mounted in Bristol East before 1910. In the election of January of that year a Labour party candidate, Frank Sheppard, came a poor third behind the Liberal and Tory with only 17 per cent of the vote. Pelling also makes the point that the appeal of Liberalism in the port-city was probably strengthened in the Edwardian period by support for Free Trade. As he says, 'the pull of Nonconformity and Free Trade in combination explain the comparative weakness of the independent labour movement in Bristol up to the First World War'.[11] The situation on the council was similar, with Tories and Liberals both sharing the bulk of electoral support. A Labour councillor was first elected in 1887, but by 1914 there were still only seven Labour members on the council.

The effects of the First World War on Bristol's politics were profound, however. On the labour side, there was a big increase in union membership, especially amongst semi and unskilled workers. Significantly, this development was dominated by the Dockers' Union, rather than by the Liberal-leaning Trades Council. This might seem surprising given the relatively small numbers of dockers in Bristol. The Dockers' Union in Bristol, however, was a branch of Tillett's London-based Dock, Wharf, Riverside and General Labourers' Union. Before the war it had built up a position on the docks which was 'unique in waterfront trades unionism at the time' as it had 'a virtual monopoly of all grades and sections of dockworkers, together with warehousemen and carters.'[12] Having achieved a near-monopoly on the docks, it was in its interest to expand its membership to other industries and trades in the city, to regulate those workers who swelled the calling-on stands at the docks when employment was scarce. Workers in other trades would also benefit from the link with the dockers as it considerably strengthened their bargaining power. In Bristol, therefore, the Dockers' Union was a genuinely 'general' union and, enthused by a dynamic young organiser in Ernest Bevin, recruited extensively outside the confines of the docks. 'By the end of the war the

[10] Howell, *British Workers*, pp. 385–387.
[11] Pelling, *Social Geography*, p. 146.
[12] Whitfield, R., 'Trade unionism in Bristol 1910–1926', in Bild, I., (ed.), *Bristol's Other History*, (Bristol, 1983), p. 78.

Dockers' Union probably contained as many members as *all* the unions of pre-war Bristol put together, and there was scarcely a trade or industry in the city that was not represented in some degree in it'. In fact the union had 40,000 members locally in 1921.[13]

Other general unions like the Gasworkers and the Workers' Union also grew in the same period. These unions, like Bevin himself, were strongly committed to the Labour party, and when the party was reorganised in 1918 they provided its strongest supporters and activists. The Bristol Dockers' Union had long been committed to independent labour politics and especially municipal politics, encouraged by the belief that the local dockers did rather better than their counterparts in other ports because the docks were municipally owned.[14] By the 1920s the Dockers had been absorbed into the Transport and General Union, which in turn was the dominant union on the merged Trades and Labour Council. The secretary of the latter body throughout the inter-war years, for example, was a member of the old Dockers' Union.[15] The contrast with another port-city, Liverpool, could not be greater. In Liverpool it was another union, the National Union of Dock Labourers, which organised dockers. This was much less a general union, which operated an exclusive recruitment policy amongst dockers only. The union remained a distant and critical ally of the Liverpool Trades Council and Labour Party in the inter-war years, seriously weakening support for the Labour party in the crucial dock-side districts of the city.[16] In Bristol, however, the post-1918 Labour party had strong trade union links, and on this solid base was able to construct a much greater degree of working-class support. In the process the tradition of Nonconformity which had fed into a working-class Liberalism was broken, and to an extent transformed into a commitment to 'Labourism'. The pre-1914 weakness of Labour noted above was thus converted into considerable strength, as the electoral data will show.

Labour's main political opponents were also affected by the impact of the Great War. The war-time government coalition was strongly supported by both Liberals and Conservatives in Bristol, and was replicated in the local council chamber. Local co-operation continued after the war ended, with both sides happy to sink their differences in the face of the rise of Labour. In parliamentary elections inter-war contests between Liberals and Conservatives were extremely rare. Similarly, when municipal elections were resumed in November 1919, 'it was understood that the Coalition arrangement made during the war period was still more or less active' and 'the two great political parties, with or without a formal agreement, have not attacked each other'.[17] Whilst the two parties retained the use of their

[13] Large and Whitfield, *The Bristol Trades Council*, pp. 15, 19; see also Whitfield, 'Trade unionism in Bristol', pp. 68–96.

[14] Howell, *British Workers*, p. 116.

[15] Large and Whitfield, *The Bristol Trades Council*, p. 18.

[16] See Davies, S., *Liverpool Labour: Social and Political Influences on the Development of the Labour Party in Liverpool, 1900–1939*, (Keele, 1996), pp. 53–69; Taplin, E.L., 'The Liverpool Trades Council, 1880–1914', in *Bulletin of the North West Group for the Study of Labour* History, no. 3, (1976); Taplin, E.L., *The Dockers' Union: A Study of the National Union Of Dock Labourers, 1889–1922*, (Leicester, 1986).

[17] *Western Daily Press*, 1 and 3 Nov. 1919.

different names, they worked closely in alliance with each other. In 1920 it was reported that 'Liberals and Conservatives did not oppose each other; on the contrary, they appeared on the same platform in wards where the seats were attacked by Labour'.[18] On only one occasion, in St George's East ward in 1919, did Liberals and Tories ever confront each other in municipal elections. From 1924 the two parties dropped their separate names for municipal purposes, and 'Liberals and Conservatives joined forces, and stood as Citizen candidates in opposition to Labour.'[19] Two interlocking points need to be borne in mind in relation to this rapid and almost effortless transformation of political forces. On the one hand the abrupt post-1918 ebbing away of working-class support for Liberalism made it more possible for the Liberal party to come to a *rapprochement* with Conservatism. Many of the more radical strands of Bristol Liberalism disappeared almost overnight, and political differences with the Tories were thus much reduced. On the other hand, the very fact that the Liberal–Conservative alliance was implemented so openly and so soon after the war no doubt alienated working-class supporters of Liberalism, thus hastening the whole process. The general tenor of the Citizens' appeal to the voters was expressed very clearly in the 1925 elections as follows:

> They declared for 'efficiency with economy' ... The main part of their programme, however, consisted of a strong protest against the 'extreme policies of the Socialists' and the 'reckless expenditure' that these policies entail. In some instances householders received by post yesterday morning a printed postcard stating that the rates in London boroughs under the Socialist control average 3s 6d in the £ more than other boroughs, and advising electors to vote against Socialism ... A noteworthy feature of the election was the issuing of a letter in support of the Citizen candidates and signed by the leaders of Liberal and Conservative members of the Council. 'A local authority', this stated, 'has certain duties to perform, and the candidate whom we ask you to support is pledged to carry out those duties efficiently and economically, and by careful administration to keep the rates as low as possible, and to bring businesslike methods to bear in every department of the Council's work. An intelligent and far-sighted policy of progress, combined with judicious expenditure of public money, is the aim of the candidate we recommend to you.'[20]

The overall effects of the post-war changes can be identified in the new balance of political forces in the city. In parliamentary elections, Labour ran a coalition Liberal close in Bristol East in 1918, and only narrowly failed to gain the seat in 1922. The constituency was finally won in 1923 and became a Labour stronghold, being one of only fifty-two seats retained nationally in the disaster of 1931. Labour

---

[18] *Western Daily Press*, 2 Nov. 1920.
[19] *Bristol Observer*, 8 Nov. 1924; Wardley, P., (ed.), *Abstract of Bristol Historical Statistics, pt. 3: Political Representation and Bristol's Elections 1700–1997*, (Bristol, 1997), p. *xvii*, wrongly states that the Citizen's party was instigated in 1926.
[20] *Western Daily Press*, 3 Nov. 1925.

also won the Central, East and North constituencies at least once in the 1920s. At the highpoint of 1929, Labour held four of the five Bristol seats, only Bristol West remaining an unshakeable Tory fortress. Liberalism receded rapidly, being relegated to the third party by the 1930s in all except Bristol North. On the council Labour made net gains of eleven seats in the three elections of 1919–1921, while the Liberals suffered a net loss of nine seats. Combined with by-election gains, this meant that Labour held twenty-one seats on the council by 1921, almost a quarter of the total of ninety-two. It should be noted that Labour in Bristol did not suffer the slump in support after the initial success of 1919 that was evident in nearly all the other county boroughs that have been analysed so far in this series of volumes. This is an indication of how strong the turn away from Liberalism towards Labour was in Bristol. Labour's share of votes won in Bristol in fact stayed steady at well over 40 per cent throughout the 1920s. In only one year in the decade, 1922, did the party experience a net loss of seats. This was an unusually consistent pattern of support. With the implementation of the Citizen's alliance in 1924, a straight confrontation along Labour–anti-Labour lines was entrenched.

Labour continued to make steady inroads on the council down to 1929, by which date it held over a third of all seats, with thirty-four councillors and aldermen. Four Labour aldermen were elected immediately after the 1929 elections, further strengthening Labour's position. The downturn in Labour's fortunes that accompanied the failures of the second Labour government was evident in the elections of 1930 and 1931, however. Labour's share of the vote fell from 54 per cent to 41 per cent between 1929 and 1930, and in 1931 hit its inter-war low of 39 per cent. While this did not result in any loss of seats in 1930, five seats went in 1931 and a further two in 1932. As in most other boroughs, though, Labour's recovery in the following two years was impressive, with its share of the vote being restored to around the 50 per cent mark. By 1934 Labour held thirty-seven seats and was getting near to challenging the Citizens' control of the council, but it was to take three years before this was accomplished. Moreover, for Labour to take power in Bristol it was necessary to carry through major changes both to the system of electing aldermen on the council and also to the ward boundaries of the borough. These changes were of such significance that it is necessary to analyse them in some detail now.

As far as aldermanic elections were concerned, for the whole of the 1920s down to 1929 Labour was heavily disadvantaged by the system. Labour had two aldermen for the whole of this period, being allowed no increase in its representation in proportion to the growing number of council seats it held. After the 1929 elections the Citizens had thirty-seven councillors to Labour's thirty-two, but with the Citizens holding twenty-one of the twenty-three aldermanic positions their majority was secure. Proportionally Labour should have been entitled to eight aldermen at this point. Labour complaints at the situation forced the Citizens into making some concessions on the issue, and Labour was allowed to fill four aldermanic vacancies, bringing its total up to six. A further Labour alderman was added after the 1933 elections, but the party still did not have its full entitlement in terms of proportionality, leading to renewed protests. Finally in April 1936 the two parties agreed to meet to resolve the problem, and the following clear arrangement was agreed to by both sides:

The Citizen Party and the Labour Party shall each be entitled to seats on the Aldermanic bench in the proportion of one seat for every three councillors being members of the respective parties at the time an election to the Aldermanic bench takes place, and seniority of service (whether continuous or intermittent) shall determine the councillors to be elected as aldermen representing the respective parties.[21]

This formal and public agreement guaranteeing fair play was highly unusual in the context of inter-war municipal politics. In no other borough examined in these volumes so far has a similar statement been found. It was even more surprising given that Labour was a serious contender for power in Bristol. In other boroughs where this was the case, manipulation of the aldermanic system for party advantage was the norm, exemplified by the experience of Birkenhead or Bootle. The first large number of aldermanic vacancies occurred after the elections in November 1936. Ironically, as the local press pointed out at the time, 'even if there were not a "gentlemen's agreement" that the five aldermen ... should be Labour members, the Labour Party have a majority of two councillors by which they could elect the new aldermen on November 9.'[22] Labour were duly allowed the five aldermen, bringing their total representation of the council to fifty-five (forty-three councillors and twelve aldermen) compared to the Citizen's fifty-seven. Labour still did not have its full proportional share, however, and when a further aldermanic vacancy occurred in the following year, Labour was ceded that as well. This brought the two sides level at fifty-six each, showing how the ruling Citizen group kept faithfully to the agreement on aldermanic elections. Even more remarkably, after Labour had tasted power for the first time in 1937, the aldermanic elections in 1938 saw Labour also sticking to the agreement. Both sides were again tied at fifty-six each, and two Citizen aldermen were due to retire, but Labour allowed two Citizen councillors to take their place to retain proportionality. As the councillors both sat for safe Citizen wards, the resultant by-elections brought the two sides back to fifty-six each.[23]

Even more important to Labour's rise to power was the revision of ward boundaries that took place in 1936. The boundaries had last been redistributed in 1906, establishing a total of twenty-three wards. By the 1930s considerable inequality in ward size had occurred due to population change, and in particular the extension of council housing.[24] Roughly 15,000 council houses were built in Bristol between the wars, which for the size of the city was not an exceptionally high figure, but which still had a considerable effect on the borough. Most of the council housing was built on new estates well outside of the town centre. The most notable of these estates were to the south of the city in Bedminster and Knowle (in

---

[21] *Western Daily Press and Bristol Mirror*, 1 Apr. 1936.

[22] *Western Daily Press and Bristol Mirror*, 3 Nov. 1936; *Bristol Observer*, 7 Nov. 1936.

[23] *Western Daily Press and Bristol Mirror*, 2 Nov. and 10 Nov. 1938.

[24] For an excellent analysis of 1920s housing developments in Bristol, see Dresser, M., 'Housing policy in Bristol, 1919–30', in Daunton, M.J., (ed.), *Councillors and Tenants: Local Authority Housing in English Cities, 1919–1939*, (Leicester, 1984); see also Dresser, M. 'People's Housing in Bristol 1870–1939', in Bild, *Bristol's Other History*, pp. 129–160.

the Bedminster East, Bedminster West and Somerset wards), to the east in Fishponds and Speedwell (in the St George's East and Stapleton wards), to the north in Horfield and Southmead (in the Horfield and Westbury on Trym wards) and to the north west along the Avon towards Avonmouth at Sea Mills and Shirehampton (also in the vast Westbury on Trym ward). Thus in 1935 while the average size of ward electorate in Bristol was just over 9,000 (see Table 3.1), there were seven wards which were well above the average. These were Bedminster East and West (13,000 and 14,000 respectively), Horfield (almost 16,000), St George's East (14,000), Somerset (almost 20,000) and Stapleton and Westbury on Trym (both 17,000).

Conversely, there were seven wards with 5,000 electors or fewer, although none of these had experienced huge loss of population. Rather they had been the beneficiaries in the 1906 revision of the convention that districts with high rateable value should be entitled to greater representation than their population figures warranted. These included in the wealthy western suburbs Clifton North (fewer than 4,000 municipal electors in 1935), Clifton South (just over 4,500), St Michael's (fewer than 6,000), and St James's (fewer than 4,500). Also in the central commercial and retail districts of the city, where most of the electors were plural voters entitled to the business vote, were the wards of Redcliff (fewer than 3,000 voters), Central East (fewer than 1,500 voters) and, smallest of all, Central West with an electorate of only 857.

It would not be true to say that the inequality of ward size worked entirely in the Citizens' favour, but overall it was fairly clear that they gained more than they lost from the pre-1936 situation. Six of the seven over-represented small wards were Citizen strongholds where Labour never won a seat between 1919 and 1935. The seventh, Redcliff, had some of the worst of the old city centre slums within it, so the business vote was not completely dominant here. Labour in fact did manage to win the ward in 1928 and 1929, but slum clearance and rehousing began to take effect in the 1930s. The electorate fell from almost 3,500 in 1929 to 2,900 by 1935, tipping the balance back in favour of the Citizens. On the other hand, three of the large under-represented wards, Bedminster East and West and St George's East were strong Labour wards. These formed part of the mainly working-class industrial belt of the city that ran from Bedminster in the south west through St Philip's, St Paul's and Easton near the city centre to St George's in the east. The other large wards, Horfield, Stapleton, Somerset and Westbury on Trym, were more marginal politically. In the early 1920s any enclaves of industry and working-class housing tended to be outweighed by more affluent suburban estates of private housing. All of these wards were sites of substantial council house development, though, so that by the late 1920s Horfield and Stapleton were mainly Labour territory, while the Labour challenge in Somerset and Westbury on Trym was far more substantial than it had been earlier.

To summarise, in 1935 the seven smallest wards had between them twenty-one councillors representing a combined electorate of 23,755, or one councillor for every 1,131 voters. All twenty-one of these councillors were Citizens in 1935. The seven largest wards had twenty-one councillors representing an electorate of 113,460, or one councillor for every 5,403 voters. Of these twenty-one, thirteen were Citizens and eleven Labour in 1935. While the large wards were more or less split evenly, to no political advantage, the small wards, which received a five-fold over-representation on the council, were all in the Citizens' favour.

The 1936 redistribution was the result of 'nine years of committee work', and ended 'a controversy that began before the [1914-18] war.[25] Labour had frequently raised the issue in the council chamber, and the disparity in ward size had become so obvious by the 1930s that the pressure for change was irresistible. The ruling Citizen's group ordered a whole-scale redistribution, even though it was almost certain to lose out by the changes. At the inquiry into the changes held by the government commissioner in March 1936, however, the Citizens tried to minimise the political damage as much as it could. A new twenty-five ward scheme to replace the existing twenty-three wards was drawn up originally by the Town Clerk, seeking to equalise ward size as far as possible. The ruling group voted down this proposal, and substituted its own twenty-seven ward scheme which to a large degree retained the inequalities of the existing system. The commissioner decided that he would accept a twenty-seven ward scheme 'in view of the great increase in the Council's work', but 'not necessarily the City Council's majority scheme'.[26] A Labour councillor protested long and hard at this decision:

> The 27-wards scheme had its birth at political headquarters. The 25-wards scheme was born in the Town Clerk's Department. This will always rankle in our minds as being an unjust and unfair proposal. No one can say the minority of the council is having a fair deal ... I will not rest content with that scheme. It still bears the anomalies and injustices which are here under the present scheme. It is a political proposal. It is designed so that the Citizen Party can continue to keep the majority in the Council.[27]

Labour had already proposed a twenty-eight ward scheme which went much further in breaking up the large suburban wards and at the same time merging the small central wards. Overnight after the first day of the inquiry the Labour party drew up another scheme for twenty-seven wards to try to derail the Citizen's plan. On the second day the solicitor representing Labour continued to criticise the direction of the inquiry, stating: 'We want electoral equality ... I suggest the group sponsoring the City Council scheme are interested in the redistribution on what would be to the best advantage of one party'. The commissioner replied: 'No – I cannot have that. You lay yourself open to a crushing retort – that you have a similar interest. I do want to exclude political considerations'. The Labour solicitor persisted in his attack, arguing for two crucial changes in particular. First, he argued that one of the smaller wards in the western suburbs should be dispensed with to make representation fairer, despite the claims for the high rateable value of this part of the city. Redland, he proposed, should be abolished and its electorate redistributed amongst the surrounding wards. Second, he suggested that a new ward of Hengrove should be created in the south, taking in parts of the suggested Somerset, Brislington and, mostly, Knowle wards. The significance of this change

25 *Western Daily Press and Bristol Mirror*, 3 Nov. 1936.
26 *Western Daily Press and Bristol Mirror*, 20 Mar. 1936.
27 *Western Daily Press and Bristol Mirror*, 19 Mar. 1936.

was that most of Hengrove's voters would be council-house dwellers who otherwise would be swamped by the more numerous voters of prosperous Knowle.[28]

The commissioner closed the inquiry with assurances that he would study the various proposals carefully. His final decisions went some way to meeting Labour's demands. He approved the inclusion of the new Hengrove ward, but he did not concur with the abolition of Redland, so that it was a twenty-eight ward scheme that was eventually instituted. The net effects of the new ward boundaries were undoubtedly in Labour's favour, as Table 3.2 shows. Labour could count on usually winning nine wards before the changes, with a further one ward which could be characterised as a Labour marginal, while the Citizens could be confident of winning thirteen wards. After the changes there were eleven safe Labour seats and a further four Labour marginals, whereas the Citizens now had twelve safe seats and one Citizen's marginal. What had been a probable in-built majority for the Citizens had been reversed in Labour's favour.

Of the new wards Windmill Hill (which effectively replaced the old Bedminster East ward), Hengrove, Brislington, Hillfields, Eastville and Avon were predominantly Labour, while only Durdham, Bishopston and Knowle could be said to be Citizen strongholds. The merging of the two Clifton wards represented three lost seats to the Citizens, while the breaking-up of the large suburban wards generally worked to Labour's favour. The old Somerset ward, almost a marginal by the mid 1930s, was carved up to produce two Labour wards (the much-reduced Somerset and Hengrove) and one for the Citizens (Knowle). Labour's old St George's East was divided in two to create Brislington, leaving two Labour strongholds where once there had been one. Large chunks were lopped off previously marginal Stapleton to create Labour-leaning Eastville and Hillfields, only partly compensated for by the fact that the smaller Stapleton was henceforth a safe Citizen seat. The old Horfield and Westbury on Trym wards, previously Citizen territory, were recast to give five wards overall. Three of these were to become Citizen strongholds (Durdham, Bishopston and the much-reduced Westbury), while the other two were to become Labour strongholds (Avon and the much-reduced Horfield).

The electoral impact of these changes was dramatic. In the first elections with the new boundaries in November 1936, Labour saw its share of the vote increase on the previous year only marginally from 49 per cent to 53 per cent. Yet Labour's representation on the council increased from thirty-six to fifty-five (after aldermanic elections and subsequent by-elections had been completed), while the Citizen's representation was virtually unchanged, going from fifty-six to fifty-seven. Labour was also helped by the fact that in five of the new wards all three new councillors were elected at once, and coincidentally all five of these were predominantly Labour-supporting. From trailing some distance behind the Citizen's, the Labour party was suddenly on the brink of power in Bristol. The confirmation of that fact occurred in the following year, but there was no doubt that the boundary revision played a large part in this transformation. It should also be stressed that in most other boroughs the years 1936–38 marked a downturn in

---

[28] *Western Daily Press and Bristol Mirror*, 20 Mar. 1936.

Labour's fortunes. In the eighteen boroughs other than Bristol analysed in the first two volumes of this series, Labour had net losses in these three years of twenty-two, seventeen and twenty seats respectively. Only in 1938 did this trend manifest itself in Bristol, with the party's vote share falling from 50 to 42 per cent and three net losses being recorded.

It should be emphasised that Labour's rise in Bristol was a reflection of real popular support in the city, and in turn a tribute to its strong organisation. It is likely that only the distortions of the ward boundaries and the aldermanic system prevented Labour from gaining power earlier. This may have been true elsewhere, but the fact that Labour in Bristol was able to force its opponents to reform both the aldermanic system and the ward boundaries was indicative of its successful tactics. The party was a model of sound organisation and moderate 'municipal socialist' policies. It had a solid trade union base allied to an effective ward and constituency structure which worked well in election campaigns. One study asserts that by 1930:

> Labour councillors and aldermen were a powerful and fully fledged opposition party on the Bristol Council. They were also on the whole a less radical group than they had been in 1919, and one which became increasingly identified ... with a somewhat narrow and bureaucratic 'labourism'.[29]

One indicator of the party's near-hegemony over working-class politics in Bristol was the almost total lack of any challenge from the Communist party. On only seven occasions between the wars did a Communist stand against Labour, which was an exceptionally low figure in a borough of Bristol's size. In St Paul's and in St Philip's South Communists stood in three successive years from 1932 to 1934, and there was also a challenge in St Philip's North ward in 1921. The best result the Communist party achieved was 10 per cent of the vote in St Philip's South in 1933. Even more unusually, there were no candidates whatever for the Communist-influenced National Unemployed Workers' Movement (NUWM). Bristol was exceptional, however, in that it was the only major city where the local Trades Council and Labour Party were the main organisers of the unemployed. The TUC and Labour Party nationally remained aloof from the organisation of the unemployed after the early 1920s, as did its affiliated Trades Councils in the localities. In Bristol, however, the Trades Council formed the Bristol Unemployed Association (BUA) in 1921, which had a number of branches throughout the city, including two for women. The BUA was more moderate in its policies and tactics than the NUWM, but it was also more influential. Only in the early 1930s did the NUWM contest the BUA's leadership of the unemployed. The BUA was so successful that when the TUC considered setting up rival unemployed committees to the NUWM in 1928 and again in 1932, it looked to Bristol as the model of organisation.[30] The unusual success of the Trades Council and Labour Party in this

[29] Dresser, 'Housing policy in Bristol', p. 165.
[30] Large and Whitfield, *The Bristol Trades Council*, pp. 22–27; see also Croucher, R., '"Divisions in the movement": the National Unemployed Workers' Movement and its rivals in comparative perspective', in Andrews, G., Fishman, N. and Morgan, K., *Opening the*

field is indicative of its deep-rooted influence in the local working-class movement.

The Labour party in Bristol also suffered from fewer of the internal divisions that damaged Labour's chances elsewhere. While moderates such as the long-serving alderman Frank Sheppard dominated the party, more radical figures were tolerated. Socialists on the left of the party such as W.H. Hennessy and Lillian Pheysey, for instance, were elected to the council from 1921, and both eventually were elected onto the aldermanic bench, in 1929 and 1933 respectively. There was a convergence of opinion within the party which had become marked by the 1930s. The municipal policies behind which all sections of the party united were chiefly as follows: the municipalisation of the chief public utilities, including the tramways, gas and water concerns, the establishment of a municipal bank, greater extension of council housing and the use of direct labour for its construction, additional educational facilities, the co-ordination of health services and the tackling of the problem of unemployment on a national basis.[31]

An issue of some interest in Bristol municipal elections was the role of women in politics. There had been a strong pre-war women's movement in Bristol, and it seems that this tradition was carried through into local politics after 1918. As the historian of women's involvement in local government before 1914 has stated, 'Bristol possessed one of the most impressive women's movements in the country.'[32] Vigorous campaigns in the city in the 1860s and 1870s over women's suffrage and the repeal of the Contagious Diseases Act were accompanied by one of the earliest attempts to organise working-class women, with the formation of the National Union of Working Women in 1874 (later called the Bristol Association of Working Women, affiliated to the Women's Protective and Provident League).[33] Later in the 1880s the Bristol Women's Liberal Association was established, the first of its kind in the country, which brought questions of women and party politics more to the fore, and by the late 1880s women's campaigns were established within the local labour movement, including the Bristol Socialist Society and the Association for the Promotion of Trade Unionism among Women. When the suffrage campaign reached its peak in the Edwardian era, both the Women's Social and Political Union and the more moderate National Union of Women's Suffrage Societies (NUWSS) had strong Bristol branches. By 1913 the NUWSS, which had earlier been closely connected with Bristol Liberalism, moved closer to the Labour Party and formed an alliance with it for electoral purposes. The East Bristol Women's Suffrage Society in particular organised working-class women, involving both the Women's Co-operative Guild and the Women's Labour League. The ILP member Walter Ayles, a Labour councillor for Easton from 1912

Books: Essays on the Social and Cultural History of the British Communist Party, (London, 1995), pp. 29–32.

[31] Western Daily Press, 2 Nov. 1920, 2 Nov. 1923, 3 Nov. 1925, 2 Nov. 1926.

[32] Hollis, P., Ladies Elect: Women in English Local Government, 1865–1914, (Oxford, 1987), p. 156.

[33] On these and later developments, see Hannam, J., '"An enlarged sphere of usefulness": The Bristol women's movement, c. 1860–1914', in Dresser and Ollerenshaw, The Making of Modern Bristol, pp. 184–209; see also Malos, E., 'Bristol women in action 1839–1919', in Bild, Bristol's Other History, pp. 97–128.

until 1922, and later for St Philip's South, put forward a Labour argument for this alliance. In 1913 he argued that the work of women was essential in the struggle for economic freedom, 'but to give this fully they must have political freedom'.[34] Once the vote was won, in Bristol 'many ex-suffragists sought to pursue their feminist policies through the Labour Party.'[35]

The impact of women in post-1918 politics in Bristol was marked. In the first municipal elections after the war in 1919 it was reported that women voted in great numbers, 'in many places in larger proportion than men.' Thus in District ward for instance, 'women voters were somewhat enthusiastic ... quite as many women as men registered their votes.' In Redcliff women voters formed the majority, and 'the women showed much more interest than the men, and treated their responsibilities in a serious manner.' In St Paul's 'women voters showed keen interest ... and it was estimated that quite 75 per cent of the votes recorded at St Agnes's were given by women.' In Somerset ward 'the surprise in regard to the voting was the large number of ladies who exercised the franchise'. Similar comments were made about succeeding elections, and it is significant that they applied to predominantly working-class wards as well as middle-class wards. Thus in 1920 in St George's East 'the feature of the election was the large number of women voters', while in St George's West 'more women polled than men'. At the same time 'women, it is said, were in the majority' in Stapleton ward. In 1923 the trend was still strong, as in the city as a whole 'women provided a very large percentage of the votes recorded, some placing the proportion as high as two-thirds of the total.'[36]

It is notable that women's participation in municipal politics in Bristol was entirely subsumed into the party battle. There were no Women's Citizen's Association candidates in the city between the wars, in contrast to such boroughs as Canterbury or Carlisle where they were nominated just after the war. It was instead the main parties who put forward women candidates in Bristol. In total women stood for Labour on thirty-nine occasions between the wars, amounting to 10 per cent of all Labour candidatures, while twenty-eight women were nominated for Labour's opponents, amounting to 6 per cent of the total. For all parties combined women stood for the council sixty-seven times, accounting for 8 per cent of the total. This was roughly in line with other large boroughs where comparable figures are available. Bristol was marginally below Birmingham, where the corresponding figures were 13, 6 and 9 per cent respectively, virtually identical with Bradford (12, 5 and 8 per cent), and slightly above Liverpool (9, 5 and 7 per cent).[37] Overall it can be said that the enthusiasm of women to participate in the political process was not matched by the willingness of parties to incorporate them fully into the political system.

Further enquiry into the figures sheds further light on this issue. On the sixty-seven occasions women candidates stood in Bristol, they were successful thirty

---

[34] Quoted in Hannam, "An enlarged sphere of usefulness", p. 203.

[35] Hannam, "An enlarged sphere of usefulness", p. 203.

[36] *Western Daily Press*, 3 Nov. 1919, 2 Nov. 1920, 2 Nov. 1923.

[37] For the Liverpool figures see Davies, S., *Liverpool Labour: Social and Political Influences on the Development of the Labour Party in Liverpool, 1900–1939*, (Keele, 1996), p. 182; for Birmingham, see volume 1 of this series, p. 228.

times, sixteen of these being victories for Labour and fourteen for Labour's opponents. The Labour party was initially, however, far less willing than the Citizens to nominate women in winnable seats. Only one female Labour councillor was elected in the whole of the 1920s, Lillian Pheysey in St Philips North in 1921, after she had been first elected in a by-election in September 1920. For the Citizens on the other hand, Miss E.H. Smith held Clifton South from 1921, Mrs E.S. Robinson-White was ensconced in Stapleton from 1924, and Miss L. Meade-King retained Central West from 1928. It was really only late in the 1930s that Labour began to put up a significant number of women in its strongholds. In 1938 Labour had a total of seven women councillors and one alderwoman, but six of these had been newly elected in the previous three years. It seems that women were beginning to play a greater part in the Labour party in these years, a trend that has been noted in other boroughs in these volumes.[38] Earlier attitudes to women in politics were less enlightened, expressed plainly in the report of the 1919 elections. Labour had nominated two women that year, but both had lost. The *Western Daily Press* commented

> The non-success of the two lady candidates, both Labour, was regarded by many as another indication that though women make useful members of the Board of Guardians, the majority of the electors 'draw the line' so far as the City Council is concerned. One experienced citizen on Saturday drew a distinction between the work of those two public bodies by saying 'the Guardians have to deal largely with the needs of women and children, but the Council have to deal mainly with docks, streets and so on.' Apparently he put health and other matters in the background.[39]

Nothing could better demonstrate the continued survival at this time of traditional nineteenth-century views on the role of women in society, despite the recent enfranchisement of women aged over thirty. The idea of 'separate spheres' for men and women, with the latter being confined to the domestic sphere concerned with children, health and the family, was still very much alive.

One final issue that is worth commenting on is the intervention in the 1919 elections of nine ex-servicemen candidates. They were connected to the myriad of groups representing the interests of ex-servicemen around the end of the First World War, the best-known of which were the National Federation of Discharged and Demobilised Sailors and Soldiers (NFDDSS – founded in 1917) and the National Association of Discharged Sailors and Soldiers (NADSS – founded 1916).[40] It is generally agreed that there was a radical edge to these organisations, and even more so to two splinter groups of the NFDDSS which were formed in 1919, the National Union of Ex-Servicemen (closely aligned to the Labour Party) and the International Ex-Services Union (a revolutionary socialist organisation centred on Glasgow). A rival body of a Conservative complexion was also

---

[38] See comments on Barnsley for instance in volume one, pp. 14–15.
[39] *Western Daily Press*, Nov. 3, 1919.
[40] For discussion of these various groups, see Wrigley, C.J., *Lloyd George and the Challenge of Labour: The Post-War Coalition 1918–1922*, (London, 1990), pp. 38–49.

established by Lord Derby, named the Comrades of the Great War. Some of these organisations later merged into the British Legion on its formation in 1921, while others faded away in obscurity. They campaigned mainly over issues such as war pensions, employment and housing for ex-servicemen in the climate of social and political tension and unrest that accompanied demobilisation at the end of the war.

Similar interventions in municipal politics to those that took place in Bristol also occurred in many other boroughs in 1919, following their precedent in parliamentary elections. The NFDDSS had first contested a Westminster seat at a by-election in Liverpool, Abercromby in June 1917, when it had gained 26 per cent of the vote against the Tory son of Lord Derby.[41] In the general election of 1918 the NFDDSS had supported a total of thirty-one candidates (three of these in Leeds also being supported by the NADSS and the Comrades). Their best performance was in Ashton under Lyne and in Liverpool, Everton, where they won over 40 per cent of the vote. Their candidates won over 70,000 votes in total, representing 13 per cent of all votes in these contests. In addition, the NADSS had been persuaded by disgruntled Tories to put forward a candidate in Sowerby in Yorkshire to oppose a Liberal who had repudiated the coalition 'coupon'. The NADSS nominee, who was a known Tory, won. He appeared to toe the Coalition line in his short parliamentary career, not standing for re-election in 1922.[42]

There were considerable local variations in these ex-servicemen groups, both in terms of their politics and their nomenclature, and the candidates in Bristol in 1919 appeared to represent a Labour-leaning descendent of one or more of the national groups. In reports on the elections they were variously described as members of the 'National General Federal Council of Ex-Servicemen', the 'British Federation of Discharged Soldiers and Sailors', and the 'National Federation of Discharged and Demobilised Sailors and Soldiers'.[43] From this it would seem most likely that they were a local alliance of NFDDSS and NADSS branches. During the campaign they approached the Labour Party to try and negotiate a pact to avoid fighting each other. General agreement could not be reached, but the ex-servicemen declared that 'they had every sympathy' with the objects of Labour's campaign, 'objects which are embodied in our programme'[44]. In one ward, St Philip's South, the ex-serviceman was given a free run against a Liberal opponent, and 'had the full support of the Labour Party in the ward'.[45] He was the only candidate to win, defeating a councillor who had been prominent on the War Pensions Committee of the council. One of the other candidates, George Daniel, was to re-appear later in the 1920s as a Labour councillor for St Philip's South.

Some of the policies of the ex-servicemen were outlined at an open-air street-corner meeting attended mostly by 'workpeople at the tobacco and other manufactories' in the Bedminster area. One speaker was reported as having

[41] For details of this contest, see Waller, P.J., *Democracy and Sectarianism: A Political and Social History of Liverpool 1868–1939*, (Liverpool, 1981), p. 280.

[42] See Craig, F.W.S., *British Parliamentary Election Results 1918–1949*, (3rd edition, Chichester, 1983), p. 527.

[43] *Western Daily Press*, 20 Oct., 25 Oct. and 3 Nov., 1919.

[44] *Western Daily Press*, 20 Oct. 1919.

[45] *Western Daily Press*, 3 Nov. 1919.

stigmatised the City Council as an antiquarian institution containing sundry ancient apostles with long white beards, who were out solely in the interests of their own class, the profit-making, rent-grabbing fraternity. All ex-service men, all widows of fighting men, were now asked to support the ex-service candidates ... He also urged the need of other reforms to reduce the price of food, and to lessen the evils of poverty and unemployment.[46]

Another speaker was the future Labour councillor George Daniel. He supported the railway workers, who were apparently numerous in the area and strong Labour supporters. They had only recently won a national rail strike to resist wage reductions and defend the eight-hour day. Daniel argued against any increase in the working day for railwaymen, saying that 'employment might be found for many people now out of work without in any way invading the eight-hour day.'[47] He also condemned the employment of women on the trams, which he said 'was only continued because the cheaper female labour increased the company's profits.'[48] While this latter comment had a basis in class politics, as blame was apportioned to the employers, it also revealed again that the notion of 'separate spheres' for the sexes was still prevalent. At another meeting candidates also put much emphasis on the need for ex-servicemen to be directly represented on the council, especially to deal with the problems of housing. As one of them put it,

> one duty of ex-servicemen in local government and other authorities would be to see that something was done to realise Mr Lloyd George's phrase that this should be 'a country fit for heroes to live in'. They did not want to come back into civil life and find that conscientious objectors were getting the most benefits accruing from the sacrifice of men who went out to the front.[49]

The reaction of Bristol's voters to these policies was mixed. The ex-servicemen candidates' share of the vote varied between 53 per cent and 3 per cent in the nine wards they contested. Between them they won 4,100 votes, equivalent to 17 per cent overall in the contested wards. It is significant, though, that by far their best performances were in the two wards where they had no Labour opposition. In St Philip's South, as already mentioned, Archie Harrison won with 53 per cent of the vote, and in St James's George Calder gained 37 per cent, in both cases in straight fights with Liberals. This suggests that their appeal was mainly to potentially

[46] *Western Daily Press*, 23 Oct. 1919.
[47] On the 1919 rail strike, see Bagwell, P.S., *The Railwaymen: The History of the National Union of Railwaymen*, (London, 1963), pp. 375–403; Howell, D., *Respectable Radicals: Studies in the Politics of Railway Trade Unionism*, (Aldershot, 1999), pp. 223–233.
[48] For details of reactions to the employment of women on trams during the First World War, see Smith, D.N., 'Trade Unions, Employers and the Development of Collective Bargaining in the Tramway and Omnibus Industry, 1889–1924', (Ph.D. thesis, University of Liverpool, 1986), pp. 198–213, 324–332; Davies, S., '"A stormy political career": P.J. Kelly and Irish Nationalist and Labour politics in Liverpool, 1891–1936', *Transactions of the Historic Society of Lancashire and Cheshire*, vol. 148, (1999), pp. 161–167.
[49] *Western Daily Press*, 25 Oct. 1919.

Labour-voting working-class voters, confirmed by the fact that their worst result of only 3 per cent was in the only predominantly middle-class ward that they stood in, Westbury on Trym. Their relative success against Liberals was also another indicator of the scale of working-class desertion from Liberalism in Bristol after 1918.

In conclusion, it is worth emphasising the strength of Labour in Bristol. The party won 47 per cent of all municipal votes cast in Bristol between the wars, a higher proportion than in any other borough in this volume, and exceeded only by Barrow and Barnsley in volume one of this series. It must be allowed that the vagaries of municipal elections, such as the proportion of no-contests or three-way contests in any borough, make these overall vote-share figures somewhat less than totally reliable. Even so it will still perhaps surprise some readers that Labour did better in Bristol than in some of its better-known northern strongholds such as Bradford or Burnley. The predominantly bucolic image of the south-west does not fit easily with the idea of Bristol as a large industrial town with a strong labour movement, indicating perhaps how misleading such images can be. Labour was well-organised and successful in Bristol, drawing on its radical Nonconformist roots. Its growth especially in the period around the First World War was due in part to a firm rejection by working-class Bristolians of their traditional Liberalism, and also to a rapid growth of 'general' trade unionism. Bristol was also, though, a good example of how the municipal electoral system could distort political realities. Labour was probably prevented from taking power earlier than 1937 by the combination of inequities in the aldermanic system and the ward boundaries. When both were reformed in 1936, then Labour was quickly able to win control of the council. Finally, it is notable that the strong pre-1914 women's movement in Bristol on the whole seems to have been less than adequately incorporated into the political process. Politics, like other aspects of public life, remained a predominantly male domain, despite female enfranchisement. There were signs that this was perhaps beginning to change by the late 1930s, before Bristol was thrown into the maelstrom of social upheaval that was to accompany the Second World War.

A guide to further reading

Newspapers

Bristol Evening Post
Bristol Observer
Bristol Times and Mirror (to 1932)
Western Daily Press (from 1932 the *Western Daily Press and Bristol Times*)

Works of reference

Wardley, P., (ed.), *Abstract of Bristol Historical Statistics, pt. 3: Political Representation and Bristol's Elections 1700–1997*, (Bristol, 1997).

Other secondary sources

Atkinson, B., *Trade Unions in Bristol: from the 1860s to 1914*, (Bristol, 1982).
Brace, K., *Portrait of Bristol*, (Second edition, London ,1976).
Croucher, R., '"Divisions in the movement": the National Unemployed Workers' Movement and its rivals in comparative perspective', in Andrews, G., Fishman, N. and Morgan, K., *Opening the Books: Essays on the Social and Cultural History of the British Communist Party*, (London, 1995), pp. 29–32.
Dresser, M., 'People's housing in Bristol 1870–1939', in Bild, I., *Bristol's Other History*, (Bristol, 1983), pp. 129–160.
Dresser, M., 'Housing policy in Bristol, 1919–30', in Daunton, M.J., (ed.), *Councillors and Tenants: Local Authority Housing in English Cities, 1919–1939*, (Leicester, 1984), pp. 156–216.
Dresser, M., 'Protestants, Catholics and Jews: religious difference and political status in Bristol, 1750–1850', in Dresser, M. and Ollerenshaw, P., (eds), *The Making of Modern Bristol*, (Tiverton, 1996), pp. 96–123.
Fleming, P., 'The emergence of modern Bristol', in Dresser and Ollerenshaw, *The Making of Modern Bristol*, pp. 1–24.
Hannam, J., '"An enlarged sphere of usefulness": the Bristol women's movement, c. 1860–1914', in Dresser and Ollerenshaw, *The Making of Modern Bristol*, pp. 184–209.
Large, D. and Whitfield, R., *The Bristol Trades Council 1873–1973*, (Bristol, 1973).
Little, B.D.G., *The City and County of Bristol: A Study in Atlantic Civilisation*, (London, 1954).
Malos, E., 'Bristol women in action 1839–1919', in Bild, *Bristol's Other History*, pp. 97–128.
Morgan, K., 'The economic development of Bristol, 1700–1850', in Dresser and Ollerenshaw, *The Making of Modern Bristol*, pp. 48–75.
Whitfield, R., 'The Labour Movement in Bristol: 1910–1939', (M.Litt. thesis, University of Bristol, 1979).
Whitfield, R., 'Trade unionism in Bristol 1910–1926', in Bild, *Bristol's Other History*, pp. 68–96.

Table 3.1 Electorates of Bristol wards before and after 1935–36
boundary changes

Ward	1935 electorate	1936 electorate
Avon	-	7,506
Bedminster	-	8,867
Bedminster East	13,747	-
Bedminster West	14,689	-
Bishopston	-	7,018
Brislington	-	7,832
Central East	1,417	-
Central West	857	-
Clifton	-	6,510
Clifton North	3,859	-
Clifton South	4,612	-
District	8,552	9,114
Durdham	-	6,387
Easton	10,467	9,777
Eastville	-	7,387
Hengrove	-	6,979
Hillfields	-	7,616
Horfield	15,826	8,232
Knowle	-	9,115
Redcliff	2,907	4,724
Redland	7,722	6,544
St Augustine's	6,298	6,074
St George's East	14,402	9,093
St George's West	9,470	8,693
St James's	4,373	5,033
St Michael's	5,730	6,718
St Paul's	6,605	6,854
St Philip's and St. Jacob's North	8,237	8,592
St Philip's and St. Jacob's South	6,833	7,146
Somerset	19,937	8,755
Southville	8,406	8,270
Stapleton	17,374	6,969
Westbury on Trym	17,485	8,341
Windmill Hill	-	8,776
Total	**209,805**	**212,922**
Average per ward	9,122	7,604

Table 3.2 Political character of Bristol wards before and after 1935–36 boundary changes[a]

1935 wards		1936 wards	
Bedminster East	**Lab**	Avon	**Lab**
Bedminster West	**Lab**	Bedminster	*Lab*
Central East	**Cit**	Bishopston	**Cit**
Central West	**Cit**	Brislington	*Lab*
Clifton North	**Cit**	Clifton	**Cit**
Clifton South	**Cit**	District	**Cit**
District	**Cit**	Durdham	**Cit**
Easton	**Lab**	Easton	**Lab**
Horfield	**Cit**	Eastville	*Lab*
Redcliff	**Cit**	Hengrove	**Lab**
Redland	**Cit**	Hillfields	**Lab**
St Augustine's	**Lab**	Horfield	*Lab*
St George's East	**Lab**	Knowle	**Cit**
St George's West	**Lab**	Redcliff	**Cit**
St James's	**Cit**	Redland	**Cit**
St Michael's	**Cit**	St Augustine's	*Cit*
St Paul's	**Lab**	St George's East	**Lab**
St Philip's and St Jacob's N	**Lab**	St George's West	**Lab**
St Philip's and St Jacob's S	**Lab**	St James's	**Cit**
Somerset	**Cit**	St Michael's	**Cit**
Southville	**Cit**	St Paul's	**Lab**
Stapleton	*Lab*	St Philip's and St Jacob's N	**Lab**
Westbury on Trym	**Cit**	St Philip's and St Jacob's S	**Lab**
		Somerset	**Lab**
		Southville	**Cit**
		Stapleton	**Cit**
		Westbury on Trym	**Cit**
		Windmill Hill	**Lab**
Total wards	23	Total wards	28
Strong Labour	9	Strong Labour	11
Marginal Labour	1	Marginal Labour	4
Strong Citizen's	13	Strong Citizen's	12
		Marginal Citizen's	1

[a] Party name in bold = strong (won all three elections before or after changes); party name in italics = marginal (won majority of three elections before or after).

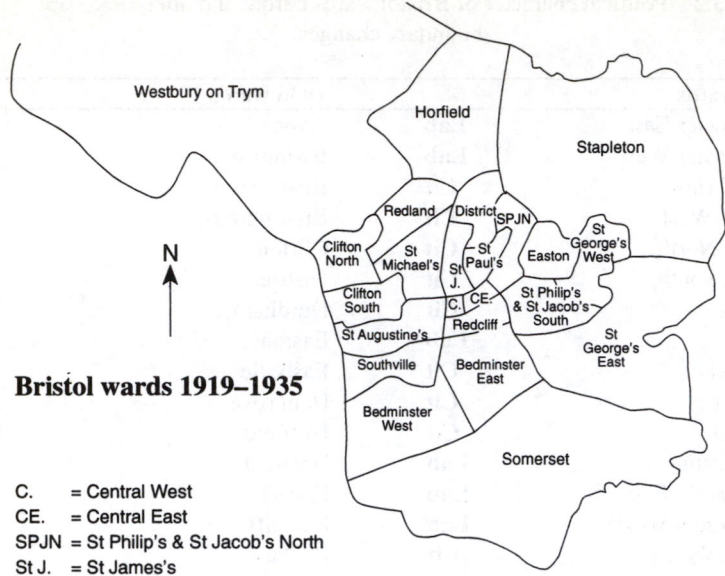

Westbury on Trym

Horfield

Stapleton

Redland District SPJN

Clifton North

St Michael's

St Paul's

Easton

St George's West

Clifton South

St J.

C. CE.

St Philip's & St Jacob's South

Redcliff

St Augustine's

Southville

Bedminster East

St George's East

Bristol wards 1919–1935

Bedminster West

Somerset

C.   = Central West
CE.   = Central East
SPJN = St Philip's & St Jacob's North
St J.   = St James's

Bristol wards 1936–1938

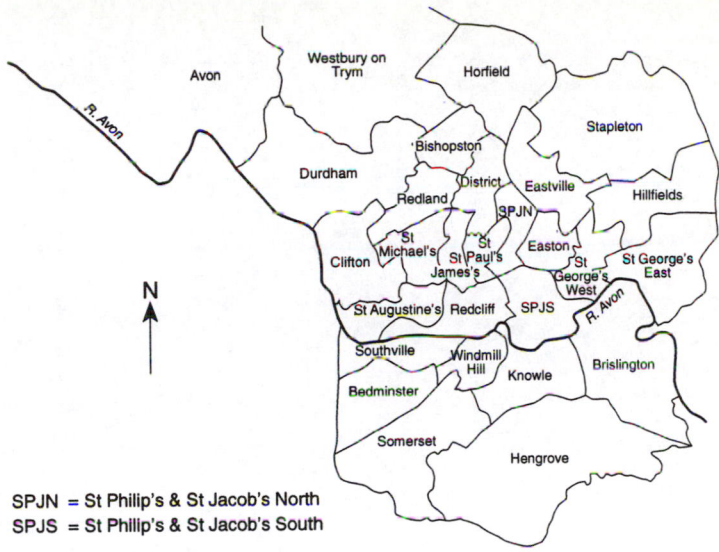

SPJN = St Philip's & St Jacob's North
SPJS = St Philip's & St Jacob's South

Persons aged fourteen and over classified by industry 1931

	Male	%	Female	%	Total	%
Metal and engineering	15,344	11.9	921	1.5	16,265	8.6
- Engineering	3,101	2.4	187	0.3	3,288	1.7
- Vehicle construction	4,791	3.7	247	0.4	5,038	2.7
Clothing	4,175	3.3	5,967	9.9	10,142	5.4
Food, drink and tobacco	11,266	8.8	10,882	18.1	22,148	11.8
- Food	5,542	4.3	4,407	7.3	9,949	5.3
- Tobacco	4,405	3.4	6,036	10.1	10,441	5.5
Paper and printing	5,906	4.6	4,521	7.5	10,427	5.5
- Printing	4,488	3.5	2,187	3.6	6,675	3.5
Building	11,722	9.1	81	0.1	11,803	6.3
Transport	18,365	14.3	466	0.8	18,831	10.0
- Railways	5,729	4.5	142	0.2	5,871	3.1
- Road	5,984	4.7	176	0.3	6,160	3.3
- Docks	3,568	2.8	52	0.1	3,620	1.9
Commerce and finance	25,595	19.9	10,330	17.2	35,925	19.1
Public admin. and defence	10,877	8.5	3,230	5.4	14,107	7.5
- Local government	7,637	5.9	2,438	4.1	10,075	5.3
Professions	3,232	2.5	3,742	6.2	6,974	3.7
Personal service	4,628	3.6	16,117	26.9	20,745	11.0
Other	17,335	13.5	3,759	6.3	21,094	11.2
Total (a)	**128,445**		**60,016**		**188,461**	
Total population (b)	185,125		211,887		397,012	
(a) as % of (b)	69.4		28.3		47.5	
Total out of work (c)	16,558		3,916		20,474	
(c) as % of (a)	12.9		6.5		10.9	
Managerial and own account	15,918	14.2	4,732	8.4	20,650	12.3
Operative	95,969	85.8	51,368	91.6	147,337	87.7
Total (excluding out of work)	111,887		56,100		167,987	

Population statistics 1931

Ward	Acres	Population	Persons/Acre	Persons/Room
Bedminster East	786	19,704	25.1	0.89
Bedminster West	1,213	26,884	22.2	0.91
Central East	109	2,876	26.4	1.02
Central West	72	999	13.9	0.91
Clifton North	443	7,869	17.8	0.58
Clifton South	239	9,246	38.7	0.68
District	342	16,740	48.9	0.69
Easton	252	20,610	81.8	0.83
Horfield	1,314	27,973	21.3	0.74
Redcliff	245	6,670	27.2	0.98
Redland	501	14,030	28.0	0.54
St Augustine's	320	14,909	46.6	0.96
St George's East	1,342	26,566	19.8	0.88
St George's West	483	20,596	42.6	0.93
St James's	133	9,655	72.6	0.87
St Michael's	267	11,249	42.1	0.68
St Paul's	160	15,492	96.8	1.01
St Philip's and St Jacob's North	246	20,026	81.4	0.99
St Philip's and St Jacob's South	269	17,014	63.2	1.04
Somerset	1,590	29,283	18.4	0.75
Southville	250	17,006	68.0	0.82
Stapleton	2,573	35,013	13.6	0.78
Westbury on Trym	6,525	26,602	4.1	0.70
Total	19,155	397,012	20.7	0.81

Overall position on the council 1919–38

	Position				Gains				Losses			
	Lab	C	L	Ind	Lab	C	L	Ind	Lab	C	L	Ind
1919	15	38	35	4[a]	6	0	0	1	0	1	6	0
1920	18	37	33	4	3	0	0	0	0	1	2	0
1921	21	36	32	3	3	1	0	0	1	2	1	0
1922	18	38	33	3	1	2	2	0	4	0	1	0
1923	18	38	33	3	0	0	0	0	0	0	0	0
	Lab	Cit			Lab	Cit			Lab	Cit		
1924[b]	18	74			1	1			1	1		
1925	20	72			3	1			1	3		
1926	23	69			3	0			0	3		
1927	26	66			3	0			0	3		
1928	28	64			2	0			0	2		
1929	34	58			4	0			0	4		
1930	38	54			0	0			0	0		
1931	33	59			0	5			5	0		
1932	31	61			0	2			2	0		
1933	32	60			1	0			0	1		
1934	37	55			4	0			0	4		
1935	36	56			0	1			1	0		
1936[c]	50*	57			-	-			-	-		
1937	58	54			2	0			0	2		
1938	56	56			1	4			4	1		

Aldermen 1919–38

1919	Lab–2, Others–21	1929	Lab–2, Cit–21
1920	Lab–2, Others–21	1930	Lab–6, Cit–17
1921	Lab–2, Others–21	1931	Lab–6, Cit–17
1922	Lab–2, Others–21	1932	Lab–6, Cit–17
1923	Lab–2, Others–21	1933	Lab–6, Cit–17
1924	Lab–2, Cit–21	1934	Lab–7, Cit–16
1925	Lab–2, Cit–21	1935	Lab–7, Cit–16
1926	Lab–2, Cit–21	1936[c]	Lab–7, Cit–16
1927	Lab–2, Cit–21	1937	Lab–13, Cit–15
1928	Lab–2, Cit–21	1938	Lab–14, Cit–14

[a] 1919 – Ind includes one Ex-Serviceman.
[b] From 1924 Liberals and Conservatives become Citizens.
[c] 1936 – five aldermanic seats vacant.

Municipal elections: winning party 1919–28

Ward	1919	1920	1921	1922	1923	1924	1925	1926	1927	1928
Bedminster East	Lab	Lab	Lab	Lab	Lab	Cit	Lab	Lab	Lab	Lab
Bedminster West	Lab	L	Coa	Lab	L	Lab	Lab	Cit	Lab	Lab
Central East	C	C	Coa	C	C	Cit	Cit	Cit	Cit	Cit
Central West	<u>C</u>	<u>C</u>	Coa	<u>C</u>	<u>C</u>	<u>**Cit**</u>	<u>**Cit**</u>	<u>**Cit**</u>	Cit	Cit
Clifton North	<u>C</u>	<u>C</u>	Coa	<u>C</u>	<u>C</u>	<u>**Cit**</u>	Cit	Cit	Cit	Cit
Clifton South	<u>C</u>	<u>C</u>	<u>**Coa**</u>	<u>C</u>	<u>C</u>	<u>**Cit**</u>	Cit	Cit	Cit	Cit
District	L	L	Coa	L	L	Cit	Cit	Cit	Cit	Cit
Easton	Lab	Lab	Coa	C	Lab	Cit	Lab	Lab	Lab	Lab
Horfield	<u>**L**</u>	L	<u>**Coa**</u>	L	L	Cit	Cit	Cit	Cit	Cit
Redcliff	C	C	<u>**Coa**</u>	C	C	Cit	Cit	Cit	Cit	Lab
Redland	<u>C</u>	<u>C</u>	Coa	<u>C</u>	<u>C</u>	<u>**Cit**</u>	Cit	Cit	Cit	Cit
St Augustine's	Lab	C	Coa	C	<u>C</u>	<u>**Cit**</u>	Cit	Lab	Cit	Lab
St George's East	Lab	L	Lab	Lab	L	Lab	Lab	Lab	Lab	Lab
St George's West	Lab	Lab	Lab	Lab	Lab	Lab	Lab	Lab	Lab	Lab
St James's	L	<u>C</u>	Coa	<u>C</u>	<u>C</u>	<u>**Cit**</u>	Cit	Cit	Cit	Cit
St Michael's	C	<u>C</u>	<u>**Coa**</u>	<u>C</u>	<u>C</u>	<u>**Cit**</u>	Cit	Cit	Cit	Cit
St Paul's	L	L	L	Lab	L	Cit	Lab	Lab	Lab	Lab
St Philip's and St Jacob's North	Lab	Lab	Lab	L	Lab	Lab	Lab	Lab	Lab	Lab
St Philip's and St Jacob's South	Ex-S	Lab	Lab	L	Lab	Lab	Lab	Lab	Lab	Lab
Somerset	L	L	Coa	L	L	Cit	Cit	Cit	Cit	Cit
Southville	L	C	Coa	<u>**L**</u>	C	Cit	Cit	Cit	Cit	Cit
Stapleton	Lab	L	Coa	Lab	L	Cit	Cit	Cit	Cit	Cit
Westbury on Trym	C	L	Coa	<u>C</u>	L	Cit	Cit	Cit	Cit	Cit

Municipal elections: party wins per year 1919–28

	1919	1920	1921	1922	1923	1924	1925	1926	1927	1928
C	8	10	17	11	10	-	-	-	-	-
Lab	8	5	5	6	5	5	8	8	8	10
L	6	8	1	6	8	-	-	-	-	-
Cit	-	-	-	-	-	18	15	15	15	13
Ind	1	-	-	-	-	-	-	-	-	-
Total	23	23	23	23	23	23	23	23	23	23
Turnout %	32.8	43.4	45.3	47.6	46.0	48.2	51.0	45.3	48.9	49.8
Labour %	44.0	44.0	43.1	48.2	47.8	44.6	44.0	48.5	45.8	49.2

Municipal elections: winning party 1929–35

Ward	1929	1930	1931	1932	1933	1934	1935
Bedminster East	Lab	**Lab**	Cit	Lab	**Lab**	Lab	**Lab**
Bedminster West	Lab	Lab	Cit	Lab	ILP	Lab	Lab
Central East	Cit	Cit	**Cit**	**Cit**	**Cit**	**Cit**	**Cit**
Central West	**Cit**	Cit	**Cit**	**Cit**	**Cit**	**Cit**	**Cit**
Clifton North	Cit	Cit	**Cit**	**Cit**	**Cit**	**Cit**	**Cit**
Clifton South	Cit	Cit	**Cit**	**Cit**	**Cit**	**Cit**	**Cit**
District	Cit	Cit	**Cit**	Cit	**Cit**	Cit	**Cit**
Easton	Lab	Lab	Cit	Lab	Lab	Lab	Lab
Horfield	Cit	Cit	Cit	Cit	Cit	Cit	Cit
Redcliff	Lab	Cit	Cit	Cit	Cit	Cit	Cit
Redland	Cit	Cit	**Cit**	**Cit**	**Cit**	**Cit**	**Cit**
St Augustine's	Lab	Lab	Cit	Lab	Lab	Lab	Lab
St George's East	Lab	Lab	Lab	**Lab**	Lab	**Lab**	**Lab**
St George's West	Lab	**Lab**	**Lab**	**Lab**	**Lab**	**Lab**	**Lab**
St James's	Cit	Cit	Cit	Cit	Cit	Cit	**Cit**
St Michael's	Cit	Cit	Cit	**Cit**	**Cit**	**Cit**	**Cit**
St Paul's	Lab	Lab	Lab	Lab	Lab	Lab	**Lab**
St Philip's and St Jacob's North	Lab	**Lab**	Lab	Lab	**Lab**	**Lab**	**Lab**
St Philip's and St Jacob's South	Lab	**Lab**	Lab	Lab	Lab	Lab	**Lab**
Somerset	Lab	Cit	Cit	Lab	Cit	Cit	Cit
Southville	Lab	Cit	Cit	Cit	Cit	Cit	Cit
Stapleton	Lab	Cit	Cit	Lab	Lab	Cit	Lab
Westbury on Trym	Cit	Cit	Cit	Cit	Cit	Cit	Cit

Municipal elections: party wins per year 1929–35

	1929	1930	1931	1932	1933	1934	1935
Lab	13	9	5	11	9	9	10
Cit	10	14	18	12	13	14	13
Ind	-	-	-	-	1	-	-
Total	23	23	23	23	23	23	23
Turnout %	38.4	41.9	51.7	46.6	44.6	49.1	49.9
Labour %	54.0	41.0	39.0	51.6	49.3	51.0	48.5

Municipal elections: winning party 1936–38

Ward	1936 (1)	1936 (2)	1936 (3)	1937	1938
Avon	Lab	-	-	Lab	Lab
Bedminster	Lab	-	-	Lab	Cit
Bishopston	Cit	-	-	Cit	Cit
Brislington	Lab	-	-	Lab	Cit
Clifton	**Cit**	-	-	**Cit**	Cit
District	**Cit**	-	-	**Cit**	**Cit**
Durdham	**Cit**	-	-	**Cit**	**Cit**
Easton	Lab	-	-	Lab	**Lab**
Eastville	Lab	Cit	Lab	Lab	Cit
Hengrove	Lab	Lab	Lab	Lab	Lab
Hillfields	Lab	Lab	Lab	**Lab**	**Lab**
Horfield	Lab	Lab	Lab	Lab	Cit
Knowle	Cit	-	-	Cit	Cit
Redcliff	Cit	-	-	Cit	Cit
Redland	**Cit**	-	-	**Cit**	**Cit**
St Augustine's	Cit	-	-	Lab	Cit
St George's East	**Lab**	-	-	**Lab**	**Lab**
St George's West	**Lab**	-	-	**Lab**	**Lab**
St James's	Cit	-	-	Cit	Cit
St Michael's	**Cit**	-	-	**Cit**	**Cit**
St Paul's	Lab	-	-	Lab	Lab
St Philip's and St Jacob's North	**Lab**	-	-	Lab	**Lab**
St Philip's and St Jacob's South	**Lab**	-	-	**Lab**	**Lab**
Somerset	Lab	Lab	Lab	**Lab**	**Lab**
Southville	Cit	-	-	Cit	Cit
Stapleton	Cit	-	-	Cit	Cit
Westbury on Trym	Cit	-	-	Cit	Cit
Windmill Hill	Lab	-	-	**Lab**	Lab

Municipal elections: party wins per year 1936–38

	1936	1937	1938
Lab	24	16	11
Cit	14	12	17
Total	38	28	28
Turnout %	**48.5**	**50.9**	**50.4**
Labour %	**53.1**	**49.8**	**41.9**

Municipal elections: party wins per ward 1919–35

Ward	Lab	Other	Total	Turnout %	Labour %
Bedminster East	15	2	17	41.0	61.6
Bedminster West	11	6[a]	17	46.8	51.6
Central East	0	17	17	50.5	22.8
Central West	0	17	17	55.4	16.1
Clifton North	0	17	17	52.8	11.9
Clifton South	0	17	17	43.0	14.1
District	0	17	17	45.7	26.7
Easton	13	4	17	48.9	56.8
Horfield	0	17	17	44.5	33.9
Redcliff	2	15	17	58.5	45.1
Redland	0	17	17	48.0	11.4
St Augustine's	9	8	17	49.9	47.6
St George's East	15	2	17	43.7	61.2
St George's West	17	0	17	44.2	72.1
St James's	0	17	17	45.4	34.6
St Michael's	0	17	17	40.8	19.3
St Paul's	12	5	17	46.7	55.1
St Philip's and St Jacob's North	16	1	17	42.8	62.3
St Philip's and St Jacob's South	15	2	17	37.9	61.7
Somerset	2	15	17	46.9	42.2
Southville	1	16	17	43.1	39.3
Stapleton	6	11	17	45.9	46.7
Westbury on Trym	0	17	17	53.0	36.6
Total	**134**	**251**	**385**	**45.8**	**46.8**

[a] Includes one ILP winner uncontested by Labour.

Seats won by Labour as a percentage of all wins 1919–35   34.8

Municipal elections: party wins per ward 1936–38

Ward	Lab	Other	Total	Turnout %	Labour %
Avon	3	0	3	62.8	56.8
Bedminster	2	1	3	48.8	51.3
Bishopston	0	3	3	51.3	31.3
Brislington	2	1	3	53.2	51.6
Clifton	0	3	3	50.3	19.1
District	0	3	3	-	-
Durdham	0	3	3	-	-
Easton	3	0	3	44.7	68.5
Eastville	3	2	5	53.5	49.3
Hengrove	5	0	5	43.9	59.5
Hillfields	5	0	5	43.4	86.5
Horfield	4	1	5	50.6	52.3
Knowle	0	3	3	50.7	36.1
Redcliff	0	3	3	56.4	34.8
Redland	0	3	3	-	-
St Augustine's	1	2	3	60.8	50.1
St George's East	3	0	3	-	-
St George's West	3	0	3	-	-
St James's	0	3	3	41.4	32.1
St Michael's	0	3	3	-	-
St Paul's	3	0	3	47.7	58.1
St Philip's and St Jacob's North	3	0	3	45.8	65.4
St Philip's and St Jacob's South	3	0	3	-	-
Somerset	5	0	5	39.7	90.2
Southville	0	3	3	53.1	38.8
Stapleton	0	3	3	50.0	39.9
Westbury on Trym	0	3	3	49.3	30.6
Windmill Hill	3	0	3	34.9	68.5
Total	**51**	**43**	**94**	**49.9**	**48.5**

Seats won by Labour as a percentage of all wins 1936–38   **54.3**

Parliamentary election results

Central constituency
(the following wards [1918 boundaries] were included in Central:
Central East, Central West, Redcliff, St Augustine's, St James's, St Paul's,
St Philip's and Jacob's South)

General election	Winner	Conservative %	Labour %	Liberal %
14 Dec. 1918	Co C	63.2 *(Co C)*	36.8	-
15 Nov. 1922	C	55.9	44.1	-
6 Dec. 1923	C	54.7	45.3	-
29 Oct. 1924	C	55.1	44.9	-
30 May 1929	Lab	44.3	55.7	-
27 Oct. 1931	C	59.6	40.4	-
14 Nov. 1935	C	52.5	47.5	-

East constituency
(the following wards [1918 boundaries] were included in East:
St George's East, St George's West, Easton [part], Somerset [part])

General election	Winner	Conservative %	Labour %	Liberal %
14 Dec. 1918[a]	Co L	-	42.8	49.6 *(CO L)*
15 Nov. 1922	NL	-	49.7	50.3 *(NL)*
6 Dec. 1923	Lab	-	53.7	46.3
29 Oct. 1924	Lab	-	58.2	41.8
30 May 1929	Lab	-	65.8	34.2
27 Oct. 1931	Lab	49.4	50.6	-
14 Nov. 1935[b]	Lab	-	59.3	-

[a] A non-coalition Liberal gained 7.6 % of the votes in 1918.
[b] A National Labour candidate gained 40.7 % of the votes in 1935.

Parliamentary election results *(continued)*

North constituency
(the following wards [1918 boundaries] were included in North:
District, St Philip's and Jacob's North, Stapleton, Easton [part])

General election	Winner	Conservative %	Labour %	Liberal %
14 Dec. 1918[a]	Co L	-	26.5	60.2 *(Co L)*
15 Nov. 1922	NL	-	35.4	64.6 *(NL)*
6 Dec. 1923	Lab	31.0	37.5	31.5
29 Oct. 1924	L	-	40.9	59.1
30 May 1929[b]	Lab	-	48.7	17.5
27 Oct. 1931	L	-	33.8	66.2
14 Nov. 1935	L	-	43.5	56.5

[a] A National Party candidate gained 13.3 % of the votes in 1918.
[b] An Independent Liberal candidate gained 33.8 % of the votes in 1929.

South constituency
(the following wards [1918 boundaries] were included in South:
Bedminster East, Bedminster West, Southville, Somerset [part])

General election	Winner	Conservative %	Labour %	Liberal %
14 Dec. 1918	Co L	-	31.8	68.2 *(Co L)*
15 Nov. 1922	NL	-	43.8	56.2 *(NL)*
6 Dec. 1923	L	-	47.3	52.7
29 Oct. 1924	L	-	48.4	51.6
30 May 1929	Lab	-	56.5	43.5
27 Oct. 1931	C	60.9	39.1	-
14 Nov. 1935	Lab	45.0	50.3	4.7

Parliamentary election results *(continued)*

West constituency
(the following wards [1918 boundaries] were included in West:
Clifton North, Clifton South, Horfield, Redland, St Michael's,
Westbury-on-Trym)

General election	Winner	Conservative %	Labour %	Liberal %
14 Dec. 1918	**Co C**	-	-	-
15 Nov. 1922	C	62.0	-	38.0
6 Dec. 1923	**C**	-	-	-
29 Oct. 1924	C	79.0	21.0	-
30 May 1929	C	53.7	25.3	21.0
27 Oct. 1931	C	83.0	17.0	-
14 Nov. 1935	C	71.0	29.0	-

Avon ward
(created in the 1936 reorganisation)

Candidate	Party	Votes	%	Electors	Turnout	Gains
1936						
F. Phippen	Lab	2,851	57.9	7,506	65.6	Lab from Cit
K.A.L. Brown	Cit	2,072	42.1			
Total votes		4,923				
1937						
H.W. Makin	Lab	2,802	57.2	7,685	63.8	Lab from Cit
K.A.L. Brown	Cit	2,098	42.8			
Total votes		4,900				
1938						
Mrs W.E. Salt	Lab	2,601	55.3	7,936	59.3	Lab from Cit
Mrs M.L. Gunning	Cit	2,104	44.7			
Total votes		4,705				

Overall Labour vote: **Overall turnout:**
1936–38   56.8%   **1936–38**   62.8%

Bedminster ward
(created from the merger of the old Bedminster East and West wards in the 1936 reorganisation)

Candidate	Party	Votes	%	Electors	Turnout	Gains
1936						
F. Berriman*	Lab	2,113	56.6	8,867	42.1	-
Miss G.M. Williams	Cit	1,623	43.4			
Total votes		3,736				
1937						
H.L. Cook*	Lab	2,440	53.0	8,986	51.2	-
A.L. Duggan	Cit	2,161	47.0			
Total votes		4,601				
1938						
A.L. Duggan	Cit	2,625	54.4	9,151	52.8	Cit from Lab
W.F. Wilkins	Lab	2,204	45.6			
Total votes		4,829				

Overall Labour vote: **Overall turnout:**
1936–38   **51.3%**   **1936–38**   **48.8%**

Bedminster East ward
(merged with Bedminster West to form the new Bedminster ward in the reorganisation of 1936)

Candidate	Party	Votes	%	Electors	Turnout	Gains
1919						
A.H. Weaver	Lab	1,834	67.7	8,102	33.5	Lab from L
T.H.J. Underdown	L	592	21.8			
J. Rogers	R	285	10.5			
Total votes		2,711				
1920						
G.L. Perkins	Lab	1,898	68.5	8,314	33.3	Lab from L
T.G. Lawrence	L	873	31.5			
Total votes		2,771				
1921						
F.E. White	Lab	1,784	54.1	8,507	38.8	Lab from Coa
E.F. Young	L	1,515	45.9			
Total votes		3,299				
1922						
A.H. Weaver*	Lab	1,795	66.5	8,643	31.2	-
T.G. Lawrence	L	905	33.5			
Total votes		2,700				
1923						
J. Curle	Lab	2,098	68.6	8,886	34.4	-
W.P. Kingston	L	960	31.4			
Total votes		3,058				
1924						
T.B. Dixon	Cit	2,251	52.9	8,940	47.6	Cit from Lab
F.E. White*	Lab	2,001	47.1			
Total votes		4,252				
1925						
F.E. White	Lab	2,316	54.9	9,010	46.8	-
R.A. Hall	Cit	1,899	45.1			
Total votes		4,215				

Bedminster East ward *(continued)*

Candidate	Party	Votes	%	Electors	Turnout	Gains
1926						
J. Curle*	Lab	2,452	61.0	8,930	45.0	-
W.S. Davis	Cit	1,569	39.0			
Total votes		4,021				
1927						
F. Wroe	Lab	2,287	56.4	8,857	45.8	Lab from Cit
Mrs Dixon	Cit	1,770	43.6			
Total votes		4,057				
1928						
F.E. White*	Lab	2,607	62.5	8,727	47.8	-
R.A. Hall	Cit	1,561	37.5			
Total votes		4,168				
1929						
F.C. Williams*	Lab	2,285	65.8	9,602	36.1	-
G.S. James	Cit	1,186	34.2			
Total votes		3,471				
1930						
F. Wroe*	Lab	Unopp.	-	9,363	-	-
1931						
A.G. Farmer	Cit	2,403	50.1	9,950	48.2	Cit from Lab
F.E. White*	Lab	2,393	49.9			
Total votes		4,796				
1932						
F.C. Williams*	Lab	3,615	69.8	11,809	43.8	-
R.N.B. Garrett	Cit	1,562	30.2			
Total votes		5,177				
1933						
C.R. Gill*	Lab	Unopp.	-	12,418	-	-
1934						
E.J. Plaisted	Lab	3,783	74.3	12,805	39.8	Lab from Cit
H.R. Hatherell	Cit	1,311	25.7			
Total votes		5,094				

Bedminster East ward *(continued)*

Candidate	Party	Votes	%	Electors	Turnout	Gains
1935						
F.C. Williams*	Lab	Unopp.		13,747	-	-

Overall Labour vote:				**Overall turnout:**		
1919–35		**61.6%**		**1919–35**		**41.0%**

Bedminster West ward
(merged with Bedminster East to form the new Bedminster ward in the reorganisation of 1936)

Candidate	Party	Votes	%	Electors	Turnout	Gains
1919						
E.C. Millard	Lab	1,195	48.7	8,980	27.3	Lab from L
T. Butler*	L	832	33.9			
S.J. White	Ex-S	425	17.3			
Total votes		2,452				
1920						
T.H.J. Underdown	L	1,819	55.8	9,257	35.2	-
S.C. Pope	Lab	1,439	44.2			
Total votes		3,258				
1921						
J. Cottle*	Coa	2,422	50.9	9,526	50.0	-
C.R. Gill	Lab	2,338	49.1			
Total votes		4,760				
1922						
C.R. Gill	Lab	2,464	50.5	9,627	50.7	-
F.J. Matthews	L	2,420	49.5			
Total votes		4,884				
1923						
T.H.J. Underdown*	L	2,277	52.8	9,785	44.1	-
C.S. Baston	Lab	2,039	47.2			
Total votes		4,316				
1924						
Dr W. Gow Cook	Lab	2,826	50.2	9,932	56.7	Lab from Cit
H.A. White	Cit	2,805	49.8			
Total votes		5,631				
1925						
C.R. Gill*	Lab	3,430	63.6	9,983	54.0	-
F.J.M. Cook	Cit	1,960	36.4			
Total votes		5,390				

Bedminster West ward (*continued*)

Candidate	Party	Votes	%	Electors	Turnout	Gains
1926						
T.H.J. Underdown*	Cit	2,397	50.6	10,379	45.7	-
F. Berriman	Lab	2,344	49.4			
Total votes		4,741				
1927						
F. Berriman	Lab	3,032	51.3	10,940	54.0	-
W.J. Kew	Cit	2,873	48.7			
Total votes		5,905				
1928						
C.R.Gill*	Lab	4,022	62.9	11,130	57.4	-
W.J. Kew	Cit	2,372	37.1			
Total votes		6,394				
1929						
C.S. Baston	Lab	3,182	57.8	12,413	44.4	Lab from Cit
T.H.J. Underdown*	Cit	2,327	42.2			
Total votes		5,509				
1930						
F. Berriman*	Lab	2,632	60.0	12,812	34.2	-
F.E. Sprackling	Cit	1,754	40.0			
Total votes		4,386				
1931						
T.T. Wills	Cit	4,270	53.6	12,907	61.7	Cit from Lab
C.R.Gill*	Lab	3,696	46.4			
Total votes		7,966				
1932						
C.S. Baston*	Lab	3,935	67.3	12,838	45.6	-
E. Luton	Cit	1,915	32.7			
Total votes		5,850				
1933						
F. Berriman*	ILP	3,412	67.2	13,928	36.4	-
H.H. Hatherell	Cit	1,662	32.8			
Total votes		5,074				

Bedminster West ward *(continued)*

Candidate	Party	Votes	%	Electors	Turnout	Gains
1934						
E.T. Pugh	Lab	3,869	52.9	14,324	51.1	Lab from C
T.T. Wills	Cit	3,449	47.1			
Total votes		7,318				
1935						
C.S. Baston*	Lab	4,276	64.6	14,689	45.1	-
A.J. Allen	Cit	2,346	35.4			
Total votes		6,622				

Overall Labour vote: **Overall turnout:**
1919–35   **51.6%**   **1919–35**   **46.8%**

Bishopston ward
(created in the 1936 reorganisation)

Candidate	Party	Votes	%	Electors	Turnout	Gains
1936						
D. Lewtas*	Cit	2,280	66.6	7,018	48.8	-
A. Jones	Lab	1,143	33.4			
Total votes		3,423				
1937						
Mrs E.M. Vevers*	Cit	2,378	66.6	7,007	50.9	-
Ms L.M. Heard	Lab	1,192	33.4			
Total votes		3,570				
1938						
H. Crook	Cit	2,749	72.4	6,993	54.3	-
Mrs B. Heard	Lab	1,047	27.6			
Total votes		3,796				

Overall Labour vote: **Overall turnout:**
1936–38   **31.3%**   **1936–38**   **51.3%**

Brislington ward
(created in the 1936 reorganisation)

Candidate	Party	Votes	%	Electors	Turnout	Gains
1936						
T.H. Martin	Lab	2,055	51.3	7,832	51.2	Lab from Cit
H.R. Lee*	Cit	1,952	48.7			
Total votes		4,007				
1937						
L.J. Blake	Lab	2,538	55.4	8,284	55.3	Lab from Cit
F.E. Fox*	Cit	2,040	44.6			
Total votes		4,578				
1938						
A.W. Wheeler	Cit	2,358	51.9	8,560	53.1	-
M. Jefferis	Lab	2,186	48.1			
Total votes		4,544				

Overall Labour vote:　　　　　　　　**Overall turnout:**
1936–38　　　　　　**51.6%**　　　**1936–38**　　　　　　　**53.2%**

Central East ward

Candidate	Party	Votes	%	Electors	Turnout	Gains
1919						
A.E. Thomas*	C	Unopp.	-	1,794	-	-
1920						
F.E. Metcalfe*	C	Unopp.	-	1,686	-	-
1921						
Dr L. Page	Coa	739	80.0	1,711	54.0	-
A.A. Brain	Lab	185	20.0			
Total votes		924				
1922						
A.E. Thomas*	C	Unopp.	-	1,749	-	-
1923						
F.E. Metcalfe*	C	Unopp.	-	1,799	-	-
1924						
R.F. Lyne	Cit	560	62.7	1,741	51.3	-
J.B. Gibbs	Ind	333	37.3			
Total votes		893				
1925						
Dr L. Page*	Cit	Unopp.	-	1,694	-	-
1926						
F.E. Metcalfe*	Cit	Unopp.	-	1,668	-	-
1927						
R.F. Lyne*	Cit	573	64.5	1,632	54.4	-
H.J. Smith	Lab	315	35.5			
Total votes		888				
1928						
Dr L. Page*	Cit	600	70.3	1,611	53.0	-
H.J. Smith	Lab	254	29.7			
Total votes		854				

Central East ward *(continued)*

Candidate	Party	Votes	%	Electors	Turnout	Gains
1929						
G.T. Plum*	Cit	512	72.9	1,732	40.5	-
G.A. Jahans	Lab	190	27.1			
Total votes		702				
1930						
R.F. Lyne*	Cit	620	73.9	1,664	50.4	-
Mrs R. Burgess	Lab	219	26.1			
Total votes		839				
1931						
R.A. Hall*	Cit	Unopp.	-	1,644	-	-
1932						
G.T. Plum*	Cit	Unopp.	-	1,555	-	-
1933						
R.F. Lyne*	Cit	Unopp.	-	1,507	-	-
1934						
R.A. Hall*	Cit	Unopp.	-	1,494	-	-
1935						
G.T. Plum*	Cit	Unopp.	-	1,417	-	-

Overall Labour vote:				**Overall turnout:**		
1919–35		**22.8%**		**1919–35**		**50.5%**

Central West ward

Candidate	Party	Votes	%	Electors	Turnout	Gains
1919						
A. McArthur*	C	Unopp.	-	1,047	-	-
1920						
S. Cox*	C	Unopp.	-	867	-	-
1921						
T. Page-Wood*	Coa	432	81.5	889	59.6	-
N.L. Lawrence	Lab	98	18.5			
Total votes		530				
1922						
A. McArthur*	C	Unopp.	-	900	-	-
1923						
S. Cox*	C	Unopp.	-	880	-	-
1924						
T. Page-Wood*	Cit	Unopp.	-	899	-	-
1925						
F. Witty*	Cit	Unopp.	-	956	-	-
1926						
S. Cox*	Cit	Unopp.	-	914	-	-
1927						
T. Page-Wood*	Cit	425	81.1	917	57.1	-
F.E.C. Habgood	Lab	99	18.9			
Total votes		524				
1928						
Miss L. Meade-King*	Cit	366	84.1	907	48.0	-
Mrs E. Saunders	Lab	69	15.9			
Total votes		435				
1929						
S. Cox*	Cit	Unopp.	-	929	-	-

Central West ward *(continued)*

Candidate	Party	Votes	%	Electors	Turnout	Gains
1930						
S.C. Humphries	Cit	468	89.0	926	56.8	-
S.C. Pope	Lab	58	11.0			
Total votes		526				
1931						
Miss L. Meade-King*	Cit	Unopp.	-	894	-	-
1932						
S. Cox*	Cit	Unopp.	-	906	-	-
1933						
S.C. Humphries*	Cit	Unopp.	-	909	-	-
1934						
Miss L. Meade-King*	Cit	Unopp.	-	892	-	-
1935						
C.G. Hutchings*	Cit	Unopp.	-	857	-	-

Overall Labour vote: **Overall turnout:**
1919–35   **16.1%**   **1919–35**   **55.4%**

Clifton ward
(Created from merger of Clifton North ward and Clifton South ward in 1936 reorganisation)

Candidate	Party	Votes	%	Electors	Turnout	Gains
1936						
W.A. Pitt*	Cit	Unopp.	-	6,510	-	-
1937						
E.W. Andrews*	Cit	Unopp.	-	6,401	-	-
1938						
Sir L.A.G. Taylor*	Cit	2,557	80.9	6,292	50.3	-
G.A.W. Allan	Lab	605	19.1			
Total votes		3,162				

Overall Labour vote: **Overall turnout:**
1936–38   **19.1%**   **1936–38**   **50.3%**

Clifton North ward
(Merged with Clifton South ward to form Clifton ward in 1936 reorganisation)

Candidate	Party	Votes	%	Electors	Turnout	Gains
1919						
M. Whitwill*	C	Unopp.		3,015	-	-
1920						
C.T. Budgett*	C	Unopp.		3,095	-	-
1921						
J.H. Inskip*	Coa	Unopp.		3,137	-	-
1922						
C.H. Hodder*	C	Unopp.		3,187	-	-
1923						
C.T. Budgett*	C	Unopp.		3,305	-	-
1924						
J.H. Inskip*	Cit	Unopp.		3,381		-
1925						
C.H. Hodder*	Cit	1,966	90.0	3,454	63.3	-
E.V. Reece	Lab	219	10.0			
Total votes		2,185				
1926						
C.T. Budgett*	Cit	1,563	85.6	3,464	52.7	-
Mrs H.M. Jahans	Lab	262	14.4			
Total votes		1,825				
1927						
J.H. Inskip*	Cit	1,816	87.9	3,568	57.9	-
Mrs Crofts	Lab	250	12.1			
Total votes		2,066				
1928						
C.H. Hodder*	Cit	1,696	85.1	3,564	55.9	-
A.W. Packer	Lab	297	14.9			
Total votes		1,993				

Clifton North ward *(continued)*

Candidate	Party	Votes	%	Electors	Turnout	Gains
1929						
H.S. Evans	Cit	1,426	87.7	3,865	42.1	-
Mrs M. Liddington	Lab	200	12.3			
Total votes		1,626				
1930						
J.H. Inskip*	Cit	1,616	92.5	3,749	46.6	-
W.J. Waring	Lab	131	7.5			
Total votes		1,747				
1931						
C.H. Hodder*	Cit	Unopp.	-	3,828	-	-
1932						
H.S. Evans*	Cit	Unopp.	-	3,781	-	-
1933						
W.T. Wright*	Cit	Unopp.	-	3,806	-	-
1934						
C.H. Hodder*	Cit	Unopp.	-	3,813	-	-
1935						
H.S. Evans*	Cit	Unopp.	-	3,859	-	-

Overall Labour vote:
1919–35   **11.9%**

Overall turnout:
1919–35   **52.8%**

Clifton South ward
(Merged with Clifton North ward to form Clifton ward in 1936 reorganisation)

Candidate	Party	Votes	%	Electors	Turnout	Gains
1919						
F.G. Mullis*	C	Unopp.	-	3,360	-	-
1920						
S.A. Shirley*	C	Unopp.	-	3,098	-	-
1921						
Miss E.H. Smith*	Coa	Unopp.	-	3,693	-	-
1922						
F.G. Mullis*	C	Unopp.	-	3,828	-	-
1923						
S.A. Shirley*	C	Unopp.	-	3,932	-	-
1924						
Miss E.H.Smith*	Cit	Unopp.	-	3,381	-	-
1925						
F.G. Mullis*	Cit	2,087	86.7	4,126	58.3	-
R.F. Reade	Lab	319	13.3			
Total votes		2,406				
1926						
R.Smith	Cit	1,467	81.7	4,202	42.7	-
R.F. Reade	Lab	329	18.3			
Total votes		1,796				
1927						
Miss E.H. Smith*	Cit	1,585	85.2	4,251	43.8	-
R.F. Reade	Lab	275	14.8			
Total votes		1,860				
1928						
F.G. Mullis*	Cit	1,688	86.1	4,279	45.8	-
A.E. Harris	Lab	272	13.9			
Total votes		1,960				

Clifton South ward (*continued*)

Candidate	Party	Votes	%	Electors	Turnout	Gains
1929						
Sir L.A.G. Taylor	Cit	1,563	87.7	4,808	37.1	-
Mrs H.M. Jahans	Lab	220	12.3			
Total votes		1,783				
1930						
Miss E.H. Smith*	Cit	1,314	87.9	4,611	32.4	-
Mrs D. Barker	Lab	181	12.1			
Total votes		1,495				
1931						
E.W. Andrews*	Cit	Unopp.	-	4,584	-	-
1932						
Sir L.A.G. Taylor*	Cit	Unopp.	-	4,571	-	-
1933						
Miss E.H. Smith*	Cit	Unopp.	-	4,515	-	-
1934						
E.W. Andrews*	Cit	Unopp.	-	4,491	-	-
1935						
Sir L.A.G. Taylor*	Cit	Unopp.	-	4,612	-	-

Overall Labour vote: **Overall turnout:**

1919–35   **14.1%**   **1919–35**   **43.0%**

District ward

Candidate	Party	Votes	%	Electors	Turnout	Gains
1919						
Sir F.W. Wills*	L	1,401	80.8	7,723	22.4	-
B.J. Hughes	R	332	19.2			
Total votes		1,733				
1920						
P. Steadman	L	2,874	79.2	7,828	46.4	-
C.A. Bamber	Lab	756	20.8			
Total votes		3,630				
1921						
W.H. Byrt	Coa	2,814	77.4	7,921	45.9	-
C.A. Bamber	Lab	821	22.6			
Total votes		3,635				
1922						
H. Haskins	L	Unopp.	-	8,017	-	-
1923						
J. Priscott	L	2,731	71.5	8,112	47.1	-
T. Jefferis	Lab	1,086	28.5			
Total votes		3,817				
1924						
W.H. Byrt*	Cit	2,840	78.3	8,113	44.7	-
T. Jefferis	Lab	788	21.7			
Total votes		3,628				
1925						
H. Haskins*	Cit	3,345	74.5	8,179	54.9	-
T. Jefferis	Lab	1,143	25.5			
Total votes		4,488				
1926						
J. Priscott*	Cit	2,630	70.6	8,032	46.4	-
T. Jefferis	Lab	1,093	29.4			
Total votes		3,723				

District ward *(continued)*

Candidate	Party	Votes	%	Electors	Turnout	Gains
1927						
W.H. Byrt*	Cit	2,977	72.5	8,014	51.2	-
T. Jefferis	Lab	1,127	27.5			
Total votes		4,104				
1928						
A.F. Moon	Cit	2,991	71.6	8,003	52.2	-
T. Jefferis	Lab	1,184	28.4			
Total votes		4,175				
1929						
J. Priscott*	Cit	2,352	63.9	8,731	42.2	-
T. Jefferis	Lab	1,330	36.1			
Total votes		3,682				
1930						
W.H. Byrt*	Cit	2,836	73.8	8,539	45.0	-
A.E. Harris	Lab	1,007	26.2			
Total votes		3,843				
1931						
A.F. Moon*	Cit	Unopp.	-	8,676	-	-
1932						
P.W. Cann	Cit	2,798	70.7	8,500	46.5	-
E. Dunster	Lab	1,157	29.3			
Total votes		3,955				
1933						
W.H. Byrt*	Cit	Unopp.	-	8,499	-	-
1934						
A.F. Moon*	Cit	2,643	64.3	8,496	48.4	-
C.H. Smith	Lab	1,465	35.7			
Total votes		4,108				
1935						
P.W. Cann*	Cit	Unopp.	-	8,552	-	-

District ward *(continued)*

Candidate	Party	Votes	%	Electors	Turnout	Gains
1936						
W.F. Cottrell*	Cit	Unopp.	-	9,171	-	-
1937						
A.F. Moon*	Cit	Unopp.	-	9,114	-	-
1938						
P.W. Cann*	Cit	Unopp.	-	9,127	-	-

Overall Labour vote:		**Overall turnout:**	
1919–35	**26.7%**	**1919–35**	**45.7%**
1936–38	**-**	**1936–38**	**-**

Durdham ward

(Created from south-west portion of Westbury on Trym ward in 1936 reorganisation)

Candidate	Party	Votes	%	Electors	Turnout	Gains
1936						
W.T. Wright*	Cit	Unopp.	-	6,387	-	-
1937						
C.H. Hodder*	Cit	Unopp.	-	6,592	-	-
1938						
H.S. Evans*	Cit	Unopp.	-	6,728	-	-

Overall Labour vote: **Overall turnout:**

1936–38   -   **1936–38**   -

Easton ward

Candidate	Party	Votes	%	Electors	Turnout	Gains
1919						
W.H. Ayles*	Lab	1,726	48.6	9,615	36.9	-
H.E.C. Cole	L	1,326	37.3			
J. Linton	Ex-S	499	14.1			
Total votes		3,551				
1920						
F.F. Clothier*	Lab	2,155	52.5	9,828	41.8	-
H.E. Connell	L	1,952	47.5			
Total votes		4,107				
1921						
H. Walker	Coa	2,642	52.0	10,086	50.3	Coa from Lab
Miss M.C. Tothill*	Lab	2,434	48.0			
Total votes		5,076				
1922						
R. Smith	C	2,943	53.0	10,134	54.8	C from Lab
W.H. Ayles*	Lab	2,609	47.0			
Total votes		5,552				
1923						
F.F. Clothier*	Lab	2,932	56.1	10,253	50.9	-
Mrs M. Walker	C	2,291	43.9			
Total votes		5,223				
1924						
H. Walker*	Cit	2,885	51.3	10,242	54.9	-
E. Dunster	Lab	2,738	48.7			
Total votes		5,623				
1925						
E. Dunster	Lab	3,059	53.8	10,288	55.2	Lab from C
R. Smith*	Cit	2,622	46.2			
Total votes		5,681				
1926						
F.F. Clothier*	Lab	3,003	63.2	10,274	46.3	-
A.G. Durbin	Cit	1,750	36.8			
Total votes		4,753				

Easton ward *(continued)*

Candidate	Party	Votes	%	Electors	Turnout	Gains
1927						
A.W. Cox	Lab	3,200	57.1	10,215	54.8	Lab from Cit
A.G. Durbin	Cit	2,400	42.9			
Total votes		5,600				
1928						
E. Dunster*	Lab	3,405	61.1	10,136	55.0	-
B.I. Johnston	Cit	2,166	38.9			
Total votes		5,571				
1929						
F.F. Clothier*	Lab	3,025	68.1	10,936	40.6	-
H. Rankin	Cit	1,415	31.9			
Total votes		4,440				
1930						
A.W. Cox*	Lab	2,718	60.0	10,690	42.4	-
R.C. Tuckett	Cit	1,812	40.0			
Total votes		4,530				
1931						
R.C. Tuckett	Cit	3,038	52.7	10,737	53.7	Cit from Lab
E. Dunster*	Lab	2,730	47.3			
Total votes		5,768				
1932						
T. Jefferis*	Lab	3,329	63.0	10,615	49.8	-
G.M. Scofield	Cit	1,953	37.0			
Total votes		5,282				
1933						
A.W. Cox*	Lab	3,370	67.0	10,595	47.5	-
H.J. Leaman	Cit	1,663	33.0			
Total votes		5,033				
1934						
E. Dunster	Lab	3,195	64.1	10,570	47.2	Lab from Cit
F.J. Burgess	Cit	1,791	35.9			
Total votes		4,986				

Easton ward *(continued)*

Candidate	Party	Votes	%	Electors	Turnout	Gains
1935						
T. Jefferis*	Lab	3,156	61.9	10,467	48.7	-
F.J. Burgess	Cit	1,943	38.1			
Total votes		5,099				
1936						
A.W. Cox*	Lab	3,103	68.9	9,777	46.0	-
G.E.I. Clements	Cit	1,398	31.1			
Total votes		4,501				
1937						
C.H. Smith	Lab	2,846	68.0	9,663	43.3	-
G.E.I. Clements	Cit	1,342	32.0			
Total votes		4,188				
1938						
T. Jefferis*	Lab	Unopp.	-	9,406	-	-

Overall Labour vote: **Overall turnout:**

1919–35	**56.8%**	**1919–35**	**48.9%**
1936–38	**68.5%**	**1936–38**	**44.7%**

Eastville ward
(created in 1936 reorganisation)

Candidate	Party	Votes	%	Electors	Turnout	Gains
1936						
H.F. Rowat	Lab	1,899	17.3	7,387	52.1	-
F.J. Burgess	Cit	1,892	17.2			
Mrs A.A. Nunn	Lab	1,848	16.8			
C.H. Smith	Lab	1,814	16.5			
W.H. Wootten	Cit	1,795	16.3			
F.N. Andrews	Cit	1,757	16.0			
Total votes		11,005				
Total voters		3,850				
(3 elected)						
1937						
Mrs A.A. Nunn*	Lab	2,015	51.3	7,526	52.2	-
R.A. Hall	Cit	1,914	48.7			
Total votes		3,929				
1938						
F.J. Burgess*	Cit	2,309	53.8	7,665	56.0	-
W. Cozens	Lab	1,986	46.2			
Total votes		4,295				

Overall Labour vote: **Overall turnout:**

1936–38   **49.3%**   **1936–38**   **53.5%**

Hengrove ward

(created from southern portion of Somerset ward in 1936 reorganisation)

Candidate	Party	Votes	%	Electors	Turnout	Gains
1936						
Mrs A.E. Nutt	Lab	2,027	19.8	6,979	50.3	-
G.T. Bullock	Lab	1,923	18.8			
P.W. Raymond	Lab	1,910	18.6			
F.G.W. Chamberlain	Cit	1,246	12.2			
W.J. Martin	Cit	1,206	11.8			
W.H. Orrom	Cit	1,169	11.4			
P.W. Hopkins	L	317	3.1			
A.L. Parry	L	232	2.3			
Mrs M.B. Elworthy	L	220	2.1			
Total votes		10,250				
Total voters		3,508				
(3 elected)						
1937						
P.W. Raymond*	Lab	2,242	64.9	7,708	44.8	-
J.T. Corthine	Cit	1,212	35.1			
Total votes		3,454				
1938						
G.T. Bullock*	Lab	1,910	56.4	8,862	38.2	-
W.J. Martin	Cit	1,476	43.6			
Total votes		3,386				

Overall Labour vote: **Overall turnout:**

1936–38   **59.5%**   **1936–38**   **43.9%**

Hillfields ward
(created in 1936 reorganisation)

Candidate	Party	Votes	%	Electors	Turnout	Gains
1936						
G.A.W. Allan	Lab	2,298	29.6	7,616	43.4	-
J. Cole	Lab	2,256	29.1			
Mrs K.A. Gleeson	Lab	2,154	27.8			
Mrs D.P. Dobson	Cit	1,049	13.5			
Total votes		7,757				
Total voters		3,304				
(3 elected)						
1937						
Mrs K.A. Gleeson*	Lab	Unopp.	-	8,096	-	-
1938						
J. Cole*	Lab	Unopp.	-	8,568	-	-

Overall Labour vote:　　　　　　　　**Overall turnout:**
1936–38　　　　　**86.5%**　　**1936–38**　　　　　　　**43.4%**

Horfield ward

Candidate	Party	Votes	%	Electors	Turnout	Gains
1919						
Dr C. Wintle*	L	Unopp.	-	8,450	-	-
1920						
W.H. Eyles*	L	2,796	67.0	8,561	48.8	-
H.J. Wilcox	Lab	1,378	33.0			
Total votes		4,174				
1921						
W.H. Curtis*	Coa	Unopp.	-	8,636	-	-
1922						
W. Bryant*	L	2,993	76.8	8,736	44.6	-
E. Brodie	Lab	903	23.2			
Total votes		3,896				
1923						
W.H. Eyles*	L	2,592	73.0	8,861	40.1	-
S.C. Pope	Lab	960	27.0			
Total votes		3,552				
1924						
W.H. Curtis*	Cit	2,671	73.5	8,977	40.5	-
S.C. Pope	Lab	964	26.5			
Total votes		3,635				
1925						
W. Bryant*	Cit	3,607	77.3	9,171	50.9	-
Miss R. Part	Lab	1,060	22.7			
Total votes		4,667				
1926						
W.H. Eyles*	Cit	2,601	63.9	9,935	41.0	-
A.E. Clarke	Lab	1,470	36.1			
Total votes		4,071				
1927						
W.H. Curtis*	Cit	3,041	64.6	10,803	43.6	-
E. Hill	Lab	1,665	35.4			
Total votes		4,706				

Horfield ward (*continued*)

Candidate	Party	Votes	%	Electors	Turnout	Gains
1928						
W. Bryant*	Cit	3,621	67.0	11,233	48.1	-
R.F. Reade	Lab	1,785	33.0			
Total votes		5,406				
1929						
W.H. Eyles*	Cit	2,713	63.7	12,421	34.3	-
R.F. Reade	Lab	1,543	36.3			
Total votes		4,256				
1930						
D. Lewtas*	Cit	3,579	56.8	13,555	46.5	-
Dr M.E.J. Packer	Lab	2,725	43.2			
Total votes		6,304				
1931						
W. Bryant*	Cit	5,374	73.5	14,355	51.0	-
Dr M.E.J. Packer	Lab	1,940	26.5			
Total votes		7,314				
1932						
R.C. Davies*	Cit	4,181	65.4	14,669	43.6	-
E.J. Plaisted	Lab	2,211	34.6			
Total votes		6,392				
1933						
D. Lewtas*	Cit	3,634	58.4	15,037	41.4	-
E.S. Bush	Lab	2,590	41.6			
Total votes		6,224				
1934						
W. Bryant*	Cit	4,299	60.3	15,389	46.3	-
L.J. Poole	Lab	2,826	39.7			
Total votes		7,125				
1935						
R.C. Davies*	Cit	4,540	62.1	15,826	46.2	-
L.J. Poole	Lab	2,769	37.9			
Total votes		7,309				

Horfield ward *(continued)*

Candidate	Party	Votes	%	Electors	Turnout	Gains
1936						
L.J. Poole	Lab	2,098	18.7	8,232	46.7	-
R.F. Reade	Lab	2,013	18.0			
J.H. Knight	Lab	1,986	17.7			
J. Powell	Cit	1,751	15.6			
F.W. Tyler	Cit	1,688	15.1			
C.A. Young	Cit	1,674	14.9			
Total votes		11,210				
Total voters		3,841				
(3 elected)						
1937						
J.H. Knight*	Lab	2,365	54.0	8,826	49.6	-
W. Gay	Cit	2,015	46.0			
Total votes		4,380				
1938						
K.A.L. Brown	Cit	2,608	50.7	9,339	55.1	Cit from Lab
R.F. Reade*	Lab	2,536	49.3			
Total votes		5,144				

Overall Labour vote: **Overall turnout:**

1919–35	**33.9%**	**1919–35**	**44.5%**
1936–38	**52.3%**	**1936–38**	**50.6%**

Knowle ward
(created from northern portion of Somerset ward in 1936 reorganisation)

Candidate	Party	Votes	%	Electors	Turnout	Gains
1936						
Miss A.M. Hall-Houghton	Cit	2,664	61.2	9,115	47.7	-
C. Merchant	Lab	1,688	38.8			
Total votes		4,352				
1937						
H.R. Lee	Cit	2,889	62.3	9,346	49.6	-
Ms M.L. Deverell	Lab	1,745	37.7			
Total votes		4,634				
1938						
T.T. Wills*	Cit	3,516	67.6	9,541	54.5	-
W. Nicholas	Lab	1,684	32.4			
Total votes		5,200				

Overall Labour vote: **1936–38** 36.1%   **Overall turnout:** **1936–38** 50.7%

Redcliff ward

Candidate	Party	Votes	%	Electors	Turnout	Gains
1919						
E.I. Neale*	C	609	51.1	3,023	39.4	-
J.H.H. Jones	Lab	582	48.9			
Total votes		1,191				
1920						
E.B. Richards*	C	858	56.8	3,011	50.1	-
J.H.H. Jones	Lab	652	43.2			
Total votes		1,510				
1921						
J.T. Francombe*	Coa	Unopp.	-	3,102	-	-
1922						
E.I. Neale*	C	1,010	58.8	3,193	53.8	-
E.G. Harding	Lab	708	41.2			
Total votes		1,718				
1923						
E.B. Richards*	C	1,035	51.4	3,282	61.3	-
A.V. Despres	Lab	978	48.6			
Total votes		2,013				
1924						
J.J. Clibbens	Cit	1,252	62.6	3,353	59.7	-
A.V. Despres	Lab	749	37.4			
Total votes		2,001				
1925						
E.I. Neale*	Cit	1,098	58.9	3,344	55.8	-
F.A. Parish	Lab	767	41.1			
Total votes		1,865				
1926						
E.B. Richards*	Cit	920	51.5	3,333	53.6	-
F.A. Parish	Lab	867	48.5			
Total votes		1,787				

Redcliff ward *(continued)*

Candidate	Party	Votes	%	Electors	Turnout	Gains
1927						
J.J. Clibbens*	Cit	1,107	54.1	3,276	62.4	-
F.A. Parish	Lab	938	45.9			
Total votes		2,045				
1928						
F.A. Parish	Lab	1,055	50.7	3,203	64.9	Lab from Cit
H.S. Evans	Cit	1,025	49.3			
Total votes		2,080				
1929						
E.G. Harding	Lab	982	52.9	3,488	53.3	Lab from Cit
E.B. Richards*	Cit	876	47.1			
Total votes		1,858				
1930						
G.S. James	Cit	1,289	57.1	3,315	68.1	-
H. Whitchurch	Lab	970	42.9			
Total votes		2,259				
1931						
A.H. Downes-Shaw	Cit	1,350	59.9	3,311	68.0	Cit from Lab
F.A. Parish*	Lab	902	40.1			
Total votes		2,252				
1932						
V.J. Robinson	Cit	1,065	54.9	3,315	58.5	Cit from Lab
E.G. Harding*	Lab	874	45.1			
Total votes		1,939				
1933						
G.S. James*	Cit	1,000	55.5	3,004	60.0	-
E.J. Plaisted	Lab	801	44.5			
Total votes		1,801				
1934						
A.H. Downes-Shaw*	Cit	986	52.8	2,945	63.4	-
E.G. Harding	Lab	882	47.2			
Total votes		1,868				

Redcliff ward *(continued)*

Candidate	Party	Votes	%	Electors	Turnout	Gains
1935						
V.J. Robinson*	Cit	1,020	55.4	2,907	63.3	-
J. Knight	Lab	821	44.6			
Total votes		1,841				
1936						
G.S. James*	Cit	1,703	63.8	4,724	56.5	-
J.T. Norman	Lab	967	36.2			
Total votes		2,670				
1937						
A.H. Downes-Shaw*	Cit	1,574	62.2	4,517	56.1	-
C.E. Slater	Lab	958	37.8			
Total votes		2,532				
1938						
V.J. Robinson*	Cit	1,690	70.0	4,270	56.6	-
A.V. Desprez	Lab	725	30.0			
Total votes		2,415				

Overall Labour vote: **Overall turnout:**

1919–35	**45.1%**	**1919–35**	**58.5%**
1936–38	**34.8%**	**1936–38**	**56.4%**

Redland ward

Candidate	Party	Votes	%	Electors	Turnout	Gains
1919						
A.J. Veale*	C	Unopp.	-	5,655	-	-
1920						
A.C. Castle*	C	Unopp.	-	5,596	-	-
1921						
J.S.G.W. Stroud*	Coa	Unopp.	-	5,614	-	-
1922						
A.J. Veale*	C	Unopp.	-	5,612	-	-
1923						
A.C. Castle*	C	Unopp.	-	5,797	-	-
1924						
A.H. Insall	Cit	Unopp.	-	5,953	-	-
1925						
A.J. Veale*	Cit	3,377	91.4	6,245	59.1	-
A.N. Ansaldo	Lab	316	8.6			
Total votes		3,693				
1926						
A.C. Castle*	Cit	2,653	88.3	6,418	46.8	-
A.H.M. Dore	Lab	350	11.7			
Total votes		3,003				
1927						
F.M. Hall	Cit	3,079	88.4	6,495	53.6	-
A.H.M. Dore	Lab	403	11.6			
Total votes		3,482				
1928						
A.J. Veale*	Cit	2,811	86.6	6,600	49.2	-
A.H.M. Dore	Lab	435	13.4			
Total votes		3,246				

Redland ward *(continued)*

Candidate	Party	Votes	%	Electors	Turnout	Gains
1929						
A.E. Wells	Cit	2,288	85.4	7,218	37.1	-
A.H.M. Dore	Lab	392	14.6			
Total votes		2,680				
1930						
F.M. Hall*	Cit	2,895	90.4	7,270	44.1	-
Miss E. Merrie	Lab	308	9.6			
Total votes		3,203				
1931						
G.I. Righton*	Cit	Unopp.	-	7,441	-	-
1932						
A.E. Wells*	Cit	Unopp.	-	7,547	-	-
1933						
F. Marshall Hall*	Cit	Unopp.	-	7,578	-	-
1934						
G.I. Righton*	Cit	Unopp.	-	7,756	-	-
1935						
A.E. Wells*	Cit	Unopp.	-	7,722	-	-
1936						
F. Marshall Hall*	Cit	Unopp.	-	6,544	-	-
1937						
G.I. Righton*	Cit	Unopp.	-	6,641	-	-
1938						
Miss G.M. Williams*	Cit	Unopp.	-	6,649	-	-

Overall Labour vote:			**Overall turnout:**	
1919–35	**11.4%**		**1919–35**	**48.0%**
1936–38	-		**1936–38**	-

St Augustine's ward

Candidate	Party	Votes	%	Electors	Turnout	Gains
1919						
T.C. Pearce	Lab	1,008	49.3	6,630	30.8	Lab from C
S.A. Shirley*	C	822	40.2			
E. Silk	Ex-S	214	10.5			
Total votes		2,044				
1920						
E.W. Savory*	C	1,543	58.0	6,550	40.6	-
E. Pike	Lab	1,117	42.0			
Total votes		2,660				
1921						
H. Livermore	Coa	2,092	69.3	6,791	44.4	-
S.C. Pope	Lab	926	30.7			
Total votes		3,018				
1922						
R. Houghton	C	1,834	62.1	6,845	43.1	C from Lab
T.C. Pearce*	Lab	1,118	37.9			
Total votes		2,952				
1923						
E.W. Savory*	C	Unopp.	-	7,052	-	-
1924						
H. Livermore*	Cit	Unopp.	-	7,126	-	-
1925						
R. Houghton*	Cit	1,901	54.0	7,223	48.7	-
A.V. Despres	Lab	1,619	46.0			
Total votes		3,520				
1926						
J. Manners	Lab	1,769	52.6	7,114	47.2	Lab from C
A.E. Maggs	Cit	1,591	47.4			
Total votes		3,360				

St Augustine's ward (continued)

Candidate	Party	Votes	%	Electors	Turnout	Gains
1927						
H. Livermore*	Cit	2,020	51.5	6,998	56.0	-
R. Neft	Lab	1,901	48.5			
Total votes		3,921				
1928						
A.V. Despres	Lab	2,019	53.1	6,932	54.8	Lab from Cit
R. Houghton*	Cit	1,782	46.9			
Total votes		3,801				
1929						
J. Manners*	Lab	1,943	54.0	7,645	47.0	-
J.W.M. Cates	Cit	1,652	46.0			
Total votes		3,595				
1930						
F.E.C. Habgood*	Lab	2,117	51.7	7,393	55.3	-
J.W.M. Cates	Cit	1,975	48.3			
Total votes		4,092				
1931						
M. McGougan	Cit	2,667	63.1	7,360	57.5	Cit from Lab
A.V. Despres*	Lab	1,562	36.9			
Total votes		4,229				
1932						
J. Manners*	Lab	1,891	50.8	6,924	53.7	-
M. Whitwill	Cit	1,830	49.2			
Total votes		3,721				
1933						
W.H. Nott	Lab	1,874	50.8	6,710	54.9	-
W.H. Orrom	Cit	1,813	49.2			
Total votes		3,687				
1934						
F. Stamp	Lab	2,000	52.1	6,571	58.5	Lab from Cit
W.H. Orrom	Cit	1,841	47.9			
Total votes		3,841				

St Augustine's ward *(continued)*

Candidate	Party	Votes	%	Electors	Turnout	Gains
1935						
J. Manners*	Lab	1,859	53.3	6,298	55.4	-
G.D. Naish	Cit	1,630	46.7			
Total votes		3,489				
1936						
R.F. Lyne*	Cit	1,792	50.1	6,074	58.9	-
Mrs F.M. Brown	Lab	1,787	49.9			
Total votes		3,579				
1937						
R.R. Cunningham	Lab	1,939	53.4	5,927	61.2	-
C. McCormack	Cit	1,691	46.6			
Total votes		3,630				
1938						
G. Talbot Plum	Cit	1,852	53.1	5,581	62.4	Cit from Lab
J. Manners*	Lab	1,633	46.9			
Total votes		3,485				

Overall Labour vote: **Overall turnout:**

1919–35	**47.6%**	**1919–35**		**49.9%**
1936–38	**50.1%**	**1936–38**		**60.8%**

St George's East ward

Candidate	Party	Votes	%	Electors	Turnout	Gains
1919						
H. Milton	Lab	2,120	56.2	10,051	37.5	-
F. Leonard	C	699	18.5			
B. Freke	L	650	17.2			
J.B. Gibbs	Ex-S	304	8.1			
Total votes		3,773				
1920						
G.B. Britton M.P.*	L	2,777	52.0	10,106	52.8	-
G. Shallard	Lab	2,563	48.0			
Total votes		5,340				
1921						
G. Shallard	Lab	2,799	52.3	10,436	51.3	Lab from Coa
H.J. Maggs*	Coa	2,554	47.7			
Total votes		5,353				
1922						
W.H. Merrick	Lab	2,821	57.5	10,522	46.7	-
R. Cornish	L	2,089	42.5			
Total votes		4,910				
1923						
H.J Maggs*	L	2,833	52.1	10,704	50.8	-
J. Manners	Lab	2,600	47.9			
Total votes		5,433				
1924						
G. Shallard*	Lab	3,389	63.2	10,751	49.9	-
D. Lewtas	Cit	1,975	36.8			
Total votes		5,364				
1925						
W.H. Merrick*	Lab	3,016	65.7	10,964	41.9	-
A. Parker	Cit	1,573	34.3			
Total votes		4,589				

St George's East ward (*continued*)

Candidate	Party	Votes	%	Electors	Turnout	Gains
1926						
A.W.S. Burgess	Lab	3,662	58.5	11,315	55.4	Lab from C
H.J. Maggs*	Cit	2,603	41.5			
Total votes		6,265				
1927						
G. Shallard*	Lab	3,285	73.0	11,602	38.8	-
Mrs Gunning	Cit	1,217	27.0			
Total votes		4,502				
1928						
W.H. Merrick*	Lab	3,285	71.0	11,818	39.2	-
J.Y. Ivens	Cit	1,345	29.0			
Total votes		4,630				
1929						
A.W.S. Burgess*	Lab	2,928	80.6	12,883	28.2	-
J.J. Dunn	Cit	706	19.4			
Total votes		3,634				
1930						
G. Shallard*	Lab	2,657	65.6	13,032	31.1	-
J.W. Watson	Cit	1,396	34.4			
Total votes		4,053				
1931						
W.H. Merrick*	Lab	3,820	57.6	13,250	50.1	-
E. Bowden	Cit	2,813	42.4			
Total votes		6,633				
1932						
H.E. Rogers*	Lab	Unopp.	-	13,470	-	-
1933						
G. Shallard*	Lab	4,150	70.3	13,647	43.3	-
W.T.P. Hassell	Cit	1,756	29.7			
Total votes		5,906				
1934						
W.H. Merrick*	Lab	Unopp.	-	13,915	-	-

St George's East ward *(continued)*

Candidate	Party	Votes	%	Electors	Turnout	Gains
1935						
H.E. Rogers*	Lab	Unopp.	-	14,402	-	-
1936						
G. Shallard*	Lab	Unopp.	-	9,093	-	-
1937						
W.A. Wilkins*	Lab	Unopp.	-	9,416	-	-
1938						
H.E. Rogers*	Lab	Unopp.	-	9,573	-	-

Overall Labour vote: **Overall turnout:**
1919–35   61.2%   **1919–35**   43.7%
1936–38   -   **1936–38**   -

St George's West ward

Candidate	Party	Votes	%	Electors	Turnout	Gains
1919						
W.A. Winchester	Lab	2,639	77.9	9,095	37.2	Lab from L
W.H. Byrt	L	747	22.1			
Total votes		3,386				
1920						
J.J. Milton*	Lab	2,631	60.0	9,137	48.0	-
H. Walker	Coa	1,751	40.0			
Total votes .		4,382				
1921						
W.H. Hennessy	Lab	2,512	58.4	9,358	45.9	Lab from Coa
W.G. Pope*	Coa	1,787	41.6			
Total votes		4,299				
1922						
W.A. Winchester*	Lab	2,746	63.6	9,360	46.1	-
D. Nicholls	L	1,570	36.4			
Total votes		4,316				
1923						
J.J. Milton*	Lab	2,995	66.5	9,466	47.6	-
D. Nicholls	L	1,512	33.5			
Total votes		4,507				
1924						
W.H. Hennessy*	Lab	3,396	69.2	9,512	51.6	-
W.G. Thatcher	Cit	1,512	30.8			
Total votes		4,908				
1925						
W.A. Winchester*	Lab	3,283	78.5	9,515	44.0	-
E.G. Clarke	Cit	901	21.5			
Total votes		4,184				
1926						
J.J. Milton*	Lab	3,317	79.3	9,473	44.2	-
Miss J. Brisland	Cit	866	20.7			
Total votes		4,183				

St George's West ward (continued)

Candidate	Party	Votes	%	Electors	Turnout	Gains
1927						
W.H. Hennessy*	Lab	3,381	78.7	9,451	45.5	-
Mrs Warren	Cit	915	21.3			
Total votes		4,296				
1928						
W.A. Winchester*	Lab	3,274	79.4	9,357	44.1	-
J.J. Dunn	Cit	848	20.6			
Total votes		4,122				
1929						
J.J. Milton*	Lab	2,934	87.1	10,160	33.1	-
G.D. Hopkins	Cit	434	12.9			
Total votes		3,368				
1930						
G.G. Adams*	Lab	Unopp.	-	9,909	-	-
1931						
W.A. Winchester*	Lab	Unopp.	-	9,839	-	-
1932						
Mrs E. Webb	Lab	Unopp.	-	9,699	-	-
1933						
G.G. Adams*	Lab	Unopp.	-	9,554	-	-
1934						
W.H. Hennessy*	Lab	Unopp.	-	9,574	-	-
1935						
W.S. Scull	Lab	Unopp.	-	9,470	-	-
1936						
G.G. Adams*	Lab	Unopp.	-	8,693	-	-
1937						
Mrs M.A. Hennessy*	Lab	Unopp.	-	8,546	-	-

St George's West ward *(continued)*

Candidate	Party	Votes	%	Electors	Turnout	Gains
1938						
W.S. Scull*	Lab	Unopp.	-	8,443	-	-

Overall Labour vote: **Overall turnout:**

1919–35	**72.1%**	**1919–35**	**44.2%**
1936–38	**-**	**1936–38**	**-**

St James's ward

Candidate	Party	Votes	%	Electors	Turnout	Gains
1919						
P.E. Gane*	L	781	62.8	4,177	29.8	-
G.W. Calder	Ex-S	463	37.2			
Total votes		1,244				
1920						
H.J. Cridland*	C	Unopp.	-	4,037	-	-
1921						
J.E. Jones	Coa	1,412	66.8	4,278	49.4	-
Miss R. Part	Lab	701	33.2			
Total votes		2,113				
1922						
P.E. Gane*	L	Unopp.	-	4,400	-	-
1923						
H.J. Cridland*	C	Unopp.	-	4,674	-	-
1924						
J.E. Jones*	Cit	Unopp.	-	4,655	-	-
1925						
P.E. Gane*	Cit	1,498	62.4	4,782	50.2	-
E. Hill	Lab	903	37.6			
Total votes		2,401				
1926						
H.J. Cridland*	Cit	1,517	62.9	4,701	51.3	-
E. Hill	Lab	895	37.1			
Total votes		2,412				
1927						
J.E. Jones*	Cit	1,286	53.5	4,687	51.3	-
S. Phippen	Lab	825	34.3			
H.G. Holt	Ind	293	12.2			
Total votes		2,404				

St James's ward (*continued*)

Candidate	Party	Votes	%	Electors	Turnout	Gains
1928						
P.E. Gane*	Cit	1,256	59.7	4,584	45.9	-
S. Phippen	Lab	849	40.3			
Total votes		2,105				
1929						
H.J. Cridland*	Cit	1,282	61.3	4,929	42.5	-
S. Phippen	Lab	811	38.7			
Total votes		2,093				
1930						
J.E. Jones*	Cit	1,291	66.6	4,764	40.7	-
G.H. White	Lab	646	33.4			
Total votes		1,937				
1931						
G.A. Martin	Cit	1,775	73.0	4,830	50.4	-
H. Whitchurch	Lab	657	27.0			
Total votes		2,432				
1932						
C.G.T. Bennett	Cit	1,261	56.3	4,787	46.8	-
H. Whitchurch	Lab	979	43.7			
Total votes		2,240				
1933						
H.A. Wall*	Cit	1,282	62.2	4,703	43.8	-
C.H. Smith	Lab	779	37.8			
Total votes		2,061				
1934						
G.A. Martin*	Cit	1,160	61.5	4,562	41.3	-
R.C. Mansfield	Lab	725	38.5			
Total votes		1,885				
1935						
R.N. Harrison	Cit	Unopp.	-	4,373	-	-

St James's ward (*continued*)

Candidate	Party	Votes	%	Electors	Turnout	Gains
1936						
H.A. Wall*	Cit	1,403	67.9	5,033	41.0	-
A.V. Despres	Lab	663	32.1			
Total votes		2,066				
1937						
G.A. Martin*	Cit	1,281	65.5	4,927	39.7	-
A.V. Despres	Lab	676	34.5			
Total votes		1,957				
1938						
R.N. Harrison*	Cit	1,455	70.1	4,784	43.4	-
P.J.R. Nash	Lab	622	29.9			
Total votes		2,077				

Overall Labour vote: **Overall turnout:**

1919–35	**34.6%**	**1919–35**	**45.4%**
1936–38	**32.1%**	**1936–38**	**41.4%**

St Michael's ward

Candidate	Party	Votes	%	Electors	Turnout	Gains
1919						
A.E. Hill*	C	917	73.6	4,986	25.0	-
C.W. Ballard	Lab	329	26.4			
Total votes		1,246				
1920						
E.J. Dunscombe*	C	Unopp.	-	4,892	-	-
1921						
H.C. Woodcock*	Coa	Unopp.	-	4,992	-	-
1922						
A.E. Hill*	C	Unopp.	-	5,051	-	-
1923						
E.J. Dunscombe*	C	Unopp.	-	5,146	-	-
1924						
J.V. Parker*	Cit	Unopp.	-	5,201	-	-
1925						
A.E. Hill*	Cit	2,113	82.4	5,290	48.4	-
W.A. Carson	Lab	450	17.6			
Total votes		2,563				
1926						
F.C. Luke	Cit	1,694	76.7	5,327	41.5	-
W.J. Ellerby	Lab	515	23.3			
Total votes		2,209				
1927						
Dr E.J. Ball	Cit	2,179	80.9	5,350	50.3	-
W.J. Ellerby	Lab	513	19.1			
Total votes		2,692				
1928						
A.E. Hill*	Cit	1,801	78.9	5,370	42.5	-
G.H. White	Lab	483	21.1			
Total votes		2,284				

St Michael's ward (continued)

Candidate	Party	Votes	%	Electors	Turnout	Gains
1929						
F.C. Luke*	Cit	1,239	73.6	5,833	28.9	-
A.W. Packer	Lab	445	26.4			
Total votes		1,684				
1930						
Dr E.J. Ball*	Cit	1,941	83.3	5,714	40.8	-
Mrs J.E. Spencer	Lab	388	16.7			
Total votes		2,329				
1931						
F.A. Webber*	Cit	2,487	89.0	5,757	48.5	-
W.J. Waring	Lab	307	11.0			
Total votes		2,794				
1932						
F.C. Luke*	Cit	Unopp.	-	5,784	-	-
1933						
A.C.K. Toms*	Cit	Unopp.	-	5,734	-	-
1934						
F.A. Webber*	Cit	Unopp.	-	5,719	-	-
1935						
F.C. Luke*	Cit	Unopp.	-	5,730	-	-
1936						
A.C.K. Toms*	Cit	Unopp.	-	6,718	-	-
1937						
F.A. Webber*	Cit	Unopp.	-	6,666	-	-
1938						
F.C. Luke*	Cit	Unopp.	-	6,619	-	-

Overall Labour vote:		**Overall turnout:**	
1919–35	**19.3%**	**1919–35**	**40.8%**
1936–38	-	**1936–38**	-

St Paul's ward

Candidate	Party	Votes	%	Electors	Turnout	Gains
1919						
A.G.O. Strong	L	1,127	46.7	6,967	34.6	-
Miss M.C. Tothill	Lab	923	38.3			
G.R. Hood	Ex-S	362	15.0			
Total votes		2,412				
1920						
W.H. Ackland*	L	1,597	57.2	6,841	40.8	
E.H. Parker	Lab	1,193	42.8			
Total votes		2,790				
1921						
J.L. Brown*	L	1,399	51.2	7,048	38.8	-
E.H. Parker	Lab	1,333	48.8			
Total votes		2,732				
1922						
E.H. Parker	Lab	1,938	51.3	7,314	51.6	Lab from L
A.G.O. Strong*	L	1,816	48.1			
L. Ward	I Lab	21	0.6			
Total votes		3,775				
1923						
W.H. Ackland*	L	2,021	53.0	7,492	50.9	-
Miss M.C. Tothill	Lab	1,794	47.0			
Total votes		3,815				
1924						
J.L. Brown*	Cit	2,011	56.3	7,510	47.5	-
Miss M.C. Tothill	Lab	1,558	43.7			
Total votes		3,569				
1925						
E.H. Parker*	Lab	2,395	59.5	7,546	53.4	-
G. Boyd	Cit	1,633	40.5			
Total votes		4,028				

St Paul's ward (continued)

Candidate	Party	Votes	%	Electors	Turnout	Gains
1926						
J.F. Bicker	Lab	2,226	60.3	7,407	49.8	Lab from Cit
W.H. Ackland*	Cit	1,463	39.7			
Total votes		3,689				
1927						
J. Owen	Lab	2,093	56.5	7,297	50.8	Lab from Cit
J.L. Brown*	Cit	1,613	43.5			
Total votes		3,706				
1928						
E.H. Parker*	Lab	2,390	65.9	7,187	50.5	-
T.E.R. Tudor-Vaughan	Cit	1,237	34.1			
Total votes		3,627				
1929						
J.F. Bicker*	Lab	1,987	68.2	7,767	37.5	-
G.H. Young	Cit	928	31.8			
Total votes		2,915				
1930						
J. Owen*	Lab	1,706	58.3	7,460	39.2	-
G.H. Young	Cit	1,221	41.7			
Total votes		2,927				
1931						
E.H. Parker*	Lab	1,967	48.9	7,542	53.4	-
G.H. Young	Cit	1,902	47.2			
G. Hitchings	Ind	157	3.9			
Total votes		4,026				
1932						
J.F. Bicker*	Lab	2,212	59.8	7,339	50.4	-
G.H. Young	Cit	1,318	35.7			
Mrs C.E. Blakeman	Com	166	4.5			
Total votes		3,696				

St Paul's ward *(continued)*

Candidate	Party	Votes	%	Electors	Turnout	Gains
1933						
J. Owen*	Lab	2,238	62.5	7,309	49.0	-
F.N. Andrews	Cit	1,225	34.2			
H. Preston	Com	118	3.3			
Total votes		3,581				
1934						
E.H. Parker*	Lab	2,220	64.8	7,072	48.5	-
F.N. Andrews	Cit	1,121	32.7			
C.H. Webber	Com	86	2.5			
Total votes		3,427				
1935						
J.F. Bicker*	Lab	Unopp.	-	6,605	-	-
1936						
J. Owen*	Lab	1,938	63.0	6,854	44.9	-
B.Y. Bartlett	Cit	1,138	37.0			
Total votes		3,076				
1937						
R.C. Mansfield*	Lab	1,911	58.6	6,543	49.8	-
B.Y. Bartlett	Cit	1,348	41.4			
Total votes		3,259				
1938						
G.H. Johnson*	Lab	1,599	52.7	6,251	48.6	-
F.W. Brunton	Cit	1,436	47.3			
Total votes		3,035				

Overall Labour vote: **Overall turnout:**

1919–35	**55.1%**	**1919–35**		**46.7%**
1936–38	**58.1%**	**1936–38**		**47.7%**

St Philip's and St Jacob's North ward

Candidate	Party	Votes	%	Electors	Turnout	Gains
1919						
A.R. Terrell	Lab	1,366	57.8	7,988	29.6	Lab from L
C.J. Thorne*	L	998	42.2			
Total votes		2,364				
1920						
E.T. Cozens	Lab	1,903	56.0	8,164	41.6	Lab from C
F. Witty*	Coa	1,493	44.0			
Total votes		3,396				
1921						
Mrs L.M. Pheysey*	Lab	1,653	49.3	8,349	40.1	-
H. Rankin	L	1,622	48.4			
W.A. Morrell	Com	77	2.3			
Total votes		3,352				
1922						
H. Rankin	L	2,019	53.5	8,473	44.5	L from Lab
A.R. Terrell*	Lab	1,752	46.5			
Total votes		3,771				
1923						
E.T. Cozens*	Lab	2,472	58.3	8,547	49.6	-
C.J. Thorne	L	1,771	41.7			
Total votes		4,243				
1924						
Mrs L.M. Pheysey*	Lab	2,412	62.9	8,679	44.2	-
J. Grigg	Cit	1,422	37.1			
Total votes		3,834				
1925						
M. Giles	Lab	2,727	59.9	8,650	52.6	Lab from Cit
H. Rankin*	Cit	1,826	40.1			
Total votes		4,553				
1926						
E.T. Cozens*	Lab	2,726	73.1	8,591	43.4	-
E.J. Ball	Cit	1,002	26.9			
Total votes		3,728				

St Philip's and St Jacob's North ward *(continued)*

Candidate	Party	Votes	%	Electors	Turnout	Gains
1927						
Mrs L.M. Pheysey*	Lab	2,647	68.2	8,483	45.7	-
F.J.M. Cook	Cit	1,232	31.8			
Total votes		3,879				
1928						
M. Giles*	Lab	2,560	69.6	8,415	43.7	-
F.J.M. Cook	Cit	1,118	30.4			
Total votes		3,678				
1929						
E.T. Cozens*	Lab	2,365	82.5	9,159	31.3	-
S. Higgs	Cit	500	17.5			
Total votes		2,865				
1930						
Mrs L.M. Pheysey*	Lab	Unopp.	-	8,913	-	-
1931						
M. Giles*	Lab	2,157	52.7	8,988	45.5	-
H.J. Leaman	Cit	1,936	47.3			
Total votes		4,093				
1932						
E.T. Cozens*	Lab	2,898	75.2	8,759	44.0	-
H.J. Leaman	Cit	954	24.8			
Total votes		3,852				
1933						
V.J. Ross*	Lab	Unopp.	-	8,668	-	-
1934						
Mrs C.M. Keel	Lab	Unopp.	-	8,488	-	-
1935						
E.T. Cozens*	Lab	Unopp.	-	8,237	-	-
1936						
V.J. Ross*	Lab	Unopp.	-	8,592	-	-

St Philip's and St Jacob's North ward *(continued)*

Candidate	Party	Votes	%	Electors	Turnout	Gains
1937						
Mrs C.M. Keel*	Lab	2,478	65.4	8,269	45.8	-
O.W. Cowlishaw	Cit	1,309	34.6			
Total votes		3,787				
1938						
J. Donovan*	Lab	Unopp.	-	7,928	-	-

Overall Labour vote:			**Overall turnout:**	
1919–35	**62.3%**		**1919–35**	**42.8%**
1936–38	**65.4%**		**1936–38**	**45.8%**

St Philip's and St Jacob's South ward

Candidate	Party	Votes	%	Electors	Turnout	Gains
1919						
A. Harrison	Ex-S	1,490	53.3	7,566	36.9	Ex-S from L
E.N. Tribe*	L	1,305	46.7			
Total votes		2,795				
1920						
E.J. Hancock	Lab	1,487	56.5	7,464	35.2	Lab from L
A.F. Moon	L	1,143	43.5			
Total votes		2,630				
1921						
G. Thompson*	Lab	1,488	73.7	7,835	25.8	-
J. Wylde	Ind	532	26.3			
Total votes		2,020				
1922						
A.F. Moon	L	1,693	47.8	7,749	45.7	L from Lab
J.R. Hughes	Lab	1,460	41.2			
J. Wylde	Ind	388	11.0			
Total votes		3,541				
1923						
E.J. Hancock*	Lab	1,884	62.7	7,919	37.9	-
C.F. Russett	C	1,121	37.3			
Total votes		3,005				
1924						
W.H. Ayles*	Lab	2,522	58.2	7,960	54.5	-
Dr L. Page	Cit	1,814	41.8			
Total votes		4,336				
1925						
R.G. Cunningham	Lab	2,560	71.4	7,992	44.8	Lab from L
C.F. Russett	Cit	1,024	28.6			
Total votes		3,584				
1926						
G. Daniel*	Lab	2,262	69.1	7,835	41.8	-
A.J. Moss	Cit	1,012	30.9			
Total votes		3,274				

St Philip's and St Jacob's South ward (*continued*)

Candidate	Party	Votes	%	Electors	Turnout	Gains
1927						
H. Stallard	Lab	2,525	70.1	7,737	46.5	-
A.J. Moss	Cit	1,076	29.9			
Total votes		3,601				
1928						
R.G. Cunningham*	Lab	2,525	72.5	7,673	45.4	-
Miss J. Brisland	Cit	959	27.5			
Total votes		3,484				
1929						
G. Daniel*	Lab	2,362	83.3	8,179	34.7	-
Mrs V.E. Pullen	Cit	473	16.7			
Total votes		2,835				
1930						
H. Stallard*	Lab	Unopp.	-	7,968	-	-
1931						
R.G. Cunningham*	Lab	2,251	60.3	7,855	47.5	-
T.D. Corpe	Cit	1,482	39.7			
Total votes		3,733				
1932						
F.A. Parish	Lab	1,446	40.6	7,473	47.7	-
G. Daniel*	I Lab	1,183	33.2			
H.R. Eastwood	Cit	717	20.1			
W.N. Paxton	Com	219	6.1			
Total votes		3,565				
1933						
D.M. Jones	Lab	2,130	90.1	7,365	32.1	-
W.N. Paxton	Com	234	9.9			
Total votes		2,364				
1934						
R.G. Cunningham*	Lab	2,061	94.5	7,189	30.3	-
W.N. Paxton	Com	120	5.5			
Total votes		2,181				

St Philip's and St Jacob's South ward (*continued*)

Candidate	Party	Votes	%	Electors	Turnout	Gains
1935						
F.A. Parish*	Lab	Unopp.	-	6,833	-	-
1936						
D.M. Jones*	Lab	Unopp.	-	7,146	-	-
1937						
Mrs F.M. Brown*	Lab	Unopp.	-	6,997	-	-
1938						
F.A. Parish*	Lab	Unopp.	-	6,692	-	-

Overall Labour vote:		**Overall turnout:**	
1919–35	**61.7%**	**1919–35**	**37.9%**
1936–38	**-**	**1936–38**	**-**

Somerset ward

Candidate	Party	Votes	%	Electors	Turnout	Gains
1919						
C.T. Enwright*	L	1,576	53.1	9,135	32.5	-
Mrs E. Anthony	Lab	1,390	46.9			
Total votes		2,966				
1920						
A.P. Keen	L	2,596	61.7	9,283	45.4	-
Mrs E. Anthony	Lab	1,614	38.3			
Total votes		4,210				
1921						
C.R. Perrett*	Coa	2,529	58.1	9,502	45.8	-
J. Astle	Lab	1,821	41.9			
Total votes		4,350				
1922						
T.J. Wise*	L	Unopp.		9,571	-	-
1923						
A.P. Keen*	L	2,715	63.3	9,677	44.3	-
F. Wroe	Lab	1,572	36.7			
Total votes		4,287				
1924						
C.R. Perrett*	Cit	2,759	66.2	9,855	42.3	-
F. Wroe	Lab	1,411	33.8			
Total votes		4,170				
1925						
T.J. Wise*	Cit	3,414	65.0	10,397	50.5	-
F. Wroe	Lab	1,836	35.0			
Total votes		5,250				
1926						
A.P. Keen*	Cit	2,561	55.8	11,122	41.2	-
S.C. Pope	Lab	2,026	44.2			
Total votes		4,587				

Somerset ward *(continued)*

Candidate	Party	Votes	%	Electors	Turnout	Gains
1927						
C.R. Perrett*	Cit	3,044	59.6	11,731	43.5	-
S.C. Pope	Lab	2,062	40.4			
Total votes		5,106				
1928						
T.J. Wise*	Cit	3,450	56.6	12,353	49.3	-
S.C. Light	Lab	2,644	43.4			
Total votes		6,094				
1929						
S.C. Light	Lab	2,622	50.1	13,956	37.5	Lab from Cit
A.P. Keen*	Cit	2,610	49.9			
Total votes		5,232				
1930						
H.R. Lee*	Cit	3,957	57.3	14,448	47.8	-
F. Stamp	Lab	2,946	42.7			
Total votes		6,903				
1931						
T.J. Wise*	Cit	5,333	70.8	15,002	50.2	-
F. Stamp	Lab	2,204	29.2			
Total votes		7,537				
1932						
S.C. Pope	Lab	3,513	50.1	15,863	44.2	-
H. Fanson	Cit	3,495	49.9			
Total votes		7,008				
1933						
H.R. Lee*	Cit	4,520	50.9	18,562	47.9	-
J.H. Knight	Lab	4,368	49.1			
Total votes		8,888				
1934						
T.J. Wise*	Cit	6,170	55.6	19,187	57.8	-
J.H. Knight	Lab	4,921	44.4			
Total votes		11,091				

Somerset ward *(continued)*

Candidate	Party	Votes	%	Electors	Turnout	Gains
1935						
T.T. Wills	Cit	6,244	57.8	19,937	54.2	Cit from Lab
S.C. Pope*	Lab	4,563	42.2			
Total votes		10,807				
1936						
A.E. Baston	Lab	2,699	31.8	8,755	39.7	
E.F. Davey	Lab	2,518	29.6			
D. Price	Lab	2,449	28.8			
C.B. Maxted	Cit	830	9.8			
Total votes		8,496				
Total voters		3,478				
(3 elected)						
1937						
D. Price*	Lab	Unopp.	-	9,278	-	-
1938						
E.F. Davey*	Lab	Unopp.	-	9,785	-	-

Overall Labour vote: **Overall turnout:**

1919–35	**42.2%**	**1919–35**	**46.9%**
1936–38	**90.2%**	**1936–38**	**39.7%**

Southville ward

Candidate	Party	Votes	%	Electors	Turnout	Gains
1919						
A.E. Dowling*	L	1,190	51.1	8,181	28.5	-
F.E. White	Lab	881	37.8			
G. Daniel	Ex-S	260	11.2			
Total votes		2,331				
1920						
F.E. Sprackling	C	1,664	58.5	8,258	34.4	-
F.E. White	Lab	1,179	41.5			
Total votes		2,843				
1921						
E. Robinson	Coa	2,790	73.8	8,455	44.7	-
E.F. Lovell	Lab	991	26.2			
Total votes		3,781				
1922						
A.E. Dowling*	L	Unopp.	-	8,520	-	-
1923						
F.E. Sprackling*	C	2,139	53.4	8,583	46.7	-
W.G. Cook	Lab	1,865	46.6			
Total votes		4,004				
1924						
F.E. Sampson*	Cit	2,535	71.2	8,631	41.2	-
S.R. Hutton	Lab	1,023	28.8			
Total votes		3,558				
1925						
H.A. White*	Cit	2,516	66.0	8,648	44.1	-
S.R. Hutton	Lab	1,295	34.0			
Total votes		3,811				
1926						
F.E. Sprackling*	Cit	1,957	60.5	8,527	37.9	-
W. Dancy	Lab	1,277	39.5			
Total votes		3,234				

Southville ward *(continued)*

Candidate	Party	Votes	%	Electors	Turnout	Gains
1927						
F.E. Sampson*	Cit	2,304	63.9	8,417	42.8	-
W. Dancy	Lab	1,301	36.1			
Total votes		3,605				
1928						
H.A. White*	Cit	2,209	56.3	8,378	46.8	-
W. Dancy	Lab	1,713	43.7			
Total votes		3,922				
1929						
W. Dancy	Lab	1,682	50.2	8,928	37.6	Lab from Cit
F.E. Sprackling*	Cit	1,671	49.8			
Total votes		3,353				
1930						
F.E. Sampson*	Cit	2,426	62.2	8,768	44.5	-
R.F. Reade	Lab	1,476	37.8			
Total votes		3,902				
1931						
H.A. White*	Cit	2,958	69.4	8,702	49.0	-
R.F. Reade	Lab	1,307	30.6			
Total votes		4,265				
1932						
T.H.J. Underdown	Cit	2,180	55.0	8,450	46.9	Cit from Lab
W. Dancy*	Lab	1,785	45.0			
Total votes		3,965				
1933						
F.E. Sampson*	Cit	2,017	55.9	8,507	42.4	-
E. Dunster	Lab	1,593	44.1			
Total votes		3,610				
1934						
A.G. Farmer	Cit	2,318	54.0	8,468	50.6	-
G.A. Burke	Lab	1,971	46.0			
Total votes		4,289				

Southville ward *(continued)*

Candidate	Party	Votes	%	Electors	Turnout	Gains
1935						
T.H.J. Underdown*	Cit	2,543	59.2	8,406	51.1	-
G.A. Burke	Lab	1,751	40.8			
Total votes		4,294				
1936						
W.S. Davies	Cit	2,708	62.9	8,270	52.1	-
H.J. Smith	Lab	1,598	37.1			
Total votes		4,306				
1937						
A.G. Farmer*	Cit	2,618	58.5	8,169	54.8	-
Ms L.M. Delaney	Lab	1,859	41.5			
Total votes		4,477				
1938						
T.H.J. Underdown*	Cit	2,638	62.5	8,039	52.5	-
W. Dancy	Lab	1,582	37.5			
Total votes		4,220				

Overall Labour vote:			**Overall turnout:**		
1919–35	**39.3%**		**1919–35**		**43.1%**
1936–38	**38.8%**		**1936–38**		**53.1%**

Stapleton ward

Candidate	Party	Votes	%	Electors	Turnout	Gains
1919						
A.W.S. Burgess	Lab	1,629	59.6	10,192	26.8	Lab from L
R. Greenough	L	1,104	40.4			
Total votes		2,733				
1920						
H.J. Newth	L	2,552	53.4	10,483	45.6	-
T.E. Lake	Lab	1,515	31.7			
F.E. Pepler	Ind	712	14.9			
Total votes		4,779				
1921						
V. Osmond	Coa	3,477	65.8	10,915	48.4	-
A.F. Read	Lab	1,807	34.2			
Total votes		5,284				
1922						
A.W.S. Burgess*	Lab	3,034	56.0	11,615	46.6	-
G. Riseley	L	2,380	44.0			
Total votes		5,414				
1923						
H.G. Newth*	L	2,878	55.8	11,894	43.3	-
F.E. White	Lab	2,278	44.2			
Total votes		5,156				
1924						
Mrs E.S. Robinson-White	Cit	3,345	63.5	12,179	43.2	-
M. Giles	Lab	1,919	36.5			
Total votes		5,264				
1925						
A.L.H. Smith	Cit	3,497	52.3	12,803	52.2	Cit from Lab
A.W.S. Burgess*	Lab	3,184	47.7			
Total votes		6,681				

Stapleton ward *(continued)*

Candidate	Party	Votes	%	Electors	Turnout	Gains
1926						
H.G. Newth*	Cit	2,756	50.5	13,154	41.5	-
L.H. Bateman	Lab	2,704	49.5			
Total votes		5,460				
1927						
Mrs E.S. Robinson-White*	Cit	3,822	54.4	13,467	52.2	-
L.H. Bateman	Lab	3,206	45.6			
Total votes		7,028				
1928						
A.L.H. Smith*	Cit	3,983	52.3	13,826	55.1	-
L.H. Bateman	Lab	3,636	47.7			
Total votes		7,619				
1929						
L.H. Bateman*	Lab	3,461	55.3	15,150	41.3	-
W.F. Cottrell	Cit	2,803	44.7			
Total votes		6,264				
1930						
Mrs E.S. Robinson-White*	Cit	3,821	56.3	15,850	42.8	-
G.A.W. Allen	Lab	2,966	43.7			
Total votes		6,787				
1931						
A.L.H. Smith*	Cit	5,474	68.5	16,283	49.1	-
G.A.W. Allan	Lab	2,516	31.5			
Total votes		7,990				
1932						
L.H. Bateman*	Lab	3,941	52.4	16,590	45.3	-
W.F. Cottrell	Cit	3,574	47.6			
Total votes		7,515				

Stapleton ward *(continued)*

Candidate	Party	Votes	%	Electors	Turnout	Gains
1933						
Ms R. Burgess	Lab	3,958	53.4	16,837	44.0	Lab from Cit
Mrs E.S. Robinson-	Cit	3,457	46.6			
White*			0.0			
Total votes		7,415				
1934						
A.L.H. Smith*	Cit	4,400	51.1	17,021	50.6	
Mrs M. Liddington	Lab	4,212	48.9			
Total votes		8,612				
1935						
L.H. Bateman*	Lab	4,509	56.0	17,374	46.4	-
R. Campbell-Kaye	Cit	3,547	44.0			
Total votes		8,056				
1936						
S.C. Humphries*	Cit	1,995	58.5	6,969	49.0	-
L.J. Blake	Lab	1,417	41.5			
Total votes		3,412				
1937						
A.L.H. Smith*	Cit	2,278	60.4	7,412	50.9	
F.J. Richmond	Lab	1,494	39.6			
Total votes		3,772				
1938						
Mrs D.P. Dobson	Cit	2,387	61.3	7,777	50.1	Cit from Lab
L.H. Bateman*	Lab	1,508	38.7			
Total votes		3,895				

Overall Labour vote: **Overall turnout:**

1919–35	**46.7%**	**1919–35**	**45.9%**
1936–38	**39.9%**	**1936–38**	**50.0%**

Westbury on Trym ward

Candidate	Party	Votes	%	Electors	Turnout	Gains
1919						
S. Humphries*	C	2,094	69.4	5,610	53.8	-
C.T. Campion	Lab	842	27.9			
W. Elphick	Ex-S	83	2.7			
Total votes		3,019				
1920						
L. Thomas	L	2,288	66.6	5,653	60.7	L from C
T.T. Howell	Lab	1,146	33.4			
Total votes		3,434				
1921						
J. Kennedy	Coa	2,132	63.4	6,116	55.0	-
T.T. Howell	Lab	1,232	36.6			
Total votes		3,364				
1922						
Sir S. Humphries*	C	2,682	62.8	6,298	67.8	-
A. Schofield	Lab	1,590	37.2			
Total votes		4,272				
1923						
L. Thomas*	L	2,372	68.7	6,712	51.5	-
A. Schofield	Lab	1,083	31.3			
Total votes		3,455				
1924						
C.T. Culverwell*	Cit	2,606	72.5	6,881	52.2	-
E. Hill	Lab	988	27.5			
Total votes		3,594				
1925						
Sir S. Humphries*	Cit	3,189	74.6	7,161	59.7	-
T.G. Howell	Lab	1,086	25.4			
Total votes		4,275				
1926						
L. Thomas*	Cit	2,420	67.3	7,552	47.6	-
D. Temblett	Lab	1,177	32.7			
Total votes		3,597				

Westbury on Trym ward *(continued)*

Candidate	Party	Votes	%	Electors	Turnout	Gains
1927						
C.T. Culverwell*	Cit	3,020	69.4	8,237	52.8	-
D. Temblett	Lab	1,332	30.6			
Total votes		4,352				
1928						
Sir S. Humphries*	Cit	3,320	61.4	9,521	56.8	-
W.J. Ellerby	Lab	2,091	38.6			
Total votes		5,411				
1929						
H.R. Griffiths	Cit	2,612	50.3	10,580	49.1	-
W.J. Ellerby	Lab	2,586	49.7			
Total votes		5,198				
1930						
F.J.M. Cook	Cit	4,279	64.9	11,477	57.5	-
E.J. Plaisted	Lab	2,316	35.1			
Total votes		6,595				
1931						
A.G. Heard*	Cit	4,874	73.9	12,481	52.9	-
E.J. Plaisted	Lab	1,725	26.1			
Total votes		6,599				
1932						
H.R. Griffiths	Cit	3,907	58.9	13,814	48.0	-
R.F. Reade	Lab	2,725	41.1			
Total votes		6,632				
1933						
F.J.M. Cook*	Cit	4,063	56.9	14,555	49.1	-
R.F. Reade	Lab	3,078	43.1			
Total votes		7,141				
1934						
A.G. Heard*	Cit	4,429	56.3	15,504	50.7	-
T. Watkins	Lab	3,436	43.7			
Total votes		7,865				

Westbury on Trym ward *(continued)*

Candidate	Party	Votes	%	Electors	Turnout	Gains
1935						
H.R. Griffiths*	Cit	5,334	58.9	17,485	51.8	-
F. Phippen	Lab	3,720	41.1			
Total votes		9,054				
1936						
F.J.M. Cook*	Cit	2,775	66.1	8,341	50.4	-
H. Orr	Lab	1,425	33.9			
Total votes		4,200				
1937						
A.G. Heard*	Cit	3,142	67.6	9,382	49.5	-
P.J.R. Nash	Lab	1,504	32.4			
Total votes		4,646				
1938						
H.R. Griffiths*	Cit	3,692	74.0	10,358	48.2	-
Mrs M. Deverall	Lab	1,300	26.0			
Total votes		4,992				

Overall Labour vote:
1919–35 36.6%
1936–38 30.6%

Overall turnout:
1919–35 53.0%
1936–38 49.3%

Windmill Hill ward
(created in 1936 reorganisation)

Candidate	Party	Votes	%	Electors	Turnout	Gains
1936						
C.R. Gill*	Lab	2,366	63.4	8,776	42.5	-
A.L.Duggan	Cit	1,363	36.6			
Total votes		3,729				
1937						
E.J. Plaisted*	Lab	Unopp.	-	8,501	-	-
1938						
F.C. Williams*	Lab	1,684	77.0	8,199	26.7	-
H. Fry	Ind	503	23.0			
Total votes		2,187				

Overall Labour vote:　　　　　　　　**Overall turnout:**
1936–38　　　　　68.5%　　　**1936–38**　　　　　34.9%

FOUR
Burnley

BURNLEY

Burnley was a county borough with a population of almost 100,000 in 1931, and was one of the main centres of cotton weaving. It was situated on the north-east edge of the Lancashire cotton textile district in the Pennine foothills, not far from the Yorkshire border. The town was largely isolated from the main areas of commercial and industrial development on the Lancashire plain until the coming of the Leeds–Liverpool Canal in 1796. Apart from being a market centre, a number of earlier features of the town's economy were to influence the borough after the First World War. Of importance were skills in handloom weaving generally and the weaving of cotton in particular, both prevalent since the early eighteenth century. The natural advantages for cotton manufacture that existed in the eighteenth century were still extant when 'cotton was king' in the Victorian age. The soft and ample water supply for power, damp climate to prevent thread breakage, and a skilled workforce, were all local advantages effectively exploited. These advantages contributed to Burnley's important position in Lancashire's burgeoning cotton export trade. Improved transportation links aided the development of the textile industries. The coming of the railway to Burnley supplemented the canal link. By 1848 the town was connected to Accrington. The next year saw further connections to Leeds and Manchester and by 1876 there was a branch line to Blackburn.

By the late nineteenth-century, the production of woollen goods and cotton spinning had given way to cotton weaving in the borough. Through borrowing and the leasing of cotton plant, Burnley, along with Nelson, was 'the last major spawning ground of self-made cotton manufacturers'.[1] At the turn of the twentieth century, with just under 100,000 looms, Burnley was said to weave a greater length of cloth than any town in the world.[2] In 1902, Burnley still had the highest number of looms for a town in England, with 79,300 being 12 per cent of the total.[3] By the early twentieth century much of Burnley weaving was devoted to producing plain calico known as 'Burnley printers'. This woven cloth was mainly for foreign markets and it was said the cloth woven before breakfast was for the domestic market, while that produced afterwards was for export. As late as 1959, Burnley was still one of the two largest weaving units of 'the weaving area' of Lancashire.[4]

Despite its major dependence on weaving, Burnley also had two other important industries. Coal had been mined locally since the fifteenth century, and by the onset of the nineteenth century Burnley had a dozen pits in the town centre alone. Local coal, a cheap and reliable resource, powered the textile mills and engineering factories and heated Burnley's homes. As late as 1948, Burnley still had six collieries within or very near its boundaries: Bank Hall, Reedley, Clifton,

---

[1] Walton, J.K., *Lancashire: A Social History, 1558–1939*, (Manchester, 1987), p. 306.
[2] Hall, B. and Spencer, K., *Burnley: A Pictorial History*, (Chichester, 1993), Introduction.
[3] Clapham, S.J., *The Cotton Industry and Trade*, (London, 1904), p. 9.
[4] Freeman, T.W., *The Conurbations of Great Britain*, (Manchester, 1959), p. 236.

Hapton Valley, Towneley Desmesne and Salterwood Drift.[5] The other nineteenth-century staple industry which was established in the borough was engineering, especially concerned with the manufacture of textile machinery. Most of the engineering works were large scale enterprises. Thus Butterworth and Dickinson had over 700 workers, while the Bankhouse Ironworks in St Peter's ward was another large employer of labour. The Bankhouse Ironworks exported Keighley Looms to world markets, especially India, China and Japan.[6] Cotton, coal and engineering were still the bedrock of Burnley's economy in the years between the wars.

All three of Burnley's main industries, however, were hit by major problems in the inter-war period, with serious repercussions for the local economy. The First World War saw the loss of markets in India, Japan and the Far East, which was a harbinger of the approaching end of Lancashire's pre-eminence in the world cotton trade. Restrictions on trade in the First World War meant that these markets were fundamentally affected, and Lancashire's exporters were unable to re-establish their dominant position there in the inter-war years. The growth of indigenous cotton industries in Japan and India was, in John Walton's words, 'to be disastrous for Lancashire in the 1920s and 1930s'.[7] After the short post-war boom, Burnley's industries faced short-time work, unemployment, the collapse of firms and a long-drawn out depression. The weaving sector of the cotton industry was the worst hit. Between 1912 and 1937–38, the output of cotton piece goods fell by nearly 60 per cent, a consequence of a 75 per cent fall in exports.[8] The attempted re-organisation of the cotton industry, which included the introduction of the six-loom system, the weaving of new types of cloth like rayon, developments in automatic looms and the introduction of new shift systems, did not bring about economic recovery in the period. In addition, Burnley's economic plight was worsened by the fact that there were also problems in the local coal industry in the 1930s, with closures leaving only six pits just over a decade after the end of this study.[9]

It has been suggested that the weaving areas of Lancashire as a whole were less successful than elsewhere at attracting new industries. Burnley did not initially qualify for Special Area Status and suffered persistent and general unemployment and insecurity in the period. Yet Walton points out that new industries in Blackburn and Burnley were 'not altogether absent' and 'offered employment to over 10,000 people between 1933 and 1938'.[10] Fogarty also points out some very modest gains were made from the mid-1930s by later use of the Special Areas legislation.[11] The borough was not the most hard-hit in the region, occupying an 'intermediate position' between towns with a handful of vulnerable large employers and those cushioned by their concentration on the home market.[12]

---

[5]   Walkerdine, R. and Treherne Jones, C., (eds), *Colliery Guardian Guide to the Coalfields*, (London, 1953), pp. 219–224.
[6]   Frost, R. *Top o' th' Town Burnley*, (Burnley, 1981), p. 20.
[7]   Walton, *Lancashire*, p. 326.
[8]   Fogarty, *Prospects*, pp. 215–216.
[9]   Hall, *Burnley*, p. 38.
[10] Walton, *Lancashire*, p. 333.
[11] Fogarty, *Prospects*, p. 206.
[12] Walton, *Lancashire*, pp. 333–337.

Nevertheless Burnley did worse than the spinning districts of Lancashire, with unemployment in the 1930s well above the national level.[13] With just over 24 per cent of all workers recorded as 'out of work' in 1931, Burnley lay seventh highest in the ranking of the eighty-three county boroughs. Indicative of Burnley's economic predicament in the period was a declining population. A population of just over 100,000 in 1921 had fallen back to 98,300 in 1931.

The most striking feature of the occupational structure of Burnley was the overwhelming importance of both cotton textiles and female labour. In 1931 over 30,000 people, just over half of the labour force of Burnley, was in textiles, mainly cotton weaving. This accounted for 73 per cent of the female workforce and 31 per cent of the male. In the ranking of the eighty-three county boroughs in these terms, Burnley was the pre-eminent borough (see appendices 7 and 8). Female labour was vital to the town's economy, emphasised as well by the fact that the female workforce amounted to almost 50 per cent of the total female population, an unusually high figure. Inevitably, the political attitudes of the weavers and their trade unions were the single most important influence on the municipal politics of Burnley. The second most important industry in the town was the male-dominated one of mining. There were over 3,200 miners, accounting for almost 10 per cent of the male labour force. In terms of the percentage of workers in this sector, Burnley was ranked number thirteen amongst the county boroughs, and it was the only Lancashire cotton town with a significant number of miners. The miners were plainly less important than the weavers in local politics, but nevertheless their presence added a distinctive flavour to the local labour movement. The third industry of Burnley was engineering, especially concerned with the manufacture of textile looms and mill furnishings. Again a predominantly male industry, over eight per cent of the male labour force was engaged in the engineering sector.

There was an unusually low percentage of the female workforce in the personal service sector in Burnley, at less than 8 per cent. In fact women in domestic service as a percentage of the total population amounted to only 2 per cent, and Burnley lay seventy-seventh in the ranking of county boroughs for that category. This was in part a reflection of the large scale of female employment available in weaving, but such a minuscule domestic sector was also an indicator of a relatively small middle class. Burnley also lay fifty-first amongst the county boroughs in terms of the 'own account' and managerial categories of the 1931 census, and again at seventy-seventh place in the rankings for professionals as a percentage of the total workforce, confirming the view that the borough only had a small middle class. There was a small upper middle class elite of mill, mine and factory owners, but they were less important in the locality than in other longer-established textile centres. As one writer has commented:

> Burnley, Nelson and Brierfield were distinct from older, larger weaving centres like Blackburn or Preston because of their high proportion of small manufacturers. The area was renowned for encouraging an ambitious tackler or shopkeeper to save up or borrow enough to rent a space in a mill, set up a few looms and employ a handful of weavers. This was called the room-and-power

---

[13] Fogarty, *Prospects*, p.220.

system, since crucial was the small manufacturer's access to the mill's steam power.[14]

The powerful influence on social and political life that the big cotton masters exerted in boroughs such as Blackburn, Bolton and Bury, as has been demonstrated elsewhere in these volumes, was noticeably less significant in Burnley. One comparative study has portrayed pre-1914 Burnley as 'progressive' with none of the 'clog Toryism' of Blackburn.[15] It should also be stressed that in general terms the workers in the weaving side of the cotton industry tended to be more radical in their trade unionism and their politics than their counterparts in spinning. The nature of the work process in mule spinning created a hierarchy amongst the workforce of spinner, 'big piecer' and 'little piecer', and the prospect of individual advancement within the hierarchy encouraged individualist attitudes. The spinners were the best organised, but tended to be highly exclusive and sectional. 'They provided a distinctive, strongly elitist element within cotton unionism'.[16] By contrast, there was a greater degree of homogeneity in terms of status and income amongst weavers, and they were more conducive to collective attitudes. The Weavers' Amalgamation espoused an inclusive recruitment policy, including the widespread unionism of the women workers in the industry. While spinners were often identified with Toryism, weavers were more often associated with a Radical Liberalism which in places such as Burnley could provide the springboard for the shift to Independent Labour and socialist politics.[17] Working-class Conservatism, with its twin poles of paternalism and deference, was much less important in Burnley than in many other cotton textile towns. Before 1914 Toryism was dominant among the surrounding gentry, some of whom like the Thursby family, were colliery owners. On the other hand the cotton masters, like the Greenwoods, Thornbers, John Grey, Hartley Emmot and the Collinge family were all prominent as leaders of Liberalism on the town council. The smaller manufacturers, however, remained distinct from the elite groups, and professionals and tradesmen provided 'the backbone of Liberalism'.[18]

Turning to the influences of cultural tradition, the strength of religious nonconformity in the area was significant. Indeed, one study sees the influence of Methodism on Burnley 'as the largest in the whole of the Manchester district.'[19] A relative shortage of public houses was noted at the end of the nineteenth century, a sure indicator of nonconformist influence. The relatively late development of weaving in Burnley and the other towns further up the valley like Nelson and Brierfield was important in this regard again. Large numbers of workers migrated into the area, attracted by the rapidly growing employment prospects, many from

[14] Liddington, J., *The Life and Times of a Respectable Rebel: Selina Cooper (1864–1946)*, (London, 1984), p. 32.
[15] Trodd, G., 'Political Change and the Working Class in Blackburn and Burnley, 1880–1914', (Ph.D. thesis, University of Lancaster, 1978), pp. 134–135.
[16] Howell, D., *British Workers and the Independent Labour Party, 1888–1906*, (Manchester, 1983), p. 54.
[17] Howell, *British Workers*, pp. 53–56.
[18] Trodd, 'Political Change', p. 181.
[19] Trodd, 'Political Change', pp. 134–135.

as far away as Cornwall and East Anglia. The greatest number, though, came from nearby, across the border from the strongly Nonconformist West Riding of Yorkshire. There were three main variants of Nonconformity locally. Wesleyan Methodism was dominated by local employers and encouraged individualism. The strong Liberal tradition of the area stemmed mainly from this source. However, the predominantly working-class Primitive Methodists and Independent Methodists bequeathed a rather different legacy to the locality. The Independents in particular, emphasising chapel democracy, self-government, temperance and self-education, were vital in encouraging a strong radicalism in the area. This radical tradition was later to be important in the developing socialist and labour movement.[20]

The presence of a sizeable number of miners in Burnley, as noted above, was also a factor of importance in the labour movement. Pelling suggests that coal-miners in Burnley made for political liberalism, and later for independent labour politics. As he points out, 'the Lancashire and Cheshire miners were early converts to independent labour politics, just because their members were divided on political questions'.[21] David Howell, the historian of Lancashire miners' unionism, explains in more detail:

> In 1900, the Lancashire Miners sent delegates to the foundation conference of the Labour Representation Committee ... Lancashire did join in May 1903, more than five and a half years before the MFGB as a whole. In the ... ballots on MFGB affiliation to the Labour Party ... Lancashire voted in favour by a majority of over two to one. This early enthusiasm for Independent Labour owed relatively little to the appeal of Socialism within the coalfield ... Labour politics was presented as a pragmatic method of ensuring the union's political influence, not a Socialist alternative but almost an apolitical one ... the coalfield never became a centre for ... left-wing developments ... Instead there dominated a cautious Labour politics.[22]

The moderation of the Lancashire region within mining trade unionism was clear, and before 1914 the Burnley miners in particular were noted as a 'volatile political force, capable of giving succour on occasions to Toryism'. Yet they also gave 'early backing to the Socialist cause',[23] and in the inter-war period the commitment of Burnley miners to the Labour party was strong. In the context of Burnley politics, the miners may have been numerous enough to tip the balance marginally in Labour's favour in the inter-war years something which could not be said about any other Lancashire textile borough. Certainly miners played an active part in the Burnley Labour party. A significant number of miners' union officials and rank and file miners stood for Labour in municipal elections, second only to textile officials and workers, as will be shown below.

[20]   Liddington, *Life and Times*, pp. 35–38.
[21]   Pelling, H., *Social Geography of British Elections 1885–1910*, (Aldershot, 1994), pp. 262 and 286; Walton, *Lancashire*, p. 299.
[22]   Howell, D., *The Politics of the NUM: A Lancashire View*, (Manchester, 1989), pp. 7–8.
[23]   Hill, J., 'Lib–Labism, socialism and Labour in Burnley, c. 1890–1918', *Northern History*, vol. 35, (1999), p. 188.

Burnley was from an early stage noted for its political radicalism. By the twentieth century the borough had the following institutions and organisations: a large Mechanics Institute, a successful building society, co-operative weaving sheds, strong Nonconformity and vibrant socialist organisations like the Social Democratic Federation (SDF) and a Socialist Party of Great Britain (SPGB) group.[24] It was a centre of activities of the SDF, the local branch being described as 'the first modern Socialist organisation in Britain'.[25] As early as 1893 an SDF member was elected as the vice-president of the Burnley Weavers' Association.[26] H.M. Hyndman stood for the SDF in the Burnley seat in the general elections of 1895, 1906 and the two elections of 1910. In his best performance, in 1906, Hyndman won almost a third of the votes cast in a three-way contest with Tory and Lib-Lab candidates. Pelling argues that Hyndman took votes mainly from the Liberals, thus making what should have been a safe Liberal seat in the pre-1914 period into somewhat of a marginal.[27] Although the SDF never had more then two councillors out of the 48 on the pre-1914 council, Hyndman's organisation played a crucial role in the local Labour movement. Walton presents the SDF as not being dogmatic and sectarian in Burnley, willing to act alongside the Independent Labour Party (ILP) and 'become very much part of the wider Labour movement'.[28] Relations between socialist politics and trade unionism were not always as simple, however, and the Lib-Lab tradition was also strong in the area. The pragmatism of the miners has already been noted, and the weavers withdrew from the Trades Council in 1904, and then revoked their financial support for SDF candidates for the council in 1909. In the same year the SDF and ILP were contesting wards against each other.[29] White however, noted the anti-socialism of the weavers as expressed by the leadership of the Textile Operatives before the First World War. He posits that the very decision to form the moderate textile operatives' organisation was an indication of the weakness of socialism among the weavers.[30]

Turning to the municipal politics of Burnley, the borough was created in 1861, and became an early exponent of 'gas and water socialism'. The borough held powers over gas, water, cemetery, baths and wash-houses by an act of 1854,[31] and the trams followed into borough control in 1901.[32] It became a county borough in 1889. Liberal control of the council was assured up to 1910. The next year the Liberals lost overall control and by 1912 the Conservatives had become the largest party in the council chamber. In 1914 Conservative strength could outvote the

[24] Trodd, 'Political Change', unnumbered.
[25] Chew, L. 'Dan Irving and socialist politics in Burnley', *North West Labour History*, no. 23, (1998/99), pp. 2–12.
[26] Liddington, J. and Norris, J., *One Hand Tied Behind Us: The Rise of the Women's Suffrage Movement*, (London, 1978), p. 44.
[27] Pelling, *Social Geography*, pp. 262–263.
[28] Walton, *Lancashire*, pp. 275, 279.
[29] Chew, 'Dan Irving', p. 7.
[30] White, J.L. *The Limits of Trade Union Militancy: The Lancashire Textile Workers 1900–1914*, (London, 1978), pp. 160–161.
[31] Bennet, W., *The History of Burnley Part 3, 1650–1850*, (Burnley, 1948), pp. 362–363.
[32] Douglas, A., *Burnley: Once Upon a Time*, (Nelson, 1976), unpaginated.

combined strength of the Liberals, SDF and ILP.[33] There had been in total eighty-two Socialist, ILP and Trades Council candidates between 1901 and 1913, of whom fifteen had been successful.[34] It was a base from which Labour could work effectively after its 1918 reorganisation. In the years immediately before the First World War there was little indication of any 'radical' Lib–Lab alliance. Instead there was a widely held belief that Conservatives and Liberals made 'common cause against the intruding Labour councillor'.[35] This 'common cause' was to have an important legacy in the period of this study.

Conservative–Liberal electoral pacts together with some co-operation in the politics of the council chamber were to be important features of inter-war municipal politics in Burnley. For the most part the council chamber was divided along the fault-lines of Socialist and anti-Socialist, with the latter controlling the borough until Labour won outright control in 1934. Overall control of the council chamber was until 1934 augmented by the two traditional party organisations using their numerical superiority to ensure that the aldermanic bench was overwhelmingly Conservative and Liberal. Until 1929, Conservatives and Liberals divided the aldermanic bench equally. In 1929 however, a concession was made to Labour's fifteen councillors and one of their number was elevated to the bench. When Labour's turn came after achieving outright control in 1934, it used its numerical superiority of councillors to increase it's own representation on the aldermanic bench. As a consequence Labour increased its aldermanic numbers from two to nine members in the three years 1935 to 1938. A harbinger of this had occurred in 1933 when flushed with the success of five gains, Labour promised 'No Quarter' in the imminent aldermanic appointments. Thus Councillor Hargreaves said in a celebratory meeting at the Labour Rooms in Grey Street that 'if there were any Aldermanic vacancies before the two years expired for the aldermanic elections, they would see who the new aldermen were'.[36] In 1938, with Labour's heavy defeat in the November elections, the boot was on the other foot. Defeat meant that three of Labour's aldermanic seats were almost certain to be lost. The combined Liberals and Conservatives outnumbered Labour's twenty-three seats on the council and revenge was sure to be exacted. Indeed, as the *Express and News* recorded, under the sub-heading 'Socialist Treatment Remembered', such retribution by Labour's opponents was predicted. Speaking on behalf of the Daneshouse Conservatives, a spokesperson declared that 'They had not forgotten the shabby treatment meted out to anti-Socialists in 1934, when ... a number of Conservative aldermen with long service had lost their seats. They resented this treatment very much, and now that the anti-Socialists had regained power, expected them to use it'.[37]

What can be said about party strength in particular wards? Widespread and abundant terraced housing across the borough had been constructed between 1855 and 1910, replacing earlier slums. Before the First World War, town houses of the well-to-do made the central wards somewhat more socially heterogeneous than

---

[33] Trodd, 'Political Change', p. 347.
[34] Trodd, 'Political Change', p. 345.
[35] Trodd, 'Political Change', p. 348–349.
[36] *Burnley News*, 1 Nov. 1933.
[37] *Express and News*, 2 Nov. 1938.

might have been expected. Nevertheless, Labour's strongest wards were mainly in central or inner-city locations where early industrialisation had occurred. St Paul's (sixteen Labour successes between the wars), Trinity (fourteen) and St Peter's (eleven) were certainly all in this category. Labour's other main stronghold, Gannow ward (fifteen successes) was also partially of this nature, taking in the western part of the old industrial centre of the town, but also extending out to the western edge of the borough. These four wards had in the 1931 census the highest number of persons per room. A significant number of colliers from the mines lived in these wards, mainly those working at the Clifton pit and Bank Hall. The greatest concentration of Burnley's textile industry was in an area known as the Weaver's Triangle. The Triangle was mainly situated in St Peter's and to a lesser extent also in St Paul's ward, by the River Brun and the Leeds–Liverpool canal. Also in St Peter's were located George Keighley's Bankhouse Ironworks and Massey's Bridge End Brewery on Westgate. The Prestige factory, opened in 1935, was built in St Peters as well. A densely populated working class ward, St Peters was referred to as having 'the greatest amount of slum property' in the 1919 elections.[38] St Peters became so solidly Labour that it became the first ward where, in 1929, Labour secured a walkover. Gannow also had large numbers of miners living within its boundaries working at the Hapton Valley pit. It was noted that in Edwardian times Gannow had twice the infant mortality rate of the adjoining middle class ward of Healey.[39] There was some Conservative strength in Gannow in the early 1920s based mainly in the suburban west of the ward. In 1928 however, 'the new housing estate at Stoops Farm, peopled for the most part by former residents of the strongly Labour ward of St Paul's, proved a decisive factor' in Gannow.[40]

The strongest Liberal wards were Healey (twenty inter-war successes), St Andrew's (eighteen) and Daneshouse (fourteen). Better quality housing existed along the Manchester Road to the south of the borough in Healey ward, while the other two Liberal strongholds were in pleasant suburbs to the north and east. As might be expected they were the wards of lowest occupancy per room, with Healey being the lowest in Burnley (0.77 per room). In 1919 the *Burnley News* said that the ward had 'always been noted for its rock solid block of Liberal votes' and insisted in being represented by 'a sound businessmen'.[41] Later in the 1932 election, the press again noted that Healey was 'the Liberal stronghold'.[42] In the 1936 election, the press noted that it was the first time in twenty-three years that the Conservatives had had the temerity to enter the field in this ward. St Andrews too was seen as 'a stronghold of Liberalism' in the 1928 election,[43] and its good housing and wealthy homes was highlighted.[44] Daneshouse too was seen in 1928

[38] *Express and Advertiser*, 5 Nov. 1919.
[39] Trodd, 'Political Change', p. 235.
[40] *Northern Daily Telegraph*, 2 Nov. 1928.
[41] *Burnley News*, 5 Nov. 1919.
[42] *Northern Daily Telegraph*, 2 Nov. 1932.
[43] *Northern Daily Telegraph*, 2 Nov. 1928.
[44] *Burnley News*, 1 Nov. 1919.

as a 'stronghold of Liberalism' for many years and indeed, up to the year 1919 it had been represented by three Liberals.[45]

Turning to the Conservatives, their strongest wards were in the east and south-eastern suburbs of Fulledge (sixteen inter-war wins) and Burnley Wood (nine wins), and in the west and south-western suburbs of Whittlefield (eleven wins), and Stoneyholme (nine wins). In terms of occupancy per room, the strongest Conservative wards tended to be below the average for the borough. One other ward had been seen as a Tory stronghold before 1914, but it assumed a much more marginal position between the wars. The Dugdale family owned Lowerhouse Mills in Lowerhouse ward, together with 300 cottages for their workers, thereby exercising paternalistic political influence.[46] Lowerhouse was still perceived as an anti-Socialist ward up to 1929, but Labour subsequently won it in most years.

The building of council houses had some effect on this pattern of political support. Burnley did not build very large numbers of such houses by the standards of the time, as will be shown below. The first council houses were built on Towneley lands in 1909, while during the First World War twenty-four workers' houses were built in St Andrew's ward in Mansergh and Killington streets. Between the World Wars, council estates were built at Rosehill in Healey ward (constructed 1919–28), at Palace House in Lowerhouse (1919 and 1928–29), at Stoops Farm in Gannow (1927–38), at Hargher Clough (1935–38), at Plane Tree in Gannow (1935–38), at Bleak House in Healey (1936–39) and at Barden and Casterton in St Andrew's ward (1929 and 1933–34 respectively).[47] The effect on Gannow ward in favour of Labour has already been noted, but it was also a factor in the trend towards Labour in Lowerhouse. In Healey and St Andrew's the council estates were swamped by extensive middle class suburbs, and they had little political effect.

Gerrymandering of ward boundaries appears to have been a factor of little importance in Burnley's politics. If anything, the ward boundaries favoured Labour marginally. Three of the strongest Labour wards, St Peters, St Paul's and Trinity had the smallest electorates, although Conservative Whittlefield was on a par. These three Labour strongholds were business and mill districts with central locations. During the inter-war period, the first two wards had falling populations and electorates, while Trinity had a slight increase in both respects. Labour's other main ward, Gannow, became solidly Labour precisely at the point its population began to rise with council house building. Most other wards saw a modest rise in electorates in the twenty year period. The solidly Liberal St Andrews was the largest ward both in area and electorate by far, and overall Conservative and Liberal wards had marginally larger electorates than the Labour strongholds. Secure in their domination up to the First World War, the traditional parties saw at first little to fear from the Labour threat, and remained well in control until the early 1930s. When Labour did come to power in the council chamber in 1934, it did so as a result of rapid, and for its opponents surprising, gains over the preceding three years. Once in power, it was hardly likely that Labour would effect

[45] *Northern Daily Telegraph*, 2 Nov. 1928; *Burnley News*, 5 Nov. 1919.
[46] Trodd, 'Political Change', p. 149.
[47] Lowe, J., *Burnley*, (Chichester, 1985), pp. 46–48.

any boundary changes, as the status quo was in its favour. There is little doubt that in this respect Burnley was an unusual county borough. The long-established ward arrangements of late-Victorian times, and the happenstance of marginal population changes, marginally aided the rise and consolidation of the local Labour Party.

What can be said of the councillors and their defeated opponents in this period? The nominations of 116 candidates for the three main parties in the elections of 1919, 1924, 1926, 1929 and 1932 have been collated. The figures show the contrast between the lower middle and middle class occupational backgrounds of the two traditional parties as opposed to the manual and trade union connections of Labour. At the upper end of the socio-economic hierarchy, the Liberals had eight company-directors and two 'gentlemen', to three Conservatives in the former but none in the latter category. In terms of small entrepreneurs, the Tories dominated, having ten small businessmen, including builders, to the Liberals three. Both the Liberals and Conservatives had three cotton manufacturers each. In the professions the Conservatives had three medical practitioners and dentists to the Liberals one, while the latter in addition had five engineers in the textile and colliery sectors. In the petit-bourgeois occupations, the Conservatives had four shopkeepers, three licensed victuallers and four skilled tradesmen (including carriage/motor body builders) to the Liberals one victualler and single skilled tradesman. Labour had none in the grouping of manufacturers, professionals and petit-bourgeois occupations, except in the somewhat less socially elevated classification of clerical and post-workers, where they had three candidates. The main group of Labour aspirants consisted of thirteen trade union officials, nearly all in weaving and mining, and five Socialist organisers. In addition, Labour nominated nine rank and file weavers and six miners and surface-workers as candidates. Another background of some importance for Labour candidates was the railways where five candidates were forthcoming. Labour also had five semi-skilled and unskilled workers outside of the key trades of weaving, mining and the railways.

Further examination of Liberalism in the borough makes apparent a continuing strength and resilience of that party in local politics. There was no 'strange death' of Liberalism in inter-war Burnley. Pre-1914 Liberalism, although losing out to Conservatism after 1910, as noted above, enjoyed both a recrudescence and consolidation of its position after 1918. It had a continuing local vibrancy down to 1934, Labour's year of triumph. Trodd suggests that although pre-1914 Liberalism showed none of the attributes of the Lancashire's often alleged 'New Liberalism', it nevertheless 'maintained wide social contacts with the working class'. Indeed 'Burnley Liberalism was tied more firmly to the respectable and politically and socially aware groups within the working class'.[48] Trodd further argues that as early as 1890, though the cotton masters ran the party, the Liberal and Labour candidates for the council, as well as leadership of the ward associations, were often run by 'a mixture of working class and shopkeepers'.[49] It is reasonable to deduce that continued working class support for Liberalism was still extant to some degree in inter-war local politics.

---

[48] Trodd, 'Political Change', pp. 106, 176–177 and 181.
[49] Trodd, 'Political Change', p. 184.

How did the Liberals maintain their position amongst both working-class and middle-class voters after 1918? One tactic was that the Liberals played down, and even attacked, the notion of class-based politics. Liberals emphasised the differences between Liberalism and Labour as well as stressing the far greater business and administrative experience of Liberal candidates. The local Press also stressed the differences between the Liberal and Labour parties in their essential beliefs. The *Burnley News*, largely a Liberal paper, frequently discussed the impact of class. Very often it gave a platform to one of the Liberal leaders, J.H. Grey. Grey appeared to be the main ideologue of the Party for well over a decade. In a meeting in 1919, Grey suggested that Labour was out to capture the municipal administration in the interest of the working class. This he viewed as an inherently 'wicked idea'. Politics should not be run in a particular class interest, even if, Grey conceded, the working class 'was the largest and most important section of that community'. Instead

> the Liberal Party stood upon a platform which had always held out an ideal that equality of opportunity should be presented to every member of the State, irrespective of class and party. He knew that they had not got equality of opportunity, but that was all the more reason why they should advocate it, and they were not giving equality of opportunity if they endeavoured to legislate avowedly and solely in the interests of a class.[50]

Consistently in the twenty years of municipal politics between the wars, Liberals in Burnley were to stress that the Labour Party was the party of narrow class interest. If it was given power, it was alleged, it would govern in a way favouring the working class rather than the community as a whole.

Liberals also levied the charge that a Labour administration would be profligate with ratepayers' money, and consequently the hard-pressed ratepayers would endure rising rate demands. Coupled with this came claims that Labour councillors were devoid of business and administrative experience. In the 1919 elections, for example, the Liberals stressed that Labour's candidates, though enthusiastic and honest, were 'without training in municipal government, without experience in administration and without any self restraint in the expenditure of money'.[51] What is noteworthy here is the subtlety of the position, for this was no straightforward anti-Red diatribe of the like seen in other boroughs at the time.

Later in the 1919 campaign, the five Liberal candidates placed a large advertisement in the *News* on polling day. In it they appealed directly to the trade unionists of the borough under the heading of 'True Citizenship or Class Interest'. Arguing that trade unions were for industrial not political purposes, the Liberals argued that if all forty-eight members of the Trades Council 'ruled' the Town Council, they would be powerless to improve the economic status of the borough's workers. Indeed the standard of life would be lowered and the rates would increase to an 'alarming extent'. The five prospective councillors went under the banner of 'a sane municipal policy' and omitted to inform their readers that they were

[50] *Burnley News*, 18 Oct. 1919.
[51] *Burnley News*, 18 Oct. 1919.

Liberal Party candidates. In the same edition of the *News*, an editorial argued that 'the best interests of community will be served by electing only men of proved experience and business capacity ... experience has shown that wherever the Socialist-Labour elements gain control of a municipality, rates rise alarmingly'.[52]

It was a traditional brand of Liberalism, with an emphasis on self-improvement and individual effort, and in which 'collectivism was anathema', that predominated in Burnley.[53] There was no rafting together of selected elements of Gladstonian Liberalism with a new emphasis on progressive social reform, wrapped in a package having a broad class appeal. Such a process could be seen in many parts of pre-First World War Lancashire.[54] This was not the case in Burnley for the simple reason that having its own popular base in the borough, there was no necessity for Liberals to have such a progressive alliance. It was also perhaps by remaining true to Gladstonian individualism that the Liberals in Burnley did not lose their lower middle and middle class constituency to the Conservative party. There may have been some diminution of working-class support for Liberalism before 1914. This can be inferred from Joe White's study of textile trade unionism. For White the four years before the War marked 'the eclipse of Lib-Labism' in the borough.[55] However, post-1918 Liberal electoral strength in the borough suggests that this 'eclipse' was not yet total enough to be fatal to the party.

There was an interesting attempt to form a 'progressive' alliance in the borough in the mid-1920s. Rought Brooks, a prominent local Liberal columnist in the *News*, tried to bridge the gap between the Liberals and Labour with the aim of shoring-up the Liberal position in local politics. In 1919 he had been foremost in the fight against Labour in his column. What he wanted then were 'men of character and business capacity.'[56] In 1924 however, Brooks argued that now the real division in politics was between Progressives and Conservatives, in which Liberal and Labour were together in the Progressive camp. He rejected the idea of the class war advocated by some Labour and Tory representatives. Brooks wished to drop the notion that politics was between Labour and anti-Labour, or as it was often put in the local Press between Socialism and Constitutionalism. He rejected what he saw as the misguided notions held dear by some Labour supporters in favour of nationalisation or municipalisation, which he pointed out, even some Liberals had adhered to in the past. Such notions, he argued, interrupted the rigours of competition in the market place which made for efficiency, as well as denuding the concept of merit and enterprise for the individual. Brooks also rejected any strong ties with Conservatives, on the grounds of the 'temperamental differences' between that party and the Progressives. Liberals could not agree with the Tories' desire to restrict public expenditure to defence, to the detriment of education and social reform. Above all, the Conservative's greatest sin was their overriding desire to support Protectionism. On the other hand the Liberals and Labour could combine on the great issue of social reform. Brooks finished with the hope that

---

[52] *Burnley News*, 1 Nov. 1919.
[53] Trodd, 'Political Change', p. 367.
[54] Clarke, P.F., *Lancashire and the New Liberalism*, (Cambridge, 1971).
[55] White, *The Limits of Trade Union Militancy*, p. 161.
[56] *Burnley News*, 18 Oct. 1919.

Labour's Socialist wing of Marxist revolutionaries would break away, leaving the non-Marxian wing in a Progressive alliance with the Liberal Party.[57]

In many respects Brooks was supporting the New Liberalism over a decade after its heyday. This was, however, a tendency that appeared little in evidence in wider Burnley Liberalism. His sentiments may have been encouraged by the events of the parliamentary by-election in Burnley in February 1924. The Liberals then had uncustomarily stood down to let Labour's Arthur Henderson take on and beat the Tory candidate in a straight fight. In the November general election of the same year, though, a Liberal candidate stood against Henderson in a three cornered contest for the Burnley seat. Brooks' call had fallen on deaf Liberal ears, while in municipal politics the Liberals and Conservatives continued to maintain electoral pacts and co-operated against Labour in the council chamber. There appears to be little doubt that such arrangements help explain Liberalism's continued strength and longevity in the municipality. Close co-operation of Burnley's Liberal and Conservative political organisations in local elections, begun in 1920, lasted throughout most of the inter-war years. This co-operation was possible because of ideological similarities, at least if compared to Labour's beliefs and policy objectives. It was also highly pragmatic, being a straightforward attempt to prevent Labour achieving power in the borough.

In some boroughs between the wars, a steady decline in Liberal candidates was mirrored by the consequent decline of Liberals. However, this was not always the case, 'as much more numerous were the towns where Conservative and Liberal combined to defeat Labour, either by a formal amalgamation or by means of an electoral pact'.[58] Occasionally formal amalgamations occurred, as in Sheffield with the Sheffield Citizens Association. In other boroughs, there were municipal alliances where an all-embracing anti-Socialist vote was the objective. Burnley was a borough with separate traditions of Liberalism and Conservatism, with many of the wards having their own flourishing Liberal and Conservative clubs. These clubs served as a focal point of politics, entertainment and sometimes, moral instruction. Thus, Burnley fits into a category of borough where no formal amalgamation of Conservatives and Liberals took place, but where there was an unofficial pact to uphold an anti-Labour front. Superficially, the position of pre-1914 Liberalism in Burnley looked both strong and independent, but it had been faced with a situation where Conservatism had gained ground in the municipal elections in the four years before 1914.[59] After 1918, something had to be done to save the party from being squeezed between the Tories and 'new' Labour. With Burnley's tradition of radical politics much more connected to Socialist organisations, and given that these organisations gave their support to Labour after 1918, it is perhaps not surprising that the local Liberal party sought some accommodation with the Conservatives.

---

[57] *Burnley News*, 25 Oct. 1924.
[58] Cook, C., *The Age of Alignment: Electoral Politics in Britain, 1922–1929*, (London, 1975), pp. 55–56.
[59] In the municipal elections between 1910 and 1914, the Liberals had fallen from 26 to 20 on the council while the Conservatives had increased from 19 to 25 members. See Trodd, 'Political Change', Table 42, p. 347.

Electoral pressure from Labour was recognised from the very first post-war election. In 1919, the Liberals had hinted at a future citizen party. A leading Liberal spokesman, in a post-election meeting at the Blind School, argued that Labour's electoral triumph in 1919 was the result of three main factors. These he outlined as, first, the tide of 'sentiment' and 'emotion' being behind Labour, second, the nature of the recent industrial unrest, and lastly the fact that 'class consciousness was being 'fanned up' by those who were behind the movement. He argued that these appeals to the electorate on a class basis would push others in a new direction. He suggested that the day was not long nigh when, if Labour continued to argue that working people were traitors to class and occupation if they did not vote for Labour, then others would have to take up the idea of a citizen party to represent the well-being of the community as a whole rather than any section within it.[60]

By the 1920 elections Labour was faced by a formal pact between the Conservative and Liberal Party organisations and this continued throughout most of the twenty year period in nearly all wards. Labour recognised this and partly blamed their electoral performance on its existence. Thus in a meeting in Burnley Trades and Labour Council in the aftermath of the election, the presiding official stated that Labour faced a new development in local politics, though this was not unexpected:

> This election had placed them in the position of having driven their opponents into one camp in their last act of desperation to which they had to flee for refuge ... They were told that there were no politics in municipal affairs – a statement that was hardly worthy of an answer in view of what had taken place. They had one candidate labelled a 'Liberal working man'. If that description did not apply to politics it could not apply to financial affairs, because he never knew a working man who had finances to be 'liberal' with. (Laughter) ... There was an oft-quoted passage
> 'Father, forgive them, O forgive,
> They know not by whom they live'.
> He would alter that and say:
> 'Forgive them Demos, O forgive,
> They think as yet by the employers
> they live'.[61]

The pact was in force throughout most of the twenty inter-war elections. It was breached in 1929 but only because of an inter-party dispute in one ward, St Andrew's. The pro-Liberal *Burnley News* reported that the Liberal loss of St Andrews was 'a direct result of the intervention of the Conservatives'.[62] The *Manchester Guardian* also noted the breach in the pact: 'A pact between the Tories and Liberals, which has been in evidence for some years, was ended this year, and one result of this was the loss of St. Andrew's ward by the Liberals to

---

[60] *Express and Advertiser*, 5 Nov. 1919.
[61] *Express and Advertiser*, 3 Nov. 1920.
[62] *Burnley News*, 2 Nov. 1929.

Labour in a three-cornered contest'.[63] In 1930 the Conservative-Liberal pact was very much back on, with the *Manchester Guardian* noting that the seven 'contests were on the anti-Labour versus Labour lines'.[64] Co-operation at Westminster with the National Government almost certainly reinvigorated the pact in Burnley. By 1932, at a Women's Section potato-pie social at the Trinity Labour club, councillor Gradwell complained that 'Liberals and Tories had now definitely joined forces against the Labour Party'.[65] In the same year the *Express* presented a quarter page spread of the anti-Socialist candidates, with photographs mixing Tories and Liberals together. In the same year the *Burnley News*, although recording both Liberal and Conservative results separately as usual, produced an additional table of Anti-Labour and Labour votes in each ward.[66] This did not however, prevent some recriminations between the two allies. The fact that St Andrew's was lost to Labour even after the reconstitution of the pact breached in 1929, was recorded with surprise by the *News* while the defeated Conservative candidate in Trinity blamed the apathy of the Liberals for his defeat 'as they could not be persuaded to come out in the rain'.[67]

Only once in the 1930s did the Conservatives and Liberals stand against each other again, as a result of a ward-level dispute in the solid Labour ward of St Paul's in 1937. The attitude at the end of the inter-war period, after Labour had gained power, was largely unchanged. In the eleven contests of 1938, the *Express and Advertiser* clearly presented the election as 'Labour' versus 'Anti-Labour'. The anti-Labour position was clear cut. Allegedly the borough was suffering from 'one-party' Labour rule and too high expenditure. This was especially so on housing and education and the question was asked as to whether the Socialists were responsible financiers. Therefore 'the towns menace is Socialism', pointed out the *Express*, and 'there are many points on which Conservative and Liberals are in agreement. Why not unite at the poll against Socialism?'[68] The pact bore fruit in 1938, with four gains to the Conservatives and one to the Liberals, all at the expense of Labour. Labour had lost control of the council, with twenty-five Liberals and Conservatives to twenty-three Labour members in the chamber. There is little doubt that the simple tactics of the pact played its part in the electoral defeat of Labour.

The pattern of Labour's development and rise to power in Burnley varied somewhat from other boroughs. As noted above, radical organisations were strongly established in Burnley before the First World War, and Hyndman had mounted a strong challenge for the parliamentary seat. Yet Labour's apparent pre-war vigour had not been translated into great strength on the council. It started the pre-war period with a small base in the council chamber, having had two Social Democratic Federation (SDF) and one Independent Labour Party (ILP) member in 1914.[69] In the inter-war years, the parliamentary seat of Burnley was won by

[63] *Manchester Guardian*, 2 Nov. 1929.
[64] *Manchester Guardian*, 3 Nov. 1930.
[65] *Burnley News*, 22 Oct. 1932.
[66] *Express and Advertiser*, 22 Oct. 1932 and *Burnley News*, 2 Nov. 1932.
[67] *Burnley News*, 2 Nov. 1932.
[68] *Express and Advertiser*, 26 Oct. 1938.
[69] Trodd, 'Political Change', p. 347.

Labour on every occasion bar 1931, when it was won by a National Liberal. The first parliamentary victory for Labour in 1918 was secured by Dan Irving, ally of Hyndman and professional socialist organiser of the SDF. Irving had made his name in the SDF and had become a councillor for that organisation, winning Gannow ward as early as 1902. He was succeeded on his death by Arthur Henderson. This impressive showing in parliamentary politics was slightly misleading, however. At every general election before 1931 there was a three-way contest between the main parties, and even in the peak year of Labour support in 1929, Henderson won with less than 50 per cent of the total poll. Nor was the parliamentary record closely mirrored in municipal elections. One clear indication of this was the fact that in 1922 Irving, at the time of course the sitting MP for Burnley, lost his council seat in Gannow ward. In more general terms, as outlined below, Labour's progress on the council was much slower than at the parliamentary level. After an initial burst of success in 1919, up to the early 1930s it never seriously threatened Liberal–Tory control of the council. From 1932 onwards, however, it made sudden and massive gains, taking power within two years. This unusual trend needs to be analysed in some depth.

Along with the party across the country in the local elections, Labour did exceptionally well in Burnley in 1919, securing six gains in the November contests, bringing its representation on the council up to nine councillors. As elsewhere these gains were achieved on a low turnout of 59 per cent, the lowest in Burnley between the wars. There may well have been some abstention of the middle class electorate in this year, although the grumble that 'our people' did not 'come out' to vote was a constant complaint by Conservatives and to a lesser extent Liberals in the declaration day speeches. Labour fell back in Burnley in 1920, its one gain being cancelled out by a loss to the Liberals. The following year Labour's share of the vote fell to 31 per cent, its lowest level between the wars, yet nevertheless it achieved two rather remarkable gains in 1921, in St Paul's and Trinity. St Paul's became a solid Labour ward in that year while Trinity was on the way to becoming one. With six net losses in 1922, though, the great advance of 1919 had been effectively reversed. The subsequent years down to 1929 saw only slow and gradual recovery. By 1928 Labour had ten councillors, still one less than it had had in 1921. The 1926 elections brought into clear relief a recurring problem for Labour, namely its lack of money to fight election campaigns. Although securing one gain amongst its four wins, Labour did not field any candidates against the Liberals that year. The reason was not because of any new amity or ideological affinity. Instead, as councillor Yates pointed out, celebrating his victory in Fulledge ward, the reason was a lack of hard cash. Supporting the General Strike, the local Labour party, said Yates, 'had made themselves responsible for the contributions of £20 a week to the miners' soup kitchens. They could not both feed and fight'.[70]

The year 1929 appeared to herald a new dawn for Labour, with four net gains bringing its total on the council to fifteen councillors, but the next two years were disappointing. The years 1930 and 1931 were years of disaster for Labour in most boroughs. The perception of Labour's handling of the national economy, followed

---

[70] *Burnley News*, 3 Nov. 1926.

by MacDonald's 'betrayal', coupled with the performance of the National Government, all told against Labour. In Burnley in Trinity ward, Labour blamed defeat in 1930 on unemployment and depression and the fact that the Labour government was getting the blame for this state of affairs.[71] The protest against Labour in Westminster however had only a limited effect on Labour's position on the council in Burnley, the party losing only one seat in both 1930 and again in 1931. To an extent this was due to the fact that Labour's unimpressive performance in Burnley in the 1920s meant that it did not have a large number of seats to defend in the early 1930s. Labour's overall share of the vote did nevertheless fall from near 50 per cent in 1929 to 42 per cent in 1930. That year the *Northern Daily Telegraph* trumpeted the 'Defeat of all Seven Socialists'.[72] But Labour's performance in 1931 saw some recovery. There were only four disputed wards, and 'little interest was taken in the contests',[73] but Labour's vote share recovered to its earlier level near 50 per cent. In two of its strongest wards Labour did exceptionally well in 1931. In St Paul's Labour held its seat with 54 per cent of the vote, having the previous year gained only 43 per cent and lost a seat to the Tories. There was a similar picture in St Peter's, with Labour holding its seat in 1931 and its vote recovering from 43 per cent to 54 per cent. There is no doubt that Labour's performance in Burnley in 1931 was relatively strong compared to nearly all the other boroughs examined in this series so far.

The years 1932–1935 proved exceptionally good for Labour in Burnley. In all contests the party won a total of 34 seats in those four years, compared to only eleven Liberal victories and a mere three for the Tories. There were twelve net gains for Labour between 1932 and 1934, propelling the party very rapidly into a position of power on the council. This is again an unusual pattern of development in Labour's strength, and requires some explanation. It is also worth noting the collapse of Tory support in this period. In the three years from 1932 to 1934 the Conservatives lost seven seats, leaving it as very much the third party on the council. It is interesting as well that having left the Burnley parliamentary seat to be contested by a National Liberal in 1931, the Tory party did not contest the seat in 1935, or for that matter in the first post-war election of 1945. The underlying strength of the Liberal tradition in Burnley, and the concomitant weakness of working-class Toryism, seems to have been especially emphasised in this period.

One possible cause of both the strong Labour showing in 1931 and the dramatic rise in Labour's support of 1932–35 may be the effect of the 'More Looms' dispute. The 'More Looms' dispute began in 1931, and rumbled on until the major lockout in the summer of 1932. The central issue of this dispute was an attempt by the mill owners to double the number of looms per weaver from four to eight, which partially slowed down the speed that the worker could operate. This industrial dispute was centred on Burnley, and had near total support from the weavers in north-east Lancashire.[74] The progress of the dispute was given

[71] *Burnley News*, 5 Nov. 1930.
[72] *Northern Daily Telegraph*, 3 Nov. 1930.
[73] *Northern Daily Telegraph*, 3 Nov. 1931.
[74] See Whittaker, B., *Review* of A. and L. Fowler, *The History of the Nelson Weavers' Association* and of Bullen, A., *The Lancashire Weavers' Union*, in *North West Labour History*, no. 10, (1984), pp. 60–62; Bruley, S., 'Women and Communism: a case study of

widespread coverage in the local press, and in 1932 in particular was a major issue at the same time as the November local elections were held.[75] The impact of the dispute on local politics must have been significant, although its precise nature is difficult to pinpoint. One consequence was an increased distrust of the workers involved for their full-time union officials, as many felt that the union did not represent them adequately through the dispute.[76] More generally, the lock-outs carried out by the employers to break the weavers' resistance must have engendered a great deal of bitterness in the locality. Heightened class consciousness was the result, and this may well have been an important factor in the rapid rise in Labour's support around this time, and also the decline in Burnley Conservatism. There is evidence too that the atmosphere surrounding the local elections of this period became more embittered, and class-based issues were stressed more strongly on all sides.[77]

For example, Labour had two important and emotive issues which they exploited with great effect in 1932: the Means Test and the government's 'false economy policy' as it was called in Burnley. Councillor Gradwell of St Paul's elaborated on both issues in a pre-election meeting, arguing that 'On both issues Labour had an over-whelming case against the government who by their actions had thrown a burden on the local rates'.[78] That same year Labour carried out a vigorous Press campaign, one of the high points being the advert in the *News* just before the November contests, hailing the electorate with: 'Smash the Means Test: VOTE LABOUR'.[79] While in many other boroughs there is evidence that Labour was becoming more moderate in its rhetoric and policies following the disasters of 1930–31, in Burnley the opposite seems to be the case. The electorate proved to be receptive to Labour's campaigns. There were contests in all twelve wards in 1932 for the first time in many years, and the Liberal-Conservative pact operated right across the borough. Thus the extent of the Labour victory was seen as a 'surprise' in the *Burnley News*. Two seismic events had occurred in the borough's politics. First, not one Conservative candidate was returned and second, Labour captured some bastions of Conservative and Liberal loyalty. With the strongly Conservative ward of Burnley Wood being gained, as well as the near solid Liberal St Andrew's, Labour in 1932 was cock-a-hoop.[80]

Labour's success continued in 1933 with five gains. It was the year too when for the first time the party achieved an overall majority of councillors over the other two parties combined. The election of Labour aldermen when vacancies occurred was now possible, giving Labour the opportunity to take overall control of the council. Even before that possibility arose, five more gains in the 1934

---

the Lancashire weavers in the depression', in Andrews, G., Fishman, N. and Morgan, K., (eds), *Opening the Books: Essays on the Social and Cultural History of the British Communist Party*, (London, 1995), pp. 64–82.

[75] See, for instance, the extensive coverage in *Burnley News*, 28 Oct. 1932.

[76] Whittaker, *Review*, p. 62.

[77] The stormy atmosphere of the time in the north-eastern Lancashire weaving towns is well described in Liddington, *The Life and Times of a Respectable Rebel*, pp. 357–383.

[78] *Burnley News*, 22 Oct. 1932.

[79] *Burnley News*, 29 Oct. 1932.

[80] *Burnley News*, 2 Nov. 1932.

elections gave Labour control. The tide began to turn in 1935, with Labour losing one of its gains from the breakthrough elections of three years previously. But after the November elections in 1935, five non-Labour aldermen were swept out, strongly bolstering Labour's position on the council.

Other examples of the bold policies Labour put forward in its rise to power in Burnley can be identified. The year before securing outright control of the council chamber, Labour carried a large advert in the *News* on behalf of their twelve candidates in the forthcoming election. It promised higher expenditure on school milk and meals, nourishment for expectant mothers, the provision of more nursery schools and lastly, the construction of more council houses. Disparaging services in the hands of the private sector, Labour implied rather than promised a greater role for municipal or public enterprise.[81] However, mindful of the concerns of middle-class rate-paying voters, after the elections the victorious Labour candidate in St Andrew's ward argued that some parts of Labour's ideals could be enacted when power was achieved 'without increasing the rates'.[82]

The construction of council houses and the use of direct labour were two central policies of Labour in Burnley, often linked together with the construction of new estates being carried out by a direct labour force. While in opposition Labour had criticised the contracting of private builders for council house construction. For example, on the Housing Committee in 1929 Labour councillors Lynch (St Peter's) and Whittaker (Gannow) advocated the use of direct labour for the construction of 176 houses to be built on four different sites. Lynch cited the examples of Yarmouth and Clithero where, he claimed, costs per unit were brought down by the use of direct labour. He also quoted Sir Alfred Mond (Lord Melchett) in parliament stating that municipal works departments kept tenders down. The Liberal alderman J.H. Grey poured scorn on this idea, and the direct works proposal was defeated for the time being.[83]

The borough built 2,140 council houses in the inter-war years up to the end of March 1939. In the ranking of council house construction shown in Appendix 16, Burnley came fifty-sixth out of the eighty-three county boroughs. With one council house built in the period for every forty-six people, the council's achievements were comparatively modest. Sub-standard housing and slum conditions were a fact of life in most of the county boroughs, especially those which had experienced early industrialisation. In this respect Burnley was no exception and Labour in opposition made housing an issue in election after election. As early as 1919, for instance, Labour was promising 1,000 new homes, rather than the 500 planned by the existing council. Labour reasoned that the additional houses would cost only an extra 1d. on the rates.[84] The issue reoccurred year after year, culminating in the especially contentious elections of 1932. Responding to fierce Labour criticism of their housing policies, the ruling Conservatives, backed by the Liberals, announced sixty new council houses, to be situated on land abutting Casterton Avenue in the solidly Liberal St Andrew's ward.[85] A Labour councillor responded, advocating

[81] *Burnley News*, 1 Nov. 1933.
[82] *Burnley News*, 4 Nov. 1933.
[83] *Burnley News*, 2 Nov. 1929.
[84] *Express and Advertiser*, 25 Oct. 1919.
[85] *Burnley News*, 26 Oct. 1932.

'slum clearance which would provide better homes for the people, and also be a means of providing for building trade operatives'.[86] By 1938, after it had been in power, the Labour party was proudly boasting that 'we have built over a thousand houses since we took over in 1934. People have been rehoused on beautiful estates'.[87] In their four years in power Labour had constructed approximately 50 per cent of all council houses built in Burnley between the wars.

One other area of expansive and innovative policies that the Labour council promoted in Burnley was in the use of public funds to attract firms and employment to the borough. The most successful example of this was the construction in 1935 of a large factory manufacturing cutlery and kitchen-ware which occupied most of Thursby Gardens. The American firm of Platers and Stampers had been attracted to the borough, and the factory, partly funded by the rates and opening in 1937, eventually became the Prestige works, remaining an important employer well into the post-1945 era.[88]

Despite its claimed successes while in office in Burnley, as in many other boroughs Labour went into a period of declining support in the late 1930s, suffering seven net losses between 1936 and 1938. Its aldermanic strength meant it was able to cling on to power until 1938, but the five losses of that year saw Labour deposed. However, it did not lose its position as the single largest party, as it did in other boroughs such as Hull, Bristol and Sunderland.[89] There is evidence that the bold policies Labour adopted in the early and mid-1930s became its Achilles heel later in the decade. Given the economic difficulties that beset local industry and the embittered atmosphere after the 'More Looms' dispute, Labour's more interventionist approach plainly had won support for a while. Labour had been willing to push up the rates in order to spend locally on alleviating unemployment, trying to attract new industries, building more council houses and increasing the use of direct labour. Attacks on Labour by its opponents as the high-spending party were, as pointed out above, commonplace throughout the inter-war years. In the 1938 elections, however, Conservatives and Liberals mounted an especially virulent campaign over this issue. Labour having been in power for four years, it was now possible for its opponents to attack its record while in office. In 1938 Labour proposed an additional charge of £17,000 a year on the rates, the equivalent of 6d in the £. Labour's proposed 1938–39 expenditure plans were for street and hospital improvements, including a children's hospital, slum clearance, recreational facilities and a new drainage system. This it was hoped would provide local employment for 'at least three or four years'.[90] The press, in stating the anti-Labour position immediately before the election, put it starkly. After the usual calls for the Liberals and Conservatives to unite, the *Express* stated that 'now is the time for strict control of Council expenditure. Insist on the Council cutting its coat according to its cloth'.[91] An unusual slant was also put on the extension of

---

[86] *Burnley News*, 22 Oct. 1932.
[87] *Express and Advertiser*, 26 Oct. 1938.
[88] Hall, *Burnley*, p. 38 and Frost, *Top o' th' Town*, p. 35.
[89] Cook, C., 'Liberals, Labour and local elections', in Peele, G. and Cook, C., (eds), *The Politics of Re-Appraisal, 1918–1939*, (London, 1975), p. 176.
[90] *Express and News*, 26 Oct. 1938.
[91] *Express and News*, 26 Oct. 1938.

council housing that had taken place under Labour. The combined anti-Labour alliance called for an end to housing estates on the outskirts of the town as 'they increase workers' 'bus fares and expenses. Why not re-house on cleared central sites?'.[92]

Given the widespread trend against Labour in other boroughs in 1938, it is difficult to establish the precise extent to which this anti-Labour campaign hit Labour in Burnley. For its opponents locally there was no doubt, however. After the rout of Labour, the *Express* headline exclaimed: 'Burnley Votes for Reduced Municipal Spending'. Councillor Parkinson, the Conservative leader of the council went even further in a triumphal meeting at Fulledge Conservative Club:

> Time after time, when they had urged economy on schemes involving great expenditure, they had been told that the Socialists had a mandate from the people. He never thought they had a mandate to go on with these extravagant schemes, and these elections had proved him right. The Socialists wanted a housing programme with 12 houses to the acre. Where were the houses going to be built under a nonsensical policy of that kind?
> The education programme was equally ridiculous. Half the school accommodation in the town was not being used, yet they insisted on building more new schools at the expense of the ratepayers. It was time that the Socialists had a rude awakening, and he could assure them that the anti-Socialists would not abuse the trust which the ratepayers had placed in them.[93]

It is necessary finally to consider the role of women in municipal politics in Burnley. It seems that women played an insignificant part on all sides in the electoral contests between the wars. Moreover, issues perceived as especially significant to women voters (such as health and child welfare) were not strongly emphasised in local elections, certainly as far as press coverage was concerned. This is surprising considering the vital role women played in the local economy, and the high degree of unionisation amongst women in the weaving industry. It is even more puzzling given the near proximity of 'red' Nelson, where the activities of militant women activists has been well documented.[94] Nevertheless, despite the huge female labour force in textiles, Burnley in its politics appeared to be very much a typically 'male' northern industrial borough, with traditional patriarchal attitudes towards the role of women in politics and society seeming to predominate. All told there were only seventeen female candidates in the period, registering eleven successes out of twenty-six contests for the council. In 1924, Mrs Marie Brown for the Conservatives, was the first woman elected to the council, achieving the breakthrough in Whittlefield. In total three women won seats on the council for the Tories. Labour fielded a woman candidate in only twelve contests, and had only one woman, Miss Gillespie, elected twice in the 1930s in Gannow ward. The Liberals put up three female candidates in the twenty-

[92] *Express and Advertiser*, 26 Oct. 1938.
[93] *Express and News*, 2 Nov. 1938.
[94] See Liddington, *The Life and Times of A Respectable Rebel*.

year period, being successful on two occasions in Stoneyholme (1931) and Healey (1937). There were also two women who stood unsuccessfully for the ILG and the Communists. All in all, only six women were elected to Burnley council in the whole inter-war period. In conclusion, it must be said that a deeper analysis of working-class politics and trade unionism in Burnley, similar to that carried out by Michael Savage for Preston, might reveal a greater involvement of women.[95]

To conclude, what were the defining features of the inter-war politics of Burnley? The relatively late development of this cotton-weaving town, its geographical isolation from the heart of cotton Lancashire, and the influence of the nearby Nonconformist tradition of the West Riding of Yorkshire, all seemed to help make Burnley distinctive. The relative absence of long-established attitudes of working-class Toryism goes some way to explaining Labour's strength here in the unpropitious soil of textile Lancashire. Liberalism survived in the inter-war years, but only by entering an alliance with Tories. There was a radical tradition in the town, and Labour was able to build on that tradition and establish a significant presence before 1914. In the inter-war years this was further developed, especially after the More Looms disputes in the early 1930s which appear to have soured employer-worker relations and increased class-combativity. Labour therefore experienced a surge of support allowing it to take control of the council, while it also appeared to have adopted a relatively radical stance at this time that seems to have suited the mood of working-class voters in the town. Nevertheless the decline of support for Labour in the late 1930s that has been noted in many other boroughs in these volumes also manifested itself in Burnley. Labour's own record of bold and expansive policies was turned against it, and the town was returned to Liberal–Tory control before war intervened.

---

[95] See Savage, M., *The Dynamics of Working-Class Politics: The Labour Movement in Preston 1880–1940*, (Cambridge, 1987). Savage argues that a shift by Labour in Preston to a more neighbourhood-based politics took place in the late-1920s. This was in part as a consequence of greater women's involvement in the party, and resulted in significant Labour gains electorally.

A guide to further reading

Newspapers

Burnley News, 1919–34
Express and Advertiser, 1919–34
Express and News, 1935–38
Manchester Guardian, 1919–38
Northern Daily Telegraph, 1919–38

Other secondary sources

Bennet, W., *The History of Burnley Part 3, 1650–1850*, (Burnley, 1948).

Bruley, S., 'Women and Communism: a case study of the Lancashire weavers in the depression', in Andrews, G., Fishman, N. and Morgan, K., (eds), *Opening the Books: Essays on the Social and Cultural History of the British Communist Party*, (London, 1995), pp. 64–82.

Chew, L. 'Dan Irving and Socialist politics in Burnley', *North West Labour History*, no. 23, (1998/99).

Davies, S. and Morley, B., *County Borough Elections in England and Wales, 1919–1938: A Comparative Analysis*, vol. 1, (Aldershot, 1999).

Douglas, A., *Burnley: Once Upon a Time*, (Nelson, 1976).

Fogarty, M.P., *Prospects of the Industrial Areas of Great Britain*, (London, 1945).

Freeman, T.W., *The Conurbations of Great Britain*, (Manchester, 1959).

Frost, R., *Top o' th' Town Burnley*, (Burnley, 1981).

Hall, B., *Burnley: A Short History*, (Burnley, 1977).

Hall, B. and Spencer, K., *Burnley: A Pictorial History*, (Chichester, 1993).

Hill, J., 'Lib–Labism, socialism and Labour in Burnley, c. 1890–1918', *Northern History*, vol. 35, (1999), pp. 185–204.

Howell, D., *British Workers and the Independent Labour Party, 1888–1906*, (Manchester, 1983), ch. 3.

Howell, D., *The Politics of the NUM: A Lancashire View*, (Manchester, 1989).

Joyce, P., *Work, Society and Politics: The Culture of the Factory in Later Victorian England*, (London, 1982).

Liddington, J. and Norris, J., *One Hand Tied Behind Us: The Rise of the Women's Suffrage Movement*, (London, 1978).

Liddington, J., *The Life and Times of a Respectable Rebel: Selina Cooper (1864–1946)*, (London, 1984).

Lowe, J., *Burnley*, (Chichester, 1985).

Pelling, H., *Social Geography of British Elections 1885–1910*, (Aldershot, 1994).

Savage, M., *The Dynamics of Working-Class Politics: The Labour Movement in Preston 1880–1940*, (Cambridge, 1987).

Trodd, G., 'Political Change and the Working Class in Blackburn and Burnley, 1880–1914', (Ph.D. thesis, University of Lancaster, 1978).

Walton, J.K., *Lancashire: A Social History, 1558–1939*, (Manchester, 1987).

White, J.L., *The Limits of Trade Union Militancy: The Lancashire Textile Workers 1900–1914*, (London, 1978).

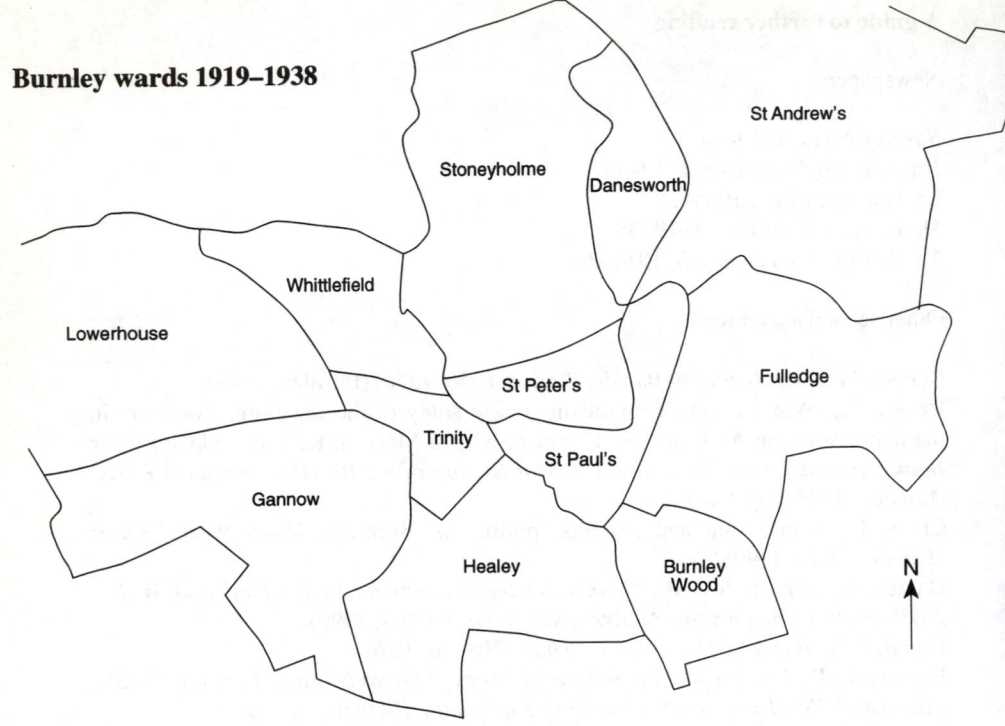

Burnley wards 1919–1938

St Andrew's

Stoneyholme

Danesworth

Whittlefield

Lowerhouse

St Peter's

Fulledge

Trinity

St Paul's

Gannow

Healey

Burnley Wood

N

Persons aged fourteen and over classified by industry 1931

	Male	%	Female	%	Total	%
Mining	3,253	9.6	10	0.0	3,263	5.4
Metal and engineering	2,784	8.2	175	0.7	2,959	4.9
- Engineering	*1,517*	*4.5*	*87*	*0.3*	*1,604*	*2.7*
Textiles	11,199	32.9	19,036	73.4	30,235	50.4
- Cotton	*10,698*	*31.4*	*18,852*	*72.7*	*29,550*	*49.3*
Transport	2,129	6.3	24	0.1	2,153	3.6
- Road	*1,391*	*4.1*	*10*	*0.0*	*1,401*	*2.3*
Commerce and finance	4,820	14.2	1,802	6.9	6,622	11.0
Public admin and defence	2,128	6.3	768	3.0	2,896	4.8
- Local government	*1,785*	*5.2*	*645*	*2.5*	*2,430*	*4.1*
Personal service	940	2.8	2,008	7.7	2,948	4.9
Others	6,776	19.9	2,108	8.1	8,884	14.8
Total (a)	**34,029**		**25,931**		**59,960**	
Total population (b)	45,978		52,280		98,258	
(a) as % of (b)	74.0		49.6		61.0	
Total out of work (c)	6,785		7,649		14,434	
(c) as % of (a)	19.9		29.5		24.1	
Managerial and own account	3,914	14.4	1,221	6.7	5,135	11.3
Operative	23,330	85.6	17,061	93.3	40,391	88.7
Total (excluding out of work)	27,244		18,282		45,526	

Population statistics 1931

Ward	Acres	Population	Persons/acre	Persons/room
Burnley Wood	360	8,102	22.5	0.82
Daneshouse	140	7,535	53.8	0.84
Fulledge	742	10,059	13.6	0.86
Gannow	476	10,762	22.6	0.90
Healey	463	8,797	19.0	0.77
Lowerhouse	517	9,970	19.3	0.83
St Andrew's	835	15,370	18.4	0.79
St Paul's	156	5,162	33.1	1.03
St Peter's	113	5,249	46.5	1.00
Stoneyholme	547	5,470	10.0	0.82
Trinity	91	6,796	74.7	0.90
Whittlefield	246	4,986	20.3	0.84
Total	**4,686**	**98,258**	**21.0**	**0.85**

Overall position on the council 1919–38

	Position			Gains			Losses		
	C	L	Lab	C	L	Lab	C	L	Lab
1919	21	18	9	0	0	6	4	2	0
1920	20	19	9	0	1	1	1	0	1
1921	18	19	11	0	0	2	2	0	0
1922[a]	22	20	5	5	2	1	1	0	7
1923	22	21	5	1	0	1	1	0	1
1924	21	21	6	0	0	1	1	0	0
1925[a]	20	19	8	0	0	1	1	0	0
1926	19	20	9	0	0	1	1	0	0
1927	20	20	8	1	0	0	0	0	1
1928	18	20	10	0	0	2	2	0	0
1929	17	16	15	1	0	5	2	3	1
1930	18	16	14	1	0	0	0	0	1
1931	19	16	13	1	0	0	0	0	1
1932	17	16	15	0	0	2	2	0	0
1933	12	15	21	0	0	5	4	1	0
1934	9	13	26	0	0	5	3	2	0
1935	9	13	26	0	1	0	0	0	1
1936[a]	7	13	27	1	1	0	0	0	2
1937	7	13	28	0	0	0	0	0	0
1938	11	14	23	4	1	0	0	0	5

Aldermen, 1919–38

1919	6-C;6-L		1929	C-6;L-5;Lab-1
1920	6-C;6-L		1930	C-6;L-5;Lab-1
1921	6-C;6-L		1931	C-6;L-5;Lab-1
1922[a]	6-C;5-L		1932	C-6;L-5;Lab-1
1923	6-C;6-L		1933	C-6;L-5;Lab-1
1924	6-C;6-L		1934	C-6;L-5;Lab-1
1925[a]	6-C;5-L		1935	C-6;L-4;Lab-2
1926	6-C;6-L		1936[a]	C-1;L-3;Lab-7
1927	6-C;6-L		1937	C-1;L-3;Lab-8
1928	6-C;6-L		1938	C-1;L-2;Lab-9

[a] One aldermanic seat vacant, 1922; 1925; 1936

Municipal elections: winning party 1919–28

Ward	1919	1920	1921	1922	1923	1924	1925	1926	1927	1928
Burnley Wood	Lab	C	C	L	**C**	C	L	C	C	**L**
Daneshouse	Lab	L	L	L	**L**	L	L	**L**	L	**L**
Fulledge	Lab	C	C	C	C	C	C	Lab	C	**C**
Gannow	**Lab**	Lab	C	C	C	Lab	C	C	Lab	Lab
Healey	L	L	L	L	**L**	L	**L**	**L**	L	**L**
Lowerhouse	Lab	L	L	C	L	L	C	**L**	**L**	**C**
St Andrew's	L	L	L	**L**	L	**L**	**L**	**L**	**L**	**L**
St Paul's	Lab	Lab	Lab	C	Lab	Lab	Lab	Lab	Lab	Lab
St Peter's	Lab	L	C	C	L	C	C	Lab	C	Lab
Stoneyholme	L	C	C	**L**	C	C	L	**C**	C	**L**
Trinity	C	C	Lab	Lab	Lab	Lab	Lab	Lab	C	Lab
Whittlefield	C	L	C	C	L	C	C	**L**	C	**C**

Municipal elections: party wins per year 1919–28

	1919	1920	1921	1922	1923	1924	1925	1926	1927	1928
C	2	4	6	6	4	5	5	3	6	3
Lab	7	2	2	1	2	3	2	4	2	4
L	3	6	4	5	6	4	5	5	4	5
Total	12	12	12	12	12	12	12	12	12	12
Turnout %	59.4	69.6	66.0	70.7	69.5	68.0	73.9	76.2	72.2	72.1
Labour %	48.1	41.0	31.2	42.9	43.4	44.6	46.5	49.4	44.9	56.5

Municipal elections: winning party 1929–38

Ward	1929	1930	1931	1932	1933	1934	1935	1936	1937	1938
Burnley Wood	C	C	**L**	Lab	Lab	L	Lab	Lab	**L**	C
Daneshouse	Lab	L	**L**	Lab	L	Lab	Lab	L	Lab	L
Fulledge	C	**C**	**C**	Lab	C	C	Lab	C	**C**	C
Gannow	Lab	**Lab**	**Lab**	Lab	Lab	Lab	Lab	**Lab**	**Lab**	Lab
Healey	**L**	**L**	**L**	L	L	L	L	L	**L**	**L**
Lowerhouse	Lab	L	**C**	Lab	Lab	Lab	**Lab**	Lab	**Lab**	C
St Andrew's	Lab	**L**	**L**	Lab	L	L	L	L	**L**	L
St Paul's	Lab	C	Lab	Lab	Lab	Lab	Lab	L	Lab	C
St Peter's	**Lab**	C	Lab	Lab	Lab	Lab	Lab	Lab	Lab	C
Stoneyholme	Lab	C	L	Lab	Lab	Lab	**Lab**	C	Lab	C
Trinity	Lab	C	C	Lab	Lab	Lab	Lab	Lab	Lab	C
Whittlefield	L	**C**	**C**	L	C	Lab	L	C	Lab	L

Municipal elections: party wins per year 1929–38

	1929	1930	1931	1932	1933	1934	1935	1936	1937	1938
C	2	7	4	0	2	1	0	3	1	7
Lab	8	1	3	10	7	8	9	5	8	1
L	2	4	5	2	3	3	3	4	3	4
Total	12	12	12	12	12	12	12	12	12	12
Turnout %	60.0	65.1	74.5	67.2	64.0	72.6	63.4	69.8	72.7	67.6
Labour %	49.7	42.1	49.3	54.4	54.0	52.8	52.8	42.8	52.7	43.0

Municipal elections: party wins per ward 1919–38

	C	L	Lab	Total	Turnout %	Labour % of all votes
Burnley Wood	9	6	5	20	73.9	47.7
Daneshouse	0	14	6	20	68.1	43.1
Fulledge	16	0	4	20	66.5	45.6
Gannow	5	0	15	20	61.8	56.6
Healey	0	20	0	20	62.3	25.0
Lowerhouse	5	7	8	20	67.4	48.9
St Andrew's	0	18	2	20	64.7	42.9
St Paul's	3	1	16	20	71.4	54.1
St Peter's	7	2	11	20	69.9	49.5
Stoneyholme	9	5	6	20	67.4	46.5
Trinity	6	0	14	20	72.9	51.7
Whittlefield	11	7	2	20	70.7	42.7
Total	**71**	**80**	**89**	**240**	**67.9**	**46.7**

Seats won by Labour as a percentage of all wins 1919–38   **37.1**

Parliamentary election results

Burnley constituency
*(all wards within the borough [1918 boundaries] were included in the
constituency)*

General election	Winner	Conservative %	Labour %	Liberal %
14 Dec. 1918	Lab	33.8 (Co C)	41.9	24.3
15 Nov. 1922	Lab	33.1	39.1	27.8
6 Dec. 1923	Lab	31.8	37.8	30.4
29 Oct. 1924	Lab	35.6	45.4	19.0
30 May 1929	Lab	33.2	46.2	20.6
27 Oct. 1931[a]	NL	-	43.0	56.2 (NL)
14 Nov. 1935	Lab	-	53.6	46.4 (NL)

[a] In 1931 a Communist candidate received 0.8% of the votes cast.

Burnley Wood ward

Candidate	Party	Votes	%	Electors	Turnout	Gains
1919						
J.A. Sampson	Lab	1,490	56.6	3,602	73.1	Lab from L
W. Morris	L	1,144	43.4			
Total votes		2,634				
1920						
W.F. Witham*	C	1,759	60.7	3,676	78.8	-
I. Eastham	Lab	1,139	39.3			
Total votes .		2,898				
1921						
J.T. Westall	C	1,588	58.3	3,695	73.7	-
J.W. Tomlinson	Lab	1,135	41.7			
Total votes		2,723				
1922						
W. Morris	L	1,475	51.8	3,642	78.2	L from Lab
J.A. Sampson*	Lab	1,372	48.2			
Total votes		2,847				
1923						
W.F. Witham*	C	Unopp.	-	3,709	-	-
1924						
J.T. Westall*	C	1,475	53.6	3,680	74.8	-
T. Harker	Lab	1,278	46.4			
Total votes		2,753				
1925						
J.H. Bracewell	L	1,591	56.5	3,714	75.8	-
T. Harker	Lab	1,224	43.5			
Total votes		2,815				
1926						
W.F. Witham*	C	1,653	56.1	3,745	78.7	-
H. Howarth	Lab	1,293	43.9			
Total votes		2,946				

Burnley Wood ward *(continued)*

Candidate	Party	Votes	%	Electors	Turnout	Gains
1927						
G.H. Heys*	C	1,501	52.8	3,751	75.8	-
J.R. Tomlinson	Lab	1,342	47.2			
Total votes		2,843				
1928						
J.H. Bracewell*	L	Unopp.	-		-	-
1929						
W.F. Witham*	C	1,353	53.0	3,992	63.9	-
Mrs M.H.	Lab	1,198	47.0			
Greenwood						
Total votes		2,551				
1930						
G.H. Heys*	C	1,550	55.8	4,009	69.3	-
A.E. Perry	Lab	1,228	44.2			
Total votes		2,778				
1931						
J.H. Bracewell*	L	Unopp.	-		-	-
1932						
H. Howarth	Lab	1,469	54.0	3,975	68.4	Lab from C
A. Ashworth	C	1,251	46.0			
Total votes		2,720				
1933						
H.J. Williams	Lab	1,475	54.1	3,983	68.5	Lab from C
G.H. Heys*	C	1,253	45.9			
Total votes		2,728				
1934						
J.H. Bracewell*	L	1,684	52.4	3,985	80.7	-
T. Harker	Lab	1,532	47.6			
Total votes		3,216				

Burnley Wood ward *(continued)*

Candidate	Party	Votes	%	Electors	Turnout	Gains
1935						
H. Howarth*	Lab	1,698	54.2	4,027	77.8	-
J.E. Hopper	C	1,435	45.8			
Total votes		3,133				
1936						
H.J. Williams*	Lab	1,481	50.8	3,997	72.9	-
W.E. Smith	C	1,433	49.2			
Total votes		2,914				
1937						
J.H. Bracewell*	L	Unopp.	-	3,957	-	-
1938						
W.E. Smith	C	1,592	55.1	3,932	73.5	C from Lab
H. Haworth*	Lab	1,299	44.9			
Total votes		2,891				

Overall Labour vote	**47.7%**		**Overall turnout**	**73.9%**

Daneshouse ward

Candidate	Party	Votes	%	Electors	Turnout	Gains
1919						
W. Eastwood	Lab	997	43.7	3,361	67.9	Lab from L
P. Heap	L	916	40.1			
T. Coates	C	369	16.2			
Total votes		2,282				
1920						
J.H. Grey*	L	1,843	74.5	3,413	72.5	-
H. Holden	Lab	632	25.5			
Total votes		2,475				
1921						
A. Green	L	1,494	73.4	3,460	58.8	-
Mrs E.E. Riley	ILG	541	26.6			
Total votes		2,035				

(ILG = Independent Labour Group, a Communist/NUWM grouping)

Candidate	Party	Votes	%	Electors	Turnout	Gains
1922						
J.T. Clegg	L	1,467	58.6	3,420	73.2	L from Lab
W. Eastwood*	Lab	1,038	41.4			
Total votes		2,505				
1923						
H. Fitzpatrick*	L	Unopp. -		3,492 -		-
1924						
A. Green*	L	1,283	56.9	3,451	65.3	-
R. Broadley	Lab	970	43.1			
Total votes		2,253				
1925						
J.T. Clegg*	L	1,315	54.3	3,483	69.5	-
Mrs E. Poppleton	Lab	1,105	45.7			
Total votes		2,420				
1926						
G. Duxbury*	L	Unopp. -		3,504 -		-

Daneshouse ward *(continued)*

Candidate	Party	Votes	%	Electors	Turnout	Gains
1927						
A. Green*	L	1,336	54.1	3,530	70.0	-
Mrs E. Poppleton	Lab	1,135	45.9			
Total votes		2,471				
1928						
J.T. Clegg*	L	Unopp.	-		-	-
1929						
H. Hargreaves	Lab	1,091	51.7	3,818	55.2	Lab from L
G. Duxbury*	L	1,018	48.3			
Total votes		2,109				
1930						
A. Green*	L	1,482	65.8	3,826	58.9	-
W. Stansfield	Lab	770	34.2			
Total votes		2,252				
1931						
J.T. Clegg*	L	Unopp.	-		-	-
1932						
H. Hargreaves*	Lab	1,405	55.2	3,766	67.6	-
A. Bullock	L	1,141	44.8			
Total votes		2,546				
1933						
A. Green*	L	1,418	53.7	3,768	70.1	-
Mrs M.A. Harpin	Lab	1,224	46.3			
Total votes		2,642				
1934						
J. Herbert	Lab	1,425	53.0	3,702	72.7	Lab from L
J.T. Clegg*	L	1,265	47.0			
Total votes		2,690				
1935						
H. Hargreaves*	Lab	1,548	58.0	3,712	71.8	-
Mrs W.H. Watson	L	1,119	42.0			
Total votes		2,667				

Daneshouse ward (*continued*)

Candidate	Party	Votes	%	Electors	Turnout	Gains
1936						
A. Green*	L	1,583	61.3	3,689	70.0	-
E. Halsall	Lab	1,000	38.7			
Total votes		2,583				
1937						
J. Herbert*	Lab	1,428	52.8	3,676	73.6	-
J. Lancaster	C	1,277	47.2			
Total votes		2,705				
1938						
J. Lancaster	L	1,489	55.7	3,656	73.2	L from Lab
H. Hargreaves*	Lab	1,186	44.3			
Total votes		2,675				

Overall Labour vote   **43.1%**   **Overall turnout**   **68.1%**

Fulledge ward

Candidate	Party	Votes	%	Electors	Turnout	Gains
1919						
J.T. Howson	Lab	1,057	52.8	4,231	47.3	Lab from C
J. Sutcliffe	C	945	47.2			
Total votes		2,002				
1920						
J.F. Walmsley*	C	1,846	58.5	4,362	72.4	-
J.W. Tomlinson	Lab	1,310	41.5			
Total votes		3,156				
1921						
A.W. Roberts	C	2,034	66.1	4,326	71.1	-
F. Robinson	Lab	1,043	33.9			
Total votes		3,077				
1922						
D. Burkin	C	1,644	61.7	4,292	62.0	C from Lab
J.T. Howson*	Lab	1,019	38.3			
Total votes		2,663				
1923						
J.H. Clegg	C	1,517	53.9	4,321	65.1	-
J.W. Tomlinson	Lab	1,297	46.1			
Total votes		2,814				
1924						
A.W. Roberts*	C	1,638	57.5	4,297	66.3	-
J.W. Tomlinson	Lab	1,212	42.5			
Total votes		2,850				
1925						
G. Parkinson*	C	1,681	54.5	4,303	71.6	-
J.S. Yates	Lab	1,402	45.5			
Total votes		3,083				
1926						
J.S. Yates	Lab	1,504	51.2	4,329	67.8	Lab from C
J.H. Clegg*	C	1,431	48.8			
Total votes		2,935				

Fulledge ward *(continued)*

Candidate	Party	Votes	%	Electors	Turnout	Gains
1927						
A.W. Roberts*	C	1,714	59.4	4,329	66.6	-
H.W. Graves	Lab	1,171	40.6			
Total votes		2,885				
1928						
G. Parkinson*	C	Unopp.	-		-	-
1929						
Dr H. Chadwick	C	1,561	55.8	4,650	60.2	C from Lab
J.F. Yates*	Lab	1,236	44.2			
Total votes		2,797				
1930						
A.W. Roberts*	C	Unopp.	-		-	-
1931						
G. Parkinson*	C	Unopp.	-		-	-
1932						
J.S. Yates	Lab	1,646	55.2	4,644	64.2	Lab from C
D. Summers	C	1,334	44.8			
Total votes		2,980				
1933						
A.W. Roberts*	C	1,423	50.0	4,638	61.3	-
Mrs M. Williams	Lab	1,422	50.0			
Total votes		2,845				
1934						
G. Parkinson*	C	1,861	51.4	4,655	77.7	-
Mrs M. Williams	Lab	1,746	48.2			
E.T. Latham	UEA	12	0.3			
Total votes		3,619				

(UEA = Unemployed Electoral Association, a Communist/NUWM grouping)

Candidate	Party	Votes	%	Electors	Turnout	Gains
1935						
J.S. Yates*	Lab	1,759	54.7	4,685	68.6	-
W.A. Hartley	C	1,454	45.3			
Total votes		3,213				

Fulledge ward (*continued*)

Candidate	Party	Votes	%	Electors	Turnout	Gains
1936						
P.J.H. Cobb	C	1,807	52.6	4,712	73.0	-
Mrs M. Williams	Lab	1,631	47.4			
Total votes		3,438				
1937						
G. Parkinson*	C	Unopp.	-	4,793	-	-
1938						
A. Webster	C	1,979	61.2	4,835	66.8	C from Lab
J.S. Yates*	Lab	1,253	38.8			
Total votes		3,232				

Overall Labour vote   **45.6%**   **Overall turnout**   **66.5%**

Gannow ward

Candidate	Party	Votes	%	Electors	Turnout	Gains
1919						
D.D. Irving MP*	Lab	Unopp.	-	3,906	-	-
1920						
L. Rippon*	Lab	1,358	57.6	3,943	59.8	-
J. Fearing	C	998	42.4			
Total votes		2,356				
1921						
R. Newbold	C	1,255	56.2	4,006	55.8	-
J. Hayes	Lab	979	43.8			
Total votes		2,234				
1922						
W.A. Hartley	C	1,288	51.5	3,934	63.6	C from Lab
D.D. Irving MP*	Lab	1,214	48.5			
Total votes		2,502				
1923						
W. Holden	C	1,396	52.1	3,959	67.7	C from Lab
L. Rippon*	Lab	1,285	47.9			
Total votes		2,681				
1924						
L. Rippon	Lab	1,325	52.2	3,946	64.4	Lab from C
R. Newbold*	C	1,215	47.8			
Total votes		2,540				
1925						
W.A. Hartley*	C	1,420	50.6	3,966	70.7	-
W. Bradley	Lab	1,385	49.4			
Total votes		2,805				
1926						
W. Holden*	C	1,600	50.7	3,993	79.0	-
W. Bradley	Lab	1,553	49.3			
Total votes		3,153				

Gannow ward *(continued)*

Candidate	Party	Votes	%	Electors	Turnout	Gains
1927						
L. Rippon*	Lab	1,448	50.4	4,031	71.3	-
C.C. Pollard	C	1,425	49.6			
Total votes		2,873				
1928						
J.R. Tomlinson	Lab	1,641	52.5	4,335	72.1	Lab from C
W.A. Hartley*	C	1,485	47.5			
Total votes		3,126				
1929						
E. Whittaker	Lab	1,737	62.9	4,730	58.4	-
J.T. Lee	C	1,023	37.1			
Total votes		2,760				
1930						
L. Rippon*	Lab	Unopp.	-		-	-
1931						
J.R. Tomlinson*	Lab	Unopp.	-		-	-
1932						
E. Whittaker*	Lab	2,155	59.4	5,190	69.9	-
J.E. Wigglesworth	C	1,475	40.6			
Total votes		3,630				
1933						
L. Rippon*	Lab	1,978	94.9	5,226	39.9	-
J. Bibby	Com	107	5.1			
Total votes		2,085				
1934						
J.R. Tomlinson*	Lab	Unopp.	-		-	-
1935						
Miss M. Gillespie*	Lab	1,864	90.0	5,422	38.2	-
W.H. Yates	ILP	208	10.0			
Total votes		2,072				

Gannow ward *(continued)*

Candidate	Party	Votes	%	Electors	Turnout	Gains
1936						
H.V. Oakes*	Lab	Unopp.	-	5,812	-	-
1937						
F. Rycroft	Lab	Unopp.	-	6,119	-	-
1938						
Miss M. Gillespie*	Lab	2,137	51.8	6,330	65.2	-
G.H. Law	C	1,991	48.2			
Total votes		4,128				

Overall Labour vote   **56.6%**   **Overall turnout**   **61.8%**

Healey ward

Candidate	Party	Votes	%	Electors	Turnout	Gains
1919						
H. Dickinson	L	1,371	63.8	3,272	65.7	-
W. Howarth	Lab	778	36.2			
Total votes		2,149				
1920						
L. Thornber*	L	1,827	70.8	3,376	76.5	-
T. Brown	Lab	755	29.2			
Total votes·		2,582				
1921						
H.R. Nuttall*	L	1,865	88.0	3,416	62.1	-
H. Archer	ILG	255	12.0			
Total votes		2,120				

(ILG = Independent Labour Group, a Communist/NUWM grouping)

Candidate	Party	Votes	%	Electors	Turnout	Gains
1922						
R. Taylor	L	1,702	74.0	3,714	61.9	-
J.W. Tomlinson	Lab	597	26.0			
Total votes		2,299				
1923						
L. Thornber*	L	Unopp.	-	3,848	-	-
1924						
H.R. Nuttall*	L	1,591	69.8	3,841	59.4	-
W. Williams	Lab	689	30.2			
Total votes		2,280				
1925						
R. Taylor*	L	Unopp.	-	3,879	-	-
1926						
J. Thornber*	L	Unopp.	-	3,926	-	-
1927						
S. Taylor*	L	1,823	68.8	3,933	67.4	-
J.H. Kerin	Lab	828	31.2			
Total votes		2,651				

Healey ward *(continued)*

Candidate	Party	Votes	%	Electors	Turnout	Gains
1928						
F.A. Simpson*	L	Unopp.	-		-	-
1929						
J. Thornber*	L	Unopp.	-		-	-
1930						
S. Taylor*	L	Unopp.	-		-	-
1931						
L. Smith	L	Unopp.	-		-	-
1932						
J. Thornber*	L	1,881	65.9	4,456	64.1	-
T.M. Walters	Lab	974	34.1			
Total votes		2,855				
1933						
S. Taylor*	L	1,683	60.6	4,455	62.3	-
J.A. Smith	Lab	1,094	39.4			
Total votes		2,777				
1934						
L. Smith*	L	1,842	61.0	4,448	67.9	-
J.A. Smith	Lab	1,178	39.0			
Total votes		3,020				
1935						
J. Howarth	L	1,639	82.7	4,685	42.3	-
J.R. Strutt	ILP	344	17.3			
Total votes		1,983				
1936						
S. Taylor*	L	1,373	48.7	4,603	61.3	-
P. Freeman-Lee	C	1,054	37.4			
E. Regan	Com	393	13.9			
Total votes		2,820				
1937						
Mrs E.A. Watson*	L	Unopp.	-	4,619	-	-

Healey ward *(continued)*

Candidate	Party	Votes	%	Electors	Turnout	Gains
1938						
J. Howarth*	L	Unopp.	-	4,647	-	-

Overall Labour vote   **25.0%**   **Overall turnout**   **62.3%**

Lowerhouse ward

Candidate	Party	Votes	%	Electors	Turnout	Gains
1919						
G. Hale	Lab	1,345	60.4	4,063	54.8	Lab from C
E. Harrison	C	882	39.6			
Total votes		2,227				
1920						
J.W. Clegg*	L	1,909	68.6	4,064	68.5	-
D. Barton	Lab	874	31.4			
Total votes		2,783				
1921						
F. Robinson	L	1,811	65.8	4,139	66.5	-
J.W. Driver	Lab	941	34.2			
Total votes		2,752				
1922						
G.W. Sherston	C	1,886	59.4	4,149	76.5	C from Lab
G. Hale*	Lab	1,289	40.6			
Total votes		3,175				
1923						
R.S. Heap*	L	1,686	54.3	4,207	73.8	-
G. Hale	Lab	1,419	45.7			
Total votes		3,105				
1924						
F. Robinson*	L	1,610	54.5	4,303	68.6	-
G. Hall	Lab	1,343	45.5			
Total votes		2,953				
1925						
G.W. Sherston*	C	1,913	57.0	4,351	77.2	-
A.M. Lott	Lab	1,445	43.0			
Total votes		3,358				
1926						
W. Crabtree	L	Unopp.	-	4,371	-	-
1927						
F. Robinson*	L	Unopp.	-		-	-

Lowerhouse ward (continued)

Candidate	Party	Votes	%	Electors	Turnout	Gains
1928						
C.C. Pollard*	C	Unopp.	-		-	-
1929						
T.P. Taylor	Lab	1,602	57.6	4,930	56.4	Lab from L
W. Crabtree*	L	1,179	42.4			
Total votes		2,781				
1930						
F. Robinson*	L	1,673	56.3	5,095	58.3	-
W. Pollard	Lab	1,296	43.7			
Total votes		2,969				
1931						
C.C. Pollard*	C	Unopp.	-		-	-
1932						
T.P. Taylor*	Lab	2,241	62.7	5,074	70.4	-
G.E. Beetham	L	1,332	37.3			
Total votes		3,573				
1933						
R. Bushby	Lab	1,857	56.6	5,043	65.0	Lab from L
F. Robinson*	L	1,423	43.4			
Total votes		3,280				
1934						
E. Sandy	Lab	2,110	60.3	5,074	69.0	Lab from C
C.C. Pollard*	C	1,391	39.7			
Total votes		3,501				
1935						
T.P. Taylor*	Lab	Unopp.	-		-	-
1936						
R. Bushby*	Lab	1,864	53.4	5,068	68.9	-
Mrs B.M. Clitheroe	C	1,629	46.6			
Total votes		3,493				

Lowerhouse ward *(continued)*

Candidate	Party	Votes	%	Electors	Turnout	Gains
1937						
E. Sandy*	Lab	Unopp.	-	5,082	-	-
1938						
Mrs M. Clitheroe	C	1,947	54.0	5,080	70.9	C from Lab
Miss E. Uttley*	Lab	1,657	46.0			
Total votes		3,604				

Overall Labour vote   **48.9%**   **Overall turnout**   **67.4%**

St Andrew's ward

Candidate	Party	Votes	%	Electors	Turnout	Gains
1919						
Dr W.F. Munro	L	2,339	58.5	6,354	62.9	-
I. Eastham	Lab	1,656	41.5			
Total votes		3,995				
1920						
W.E. Thornber	L	2,281	52.0	6,380	68.7	L from Lab
H. Lees*	Lab	2,102	48.0			
Total votes		4,383				
1921						
J.H. Heap	L	2,820	58.5	6,452	74.8	-
H. Lees	Lab	2,004	41.5			
Total votes		4,824				
1922						
Dr W.F. Munro*	L	Unopp.	-		-	-
1923						
J.R. Clark	L	3,038	69.6	6,466	67.6	-
R. Haworth	Lab	1,330	30.4			
Total votes		4,368				
1924						
J.H. Heap*	L	Unopp.	-	6,526	-	-
1925						
Dr W.F. Munro*	L	Unopp.	-	6,525	-	-
1926						
J.R. Clark*	L	Unopp.	-	6,587	-	-
1927						
J.H. Heap*	L	Unopp.	-		-	-
1928						
Dr W.F. Munro*	L	Unopp.	-		-	-

St Andrew's ward (continued)

Candidate	Party	Votes	%	Electors	Turnout	Gains
1929						
H. Preston	Lab	1,644	37.5	7,142	61.4	Lab from L
J.R. Clark*	L	1,511	34.5			
J. Pickup	C	1,230	28.1			
Total votes		4,385				
1930						
J.H. Heap*	L	Unopp.	-		-	-
1931						
Dr W.F. Munro*	L	Unopp.	-		-	-
1932						
H. Preston*	Lab	2,218	50.6	7,513	58.4	-
T. Duxbury	L	2,169	49.4			
Total votes		4,387				
1933						
J.H. Heap*	L	2,391	52.1	7,509	61.1	-
W. Yates	Lab	2,197	47.9			
Total votes		4,588				
1934						
H. Nutter	L	2,606	50.7	7,685	66.9	-
W. Yates	Lab	2,535	49.3			
Total votes		5,141				
1935						
J.T. Clegg	L	2,752	51.3	8,086	66.3	L from Lab
H. Preston*	Lab	2,611	48.7			
Total votes		5,363				
1936						
M. Greenwood	L	3,051	57.2	8,174	65.2	-
J. Harrison	Lab	2,280	42.8			
Total votes		5,331				
1937						
H. Nutter*	L	Unopp.	-	8,217	-	-

St Andrew's ward *(continued)*

Candidate	Party	Votes	%	Electors	Turnout	Gains
1938						
J.T. Clegg*	L	3,433	67.6	8,325	61.0	-
F. Connor	Lab	1,643	32.4			
Total votes		5,076				

Overall Labour vote   **42.9%**   **Overall turnout**   **64.7%**

St Paul's ward

Candidate	Party	Votes	%	Electors	Turnout	Gains
1919						
S. Lynch	Lab	716	62.0	2,242	51.5	Lab from C
R. Lawrie	C	439	38.0			
Total votes		1,155				
1920						
J.W. Gradwell	Lab	907	55.0	2,493	66.1	Lab from C
J. Catlow	C	741	45.0			
Total votes		1,648				
1921						
T. Brown	Lab	946	50.6	2,519	74.2	Lab from C
W. Eastwood	C	924	49.4			
Total votes		1,870				
1922						
W. Eastwood	C	1,019	52.4	2,473	78.6	C from Lab
R. Broadley	Lab	924	47.6			
Total votes		1,943				
1923						
J.W. Gradwell*	Lab	1,027	53.4	2,499	77.0	-
S. Collison	C	896	46.6			
Total votes		1,923				
1924						
T. Brown*	Lab	930	51.4	2,476	73.1	-
S. Collison	C	881	48.6			
Total votes		1,811				
1925						
R. Broadley	Lab	1,041	53.7	2,451	79.0	Lab from C
W. Eastwood*	C	896	46.3			
Total votes		1,937				
1926						
J.W. Gradwell*	Lab	1,023	52.4	2,482	78.6	-
H. Durkin	C	929	47.6			
Total votes		1,952				

St Paul's ward *(continued)*

Candidate	Party	Votes	%	Electors	Turnout	Gains
1927						
J.W. Tomlinson*	Lab	922	52.9	2,422	72.0	-
G.C. Lancaster	C	775	44.4			
J.R. Strutt	Ind	47	2.7			
Total votes		1,744				
1928						
R. Broadley*	Lab	965	62.7	2,328	66.2	-
A. McCluggage	C	575	37.3			
Total votes		1,540				
1929						
J.W. Gradwell*	Lab	801	53.9	2,486	59.8	-
H. Collison	C	659	44.3			
Mrs A. Hargreaves	Com	27	1.8			
Total votes		1,487				
1930						
G.C.A. Huffner	C	810	52.1	2,346	66.3	C from Lab
J.W. Tomlinson*	Lab	669	43.0			
H. Mannion	Com	77	4.9			
Total votes		1,556				
1931						
R. Broadley*	Lab	918	54.4	2,334	72.2	-
J. Whitham	C	768	45.6			
Total votes		1,686				
1932						
J.W. Gradwell*	Lab	1,088	60.9	2,348	76.1	-
G.W. Steen	C	700	39.1			
Total votes		1,788				
1933						
W. Heys	Lab	1,113	62.4	2,332	76.5	Lab from C
G.C.A. Haffner*	C	670	37.6			
Total votes		1,783				

St Paul's ward (continued)

Candidate	Party	Votes	%	Electors	Turnout	Gains
1934						
R. Broadley*	Lab	1,052	64.9	2,202	73.6	-
G. Cook	C	568	35.1			
Total votes		1,620				
1935						
J.W. Gradwell*	Lab	886	57.5	2,091	73.6	-
J.H. Brotherton	C	602	39.1			
T. Tickle	ILP	52	3.4			
Total votes		1,540				
1936						
H. Massey	L	645	51.2	1,821	69.2	L from Lab
W. Woodhead	Lab	615	48.8			
Total votes		1,260				
1937						
H. Hudson*	Lab	665	50.7	1,734	75.7	-
S. Pickard	C	373	28.4			
C. Cavanagh	L	274	20.9			
Total votes		1,312				
1938						
J.H. Brotherton*	C	566	59.2	1,469	65.1	-
J. Hartley	Lab	390	40.8			
Total votes		956				

Overall Labour vote   **54.1%**   **Overall turnout**   **71.4%**

St Peter's ward

Candidate	Party	Votes	%	Electors	Turnout	Gains
1919						
J. Leeming	Lab	518	51.2	2,080	48.7	Lab from C
T. Pierson	C	494	48.8			
Total votes		1,012				
1920						
J. Whewell*	L	793	53.6	2,217	66.7	-
R. Broadley	Lab	686	46.4			
Total votes		1,479				
1921						
J. Bestwick	C	905	63.7	2,254	63.0	-
A. Hoyle	Lab	515	36.3			
Total votes		1,420				
1922						
D. Prattley	C	843	55.5	2,215	68.6	C from Lab
J. Leeming*	Lab	676	44.5			
Total votes		1,519				
1923						
J. Whewell*	L	851	55.9	2,279	66.8	-
M.H. Brogan	Lab	671	44.1			
Total votes		1,522				
1924						
J. Bestwick*	C	932	62.2	2,244	66.8	-
T. Wallworth	Lab	566	37.8			
Total votes		1,498				
1925						
D. Prattley*	C	871	53.1	2,254	72.8	-
W. Eastwood	Lab	770	46.9			
Total votes		1,641				
1926						
J.A. Sampson*	Lab	844	51.4	2,258	72.8	-
W. Ingham	C	799	48.6			
Total votes		1,643				

St Peter's ward (continued)

Candidate	Party	Votes	%	Electors	Turnout	Gains
1927						
J. Bestwick*	C	921	55.8	2,233	73.9	-
J. Lynch	Lab	729	44.2			
Total votes		1,650				
1928						
J. Lynch	Lab	870	52.7	2,245	73.5	Lab from C
D. Prattlet*	C	781	47.3			
Total votes		1,651				
1929						
J.A. Sampson*	Lab	Unopp.	-		-	-
1930						
J. Bestwick*	C	902	56.7	2,398	66.4	-
W. Woodhead	Lab	690	43.3			
Total votes		1,592				
1931						
J. Lynch*	Lab	981	54.2	2,365	76.5	-
J.D. Towers	C	828	45.8			
Total votes		1,809				
1932						
J.A. Sampson*	Lab	974	57.9	2,362	71.2	-
H. Hartley	C	708	42.1			
Total votes		1,682				
1933						
G. Hale*	Lab	989	55.4	2,369	75.3	-
H. Hartley	C	795	44.6			
Total votes		1,784				
1934						
J. Lynch*	Lab	1,080	62.9	2,288	75.0	-
J. Blakeley	C	636	37.1			
Total votes		1,716				

St Peter's ward (continued)

Candidate	Party	Votes	%	Electors	Turnout	Gains
1935						
J.A. Sampson*	Lab	848	54.0	2,068	76.0	-
J. Bestwick	C	678	43.2			
E. Heyworth	ILP	45	2.9			
Total votes		1,571				
1936						
G. Hale*	Lab	784	52.8	2,018	73.5	-
J. Bestwick	C	700	47.2			
Total votes		1,484				
1937						
L. Ingham	Lab	690	54.9	1,794	70.1	-
T.B. Parker	C	567	45.1			
Total votes		1,257				
1938						
E. Brooks	C	682	56.1	1,756	69.2	C from Lab
Mrs M.A. Battle*	Lab	534	43.9			
Total votes		1,216				

Overall Labour vote   **49.5%**   **Overall turnout**   **69.9%**

Stoneyholme ward

Candidate	Party	Votes	%	Electors	Turnout	Gains
1919						
J. Knape	L	745	54.6	2,289	59.6	-
J.W.Briggs	Lab	620	45.4			
Total votes		1,365				
1920						
J. Sutcliffe	C	1,030	61.9	2,353	70.7	-
J. Lynch	Lab	634	38.1			
Total votes		1,664				
1921						
R. Place*	C	1,067	79.7	2,358	56.8	-
I. Ransom	ILG	272	20.3			
Total votes		1,339				

(ILG = Independent Labour Group, a Communist/NUWM grouping)

Candidate	Party	Votes	%	Electors	Turnout	Gains
1922						
J. Knape*	L	Unopp.	-		-	-
1923						
J. Sutcliffe*	C	862	57.2	2,359	63.9	-
G. Knowles	Lab	645	42.8			
Total votes		1,507				
1924						
R. Place*	C	946	62.8	2,354	64.0	-
A. Faraday	Lab	561	37.2			
Total votes		1,507				
1925						
T. Clegg*	L	851	55.8	2,364	64.6	-
T. Wallwork	Lab	675	44.2			
Total votes		1,526				
1926						
J. Sutcliffe*	C	Unopp.	-	2,385	-	-

Stoneyholme ward *(continued)*

Candidate	Party	Votes	%	Electors	Turnout	Gains
1927						
R. Place*	C	870	51.7	2,388	70.5	-
J. Smith	Lab	814	48.3			
Total votes		1,684				
1928						
T. Clegg*	L	Unopp.	-		-	-
1929						
W. Sutcliffe	Lab	775	52.2	2,569	57.8	Lab from C
F. Riding	C	710	47.8			
Total votes		1,485				
1930						
S. Fearnehough*	C	950	53.1	2,560	69.9	-
G. Hale	Lab	840	46.9			
Total votes		1,790				
1931						
Mrs M. Whitehead*	L	1,036	56.1	2,559	72.2	-
G. Hale	Lab	811	43.9			
Total votes		1,847				
1932						
W. Sutcliffe*	Lab	1,109	60.4	2,559	71.8	-
R. Collinge	C	728	39.6			
Total votes		1,837				
1933						
A.E. Brown	Lab	1,030	57.4	2,531	70.8	Lab from C
S. Fearnehough*	C	763	42.6			
Total votes		1,793				
1934						
L. Thompson	Lab	1,166	64.7	2,576	70.0	Lab from L
Mrs M. Whitehead*	L	637	35.3			
Total votes		1,803				
1935						
W. Sutcliffe*	Lab	Unopp.	-		-	-

Stoneyholme ward *(continued)*

Candidate	Party	Votes	%	Electors	Turnout	Gains
1936						
T. Holt	C	960	51.1	2,458	76.4	C from Lab
A.E. Brown*	Lab	917	48.9			
Total votes		1,877				
1937						
L. Thompson*	Lab	962	53.6	2,545	70.5	-
E. Stevenson	C	832	46.4			
Total votes		1,794				
1938						
Miss A. Fearnehough*	C	944	55.2	2,541	67.3	-
C. Walton	Lab	765	44.8			
Total votes		1,709				

Overall Labour vote   **46.5%**   **Overall turnout**   **67.4%**

Trinity ward

Candidate	Party	Votes	%	Electors	Turnout	Gains
1919						
A.E. Glashan	C	865	56.8	2,959	51.4	-
H. Shapcott	Lab	657	43.2			
Total votes		1,522				
1920						
T. Blackledge	C	1,061	54.0	3,000	·65.5	-
H. Shapcott	Lab	905	46.0			
Total votes		1,966				
1921						
A. Foster	Lab	1,039	51.8	3,074	65.2	Lab from C
W. Parker*	C	965	48.2			
Total votes		2,004				
1922						
J. Proctor	Lab	1,289	55.0	3,074	76.3	Lab from C
Dr A.C. Glashan*	C	1,056	45.0			
Total votes		2,345				
1923						
H. Lees	Lab	1,204	51.9	3,109	74.7	Lab from C
T.C. Blackledge*	C	1,118	48.1			
Total votes		2,322				
1924						
A. Foster*	Lab	1,208	53.4	3,084	73.4	-
J. Fearing	C	1,055	46.6			
Total votes		2,263				
1925						
J. Proctor*	Lab	1,329	53.1	3,109	80.5	-
R.L. Todd	C	1,175	46.9			
Total votes		2,504				
1926						
H. Lees*	Lab	1,278	50.3	3,108	81.7	-
R.L. Todd	C	1,262	49.7			
Total votes		2,540				

Trinity ward *(continued)*

Candidate	Party	Votes	%	Electors	Turnout	Gains
1927						
R.L. Todd	C	1,343	50.2	3,156	84.8	C from Lab
A. Foster*	Lab	1,333	49.8			
Total votes		2,676				
1928						
A. Foster	Lab	1,436	60.5	3,147	75.4	-
H.N. Brown	C	938	39.5			
Total votes		2,374				
1929						
E. Broderick	Lab	1,204	52.6	3,397	67.4	-
Mrs M.R. Wood	C	1,084	47.4			
Total votes		2,288				
1930						
R.L. Todd*	C	1,457	60.1	3,369	71.9	-
R. Howarth	Lab	966	39.9			
Total votes		2,423				
1931						
C. Heyworth	C	1,372	53.8	3,342	76.4	C from Lab
A. Foster*	Lab	1,180	46.2			
Total votes		2,552				
1932						
E. Brodrick*	Lab	1,396	57.1	3,332	73.4	-
C. Clampett	C	1,050	42.9			
Total votes		2,446				
1933						
A. Lord	Lab	1,244	50.7	3,325	73.8	Lab from C
R.L. Todd*	C	1,211	49.3			
Total votes		2,455				
1934						
J. Nicholls	Lab	1,358	53.7	3,253	77.8	Lab from C
R.L. Todd	C	1,173	46.3			
Total votes		2,531				

Trinity ward *(continued)*

Candidate	Party	Votes	%	Electors	Turnout	Gains
1935						
E. Brodrick*	Lab	1,482	62.7	3,249	72.8	-
R. Hudson	C	882	37.3			
Total votes		2,364				
1936						
L. Haworth	Lab	1,188	51.6	3,202	72.0	-
R. Hudson	L	1,116	48.4			
Total votes		2,304				
1937						
W. Almond	Lab	1,188	53.2	3,123	71.5	-
H. Uttley	C	1,044	46.8			
Total votes		2,232				
1938						
R. Hudson*	C	1,118	51.3	3,129	69.7	-
J. Chew	Lab	1,062	48.7			
Total votes		2,180				

Overall Labour vote **51.7%** **Overall turnout** **72.9%**

Whittlefield ward

Candidate	Party	Votes	%	Electors	Turnout	Gains
1919						
J. Heaton	C	747	55.5	2,073	64.9	-
J.W. Driver	Lab	598	44.5			
Total votes		1,345				
1920						
A.B. Crossley	L	910	64.6	2,092	67.3	-
F. Robinson	Lab	498	35.4			
Total votes		1,408				
1921						
T. Kershaw*	C	904	76.8	2,093	56.2	-
W. Sugden	ILG	273	23.2			
Total votes		1,177				

(ILG = Independent Labour Group, a Communist/NUWM grouping)

Candidate	Party	Votes	%	Electors	Turnout	Gains
1922						
W. Buchanan	C	944	61.1	2,106	73.4	-
J.E.P. Jowett	Lab	601	38.9			
Total votes		1,545				
1923						
T. Whittaker	L	970	63.3	2,141	71.6	-
J.E.P. Jowett	Lab	562	36.7			
Total votes		1,532				
1924						
Mrs M. Brown	C	873	53.1	2,147	76.6	-
J.A. Sampson	Lab	772	46.9			
Total votes		1,645				
1925						
W. Buchanan*	C	986	59.5	2,137	77.6	-
J.J. Rigby	Lab	672	40.5			
Total votes		1,658				
1926						
T. Whittaker*	L	Unopp.	-	2,169	-	-

Whittlefield ward *(continued)*

Candidate	Party	Votes	%	Electors	Turnout	Gains
1927						
Mrs M. Brown	C	958	59.4	2,198	73.3	-
E.S. Eldridge	Lab	654	40.6			
Total votes		1,612				
1928						
W. Buchanan*	C	Unopp.	-		-	-
1929						
T. Whittaker*	L	753	53.1	2,373	59.7	-
W. Glenn	Lab	664	46.9			
Total votes		1,417				
1930						
Mrs M. Brown*	C	Unopp.	-		-	-
1931						
W.A. Hartley	C	Unopp.	-		-	-
1932						
G. Duxbury*	L	811	52.0	2,383	65.5	-
G. Hale	Lab	750	48.0			
Total votes		1,561				
1933						
Mrs M. Brown*	C	871	50.7	2,415	71.2	-
T. Maxfield	Lab	848	49.3			
Total votes		1,719				
1934						
T. Maxfield	Lab	1,015	56.0	2,397	75.6	Lab from C
W.A. Hartley*	C	784	43.2			
I. Ransom	UEA	14	0.8			
Total votes		1,813				

(UEA = Unemployed Electoral Association, a Communist/NUWM grouping)

Candidate	Party	Votes	%	Electors	Turnout	Gains
1935						
G. Duxbury*	L	882	51.5	2,396	71.5	-
J. Hartley	Lab	832	48.5			
Total votes		1,714				

Whittlefield ward *(continued)*

Candidate	Party	Votes	%	Electors	Turnout	Gains
1936						
Mrs M. Brown*	C	1,053	56.0	2,360	79.7	-
J. Hartley	Lab	827	44.0			
Total votes		1,880				
1937						
T. Maxfield*	Lab	894	50.8	2,353	74.8	-
W.E. Smith	C	867	49.2			
Total votes		1,761				
1938						
G. Duxbury*	L	1,005	59.2	2,363	71.8	-
Miss A. Proctor	Lab	692	40.8			
Total votes		1,697				

Overall Labour vote   **42.7%**   **Overall turnout**   **70.7%**

FIVE
Burton-upon-Trent

BURTON-UPON-TRENT

Burton-upon-Trent began its existence as an eleventh-century Saxon abbey. With local water of excellent quality and in plentiful supply, its staple industry, brewing, was long established by the seventeenth century. The success of Burton's ales was based on the use of local hard water from Keuper marl.[1] Location was also important. Situated on the River Trent, Burton was at the centre of a communications apex that linked the Midlands to the Humber and the port of Hull. By the early nineteenth century, Burton was a centre for the export of manufacture goods from the Midlands to the Baltic, and was an important market and commercial centre.[2] In the Victorian era the town's breweries and associated industries were dominant, and Burton became Britain's 'premier brewing centre after 1840'.[3] As far back as 1777 William Bass had established the world's largest brewery in Burton. In 1860 the *Burton Weekly News* could say with pride, 'Look at our monster breweries, employing thousands of hands in the manufacture of our staple commodity, and sending it to almost every part of the habitable globe ... Thus Burton has attained an eminence which perhaps no other town in the Kingdom, of similar population, has done'.[4] From 1870 onwards, with its twenty-six breweries, 104 malthouses, seventy-six ale stores and twenty cooperages, Burton was almost a one-industry town.[5] By then the firm of Bass, Ratcliff and Gretton was by far the largest amongst the brewing concerns of the borough. In 1888, Bass employed 2,760 workers, while Allsopp and Sons (1,750 workers), Worthington (470), Mann, Crossman and Paulin (450), and T.F. Salt (400) were also significant.[6] Based on the growth of brewing, the population of Burton grew from 8,000 in 1841 to 50,000 by 1901, but stagnated thereafter, being less than 50,000 in 1931. Burton was in fact the third-smallest county borough in England and Wales, and remained almost a one-industry town in the inter-war period.

The second most significant industry in the borough was that of railways. Burton's earlier position as a centre of communications via the Trent was augmented in the 1860s by its strategic importance as a railway junction. It became a network centre for the Midland Railway and the London and North Western Railway, and by the time it had acquired county borough status in 1901 it could be accurately described as 'a town of railways and beer'.[7] The breweries had their own light rail systems linking them to the main lines and Burton was criss-crossed by level crossings. There was also some engineering in the borough, including the manufacture of brewery equipment and light locomotives. The firm of Thornwill and Warham, starting by supplying the Burton brewers, grew to export

---

[1]   Freeman, T.W., *The Conurbations of Great Britain*, (Manchester), p. 255; Owen, C.C., *The Development of Industry in Burton upon Trent*, (Chichester, 1978), p. 3.
[2]   Owen, C., *Burton upon Trent: The Illustrated History*, (Derby, 1994), pp. 46–56.
[3]   Owen, *Burton ... The Illustrated History*, p. 84.
[4]   Quoted in Owen, *Burton ... The Illustrated History*, p. 89.
[5]   Owen, *Burton ... The Illustrated History*, p. 84.
[6]   Stuart, D., *County Borough: the History of Burton upon Trent 1901–1974, Part 2 1914–1974*, (Burton upon Trent, 1977), p. 23.
[7]   Owen, *Burton ... The Illustrated History*, p. 83.

locomotives to mines and breweries all over the world. The manufacture of textiles and clothing was also significant in the nineteenth century, especially as far as female employment was concerned, although these sectors were in recession by the inter-war period.

The borough's long economic decline began in the twentieth century. The end of the Victorian age saw the master brewers of Burton, and their huge limited liability companies, begin to suffer a variety of economic difficulties. These difficulties lasted throughout the Edwardian and inter-war years. Increased competition from foreign and domestic brewers, together with the impact of a vociferous temperance lobby meant that local output fell dramatically in the Edwardian years. Mergers, liquidations and falling output in the brewing industry prompted the borough to establish a Commercial and Development Committee to attract new industries as early as 1907. The First World War depressed the Burton staple still further with the town's total output falling from over 30 million barrels in 1914 to under 14 million by 1918. After the war production rose briefly between 1919 and 1921, but then fell back again from 1923. Bass's production fell from 1.5 million barrels in 1921 to just over a million between 1923 and 1927. As well as reduced demand, Burton's brewers faced escalating excise duties. Between the years 1919 and 1921, Bass and Co.'s excise payments went up from £1.4 million to £6.9 million. Although Ind Coope was expanding by way of predatory take-overs of other firms, jobs were invariably lost. In 1926 even the giant Charrington and Co closed its Burton brewery.[8] In 1926 Bass and Worthington merged, while Ind Coope became associated with both Robinsons and the Burton Brewery Company.[9] Many brewery workers were thrown out of work as a result of these mergers, and unemployment in the borough grew.

It has been claimed that the earlier prosperity of the brewing industry generated 'an air of complacency amongst the local politicians.' Moreover the brewing companies of the early twentieth century had 'a vested interest in limiting other economic activities that might compete for local labour and also raise the level of wages. By their ownership of large areas of land, especially close to the town centre, they were able to exert a powerful influence over alternative forms of industrial and commercial development'.[10] Large areas of the town were reserved for the supply of water and suburban growth, the former being reasonable given the importance of water to the brewers, the latter less so given the population stagnation of the inter-war years. As to the charge that the brewing industry restricted competition for labour, this is difficult to document.[11] Nevertheless the Commercial Development Committee of the council had some success. Firms were established converting brewing by-products to animal and human foodstuffs. Malting firms were established before the First World War, two of the most important being English Grains and the Marmite Food Extract Company. In a council meeting in 1919, a councillor listed the main economic activities of the borough:

---

[8] Owen, *Burton ... The Illustrated History*, p. 145.

[9] Stuart, *County Borough*, p. 34 and 36.

[10] Owen, *Burton ... The Illustrated History*, p. 146–147.

[11] Stuart, *County Borough*, p. 124.

The staple industry of Burton-upon-Trent is brewing, but during the past six or seven years, a number of other trades have been introduced to the town, such as net mending, constructional engineering, toy making, clothing, hosiery, rubber, light castings, aircraft etc., and works are in progress or are contemplated for the manufacture of fertilisers, cattle food, paper, boots and lace.[12]

After the First World War, the Development Committee played a role in attracting two rubber companies, Pirelli Ltd. (in 1929) and British Tyre and Rubber (1930), both in Derby Road. Other inter-war diversification was the establishment of the Eatough shoe factory (1921), Cyclops Engineering (1918), the Burton Box Company (1924), Cross and Blackwell Preserved Food Company (1921) and finally, the Branston Artificial Silk Company (1927). The last concern epitomises Burton's inter-war economic fortunes outside of brewing. It built up to near 500 employees, but by 1930, it had ceased production and closed.[13] The general economic picture after 1921 was fraught. The early post war optimism based on the upturn in production in brewing and the hopes for diversification were only partially realised.

The industry tables of the 1931 census very much reflected the industrial structure of Burton. Over 5,000 men, amounting to over 30 per cent of the male labour force, were employed in the drink category, and 6 per cent of women workers were also found in this category. This was by far the highest proportion of workers in the brewing industry amongst all the county boroughs. Transport was the second most important sector for male employment, mainly comprising of railway workers who accounted for 8 per cent of male workers. Burton lay tenth amongst the county boroughs in terms of the percentage of the male workforce employed in the railway industry (see Appendix 11). Metal and engineering also accounted for over 8 per cent of the male workforce. There was an equivalent proportion of women employed in textiles, and also in the manufacture of clothing. The manufacture of tyres and other rubber products was picking up in the 1930s, but by 1931 it accounted for less than 4 per cent of the total workforce. The largest sectors of female employment were personal service (30 per cent) and commerce and finance (18 per cent), but the relatively high level of women in manufacturing is also noteworthy. In total over 30 per cent of women workers were employed in the textiles, clothing, drink and rubber industries. With over one-fifth of the total workforce in the commerce and finance and public administration and defence sectors, there was also a substantial lower middle class of clerical and white-collar workers. There was not a massive middle-class higher up the social scale, however, as shown in the key indicators from the 1931 census. Burton was forty-second amongst the eighty-three county boroughs in terms of female domestic servants as a proportion of the total population, fifty-second in terms of the proportion of professionals in the workforce, and sixty-seventh in terms of the proportion defined as self-employed or employed in a managerial capacity. A survey of the town's housing stock in 1919 designated 9,837 of the 11,461 houses

---

[12] *Burton Daily Mail*, 4 Nov. 1919.
[13] Stuart, *County Borough*, p. 124–128.

within the borough as 'working class'.[14] This was a predominantly working-class borough, without a numerous local elite prevailing socially and politically. Instead it was the breweries as the dominant local interest which dominated Burton.

As early as the middle of the nineteenth century, for instance, brewers from the Bass, Worthington, Allsopp and Mann families had replaced landed magnates like the Paget family (Marquises of Anglesey) in municipal affairs. In the first group of twenty-seven commissioners responsible for the administration of the town from 1853, eleven were from the brewing industry.[15] When Burton became a municipal borough in 1878 the first mayor was a member of the Worthington dynasty of brewers, and three of the first eight aldermen were also members of brewing families. It was not just the brewery owners, however, who made up the brewing interest, but the brewery workers as well. It is arguable that there was a distinct form of working-class conservatism which was influential in Burton, based on the attitudes of the brewery workers. The use of the lower-case for conservatism here is deliberate, for though there is no doubting the Conservative party's close connections to the brewing industry, the conservatism of Burton embraced a wider political spectrum. The brewers could be harsh in their treatment of their employees when challenged, but usually a live-and-let-live relationship between workers and employers prevailed, as long as the workers played the game largely according to the bosses' script. This contributed to a lack of worker militancy. The influence of the brewery employers provided a transmission belt of authority, values and ideological and cultural attitudes. Moreover in an almost one-industry town employees in the brewing industry crossed the employers at their peril. The sack and blacklisting could mean the end of a working career in the locality, as well as the loss of the grace-and-favour pension from the brewery.

Turning now to electoral politics, in parliamentary terms as Pelling has commented, the Burton division before the First World War was 'determined to have a brewer as its representative irrespective of party labels.'[16] This cavalier attitude to party differences reiterates the point that the conservatism of Burton was almost non-party, and could incorporate not only Liberalism, but later on Labour as well in the municipal sphere, as will be demonstrated below. Thus Sir Arthur Bass (later Lord Burton) and then Sydney Evershed, both connected to prominent breweries, successively represented the borough between 1885 and 1900 as Liberals. This was despite the traditional hostility towards the drink trade of those sections of Liberalism linked to Nonconformity and temperance. The Liberal party was in fact weak in Burton, but the personal choice of Bass and Evershed for Liberalism was insignificant compared to the fact they were effectively the nominees of the breweries, so much so that they were unopposed in the general elections of 1886, 1892 and 1895. Evershed was succeeded in 1900 by another brewer, Major R.F. Ratcliff, standing as a Liberal Unionist against the Liberals. The influence of Joseph Chamberlain radiating out from Birmingham can be detected here. Burton lay within the area sometimes referred to as

---

[14] Owen, *Burton ... The Illustrated History*, p. 153.
[15] Owen, *Burton ... The Illustrated History*, p. 99.
[16] Pelling, H., *Social Geography of British Elections, 1885–1910*, (Aldershot, 1994), p. 194.

'Chamberlain's Duchy', where he was given a free hand to organise Liberal Unionism.[17] Ratcliff continued to hold the seat comfortably against Liberal opponents up to 1914, effectively signifying the end of the Liberal party as any sort of force in the borough. A Coalition Conservative took over unopposed in 1918, and as a Conservative held the seat until 1943. Labour contested the seat for the first time in 1924, but never won more than the 30 per cent of the poll it achieved in 1929.

As far as municipal elections were concerned, Burton had become a county borough in 1901, at which date the boundaries of the eight wards which pertained between the wars were established.[18] In the inter-war years the council was run by an alliance of 'independents' which steadfastly stuck to the assertion that municipal politics was a non-party affair. The conservatism that lay behind this grouping was obvious, and it had only weak opposition from the only organised party on the council, Labour. Summarising the pattern of political support over time, Labour did well in 1919 and 1920, making two gains in both years, taking their total representation on the council to seven. This was the highpoint for Labour between the wars, maintained in 1922 while none of the early gains came up for re-election. In the following six years, however, a series of losses saw Labour reduced to a rump of only three councillors, a position that was to remain static for the rest of the period. Two linked points need to be made about this situation. First, as will be shown below, Labour was drawn in to a political rapprochement with the independents on the council, whereby a small number of Labour councillors were effectively allowed to sit on the council and to an extent play a part in the administration of the borough. Second, as a consequence of this, very few seats were contested after the early 1920s. Labour in fact made no challenge on independent-held seats after 1931, and its own three councillors were given a free run in all elections after 1929. An independent councillor referring to the pre-1914 council remarked that 'there were no politics in the council, and ... no political question had ever cropped up'.[19] This applied almost as much to the situation in the 1930s, and there is little, therefore, that can be said about trends in political support in Burton.

It is also the case that the spatial pattern of political support in Burton requires little comment. This was a small borough, with no great variations in housing type between wards. The population statistics for wards in the 1931 census show this clearly, with all the wards having a relatively low person per room figure varying between 0.72 and 0.83. With so few contests, it is hard to pinpoint strongholds, but it is clear that Burton ward covered the city centre and included most of the commercial premises and many of the large breweries. It had the smallest population with relatively few residents and most of the plural voters. Labour therefore never contested this ward between the wars, and had virtually no success other than in non-contests in four other wards, Horninglow to the north and Shobnall, Uxbridge and Broadway in the west and south of the borough. Labour's only real strength lay in Victoria ward to the north-west, which it won four times

[17] Pelling, *Social Geography*, p. 183.
[18] *The Municipal Yearbook*, 1910, p. 43.
[19] *Burton Daily Mail*, 29 Oct. 1920.

in contested elections. Labour also won some victories in Stapenhill and Winshill wards to the south and east before the electoral truce set in. In each of these last three wards Labour was allowed one uncontested councillor after 1929.

Turning to the analysis of the main groupings on the council, the Independents who controlled inter-war Burton sought to take the politics out of the administration of local affairs, and appeared to succeed to a greater extent than in most other county boroughs. That this might hide a self-seeking motive did not diminish its power and effectiveness as a model of politics. Conservatives effectively ran Burton in the inter-war years, though usually under an Independent flag or very occasionally under some other such as 'Ratepayer'. A Ratepayer candidate in 1921 argued for policies that were indistinguishable from those of other Independents, namely 'the cutting down of expenses' to keep the rates low and to prevent money being 'squandered'.[20] At the same time Independents claimed to stand above class interest in the wise administration of the borough. Thus the candidate above asserted that he 'had the interest of Labour at heart as much as any Labour man in Burton today'.[21] Another Independent, and brewery director, echoed the same point in 1926: 'they did not want any politics in municipal affairs. We do not want men who represent one section of the community only. I stand for all classes and no particular interests.'[22] A third independent in the same year accused Labour of being unpatriotic and being 'touched with the red flag', and asserted:

> As a working man who had worked from the bottom of the ladder, and an old trade union secretary, he absolutely objected to the Socialist society calling themselves working men and the only class that represented working men. Liberals and Conservatives had as much right to call themselves members of the Labour Party as Socialists had.[23]

Eleven years later another Independent argued that he was a businessman representing no particular class or party, while defending the brewing interest enthusiastically.[24] The note of patriotism struck above was also reiterated by a candidate when he said:

> another important point was his colours, a very important item with the fair sex, and extremely so in this case. His colours were red, white and blue, the good old Union Jack, which they must keep flying over the Town Hall as a token of loyalty to the King and fidelity to the British Empire.[25]

Coupled with these points, Independent councillors persistently reminded the electorate of the importance of the brewing interest to the borough. Thus, a

---

[20] *Burton Daily Mail*, 26 Oct. 1921.
[21] *Burton Daily Mail*, 26 Oct. 1921.
[22] *Burton Daily Mail*, 30 Oct. 1926.
[23] *Burton Daily Mail*, 27 Oct. 1926.
[24] *Burton Daily Mail*, 26 Oct. 1937.
[25] *Burton Daily Mail*, 27 Oct. 1926.

brewery director and councillor defended the brewers as 'the life-blood' of the borough, and pointed out that the brewers

> were directly funding their own rates and indirectly funding the rates of the majority of householders. If the brewers did not find work, wages and salaries for the householders, how could the householders pay their rates ... As an Independent candidate I claim to represent the brewery workers and the staple industry, and when you go to the poll on Monday do not forget that small insignificant word 'Beer'.[26]

The issue of the rates, the key source of council finance, was the one area where the ruling group on the council and the brewing industry could fall out. The brewers did not always get their way in disputes with the corporation, despite the close ties that existed. The Town Clerk, for instance, noted in February 1928 that Bass and Co. had won from the Assessment Committee 'big reductions' in their rates in respect of their premises recently acquired from Salt and Co. Two years later, in April 1930, he noted that councillors were 'delighted' when the council won a judgement with costs against Bass who were again appealing against the level of their rates.[27] Despite this sort of isolated occurrence, of course, the dominant influence of the breweries amongst the ranks of the Independents could not be gainsaid.

The occupational background of the men and women who contested the November elections brings into clear relief the importance of the brewing industry in Burton. Directors of the breweries were certainly more prominent in the Victorian age, but together with others connected to the industry they were still influential in the inter-war years.[28] A survey of occupations of candidates for the council in six separate years between 1919 and 1937 confirms this.[29] In these years there were thirty-nine Independent candidatures. Twelve were company directors or owners of firms, of which five were brewers or directors of breweries. There were also four professionals and managers (one clearly connected to brewing), ten in the small businessman, shopkeeper or tradesmen category, three clerical workers (two in brewing), eight retired and two unspecified women candidates. Overall, of nineteen candidatures for the Labour party, seven were trade union officials with four of these being listed as brewery employees. There were also four skilled workers (including an engine driver), two married women, a brewery foreman, a cattle dealer, a tailor's cutter, a van driver, an unskilled labourer, and an unemployed man. Five of the nineteen were directly employed by the breweries, although some of the unspecified skilled workers could also have been employed in the industry.

Turning now to the Labour party in Burton, the party's response to the 'no politics in the council' approach of the Independents was muted. At one Labour meeting in 1929, a supporter suggested that 'independents used that title because

[26] *Burton Daily Mail*, 30 Oct. 1926.
[27] Stuart, *County Borough*, pp. 50–51.
[28] Owen, *Burton ... The Illustrated History*, p. 99.
[29] Collated from the declaration of candidates in the *Burton Daily Mail* for the years 1919, 1920, 1921, 1926, 1929 and 1937.

they were ashamed of their party.' The Burton parliamentary constituency was then described as 'die-hard Tory', and the Labour candidate stated that '"Independent" candidates were, with few exceptions, a sub-division of the Conservative Party'.[30] Such candid comment was very rare in Burton, and non-existent after 1929 when Labour was increasingly drawn in to the orbit of the ruling independent group. This development can only be understood by examining the overall weakness and also the prevailing political moderation of Labour in Burton.

The Burton Labour party was not formed until 1920 and its membership for most of the 1920s hovered around the hundred mark. It reached 180 members in 1929 and 1930, and 531 in 1931. Thereafter it declined, with around 240 members between 1932 and 1934 and 115 in 1935, before recovering somewhat to 270 in 1938. There was also a branch of the Independent Labour Party active in the borough.[31] The Workers Union, whose membership was largely based in the breweries, was the mainstay of Burton Labour, and a force for moderation in the party. The union supplied many of the officials and activists of the local party. The Workers Union, which became part of the Transport and General Workers Union (TGWU) in 1928–29, was the third largest general union after the First World War. It had been formed by Tom Mann in 1898, and it had its main strength amongst semi-skilled workers in the engineering industry, and had built up its membership especially in the Midlands in areas which traditionally had experienced low levels of unionisation. By 1919 it had become very moderate and entirely reformist.[32] The semi-skilled brewery workers it recruited in Burton, although by no means belonging to the aristocracy of labour, were better-paid and had better benefits than unskilled and casual workers. The union in Burton was intimately connected to the fortunes of the great brewery firms, and played its part in shaping a moderate and conservative approach to local politics.

The industrial and political atmosphere of the breweries was not conducive to radicalism. Union organisation and political activity in support of Labour was necessarily surreptitious amongst brewery workers. Valuable oral testimony collected amongst them shows that 'brewery workers who had Labour sympathies did not always advertise their political views'. One worker recounted how Billy Hutson, the Labour councillor and Workers Union official, had to collect the union dues of the ale-loading gangs in a secretive manner. He also recalled:

> There was a foreman who could sack a man at a minute's notice ...
> They only tolerated people who behaved themselves. But my
> father worked for fifteen years at Salt's and about thirty at Bass's,
> collected the tuppences. He got very bad on his feet and when he
> retired he didn't get the ten bob a week they used to give brewery
> labourers. When I went down to ask why they said 'Your father

---

[30] *Burton Daily Mail*, 22 Oct. 1929.
[31] Stuart, *County Borough*, p. 214–215.
[32] On the Workers' Union, see Hyman, R., *The Workers' Union*, (Oxford, 1971).

made enough out of the union.' Of course it finished up a swearing match. After that I couldn't get a job inside Burton.[33]

Another brewery worker said that to challenge the political interest of the brewery owners 'required courage'. When he posed a difficult question to a Conservative candidate at a meeting, he was spat at and shouted down, and taunted, 'we know who you are. You won't keep your job long'. He revealed that 'you mightn't get much promotion in the brewery if you didn't work for the Conservative Party ward organisations'.[34] Such testimony is evocative of the industrial and political atmosphere prevailing in Burton.

It is hardly surprising, therefore, that industrial and political moderation was the watchword of the brewery workers. The General Strike of May 1926 in Burton illustrated this very well. There were only 456 miners left in Burton in 1921, mostly resident in Stapenhill and employed mainly at the Bretby pit.[35] The brewery workers did not strike in support of the locked-out miners, although others did in Burton, most notably the tramwaymen and railwaymen. Brewery engineers who were members of the Amalgamated Engineering Union also stayed at work despite being called out by their union. During the lock out of the miners after the strike was over, a relief fund for their families was organised in the borough. It was subscribed to by most local unions, but in the breweries only the coopers were notably generous. A Labour party member recalled:

> There was quite a strong comradeship developed among the people, though they didn't like the brewery workers because the brewery workers never gave them any support, you see, they carried on working at the breweries.[36]

As the lock-out wore on the breweries had difficulty in getting enough coal to keep the industry going. Desperate miners and others dug out coal from shallow pits on Gresley Common and sold it on the spot to the brewers, thus undermining the position of the Miners' Federation. The brewers also thoughtfully provided beer to them. When the miners' leader A.J. Cook personally came down to appeal to those on Gresley Common to desist, the 'three parts drunk' crowd swore at him and refused to listen. Cook apparently departed in tears.[37]

The local leaders of the brewery workers were also the dominant figures in Burton Labour party, and their moderate industrial leadership was matched by their moderation in politics. Billy Hutson was a brewery employee and secretary of the local Workers Union, and later secretary of No. 2 branch of the TGWU, while J.W. Clark was a Workers Union official and later Divisional Organiser of the TGWU. Clark was a Labour councillor from 1919 and Hutson from 1920, both of them unopposed after 1929. By the mid 1920s Clark was to become chairman of the Housing Committee on the council, while later Hutson was to become chairman of the Health Committee and the Small Holdings and Allotments

---

[33] Stuart, *County Borough*, p. 216.
[34] Stuart, *County Borough*, p. 216–217.
[35] Stuart, *County Borough*, p. 106.
[36] Stuart, *County Borough*, pp. 107–112.
[37] Stuart, *County Borough*, pp. 112–113.

Committee. John Jones, the other unopposed Labour councillor in the 1930s, was also vice-chairman of the Public Assistance committee. Hutson was elected Mayor of the borough in 1932–33 and Clark in 1937–38.[38] A sign of the goodwill of the breweries for Hutson by then, despite his earlier secret collecting of union dues, was the fact that while he served as mayor he was given the year off on full pay.[39] Both Hutson and Clark were elevated to the aldermanic bench after the Second World War. Both were well respected by the Independent councillors of the ruling bloc. In the low-key affair that stood for inter-war municipal politics in Burton, Labour councillors were invited by the Independents past the portals of power, despite the paucity of their numbers, as long as they were moderate enough to be safely tolerated.

Labour's co-option into the ranks of the ruling bloc in Burton was achieved over the period between 1919 and 1929. In the early 1920s the party still had some radical pretensions, as shown in a speech made in 1920 by Major Coleman, M.A. of Denstone college. Under the headline of 'Red Flags over Breweries', the local newspaper reported him as saying that the workers of Burton should

> throw in their lot with Labour throughout the world, because throughout the world the working classes were not satisfied with their rulers. A few weeks ago he was in the port of Genoa and saw red flags flying over great buildings and shipbuilding yards ... It would be a little relief to the colour scheme of Burton to see a few red flags flying on the chimneys of the breweries ... They were told ... that they could only trust the people to rule the country properly, who had a stake in the country. This was a delightful phrase, but it did not mean much. It was absurd to say the international capitalist had more stake in the country than the meanest and lowest working man ... Labour candidates, whether municipal or parliamentary, could not hope to compete with two quarts of beer per diem. When the breweries were nationalised and decorated with red flags, and black ones here and there for variety, it might be possible to give three quarts of beer instead of two, and those who did not want beer, allow them the money equivalent which was not now allowed.

The speech was frequently 'punctuated with applause', and the meeting finished with a resolution calling upon 'the workers to organise politically as they had done industrially, believing they can only bring about their emancipation by doing so.'[40] This rhetoric was unusual in Labour circles in Burton, and more typical was the speech made by one of the Labour candidates in 1920, who argued that 'though they had to fight for everything labour obtained he believed that the spirit of antagonism towards them as trade unionists was gradually withering away.'[41] Another candidate argued that a large amount of the rates had been 'contributed by

---

[38] *Burton-on-Trent Directory for 1932*, p. 23; *Burton-on-Trent Street Directory for 1937–38*, pp. 3 and 15.
[39] Stuart, *County Borough*, p. 272.
[40] *Burton Daily Mail*, 1 Nov. 1920.
[41] *Burton Daily Mail*, 30 Oct. 1920.

their class', so 'Labour should be better represented as there had not been sufficient consideration shown in matters which affected the workers'.[42] Some of their political opponents began to concede this last point. Thus in 1926 an Independent stated

> No sensible man objects to Labour on the Town Council. Any reasonable man thinks all parties should be represented, and at the last election I did what I could to get the return of a Labour candidate, my friend Jackie Jones, now I suppose Mr. Councillor John Jones, but I always think of him as little Jackie Jones, of Gresley Rovers, a good sport and a topping little fellow.[43]

Some Labour representatives were personally absorbed into the governing bloc of the borough. George Sanders, for instance, was elected under the 'Labour and Co-operative' banner in Victoria ward in 1919. He was returned unopposed simply as a 'Co-operative' candidate in 1922, and from 1925 sat as an 'Independent' councillor. For others the process was more subtle. Open electoral conflict between Labour and its opponents took place for the last time in the late 1920s. In 1928 Labour's Joe Clark was unseated in Winshill ward by an Independent, largely due to the accusation that the rates had gone up, and Clark as a de facto member of the administration of the council could be held responsible. His opponent was plainly a rogue 'Independent' outside of the ambit of the ruling group, while Clark could by now be portrayed very much as an insider. In the following year Clark got back onto the council by defeating another of the sitting Independents in the ward. A supporter of his opponent regretted that Clark was forcing a contest, and that the contest

> was being conducted on party lines. He deeply regretted that politics had crept into municipal affairs, for municipal matters were on an entirely different plane from Parliamentary business. He believed, however, that there was still as substantial body of ratepayers who would not let politics be their sole guide, but would look at the election from the right standpoint as to whom was the best man to represent their interests.[44]

Nevertheless at the same meeting an Independent councillor said that 'he had supported a Labour candidate the other night'. After this date such intrusion of 'politics' into municipal affairs was effectively avoided. Labour unsuccessfully stood against the rogue Independent who had deposed Clark when he came up for re-election in 1931, but party politics in any meaningful sense had ceased to operate.

Given its small size the germane fact is that Labour was awarded both position and some influence in Burton. No doubt the paternalism of the dominant brewing interest, although harsh in respect of organised Labour in the workplace, could see an advantage in tolerating the small and moderate Labour group in the borough's

---

[42] *Burton Daily Mail*, 23 Oct. 1920.
[43] *Burton Daily Mail*, 30 Oct. 1926.
[44] *Burton Daily Mail*, 26 Oct. 1929.

local politics. Accommodation contributed to the apolitical tenor of the borough, and drew Labour into the orbit of Independent administration, thereby defusing any residual radicalism. Labour for its part gained some power from this arrangement. In return attacks on Independents and their policies, and vice versa on Labour, were extremely muted at election time. Rarely were there *ad hominin* attacks, still less disputes over policy. Much more often, Labour councillors defended the council's record. Attitudes towards housing policy illustrate this very well.

The Labour party made housing something of an issue in 1919 and the early 1920s, before it had been absorbed into the ruling bloc on the council. The pre-war corporation had built only eight-eight 'workmen's dwellings'.[45] Just over 1,000 council houses were built in the inter-war years, amounting to one house built for every forty-seven people, a relatively modest ratio making Burton fifty-seventh amongst the county boroughs in this regard. (see Appendix 16). Over 700 council houses were built between 1925 and 1929, mainly in Horninglow ward and also in Winshill and Stapenhill. In the 1930s council house building slackened off with the largest development again in Horninglow, and smaller projects in Stapenhill, Victoria and Broadway wards. The council did not succumb to Labour calls for the employment of direct labour and all the council houses were constructed by local firms.[46] Between 1930 and 1940 more than twice as many private as corporation dwellings were constructed, the main private developments being in Horninglow, Stapenhill, Victoria and Winshill wards.[47]

For most of the period housing was an issue raised by Labour and Independents alike. Points about the quality and quantity of council housing, and occasionally the need for slum clearance, were raised, and Labour had no monopoly on these criticisms of council housing policy. The commonest complaint was the high rent of council properties for working-class people. Thus in 1926 Billy Hutson could say

> The houses the corporation are building were outside the scope of the ordinary working men and women. (Hear, hear). In saying that he was not decrying the local housing committee. Circumstances prevailed that forced the committee into the position of complying with the laws, and he had heard that in some cases only a few coppers were left out of £1 a week when rent, rates and other charges were met.[48]

Hutson's exoneration of the Housing Committee on the question shows the high level of co-operation between the ruling Independents and Labour that had already been developed. Joe Clark was the chair of the Housing Committee at this stage, and Hutson could not be too critical of his colleague. It was actually an Independent who in the same election mounted a much stronger attack on the council's record on public housing. His main complaint was about high building

[45] *The Municipal Yearbook*, 1910, p. 43.
[46] Stuart, *County Borough*, p. 167., and Owen, *Burton ... The Illustrated History*, p. 153.
[47] Stuart, *County Borough*, p. 168.
[48] *Burton Daily Mail*, 26 Oct. 1926.

costs, low density of building, and therefore unrealistically high rents for working people. He 'objected to the type of building put up for working men to live in. It was a scandal when a man had to pay a third of his wage for a place to lay his head'.[49] A few days later, the Labour Chairman of the Housing Committee replied with a defence of the ruling group on the council, outlining national guidelines on housing density and the detail of building costs.[50] Three years later in 1929, a Labour candidate could say that 'we should be thankful that we have a local authority that had built houses', and that he 'did not think that the houses could be let at a lower rental, because he did not think the cost should be spread over the ratepayers as a whole'. He did, however, advocate the adoption of a direct building department.[51] The use of direct labour, usually linked to schemes of unemployment relief, was a constant Labour policy issue throughout the 1920s. Given the fact that Labour became very much an insider in terms of housing policy, its lack of success in implementing this favoured panacea shows the limits of its influence on the council, and the real control exerted by the independents.

The final question to be considered in relation to the municipal politics of Burton is the part played by women. Women candidates were very rare, with women standing in all on only eleven occasions between the wars. This represented only 5 per cent of the 204 candidatures in the period. Labour fielded a woman candidate only twice, and on a further two occasions women stood for the Co-operative party. Women stood as Independents seven times, but the only woman to win election to the council between the wars was Mary Goodger in Uxbridge ward in uncontested elections between 1925 and 1934. Goodger was the sister of the Clerk of the Magistrates, and a benefactor of the town in terms of both sales and gifts of land.[52] She was Burton's first female mayor in 1931–32. Overall, then, women seemed to have been allowed very little scope in local politics. This is perhaps not unexpected, given the influence of the brewing industry. Beer was a male-dominated product not only in terms of those who produced it but also largely in terms of those who consumed it at this time.[53]

Nevertheless women were treated as a group of electors that deserved special attention, especially after the enfranchisement of women over the age of twenty-one in 1918. Labour's candidate in Winshill, Joe Clark, held a meeting for women in the 1919 election. He was opposed by a female Independent candidate, so he perhaps thought it expedient to address a 'women only' meeting. Claiming that he had supported votes for women 'for many years', Clark said that he did not object to his opponent on 'the ground of sex', but he did not consider her a 'working woman, and one who would know the requirements of the erection of a working man's house'. He emphasised the need for better design of council houses, and for women to be consulted on these questions, as well as improvements in sanitary conditions to raise the standard of health amongst children. Miss Weaver, an organiser for the Workers Union, said that 'women had been kept at home, and never been led to understand that they ought to take part in the picking of a

[49]   *Burton Daily Mail*, 27 Oct. 1926.
[50]   *Burton Daily Mail*, 28 Oct. 1926.
[51]   *Burton Daily Mail*, 22 Oct. 1929.
[52]   Stuart, *County Borough*, p. 63 and pp. 258–259.
[53]   Stevenson, J., *British Society 1914–1945*, (Harmondsworth, 1984), p. 383.

municipal candidate'. Susan Stack, Clark's opponent, later defended herself publicly as a working woman and married to a weaver, living in a typical weaver's home, who had 'always lived among the workers'. In another Labour meeting, Billy Hutson rather undermined the efforts of his colleague to win the support of women voters by urging the sacking of women 'who were not employed in their particular work prior to the war' to make way for ex-servicemen. The Chamber of Trade candidate in Stapenhill ward was not so harsh as Hutson, allowing that 'the widows of soldiers should not be displaced by men. (Hear, hear.)'.[54]

The Independents also arranged women-only meetings. Councillor Hutchinson, defending Victoria ward in 1921, attended one such 'composed exclusively of ladies' and presided over by a woman. Outlining his credentials as the champion of women, Hutchinson said that he had supported votes for women, that he had nominated a woman for the council during the recent war, and expected votes for women over the age of twenty-one to be implemented soon. The main focus of his speech, however, was on the question of the rates. Hutchinson believed that 'women were as much, if not more, concerned than men in the question of the rates, because they had to manage a household', and he pledged 'a big reduction in the rates'. Shortly, the doors were 'thrown open to the whole of the electors and the attendance was much more satisfactory'.[55] Overall, it can be seen that women in Burton were treated as a group of electors with special concerns related primarily to the domestic sphere of home and family.

In conclusion, a number of points can be made concerning municipal elections and politics in Burton. The borough in the inter-war years lacked orthodox party conflict in elections to the council chamber. The reasons for this lay partly in the central role of the breweries in the life of the borough, partly in the weakness of the local Labour Party. Labour was so weak numerically, and so moderate, that its councillors could be invited into the inner circles of local government by the ruling group, amongst whom in turn there existed little difference between Conservatives and Independents. In these respects Burton was much more akin to the smaller local authorities than most of the other county boroughs. Labour's acceptance of the embrace of the dominant Independents gave it some advantages, allowing it some input into policy, especially over housing. Ultimately of course the Independents had the power, and Labour could only achieve what was acceptable to its masters. By being drawn into the orbit of power, Labour also served to legitimise the actions and policies of the ruling Independents. Party battles were few and far between and there was almost literally 'no politics in the council' in Burton.

---

[54] *Burton Daily Mail*, 23, 24 and 29 Oct. 1919.
[55] *Burton Daily Mail*, 26 Oct. 1921.

A guide to further reading

Newspapers

Burton Daily Mail
Burton Evening Gazette

Works of reference

Burton on Trent Directory , 1932 and 1934.
Burton on Trent Street Directory, 1937–38.

Other secondary sources

Owen, C.C.,*The Development of Industry in Burton upon Trent*, (Chichester, 1978).
Owen, C., *Burton upon Trent: The Illustrated History*, (Derby, 1994).
Stuart, D., *County Borough: the History of Burton upon Trent 1901–1974, Part 2 1914–1974*, (Burton-upon-Trent, 1977).

Burton-upon-Trent wards 1919–1938

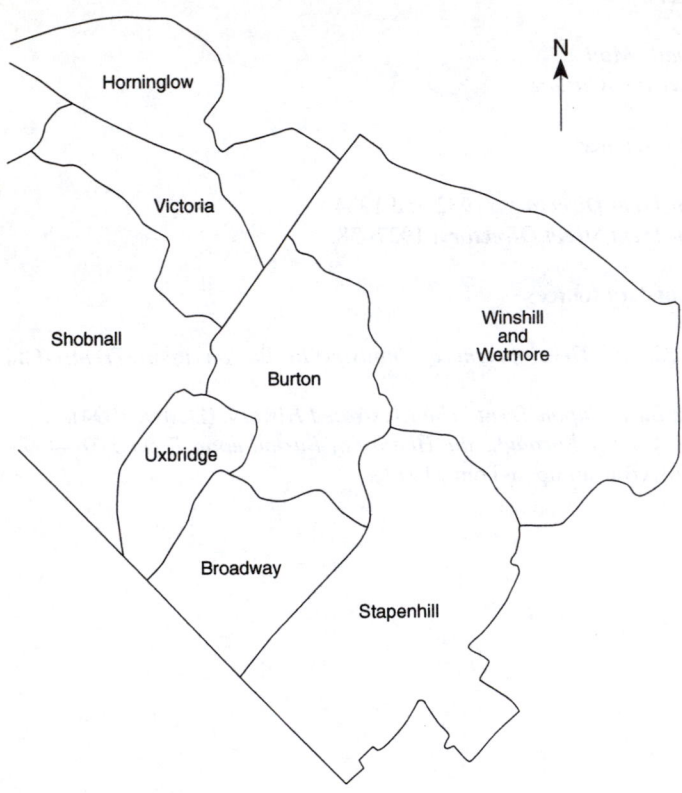

Horninglow

Victoria

Shobnall

Burton

Winshill
and
Wetmore

Uxbridge

Broadway

Stapenhill

N

Persons aged fourteen and over classified by industry 1931

	Male	%	Female	%	Total	%
Metal and engineering	1,419	8.5	163	3.0	1,582	7.1
Textiles	187	1.1	443	8.1	630	2.8
Clothing	290	1.7	444	8.2	734	3.3
Food, drink and tobacco	5,616	33.6	452	8.3	6,068	27.4
- Drink	*5,247*	*31.4*	*347*	*6.4*	*5,594*	*25.2*
Building	1,124	6.7	9	0.2	1,133	5.1
Other manufacturing	605	3.6	317	5.8	922	4.2
- Rubber	*505*	*3.0*	*301*	*5.5*	*806*	*3.6*
Transport	1,641	9.8	56	1.0	1,697	7.7
- Railways	*1,340*	*8.0*	*49*	*0.9*	*1,389*	*6.3*
Commerce and finance	2,206	13.2	984	18.1	3,190	14.4
Public admin.and defence	966	5.8	435	8.0	1,401	6.3
- Local government	*762*	*4.6*	*372*	*6.8*	1,134	5.1
Personal service	416	2.5	1,635	30.0	2,051	9.3
Others	2,251	13.5	505	9.3	2,756	12.4
Total (a)	**16,721**		**5,443**		**22,164**	
Total population (b)	24,303		25,183		49,486	
(a) as % of (b)	68.8		21.6		44.8	
Total out of work (c)	2,216		458		2,674	
(c) as % of (a)	13.3		8.4		12.1	
Managerial and own account	1,509	10.4	472	9.5	1,981	10.2
Operative	12,996	89.6	4,513	90.5	17,509	89.8
Total (excluding out of work)	14,505		4,985		19,490	

Population statistics 1931

Ward	Acres	Population	Persons/acre	Persons/room
Broadway	290	5,663	19.5	0.74
Burton	429	4,308	10.0	0.83
Horninglow	477	7,486	15.7	0.72
Shobnall	776	6,250	8.1	0.76
Stapenhill	790	5,740	7.3	0.78
Uxbridge	180	7,590	42.2	0.81
Victoria	250	6,227	24.9	0.72
Winshill and Wetmore	1,011	6,222	6.2	0.75
Total	**4,203**	**49,486**	11.8	**0.76**

Overall position on the council, 1919–38

	Position		Gains		Losses	
	Ind	Lab	Ind	Lab	Ind	Lab
1919	27	5	0	2	2	0
1920	25	7	0	2	2	0
1921	25	7	0	0	0	0
1922	26	6	1	0	0	1
1923	26	6	0	0	0	0
1924	27	5	1	0	0	1
1925	27	5	1	1	1	1
1926	28	4	1	0	0	1
1927	28	4	0	0	0	0
1928	29	3	1	0	0	1
1929	29	3	0	1	1	0
1930	29	3	0	0	0	0
1931	29	3	0	0	0	0
1932	29	3	0	0	0	0
1933	29	3	0	0	0	0
1934	29	3	0	0	0	0
1935	29	3	0	0	0	0
1936	29	3	0	0	0	0
1937	29	3	0	0	0	0
1938	29	3	0	0	0	0

Aldermen 1919–38

Independents held all aldermanic seats 1919–1938.

Municipal elections: winning party 1919–28

Ward	1919	1920	1921	1922	1923	1924	1925	1926	1927	1928
Broadway	Nfds	**Fr S**	**Ind**	Ind	**Ind**	**Ind**	**Ind**	**Ind**	**Ind**	**Ind**
Burton	Ch T	**Ind**	**Ind**	Ind	**Ind**	**Ind**	**Ind**	Ind	**Ind**	**Ind**
Horninglow	Lab	Ind	Ind	Ind	**Ind**	**Ind**	**Ind**	**Ind**	Ind	**Ind**
Shobnall	Ind	Ind	**Ind**	**Ind**	**Ind**	**Ind**	Ind	**Ind**	**Ind**	**Ind**
Stapenhill	**Ch T**	**Ind**	**Lab**	**Ind**	**Ind**	**Lab**	Lab	Ind	**Ind**	**Lab**
Uxbridge	**Lab**	Lab	Ind	**Lab**	**Lab**	Ind	**Ind**	Ind	**Ind**	**Ind**
Victoria	Lab	Lab	Ind	**Lab**	**Lab**	**Ind**	Ind	Lab	**Ind**	**Ind**
Winshill and Wetmore	Lab	R	Ind	**Lab**	**Ind**	**Ind**	**Lab**	**Ind**	**Ind**	Ind

Municipal elections: party wins per year 1919–28

	1919	1920	1921	1922	1923	1924	1925	1926	1927	1928
Ind	4	6	7	5	6	7	6	7	8	7
Lab	4	2	1	3	2	1	2	1	0	1
Total	8	8	8	8	8	8	8	8	8	8
Turnout %	**50.0**	**59.9**	**59.9**	**68.6**	-	**60.0**	**66.0**	**60.9**	**65.0**	**75.0**
Labour %	**36.7**	**30.6**	**14.5**	**22.7**	-	**33.6**	**40.1**	**46.0**	-	**45.1**

Municipal elections: winning party 1929–38

Ward	1929	1930	1931	1932	1933	1934	1935	1936	1937	1938
Broadway	Ind	**Ind**	**Ind**	**Ind**	**Ind**	**Ind**	**Ind**	**Ind**	Ind	**Ind**
Burton	**Ind**	**Ind**	**Ind**	**Ind**	**Ind**	**Ind**	**Ind**	**Ind**	**Ind**	**Ind**
Horninglow	Ind	Ind	Ind	**Ind**	**Ind**	**Ind**	**Ind**	**Ind**	**Ind**	**Ind**
Shobnall	**Ind**	**Ind**	**Ind**	**Ind**	**Ind**	**Ind**	**Ind**	**Ind**	**Ind**	**Ind**
Stapenhill	Ind	**Ind**	**Lab**	**Ind**	**Ind**	**Lab**	**Ind**	**Ind**	**Lab**	**Ind**
Uxbridge	Ind	Ind	**Ind**	**Ind**	**Ind**	**Ind**	**Ind**	**Ind**	Ind	**Ind**
Victoria	Lab	**Ind**	**Ind**	**Lab**	**Ind**	**Ind**	**Lab**	**Ind**	**Ind**	**Lab**
Winshill and Wetmore	Lab	**Ind**	Ind	**Lab**	**Ind**	**Ind**	**Lab**	**Ind**	**Ind**	**Lab**

Municipal elections: party wins per year 1929–38

	1929	1930	1931	1932	1933	1934	1935	1936	1937	1938
Ind	6	8	7	6	8	7	6	8	7	6
Lab	2	0	1	2	0	1	2	0	1	2
Total	8	8	8	8	8	8	8	8	8	8
Turnout %	**51.7**	**46.4**	**42.2**	-	-	-	-	-	**48.9**	-
Labour %	**40.8**	**34.6**	**23.7**	-	-	-	-	-	-	-

Municipal elections: party wins per ward 1919–38

	Ind	Lab	Total	Turnout %	Labour % of all votes
Broadway	20	0	20	49.3	7.7
Burton	20	0	20	54.5	6.8
Horninglow	19	1	20	57.4	27.0
Shobnall	20	0	20	64.2	33.3
Stapenhill	13	7	20	63.7	-
Uxbridge	16	4	20	51.4	31.4
Victoria	11	9	20	56.2	36.4
Winshill and Wetmore	13	7	20	64.8	37.9
Total	**132**	**28**	**160**	**57.0**	**30.8**

Seats won by Labour as a percentage of all wins 1919–38   **17.5**

Parliamentary election results

Burton constituency
*(all wards within the borough [1918 boundaries] were included in the
constituency, along with the urban district of Uttoxeter and the rural
districts of Stafford (part), Tutbury and Uttoxeter)*

General election	Winner	Conservative %	Labour %	Liberal %
14 Dec. 1918	**Co C**	-	-	-
15 Nov. 1922	**C**	-	-	-
6 Dec. 1923	**C**	-	-	-
29 Oct. 1924	C	74.2	25.8	-
30 May 1929	C	52.6	30.3	17.1
27 Oct. 1931	C	74.7	25.3	-
14 Nov. 1935	C	74.5	25.5	-

Broadway ward

Candidate	Party	Votes	%	Electors	Turnout	Gains
1919						
A.W. Bennett	Nfds	636	59.5	2,313	46.2	-
C.M. Livens	Ind	433	40.5			
Total votes		1,069				
1920						
A.J. Thornley*	Fr S	Unopp.	-		-	-
1921						
G. Hill*	Ind	Unopp.	-		-	-
1922						
A. Fox	Ind	1,176	76.8	2,345	65.3	Ind from Nfds
H. Holmes	Lab	356	23.2			
Total votes		1,532				
1923						
A.J. Thornley*	Ind	Unopp.	-		-	-
1924						
C.M. Livens	Ind	Unopp.	-		-	-
1925						
A. Fox*	Ind	Unopp.	-		-	-
1926						
G.E. Rider*	Ind	Unopp.	-		-	-
1927						
C.M. Livens*	Ind	Unopp.	-		-	-
1928						
A. Fox*	Ind	Unopp.	-		-	-
1929						
G.E. Rider*	Ind	505	74.9	2,308	29.2	-
M. Codling	Ind	169	25.1			
Total votes		674				

Broadway ward *(continued)*

Candidate	Party	Votes	%	Electors	Turnout	Gains
1930						
G. Smith*	Ind	Unopp.	-		-	-
1931						
A. Fox*	Ind	Unopp.	-	2,521	-	-
1932						
G.E. Rider*	Ind	Unopp.	-		-	-
1933						
D.R. Fergusson*	Ind	Unopp.	-		-	-
1934						
J.H. Kirk*	Ind	Unopp.	-		-	-
1935						
G.E. Rider*	Ind	Unopp.	-		-	-
1936						
D.R. Fergusson*	Ind	Unopp.	-		-	-
1937						
W.P. Wibberley	Ind	704	52.0	2,429	55.8	-
S.G. Edwards	U	429	31.7			
Mrs A. Chadwick	Coop	222	16.4			
Total votes		1,355				
1938						
G.E. Rider*	Ind	Unopp.	-		-	-

Overall Labour vote   **7.7%**   **Overall turnout**   **49.3%**

Burton ward

Candidate	Party	Votes	%	Electors	Turnout	Gains
1919						
W. Lean	Ch T	268	55.7	1,743	27.6	-
J.R. Cain	Ind	213	44.3			
Total votes		481				
1920						
J.D. Robertson	Ind	Unopp.	-		-	-
1921						
W.D. Johnson*	Ind	Unopp.	-		-	-
1922						
L.T. Peach	Ind	883	58.6	1,896	79.4	-
W. Lean*	Ind	623	41.4			
Total votes		1,506				
1923						
J.D. Robertson*	Ind	Unopp.	-		-	-
1924						
W.D. Johnson*	Ind	Unopp.	-		-	-
1925						
L.T. Peach*	Ind	Unopp.	-		-	-
1926						
F.G. Thompson	Ind	805	79.7	1,863	54.2	-
H.W. Brewin	Lab	205	20.3			
Total votes		1,010				
1927						
W.D. Johnson*	Ind	Unopp.	-		-	-
1928						
W.P. Stanley	Ind	Unopp.	-		-	-
1929						
F.G. Thompson*	Ind	Unopp.	-		-	-

Burton ward *(continued)*

Candidate	Party	Votes	%	Electors	Turnout	Gains
1930						
W.D. Johnson*	Ind	Unopp.	-		-	-
1931						
W.P. Stanley*	Ind	Unopp.	-	2,066	-	-
1932						
F.G. Thompson*	Ind	Unopp.	-		-	-
1933						
H.S. Lance*	Ind	Unopp.	-		-	-
1934						
W.P. Stanley*	Ind	Unopp.	-		-	-
1935						
F.G. Thompson*	Ind	Unopp.	-		-	-
1936						
H.S. Lance*	Ind	Unopp.	-		-	-
1937						
W.P. Stanley*	Ind	Unopp.	-		-	-
1938						
F.G. Thompson*	Ind	Unopp.	-		-	-

Overall Labour vote   **6.8%**   **Overall turnout**   **54.5%**

Horninglow ward

Candidate	Party	Votes	%	Electors	Turnout	Gains
1919						
C. Robinson	Lab	770	51.1	2,772	54.4	Lab from Ind
A.E. Baldock	Ind	738	48.9			
Total votes		1,508				
1920						
A. Brooks*	Ind	1,461	77.7	2,839	66.3	-
T. Keeling	Lab	420	22.3			
Total votes		1,881				
1921						
J.W. Campion	Ind	810	39.7	2,846	71.7	-
J. Harper	Ind	801	39.3			
D.W. Ford	Lab	429	21.0			
Total votes		2,040				
1922						
J. Harper	Ind	1,084	59.2	2,856	64.1	Ind from Lab
C. Robinson*	Lab	747	40.8			
Total votes		1,831				
1923						
A. Brooks*	Ind	Unopp.	-		-	-
1924						
J.W. Campion*	Ind	Unopp.	-		-	-
1925						
J. Harper*	Ind	Unopp.	-		-	-
1926						
A. Brooks*	Ind	Unopp.	-		-	-
1927						
J.W. Campion*	Ind	1,215	65.7	2,845	65.0	-
J. Sheratt	Ind	634	34.3			
Total votes		1,849				
1928						
J. Harper*	Ind	Unopp.	-		-	-

Horninglow ward *(continued)*

Candidate	Party	Votes	%	Electors	Turnout	Gains
1929						
G.L. Mee*	Ind	880	51.9	3,258	52.1	-
H. Allcock	Lab	563	33.2			
Mrs Johns	Ind	253	14.9			
Total votes		1,696				
1930						
J.W. Campion*	Ind	1,233	71.1	3,562	48.7	-
H. Allcock	Lab	502	28.9			
Total votes		1,735				
1931						
J.S. Harper*	Ind	1,159	75.7	3,536	43.3	-
T. Turner	Lab	372	24.3			
Total votes		1,531				
1932						
G.L. Mee*	Ind	Unopp.	-		-	-
1933						
J.W. Campion*	Ind	Unopp.	-		-	-
1934						
J. Harper*	Ind	Unopp.	-		-	-
1935						
G.L. Mee*	Ind	Unopp.	-		-	-
1936						
A. Bamford	Ind	Unopp.	-		-	-
1937						
J. Harper*	Ind	Unopp.	-		-	-
1938						
G.L. Mee*	Ind	Unopp.	-		-	-

Overall Labour vote		**27.0%**		**Overall turnout**		**57.4%**

Shobnall ward

Candidate	Party	Votes	%	Electors	Turnout	Gains
1919						
A. Elliott*	Ind	706	51.6	2,368	57.8	-
C. Gilson	Nfds	359	26.2			
W. Hutson	Lab	303	22.1			
Total votes		1,368				
1920						
W.H. Giles	Ind	1,167	73.6	2,452	64.7	-
C. Gilson	Lab	419	26.4			
Total votes		1,586				
1921						
T. Ross*	Ind	Unopp.	-		-	-
1922						
A. Elliott*	Ind	Unopp.	-		-	-
1923						
W.H. Giles*	Ind	Unopp.	-		-	-
1924						
R. McCreath	Ind	Unopp.	-		-	-
1925						
A. Elliott*	Ind	887	51.5	2,464	69.9	-
W. Evans	Lab	835	48.5			
Total votes		1,722				
1926						
W.H. Giles*	Ind	Unopp.	-		-	-
1927						
R. McCreath*	Ind	Unopp.	-		-	-
1928						
F.O.N. Hurdle*	Ind	Unopp.	-		-	-
1929						
W.H. Giles*	Ind	Unopp.	-		-	-

Shobnall ward *(continued)*

Candidate	Party	Votes	%	Electors	Turnout	Gains
1930						
R. McCreath*	Ind	Unopp.	-		-	-
1931						
F.O.N. Hurdle*	Ind	Unopp.	-	2,691	-	-
1932						
W.H. Giles*	Ind	Unopp.	-		-	-
1933						
R. McCreath*	Ind	Unopp.	-		-	-
1934						
F.O.N. Hurdle*	Ind	Unopp.	-		-	-
1935						
A. Fidkin*	Ind	Unopp.	-		-	-
1936						
R. McCreath*	Ind	Unopp.	-		-	-
1937						
J.H. Smith	Ind	Unopp.	-		-	-
1938						
A. Fidkin*	Ind	Unopp.	-		-	-

Overall Labour vote   **33.3%**   **Overall turnout**   **64.2%**

Stapenhill ward

Candidate	Party	Votes	%	Electors	Turnout	Gains
1919						
W.R. Thornley	Ch T	Unopp.	-		-	-
1920						
A.H. Yeomans*	Ind	Unopp.	-		-	-
1921						
J. Wilkinson*	Lab	Unopp.	-		-	-
1922						
W.R. Thornley*	Ind	Unopp.	-		-	-
1923						
A.H. Yeomans*	Ind	Unopp.	-		-	-
1924						
J. Wilkinson*	Lab	Unopp.	-		-	-
1925						
J. Jones	Lab	1,101	74.7	2,124	69.4	Lab from Ind
Mrs K.E. Brittain	Ind	372	25.3			
Total votes		1,473				
1926						
T.H. Walters	Ind	778	53.6	2,222	65.3	-
C. Gibson	Lab	673	46.4			
Total votes		1,451				
1927						
T.F. Lewis*	Ind	Unopp.	-		-	-
1928						
J. Jones*	Lab	Unopp.	-		-	-
1929						
T.H. Walters*	Ind	847	64.7	2,305	56.8	-
C.E. Royle	Lab	463	35.3			
Total votes		1,310				

Stapenhill ward *(continued)*

Candidate	Party	Votes	%	Electors	Turnout	Gains
1930						
T.F. Lewis*	Ind	Unopp.	-		-	-
1931						
J. Jones*	Lab	Unopp.	-	2,599	-	-
1932						
T.H. Walters*	Ind	Unopp.	-		-	-
1933						
T.F. Lewis*	Ind	Unopp.	-		-	-
1934						
J. Jones*	Lab	Unopp.	-		-	-
1935						
T.H. Walters*	Ind	Unopp.	-		-	-
1936						
T.F. Lewis*	Ind	Unopp.	-		-	-
1937						
J. Jones*	Lab	Unopp.	-		-	-
1938						
T.H. Walters*	Ind	Unopp.	-		-	-

Overall Labour vote   -   **Overall turnout**   **63.7%**

Uxbridge ward

Candidate	Party	Votes	%	Electors	Turnout	Gains
1919						
W. Austin	Lab	Unopp.	-		-	-
1920						
B.T. Curtis	Lab	782	54.1	2,935	49.3	Lab from Ind
L. Radford*	Ind	664	45.9			
Total votes		1,446				
1921						
J.W.A. Basnett*	Ind	1,189	72.9	2,900	56.3	-
A.E. Ingledew	Nfds	443	27.1			
Total votes		1,632				
1922						
W. Austin*	Lab	Unopp.	-		-	-
1923						
B.T. Curtis*	Lab	Unopp.	-		-	-
1924						
L. Radford	Ind	1,214	66.4	3,045	60.0	Ind from Lab
J. Tivey	Lab	613	33.6			
Total votes		1,827				
1925						
Miss M. Goodger	Ind	Unopp.	-		-	Ind from Lab
1926						
F.J. Coxon	Ind	1,038	54.0	3,059	62.8	Ind from Lab
B.T. Curtis*	Lab	883	46.0			
Total votes		1,921				
1927						
L. Radford*	Ind	Unopp.	-		-	-
1928						
Miss M. Goodger*	Ind	Unopp.	-		-	-

Uxbridge ward *(continued)*

Candidate	Party	Votes	%	Electors	Turnout	Gains
1929						
A. Harrison	Ind	789	56.9	3,064	45.3	-
T. Burchill	Lab	598	43.1			
Total votes		1,387				
1930						
J. Sherratt	Ind	852	58.6	3,302	44.0	-
Mrs H. Causer	Lab	601	41.4			
Total votes		1,453				
1931						
Miss M. Goodger*	Ind	Unopp.	-	3,393	-	-
1932						
A. Harrison*	Ind	Unopp.	-		-	-
1933						
J. Sherratt*	Ind	Unopp.	-		-	-
1934						
Miss M. Goodger*	Ind	Unopp.	-		-	-
1935						
A. Harrison*	Ind	Unopp.	-		-	-
1936						
J.T.H. Jackson	Ind	Unopp.	-		-	-
1937						
C.H. Dobson	Ind	719	51.2	3,219	43.6	U from Ind
Mrs E. Martin	Coop	686	48.8			
Total votes		1,405				
1938						
A. Harrison*	Ind	Unopp.	-		-	-

Overall Labour vote	**31.4%**			**Overall turnout**		**51.4%**

Victoria ward

Candidate	Party	Votes	%	Electors	Turnout	Gains
1919						
G. Sanders*	Lab	567	52.7	2,535	42.4	-
H.W. Brewin	Nfds	509	47.3			
Total votes		1,076				
1920						
W. Hutson	Lab	783	50.9	2,641	58.2	Lab from Ind
J.R. Johnson	Ind	755	49.1			
Total votes		1,538				
1921						
W.G. Hutchinson*	Ind	1,053	70.9	2,638	56.3	-
A.R. Cardy	Nfds	433	29.1			
Total votes		1,486				
1922						
G. Sanders*	Coop	Unopp.	-		-	-
1923						
W. Hutson*	Lab	Unopp.	-		-	-
1924						
R.H. Dove	Ind	Unopp.	-		-	-
1925						
G. Sanders*	Ind	1,129	69.0	2,728	60.0	-
W. Lean	Ind	507	31.0			
Total votes		1,636				
1926						
W. Hutson*	Lab	1,073	60.3	2,977	59.8	-
J. Arnold	Ind	706	39.7			
Total votes		1,779				
1927						
R.H. Dove*	Ind	Unopp.	-		-	-
1928						
G. Sanders*	Ind	Unopp.	-		-	-

Victoria ward *(continued)*

Candidate	Party	Votes	%	Electors	Turnout	Gains
1929						
W. Hutson*	Lab	900	55.7	2,726	59.3	-
A.F. Whetton	Ind	717	44.3			
Total votes		1,617				
1930						
A.F. Whetton	Ind	Unopp.	-		-	-
1931						
G. Sanders*	Ind	Unopp.	-	3,053	-	-
1932						
W. Hutson*	Lab	Unopp.	-		-	-
1933						
A.F. Whetton*	Ind	Unopp.	-		-	-
1934						
G. Sanders*	Ind	Unopp.	-		-	-
1935						
W. Hutson*	Lab	Unopp.	-		-	-
1936						
A.F. Whetton*	Ind	Unopp.	-		-	-
1937						
G. Sanders*	Ind	Unopp.	-		-	-
1938						
W. Hutson*	Lab	Unopp.	-		-	-

Overall Labour vote   **36.4%**   **Overall turnout**   **56.2%**

Winshill and Wetmore ward

Candidate	Party	Votes	%	Electors	Turnout	Gains
1919						
J.W. Clark	Lab	912	63.0	2,170	66.7	Lab from Ind
Mrs S. Stack	Ind	536	37.0			
Total votes		1,448				
1920						
R.A. Hatfield	R	1,102	78.7	2,245	62.4	-
W.H. Coltman	Nfds	298	21.3			
Total votes		1,400				
1921						
J.T. Adams	Ind	694	58.5	2,205	53.8	Ind from Lab
C.H. Goodall	Lab	492	41.5			
Total votes		1,186				
1922						
J.W. Clark*	Lab	Unopp.	-		-	-
1923						
R.A. Hatfield*	Ind	Unopp.	-		-	-
1924						
J.T. Adams*	Ind	Unopp.	-		-	-
1925						
J.W. Clark*	Lab	Unopp.	-		-	-
1926						
R.A. Hatfield*	Ind	Unopp.	-		-	-
1927						
J.T. Adams*	Ind	Unopp.	-		-	-
1928						
S.R. Sharp	Ind	1,029	54.9	2,500	75.0	Ind from Lab
J.W. Clark*	Lab	846	45.1			
Total votes		1,875				

Winshill and Wetmore ward *(continued)*

Candidate	Party	Votes	%	Electors	Turnout	Gains
1929						
J.W. Clark	Lab	893	53.1	2,524	66.6	Lab from Ind
R.A. Hatfield*	Ind	788	46.9			
Total votes		1,681				
1930						
J.T. Adams*	Ind	Unopp.	-		-	-
1931						
S.R. Sharp*	Ind	1,387	76.8	2,859	63.2	-
Mrs H. Causer	Lab	419	23.2			
Total votes		1,806				
1932						
J.W. Clark*	Lab	Unopp.	-		-	-
1933						
J.T. Adams*	Ind	Unopp.	-		-	-
1934						
G.H.F. White	Ind	Unopp.	-		-	-
1935						
J.W. Clark*	Lab	Unopp.	-		-	-
1936						
J.T. Adams*	Ind	Unopp.	-		-	-
1937						
G.H.F. White*	Ind	Unopp.	-		-	-
1938						
J.W. Clark*	Lab	Unopp.	-		-	-

Overall Labour vote   **37.9%**   **Overall turnout**   **64.8%**

SIX
Bury

BURY

Up to the mid-eighteenth century Bury was a market town and a centre for tanning, paper-making and the manufacture of woollen cloth and felt hats.[1] The subsequent development of the cotton industry made Bury a centre of economic importance to Lancashire. In the high and late Victorian age Bury's cotton industry was a power in the world market. Although Bury lay within the Manchester conurbation, it was not a mere extension of that cotton metropolis. Securing early canal and rail links, Bury had many advantages of lying within Manchester's economic orbit. As 'an old market town' however, by the twentieth century, Bury had 'a well developed commercial focus', allied to a 'strongly independent corporate life and robust local patriotism'.[2] Cotton spinning with dying and bleaching had become the central core of the town's economy by the mid-nineteenth century. Though in the spinning belt, Bury had a more balanced cotton industry than some other Lancashire towns, and the borough was also an 'outpost of weaving in the Manchester area'.[3] In 1931 cotton spinning and weaving employed over 13 per cent of males and 46 per cent of females in the borough, and the textile category as a whole including dying and finishing employed a quarter of all men and over half of all women aged fourteen and over. Linked to textiles, the manufacture of clothing was important with over 10 per cent of employed women in this sector. Unsurprisingly Bury was high in the ranking of textile towns, lying seventh in terms of the percentage of the total labour force in textiles, and eighth in terms of the female labour force (see appendices 7 and 8). Cotton and engineering had a close relationship in pre-Depression Lancashire, and by the early twentieth century engineering was gaining ground on cotton as the town's main staple.[4] This was an important sector of skilled manual work for men, accounting for over 12 per cent of the male workforce. Bury was ranked fourteenth of the county boroughs in the engineering category. The engineering plants mainly produced textile machinery, mill furnishings and paper-making machinery. One specialism of engineering was the construction of ambulances by the firm of Wilson and Stockhall. Paper-making was a traditional industry in the area and this industry of largely male employment changed and became notable for its significant proportion of female labour in the twentieth century. There was also the important slipper works of J.H. Parker which was a large employer of both male and female labour, and more generally Bury also had a substantial boot and shoe industry.[5] The manufacture of rayon and hats

---

[1]   Bannister, J., *From Parish to Metro: Two Centuries of Local Government in a Lancashire Town*, (Bury, 1974), pp. ix–x.
[2]   Freeman, T.W., Rodgers, H.B. and Kinvig, R.H., *Lancashire, Cheshire and the Isle of Man*, (London, 1966), pp. 218–220.
[3]   Walton, J., *Lancashire: A Social History, 1558–1939*, (Manchester, 1987), p. 199; Freeman, Rodgers and Kinvig, *Lancashire, Cheshire and the Isle of Man*, p. 219; Fogarty, M.P., *Prospects of the Industrial Areas of Great Britain*, (London, 1945), p. 220.
[4]   Pelling, H., *Social Geography of British Elections 1885–1910*, (London, 1967), p. 240.
[5]   Fogarty, *Prospects of the Industrial Areas*, p. 220.

was also important while a further element of diversification was the survival of woollen manufacture.[6]

In the petite bourgeois and middle class occupations, Bury had a reasonably developed commercial and financial sector which employed over 11 per cent of the total workforce, while public administration and defence – including local government – was also worthy of note. A small but established lower middle class existed. Higher up the social scale there was also a small upper middle class, largely the owners of the mills and engineering plants together with the lawyers and other professionals who serviced them. 11 per cent of the workforce was found in the managerial and own account categories, and in these terms Bury was ranked only fifty-eighth amongst the county boroughs. It was also ranked at fifty-ninth in terms of the professional category (see Appendices 4 and 5). In addition, with female domestic servants making up only 2 per cent of the total population, Bury was plainly a town with only a small middle class. Overall, Bury was predominantly a working-class town, and as with other textile towns, women workers were especially significant in comparison to most other boroughs.

Bury's economy was, along with the other cotton towns of Lancashire, hit by the impact of the First World War. The cotton industry slumped due to the loss of Far Eastern markets, a process aided by the export of textile machinery from the town, and was further decimated by the Depression after 1929. The town's second industry, engineering, was also affected adversely by the inter-war travails of the British economy, though not so dramatically as textiles. With Lancashire's cotton industry in decline the economic base of cotton towns needed to change. But as the Manchester area had some economic bright spots, Lancashire was not included in the Special Areas act of 1934, even though the weaving districts were as hard hit as South Wales, Durham and Tyneside and West Cumberland. Thus no central government funds were forthcoming to bring in new industry. However, Bury was less hard hit than other cotton towns, as it did not have an overwhelming reliance on only one or other of the spinning or weaving sectors, and in other ways also had a more diversified local economy. This enabled the borough to endure fierce international competition and world-wide depression somewhat better than other parts of cotton Lancashire. This resulted in comparatively fewer unemployed, less economic dislocation and a slightly more managed decline. By November, 1930 there were 883 persons in Bury receiving relief and a further 600 benefiting from outdoor relief. By the official figures, 15.7 per cent were unemployed in 1929 and that had risen to 27.9 per cent by December 1930. In the ranking of boroughs in terms of unemployment derived from the 1931 census, Bury, with 16.9 per cent of the workforce defined as out of work, suffered less than Preston (18.6 per cent), Oldham (22.8 per cent), Burnley (24.1 per cent) and especially Blackburn (32.7 per cent). Only Rochdale, Manchester and Bolton fared marginally better in cotton Lancashire. There was also some recovery later in the decade. Bury unemployment 'returned to about the average of the county as a whole by 1936 and 1937', and one study saw 'most of the spinning district ... at a certain moderate level of prosperity at the peak of the trade cycle' by 1937.[7] The inter-war economic trends

---

[6]   Freeman, Rodgers and Kinvig, *Lancashire, Cheshire and the Isle of Man,* pp. 219.
[7]   Fogarty, *Prospects of the Industrial Areas,* p. 220.

were reflected in the population growth of the borough. Bury had a population of 52,000 when it became a county borough in 1888, but the borough's hey-day as a growing and dynamic centre of economic activity had passed by 1914, and by the inter-war period the population of the town was more or less static around 56,000.

Bury was also a strongly Anglican town, which had some influence on political developments. Mid-Victorian Bury's ruling elite was 'steadfastly Anglican', and the strength of Anglican and Tory feeling was shown by the fact that the town had no Board Schools before 1914.[8] This tradition was carried over into the 1930s, with the council being noted for its parsimonious attitude to education.[9] This is not to say that Nonconformity was absent in Bury. In the 1851 religious census over 50 per cent of worshippers were classified as Dissenters, and the Nonconformist tradition was reflected by the late nineteenth century in a shortage of public houses.[10] There were also a significant number of Methodist schools in the borough,[11] and the Temperance Union and Band of Hope were prominent. Nonconformity provided a basis for Liberalism in the borough, which was reflected in Liberal positions on education in inter-war politics, as will be shown below. Nevertheless, Nonconformity was subordinate to Anglicanism in Bury. The schisms in Methodism weakened its influence, and more radical strands such as the Primitive and Independent Methodists were insignificant. The contrast with another cotton-spinning town, Rochdale, where a strong Nonconformist tradition produced a dominant Liberalism, is apparent.[12] Even more striking is the contrast with the weaving town of Burnley, where radical Nonconformity fed into a socialist tradition.[13]

Turning to the local government of Bury, the town became incorporated as a municipal borough in 1876. A notable feature of the town was the influence of the Lancashire landed magnates, the Stanley's, and the Earl of Derby's agent played a prominent part in the negotiations with the Privy Council Inquiry that established the new borough status. The ward structure of the borough was established at this time and these arrangements persisted largely unchanged until 1934 when Unsworth ward was added. There were five wards originally, Church, East, Elton, Moorside and Redvales. A double-member ward structure was established with six councillors and two aldermen representing each ward, two of the six coming up for election each November. The ubiquitous Stanleys were again involved in the elevation of the municipality to county borough status in 1888, Lord Derby selling land to Bury to facilitate an extension of the boundaries. By the early twentieth century, the corporation was responsible for the usual range of services, including the provision of education, electricity, gas, leisure facilities, some health services, and even some responsibility for unemployment. The borough was extended in

[8]   Joyce, P., *Work, Society and Politics: The Culture of the Factory in Later Victorian England*, (London, 1982), p. 14, and Pelling, *Social Geography*, p. 255.
[9]   Bannister, *From Parish to Metro*, p. 70.
[10]   Walton, *Lancashire*, pp. 184, 299.
[11]   Bannister, *From Parish to Metro*, p. 71.
[12]   Pelling, *Social Geography*, p. 255.
[13]   See chapter 4 in this volume.

March 1933, creating the additional ward of Unsworth.[14] The extension added two councillors to the council, and a further councillor and an Alderman in 1936, Unsworth becoming the only ward in Bury where only one councillor was re-elected each year.

In parliamentary elections Bury returned only Liberal MPs until 1867, but by the twentieth century the borough had become a Tory bastion, and in the seven inter-war general elections returned none but Conservative members. In 1929, Labour's peak between the wars, forty-one Lancashire seats were won by Labour, but in Bury Labour failed to disturb Tory dominance. As Walton in his history of Lancashire points out, Conservatives were driven back to 'their strongholds of Liverpool, the Manchester suburbs, the seaside resorts and (for inscrutable reasons which require investigation) Bury'.[15] This picture of rock-solid Tory support in Bury was reflected in municipal elections as well, and the 'inscrutable' reasons for this are the main focus of this chapter. After incorporation in 1876 the Liberal party had initially dominated the council, securing twenty-three of the thirty seats in the November elections, the remaining seven being Conservatives. All ten aldermen were initially Liberals, and the party continued to govern the municipality until the 1890s. Liberal Unionism in alliance with Conservatism then ended outright Liberal control, and the Conservative party had become by 1911 the strongest party in the borough. On paper Conservatism existed in near parity with the Liberals on the council for much of the inter-war period and then pulled away and achieved numerical supremacy in 1937 and 1938. The Liberals were the largest party in the council chamber briefly between 1920 and 1923, and not until 1938 could the Conservatives, if they had so wished, have assumed outright control of the council. This sharing of power with Liberalism was very much a tactical ploy, however. For the whole of the period the Liberals and Conservatives co-operated in the running of the borough, with electoral pacts and semi-official collaboration operating throughout to the benefit of both, as will be shown below.

Working-class Toryism and employer paternalism were as strong in Bury as in any other borough in the Lancashire cotton district. Factors of working-class support for the owners of the cotton mills and the other large manufacturing concerns was a fact of life in the municipal politics of inter-war Bury, and the employers loomed large as substantial and influential men in the affairs of the borough. As early as 1868, Joyce points to relations between the Liberal and Tory parties being 'particularly gentlemanly' in Bury.[16] In the last third of the nineteenth century, he portrays a 'technologically stable' factory town with a tight-knit ruling elite', with 'Tory and Anglican loyalties' that made the borough an example of 'indigenous, early established, business Toryism'.[17] Industrial employers became well established and with the patrician Stanleys influenced Bury and its people. By owning the core of the locale – not only the means of production in the mills and factories, but also much of the housing stock – the social elite imparted to the

---

[14] *Bury Times*, 4 Nov. 1933; Unsworth's first November elections were in 1934. Two councillors assumed office in March 1933, and the seats were not contested in November, 1933.

[15] Walton, *Lancashire*, p. 349.

[16] Joyce, *Work, Society and Politics*, p. 218.

[17] Joyce, *Work, Society and Politics*, p. 14.

neighbourhood its character, 'shaping its sense of place, and proclaiming this to the town.'[18] Even though limited liability companies controlled 50 per cent of local firms in Bury by the inter-war period, the cottonocracy and other large employers continued to exert a strong influence on Bury's politics, in a similar fashion to that shown in Blackburn and Bolton.[19] Tory and Liberal control had its origins in the nineteenth-century industrial structure of the town, the centrality of King Cotton, and the organisation of the mill. For many reasons, including the obvious electoral ones, but also due to wider considerations of status and control, both traditional parties maintained close social contacts with the working class.[20] Never amounting to crude manipulation, the transmission-belt of working-class Toryism and employer paternalism was oiled by both the operation of ideology and solid material interest. Such factors were based on the firm footing of inter-locking networks of social and cultural ties which served both Conservative and Liberal employer and propertied interests. Joyce points also to the important role of the overlookers in the cotton industry. The overlookers, though the bosses' men and probably chosen for their political bias, looked after the workers' interests too. These influential figures exerted leadership and influence through running the committees of the Co-op, friendly societies and chapel.[21] As will be seen below, in Bury the Co-operative movement was particularly influential.

As a symbol of the Conservative heritage, the statue of Sir Robert Peel stood in the Market Place. He was still regarded as Bury's most famous 'son',[22] but he could by no stretch of the imagination be regarded as a paternalist. More typical was Blackburn's Tory MP, W.H. Hornby, who plainly personified the paternalism and appeal to the local working class of Lancashire textile Conservatism. Hornby's place in Bury was taken by the far more patrician Stanley family, indicating another important prop in the Tory control of the borough, the interlinking of landed and industrial interests. The Stanleys were patrons in Bury on a grand scale. In the mid-Victorian period the Stanleys' close attention to local interests enhanced their popularity in the town. Visiting Bury in 1857, the future fifteenth Earl of Derby noted in his journal: 'Although the town has 40,000 inhabitants with an immense trade, I found remaining an almost feudal respect for our family'.[23] The Stanleys were a patrician dynasty 'jealously guarding' their influence in the borough, with the fifteenth earl promoting the concept of 'Tory Democracy'. These magnates understood the importance of securing support beyond the elite. As the 'Kings of Lancashire', the Stanleys believed that 'working men and tenants' should show 'respect, affection and deference' to their 'employers and

---

[18] Joyce, *Work, Society and Politics*, p. 123.
[19] On Blackburn and Bolton, see chapters 6 and 8 in Volume One of this series.
[20] For detailed discussion of working-class Toryism, see Joyce, *Work, Society and Politics*; Kirk, N., *Labour and Society in Britain and the USA, Volume 2: Challenge and Accommodation, 1850–1939*, (Aldershot, 1994); Nordlinger, E.A., *The Working Class Tories: Authority, Deference and Stable Democracy*, (Worcester and London, 1967); and Trodd, G., 'Political Change and the Working Class in Blackburn and Burnley, 1880-1914', (Ph.D. Thesis, Lancaster University, 1978).
[21] Joyce, *Work, Society and Politics*, pp. 154, 100–103.
[22] North West Civic Trust, *The Treasures of Lancashire*, (Manchester, 1989), p. 236.
[23] Joyce, *Work, Society and Politics*, p. 6.

landlords', and worked actively to promote and sustain such attitudes.[24] Typically, in the late nineteenth century, the family had given land for Bury's infirmary. They continued to show their favour well into the twentieth century, with strategic leases and outright gifts to the council.[25] Their high standards for construction on their land prevented 'jerry building' in the early twentieth century.

Their influence locally was not always viewed favourably, though. In the 1890s they were accused of blocking the development of the town by not releasing land for development, and their landed grip prevented speculative builders from constructing worker's housing, as a 1903 report shows. In that year Alderman Ashworth, a builder, complained that he would receive only a three and a half per cent return on capital in Bury while his Bolton working-class housing stock yielded six per cent. Lord Derby managed the unusual feat of falling foul both of local builders and of the Bury Socialists and Bury Christian Socialist Union on the housing issue.[26] For the first quarter of the twentieth century, as well, the rating question and the position of the Stanleys vexed the Corporation. As there were no rates on empty property, and much lower rates on land, 'Lord Derby therefore paid very low rates and received large ground rents'.[27] It was alleged locally that the land question caused the Tory defeats in both parliamentary elections of 1910.[28] Nevertheless, successive generations of the family were intimately involved in the affairs of the council. Their political home was not consistently Tory, as some of the dynasty had veered towards Liberalism over the decades, but via Unionism they had been firmly ensconced in the Conservative camp by 1918. The patronage of the Stanleys influenced Bury Conservatism in the inter-war period, and neither Tory nor Liberal councillors wilfully sought to offend Stanley interests. The family were not immune to criticism, but only Labour might have made an issue of Stanley power. If they did so, it was not overt and certainly not articulated at the local elections. Local press coverage of the Stanleys was invariably positive.

Many of the inter-war records of the Bury and Radcliffe Conservative Association have survived, and they are illuminating on the workings of Toryism in the borough. In April 1919 the local Conservative association formed a Labour Committee, showing the importance the Tories placed on winning working-class support in the face of the growth of the Labour party. The minute books of this committee provide a fascinating insight into Tory attempts to continue to hold on to long-established working-class support. Each Conservative club had two representatives on the committee, showing the importance of the clubs in the social and political organisation of working-class Toryism, as will be shown below. There was also one delegate from the Workingmen's Unionist Association Committee in each ward, showing the depth of political organisation in the locality. The committee was charged with organising working-class support at municipal as well as Westminster elections, including canvassing for working-class voters in the November elections. The Labour Committee had been set up 'to

[24] Joyce, *Work, Society and Politics*, p. 299.
[25] Bannister, *From Parish to Metro*, pp. 40–41.
[26] Bannister, *From Parish to Metro*, pp. 76–79.
[27] Bannister, *From Parish to Metro*, p. 80.
[28] Pelling, *Social Geography*, p. 256.

increase party representation in trade unions and co-operatives',[29] and its other main objective was to penetrate and organise within such working-class bodies. The Co-operative Society in Bury played a large role in working-class life, and Tory efforts to intervene in it were constant and well-organised. Thus in August 1920, the Tories launched a campaign to stop the Bury Co-operative movement from affiliating with the local Labour party.[30] The Conservative Association Labour Committee also organised slates of Tory supporters for elections within Co-operative societies, and actively supported and campaigned for them.[31] The local Conservative Association also attempted to organise within the trade unions. For instance, the Bury Tories mounted a campaign against a *Daily Herald* plan to raise £200,000 from the trade union movement to establish a Manchester edition of this overtly Labour newspaper. The Conservatives opposed the action under the guise of it being a 'seizure' of trade union funds. A minute of the Labour Committee argued that the *Herald* plan would be opposed 'as long as that organ pursues its present policy of advocating direct or industrial action, expounding Bolshevist propaganda, and fanning the flames of revolutionary fanaticism'.[32] The executive committee of the Bury and Radcliffe Conservative and Unionist Association also reflected the importance of working-class participation in the party. The chair, treasurer and secretary of each ward organisation was represented, plus an occasional extra representative, but always 'one or more labour representatives'. Thus Church, Redvale and East wards had one labour representative, while Elton and Moorside had two.[33]

Another important aspect of political and social organisation in Bury for both the Conservative and Liberal parties were the political clubs, as mentioned above. These clubs served as a focal point of politics, entertainment and sometimes, moral instruction. The main Conservative clubs were the Salisbury and the Walmersby (in Moorside ward), the Unionist (in Church ward), and the Blackford Bridge, the Rock and the Stanley (in Redvales ward). In addition the Tories had a Women's Unionist Association and a Primrose League branch. The Liberals, if anything had a more vibrant club organisation. Some of their clubs carried the great names of nineteenth century Liberalism: the Gladstone (East ward), the Cobden and the Trevelyan (Church ward). Also active were the Blackford Bridge, Philip's and the Fishpool Liberal Club. These firmly entrenched organisations aided the strong performance of the Conservatives and Liberal parties throughout the twenty years of elections. The Labour party realised the advantage the other two parties had with their clubs and bemoaned their own lack of them. At a post-election inquest in Peter Street, the Labour headquarters in 1920, the party chairman, Mr. F. Anderson said Labour 'had to recognise that the other parties had clubs, and worked inside those clubs.'[34]

---

[29] *Minutes of the Bury Conservative Association Labour Committee*, [BCLC], GCP/C/2/1, 1920–1929, Bury Record Office.
[30] [BCLC], GCP/C/2/1, 19 Aug. 1920.
[31] [BCLC], GCP/C/2/1, 24 Jun. 1920 and 27 Apr. 1926.
[32] [BCLC], GCP/C/2/1, 19 Nov. 1920.
[33] *Minutes of the Bury and Radcliffe Conservative Association*, GCP/C/1/3, 26 Feb. 1936.
[34] *Bury Times*, 3 Nov. 1920.

A further factor in popular Conservatism was the stress on the patriotic appeal to 'the people'.[35] This patriotic appeal certainly seemed stronger in Bury than in the other cotton towns. The continued inter-war hold on the popular imagination of the Gallipoli Sunday parades in Bury was evidence of this. Gallipoli Sunday was still being commemorated in Bury in the 1990s.[36] The borough was also a major depot of the Lancashire Fusiliers, which may have helped to reinforce this patriotism. The fact that Bury was predominantly Anglican, as mentioned above, was also relevant. The overtly anti-Catholic Protestantism of the nineteenth-century cotton districts was of course much more muted by the inter-war period, but it was an element in the appeal of Toryism to working-class voters. It also played some part in the important development of Liberal Unionism in Bury. Liberal Unionism in Bury was reckoned to be second only to that of Birmingham in terms of vitality, political success and overall strength.[37] It operated at both the parliamentary and municipal level, and took hold locally when in 1885 the Liberal MP, Sir Henry James became a Liberal Unionist. He was popular for his work on behalf of trade unionists and it was he who made the claim that next to Birmingham, 'Bury contains more Liberal Unionists than any other constituency'.[38] The unique strength of Liberal Unionism in a Lancashire municipality combined with a strongly entrenched Conservative presence produced, as in Birmingham, a powerful political force. By the 1890s 'the Council was becoming more Conservative in membership – Liberal Unionists in alliance with Conservatives outnumbered Gladstonian Liberals in 1893'.[39] Fourteen Tories and six Liberal Unionists could control the council chamber, faced with fourteen Liberals.

Co-operation between Conservatives and Liberal Unionists was then firmly established by the early twentieth century. After the First World War the combined Conservative and Liberal Unionists now co-operated politically with the remaining descendants of the Gladstonian wing of Liberalism, as indicated above, to further cement its power. The local press between the wars referred consistently to the Conservative party in municipal politics as simply the 'Unionists', as also was the case in Birmingham. Liberalism survived locally through this arrangement. In what was a distinctly Conservative borough this made political sense for the Liberal party. Cooperation was helped by a minimum of ideological and political differences existing between the two parties. Both stood above all for the free market and private property. This was translated into a defence of the ratepayers 'true' interests by the advocating of 'small government'. Minimum government, ostensibly in the interest of the freedom of the individual, involved a resistance to any perceived unnecessary expenditure of ratepayers' money. The defence of public order in the face of another perceived threat, that of the unemployed, was another area of mutual agreement.

Disputes between the Liberals and Tories were rare. One issue that could divide them was tariff reform. For instance, in the lead-up to the 1926 elections, the

---

[35] Kirk, *Labour and Society*, pp. 188–189, 195 and 196.
[36] Hudson, J. *Bury in Old Photographs*, (Stroud, 1993), pp. 74–77.
[37] For a discussion of Unionism in Birmingham see chapter 5 in Volume One of this series.
[38] Pelling, *Social Geography*, p. 255.
[39] Bannister, *From Parish to Metro*, p.73.

Liberal candidate in Moorside, Othello Whitehead, opined 'that the only difference between Conservatives and Liberals was that the former represented the dividend seekers'. James Latham, the Conservative agent entered the fray to defend his party. He suggested that 'he did not wish at that moment to enter into the question of Free Trade and Tariff Reform but supposing the Conservatives did represent the dividend seekers, they preferred that the dividends should be earned by British workmen rather than by foreign workers whose goods might be imported in to this country at a cheap rate'.[40] The disagreement, however, did not pose a serious problem for the two parties who put up a candidate each for the two seats in Moorside, and won both comfortably. Religion could also cause some division. In 1919, for example, when the defending Liberal councillor in Moorside, Thomas Rigby, lost his seat, he believed that the issue of religious education was the cause of his defeat. Speaking at the Primitive Methodist school in Walmersley Road, he said that he had supported the Fisher Act wanting 'education on a democratic basis' in order to give children of the working class the same opportunities as children of the well-to-do.[41] In general Liberals also argued for more expenditure on education than the Tories in Bury. Oscar Hall, a successful Liberal in 1920, argued for rate expenditure on education. Secondary education, Hall argued, should not depend on whether or not children's parents could afford the fees. Instead, said Hall, 'the most we can do for any of them is to provide an opportunity'.[42] Again in 1926, the Liberal candidate in Moorside asserted that Liberals wanted clean, healthy schools, efficient teachers and smaller classes, together with playing fields for elementary schools.[43]

But these disagreements were isolated occurrences. Usually cooperation between Unionism and Liberalism was seen as straightforward common-sense. Thus the sitting Liberal in East ward in 1925, Dr L.W. Johnson, saw the election as a simple case of anti-socialism versus socialism. Here the two Liberal candidates sought to rally not only Conservatives to the Liberal cause, 'but also Labour men as distinct from socialists'.[44] Labour plainly recognised the combination of forces it was faced with. Thus in the East ward inquest in 1924, a Labour speaker said that with the withdrawal of the Conservative candidate, Tory voters had been requested to vote for the Liberal candidates. He believed that few had done so, but there is no way of telling whether he was correct.[45] A speech in 1928 by a Liberal councillor, Thomas Evans, pointed to even closer future co-operation between the two parties. Evans, holding an inquest over Labour topping the poll against two Tories, argued that the 'forces of destruction', in other words Labour, were poised against the forces of 'construction'. Evans continued: 'there was red, white and blue in the Union Jack, there was no yellow. The time was not far distant when a little sanity must be displayed in the ranks of the Liberals and Conservatives, and they must unite their forces against the forces of destruction'.[46]

[40] *Bury Times*, 23 Oct. 1926.
[41] *Bury Times*, 5 Nov. 1919.
[42] *Bury Times*, 27 Oct. 1920.
[43] *Bury Times*, 30 Oct. 1926.
[44] *Bury Times*, 4 Nov. 1925.
[45] *Bury Times*, 4 Nov. 1924.
[46] *Bury Times*, 3 Nov. 1228.

From the onset of the post-war elections in 1919, electoral pacts between Liberals and Tories were effective. In that year, in Redvales, the Conservatives did not oppose the return of two Liberals, including the mayor. In East ward again, a Tory stood down to facilitate the electoral progress of two well qualified Liberals.[47] In Church ward, on the other hand, a Liberal and a Tory stood in tandem for the two seats. In only one ward, Moorside, were the two parties in conflict, a Liberal and two Tories competing for the two available seats. In the following year Liberals and Tories were in opposition in three wards, but after this such conflicts were extremely rare. In the one hundred contests that took place between the wars in the five double-member wards, a Liberal and a Conservative were elected in tandem on fifty-seven occasions, and one of the parties stood down in favour of the other in another twenty-four contests. In addition, the two parties never clashed in the new ward of Unsworth from 1933.

The main opponent to the two ruling parties was, of course, the Bury Labour party. It was, however, a weak force working in a hostile environment. The Bury labour movement had a distant heritage of radicalism. The Chartists had been active in Bury, and a crowd of their supporters were noted for attacking a detachment of London police sent up to the town by the new rail link in 1839.[48] This radicalism however, lay three generations in the past, and had been largely replaced by the moderation of the cotton operatives in the twentieth century. The spinners in particular were noted for their moderate politics. The organisation of work in mule spinning was conducive to individualist attitudes, as has been outlined elsewhere in this volume.[49] Spinners were the most comprehensively unionised, but their union was exclusive and sectional. 'They provided a distinctive, strongly elitist element within cotton unionism'.[50] The weavers in general were more radical, especially in the Burnley and Nelson area in the north-east of Lancashire. But the conservatism of the weaver's union leaders in Bury has been noted. Their leadership did not point to 'a strong penchant for industrial militancy or political radicalism on the part of the weavers in those districts, which, in political terms, seemed to have been rather somnolent places'.[51] The cotton unions as a whole through the United Textile Factory Workers' Association voted to affiliate to the Labour Representation Committee in late 1902. The weavers were over four to one in favour, the spinners nearer three to one, but overall the decision was taken in a spirit of 'pragmatic independence'.[52] Cotton workers needed representation in parliament to defend them in an unfavourable industrial and political climate, not to advance socialism. The primacy of economistic goals was the norm for cotton unions. The three largest cotton unions contracted out of paying the political levy to Labour as a consequence of the Trade

---

[47] *Bury Times*, 5 Nov. 1919.
[48] Gooderson, P.J., *A History of Lancashire*, (London, 1980), p. 140.
[49] See chapter 4 (Burnley), p. 310, in this volume.
[50] Howell, D., *British Workers and the Independent Labour Party, 1888–1906*, (Manchester, 1983), p. 54.
[51] White, J.L., *The Limits of Trade Union Militancy: The Lancashire Textile Workers 1910–1914*, (London, 1978), p. 97.
[52] Howell, *British Workers and the Independent Labour Party*, p. 67.

Union Act of 1913.[53] Cotton workers did not want their funds used for political purposes. Given the strength of working-class Conservatism, as well as the survival of Liberalism into the inter-war period, the Labour party in Bury was always operating on unfavourable terrain, as the election results bore out.

Turning then to the spatial distribution of political support, the first point to note is that Bury was divided up so that most of the wards took in a portion of the central and industrial districts of the town. There was only one central ward, Church, and only one solely suburban ward, Unsworth, after it was added to the borough in 1933. This basic pattern was preserved when the boundaries were redrawn in 1936, as will be shown below. There was little distinction between inner city and suburban wards in Bury, therefore. Elton ward, for instance, included the western suburbs, and it also had some military influence, being the site of the Wellington barracks, However, Elton also had a number of important industrial concerns within its boundaries. Along the Tottington Road to the north-west were situated the Woolfold dye and bleach works and paper mills, as well as cotton mills and engineering works. To the south-west, along the Bolton Road and the banks of the River Irwell, were numerous cotton mills, including the Wellington mills, Albion mills and Egyptian mills, and iron-works such as the Atlas works and the Irwell forge and rolling mills. It is doubtful if suburban voters were in the majority in Elton ward, but their influence combined with working-class Toryism ensured that Labour won few seats here. At Labour's high-points, around 1928–29 and 1934–35, the party picked up one of the two seats, but otherwise the Tories and Liberals dominated the ward. East ward presented a similar picture, despite having an electorate dominated by 'chiefly a working class element'.[54] It was second only to Church ward in terms of density per acre and high room occupancy. Liberals and Tories ruled the ward for the most part, Labour again only picking up single seats in its best years. Moorside and Redvales wards were more firmly middle-class, and Labour's overall share of the vote, around 20 per cent in both, reflected the party's weakness here.

Before the boundary revisions of 1936, the sole central ward of Church was by far the smallest both in terms of acreage and population. Church housed the poorest amongst the borough's population, being noted for its high infant mortality rates by the medical officer both in the 1890s and again in 1926.[55] It also had the densest population with over 24 persons per acre in 1931, and the highest number of persons per room. The Mosses district of the ward was noted as solid Labour territory in the local Press.[56] This was Labour's strongest ward in the town, but it was still hardly a stronghold. Labour won twelve seats here of the forty contested in November elections between the wars, and overall won 34 per cent of the votes cast. What appears to be a clear example of Liberal paternalism can be seen in Church, where Oscar Hall, the head of a large works employing hundreds of people, was elected in 1920 and 1923, although he was ousted by Labour in 1926.

---

[53]   White, *The Limits of Trade Union Militancy*, pp. 147–152.
[54]   *Bury Times*, 5 Nov. 1919.
[55]   Bannister, *From Parish to Metro*, pp. 63 and 72.
[56]   *Bury Times*, 3 Nov. 1923.

Somewhere in the region of 2,500 council houses were constructed between the wars in Bury. For a borough of its size this was a considerable housing programme (see Appendix 16), and represented quite extensive movement of population. This had little significant political impact, however. As shown above, there was no great concentration of working-class voters in inner-city wards to provide Labour strongholds in the town. Equally important, the new housing estates were scattered in the various wards, and their population was far outweighed by the pre-existing inhabitants. So the dispersal of population had little or no discernible effect on the support for the parties in each ward. The spatial geography of political support in Bury could have been affected far more by the redistribution of ward boundaries that took place in 1936. In fact, the effects provide an interesting example of gerrymandering.[57] There had been no major revision of the boundaries since the creation of the borough in the 1870s, and inevitably the subsequent six decades of population growth and movement had caused inequalities in terms of ward electorates. Church ward in 1935 had only 2,000 voters, whereas East, Moorside and Redvales wards had over three times as many, and Elton over four times. The recently added Unsworth ward had just over a thousand voters, and even though it had only two councillors compared to the six in other wards, it was still considerably over-represented on the council. Overall the situation was probably favourable to Labour – its strongest ward, Church, was over-represented, while its opponents' areas of strength were underrepresented.

A sub-committee was appointed in June 1935 to consider revisions, and the Town Clerk was instructed to draw up plans. He put his preferred option to the members of the sub-committee in October. In essence he proposed to enlarge Church ward to take in most of the central districts of the borough, which would also have the effect of reducing the population in each of the surrounding wards. Unsworth was also to be enlarged by taking in some of the southern edge of Redvales ward. Under the Town Clerk's proposals Church was likely to become a more solid Labour ward, while the other wards would be more suburban in character, and therefore presumably more solid anti-Labour territory. A Conservative member of the sub-committee, Alderman Smith, proposed a substantial amendment to the plans, however. A large portion of Redvales ward on the south-west of the town would be transferred to Church ward, while another part of Church to the south-east would go to Redvales. Also, the northern section of Church ward would be placed in Moorside ward. The net effect of these amendments were quite clear. Church would be far more marginal, as the working-class areas in the middle of the town would be reduced and a large chunk of suburbia would be added. On the other hand, the small portions of the central districts added to Moorside and Redvales would have little impact on those wards, being swamped by the suburbs in each case. Alderman Smith's amendment was carried by the sub-committee consisting of four Tories, three Liberals and two Labourites.

---

[57] The details of the redistribution described here can be found in Bury Record Office in the *Minutes* of Bury Council, (ABU/T28), 20 Jun. 1935, (minute no. 390), 10 Oct. 1935, (minute no. 440), 30 Oct., 1935, (minute nos. 438–441), 7 May 1936, (minute nos. 570–571); *Bury Times*, 4 Apr., 1936.

A public enquiry to discuss the plans was held in the following April, at which Labour lodged a barrage of criticisms. Cecil Heap, chair of the Bury Labour party, said the council had 'merely tinkered with the present position', and had 'juggled with portions of the wards'. Mr Warburton, secretary of the local party, demanded that any alternative plans considered by the sub-committee should be considered at the enquiry, but the Commissioner ruled that the Town Clerk did not have to do so. The Town Clerk himself merely stated that he had prepared 'about half a dozen schemes'. Warburton pointed out one of the most obvious absurdities of the scheme: 'Isn't Church ward going to stretch from one end of the town to the other?' The Labour party advocated a much more radical change of switching to a larger number of smaller, three-member wards, and claimed it had submitted such a plan to the Council but had been ignored. A Labour councillor also objected that 'the councillors themselves had never been given an adequate opportunity of discussing the scheme', but a Tory denied that the scheme had been 'hurried'.

Labour's objections were to no avail, and the plans came before the full council for ratification in May 1936. They were passed by twenty votes to fourteen, Tories voting solidly for, Labour unanimously against, while Liberals and Independents were divided. It is plain that party advantage rather than individual security motivated Conservative councillors. If anything the amended plan made the sitting Tories in Redvales and Moorside slightly less safe, but all of them voted in its favour. It is significant that in the succeeding three years of elections before the war, Labour lost two of its three seats in Church ward. It could be argued that the trend was against Labour anyway, four other seats being lost in the same period. Nevertheless the boundary changes certainly made the situation worse for Labour, and the Tories in particular had used them to bolster their already strong position.

Turning now to the detail of the inter-war municipal elections, it should be stated that the double-member system that applied to wards in Bury, combined with the fact that often parties only stood for one of the two available seats, means that interpretation of the percentages of the votes that parties won is difficult. It is best perhaps to concentrate on the seats actually held by parties to assess party performance. In these terms, it is notable that Liberals and Tories maintained a rough parity on the council through the 1920s, although the Liberal position was artificially boosted through these years by the fact that Liberals held most of the aldermanic seats. Liberal strength then fell away temporarily in 1930, and more consistently declined in the late 1930s, suggesting that Conservatism was beginning to be the dominant force in the alliance. The Labour position on Bury council was weak throughout the inter-war years. It started from a very small base of two councillors in 1919, made little progress in the years up to 1925, and then showed some growth from 1926 to 1930, increasing its representation on the council to eight in 1930, including one alderman. Labour surprisingly made two gains in 1930, a year where elsewhere it suffered many losses, but in 1931 Bury reverted to the national trend, with two Labour losses. Two more losses in 1932 saw Labour fall back to only two councillors plus an alderman, but recovery in the mid 1930s enabled Labour to hit its inter-war peak of nine out of the total of forty-four on the council in 1936. Subsequently Labour suffered the late-1930s slump in its support that was experienced in many other boroughs, worsened in Bury as suggested above by the impact of ward boundary changes. By 1938 Labour had only two councillors left, no more than it had had in 1919. The fact that it was now over-represented on the aldermanic bench meant that the Labour party had four representatives on Bury council, but its real political strength was plainly minimal. As in many other boroughs, Labour's position in 1938 gave no hint of the dramatic way it was to advance electorally after the Second World War. In the 1945 general election the Tory majority in Bury was cut to only 110 votes, and in the municipal elections later that year, Labour made an unprecedented twelve gains, seven from the Conservatives and six from the Liberals, and raised its representation in the council chamber to sixteen members.[58]

The use of the aldermanic system to bolster party strength on the council was never a significant factor in inter-war Bury. Labour did at times protest against the system, although it was never badly disadvantaged by it, and positively benefited from it in the late 1930s. In 1919 for instance a Labour candidate queried the very existence of aldermen, asking 'why should a man become an alderman after a term of years and not have to go before the ratepayers'.[59] Ten years later in 1929, the unfairness of the aldermanic system was one of the main election topics, and the Labour agent complained

> The only qualification for an Alderman, so far as Bury was concerned, was Anno Domini. It was not ability that put a man there, but old age ... Labour had not had its chance to possess the qualification of longevity. The time had come when it should have better representation. It was its right, not because of long service but because it was a political power in the Council. Labour had a right to equality.[60]

Such complaints died away in the 1930s as Labour's strength in the council became increasingly dependent on it retaining its aldermen.

The occupations of municipal candidates in Bury brings into clear relief the class distinctions between Labour and their opponents. In a sample of five separate years between 1922 and 1938 there were a total of seventy-four candidates for the three main parties.[61] Amongst twenty-eight Conservative candidatures there were nine small businessmen, four manufacturers (none in cotton), three professionals (all engineers), one 'gentleman', one company director, one manager, two insurance agents, five retired, one skilled worker and one unspecified woman. The twenty-one Liberal candidatures also included nine small businessmen, plus three manufacturers (two in wool, one in cotton), six retired, one clerk, one manual worker and one unspecified woman. For Labour there were twenty-five candidatures, of which eight were filled by manual workers, four by trade union officials and four by railway workers. There were also five unspecified women, plus two small businessmen, one insurance agent and one retired. The class distinctions between Labour and non-Labour candidates were clear. What is also noteworthy is the falling away of the cotton and engineering industrialists who had

[58]   Bannister, *From Parish to Metro*, p. 103.
[59]   *Bury Times*, 25 Oct. 1919.
[60]   *Bury Times*, 26 Oct. 1929.
[61]   Collated from the declaration of candidates in the *Bury Times* in 1922, 1926, 1929, 1934 and 1938.

served on the council before the First World War, a phenomenon noted in other textile towns in the period.[62] The other feature of importance is the fact that small businessmen made up more than one-third of all Tory and Liberal candidates.

There were a number of political issues that predominated in the discourse of inter-war municipal elections in Bury. Housing was one of the most prominent. As mentioned earlier, roughly 2,500 council houses were constructed in Bury between the wars, a ratio of one house for every twenty-three people, making the borough nineteenth amongst the eighty-three county boroughs in these terms (see Appendix 16). The extensive surviving Victorian housing stock was regarded as sub-standard by the 1920s. Edwardian maps show the survival of back-to-backs and widespread terraced housing. This mostly dated from the period of greatest expansion sixty to seventy years earlier. Sub-standard and inappropriate housing was a major issue before the First World War. This was borne out by Bury having one of the highest infant mortality rates in the country in 1909, standing at 129 per thousand.[63] Although there was encouragement from central government with the subsidy acts of 1923 and 1924, little utilisation was immediately effected by the council. Only 167 houses were built between 1919 and 1923. Of these 92 were on the council estate of Walmersley, although the contractor, the Bury House Building Company collapsed shortly after.[64] It is claimed that later in the 1920s, 'the town had a good record in housing ... providing employment and housing for the working man'.[65] In October 1932, the Liberal councillor, Othello Whitehead, pointed out that the council had built by then 1,916 houses out of the 16,000 in the borough, while private firms had delivered only 339 in the same period. In 1932 itself the council built 514 houses, while private developers managed only 114, but in 1933 only 44 municipal houses were constructed while private enterprise built 76 units, suggesting the end of the main phase of council-house building as central government subsidies dried up.[66]

Labour invariably argued for more expansive construction projects. A Labour candidate in 1919 argued that the council should build houses for £500 each, charge 10s. a week rent, and 'in twenty years they would have paid for themselves, and in another ten years they could have paid interest on the capital borrowed, and the houses could have become the property of the Corporation'.[67] Another candidate argued that it was the duty of the council to provide housing. There had been a 'big agitation' for municipal housing but projects had been stopped by a 'preponderance of property owners on the Council'.[68] Tories and Liberals urged caution at one end of the spectrum to 'economy' at the other. Sometimes the Liberals seemed more careful than the Tories. Thus a Liberal in 1919 called for 'economy and efficiency', and argued that the rates should not be raised unless 'absolutely necessary'.[69] Again in 1922 the Liberals called for 'reining in' the

[62] See chapter 8 in Volume One of this series.
[63] Bannister, *From Parish to Metro*, p. 74.
[64] Bannister, *From Parish to Metro*, pp. 78–79.
[65] Bannister, *From Parish to Parish*, pp. 76–80.
[66] Bannister, *From Parish to Parish*, p. 97.
[67] *Bury Times*, 25 Oct. 1919.
[68] *Bury Times*, 1 Nov. 1919.
[69] *Bury Times*, 27 Oct. 1919.

rates.[70] The Tories usually had a similar view on housing as the Liberals. Occasionally however, they advocated house ownership in the electioneering period. For example the Tory agent in 1926 said that the policy of the Conservative party 'was to encourage the ratepayers to become the owners of their own homes'. He added that the council currently build houses that the 'artisans did not like'. What was needed, he added, was cheaper houses working men could afford to pay for 'without being compelled to cultivate a large plot of land.' He finished by advocating lower-cost housing as such dwellings would be cheaper to let 'at an economic rent'.[71]

Conservatives and Liberals insisted on economy, efficiency and 'value for money' for the ratepayers in the construction of municipal housing. They had their way when it came to the rates, keeping them low throughout the 1930s.[72] In the main both the Liberals and Tories insisted on 'fair rents', which in effect meant as near an economic rent as was feasible. A Liberal in 1919, responding to a Housing Committee view that to build new houses to existing standards would cost £1,000 per unit, said he wanted houses for those who served in the recent war up to standard, but Bury would not spend £1,000 per house. Instead the corporation would build cheaper houses. The problem was that central government subsidies did not meet the full cost of building and renting. Westminster he said, 'thought we should charge as near as possible an economic rent. Working men could not pay 15s or 16s a week, and with central government responsible for only 75 per cent of the loss, the ratepayers were 'responsible for the other 25 per cent'. The Liberal argued that 'to subsidise the rents would be a mischievous policy and unsound finance. (Hear, hear). No man, when he had paid the rent of his own house ought to be called upon to help pay the rent of another man. (Hear, hear)'.[73]

Nevertheless the need for council housing was agreed upon by all sides, especially in the decade between the mid 1920s and the mid 1930s. Encouraged by central-government subsidies, a Liberal and Tory-controlled council, which was never seriously threatened by the rise of Labour, built housing on an extensive scale. The quality of housing, the level of rents and the conditions of letting became Labour's main cause at elections. Thus Labour wanted the council to drop the requirement of tenants to pay a £1 deposit on first entering a council property, the issue coming up frequently.[74] Labour also increasingly called for slum clearance in the 1930s as it attracted government grants. Labour though was outraged at the compensation paid to property owners. Slum landlords, Labour argued, should not be compensated. Thus in 1934, a Labour councillor criticised the council for compensating property-owners whose houses

> had been condemned as unfit for human habitation ... A butcher
> selling bad meat isn't compensated ... he is lucky if he is not
> prosecuted ... Why ... should landlords, who had allowed their

[70] *Bury Times*, 1 Nov. 1922.
[71] *Bury Times*, 23 Oct. 1926.
[72] Bannister, *From Parish to Metro*, pp. 86.
[73] *Bury Times*, 25 Oct. 1919.
[74] *Bury Times*. 27 Oct. 1934.

property to fall into a state of disrepair, and yet claimed high rents, be compensated?[75]

Another Labour candidate went further, advocating that 'it would be a wise policy for all rented houses in the town to be controlled by the Council'.[76] It was not until 1935 that the first major slum clearance areas were named by the Council.[77]

The Labour party in Bury also raised the issue of direct labour to solve the problems of housing and at the same time relieve unemployment. The employment of direct labour in constructing other public works was also advocated. Tom Birch, the Labour candidate in Redvales, saw direct labour as the answer to Bury 'falling behind' in municipal housing.[78] Again in 1929, the Labour agent advocated the use of direct labour both to build houses under the Wheatley Act of 1924 and to tackle the problem of unemployment. He pointed out that the Liberal and Tory ruling majority had ignored the wishes of the (Labour) Lord Privy seal who had appealed for the unemployed to be taken on by councils for municipal projects.[79] Labour then was very much the party of interventionism. The controlling group were invariably opposed to the use of direct labour. Occasionally though, the corporation was prepared to take up unemployed labour on short-term, temporary relief schemes, as in 1929 when mass unemployment was growing. The Liberals were confident enough to make an election issue out of it, one councillor referring approvingly to work schemes in operation to construct tennis courts and putting greens, and further proposing a playing field scheme off Chesham Road.[80] A Tory councillor, Thomas Steen, went as far as to propose the adoption of a direct labour department in 1931. He managed to get the council to debate the issue, arguing that 'the scheme would be more likely to help men regain their manhood, because they would be able to see something at the end of it, something that would take men from the slums and give them homes'.[81] His proposal was rejected, however. In 1934 the Public Assistance Committees run by councils were replaced by Unemployed Assistance Boards, which were less subject to local influence. As a result direct labour became less of an issue, but on the other hand the 1934 Act provided for task work with low rates of pay. On this issue at least the Communist party, the NUWM and Bury Labour party were in agreement, all arguing against task work.

From 1931 'the spectre of unemployed violence' was referred to in Bury.[82] This probably overdramatises the campaigns on behalf of the unemployed, but there were a number of demonstrations organised by the NUWM in the borough after this date, as well as the intervention of NUWM candidates in municipal elections. Opposition to the operation of the Means Test became a focus for Labour and NUWM candidates, and 1934 saw the culmination of these campaigns when

[75] *Bury Times*, 27 Oct. 1934.
[76] *Bury Times*, 27 Oct. 1934.
[77] Bannister, *From Parish to Metro*, pp. 97.
[78] *Bury Times*, 27 Oct. 1920.
[79] *Bury Times*, 26 Oct. 1929.
[80] *Bury Times*, 19 Oct. 1929.
[81] Bannister, *From Parish to Metro*, p. 88.
[82] Bannister, *From Parish to Metro*, p. 102.

unemployment became a major issue. Even before electioneering was under way, on 6 October 1934, the Council refused to meet with a deputation of the unemployed.[83] Then in the week before the election the breaking of the plate glass windows of the herbalist store owned by the mayor hit the headlines. In the *Bury Times*, under the headline of 'Communism Condemned', the mayor claimed to have been shadowed for several months by two or three unemployed men on the way to his appointments, and that an attempt had been made to poison his dog. He charged that his persecution was because he was part of a Council that had recently banned demonstrations by the unemployed. He had been asked to suspend task work for the unemployed over the holiday period in the summer, but had refused to do so. He also said he had been asked by the NUWM if their members would be given the first choice of work if it became available in corporation departments. He had declined to discuss their proposal, and asked

> Think what would have happened had the request been acceded to! The unemployed of Bury would have been intimidated into joining the NUWM. I am not going to be responsible for forcing local unemployed into Communism ... demonstrations and disturbances cannot be tolerated in a well-ordered society. A stop must be put to them, and if stern measures have to be applied I shall see that they are applied.

The NUWM denied any involvement in these events. The secretary of the Bury branch stated

> The whole idea is one designed to discredit our organisation before the municipal elections for which we have nominated candidates ... We could not hope to win the support of the electors if we pursued such methods as a protest against the treatment meted out to us by the Town Council.[84]

The thrown paving stone also caused trouble for the Labour party. George Dyke, Labour's candidate in East ward, made one of many speeches by his party's representatives on the subject. While exonerating the NUWM and the general mass of unemployed, he blamed 'some poor individual on the brink of starvation', adding that it was 'one of the things which puts the clock back for the working class'. Of further interest was Dyke's view that unemployment could not be solved at the level of municipal government. Instead

> Unemployment would never be cured by municipal pills. The pain might be alleviated, but to get rid of the complaint it was necessary to have an operation. The remedy for unemployment was the sending of more Socialist members to Westminster.[85]

Another Labour candidate in 1934 asserted the importance of winning municipal control, though. He pointed out that Bury still had five or six thousand unemployed and that the present Council was failing to tackle the problem. The

---

[83] Bannister, *From Parish to Metro*, p. 89.
[84] *Bury Times*, 24 Oct. 1934.
[85] *Bury Times*, 27 Oct. 1934.

ruling Tories and Liberals had responded with the tired old formula of 'cutting down the rates'. He added that

> Labour was determined to use every legitimate weapon to usher in a new form of society. We have a lasting remedy for the problem of unemployment and its concomitants – misery, poverty, and despair – if we can only secure such representation on the local Councils as will enable us to proceed with our programme.[86]

The audience at this meeting was, in his own words, 'lamentably small', however, and Labour found that rousing the electorate was hard going.

In the 1934 elections the Communist party tried to get political co-operation with Labour over various issues including unemployment. This was very much in line with the Popular Front policies adopted by Communist parties internationally at this time. The party sought to secure the withdrawal of Labour's candidates in East and Redvales wards in favour of two NUWM candidates. Some agreement between Labour and the NUWM over the issue of task work had already been achieved, as noted above, and the Bury Communist party issued the following statement:

> The Labour candidates have agreed to support the following programme:-
> (1) To work for United Action against Fascism and War.
> (2) To take no part in the operation of Part 1 of the Unemployment Act. To fight for relief for all who refuse to enter the slave camps.
> (3) To fight the operation of task work and the Means Test.
> (4) To fight the Sedition Bill.

At a public meeting in the Co-operative Hall on 28 October the Bury Labour party 'emphatically rejected the approaches' of the Bury Communist party. Cecil Heap, the presiding officer and member of the Bury Labour party executive, said that the manifesto put forward by the Communists 'would have the whole-hearted support' of the Labour party, but no pact would be entered into. He then turned round the Communist request, advising NUWM members that if they wished to assist the Labour candidates in the implementation of this programme, then they should join the Labour party. The secretary of Bury Labour party, James Walsh, pointed out that successive TUC conferences had 'ostracised' the Communist party, and 'the proposed pact could not be contemplated for one moment'. The prospective Labour candidate for Whitehaven, Frank Anderson, went further, claiming the Communist suggestion of a 'united front' was nothing short of hypocrisy, and 'a form of propaganda often pursued by these movements for utilising our meetings for their own purposes'.[87] No more was heard of a Communist–Labour pact after this meeting.

The council's response to unemployment was, as already stated, usually very cautious. The need to attract new industries to offset economic decline was usually

---

[86] *Bury Times*, 27 Oct. 1934.
[87] *Bury Times*, 31 Oct. 1934.

prevented by the ruling Tory and Liberal councillors' desire to maintain strict financial control and keep the rates as low as was politically feasible. Some action was taken in 1932 when the Corporation agreed to spend a halfpenny rate (up to a 1d. was allowed) to aid the objectives of the Lancashire Industrial Development Committee and Bury Industrial Committee.[88] The ruling group, however, would not even authorise expenditure to advertise in a *Manchester Guardian* supplement designed to attract new industries. Keeping the rates low was itself often advocated as the main way for the council to reduce unemployment. In 1929, for example, the Liberal candidate Othello Whitehead argued that if the rates remained low then Bury would be able to attract new industries and relieve unemployment.[89] Bury maintained through the inter-war period one of the lowest rates among the county boroughs. Teachers' salaries were cut between 1931 and 1935 and the borough did not pay the Burnham rate. Also local government workers' pay in Bury was lower than the voluntary Whitby Council norm.[90] Such local parsimony meant that few public works such as roads, schools and libraries were financed through the rates. In inter-war Bury it was rather the re-naming of streets that was proclaimed as a great municipal advance. Without irony the Liberal leader Alderman Evans could suggest that the programme of street re-naming was 'the most striking evidence that we have banned municipal inertia from which in the past, the town has suffered so long'.[91]

One final issue that warrants attention is the involvement of women in the municipal politics of Bury. As with the other textile towns, the significance of women in the local economy meant that they might have been expected to play a greater role in public life than elsewhere. The co-operative movement, which had a substantial female membership and involvement, also occupied an important place in Bury. Through its strong links with Labour it might also have encouraged women's involvement in local politics. The evidence of the number of women candidates in Bury seems to bear out these expectations. Women stood as candidates on twenty-four occasions between the wars, representing 7.5 per cent of all candidatures. This was an unexceptional rate of female participation, being slightly above the average for all nineteen boroughs covered in the first two volumes in this series. However, seventeen of the women candidatures in Bury were for Labour, accounting for almost 19 per cent of the total Labour candidatures. This was in fact the highest proportion of women standing for Labour in any of the boroughs dealt with in the series so far. Two women, Mrs Ethel Goodall in Church ward in 1928–31 and 1934–38, and Mrs Isabel Bottomley in Elton in 1934–37, sat on the council for Labour, and it is clear that women did count for something in the Bury Labour party and Labour group on the council. The first woman to be elected to the council, however, was Miss Jane Taylor for the Conservatives in Moorside ward in 1919. She was the daughter of Thomas Taylor, a founder of a notable firm of dyers, and she was treasurer of the Women's Unionist Association and a member of the Primrose League. The only other Tory

---

[88]   Bannister, *From Parish to Metro*, p. 87.
[89]   *Bury Times*, 19 Oct. 1929.
[90]   Bannister, *From Parish to Metro*, p. 103.
[91]   Bannister, *From Parish to Metro*, p. 87.

woman to enter the council was in 1936 in Church ward when Mrs Taylor, the wife of former councillor Richard Taylor, was elected. Whether she was also related to the earlier Councillor Jane Taylor is not known. One Liberal woman, Miss Sarah Fletcher, also sat for Church ward in 1931–34. One unsuccessful candidate for the Women's Citizens Association (WCA) appeared in 1920.

What were perceived as women's issues, those most directly affecting home life and child welfare, did enter the political discourse. Housing, health and education were the main areas that successful women candidates appeared to be interested in. Sometimes sympathetic men would also raise these issues on behalf of women. Hence Labour's Ezra Collen, in Church ward in 1919, argued that every ward should have baths and a public washhouse to lessen the hours of work 'for the womenfolk'.[92] The Bury WCA put up no candidates in 1919, but it posed a series of questions to the candidates of the three main parties. These asked if they supported a range of measures including pensions for civilian widows with dependent children 'free from the taint of the Poor Law', the appointment of a Women's Housing Advisory Committee to consider new houses from the 'point of view of health and convenience of the housewife', equal pay for women as council employees, and the appointment of women police.[93] Another echo of these issues surfaced once more in 1934, when a Labour activist, Miss Frances Edwards, appealed to women electors saying they should rid 'themselves of their apathy towards municipal and national elections.' She continued, 'Women are the mothers of the citizens, and your duty is to prepare for the heralding in of a new social order.'[94] The obstacles to women progressing in local politics were alluded to, however, in 1936 when Conservatives rejoiced at Mrs Taylor's election. She said that 'the women of Church ward had received no encouragement to work for her at first', and added that she would not have been surprised if she had been at the bottom of the poll because of the 'adversities' she had had to face.[95]

To conclude, what were the main defining features of the inter-war politics of Bury? One was the enduring strength of Conservatism, by no means untypical of the cotton towns, but in Bury's case even more impressive. Bury's diversified local economy survived the Depression better than most of industrial Lancashire, and the relative economic security this produced may have helped to generate allegiance to Toryism. Of even greater importance was the apparent survival of the heritage and traditions of political loyalties from the past. Bury's nineteenth-century industrial structure at the pinnacle of the Lancashire cotton industry was conducive to the phenomenon of working-class Toryism, especially amongst the notably moderate spinners. In a strongly Anglican context, Victorian patterns of behaviour proved resilient nearly a generation after the founding of the Labour party. It has also been noted here how the Conservative organisation in Bury worked consciously to penetrate and influence working-class organisations, such as the Co-operative movement, and to generate working-class support in general.

[92] *Bury Times*, 25 Oct. 1919.
[93] *Bury Times*, 25 Oct. 1919.
[94] *Bury Times*, 31 Oct. 1934.
[95] *Bury Times*, 4 Nov. 1936.

Through its network of social clubs as well, Bury Toryism actively created and reinforced political support from large sections of the inter-war working class.

The second feature of note is the strength of Liberal Unionism in Bury and the close electoral co-operation the Liberals had with the Conservative party. While Liberal Unionism after 1918 was fully absorbed into the Tory party, the remnants of Bury Liberalism remained nominally independent all the way through the inter-war era and maintained a significant presence on the council. However, this survival was within the confines of an anti-Labour alliance with Conservatives. The level of co-operation extended beyond the round of elections to the day-to-day management of the town in the council chamber. The continued success of both parties at the elections suggests that a majority of the electorate was at least moderately content with their administration. The council's house-building strategy, although criticised, seems to have delivered at least the minimum that many of the rate-payers desired. Keeping the rates as low as was feasibly possible, with the aim of 'economy with efficiency' in the interests of 'good government', was the base-level of Tory and Liberal agreement.

Finally the Labour party, based upon the solid moderation of the spinners' union, never posed a serious electoral threat to Conservative and Liberal dominance in Bury during the whole period. Labour's marginalisation was very much a consequence of the town's traditions. Employer authority and continuing working-class support for the Conservatives hamstrung the party. Labour attempted to counterpose themes of social and economic justice, and protested about inter-war problems such as unemployment and the operation of the Means Test, but with little success. Labour's position was also made more difficult by the gerrymandering of ward boundaries when they were revised in 1936. Although the Tories and Liberals hardly needed this boost to their municipal strength, they nevertheless forced through changes which were plainly to their advantage, despite loud complaints by Labour. In the end Bury provided a near-perfect working model of inter-war working-class Conservatism in action.

A guide to further reading

Newspapers

Bury Times
Manchester Guardian

Secondary sources

Bannister, J., *From Parish to Metro: Two Centuries of Local Government in a Lancashire Town*, (Bury, 1974).

Barrett, H., *Bury as it was ...*, (Nelson, 1976).

Cook, C., *The Age of Alignment: Electoral Politics in Britain, 1922–1929*, (London, 1975).

Fogarty, M.P., *Prospects of the Industrial Areas of Great Britain*, (London, 1945).

Freeman, T.W., Rodgers, H.B. and Kinvig, R.H., *Lancashire, Cheshire and the Isle of Man*, (London, 1966).

Gooderson, P.J., *A History of Lancashire*, (London, 1980).

Howell, D., *British Workers and the Independent Labour Party, 1888–1906*, (Manchester, 1983), ch. 3, pp. 52–68.

Hudson, J., *Bury in Old Photographs*, (Stroud, 1993).

Joyce, P., *Work, Society and Politics: The Culture of the Factory in Later Victorian England*, (London, 1982).

Kirk, N., *Labour and Society in Britain and the USA, Volume 2: Challenge and Accommodation, 1850–1939*, (Aldershot, 1994).

North West Civic Trust, *The Treasures of Lancashire*, (Manchester, 1989).

Pelling, H., *Social Geography of British Elections, 1885–1910*, (Aldershot, 1994).

Walton, J., *Lancashire: A Social History, 1558–1939*, (Manchester, 1987).

White, J.L., *The Limits of Trade Union Militancy: The Lancashire Textile Workers 1910–1914*, (London, 1978).

Bury wards 1919–1933

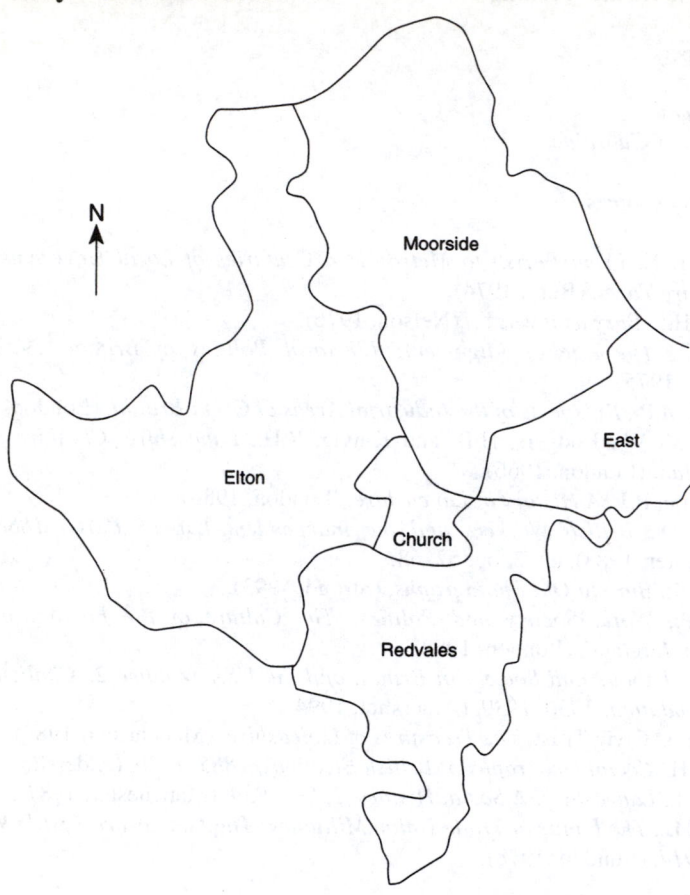

N

Moorside

East

Elton

Church

Redvales

Bury wards 1934–1938

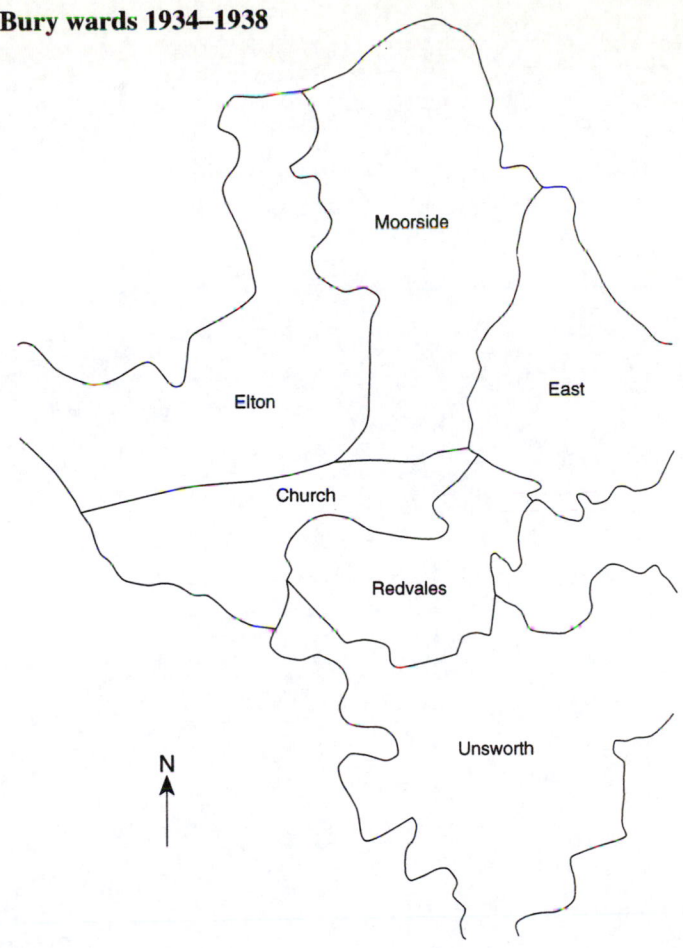

Moorside

Elton

East

Church

Redvales

Unsworth

N

Persons aged fourteen and over classified by industry 1931

	Male	%	Female	%	Total	%
Metal and engineering	2,460	12.5	103	0.8	2,563	7.9
- Engineering	1,725	8.8	59	0.5	1,784	5.5
Textiles	5,000	25.5	6,884	54.0	11,884	36.7
- Cotton	2,570	13.1	5,913	46.4	8,483	26.2
- Dyeing, finishing, etc.	1,778	9.1	366	2.9	2,144	6.6
Clothing	1,251	6.4	1,356	10.6	2,607	8.1
Paper and printing	1,234	6.3	609	4.8	1,843	5.7
- Paper making	997	5.1	361	2.8	1,358	4.2
Building	1,264	6.4	12	0.1	1,276	3.9
Transport	1,376	7.0	40	0.3	1,416	4.4
Commerce and finance	2,522	12.8	1,139	8.9	3,661	11.3
Public admin. and defence	1,397	7.1	562	4.4	1,959	6.0
- Local government	938	4.8	496	3.9	1,434	4.4
Personal service	571	2.9	1,166	9.1	1,737	5.4
Other	2,565	13.1	874	6.9	3,439	10.6
Total (a)	19,640		12,745		32,385	
Total population (b)	**26,150**		**30,032**		**56,182**	
(a) as % of (b)	75.1		42.4		57.6	
Total out of work (c)	2,990		2,490		5,480	
(c) as % of (a)	15.2		19.5		16.9	
Managerial and own account	2,230	13.4	726	7.1	2,956	11.0
Operative	14,420	86.6	9,529	92.9	23,949	89.0
Total (excluding out of work)	16,650		10,255		26,905	

Population statistics 1931

Ward	Acres	Population	Persons/acre	Persons/room
Church	226	5,596	24.8	1.05
East	791	11,836	15.0	0.92
Elton	2,081	14,105	6.8	0.82
Moorside	1,687	14,044	8.3	0.81
Redvales	1,140	10,601	9.3	0.76
Total	**5,925**	**56,182**	**9.5**	**0.84**

Overall position on the council 1919–38

	Position				Gains				Losses			
	C	Lab	L	Ind		C	Lab	L	Ind		C	Lab	L	Ind
1919	19	2	18	1		1	1	1	0		1	0	2	0
1920	17	3	19	1		0	1	1	0		2	0	0	0
1921	17	3	19	1		0	0	0	0		0	0	0	0
1922	17	3	19	1		0	0	0	0		0	0	0	0
1923	17	3	19	1		1	1	0	0		1	1	0	0
1924	18	3	18	1		2	0	0	0		0	0	2	0
1925[a]	18	3	17	1		1	0	1	0		1	0	1	0
1926	17	5	17	1		0	2	1	0		1	1	1	0
1927	17	5	17	1		0	0	0	0		0	0	0	0
1928	16	6	16	2		1	2	0	0		2	0	1	0
1929	18	6	15	1		0	1	1	0		1	1	0	0
1930	18	8	12	2		1	2	0	0		1	0	2	0
1931	18	6	15	1		1	0	2	0		1	2	0	0
1932	19	3	17	1		1	0	1	0		0	2	0	0
1933[b]	18	3	18	3		0	0	1	0		1	0	0	0
1934	18	6	15	3		0	3	0	0		1	0	2	0
1935	17	8	14	3		0	2	1	0		2	0	1	0
1936[c]	17	9	14	4		1	0	0	1		1	1	0	0
1937	22	6	13	3		2	0	0	0		0	2	0	0
1938	25	4	13	2		4	0	0	0		0	3	1	0

Aldermen 1919–38

1919	C–4, L–5, Ind–1	1929	C–2, L–6, Ind–1, Lab–1
1920	C–4, L–5, Ind–1	1930	C–2, L–6, Ind–1, Lab–1
1921	C–4, L–5, Ind–1	1931	C–1, L–7, Ind–1, Lab–1
1922	C–4, L–5, Ind–1	1932	C–2, L–6, Ind–1, Lab–1
1923	C–4, L–5, Ind–1	1933	C–2, L–6, Ind–1, Lab–1
1924	C–3, L–6, Ind–1	1934	C–3, L–5, Ind–1, Lab–1
1925[a]	C–3, L–5, Ind–1	1935	C–3, L–5, Ind–1, Lab–1
1926	C–3, L–5, Ind–1, Lab–1	1936[c]	C–3, L–5, Ind–1, Lab–2
1927	C–3, L–5, Ind–1, Lab–1	1937	C–4, L–4, Ind–1, Lab–2
1928	C–2, L–6, Ind–1, Lab–1	1938	C–3, L–5, Ind–1, Lab–2

[a] 1925 – 1 aldermanic vacancy.

[b] 1933 – 2 extra councillors allocated for Unsworth ward.

[c] 1936 – 1 extra alderman and 1 extra councillor allocated for Unsworth ward.

Municipal elections: winning party 1919–28

Ward	1919	1920	1921	1922	1923	1924	1925	1926	1927	1928
Church (1)	C	Lab	L	C	L	L	Lab	Lab	L	Lab
Church (2)	Lab	L	C	Lab	C	C	C	C	C	C
East (1)	L	C	L	**L**	**C**	L	L	C	**L**	L
East (2)	L	C	L	**L**	**C**	L	L	Lab	**L**	C
Elton (1)	**Lab**	L	L	**C**	**L**	C .	C	**L**	C	Ind
Elton (2)	**C**	C	L	**C**	**C**	L	C	**C**	L	Lab
Moorside (1)	C	**C**	C	C	**C**	**C**	L	L	**C**	L
Moorside (2)	C	**Lab**	L	C	**Lab**	**L**	C	C	**L**	C
Redvales (1)	L	C	L	L	**L**	L	C	L	L	C
Redvales (2)	L	L	L	L	**Lab**	C	L	Lab	C	L
Unsworth	-	-	-	-	-	-	-	-	-	-

Municipal elections: party wins per year 1919–28

	1919	1920	1921	1922	1923	1924	1925	1926	1927	1928
C	4	5	2	5	5	4	5	4	4	4
Lab	2	2	0	1	2	0	1	3	0	2
L	4	3	8	4	3	6	4	3	6	3
Ind	0	0	0	0	0	0	0	0	0	1
Total	10	10	10	10	10	10	10	10	10	10
Turnout %	**42.8**	**45.1**	**45.7**	**39.1**	**64.9**	**40.7**	**46.6**	**48.3**	**46.2**	**52.8**
Labour %	**21.8**	**23.0**	**23.9**	**19.3**	**45.1**	**13.5**	**16.3**	**28.9**	**26.0**	**27.1**

Municipal elections: party wins per ward 1919–38

Ward	C	Lab	L	Ind	Total	Turnout %	Labour % of all votes
Church	19	12	9	0	40	47.5	34.2
East	13	3	23	1	40	38.8	24.6
Elton	23	5	11	1	40	40.1	27.3
Moorside	23	2	15	0	40	43.1	19.3
Redvales	16	5	19	0	40	44.8	21.4
Unsworth	1	1	0	3	5	43.8	37.6
Total	**95**	**28**	**77**	**5**	**205**	**42.5**	**24.9**

Seats won by Labour as a percentage of all wins 1919–38   **13.7**

Municipal elections: winning party 1929–38

Ward	1929	1930	1931	1932	1933	1934	1935	1936	1937	1938
Church (1)	Lab	C	L	C	L	Lab	Lab	C	C	C
Church (2)	C	Lab	C	L	Lab	C	C	L	Lab	C
East (1)	C	L	C	C	**L**	L	L	L	C	L
East (2)	L	Lab	L	L	**C**	Lab	C	Ind	L	C
Elton (1)	L	C	C	L	C	C	Lab	C	C	C
Elton (2)	Lab	C	L	C	C	Lab	L	C	C	C
Moorside (1)	L	C	**L**	L	L	**L**	L	C	L	C
Moorside (2)	C	C	**C**	C	C	**C**	C	L	C	L
Redvales (1)	C	L	C	C	L	C	Lab	L	L	C
Redvales (2)	Lab	C	L	Lab	C	L	C	C	C	C
Unsworth	-	-	-	-	-	Ind	**Ind**	Lab	Ind	C

Municipal elections: party wins per year 1929–38

	1929	1930	1931	1932	1933	1934	1935	1936	1937	1938
C	4	6	5	5	5	4	4	5	6	9
Lab	3	2	0	1	1	3	3	1	1	0
L	3	2	5	4	4	3	3	4	3	2
Ind	0	0	0	0	0	1	1	1	1	0
Total	10	10	10	10	10	11	11	11	11	11
Turnout %	**40.6**	**46.4**	**44.4**	**36.4**	**29.1**	**34.8**	**46.6**	**34.2**	**39.9**	**47.6**
Labour %	**31.3**	**22.0**	**19.1**	**23.9**	**11.5**	**24.5**	**32.1**	**25.9**	**28.1**	**32.9**

Parliamentary election results

Bury constituency
(all wards within the borough [1918 boundaries] were included in the constituency, along with the urban district of Tottington)

General election	Winner	Conservative %	Labour %	Liberal %
14 Dec. 1918	C	45.9	22.7	31.4 *(Co L)*
15 Nov. 1922	C	41.2	36.7	22.1
6 Dec. 1923	C	40.3	36.1	23.6
29 Oct. 1924	C	46.9	36.1	17.0
30 May 1929	C	42.1	37.5	20.4
27 Oct. 1931	C	70.3	29.7	-
14 Nov. 1935	C	49.4	34.4	16.2

Church ward

Candidate	Party	Votes	%	Electors	Turnout	Gains
1919						
T.B. Smith*	C	503	43.9	2,314	40.8	1 Lab from L
E. Collen	Lab	382	33.3			
F. Howarth*	L	261	22.8			
Total votes		1,146				
Total voters		945				
1920						
H. Ashworth	Lab	490	24.9	2,340	44.7	1 Lab from C
O.S. Hall	L	456	23.2			1 L from C
J. Colbeck*	C	385	19.6			
J. Sharp*	C	374	19.0			
Miss E. Johnstone	WCA	264	13.4			
Total votes		1,969				
Total voters		1,046				
1921						
T. Evans	L	648	37.5	2,380	50.1	-
J.B. Salter	C	543	31.4			
G.H. Purcell	Lab	536	31.0			
Total votes		1,727				
Total voters		1,193				
1922						
J.D. Lepp	C	534	36.5	2,383	42.4	-
E. Collen*	Lab	497	34.0			
W. Talbot	L	432	29.5			
Total votes		1,463				
Total voters		*1,009*				
1923						
O.S. Hall*	L	769	28.2	2,441	64.9	
J.H. Pilling	C	729	26.7			C from Lab
H. Ashworth*	Lab	670	24.6			
H.H. Griffiths	Lab	560	20.5			
Total votes		2,728				
Total voters		1,583				

Church ward (continued)

Candidate	Party	Votes	%	Electors	Turnout	Gains
1924						
T. Evans*	L	738	37.5	2,610	51.7	-
J.B. Salter*	C	621	31.5			
H. Ashworth	Lab	611	31.0			
Total votes		1,970				
Total voters		1,350				
1925						
E. Collen*	Lab	610	36.8	2,620	52.9	-
J.D. Lepp*	C	582	35.1			
T. Whitworth	L	467	28.1			
Total votes		1,659				
Total voters		1,385				
1926						
F. Heap	Lab	615	39.5	2,613	47.3	Lab from L
J. Pilling*	C	488	31.3			
O.S. Hall*	L	454	29.2			
Total votes		1,557				
Total voters		1,237				
1927						
T. Evans*	L	722	38.1	2,552	55.0	-
J.B. Salter*	C	617	32.6			
Mrs E. Goodall	Lab	554	29.3			
Total votes		1,893				
Total voters		1,404				
1928						
Mrs E. Goodall	Lab	781	34.2	2,569	60.3	Lab from C
J.D. Lepp*	C	763	33.4			
W.H. Rodwell*	C	739	32.4			
Total votes		2,283				
Total voters		1,550				

Church ward (*continued*)

Candidate	Party	Votes	%	Electors	Turnout	Gains
1929						
F. Heap*	Lab	683	39.6	2,663	48.1	-
J. Hayward	C	605	35.1			
L. Myers	L	373	21.6			
J.E. Walsh	Com	62	3.6			
Total votes		1,723				
Total voters		1,280				
1930						
T. Evans*	C	572	34.6	2,508	42.3	
J. Heenighan	Lab	555	33.6			Lab from C
J.B. Salter*	C	525	31.8			
Total votes		1,652				
Total voters		1,061				
1931						
Miss S.A. Fletcher	L	725	34.3	2,367	60.4	L from Lab
R. Taylor	C	687	32.5			
Mrs E. Goodall*	Lab	618	29.2			
Albert Hardman	Nuwm	84	4.0			
Total votes		2,114				
Total voters		1,430				
1932						
J. Hayward*	C	572	31.7	2,212	50.4	
W. Cragg	L	465	25.8			L from Lab
Mrs E. Goodall	Lab	456	25.3			
C. Heap	Lab	309	17.1			
Total votes		1,802				
Total voters		1,114				
1933						
J.A. Crawshaw*	L	411	34.5	2,079	41.7	-
J. Heenighan*	Lab	401	33.6			
W. Halpin	C	381	31.9			
Total votes		1,193				
Total voters		866				

Church ward *(continued)*

Candidate	Party	Votes	%	Electors	Turnout	Gains
1934						
Mrs E. Goodall	Lab	468	37.0	2,124	48.5	Lab from L
W. Halpin	C	463	36.6			
Miss S.A. Fletcher*	L	333	26.3			
Total votes		1,264				
Total voters		1,031				
1935						
H. Ashworth	Lab	509	37.9	2,090	49.3	Lab from L
F. Aspinall	C	465	34.6			
W. Cragg*	L	369	27.5			
Total votes		1,343				
Total voters		1,030				
1936						
Mrs R. Taylor	C	973	38.6	5,722	34.1	C from Lab
J.A. Crawshaw*	L	915	36.3			
J. Heenighan*	Lab	635	25.2			
Total votes		2,523				
Total voters		1,952				
1937						
W. Halpin*	C	1,155	37.0	5,457	43.0	-
Mrs E. Goodall*	Lab	1,057	33.9			
S.A. Fletcher	L	907	29.1			
Total votes		3,119				
Total voters		2,344				
1938						
F. Aspinall*	C	1,106	25.5	5,389	45.4	
F. Jackson	C	1,020	23.5			C from Lab
G. Dykes	Lab	786	18.1			
Mrs G. Skinner	Lab	732	16.9			
E. Howcroft	L	697	16.1			
Total votes		4,341				
Total voters		2,449				

Overall Labour vote		**34.2%**		**Overall turnout**		**47.5%**

East ward

Candidate	Party	Votes	%	Electors	Turnout	Gains
1919						
Dr L.W. Johnson	L	1,300	46.1	4,742	36.8	L from C
F. Ashworth*	L	954	33.8			
F. Heap	Lab	567	20.1			
Total votes		2,821				
Total voters		1,746				
1920						
J.J. McGough*	C	719	27.6	4,777	38.2	-
F .Jackson*	C	701	26.9			
T. Rigby	L	689	26.4			
Mrs J. Darlington	Lab	500	19.2			
Total votes		2,609				
Total voters		1,827				
1921						
W.H. Waterhouse	L	1,116	37.3	4,776	39.6	-
T. Rigby	L	1,096	36.7			
Mrs J. Darlington	Lab	776	26.0			
Total votes		2,988				
Total voters		1,891				
1922						
Dr L.W. Johnson*	L	Unopp.	-	4,767	-	-
R.B. Hall	L	Unopp.				
1923						
J.J. McGough*	C	Unopp.	-	4,849	-	-
F. Jackson*	C	Unopp.				
1924						
T. Rigby*	L	1,340	38.6	4,861	43.6	-
W.H. Waterhouse*	L	1,196	34.5			
F.H. Edwards	Lab	933	26.9			
Total votes		3,469				
Total voters		2,121				

East ward *(continued)*

Candidate	Party	Votes	%	Electors	Turnout	Gains
1925						
Dr L.W. Johnson*	L	1,651	40.4	4,970	52.3	-
R.B. Hall*	L	1,419	34.7			
F.H. Edwards	Lab	1,020	24.9			
Total votes		4,090				
Total voters		2,598				
1926						
T. Hoyle*	C	852	31.6	4,950	41.2	
W. Johnston	Lab	834	30.9			Lab from C
F. Jackson*	C	827	30.7			
D. Pickles	Ind	182	6.8			
Total votes		2,695				
Total voters		2,040				
1927						
T. Rigby*	L	Unopp.	-	5,067	-	-
W.E. Turner	L	Unopp.				
1928						
Dr L.W. Johnson*	L	1,179	31.8	5,060	50.3	
J. Wild	C	875	23.6			C from L
T. Holt	Lab	830	22.4			
R.B. Hall*	L	818	22.1			
Total votes		3,702				
Total voters		2,545				
1929						
T.Hoyle*	C	841	33.5	5,335	36.0	
D.Pickles	L	837	33.3			L from Lab
T.Holt	Lab	834	33.2			
Total votes		2,512				
Total voters		1,918				

East ward *(continued)*

Candidate	Party	Votes	%	Electors	Turnout	Gains
1930						
W.E. Turner*	L	1,253	28.9	5,749	53.3	
T. Holt	Lab	1,112	25.7			Lab from L
L.H. Lomas	C	1,068	24.6			
R.B. Hall	L	900	20.8			
Total votes		4,333				
Total voters		3,063				
1931						
W.K. Heaton	C	1,452	48.8	5,707	38.3	
L. Myers	L	1,026	34.5			L from C
Alfred Hardman	Lab	496	16.7			
Total votes		2,974				
Total voters		2,185				
1932						
T. Hoyle*	C	892	41.2	5,603	28.0	
D. Pickles*	L	704	32.5			
R.B. Hall	Ind	570	26.3			
Total votes		2,166				
Total voters		1,567				
1933						
J.M. Arnot*	L	Unopp.	-	6,124	-	-
G. Partington*	C	Unopp.				
1934						
L. Myers*	L	867	46.9	6,303	24.5	
G. Dykes	Lab	638	34.5			Lab from C
A. Bell	Nuwm	344	18.6			
Total votes		1,849				
Total voters		1,543				
1935						
J. Duckworth	L	1,141	28.4	6,393	39.2	L from C
T. Hoyle*	C	1,041	25.9			
R.B. Hall*	C	948	23.6			
Mrs F. Furlong	Lab	893	22.2			
Total votes		4,023				
Total voters		2,504				

East ward *(continued)*

Candidate	Party	Votes	%	Electors	Turnout	Gains
1936						
J.M. Arnot*	L	702	30.4	6,027	23.4	
R.B. Hall	Ind C	702	30.4			Ind from C
G. Partington*	C	519	22.5			
P. Taylor	Lab	384	16.6			
Total votes		2,307				
Total voters		1,411				
1937						
W. Elliott	C	869	35.6	6,045	32.2	C from Lab
J. Clapham	L	804	32.9			
G. Dykes*	Lab	771	31.5			
Total votes		2,444				
Total voters		1,946				
1938						
J. Duckworth*	L	1,496	34.7	5,902	49.4	-
F. Riley*	C	1,363	31.6			
J. Robinson	Lab	751	17.4			
J. Golding	Lab	697	16.2			
Total votes		4,307				
Total voters		2,914				

Overall Labour vote   **24.6%**   **Overall turnout**   **38.8%**

Elton ward

Candidate	Party	Votes	%	Electors	Turnout	Gains
1919						
W. Nabb	Lab	Unopp.	-	5,461	-	-
A. Hopkinson	C	Unopp.				
1920						
J. Battersby*	L	1,269	30.4	5,549	42.3	-
J. Cox	C	1,179	28.3			
J.W. Harrison*	C	866	20.8			
W. Jones	Lab	854	20.5			
Total votes		4,168				
Total voters		2,346				
1921						
A.E. Boyden*	L	1,443	40.6	5,600	37.0	-
A.E. Gee	L	1,278	36.0			
A. Pilling	Lab	829	23.4			
Total votes		3,550				
Total voters		2,073				
1922						
J.L. Lord*	C	Unopp.	-	5,589	-	-
W.N. Nuttall	C	Unopp.				
1923						
J. Battersby*	L	Unopp.	-	5,692	-	-
J. Cox*	C	Unopp.				
1924						
S. Wood	C	975	41.4	5,752	28.4	C from L
A.E. Gee*	L	700	29.7			
F. Pearson*	L	680	28.9			
Total votes		2,355				
Total voters		1,631				
1925						
J. Lord*	C	1,491	38.2	5,867	44.0	-
S. Pickering*	C	1,328	34.1			
H. Ashworth	Lab	1,080	27.7			
Total votes		3,899				
Total voters		2,580				

Elton ward *(continued)*

Candidate	Party	Votes	%	Electors	Turnout	Gains
1926						
W. Judge*	L	Unopp.	-	6,122	-	-
T. Smethurst	C	Unopp.				
1927						
H. Potts	C	1,215	39.6	6,232	39.6	-
A.E. Gee*	L	934	30.4			
J. McGurk	Lab	923	30.0			
Total votes		3,072				
Total voters		2,470				
1928						
J.L. Lord*	Ind	1,872	42.3	6,368	51.0	
J. McGurk	Lab	1,456	32.9			Lab from C
S. Pickering*	C	1,093	24.7			
Total votes		4,421				
Total voters		3,248				

*(Lord was supported by both Tory and Liberal parties, and was termed an
'Independent Conservative' in the* Manchester Guardian*; he later reverted
to the Conservative label)*

Candidate	Party	Votes	%	Electors	Turnout	Gains
1929						
W. Judge*	L	1,250	37.7	6,880	37.2	
E.C. Collen	Lab	1,071	32.3			Lab from C
T. Smethurst*	C	997	30.0			
Total votes		3,318				
Total voters		2,560				
1930						
S. Braddock	C	1,438	32.6	6,878	40.4	C from L
J. Whitehead	C	1,332	30.2			
Alfred Hardman	Lab	937	21.2			
A.E. Gee*	L	705	16.0			
Total votes		4,412				
Total voters		2,780				

Elton ward (*continued*)

Candidate	Party	Votes	%	Electors	Turnout	Gains
1931						
C.S. Goodwill	C	1,600	40.5	7,136	41.6	C from Lab
R. Foden	L	1,531	38.7			
Mrs I.M. Bottomley	Lab	823	20.8			
Total votes		3,954				
Total voters		2,966				
1932						
W. Judge*	L	1,625	38.1	7,508	37.3	
T. Wilcock	C	1,196	28.0			C from Lab
Mrs I.M. Bottomley	Lab	731	17.1			
E.C. Collen*	Lab	712	16.7			
Total votes		4,264				
Total voters		2,800				
1933						
S. Braddock*	C	1,136	31.1	7,659	29.6	-
J. Whitehead*	C	1,006	27.6			
E.C. Collen	Lab	766	21.0			
J. Hurst	L	739	20.3			
Total votes		3,647				
Total voters		2,264				
1934						
R. Ramsbottom	C	1,177	28.6	7,819	34.5	
Mrs I.M. Bottomley	Lab	1,074	26.1			Lab from L
F. Smith	C	1,054	25.6			
R. Foden*	L	805	19.6			
Total votes		4,110				
Total voters		2,696				
1935						
F. Davenport	Lab	1,607	36.0	7,945	42.7	Lab from C
W. Judge*	L	1,433	32.1			
T. Wilcock*	C	1,430	32.0			
Total votes		4,470				
Total voters		3,392				

Elton ward *(continued)*

Candidate	Party	Votes	%	Electors	Turnout	Gains
1936						
J. Whitehead*	C	1,346	41.2	5,287	39.3	-
F. Smith	C	1,183	36.2			
L. Jack	Lab	740	22.6			
Total votes		3,269				
Total voters		2,078				
1937						
C.S. Goodwill	C	1,357	37.0	5,494	45.1	C from Lab
R. Ramsbottom*	C	1,243	33.9			
Mrs I.M. Bottomley*	Lab	1,065	29.1			
Total votes		3,665				
Total voters		2,476				
1938						
S. Lord	C	1,479	25.6	5,637	56.0	C from Lab
L.B. Jones	C	1,393	24.1			C from L
Mrs I.M. Bottomley	Lab	1,204	20.8			
A. Dawson	Lab	1,106	19.1			
J. Killelea	L	600	10.4			
Total votes		5,782				
Total voters		3,154				

Overall Labour vote		**27.3%**		**Overall turnout**		**40.1%**

Moorside ward

Candidate	Party	Votes	%	Electors	Turnout	Gains
1919						
J. Smith*	C	1,343	29.9	5,770	48.6	
Miss J. Taylor	C	1,217	27.1			C from L
T.Rigby*	L	1,142	25.4			
Mrs Darlington	Lab	797	17.7			
Total votes		4,499				
Total voters		2,807				
1920						
A. Redford*	C	Unopp.	-	5,826	-	-
A.E. Lees	Lab	Unopp.				
1921						
J. Hill*	C	1,740	42.3	5,865	53.1	-
P. Stock*	L	1,437	34.9			
S. Goddard	Lab	938	22.8			
Total votes		4,115				
Total voters		3,116				
1922						
J. Smith*	C	1,395	36.7	5,880	38.5	-
Miss J. Taylor*	C	1,340	35.2			
S. Goddard	Lab	1,069	28.1			
Total votes		3,804				
Total voters		*2,263*				
1923						
A. Redford*	C	Unopp.	-	6,082	-	-
A.E. Lees*	Lab	Unopp.				
1924						
J. Hill*	C	Unopp.	-	6,136	-	-
P. Stock*	L	Unopp.				
1925						
A. Schofield	L	1,962	42.4	6,184	44.5	L from C
J. James*	C	1,345	29.1			
G. Heywood*	C	1,320	28.5			
Total votes		4,627				
Total voters		*2,753*				

Moorside ward (*continued*)

Candidate	Party	Votes	%	Electors	Turnout	Gains
1926						
O.L.W. Whitehead	L	2,070	47.0	6,337	56.9	L from Lab
T. Steen	C	1,379	31.3			
S. Goddard	Lab	957	21.7			
Total votes		4,406				
Total voters		3,604				
1927						
J. Hill*	C	Unopp.	-	6,415	-	-
P. Stock*	L	Unopp.				
1928						
A. Schofield*	L	1,953	40.7	6,719	52.0	-
J. James*	C	1,761	36.7			
C. Collen	Lab	1,083	22.6			
Total votes		4,797				
Total voters		3,497				
1929						
O.L.W. Whitehead*	L	1,783	43.3	7,215	40.3	-
T. Steen*	C	1,229	29.8			
Ms H. Duckworth	Lab	1,107	26.9			
Total votes		4,119				
Total voters		2,910				
1930						
E.W. Andrew*	C	1,769	33.7	7,109	45.3	-
H.G. Pierce	C	1,352	25.8			
Miss S. Fletcher	L	1,267	24.2			
H. Ashworth	Lab	858	16.4			
Total votes		5,246				
Total voters		3,222				
1931						
A. Schofield*	L	Unopp.	-	7,163	-	-
J. James*	C	Unopp.				

Moorside ward (continued)

Candidate	Party	Votes	%	Electors	Turnout	Gains
1932						
O.L.W. Whitehead*	L	1,464	48.1	7,052	30.0	-
T. Steen*	C	1,136	37.3			
J. Rigby	Lab	443	14.6			
Total votes		3,043				
Total voters		2,119				
1933						
J. Hamer	L	1,106	37.6	7,074	26.1	L from C
H.G. Pierce*	C	953	32.4			
W. Dearnley	C	883	30.0			
Total votes		2,942				
Total voters		1,844				
1934						
A. Schofield*	L	Unopp.	-	7,211	-	-
J. James*	C	Unopp.				
1935						
O.L.W. Whitehead*	L	1,932	37.3	7,352	50.9	-
J.H. Preston	C	1,930	37.3			
J.E. Walsh	Lab	1,319	25.5			
Total votes		5,181				
Total voters		3,742				
1936						
S. Ratledge	C	1,183	42.9	6,412	35.4	-
J. Hamer*	L	954	34.6			
T. Deakin	Lab	619	22.5			
Total votes		2,756				
Total voters		2,269				
1937						
A. Schofield*	L	1,538	40.7	6,453	40.3	-
W.K.Heaton*	C	1,490	39.4			
J. Robinson	Lab	752	19.9			
Total votes		3,780				
Total voters		2,601				

Moorside ward (*continued*)

Candidate	Party	Votes	%	Electors	Turnout	Gains
1938						
J.H. Preston*	C	1,677	41.9	6,504	44.4	-
O.L.W. Whitehead*	L	1,472	36.8			
C. Wilcox	Lab	856	21.4			
Total votes		4,005				
Total voters		2,889				

Overall Labour vote		**19.3%**		**Overall turnout**		**43.1%**

Redvales ward

Candidate	Party	Votes	%	Electors	Turnout	Gains
1919						
Sir J. Hacking*	L	1,337	41.3	4,671	42.6	-
J. Turner*	L	1,141	35.2			
T. Birch	Lab	762	23.5			
Total votes		3,240				
Total voters		1,990				
1920						
J. Barrett	C	1,173	36.8	4,682	55.8	-
S.H. Wilkinson*	L	1,150	36.1			
T. Birch	Lab	861	27.0			
Total votes		3,184				
Total voters		2,611				
1921						
T. Hartley*	L	1,741	43.6	4,712	50.7	-
K. Kay	L	1,434	35.9			
T. Birch	Lab	817	20.5			
Total votes		3,992				
Total voters		2,388				
1922						
J. Turner*	L	1,148	38.1	4,683	38.3	-
D. Pickles	L	1,059	35.1			
J.H. Ashworth	C	809	26.8			
Total votes		3,016				
Total voters		*1,795*				
1923						
S.H. Wilkinson*	L	Unopp.	-	4,733	-	-
T. Birch	Lab	Unopp.				Lab from C
1924						
T. Hartley*	L	1,581	44.5	4,783	46.4	
H. Hill	C	986	27.8			C from L
A. Schofield	L	982	27.7			
Total votes		3,549				
Total voters		2,221				

Redvales ward *(continued)*

Candidate	Party	Votes	%	Electors	Turnout	Gains
1925						
J. Nichols	C	1,185	36.5	4,941	43.3	C from L
J. Eastham*	L	1,067	32.9			
D. Pickles*	L	991	30.6			
Total voters		3,243				
1926						
S.H. Wilkinson*	L	1,003	35.0	5,110	45.0	-
T. Birch*	Lab	936	32.7			
S. Ratledge	C	925	32.3			
Total votes		2,864				
Total voters		2,301				
1927						
W. Hartley	L	1,415	44.5	5,131	49.9	-
H. Hill*	C	1,117	35.1			
J.W. Walker	Lab	650	20.4			
Total votes		3,182				
Total voters		2,560				
1928						
J. Nichols*	C	1,454	39.7	5,149	54.8	-
J. Eastham*	L	1,252	34.2			
J. Heenighan	Lab	956	26.1			
Total votes		3,662				
Total voters		2,820				
1929						
E. Riddel*	C	1,479	44.5	5,482	46.4	-
T. Birch*	Lab	990	29.8			
W.K. Heaton	L	858	25.8			
Total votes		3,327				
Total voters		2,541				
1930						
W. Hartley*	L	1,443	40.8	5,421	50.2	-
H. Hill*	C	1,352	38.2			
C. Heap	Lab	742	21.0			
Total votes		3,537				
Total voters		2,721				

Redvales ward *(continued)*

Candidate	Party	Votes	%	Electors	Turnout	Gains
1931						
J. Nichols*	C	1,742	43.1	5,464	47.7	-
J. Eastham*	L	1,612	39.9			
C. Heap	Lab	553	13.7			
J.E. Walsh	Com	133	3.3			
Total votes		4,040				
Total voters		2,604				
1932						
E. Riddel*	C	1,644	41.9	6,004	45.3	-
T. Birch*	Lab	1,062	27.1			
P. Kaighin	L	1,051	26.8			
Albert Hardman	Nuwm	166	4.2			
Total votes		3,923				
Total voters		2,720				
1933						
W. Hartley*	L	1,223	50.6	6,070	27.9	-
H. Hill*	C	904	37.4			
Albert Hardman	Nuwm	292	12.1			
Total votes		2,419				
Total voters		1,694				
1934						
J. Nichols*	C	1,344	39.3	6,260	36.6	-
J. Eastham*	L	1,174	34.3			
J.E. Walsh	Lab	603	17.6			
Albert Hardman	Nuwm	297	8.7			
Total votes		3,418				
Total voters		2,293				
1935						
T. Birch*	Lab	1,960	41.3	6,382	53.3	-
E. Riddel*	C	1,614	34.0			
G. Blake	L	1,177	24.8			
Total votes		4,751				
Total voters		3,399				

Redvales ward *(continued)*

Candidate	Party	Votes	%	Electors	Turnout	Gains
1936						
W. Hartley*	L	1,207	38.8	6,298	37.8	-
H. Hill*	C	992	31.9			
E. Duxbury	Lab	911	29.3			
Total votes		3,110				
Total voters		2,379				
1937						
T. Toon	L	1,407	42.3	6,319	39.5	-
J. Nichols*	C	1,206	36.2			
I. Howarth	Lab	717	21.5			
Total votes		3,330				
Total voters		2,498				
1938						
E. Riddel*	C	1,597	30.3	6,371	45.0	-
J.W. Clark*	C	1,415	26.9			
H. Haslam	Lab	786	14.9			
I. Howarth	Lab	736	14.0			
R. Lord	L	729	13.9			
Total votes		5,263				
Total voters		2,870				

Overall Labour vote   **21.4%**   **Overall turnout**   **44.8%**

Unsworth ward
(added by extension of the borough in 1932 –33)

Candidate	Party	Votes	%	Electors	Turnout	Gains
1933						
(2 Ind candidates elected unopposed in March; no election in November)						
-	-	-	-	1,138	-	-
1934						
T. Taylor*	Ind	385	56.5	1,166	58.5	-
H. Grimshaw	Ind	297	43.5			
Total votes		682				
1935						
W. Ainsworth	Ind	Unopp.	-	1,149	-	-
1936						
Alfred Hardman	Lab	430	50.6	2,218	38.3	-
P.G. Coulton	C	419	49.4			
Total votes		849				
1937						
T. Taylor*	Ind	577	57.1	2,470	40.9	-
R. Haines	Lab	434	42.9			
Total votes		1,011				
1938						
H. Milburn	C	649	54.7	2,659	44.6	C from Lab
W. Ainsworth*	Lab	538	45.3			
Total votes		1,187				

(Ainsworth had stood previously as an Independent, but had changed allegiance to Labour for this election)

Overall Labour vote   **37.6%**   **Overall turnout**   **43.8%**

SEVEN
Canterbury

CANTERBURY

The major city of the county of Kent in south-east England, Canterbury became a county borough in 1888 under the provisions of the Local Government Act of that year. Although close to London, being sixty-one miles away by rail and fifty-five by road, with good communications to the capital, Canterbury was on most indicators by far the least significant of the eighty-three county boroughs of the inter-war era. This was certainly so in terms of population and economic importance. With a population of 24,900 in 1901, for thirty years there was zero growth, and the census of 1931 recorded a fall of over 400 inhabitants over the previous ten years. Chester, one higher in the population ranking of county boroughs, had nearly double Canterbury's population in the period.

For over two thousand years the site of Canterbury has been a place of habitation. A Celtic, Roman and Saxon settlement in turn, Canterbury became the font of Saxon, Norman and then English Christianity. Although both earlier Celtic and Roman names entered the record, it was the Saxon *Cant-wara-byrig*, the burgh of the men of Kent, from which the name Canterbury derived.[1] Canterbury remained an important centre of pilgrimage in the middle ages and then became the spiritual heart of the Anglican communion from the Henrician Reformation. Anglican conservatism, which seemed to pervade the politics in the period of this study, kept the borough in somnolent torpidity for generations. At the time of the Great Reform Bill however, local reformers sullied this clerical and conservative reputation, by showing their displeasure with Archbishop Howley who was opposing Whig plans. Howley was greeted by the citizens by 'a torrent of hissing, howling and groans, followed by mud, rotten eggs, and stones, falling around as thick as blackberries'.[2] Radicalism however, was not a feature of the borough's local politics in the first half of the twentieth century.

Turning to nineteenth century Canterbury's parliamentary elections, these were regarded as riddled with corrupt practices, so much so that a Royal Commission of Enquiry was established in 1853.[3] The Redistribution of Seats Act of 1885 reduced the parliamentary representation to one. Indeed between 1878 and 1885, the city was penalised by parliamentary disenfranchisement.[4] Under the Representation of the People Act of 1918, Canterbury was disenfranchised as a separate borough and gave its name to the county division. Between the two world wars, the Canterbury division of Kent returned Conservative members to Westminster without a break. This was a continuation of the past with Canterbury at the hub of a Tory stronghold. Pelling noted that this division of Kent was 'the safest Conservative seat of all' with only three contests against the sitting Tory member between 1885 and 1910.[5] Indeed Pelling further commented that with such strong ecclesiastical and military influences (it was the home of the East Kent Regiment, the Buffs),

---

[1] Gardiner, D., *Canterbury: The Story of the English Towns*, (London, 1923), p. 15.
[2] Gardiner, *Canterbury*, p. 118.
[3] Gardiner, *Canterbury*, p. 121.
[4] Gardiner, *Canterbury*, p. 121.
[5] Pelling, H., *Social Geography of British Elections, 1885–1910*, (Aldershot, 1994), p. 76.

Canterbury 'could hardly be other than Conservative'.[6] After the First World War, on five occasions the Conservatives secured over 70 per cent of the poll. When Sir W.A. Wayland recorded a lowly 56 per cent in 1929 it was as an Independent Conservative. Wayland soon returned to the official Conservative fold. In parliamentary terms then Canterbury was a solidly Conservative borough. No doubt this helped to shape its municipal politics.

Early Victorian Canterbury was known for the corruption of its municipal government. At least the 1835 Municipal Corporations Act partly cleaned up the city corporation, 'regulated the whole civic machinery, and fixed the number of aldermen at six with eighteen councillors, elected from three wards.'[7] The three new municipal wards of Dane John, Northgate and Westgate replaced the six ancient wards of Worthgate, Northgate, Westgate, Burgate, Queningate, and Ridingate, each named from one of the entrance gates. This structure was to remain in place throughout the period of this study. It was, however, Canterbury's special historic and traditional significance, namely the 'greatness and endurance of its ecclesiastical rank as the chief city of the English Christian world', that secured its county borough status.[8] With its additional significance as the capital of East Kent, 'the Mother of England' to its Victorian burghers, became a county borough in 1888.[9]

As a county borough Canterbury was an anomaly in terms of population and economic significance to the nation. This point necessitates some discussion of the borough's relationship with its county, Kent. With its three wards having a combined municipal electoral roll of 9,089 in 1919, the city only secured its one parliamentary seat by being a part of the county constituency, the Canterbury division of Kent having over 31,000 parliamentary electors in 1918. The discrepancy between these electorates cannot be accounted for by the differences between the inter-war municipal and parliamentary franchises, with roughly one-fifth of parliamentary electors being denied the municipal vote.[10] This brings into clear relief Canterbury's insignificance in terms of its voting power in the constituency overall. It was with some difficulty that Canterbury had managed to retain its separate identity from the county of Kent in 1888. Between the wars it had a continual struggle to keep control of its status and its various administrative responsibilities. Given Canterbury's low population and financial resources, maintaining its position as a county borough was a difficult and perennial problem. The administration of police and education were both contentious issues in the tussle between the city and the county. In the 1920 municipal elections, for example, the question of the amalgamation of the city police force with that of Kent became one of the three main election issues. A councillor sounded a typically defiant note in his victory address at the declaration of the poll in 1920: 'For one thing, I am not going to sacrifice the privileges or be a party to barter

---

[6]   Pelling, *Social Geography*, p. 81.
[7]   Gardiner, *Canterbury*, p. 121.
[8]   *Kelly's Directory of Canterbury, Whitstable, Herne Bay and Neighbourhood*, 22nd. Edition, (London, 1934), p. A12.
[9]   Boyle, J., *Portrait of Canterbury*, (London, 1974), p.31. *Ave Mater Angliae* – Hail, Mother of England – was the Victorian motto of the borough.
[10]   See notes at the end of this volume, p. 677.

away the rights of this ancient City.[11] Another major issue of that election was whether the new scheme of education under the Act of 1918 should be formulated by the District Education Board or the Canterbury Education Committee.[12] Keeping Kent at bay was one of the leitmotivs of inter-war municipal politics. In terms of the police, fire, education, housing, roads and other ancillary services, independence was maintained, although some services were shared with Kent. On the administrative side of council services, as well as the police, fire and education departments, Canterbury maintained a cemetery, mental hospital, markets, museum, library, and a school of art. It also had an important asset in terms of a municipal electricity works.[13] Given the lack of economies of scale, whether the satisfaction of political control resulted in loss of efficiency and less munificent local services is an open question.

There was only one extension of the borough in the period of this study and it added little by way of population. The Canterbury Extension Act of 1933 altered and extended the boundaries as from April 1934 so as to include the parishes of St Dunstan Without, Hackington, Harbledon and Thannington Without.[14] This did not alter the basic three-ward structure, with Dane John, Northgate, and Westgate wards remaining in place. Each ward had six councillors, two per ward coming up for election each year. In addition there were six aldermen elected by the council for six years. As might be expected this made for the smallest number of county borough legislators, with a full council of twenty-four members, from whom the mayor and a sheriff were chosen. The extension added to the physical area of Dane John and mainly Westgate, but increased the electoral roll of either ward only very marginally. In physical size, population, economy and politics, inter-war Canterbury was more akin to the urban and rural district councils than the county boroughs. In many of the smaller authorities formal political activity was insignificant, and party politics and party competition were minimal too in Canterbury. The council chamber was dominated by Independents between the wars, and party battles were few and far between in what was essentially a middle-class city. Thus unlike most of the county boroughs of the period, there is not a great deal that can be deduced from the city's politics that can inform wider political analysis.

As might be expected, the socio-economic structure of Canterbury influenced both the political culture and specific focus of policy issues in the municipality. The proximity of London and the Kent coal field to the south appeared to have had little direct impact on the borough. Yet as early as 1830 the railway had arrived, connecting Canterbury, the Kentish coal field and London. Coal was carried by goods trains via Canterbury to Whitstable and then in hoys along the Thames to the capital. The importance to the town of trade with its hinterland in wool, flour and above all hops has been noted, which with the allied brewing industry kept Victorian Canterbury alive.[15] The near absence of industrial production further

---

[11] *Kentish Gazette and Canterbury Press*, 6 Nov. 1920.

[12] *Kentish Gazette*, 16 Oct. 1920.

[13] *The Municipal Yearbook and Public Services Directory*, (London, 1923), p. 42.

[14] *The Municipal Yearbook and Public Services Directory*, (London, 1935), p. 87.

[15] Gardiner, *Canterbury*, p. 115.

north in the county appears to apply to Canterbury too in the period of this study.[16] The industry tables of the 1931 census show a borough dominated by commerce and finance (23.3 per cent) and public administration and defence (12.6 per cent). In the former category female labour was as important in overall percentage terms as the male contribution. This was so too in terms of local government employment, with approximately a five per cent contribution by both sexes. Thus nearly 36 per cent of the labour force was classified as being in these two broad sectors, a category rivalled only by personal service (an overall 18 per cent). Personal service was dominated by female labour, there being nearly four times as many women as men in this category. Personal service by women, with 47 per cent of the female labour force so employed, was high in relation to other county boroughs. With female domestic servants at 6 per cent of the whole population, Canterbury stood tenth in the ranking of county boroughs in this category. This was an indicator of high social class, and other such indicators confirmed this.[17] The borough was ranked ninth in terms of the proportion in the professionals category and eleventh in the own account and managerial categories. On the other hand in the population tables of the census Canterbury averaged a very low 0.72 persons per room, making it sixty-ninth amongst the county boroughs. All of these statistics suggest a preponderance of people of high social class in the city. The comparatively large percentage classified as professionals is noteworthy and requires further comment. Two features stand out. First, there were a large number of women in this category, with over 8 per cent of women classified as professionals. Only six other boroughs had a higher percentage of female professionals than this. What jobs did these women do? The industry tables do not give this information, but teaching in all sectors and levels was usually an important form of professional employment for women. Canterbury provided some services for the county for which the city was reimbursed and this probably boosted the numbers employed in teaching.[18] Second, the number of male professionals was enhanced by a preponderance of clergymen and others associated with the administration of the church, given the city's role at the centre of the hierarchy of the Anglican church.

From this data a profile emerges of Canterbury being dominated by commerce, finance and the service sector, with high employment of women in the professional and domestic labour categories. This suggests a relatively affluent borough, with a comfortable middle class. Together with a lower middle class of shop keepers and small businessmen and further down the class scale, shop assistants, the social structure of Canterbury appears straightforward. The picture of relative affluence and economic well-being is further reinforced by the relatively low levels of unemployment in the borough in the 1930s. Thus in the 1931 census only 7 per cent of the workforce was recorded as out of work, a very low figure placing Canterbury at seventy-eighth amongst the eighty-three county boroughs. Fogarty, constructing an average monthly unemployment total for 1932 from monthly

---

[16] Fogarty, M.P., *Prospects of the Industrial Areas of Great Britain*, (London, 1945), p. 425.
[17] See the appendices in this volume, pp. 685–687.
[18] Boyle, *Portrait of Canterbury*, p. 182.

returns, produced a figure of just under 10 per cent. The city did, however, have a substantial minority of working-class people. These included just over 250 miners and quarrymen, 3.6 per cent of the male labour force. Just over 4 per cent of the workforce was also employed in the food, drink and tobacco industries, linked to the processing of the products of Canterbury's agricultural hinterland. Male employment was also significant in metal and engineering, building, transport, and agriculture. The social profile drawn of middle class comfort must then be modified to an extent. A significant proportion of men, and some women, employed in manual labour existed. This fact, together with the running political sore of the housing issue at the November elections, did cast a shadow on an image of uniform gentility and prosperity.

Turning to the municipal politics of Canterbury between the wars, it should be stressed at the outset that the near absence of party politics and the infrequency of elections mean that comment and analysis must be necessarily brief. Available data of electors registered by wards is fragmentary but enough is available to indicate a rough and ready electoral equality between the wards. Thus Dane John and Northgate both increased from a little over 3,500 electors to near 4,500 in the 1930s, while Westgate had a slightly smaller population with roughly 2,500 electors in 1925, the last available figure. There is no evidence here of gerrymandering, nor would the ruling Independents have required such chicanery given their numerical dominance of the council chamber. With the whole of the borough being divided into only three wards, any variations in terms of the social class and housing type of different areas would tend not to be reflected in differences between the wards. Small pockets of sub-standard working-class housing would be swamped by the larger affluent districts in each ward. So despite housing being one of the main electoral issues in the borough, ward differences in the persons per room figures were minimal. All three wards had relatively low averages, varying between 0.66 persons per room in Dane John to 0.78 in Northgate.

If the election results are examined on a ward basis, a situation of overall electoral apathy and absence of political competition emerges. On three occasions, in 1924, 1926 and 1936, no elections took place at all in the borough, and on eleven occasions there was an election in only one of the wards. In only three years, 1919, 1921 and 1925, were all three wards contested. Of a possible sixty elections in the three wards over the twenty year period, only twenty-six required the electors to cast their votes. It was also the case that in those elections, apart from a small number of Women's Citizens Association (WCA) and National Unemployed Workers' Movement candidates in the early years, only Labour stood on a party label before 1934. Labour in fact stood candidates on seventeen occasions in all (once uncontested), and only once succeeded in winning in a contested election.

These general points applied most to Westgate, which with a mix of suburban and semi-rural settlement provided the Independents with totally safe seats which were seldom contested, there being only five contests in total between the wars. All of these contests occurred in the years up to 1925, Labour fighting the ward three times unsuccessfully. Apart from the success of the Women Citizens' Association in 1919, all others elected in Westgate were Independents who refrained from the use of party labels. Labour's only council success was in Dane John ward in 1933 when Sidney Palmer became the borough's first and only Labour councillor before the Second World War. Dane John was contested on eight occasions in all, with the Conservative party only emerging as an official and named electoral force in 1934. The adoption of official Conservative candidates appears to have begun only when Labour party competition became more sustained, and especially after Labour had managed to win a seat. Even then the party battle was still restrained. Despite Labour candidates being soundly defeated by Conservatives in the two years after Palmer's victory, he was allowed a free run when he came up for re-election in 1936. This was tantamount to a 'grace and favour' appointment by the ruling group, being a paternalistic concession to the 'demands of labour'. A WCA candidate also won a seat in Dane John in 1919, but otherwise unlabelled independent candidates held sway until the mid 1930s. Political activity was greatest in the third ward, Northgate, where there were thirteen contested elections between the wars. The Tories also appeared in name here from 1934, and again apart from a WCA winner in 1919 all other winners were unlabelled independents.

Inter-war municipal politics in Canterbury were marked by an apolitical ethos, where largely middle-class small traders, shopkeepers and professionals were elected in the stated interests of the ratepayers by predominantly affluent middle-class electorates. These 'Independents' were allegedly non-partisan, but as was the case in some other county boroughs of the era, the Independent umbrella masked an innate Conservatism. With small businessmen to the fore as councillors, the Independents tried to ensure non-party politics. This worked in the main to stifle political debate, very often on the issues of social deprivation and unemployment. Certainly ideological conflict was kept at a minimum by their paramount position. The watchwords of these Independents were 'economy' and 'efficiency' in the interests of the ratepayers. Canterbury's conservatism was understated and all-pervading and informed both ideological belief and political action. This produced an atmosphere of inertia and immobilisation in borough politics perhaps only enlivened by a few mavericks within the 'independent' ranks.

One councillor, Mrs Lucy Wells, testified to the undoubted Independent control of the inter-war council. Mrs Wells was elected to the Westgate ward under the auspices of the Women Citizens' Association in 1919. Thereafter she sat as an Independent, becoming an alderwoman in 1931 and the first female mayor of Canterbury in 1939–40. Describing herself as an Independent member of the council and looking back to before the Second War, Lucy Wells said: 'We [i.e., Independents] had control of everything in those days. Police force, fire service, health, education, roads, and survey and finance, to say nothing of sewage'.[19] As has been noted in other county boroughs, independents both despised and resented what they saw as the intrusion of party politics into municipal government. The local press, the *Kentish Gazette & Canterbury Press* agreed with them in an article on the forthcoming election of 1920:

> In the past the election of municipal representatives on the Party ticket was undoubtedly a serious blot upon the municipal life of

---

[19] Williamson, C.E., *Come Along With Me*, (London, 1971), pp. 63–64.

our country. Today in Canterbury – as in many other places – this bad old system has practically disappeared and it is to be hoped forever. The independent candidate has, we believe, at long last come into his own – and individual merit and character now constitute the crucial test.[20]

These non-party men and women believed that independent candidates, with at least some modest means, should run the corporation in an even-handed and judicious manner. Rates should be kept low in the interests of the ratepayers. Economy should run hand in glove with efficiency to provide the best possible local services for the lowest possible outlay from the public purse. The very notion of party organisation and discipline was far removed from their political lexicon. One noted Independent who fitted the maverick disposition noted above, was J.C.B. Stone. Councillor Stone (1863–1957) served continuously on the council for Westgate ward from 1899 until after the Second World War, being returned unopposed a record seventeen times. Only once in the period of this study was he forced to go to the hustings, in 1920 when he topped the poll after Labour had had the temerity to stand a candidate against him. Stone had a tailor's shop and was possibly an extreme exponent of the Independent position. He was a member of the Board of Guardians and an expert on the poor law, rating and assessment, and chairman of the watch committee for many years. By the 1930s he was the 'father of the council'. As a true independent however, he could not allow himself to be put forward for the honour of being alderman or mayor as he 'refused to be placed in a position which made him dependent on his fellow councillors.[21] In his pre-election advert for 1920, Stone could write of himself:

> It is perhaps only fair to myself that I should say that were I merely desirous of occupying a seat on your council, I could have been elected to the Aldermanic bench years ago. I, however, preferred to leave myself in your hands and the feeling that I had the people behind me has given me greater freedom of action than would have been the case had I owed my position to those with whom I am not always in agreement.[22]

Stone's last act of notoriety in a long list was an arrogant snub to the Minister of Town and Country Planning in Atlee's government, Lewis Silkin. When Silkin visited the borough, Stone organised a council boycott, with councillors refusing to meet the minister. Stone went even further, releasing a speech to the press that fellow councillors had deemed too insulting.[23]

Canterbury's councillors were drawn, as might be expected, largely from the same occupational and social backgrounds. There were two main categories of employment, shopkeepers and professionals. These categories, together with the well-off retired, formed the backbone of the council. The first post-war election in 1919 was unusual having three married women, as well as a company director,

---

[20] *Kentish Gazette*, 16 Oct. 1920.
[21] Boyle, *Portrait of Canterbury*, p. 140.
[22] *Kentish Gazette*, 23 Oct. 1920.
[23] Boyle, *Portrait of Canterbury*, p. 141.

manufacturer and a church official elected. The unsuccessful Labour candidates were an insurance agent, post office worker, and surprisingly, an art dealer.[24] Thereafter the successful candidates were remarkably similar in occupational background over the two decades. In 1924, there were three small businessmen, namely a pawnbroker, flour factor and a baker, two retired males: a naval officer and a sanitary inspector, and an insurance agent. The role of insurance agent was a typical occupation of inter-war Labour candidates. It is worth noting that J.F. Lamb, the insurance agent in question, had fought Westgate unsuccessfully in 1919 on the Labour ticket. The next year he dropped the Labour label and in 1921 he secured an electoral victory as an 'independent'. Again, if a 1930s survey of candidates is examined, a similar picture emerges. In 1937 for example, three shopkeepers (one retired), a licensed victualler, a solicitor and retired civil servant entered the council. The occupational structure of the council was similar to other smaller southern county boroughs at the time, such as Bath and Bournemouth, except perhaps in one particular. The importance of the church in the borough was reflected in the fact that two clergymen held seats on the council, the Rev S.G. Wilson sitting for Dane John ward between 1926 and 1935, and the Rev E.H. Sheppard for Northgate between 1926 and 1938. It should be noted that ministers of religion were legally allowed to stand for political office only from 1925. It is also of interest that while Wilson was predictably an Anglican, Sheppard was a Catholic priest. Plainly there was an ecumenical tinge to the ranks of the Independent councillors.

The Labour party was extremely weak in the borough. The party's profile in local politics was virtually non-existent between the unsuccessful electoral forays of the early 1920s and the greater success after 1931. The three Labour candidates in 1919 all performed poorly, the most successful obtaining only 260 votes in Dane John. The Labour candidates produced a joint electoral statement in a press advert to the electors. Stating that they had been asked to stand at the request of the Canterbury Trades and Labour Council, their manifesto provided some insight into Labour's concerns in the borough. Evening council meetings, a demand that the council should become a model employer always ready to confer with the trade unions, preferential treatment of ex-servicemen for council employment, the tightening up of legislation against profiteering were all given prominence. Education was also an issue, Labour arguing that advantage should be taken of the new Education Act to enhance all possible opportunities for children. Finally, the three candidates touched on the issue of housing, the major issue of the borough over the twenty-year period. Labour pointed out that the Ministry of Labour had placed Canterbury on the 'Black List' because of the council's delay in implementing the Housing Scheme.[25]

Later in 1932 Sidney Palmer, who had been an accountant of thirty years standing and was now a fruit grower, secretary of the Canterbury Labour party and a JP, proffered his electoral platform. His main emphasis appears to have been on council-inspired public works, though this message was couched in vague terms:

---

[24] *Kentish Gazette*, 1 Nov. 1919.
[25] *Kentish Gazette*, 18 Oct. 1919.

> As will be seen from his address Mr. Palmer makes a strong claim
> that while there is a great deal of profitable work to be done and
> men willing and anxious to do it, yet the community are failing to
> organise to bring the men and the work together.[26]

In his next successful election in 1933, Palmer emphasised housing and slum clearance, denouncing the city council's five year plan as 'entirely inadequate', as well as urging the construction of a by-pass road. Once again it appears that public works were being advocated, though again *sotto voce*.[27]

Why was Labour so very weak, even when compared to other comparable southern county boroughs of the period?[28] The Labour party appears to have come late to the borough in terms of establishing itself electorally. A small working class in a predominantly middle class population with a strong conservative ethos did not help. Trade unions had little presence in the borough. There was a Trades and Labour Council, which in the 1926 General Strike appears to have been successful in mobilising support. The proximity of the Kent miners may have helped to engender some sympathy in this case. It was reported that 'the organisation here was perfect', and that there was 'no weakening whatever; our difficulty was to keep the men not involved at work.'[29] This was exceptional, however, and poor organisation and a lack of a vibrant trade union membership and thus support for the party seems to have been the case. All this derived from the borough's economic structure. There were no big employers of labour and little in the way of light engineering. Working people were employed in small enterprises and their social and political weight was small. There were a significant number of shop assistants, but these were perceived as being far higher up the class structure then than they are now. With their self-perception as lower middle class, these and other white collar workers did little to assuage Labour's electoral weakness. There is no doubt that the case of Canterbury supports the view that 'on the whole, and in southern Britain in particular, the Labour Party failed to establish an alternative political culture to the dominant Conservative and Anglican-influenced one of much of the countryside.'[30]

The Conservative party was of course nominally absent in the local political arena, at least until their emergence in 1934. That is however, not to say that the Conservative party was weak in Canterbury. Many of the Independents were Conservatives, and the Independents dominated the town with a largely Conservative agenda and policies which Conservatives would have approved of. The ease with which some Independents became Conservatives once faced by a more organised threat from Labour is noteworthy. E.H. Sheppard in Northgate, and

---

[26] *Kentish Gazette*, 29 Oct. 1932.

[27] *Kentish Gazette*, 28 Oct. 1933.

[28] On Labour's success in some small towns and rural areas, especially in the immediate post-First World War years, see Wrigley, C.J., 'Explaining why so many as well as so few: some aspects of the development of the Labour party in small towns and rural areas', *Journal of Regional and Local Studies*, vol. 10, no. 1, (1990), pp. 17–22.

[29] Burns, E., *The General Strike May 1926: Trades Councils in Action*, (London, 1975), p. 109.

[30] Wrigley, 'Explaining why so many', p. 21.

Messrs. Withwick, Kingsford and Thompson in Dane John had all stood as aspiring Independents or had been Independent councillors, before flying under the Conservative flag after 1934. Given the middle-class electoral hold on Canterbury and the absence of an effective Labour party, there was no need for the usual 'Anti-Socialist' alliance to operate. In other boroughs such alliances between Conservatives and Liberals, and sometimes Independents and various Rate-payers groups had come into being, but such an arrangement was unnecessary in Canterbury. It is interesting to note that the pre-election address of Canon E.H. Sheppard and Percy Botting, the Conservative candidates for Northgate in 1938, was virtually the same as that of the Independents in previous years. They urged 'that the strictest economy should be observed in our local public expenditure.....we are strongly of the opinion that several of the costly schemes contemplated by the Council should be deferred until a more appropriate time......Our policy in short, is one of Wise Spending and Ordered Progress'. The only different note struck was that economy was urged for one new reason – the burdens placed 'upon the nation by the all-important Defence and A.R.P. Programmes'. Despite Labour having only one supporter in the council chamber, the Conservative candidates nevertheless appealed for support 'in opposition to the Socialist policies of reckless and wasteful spending, which in many parts of the country has had such disastrous consequences'.[31]

The appearance of the Women's Citizens Association (WCA) in the 1919 elections in Canterbury requires some comment. All three women candidates for this organisation were elected in that year, each taking second place in their respective wards in the city. The WCA, which had been founded in 1913, after the First World War formed one of the remaining elements of the feminist movement that had not been absorbed into the main political parties. It was of a 'largely middle-class and non-party character', and one of its main objectives was 'encouraging women to participate in local government'.[32] The three women placed a common electoral advert to the voters in the *Kentish Gazette*. Their main manifesto point was the repair of houses to ensure healthy homes together with taking advantage of Government subsidies to build houses on healthy sites. They also proposed better educational opportunities for children possibly in co-operation with Kent County Council. Promising to get full value 'for the ratepayers money', they urged that the Corporation should become a 'fair house' in terms of rates of pay and hours of work for employees.[33] It is also curious that a local magistrate stood unsuccessfully under the banner of the 'Canterbury Men's Citizens Association' in Dane John ward 1919. The provenance of this body and its links, if any, with the WCA is unclear.

In the middle-class context of Canterbury, the WCA was probably an especially moderate wing of the feminist movement, and was soon submerged with the other Independents on the council, as the case of Lucy Wells above demonstrated. In Canterbury at least the WCA also seems to have had some affinity with the Middle

---

[31] *Kentish Gazette*, 29 Oct. 1938.
[32] Pugh, M., *Women and The Women's Movement in Britain 1914–1959*, (London, 1992), p. 51; for more on the WCA, see chapter nine in this volume on Carlisle, pp. 602–604.
[33] *Kentish Gazette*, 18 Oct. 1919.

Classes Union (MCU), a branch of which was formed in Canterbury in 1921. Such unions sprang up across the country in the years between 1919 and 1922, indicative of a feeling of insecurity amongst the lower middle class in this period of heightened class consciousness. The threat of socialism and the organised working class, rising taxation and a fall in lower middle-class incomes relative to prices during the war had all contributed to this insecurity. It was accompanied by an idea that the major parties were failing the 'little man', 'who is of the opinion that his interest and his liberty are not safe-guarded by organised labour on one side and federated capital on the other', as one of the leaders of the MCU put it. As he went on to say, it was 'clear to the middle-class man that the party rosette, put away in a drawer against the next election, must now be left to the moth'.[34] Such sentiments were short-lived, and it was the Conservative party's success nationally in restoring the faith and political loyalty of these disgruntled citizens that was at the heart of its electoral strength between the wars in places like Canterbury. The local MCU chairman, Arthur Wells, complained at a meeting about heavy taxation of the middle classes which, together with the influence of the trade unions, was, he claimed, harming the well-being of the country. He then stated that the ladies present should belong to the MCU and as well 'join and take an active interest in' the Women's Citizens Association.[35] In the event his blandishments were plainly rejected as unnecessary, as all found succour in the Conservatism that dared not speak its name, the 'Independents' of Canterbury.

It is interesting that in Canterbury women seemed to be better represented in the political process than in many of the other boroughs considered so far in these volumes. The merging of the feminist movement into the non-party milieu seemed to enable women more easily to be put forward as candidates for the municipal elections. Equally the Labour party seemed to respond by choosing women amongst its candidates. Twelve out of the total of 140 candidatures between the wars were women (almost 9 per cent), and women were candidates twice amongst Labour's seventeen candidatures. Moreover, the success rate of the non-Labour women candidates was 100 per cent, so the number of women who actually got onto the council was also high. In total seven women sat as councillors at one time or another between 1919 and 1938, which in a council of only twenty-four in total represented quite a significant feminine presence compared to many other boroughs. Whether that presence had a significant influence on the business of the council is unclear. It is possible, however, that it was one reason why the question of housing, which was seen traditionally as coming within the 'domestic sphere' appropriate to women, was so often highlighted and relatively generously dealt with.

Housing, or rather the standard and dearth of it, occurred as a constant political issue in the November elections. Suggesting that the issue itself was one of political contention perhaps over-states the case. Most aspirants to the council agreed that housing should be high on the political agenda. Any differences that

[34] Quoted in Waites, B., *A Class Society at War: England 1914–18*, (Leamington Spa, 1987), pp. 53–54; on the lower middle-class revolt and the background to the MCU see also pp. 24–29, 47–54, 81–91, 240–264; see also Morgan, K.O., *Consensus and Disunity: The Lloyd George Coalition Government 1918–1922*, (London, 1979), pp. 236–254, 298–301.
[35] *Kentish Gazette*, 15 Oct. 1921.

seem to have arisen were over how far the rate-payers should have to go in helping to finance the correction of what was seen as the most obvious social ill in Canterbury. In all housing was an important issue in eleven of the twenty November elections between the wars, and on two occasions, in 1919 and 1925, it was by far the major issue. The press reported that the usual demands were for slum clearance, taking advantage of government Housing Acts and the construction of more houses for both sale and rent. Nearly all candidates put new and improved housing at the top of their manifestos in the 1919 election, but it was in the 1925 election that the issue of housing received its biggest billing in the inter-war period, two editions of the local press giving housing prominence. Thus 'Housing Question the Dominating Issue' and 'Houses to Let the Paramount Issue' were both sub-headlines to the reports on the municipal elections in successive weeks.[36] Housing was viewed as a social ill and a cause for concern for the prospects of the local economy. The *Kentish Gazette* believed

> the housing shortage in Canterbury is probably as acute as in almost any other place of its kind in the South of England ... Numerous instances may be cited of two, three and even four families occupying a single house, and of people living in lodgings because they are unable to get the accommodation they require. The numbers of men who flock in by train and 'bus in the mornings to follow their vocations in the city afford further evidence of the grievous nature of the shortage. Apart from social and humanitarian considerations, there is a big business side to the question. It cannot be other than detrimental to the city that the money which many persons earn in Canterbury should be spent in the maintenance of their families elsewhere. The difficulties which the Council have had to encounter in the past will be generally acknowledged, but the time has now arrived when a determined effort must be made to effectively grapple with, and find a solution for, the serious condition of affairs which prevails. Public opinion, if it bestirs itself, is a very potent force, and we believe it is the intention of the electors of Canterbury in the next few weeks to exercise their powers in impressing upon the City Council that they expect a 'move-on' to be made in this vitally important question. The *Kentish Gazette* has recently given prominence to various schemes for providing the much needed houses which may be let at an economic rent which working class families can afford to pay. This would be the best possible solution of the problem that can be found: but even if it be deemed impossible to erect houses to be let as an economic proposition – and this is certainly open to question – some scheme must be instituted (even if it involves a little assistance from the rates and taxes) to put an end to the present intolerable position of affairs.[37]

[36] *Kentish Gazette*, 17 and 24 Oct. 1925.
[37] *Kentish Gazette*, 17 Oct. 1925.

Invariably Labour, and sometimes prospective Independent councillors, saw the council's housing schemes as inadequate.[38] On occasions candidates recommended themselves by their record in the deliberations of the council on housing. Thus, in his victory speech during the declaration of the poll, C. Phillips proclaimed: 'You wanted houses, and you have got some – ("hear, hear"): and you will get some more if they are required. (Applause.).'[39] The local press entered a note of realism as to the probable impact of councillors who had trumpeted the housing issue once they were in the council chamber, commenting in 1925:

> The question of housing in general and of houses to let in particular ... entirely overshadows and obscures every other issue. It is significant that all the candidates, old and new, are going to subject its due prominence in their election addresses. To make a dead set against the former members who happen to be seeking the suffrages of the electors at this time – because of any 'act of omission' which the Council as a whole may be deemed to have committed – would be both illogical and unfair. It is well to bear in mind that whatever the outcome of the election, the change in personnel of the Council will be so small that, so far as numbers go, it cannot greatly alter the decisions of that body. The opportunity however, is now offered for the electors to strongly impress their wishes upon the candidates ... so that the Councillors who are returned will be able to give a clear expression of the will of the citizens on this vitally important matter. On November 4, a thoroughly representative and non-party delegation, headed by the Dean of Canterbury is to wait upon the new Council, at its first meeting, to press for a larger housing programme, and particularly for the provision of houses to let. Public opinion in Canterbury can do much in the meantime to ensure the success of this appeal to the City Fathers'.[40]

On other occasions of course, the press endeavoured to trumpet the achievements of the Independent-controlled council. In the build up to the 1929 election, the *Kentish Gazette* thanked Councillor Hooker and the Housing Committee on behalf 'of the citizens for having, by the provision of between 300 and 400 new houses relieved a large part of the housing problem in the city'.[41] Finally, a Conservative demonstrated his faith in individual initiative and private enterprise helping to solve the housing problem. In the 1934 election J. Couper Davie, the sitting candidate in Northgate ward, advised the press on nomination day that he had 'carried out a housing scheme of his own at Old Park Avenue, all the houses having been readily let'. Without irony, he went on to say he was 'a staunch advocate of economy and basic soundness in local administration'.[42] This left little doubt that the borough's housing problems should be solved by entrepreneurs and

[38] *Kentish Gazette*, 28 Oct. 1933.
[39] *Kentish Gazette*, 5 Nov. 1927.
[40] *Kentish Gazette*, 24 Oct. 1925.
[41] *Kentish Gazette*, 26 Oct. 1929.
[42] *Kentish Gazette*, 27 Oct. 1934.

advocates of private enterprise like himself, rather than by the expenditure of public funds.

If there was a difference in policy over housing, it was straightforward. The Independents wanted 'economy and efficiency' to ensure that the ratepayers got 'good value for money', while the handful of Labour candidates emphasised a more 'generous' (or in their opponents eyes, 'profligate') attitude to public expenditure. From the returns of the county boroughs made to the *Municipal Yearbook*, it can be seen that Canterbury council constructed 786 houses up to 31 March 1939. With one house built for every thirty-one people in the borough, this was quite generous provision, with Canterbury being thirty-sixth amongst the county boroughs in this regard. For a relatively affluent town this was surprisingly high, but there were few reserves of housing to let and inter-war Canterbury did have a substantial housing problem. Local authority action was needed as the private sector will often meet a market demand but rarely, if ever, a social need.

In other county boroughs, major employers like shipyards (Barrow), cotton mills (Bolton, Blackburn), or collieries (Barnsley), owned and managed a substantial housing stock. In Canterbury, the role of the Anglican church requires further investigation as a possible owner of housing. Christ Church Cathedral certainly owned substantial holdings, mostly of commercial property. These were mainly in the Cathedral Precinct and the boundaries of the Precinct. Thus the far end of Burgate, Broad Church, Sun and Palace Streets were in the gift of the Church. Many of these properties were shops with substantial numbers of people living above the premises. There were many houses for domicile owned by the Cathedral in the Precinct too, but these were let to existing and retired clergy. As a separate landlord, it is possible that the Church or Ecclesiastical Commissioners (of the Church of England) owned some properties, but there is little evidence of this being the case in Canterbury. Certainly the press did not raise the role of the Church as a landlord and neither did the aspiring councillors. Apart from the Dean of Canterbury leading the November 1925 delegation to the council on the housing issue, it appears that the Church was not greatly involved in the controversy.[43] The inter-war Church of England was still largely the 'Conservative party at prayer', although in Canterbury itself it perhaps quietly prayed along with the Independents.

Few other issues exercised the minds of the electorate as much as housing. By-pass roads and, ironically, political apathy were two other November issues that did emerge periodically. The *Kentish Gazette* commented in 1927:

> On the eve of the Canterbury municipal elections a strange quiet pervades the public life of the City, though in matters pertaining to the zest for pleasure and amusement there is every evidence of activity. In days not far distant things were very different. Then feeling ran high and controversies of an embittered personal character held sway. We are glad that the elections in these times are no longer fought on the old personal issues, but we are constrained to question whether the pendulum has not swung too far in the opposite direction. Honest differences of opinion on

[43] *Kentish Gazette*, 24 Oct. 1925.

matters of high principle are, surely, to be encouraged rather than discounted and make for a healthy tone to our local self government.[44]

This lament highlighted the all-pervading atmosphere of inter-war municipal politics in Canterbury, one of apathy and complacency.

To conclude, the exceptionally small size of Canterbury made it unusual amongst the county boroughs. As in many other small authorities, political conflict was at a low level of intensity, and an apolitical ethos was fostered that, at least in Canterbury, suited the Independents. It was also an environment that allowed for some participation by women in the political process. After the slight alarums of the immediate post-war years, a largely comfortable middle-class electorate was content to let the Independents govern with the watchwords of economy and efficiency. Relatively low unemployment helped reinforce middle-class satisfaction with their small businessmen and professional representatives in the council chamber. Party labels were virtually non-existent in the inter-war period, though the local press pointed to a different picture before 1914.[45] The central position of the Church of England was both responsible for the city's local government status and reinforced its distinctiveness. There are some grounds for suggesting that a clerical conservatism, part of the contemporary Anglican ethos, informed the local politics of the borough. To what extent the Church aided the Independent control of Canterbury, or gave some succour to the mid 1930s emergence of the Conservative party, is a question that requires further research. By contrast the Labour party had a low profile in Canterbury. There was only a small and poorly organised working class, whose political weight in the borough was slight. Labour's one solitary councillor from 1933 onwards must have been a lonely figure. It seems that his continuation on the council was a sop granted in a paternalistic fashion by the natural rulers of the city to the 'labour interest'. Finally the issue of housing did show that social inequality and a degree of relative poverty existed in Canterbury. The Independent-controlled council, given the number of houses built, could be said to have directly addressed this question. This was done, however, always with an eye to resources, 'economy' and the desire not to offend the ratepayers. Overall, the 'Mother of England', as seen through the prism of over half a century, emerges as a comfortably middle-class, stern parent who provided houses for its offspring and successfully warded off the threatened incursions of the county of Kent.

[44] *Kentish Gazette*, 22 Oct. 1927.
[45] *Kentish Gazette*, 16 Oct. 1920.

A guide to further reading

Newspapers

Kentish Gazette and Canterbury Press

Works of reference

Kelly's Directory of Canterbury, Whitstable, Herne Bay and Neighbourhood, 22nd edition, (London, 1934).
The Municipal Yearbook and Public Services Directory, (London, 1919–1939).

Secondary sources

Bateman, A., *Victorian Canterbury*, (Bucks., 1991).
Boyle, J., *Portrait of Canterbury*, (London, 1974).
Gardiner, D., *Canterbury: The Story of the English Towns*, (London, 1923).
Fogarty, M.P., *Prospects of the Industrial Areas of Great Britain*, (London, 1945).
Lincoln, E.F., *The Story of Canterbury*, (London, 1955).
Lyle, M., *Canterbury*, (London, 1994).
Pelling, H., *Social Geography of British Elections, 1885–1910*, (Aldershot, 1994) pp. 60–86.
Williamson, C.E., *Come Along With Me*, (London, 1971).

Canterbury wards 1919–1938

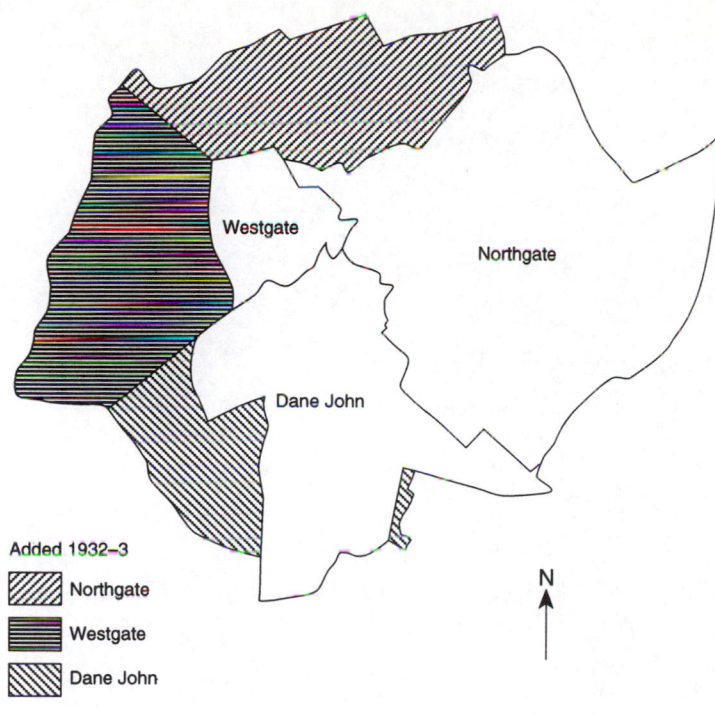

Westgate

Northgate

Dane John

Added 1932–3

Northgate

Westgate

Dane John

N

Persons aged fourteen and over classified by industry 1931

	Male	%	Female	%	Total	%
Agriculture	557	7.0	69	2.1	626	5.5
Metal and engineering	567	7.1	17	0.5	584	5.2
Building	838	10.5	9	0.3	847	7.5
Transport	643	8.0	38	1.2	681	6.0
- Road	*475*	*5.9*	*34*	*1.0*	*509*	*4.5*
Commerce and finance	1,845	23.0	782	23.8	2,627	23.3
Public admin. and defence	1,192	14.9	235	7.2	1,427	12.6
- Defence	*497*	*6.2*	*13*	*0.4*	*510*	*4.5*
- Local Government	*450*	*5.6*	*166*	*5.1*	*616*	*5.5*
Professions	303	3.8	283	8.6	586	5.2
Personal service	467	5.8	1,564	47.7	2,031	18.0
Other	1,599	20.0	285	8.7	1,884	16.7
Total (a)	**8,011**		**3,282**		**11,293**	
Total population (b)	11,488		12,958		24,446	
(a) as % of (b)	69.7		25.3		46.2	
Total out of work (c)	632		155		787	
(c) as % of (a)	7.9		4.7		7.0	
Managerial and own account	1,306	17.7	434	13.9	1,740	16.6
Operative	6,073	82.3	2,693	86.1	8,766	83.4
Total (excluding out of work)	7,379		3,127		10,506	

Population statistics 1931

Ward	Acres	Population	Persons/acre	Persons/room
Dane John	1,265	8,458	6.7	0.66
Northgate	2,254	9,794	4.3	0.78
Westgate	456	6,194	13.6	0.71
Total	**3,975**	**24,446**	**6.1**	**0.72**

Overall position on the council 1919–38

	Position		Gains		Losses	
	Others	Lab	Others	Lab	Others	Lab
1919	24	0	0	0	0	0
1920	24	0	0	0	0	0
1921	24	0	0	0	0	0
1922	24	0	0	0	0	0
1923	24	0	0	0	0	0
1924	24	0	0	0	0	0
1925	24	0	0	0	0	0
1926	24	0	0	0	0	0
1927	24	0	0	0	0	0
1928	24	0	0	0	0	0
1929	24	0	0	0	0	0
1930	24	0	0	0	0	0
1931	24	0	0	0	0	0
1932	24	0	0	0	0	0
1933	23	1	0	1	1	0
1934	23	1	0	0	0	0
1935	23	1	0	0	0	0
1936	23	1	0	0	0	0
1937	23	1	0	0	0	0
1938	23	1	0	0	0	0

Aldermen 1919–38

Independents held all aldermanic seats 1919–38.

Municipal elections: winning party, 1919–28

Ward	1919	1920	1921	1922	1923	1924	1925	1926	1927	1928
Dane John (1)	O	**O**	O	**O**	**O**	**O**	O	**O**	**O**	O
Dane John (2)	O	**O**	O	**O**	**O**	**O**	O	**O**	**O**	O
Northgate(1)	O	O	O	O	O	**O**	O	**O**	O	**O**
Northgate (2)	O	O	O	O	O	**O**	O	**O**	O	**O**
Westgate(1)	O	O	O	O	**O**	**O**	O	**O**	**O**	**O**
Westgate(2)	O	O	O	O	**O**	**O**	O	**O**	**O**	**O**

Municipal elections: party wins per year 1919–28

Wins	1919	1920	1921	1922	1923	1924	1925	1926	1927	1928
Other	6	6	6	6	6	6	6	6	6	6
Lab	0	0	0	0	0	0	0	0	0	0
Total	6	6	6	6	6	6	6	6	6	6
Turnout %	**48.8**	**46.5**	**31.6**	**37.1**	**15.3**	**-**	**45.9**	**-**	**32.8**	**29.0**
Labour %	**9.0**	**22.8**	**-**	**-**	**-**	**-**	**7.8**	**-**	**-**	**14.0**

Municipal elections: party wins per ward 1919–38

Wins	Other	Lab	Total	Turnout %	Labour %
Dane John	38	2	40	41.1	16.9
Northgate	40	0	40	33.6	12.0
Westgate	36	0	36	57.1	13.9
Total	**114**	**2**	**116**	**39.1**	**14.1**

Seats won by Labour as a percentage of all wins 1919–38   **1.72**

Municipal elections: winning party, 1929–38

Ward	1929	1930	1931	1932	1933	1934	1935	1936	1937	1938
Dane John (1)	O	O	O	O	O	O	O	O	O	O
Dane John (2)	O	O	O	O	Lab	O	O	Lab	O	O
Northgate(1)	O	O	O	O	O	O	O	O	O	O
Northgate (2)	O	O	O	O	O	O	O	O	O	O
Westgate(1)	O	O	O	O	-	-	O	O	O	O
Westgate(2)	O	O	O	O	-	-	O	O	O	O

Municipal elections: party wins per year 1929–38

Wins	1929	1930	1931	1932	1933	1934	1935	1936	1937	1938
C	6	6	6	6	3	4	6	5	6	6
Lab	0	0	0	0	1	0	0	1	0	0
Total	6	6	6	6	4	4	6	6	6	6
Turnout %	11.7	23.1	37.3	43.1	47.2	53.1	40.7	-	43.9	44.6
Labour %	-	-	17.1	24.4	33.4	22.4	23.8	-	21.5	23.7

Parliamentary election results

Canterbury constituency
*(all wards within the borough [1918 boundaries] were included in the
constituency, along with the urban districts of Herne Bay and
Whitstable, and the rural districts of Blean, Bridge, Elham and
Faversham [part])*

General election	Winner	Conservative %	Labour %	Liberal %
14 Dec. 1918	Co C	80.8 *(Co C)*	19.2	-
15 Nov. 1922	C	71.2	28.8	-
6 Dec. 1923	C	58.4	-	41.6
29 Oct. 1924	C	70.3	-	29.7
30 May 1929	C	56.7	13.9	29.4
27 Oct. 1931	C	83.7	16.3	-
14 Nov. 1935	C	74.3	25.7	-

Dane John ward

Candidate	Party	Votes	%	Electors	Turnout	Gains
1919						
J.F. Finch		883	32.0	3,556	52.4	-
Mrs L. Prentice	WCA	850	30.8			
J.G. Johnson*		429	15.5			
E.G. Hammond	MCU	254	9.2			
G.T. Mills		197	7.1			
E.E. Taylor	Lab	148	5.4			
Total votes		2,761				
Total voters		1,862				
1920						
R.H. Arrowsmith*		Unopp.	-		-	-
W. Hunt*		Unopp.				
1921						
P.R. Flinn*		517	45.8	3,812	18.3	
E.V. Dean*		450	39.8			
J.J. Galvin	Nuwm	163	14.4			
Total votes		1,130				
Total voters		696				
1922						
Col. Fellows		Unopp.	-		-	-
W. Cozens		Unopp.				
(no initials given for Colonel Fellows)						
1923						
H.J. Belsey*		Unopp.	-		-	-
G.M. Kingsford		Unopp.				
1924						
W.V. Howard		Unopp.	-		-	-
J.G. Johnson		Unopp.				
1925						
E.G. Noble		969	39.6	4,279	42.9	-
A.E. Galloway		812	33.2			
W. Cozens*		664	27.2			
Total votes		2,445				
Total voters		1,835				

Dane John ward *(continued)*

Candidate	Party	Votes	%	Electors	Turnout	Gains
1926						
Rev S.G. Wilson*		Unopp.	-		-	-
G. Kingsford*		Unopp.				
1927						
W.V. Howard*		Unopp.	-		-	-
J.G. Johnson*		Unopp.				
1928						
E.G. Noble*		1,190	52.7	*4,330*	29.0	-
H. Harrison		521	23.1			
A. Graham Porter	Lab	315	14.0			
C. Guy		232	10.3			
Total votes		2,258				
Total voters		*1,254*				
1929						
Rev S.G. Wilson*		Unopp.	-		-	-
G.M. Kingsford*		Unopp.				
1930						
W.V. Howard*		Unopp.	-		-	-
J. Partridge*		Unopp.				
1931						
E.G. Noble*		Unopp.	-		-	-
N.H. Wightwick		Unopp.				
1932						
Rev S.G. Wilson*		1,199	40.6	4,400	43.1	
G.M.Kingsford*		1,036	35.1			
S. Palmer	Lab	720	24.4			
Total votes		2,955				
Total voters		1,898				

Dane John ward *(continued)*

Candidate	Party	Votes	%	Electors	Turnout	Gains
1933						
J. Partridge*		1,107	36.7	4,300	47.2	
S Palmer	Lab	1,009	33.4			Lab from
J.B. Thompson		904	29.9			Other
Total votes		3,020				
Total voters		2,029				
1934						
J.B. Thompson*	C	1,472	40.3	4,300	54.5	-
H.H. Withwick*	C	1,444	39.5			
Mrs G. Keable	Lab	736	20.2			
Total votes		3,652				
Total voters		2,345				
1935						
G.M. Kingsford*	C	1,216	38.6	*4,300*	40.7	
E.R James	C	1,186	37.6			
Mrs G. Keable	Lab	749	23.8			
Total votes		3,151				
Total voters		1,751				
1936						
Mrs M.E. Hews		Unopp.	-		-	-
S. Palmer*	Lab	Unopp.				
1937						
H.H. Withwick*		Unopp.	-		-	-
A.E. Hammond		Unopp.				
1938						
E.R. James*		Unopp.	-		-	-
A.W. Fowler*		Unopp.				

Overall Labour vote   **16.9%**   **Overall turnout**   **41.1%**

Northgate ward

Candidate	Party	Votes	%	Electors	Turnout	Gains
1919						
J. McClemens*		593	31.1	3,217	40.1	-
Mrs D. Gardiner	WCA	509	26.7			
C. Phillips		476	24.9			
T.J. Collins	Lab	199	10.4			
W.H. Powell		131	6.9			
Total votes		1,908				
Total voters		1,289				
1920						
W.J. Russell*		443	25.3	3,447	38.3	-
J.G. Johnson		396	22.6			
A.E. Vandersteen		371	21.2			
H.F. Bates	Lab	290	16.5			
E.G. Hammond		254	14.5			
Total votes		1,754				
Total voters		1,320				
1921						
C. Phillips*		618	43.3	3,545	25.1	-
A.E. Vandersteen		523	36.6			
H. Hulse	Nuwm	287	20.1			
Total votes		1,428				
Total voters		891				
1922						
Maj. Thirlwall		640	33.8	3,731	28.2	-
F.A. Parry		556	29.4			
J. McClemens*		402	21.2			
Mrs D. Gardiner		294	15.5			
Total votes		1,892				
Total voters		1,051				
(no initials given for Major Thirlwall)						
1923						
W.R. Pierce		409	38.0	3,917	15.3	-
W.J. Russell*		392	36.4			
J.G. Johnson*		275	25.6			
Total votes		1,076				
Total voters		598				

Northgate ward *(continued)*

Candidate	Party	Votes	%	Electors	Turnout	Gains
1924						
C. Phillips*	Unopp.	-		-		-
A.E. Vandersteen*	Unopp.					
1925						
H.G. Mount		1,006	46.6	4,290	40.7	-
F.A. Parry*		618	28.6			
J.W. Edwards*		536	24.8			
Total votes		2,160				
Total voters		1,744				
1926						
W.R. Pierce*	Unopp.	-		-		-
Rev E.H. Sheppard*	Unopp.					
1927						
C. Phillips*		760	37.5	4,035	32.8	-
A.E. Vandersteen*		688	33.9			
C. Skam		358	17.6			
H. Funnell		223	11.0			
Total votes		2,029				
Total voters		1,323				
1928						
E.R. Crow	Unopp.	-		-		-
Mrs V.M. Williamson	Unopp.					
1929						
Rev E.H. Sheppard*		353	40.5	*4,151*	11.7	-
C. Guy		264	30.3			
A. Graham Porter		255	29.2			
Total votes		872				
Total voters		484				

(Porter ran as an independent, not for Labour as he had done in 1928 in Dane John ward)

Northgate ward *(continued)*

Candidate	Party	Votes	%	Electors	Turnout	Gains
1930						
A. Baynton		1,019	58.2	*4,209*	23.1	-
C. Phillips*		541	30.9			
A.E. Vandersteen*		190	10.9			
Total votes		1,750				
Total voters		972				
1931						
Mrs V.M. Williamson*		1,374	44.5	*4,267*	37.3	-
E.R. Crow*		1,183	38.3			
H.E. Dawkins	Lab	315	10.2			
F. Harbottle	Lab	214	6.9			
Total votes		3,086				
Total voters		1,591				
1932						
Rev E.H. Sheppard*		Unopp.	-		-	-
F.C. Lefevre		Unopp.				
1933						
A. Baynton*		Unopp.	-		-	-
C. Phillips*		Unopp.				
1934						
J. Couper-Davie*	C	1,285	37.8	*4,441*	51.7	-
J. Holloway	C	1,276	37.5			
S. Hopton	Lab	841	24.7			
Total votes		3,402				
Total voters		2,297				
1935						
Rev E.H. Sheppard*		Unopp.	-		-	-
F.C. Lefevre*		Unopp.				
1936						
A. Baynton*		Unopp.	-		-	-
W.F. Simpson*		Unopp.				

Northgate ward *(continued)*

Candidate	Party	Votes	%	Electors	Turnout	Gains
1937						
J.T. Holloway*	C	1,333	40.1	4,616	43.9	-
R.H.W.V Surtees*	C	1,274	38.4			
J.E. Finn	Lab	714	21.5			
Total votes		3,321				
Total voters		2,026				
1938						
Rev E.H. Sheppard*	C	1,314	38.6	4,727	44.6	
P. Botting*	C	1,287	37.8			
J.E. Finn	Lab	806	23.7			
Total Votes		3,407				
Total Voters		2,108				

Overall Labour vote   **Overall turnout**   **33.6%**

Westgate ward

Candidate	Party	Votes	%	Electors	Turnout	Gains
1919						
H.G. James		841	40.9	2,316	55.4	-
Mrs L.G. Wells	WCA	508	24.7			
T. Wood*		446	21.7			
J.F.Lamb	Lab	260	12.7			
Total votes		2,055				
Total voters		1,284				
1920						
J.G.B. Stone*		750	39.2	2,433	58.2	-
G.R. Barrett		614	32.1			
J.F. Lamb	Lab	549	28.7			
Total votes		1,913				
Total voters		1,416				
1921						
C. Richardson*		949	41.0	2,466	61.4	-
J.F Lamb		514	22.2			
H.J. Goulden		427	18.5			
Ms A. Gibson		231	10.0			
C. Sanderson		191	8.3			
Total votes		2,312				
Total voters		1,513				
1922						
Mrs L.G. Wells*		646	32.7	*2,484*	50.4	-
F. Hooker		612	31.0			
J.W. Edwards		591	29.9			
T. Potten		128	6.5			
Total votes		1,977				
Total voters		1,252				
1923						
G.R. Barrett*		Unopp.	-		-	-
J.G.B Stone*		Unopp.				
1924						
C. Richardson*		Unopp.	-		-	-
J.F. Lamb		Unopp.				

Westgate ward *(continued)*

Candidate	Party	Votes	%	Electors	Turnout	Gains
1925						
Mrs L.G. Wells*		877	38.4	2,540	59.9	-
F. Hooker*		810	35.4			
W.A. Terry	Lab	598	26.2			
Total votes		2,285				
Total voters		1,521				
1926						
G.R. Barrett*		Unopp.	-		-	-
J.G.B. Stone*		Unopp.				
1927						
C. Richardson*		Unopp.	-		-	-
J.F. Lamb*		Unopp.				
1928						
Mrs L.G. Wells*		Unopp.	-		-	-
F. Hooker*		Unopp.				
1929						
J.G.B. Stone*		Unopp.	-		-	-
F Wood*		Unopp.				
1930						
J.F. Lamb*		Unopp.	-		-	-
C.P. Mason		Unopp.				
1931						
F. Hooker*		Unopp.	-		-	-
J.W. Edwards		Unopp.				
1932						
J.G.B. Stone*		Unopp.	-		-	-
F. Wood*		Unopp.				

1933
No election held – boundary extension.

1934
No election held – boundary extension.

Westgate ward *(continued)*

Candidate	Party	Votes	% Electors	Turnout	Gains
1935					
J.W. Edwards*	Unopp.	-		-	-
H. Harrison*	Unopp.				
1936					
W.J. Dray*	Unopp.	-		-	-
Mrs C. Williamson*	Unopp.				
1937					
J.G.B. Stone*	Unopp.	-		-	-
H. Rigden*	Unopp.				
1938					
H. Harrison*	Unopp.	-		-	-
J.M. Symns*	Unopp.				

Overall Labour vote   **13.9%**   **Overall turnout**   **57.1%**

EIGHT
Cardiff

CARDIFF

The county borough of Cardiff (in Welsh, *Caerdydd*) in the inter-war years was a major regional centre and the commercial capital of south Wales.[1] With a population of over 223,000 in 1931, Cardiff was the most important urban centre in Wales and the seventeenth largest of the county boroughs. In the nineteenth century, Cardiff's location on the river Taff and its tributaries meant that it became the focal point for the development of both the iron working and coal mining of Glamorgan.[2] Its economic fortunes lay in the export of the coal and iron ore together with the output of the highly developed heavy industry of its valley hinterlands. In the first half of the nineteenth century the borough's growth rested on the port trade in iron ore. However, by the mid nineteenth century Cardiff was of prime importance to the British economy and to the expanding global trade in coal. Cardiff's Victorian prosperity was based on the mining and exploitation of the fine quality steam coal of the Rhondda valley from the 1860s. The other valleys of South Wales were then developed and linked to the port of Cardiff by a highly developed railway system that ran into the dockside. Transport was 'the *raison d' être* of the town – the transfer of coal from the railway wagons to ships'.[3] To the wider world the coal of the South Wales valleys was known as 'Cardiff Coal'. Cardiff's industries, and those in its hinterland, also provided a large proportion of the iron rails of the developing railway networks of the world. By the 1880s the port of Cardiff ranked with Liverpool and London in terms of tonnage cleared and dominated the coal export trade of both the British Empire and the world.[4] Cardiff's economic strength lasted up to the First World War and then went into decline.

A handbook of 1919 noted the prime economic functions of Cardiff and linked the fortunes of the borough with its major benefactors and political magnates, the Stuart dynasty, Marquesses of Bute:

> The story of the development of the South Wales Coalfield is interlaced with the history of the magnificent docks at Cardiff, and the various railways, with many mineral lines threading their way up the mining valleys and radiating from the common centre of the Port of Cardiff. All this was made possible by the late Marquess of Bute and the trustees during his minority.[5]

This eulogistic view of the Butes and their purported benevolent influence on the economic development of Cardiff has not gone unchallenged. Martin Daunton has contested the view that these landed-magnates-turned-dock-owners were in fact the

[1] Freeman, T.W., *The Conurbations of Great Britain*, (Manchester, 1959), pp. 205 and 293.

[2] Morgan, P.H., 'Building Use and Social Change in the Inner City: A Case Study of Cardiff, 1850–1950', (Ph. D. thesis, University of Wales, Aberystwyth, 1985), p. 238.

[3] Daunton, M.J., *Coal Metropolis: Cardiff 1870–1914*, (Leicester, 1977), p. 181.

[4] Daunton, *Coal Metropolis*, p. 7; Freeman, *The Conurbations of Great Britain*, p. 292.

[5] Willson Lloyd, D., *Cardiff 1919: A Commercial and Industrial Centre*, (Cardiff, 1919), p. 132.

'makers of modern Cardiff'. Bute ownership of the Bute Ship Canal (later West Dock) was at variance with the pattern of development of docks in the rest of Britain, where ownership was by harbour trusts or public companies. Although Bute stewardship might have given the borough initial advantages over rivals, the long-term development of Cardiff was retarded. Low returns from the docks drained the Bute Estate, and during the minority of the third Marquess much-needed further dock development was held up.[6] The Roath Docks were constructed too late to secure economic advantage to the city and were soon redundant. The Cardiff Railway Company, constructed by 1912, was also an almost immediate failure. In addition, the shipowners, who were an important part of the economic elite, were critical of Bute stewardship. Thus in 1906 a coal owner could say that 'so far from Lord Bute being creator of Cardiff, the docks in the hands of a private individual have greatly retarded the progress of the port'.[7] Corporation ownership too would have benefited the borough and its rate-raising power. According to contemporary critics in the early twentieth century, Bute ownership of the leasehold of vast tracts of land in Cardiff also held back growth. The marquesses therefore stood in the path of the further economic development of the city as an industrial centre. The Butes wanted no economic rivals to their enterprises, or, for that matter, rival sources of employment that might raise wages. Thus shortly before the First World War, the proposed construction of a new Cammel Laird plant, which would have employed 6,000 workers, came to naught.[8] In sum, the nineteenth-century Bute heritage for Cardiff was a poisoned chalice:

> The Bute Docks were the very life of Cardiff, but also in a way its weakness. Cardiff depended upon the continued growth and modernity of its docks for its continued prosperity; the coal trade demanded cheap and efficient docks but was not necessarily concerned if they were at Cardiff; the Bute estate was the sole provider of docks at Cardiff but found it increasingly difficult to supply the docks required by the coal trade and for the continued growth of Cardiff. This was the central weakness of the position of Cardiff before 1914'.[9]

Bute political influence in Cardiff was also potent, but it was on some accounts much reduced by the 1870s, and certainly in steep decline by 1918.[10] In terms of economic development, however, if the Butes held Cardiff back, wider forces had severe consequences for the borough after 1918. It was the loss of global markets for Welsh steam coal, caused both by increased international competition and by

[6]   Daunton, M.J., 'Examines the phenomenal nineteenth-century growth of the harbour facilities in Cardiff', in Williams, S, (ed.), *The Cardiff Book,* Volume 1, (Barry, 1973), p. 113.

[7]   Quoted in Daunton, 'Examines the phenomenal nineteenth-century growth', p. 111–114.

[8]   Davies, J. *Cardiff and the Marquesses of Bute,* (Cardiff , 1981), p. 211.

[9]   Daunton, 'Examines the phenomenal nineteenth-century growth', p. 114.

[10]   Daunton, *Coal Metropolis,* p. 198; Davies, J., 'Aristocratic town-makers and the coal metropolis: the marquesses of Bute and Cardiff, 1776 to 1947', in Cannadine, D., (ed.), *Patricians, Power and Politics in Nineteenth Century Towns,* (Leicester, 1982), pp. 56–58.

the wide-spread adoption of oil-fired marine turbines in the shipping industry, that led to the borough's difficulties in the inter-war years.

The industry tables of the 1931 census provide insight into the borough's socio-economic structure. The service, finance and administrative functions of Cardiff were clearly preponderant in the inter-war years. Over 30 per cent of the labour force were engaged in the commerce and finance and public administration and defence categories. Some manual occupations would be included in this classification, but these figures confirm that Cardiff had a substantial middle class and petite bourgeoisie. Nearly a quarter of the male labour force was located in the transport sector of the local economy. Of these, nearly 8 per cent were in the rail industry, with a similar percentage in water-borne transport, and 4.5 per cent in the docks. Cardiff was ninth in the ranking of the county boroughs in terms of the percentage of the workforce in docks and water transport. As might be expected for this era there was a low representation of female labour in the transport sector. Heavy industry also played a significant role in the local economy, with over 13 per cent of males in the metal and engineering category. 8,500 men and women were in the food, drink and tobacco category, comprised mainly of portside processing industries, accounting for just under 7 per cent of the female workforce. Over 6 per cent of male workers were also employed in the building trades.

The largest single category of employment for women was personal service, with nearly 10,000 employed, over one-third of the total female workforce. This was a good indicator of the strength of the middle class in the municipality in this period. Cardiff was seventeenth in the ranking of the eighty-three county boroughs in terms of female domestic servants as a percentage of the total population, fifteenth in terms of the percentage of its workforce in the professional category, and eighteenth in terms of the percentage in the own account and managerial categories, all indicators confirming the existence of a substantial administrative, professional and trading bourgeoisie, as well as an artisanal and shop-owning small middle class. In addition, the city had a large, heterogeneous working class, with a 'multiplicity of trades'.[11] These manual groups ranged from skilled workers in engineering and the steel industry, to semi-skilled cadres in a wide range of industries, to the predominantly casually employed and unskilled portside workforce.

Overall, Cardiff's social structure was one of approximate equilibrium between the classes. A large manual working class was faced by an equally numerous and established middle class which included a substantial petite bourgeoisie. The even balance of social forces was an important factor in local politics, and perhaps put a limit on the progress the Labour party might have been expected to make in the inter-war years. It would be wrong too to over-estimate the importance of the heavy industries as a base of support for Labour in Cardiff. The borough's port and regional functions outweighed its heavy metallurgical industries.[12] As one commentator has pointed out, 'Cardiff has never been an industrial city in the sense that one industry or a small range of industries has formed the backbone of

[11] Morgan, K.O., *Rebirth of a Nation: Wales 1880–1980*, (Oxford, 1981), p. 277.
[12] Fogarty, M.P., *Prospects of the Industrial Areas of Great Britain*, (London, 1945),   p. 105; and Willson Lloyd, *Cardiff 1919*, pp. 105–106.

its economy'.[13] It was as much an administrative and commercial city as an industrial one, being an important retail and shopping centre for the surrounding region.[14] This produced a borough which had significant numbers of white-collar workers living in the majority of wards in the city, which in turn had important positive implications for the potential strength of Liberalism and Conservatism in the locality.

Cardiff's economic performance between the wars requires some comment as the decline of its key coal trade and the onset of the world depression were to have political repercussions in the municipal arena. Ten and a half million tons of coal and coke were exported in 1914, but by 1921 less than four million tons were exported, recovering to over eight and a half million tons in 1923. The recovery was however temporary, with less than three million tons exported in 1926, rallying later to a level of less than five million tons by 1932, and nearly five and a half million tons by 1937.[15] This decline of the coal trade hit the docks and associated transport industries hard, and precipitated some rationalisation, most notably with the Bute Docks being amalgamated with the Great Western Railway Company (GWR) in 1921.[16] Four railway companies had previously employed Cardiff labour, the Barry, the Cardiff, the Taff Vale and the Rhymney. These had all been merged under the auspices of the GWR by 1922. The GWR had effectively replaced the Butes as the patrons of the city by then, employing over 8,500 people locally. The company contributed £86,200 in rates, 11 per cent of the rateable value of the city, and its directors always had the ear of city hall. One GWR manager became mayor in the late 1920s. When Sir Felix Pole, head of the GWR, addressed the Business Club of the South Wales Institute of Engineers in 1928, it was a lock out. As one commentator has noted, 'the Cardiff bourgeoisie clearly recognised the sound of their master's voice'.[17]

The effect of the drastic decline of the coal trade and economic rationalisation was mass unemployment in Cardiff. With over 17 per cent classified as out of work in the 1931 industry tables, Cardiff was ranked seventeenth of the county boroughs in this league table of social misery. The lack of employment opportunities for women outside of domestic service also meant there was much hidden unemployment. In Cardiff there were 'no more than 22 insured women and girls in 1938 for every 100 males, as against the national proportion of 40'.[18] In terms of help from central government Cardiff received little. In the 1930s the borough was unlucky to be excluded from Special Area Status. Westminster's decision was difficult to justify for it was apparent 'that Cardiff ... formed part of the same economic unit as the neighbouring depressed area, and for the purposes

[13]   Evans, N., 'Cardiff's Labour tradition', *Llafur,* vol. 4, no. 2, (1985), p. 87.

[14]   Fogarty, *Prospects,* p. 105; and Willson Lloyd, *Cardiff 1919,* p. 29.

[15]   Rees, W., *Cardiff: A History of the City,* (Cardiff, 1962), p. 150; *Cardiff Year Books* and *South Wales Transport Commission,* (1948), both quoted in Jones, R.G., 'Butetown Cardiff: Change in a Dockland Community from the early Nineteenth Century to the Present', (MA thesis, University of Keele, 1980), pp. 76–77.

[16]   British Association for the Advancement of Science, *Cardiff 1960,* (Cheltenham and London, 1960), p. 48.

[17]   Evans, 'Cardiff's Labour tradition', pp. 79–80.

[18]   Fogarty, *Prospects,* p. 100.

of economic planning the economic unit should have in any case have been treated as a whole'.[19] In its percentage of unemployed, Cardiff in the 1930s was as hard-hit as Dundee, which in Scotland was seen as a depressed area. Although the borough was prosperous by Welsh standards, Fogarty was correct in emphasising that Cardiff 'experienced unemployment well above the level for Great Britain as a whole'.[20]

Inter-war Cardiff was depressed, then, but there were some off-setting factors. If 'the rise of Cardiff was inseparably linked with the fortunes of the coal trade', it was fortunate that the city's economy had to an extent diversified into other areas by the early twentieth century.[21] Ship repair had been given a enormous boost with Antwerp and Rotterdam being out of commission in the First World War. A 1920 study placed Cardiff as 'the principal ship repairing centre of the world' and probably the first in the ownership of cargo ships in the 'tramp' class.[22] Metallurgical industries closely related to the borough's port functions and the proximity of the coal and iron of the Valleys has also developed. In the mid 1930s, 500,000 tons of pig iron, 600,000 tons of steel and 500,000 tons of rolled products and castings were being produced.[23] There was also patent fuel production, the Portland cement industry, as well as silica and firebrick production, all utilising local raw materials. Large employers outside the docks included the Dowlais Cardiff Steel Works, the iron works of Guest, Keen and Baldwins, and the flour and bread producers Spillers and Bakers. Additionally, in an age of municipal enterprise, with the council running a number of utilities including the tramways and the supply of electricity and water, over 2,100 men and women were council employees in 1919.[24] This municipal enterprise provided substantial relief for the ratepayers of Cardiff.[25] Municipal socialism might have been publicly frowned upon by the Liberal and Tories in charge of the city, but bigger government and the extension of the services of local government was the order of the day. It also brought higher employment levels in both white-collar and manual occupations.

The broader culture of the *locale* before 1914 helps provide the context for the contests in the municipal arena. Both religious affiliation and ethnicity played at least some role in the formation of attitudes to policies and politics generally. Before 1914 religious affiliation in Cardiff was a potent force, although the influence of religion was diminishing in the inter-war period. A study of the history of Nonconformity in Cardiff draws a picture of thriving communities outside of the local Anglican communion, the Church of Wales. In 1900 these included 2,512 Congregationalists, 3,077 Wesleyans, 4,390 Baptists, 2,370 Calvinistic Methodists and 3,011 'other denominations'.[26] There were also 15,000

[19] Fogarty, *Prospects,* p. 454.
[20] Fogarty, *Prospects,* pp. 87 and 101–103.
[21] Freeman, *The Conurbations of Great Britain,* p. 292.
[22] Hallett, H.M., (ed.). *British Association Cardiff Meeting 1920, Handbook to Cardiff and the Neighbourhood,* (Cardiff, 1920), pp. 157–158.
[23] Rees, *Cardiff,* p. 166.
[24] Willson Lloyd, *Cardiff 1919,* p. 69.
[25] Evans, 'Cardiff's Labour tradition', p. 82.
[26] Austin Jenkins, J. and Edwards James, R., *The History Of Nonconformity in Cardiff,* (Cardiff and London, 1901), pp. 217–221.

Catholics, largely of Irish extraction, resident by the end of the nineteenth century.[27] Also of note were the Roman Catholic 'predilections' of the third and forth Marquesses of Bute.[28] Thus the leaders of local Toryism were not the usual bastions of the established Church. On the whole Nonconformity in Cardiff seems to have reinforced Liberalism. From 1885 to 1914 the single member parliamentary seat had been held by a Liberal in most general elections, although usually by a narrow margin, and Tories took the seat in 1895 and again in December 1910. Later commentators, such as the Labour leader and Cardiff MP James Callaghan, also referred to the natural association of 'chapel' with the early Labour movement.

Certainly politics in Cardiff before 1914 were intimately bound up with religious questions. Adamsdown ward was seen as very much a Catholic ward around 1900, and a member of the Irish Catholic League stood as a Trades Council candidate for the council in 1898. The political presence of Catholicism in South and Grangetown wards had also been noted in 1885, and the Catholic vote was influential in a number of elections.[29] In the 1906 elections religious issues were paramount, especially concerning the control of education.[30] Again in the 1913 elections a 'purity crusade' with strong religious overtones promoted Sabbatarianism, temperance and the curbing of prostitution, and took precedence over other social issues.[31] Disputes between the dominant Nonconformists and Catholics in Cardiff also took place between the wars. During the 1924 elections for example, a meeting of the Cardiff Board of Guardians was disturbed by an argument over the prayer used at the opening of the new Infants' Home headquarters.[32] Again temperance, so intimately connected to nonconformity, and to a degree still to Liberalism, was an issue in the 1925 election in Gabalfa ward, with an independent candidate entering the fray over the issue of liquor licensing.[33] Education remained the main bone of contention with religious connotations in local politics, however.

Nationality and race were also aspects of Cardiff society that need to be considered. Cardiff was one of only four Welsh county boroughs at this time (the others being Merthyr, Newport and Swansea), and was to become the capital of Wales in 1955. Yet the 'Welshness' of Cardiff was not strongly articulated, and it had only minor political significance in this period. The speaking of Welsh in Cardiff was 'confined to a small minority' by 1931,[34] and the descendants of many of its inhabitants had been relatively recent migrants from Ireland, England and elsewhere. The Cardiff *Cymmrodorion* Society (a body dedicated to the restoration of Welsh language and culture) sometimes put a questionnaire to municipal candidates on Welsh issues. In Splott ward in 1921 both the Coalition

[27]   Rees, *Cardiff*, p. 154.
[28]   Davies, *Cardiff*, p. 212.
[29]   Pelling, H., *Social Geography of British Elections 1885–1910*, (London, 1967), p. 353.
[30]   Daunton, M.J., 'Aspects of the Social and Economic Structure of Cardiff, 1870–1914', (Ph.D. thesis, University of Kent at Canterbury, 1974), p. 307.
[31]   Daunton, 'Aspects', p. 492.
[32]   *Western Mail*, 3 Nov. 1924.
[33]   *Western Mail*, 3 Nov. 1925.
[34]   Morgan, *Rebirth of a Nation*, p. 244.

Conservative and Labour hopefuls replied that they supported the teaching of Welsh in schools, both also saying they favoured Home Rule for Wales. In the Tory's opinion Welsh language lessons should only be voluntary, though, as should the speaking of Welsh in the council chamber. The Labour candidate thought Welsh lessons should be compulsory, but only after a plebiscite of the people had agreed to it, and only after that might Welsh 'make its presence felt in the council.'[35] Welsh nationalism as an organised political force was virtually non-existent. Only once in parliamentary or municipal elections between the wars did a Plaid Cymru candidate ever appear (the party was only formed in 1925), in Plasnewydd ward in 1935, when Miss C.M. Hughes polled 197 votes, or 5.7 per cent of the poll. Pelling points to pre-1914 political behaviour in Cardiff in general elections as corresponding 'to no distinctly Welsh pattern, or for that matter to any pattern naturally to be associated with a particular class or industry'.[36]

Cardiff was distinctive, though, in having a significant black population at this time. This population was concentrated in Butetown straddling the Adamsdown and South wards. Here as many as 2,000 seamen jumped ship in any one year, many of them non-British. Some of them settled in the area, and their descendants formed the black community in what became known to journalists and authors at least as Tiger Bay. A local journalist wrote of the area that 'Chinks and Dagos and Levantines slippered about the faintly evil ways that ran off Bute Street'.[37] Such racist press comment probably contributed to the race strife in the borough before and after the First World War. In the dock strike of 1911, Chinese laundries and lodging houses were attacked, with rumours that Chinese strike-breakers were to be brought into Cardiff.[38] With rising unemployment in 1918–19, mobs of indigenous whites rioted for several days in June 1919. Property was destroyed and one person was killed.[39] The state responded to this race riot and similar riots around the same time in Liverpool, Newport and elsewhere, with the Aliens Order of 1920, and a Special Restriction (Coloured Alien Seaman) Order in 1925, restricting employment for non-whites. The size of the black population in Cardiff was not large enough to constitute a significant political force in electoral terms, but it was large enough to have an effect on the culture, black and white, of the *locale*. The events of 1919 can be seen as indicators of worsening economic conditions for the local working class, but on a broader canvas they illustrated racist attitudes to black people which were reflected in wider political beliefs. Trade Unions and some Labour party branches were as discriminatory on the grounds of race as any other sector of society. In Splott ward for example, in the 1923 elections, the Cardiff Labour party passed a motion 'condemning the

[35] *Western Mail*, 26 Oct. 1921.
[36] Pelling, *Social Geography*, p. 353.
[37] Quoted in Morgan, 'Building Use', p. 264.
[38] Leng, P.J., *The Welsh Dockers*, (Ormskirk, 1981), p. 59.
[39] On the 1919 riots see Evans, N., 'The South Wales race riots of 1919', *Llafur*, vol. 3, no. 1, (1980), pp. 5–29; 'Regulating the reserve army: Arabs, blacks and the local state in Cardiff, 1919–1945', *Immigrants and Minorities*, vol. 4, no. 2, (1985), pp. 68–115; on the black community in Cardiff, see also Tabili, L., *'We Ask For British Justice': Workers and Racial Difference in Late Imperial Britain*, (Ithaca and London, 1994), pp. 135–160.

employment of "coolies and Arabs" at miserable wages while white British sailors were idle and starving'.[40]

Turning now to the politics of the borough, in terms of Westminster elections Cardiff had three constituencies from 1918, Central, East and South. All three constituencies were won by Labour in its high tide of success in 1929, but this was hardly representative of the inter-war pattern. South was won by Labour on only one other occasion in 1923, by the son of the national Labour figure Arthur Henderson, but otherwise was Tory-held. Before 1929 the Central division had been solidly Tory, and from 1931 a Labour deserter in the National Coalition held the seat. The East division returned Liberals and Conservative alternately between 1918 and 1924, and after Labour's win in 1929 the Conservatives took it. Overall the inter-war parliamentary record suggests that the borough was far from a Labour stronghold, and Liberalism and Toryism in the 1920s, and Toryism alone in the 1930s, were the dominant political forces.

The municipal elections tend to confirm this assessment. Cardiff became a county borough in 1888 and a city in 1905.[41] In 1919 it was comprised of ten wards each returning three councillors, with ten aldermen making up the total of forty members on the council. A boundary extension in 1922 brought within the county borough the ecclesiastical city of Llandaff as well as substantial outlying districts for further housing development.[42] These additional territories were parts of Michealston, St Fagan's, Whitchurch, Llanishen and Lanedern.[43] A further four wards were created, Llandaff, Gabalfa, Penylan and Plasnewydd, but Penylan and Plasnewydd were created partly from the abolition of Park ward, giving a total of thirteen wards and fifty-two members of the council. In 1936 a new ward, Ely, was carved out of Llandaff ward because of the construction of the huge new council estate from which the ward received its name. The council then consisted of fourteen wards, and fifty-six members.

As far as the socio-spatial distribution of political support in the borough was concerned, the situation of the borough on the Bristol Channel was an important influence. With the docks and industrial developments being sited mainly along the Channel and at the mouth of the river Taff, working-class housing was mostly clustered near here. Further out to the north and west, middle-class suburban housing predominated, a 'band of clerkdom' in one description, 'the leafy suburbs of north Cardiff' in another.[44] Extensive council-house development in Ely rather altered the picture on the western edge of the borough in the 1930s, however, as will be seen below. Llandaff, Gabalfa, Penylan, Roath and Plasnewydd formed an outer ring of wards which were mostly anti-Labour. To these could be added on the predominantly anti-Labour side Central and Riverside wards in the city centre, set some way back from the dockside, where substantial numbers of business voters and some superior housing, especially in Riverside, outweighed pockets of working-class housing. South ward was socially mixed, although predominantly

[40]   Evans, 'Cardiff's Labour tradition', p. 86.
[41]   Wheatley, J.L., 'Cardiff and its municipal government', in Hallett, *British Association 1920*, p. 64.
[42]   British Association for the Advancement of Science, *Cardiff 1960*, p. 6.
[43]   Rees, *Cardiff*, p. 152.
[44]   Evans, 'Cardiff's Labour tradition', p. 80; Morgan, *Rebirth of a Nation*, p. 291.

working-class. It had some middle-class streets in the south-west corner of the borough adjoining the river Ely and the affluent suburbs of Penarth beyond the borough boundary, but it was also referred to as the 'Docks district'[45]. Labour won here on five occasions between the wars, but it was called a 'Conservative ward' in 1932.[46] There was a noted volatility to the political feeling of this ward, and frequent Communist and NUWM interventions in elections, suggesting that the dockers were not as steadfast in their support for Labour as some other working-class occupational groups, as will be discussed further below.[47] The persons per room figures from the 1931 census showed some correspondence to the political complexion of these wards, although they were by no means a perfect fit. Penylan, Plasnewydd, Riverside and Roath had the lowest room-occupancy figures in the borough in the 0.67–0.76 range, well below the Cardiff average of 0.86, but South was high at 1.01, demonstrating again its distinctive political character. Gabalfa and Llandaff were both slightly above the average at 0.90–0.91, reflecting the development of council housing estates there.

Labour support was concentrated in a handful of wards. The dockside wards of Adamsdown and Splott were Labour's strongest. These two wards were populated by dockers, seafarers and other portside manual workers, but there were also considerable numbers of steelworkers and other skilled workers here, with the Dowlais steelworks straddling the two wards. Adamsdown in the late nineteenth century had been home to Irish migrants,[48] as well as the black population mentioned above, while Splott was described in 1932 as 'for years a Socialist stronghold'.[49] Slum clearance and the small Splott housing scheme planned in 1925 did little to change its Labour loyalty. Across the river Taff was the slightly more mixed working-class ward of Grangetown, containing significant numbers of railway employees and factory workers. Labour was also fairly strong here, winning twelve of the twenty inter-war contests. Adjoining the city centre to the west and north were the more marginal Canton and Cathays wards, both of which contained significant pockets of working-class housing. Cathays was apparently 'dominated' by railwaymen,[50] but it also included the municipal buildings, including City Hall, the Law Courts and the University. Ernie Gough, a GWR inspector and future Lord Mayor, held this ward for Labour in the 1920s, while W.R. Williams, the GWR manager in Cardiff, held one of the other Cathays seats for the Liberals.[51] The high persons per room figures for Adamsdown, Grangetown

[45] *Western Mail*, 26 Oct. 1921.

[46] *Western Mail*, 1 Nov. 1932.

[47] On the distinctiveness or otherwise of the politics of dock workers, see Adams, T., Labour and the First World War: economy, politics and the erosion of local peculiarity', *Journal of Regional and Local Studies*, (1990), pp. 33-40; Davies, S., *Liverpool Labour: Social and Political Influences on the Development of the Labour Party in Liverpool, 1900–1939*, (Keele, 1996), pp. 197–231; on divisions in the Cardiff dock labour force that worked against a strong Labour stance in politics, see Daunton, *Coal Metropolis*, pp. 184–185.

[48] Daunton, 'Aspects', p. 427.

[49] *Western Mail & South Wales News*, 1 Nov. 1932.

[50] Evans, 'Cardiff's Labour tradition', p. 82.

[51] Evans, 'Cardiff's Labour tradition', p. 82.

and Splott, in the narrow range of 0.98 to 1.01, did reflect the working-class nature of these wards, while Canton and Cathays were more in the middling range suggesting their mixed social character.

It has been claimed that Cardiff 'had never been as hopeful territory for Labour as had been the more homogeneous and sociologically closer-knit' valley towns of South Wales.[52] The pattern of support outlined here plainly confirms this, showing that Labour was the minority political force, which in a good year might hope to win six of the thirteen wards, but normally could only be confident of winning three or four. The development of a small council-housing estate in Gabalfa had no political impact on this picture, but the much larger Ely estate in Llandaff was significant. Llandaff's electorate grew from 5,000 to 15,500 in little more than a decade, and by the late 1920s Labour was winning the ward in good years. The ward was split in two in 1936, the Ely portion becoming a new Labour stronghold, the remaining parts of Llandaff reverting to its earlier anti-Labour complexion. Overall though this change if anything reduced Labour's position, one Labour and one anti-Labour ward replacing what had become a predominantly Labour seat by the mid 1930s.

Conservative–Liberal pacts against Labour in municipal politics were an important factor in reinforcing Labour's electoral weakness, but the development of these pacts was not entirely straightforward. Independents and Ratepayers also stood for election at times, and it was not until 1928–29 that a formal Anti-Socialist alliance was formed. A harbinger of co-operation occurred much earlier in 1903. Under the slogans of 'economy with efficiency' Tories and Liberals came together in the council, supporting a 'sound and wholesome policy of retrenchment while at the same time not interfering with the efficiency of local government'.[53] In 1920 and 1921 local Conservatives and Liberals also stood together as Coalition candidates while the wartime Coalition government effected by Lloyd George survived at Westminster. Liberals and Tories adopted a supposedly apolitical stance, with a coalition candidate in Cathays ward in 1921 claiming that 'although he was the nominee of the Liberal and Conservative parties, he regarded himself as an independent candidate. Politics in a municipal matter would be an absurdity'.[54] Co-operation was not perfect, however. In 1921 the virulently anti-Labour *Western Mail* noted:

> The leaders of the Liberal and Conservative parties are working in thorough and cordial harmony in all the wards to which reference has been made, but there are evidences, particularly in the Canton ward, that this co-operation of the two parties is not understood by the rank and file. No effort should be spared, in the last hours of preparation for the poll, to inform all adherents of the Liberal and Conservative parties that Mr C.F. Sanders is the joint party

[52] Morgan, *Rebirth of a Nation*, p. 277, p. 291.
[53] Quoted in Daunton, *Coal Metropolis*, p. 175.
[54] *Western Mail*, 26 Oct. 1921.

candidate, and that, in the interests of good government, every ratepayer should give him support in the polling booth.[55]

In Park ward also, an Independent Conservative broke with the coalition and stood against the sitting Liberal. The *Western Mail* reiterated,

> If the adherents of the old political associations will but pull together and vote solidly to-morrow the risk of further thoughtless squandering of rates will be averted. If they do not do so there will be a rude awakening when it is too late, and the government of our municipalities has passed to people who have little aptitude or ability for the task.[56]

Between 1922 and 1928 informal anti-Labour pacts held sway in most wards, although there were occasional breakdowns in co-operation. Their significance in reducing Labour chances of winning more marginal wards can be demonstrated by one such breakdown in Cathays ward in 1926. A three-way contest there led to Labour, with 44.6 of the poll, unseating a Liberal. Under the headline of 'Cardiff blunder leads to a gain for the Socialists', the *Western Mail* complained,

> Cardiff provided another object lesson in the folly of the older parties, who are anti-socialists, failing to realise that the prime consideration in the municipal elections was the defeat of the socialist candidates ... The Conservative members of the city council were unanimous in their advice to their party in Cathays to fall in with the wise policy of an anti-Socialist combination, but a Cathays group that put party politics in municipal affairs before the general interest of the rate-payers declined that advice with the result that a present of the seat has been made to the Socialists.[57]

By 1928, with Labour having made nine gains over the previous two years, the need for a more formal pact was highlighted:

> No time should now be lost in organising the city systematically against the menace of Socialist domination. This can only be done successfully by an earnest pact between the anti-Socialist groups and a determination to vote on a non-political party ticket.[58]

The formal pact that came into operation at the 1929 elections was more solid, encompassing Liberals, Tories, Ratepayers and Independents. It was broken only occasionally, mainly when Independents and Ratepayers both stood ensuring three-way contests.

The anti-Labour forces in Cardiff attacked Labour over its supposed 'extremism', and over its imagined profligacy with the rates if it ever got into power. One of the most favoured taunts was to accuse Labour candidates of being Communists, or that they were in the grip of alien powers and 'extremists'. The

---

[55] *Western Mail*, 31 Oct. 1921.
[56] *Western Mail*, 31 Oct. 1921.
[57] *Western Mail*, 2 Nov. 1926.
[58] *Western Mail & South Wales News*, 2 Nov. 1928.

Labour party in inter-war Cardiff did have genuine problems of factionalism and infiltration from the left, especially the Communists, which were much exaggerated in election campaigns and in the pages of the *Western Mail*. Thus in Grangetown ward in 1921 the Coalition candidate asked,

> I am still waiting for my opponent's reply to my question: 'Is he a Communist. If not, does he spend a great deal of his time in reading Communist literature?' ... Do the electors of this ward want to be represented by a member of a party who are preaching revolution, and who are doing all they can to incite riots and disorder?[59]

In the same year the Coalition candidate in Cathays ward claimed that modern youth were having their minds 'poisoned' by the Communists. In an address to the women electors of Cathays entitled 'Protect your Homes', he quoted a Communist school text-book that George Orwell was to comment upon a generation later in a 1940 *Horizon* article.[60] Orwell remembered a Communist tract circulating around 1920–21, the wording of which was practically identical to that quoted with disapproval in Cathays ward:

> No boy Socialist can become a boy scout because he has to salute
> the Union Jack, and that is an emblem of oppression and slavery.
> Thou shalt not be a patriot, because a patriot is an international
> blackleg.
> Is it true that God has ever been revealed? Since there is no God,
> he could not reveal himself.

The purveyors of this tract, it was claimed, 'sought to provoke sedition, treason and revolution'.[61] How much this sort of scare-mongering worked is questionable, but the Coalition candidate in this case won by over 2,000 votes in a ward where Labour performed moderately well in the 1920s as a whole.

Counterposed to the extremism and profligacy of Labour, the anti-Labour forces promised that if they were entrusted with the stewardship of Cardiff, the outcome would be felicitous for the electorate. Only they would ensure the rates were kept down, and give 'value for money' to the hardpressed ratepayers. They made a virtue of the fact that many of them were businessmen, with 'business' values. As has been suggested elsewhere, 'tradesmen were well known locally and competition with a shopkeeper was not always something Labour could overcome'.[62] Thus the Coalition victor in Grangetown in 1921 said that Labour would hit the majority of electors, 'and especially the small tradesmen', who will 'find burdens placed upon them, in the shape of the rates, more than they will be able to bear'.[63] This kind of appeal had hardly changed over a decade later. In Plasnewydd ward before the 1932 elections, the Independent candidate emphasised

---

[59] *Western Mail*, 1 Nov. 1921.
[60] Orwell, G., 'Boys weeklies', in *The Penguin Essays of George Orwell*, (Harmondsworth, 1984), p. 105.
[61] *Western Mail*, 27 Oct. 1921.
[62] Evans, 'Cardiff's Labour tradition', p. 82.
[63] *Western Mail*, 26 Oct. 1921.

that 'for years he had been strongly favouring economy'; in future he could promise 'value for money' as well as providing 'better opportunities to examine estimates and scrutinise expenditure'.[64] Again in 1929 it was claimed:

> The progress of Mr. Frederick Jones, the wellknown docksman in the South Ward augers well for the movement to secure more business brains in local government. In addition to being a large employer of labour, Mr. Jones has a practical knowledge of engineering matters. The corporation owns over a million pounds worth of engines, boilers and machinery, and can well benefit from the services of men of practical knowledge and experience. The Socialist candidate in the South Ward has neither business nor municipal administrative experience, but he has contested several elections unsuccessfully.[65]

Turning to the development of the Labour party in Cardiff now, it needs to be reiterated that, in the words of Duncan Tanner, 'Labour politics in the coastal seats of south and north Wales were in some ways very different from Labour politics in the coalfields.[66] Nowhere was this more true than in Cardiff, which was a world away from the 'Little Moscows' of the South Wales valleys which have tended to be the focus of much Welsh labour history. Little has been written specifically on the Cardiff Labour party between the world wars, although at least one new major study of Labour in Wales will help to fill the gap.[67] As for pre-1914 development, Lib-Lab councillors were elected in Cardiff's municipal elections in the 1890s, at the same time as in other similar urban authorities. In the early 1890s the Fabians were established in the Cardiff area and by 1897 the Social Democratic Federation had seventy members. The Cardiff ILP by 1905 could claim substantial numbers. However they had only ninety on the books, many of whom had not paid their subscriptions.[68] The Trades Council, formed after the 'new unionist' strikes of 1889–90, had 4,000 members by 1902, with a wide range of affiliated unions reflecting the 'extraordinary diversity of trades' in Cardiff.[69] The Trades Council had close links with the Liberal party before 1914, however, such support for Liberalism preventing J. H. Thomas, the railwayman's organiser, winning Splott ward in 1908.[70] By 1912, there were thus no working-class councillors in Cardiff.

Cardiff had, nevertheless, been a focal point of the waterfront strife of the 'new unionism' period. It was also the locus of the Taff Vale strike and the notorious judgement against trade unionism in 1901 that did so much to encourage unions to affiliate to Labour. Yet, as Daunton says, 'the labour movement in Cardiff was slower than in other areas in south Wales, and slower than many other urban areas

---

[64] *Western Mail*, 1 Nov. 1932.

[65] *Western Mail & South Wales News*, 28 Oct. 1929.

[66] Tanner, D.M., 'The pattern of Labour politics', in Tanner, D.M., Williams, C.M. and Hopkin, D.R., (eds), *The Labour Party in Wales*, (Cardiff, 2000), ch. 5.

[67] Tanner, Williams and Hopkin, *The Labour Party in Wales*.

[68] Hopkin, D., 'The rise of Labour in Wales 1890–1914', *Llafur*, vol. 6, no. 3, (1994), pp. 120–141.

[69] Morgan, *Rebirth of a Nation*, p. 75.

[70] Evans, 'Cardiff's Labour tradition', p. 79.

of the same size, in making a successful move from Lib-Labism to an independent political stance'.[71] He stresses the importance of the local occupational structure in this. Important sectors were imbued with a moderate stance. In terms of the local labour market and industrial relations, the opportunity for a strong Labour movement and Party in the borough was undermined:

> The main characteristics of the working class in Cardiff were fragmentation and a heterogeneous experience of industrial relations. No single occupation was able to give a lead. Further, in the sectors characterised by bad labour relations and militancy, fragmentation of the workforce made continued organisation extremely difficult, so that after a brief spell of activity the movement collapsed into quiescence with no basis for political action. On the other hand, those who had a favourable position in the labour market and could maintain continuity of organisation, secured recognition and had little incentive to renounce moderation. The occupational structure of Cardiff was loosely articulated, so that events on one sector set up only limited repercussions in other groups.[72]

Of particular note were the pre-1914 union divisions on the waterfront. The docks were substantial employers of male labour and a potential source of support for an independent Labour party by way of the Dockers union. Two of the main sectors of the workforce were the coal trimmers and the coal tippers, elite groups with specialised skills and enhanced bargaining power. Unfortunately for the nascent Labour movement, the Dockers union lost control of the trimmers and the tippers. The trimmers formed their own union, the Cardiff Coal Trimmers Union in 1888, while the tippers became part of the Amalgamated Society of Railway Servants (ASRS). Even worse for the development of an independent Labour politics, the trimmers for sectional reasons emphasised 'moderation and respectability' in Daunton's words. Before 1914 they refused to give any assistance to the Dockers Union or to join the Transport Workers Federation. When the Transport and General Workers Union was formed in January 1922, the trimmers voted against amalgamation with the other unions, even though their own Executive Committee favoured such a move.[73] In terms of Cardiff's labour relations, these moderate union leaders opened themselves to the charge of collaboration.[74] Daunton also points to disunity in the ASRS, 'split by companies, by grades, and geographically along the line'. The Dockers Union therefore did not command either the waterfront or the coal trade.[75] J.H. Thomas of the ASRS, and Ernest Bevin of the Dockers union, both prominent in the Cardiff area, had had no success in calls for a Labour representation separate from local Liberalism before the First World War. Instead the Coal trimmers and their leader Samuel Fisher controlled the Trades Council. From such leadership a policy of moderation prevailed. Indeed

[71] Daunton, *Coal Metropolis*, p. 178.
[72] Daunton, *Coal Metropolis*, p. 181.
[73] Leng, *Welsh Dockers*, p. 93.
[74] Daunton, M., 'The Cardiff Coal Trimmers Union', *Llafur*, vol. 2, no. 3, (1978), p. 21.
[75] Daunton, *Coal Metropolis*, pp. 184–187.

Fisher was a leading Liberal, while the five Lib-Lab councillors before 1914 were also from moderate labour cadres.[76] Although the Cardiff Coal Trimmers only had a membership of 1,899 in 1918, their influence was pervasive and indicative of a moderation in sections of the wider Cardiff labour movement.[77]

As has already been made clear, the balance of the classes was unfavourable to Labour in what was an administrative and service centre as well as an industrial city, and Cardiff was not a borough with a predominant manual working class in one major industry like steel, coal, or in a small group of industries. The major unions favoured Liberalism locally before 1914 and largely remained a moderating influence on Labour in Cardiff after 1918. The moderate unions found at least rhetorical backing from the Liberal Party, but given the domination of what Daunton argues was 'Old Liberalism' in borough politics, Lib-Labism gained little by way of social reform.[78] The 'New Liberalism' advocating social reform had been far less influential in the Liberal party or the council chamber. With its emphasis on temperance, Sabbatarianism, Nonconformity and above all the Gladstonian shibboleth of sound finance, 'Old Liberalism' gave little of substance to its working-class supporters. Yet the leaders of the manual working class were not predisposed to rebel against the Liberal leadership before 1914. Only after 1918 did the 'resentment' of the union leaders build up 'until a fracture occurred'.[79] The consequences of the failures of Lib-Labism in Cardiff's politics were to contribute to Labour's breakthrough in 1919. Despite big gains for Labour in the 1919 elections, though, the auguries for the party were still less than auspicious in Cardiff. As Neil Evans has pointed out, pre-1914 radical and anti-landlord Liberalism had accommodated itself to Bute influence, while the middle class had moved closer to Toryism. The merger of the Trades Council and the Labour party in 1914 provided a stronger organisational base for Labour, but a weak political tradition meant that inter-war Cardiff provided some of the least promising ground for Labour.[80]

Labour's electoral performance was not helped either by the existence of an unremittingly antagonistic local press, in particular the *Western Mail*. Most newspaper proprietors were not the friends of the Labour party in the inter-war years, but occasionally local newspapers strove for at least a degree of even-handedness in their reporting of the local elections. This was certainly not the case with the *Western Mail*. Fairness and balance in the reporting of politics were entirely absent from this newspaper. The tenor of the political comment delivered in the columns of the *Mail* was hysterically anti-Labour. Throughout the inter-war period it was in favour of municipal electoral pacts between anti-Labour candidates. In the general elections however, the *Mail* revealed its true colours as invariably Tory. Thus in the 1922 parliamentary elections, the *Mail* turned on the Liberals who were 'not to be trusted', and had 'compromised with the Socialists'.[81] Unfortunately for those interested in the analysis of local politics, the *Mail's*

[76] Daunton, *Coal Metropolis*, pp. 189–195.
[77] Leng, *Welsh Dockers*, p. 82.
[78] Daunton, *Coal Metropolis*, pp. 174–175.
[79] Daunton, *Coal Metropolis*, pp. 206.
[80] Evans, 'Cardiff's Labour tradition', pp. 87–88.
[81] *Western Mail*, 2 Nov. 1922.

reporting of the municipal elections after the early 1920s was also as scant as it was politically slanted. Headlines such as 'Extremists' Effort to Gain Ascendance', 'The Issue at the Elections: The Danger of Labour Domination: Need for Businessmen at Cardiff', 'A Warning to the Electors: Labour's Arrogance in South Wales', 'A Typical Extreme Outrage: Dirty Dodge on the Eve of the Poll', 'Despicable Labour Lie at Cardiff', and 'The Menace of Labour', and a sneering piece entitled 'The Eloquence of a Socialist', all show the blatant anti-Labour stance of the *Western Mail*.[82]

Other local forces also worked against Labour in Cardiff. The Middle Classes Union (MCU) was an anti-Labour pressure group that had an impact on the November elections in the early 1920s. The MCU was an organisation attempting to mobilise and organise the middle class in these years. Invariably it posed as the defender of the ratepayers' interest in terms of keeping the rates low, the elimination of 'waste', and the promotion of 'efficiency' and 'value for money' in local government. It also condemned trade unions and strikes. There had been a similar body, the Citizen's Association, in Cardiff in the immediate pre-1914 elections. In the 1920 elections, an MCU speaker urged the middle class to stand up and fight 'extremists'. In particular the enemy was the Labour party, strikers and that 'striker's charter', the Trades Disputes Act of 1906:

> The Labour party was preaching a class warfare at the call of the extreme section, and the business of the country had to be carried on under the heavy cloud of perpetual strikes, which brought losses upon the middle classes, for which they had no compensation whatsoever ... There was little hope of redress until all strikes were declared by statute to be illegal ... the Trades Disputes Act, which was of no real benefit to the workers themselves, had been called the "Magna Charta of Syndicalism and Anarchy".[83]

Again in 1921, just before the election, a circular went out from the MCU, listing their approved candidates, five Coalitionists and a Liberal. A pre-election MCU meeting also announced that the Cardiff branch membership was up to 1,412, an increase of 762 on the previous year.[84]

A brief survey of the pattern of electoral results over the inter-war period is of value at this point. Labour performed well in 1919, making four gains, bringing its total membership up to five out of the total of forty. This represented a breakthrough for Labour in Cardiff, marking the break with Lib-Labism noted above, but Labour was still well behind the seventeen Tories and fifteen Liberals in the council chamber. Labour's success was achieved on a turnout of 42.6 per cent across the municipality, the lowest level in the whole twenty-year period between the wars. Turnout increased markedly to 55 per cent in 1920, and remained relatively high for the rest of the decade, usually exceeding 50 per cent. From 1920 to 1925 Labour's share of the vote remained low, fluctuating between

---

[82] *Western Mail*, 2 Nov. 1920; 29 Oct. 1921; 31 Oct. 1921; 1 Nov. 1921; 28 Oct. 1929.
[83] *Western Mail*, 2 Nov. 1920.
[84] *Western Mail*, 26 and 29 Oct. 1921.

26.6 per cent and 34.8 per cent, and its representation on the council had only increased by one by 1925. The four elections from 1926 to 1929 were years of big Labour gains in most boroughs across the country, and Labour in Cardiff shared in the party's good fortune. The party's share of the vote increased sharply in 1926 to 50.2 per cent, reflecting perhaps the radicalising effect of the 1926 General Strike and the bitter lockout of the miners in the nearby valleys. Labour's vote share remained in the mid to high 40s range in the following three years, and as a consequence the party made eleven net gains between 1926 and 1929. With nineteen of the fifty-two seats on the council by 1929, and two Labour aldermen to be added soon after, Labour seemed within reach of power.

As in every other borough, the elections of 1930–31 were disastrous for Labour, primarily due to the failures of the second Labour government and its collapse in 1931. Labour lost four seats both in 1930 and 1931, and its share of the vote fell to 41.3 per cent in 1930 and 32.7 per cent in 1931. Especially noteworthy in 1930 was Labour's loss in Grangetown, where the party had not been defeated since 1921. Here the defending councillor, who was also the MP for Breconshire and Radnorshire, was beaten by over 500 votes. Labour also did not receive the benefit of a moratorium on local elections, introduced in some other local authorities for reasons of economy in the early 1930s. All seats were contested in 1930, and Labour was given one walk-over in 1931, so there was no cushioning of the blow of its slump in popularity.

However, as elsewhere Labour in Cardiff recovered rapidly in 1932, its share of the vote jumping back up to 48.2 per cent, although it made no net gains on the very good results of three years before. Yet its performance for the rest of the 1930s was disappointing. One writer has argued that 'the tide had definitely ebbed and Labour was now on the defensive'.[85] Labour's share of the vote fell back to 40.2 per cent in 1933, and stayed in the low 40s for the rest of the decade. Labour made moderate gains in each year between 1933 and 1936, but in the first two years it was only partially recovering the big losses of 1930–31. Labour had twenty representatives on the council in 1936, its highest number between the wars. It must be remembered, however, that three councillors and an alderman had been added to the council by the creation of Ely ward, so proportionally Labour's representation was no better than it had been in 1929. After 1936 Labour fell away, with one loss in each of the 1937 and 1938 rounds of elections, as well as by-election losses, leaving the party with only fifteen representatives out of the total of fifty-six in the council chamber. It seems possible that internal divisions within the party that emerged after the 1936 contests had an adverse effect on Labour's electoral performance. On the other hand it should be pointed out that Labour did badly in most other boroughs in the late 1930s, so Cardiff was perhaps simply reflecting a national trend. Whether the causes were local or national, Labour ended the inter-war years in low spirits, very far from gaining power in Cardiff.

The internal divisions in Labour of the late 1930s had been manifested earlier as well, and their possible impact needs to be considered. Disagreements between the Independent Labour Party (ILP) and the rest of the party were mooted in the

---

[85] Evans, 'Cardiff's Labour tradition', p. 82–83.

early 1920s. The *Western Mail*, with typical hyperbole, amplified these differences for its own purposes, claiming

> The ILP was the same as the Communist Party and the Syndicalist Party. They were absolutely incompetent to govern, not only the affairs of the city, but of a rural parish.[86]

The 'factionalism' of the 1920s, where 'extremists' and 'moderates' vied for influence, was not merely a figment of the *Western Mail's* fevered imagination, however. In 1921 there was a damaging split in Adamsdown ward that was linked not only to politics but also to religious differences. The ward Labour party decided to stand a candidate against the incumbent Coalition member and Lord Mayor-elect, Harold Turnbull. Turnbull was popular due to his efforts in promoting unemployed relief work in the ward, and a faction of the ward Labour party thought he should be given a walk-over. Three representatives of the ward on the Executive of the South divisional party had resigned in protest, all of them Catholics, one of whom alleged the incident was 'causing a break-up of the Adamsdown Labour party'. It was reported that 'Catholics ... who were formerly allied to the Labour cause are so disgusted at the ungracious treatment thus meted out to the Lord Mayor-elect that he is sure of their whole-hearted support.'[87] Labour lost the election on an unusually high turnout, gaining only 38.9 per cent of the votes cast, by far its worst performance between the wars in this ward, suggesting that Labour voters did desert to the opposition in significant numbers. The schism was healed subsequently, and Labour never lost the ward again.

A further indication of disquiet in Labour's ranks emerged in 1930, when four of Labour's leaders on the council lost their seats. The remaining Labour councillors appeared not unduly upset, as they were apparently 'tired of their self-appointed leaders'. It was reported that

> the four old Socialist members who were defeated were the four who arrogated to themselves the position of leaders of the Labour group on the city council, and it is no secret that the defeat of Messrs. Robson, Williams, Phillips and Freeman will be welcomed in no quarter more heartily – albeit mutely – than in the ranks of the remaining sixteen Socialist members of the council.[88]

Labour was also opposed at times by rivals on the left. After it had disaffiliated from the Labour party nationally in 1932, the ILP opposed Labour in Roath in 1933. From the late 1920s Communists also stood against Labour in working-class wards, in the spirit of the Comintern formula of social fascism, which saw Labour as the ally of the class enemy and 'the moderate wing of Fascism'.[89] Later in the 1930s however, links between some sections of Labour and the Communist party undoubtedly existed. The Trades and Labour Council was a centre of influence and social life for activists and the local Labour movement generally, and it provided

---

[86] *Western Mail*, 26 Oct. 1921.
[87] *Western Mail*, 26 and 29 Oct. 1921.
[88] *Western Mail and South Wales News*, 3 Nov. 1930.
[89] Stalin, J.V., quoted in Smith, D., *Left and Right in Twentieth Century Europe*, (London, 1973), p. 103.

contacts between members of different factions of the left. These links increased in the 1930s in the era of the Popular Front, although it should be noted that the Communist party was weak in Cardiff.[90] By the later 1930s the Communist party and Socialist League had permeated Labour at constituency level in Cardiff, and the Communists, much stronger of course in the Valleys, were attempting to capture the Welsh Labour party machine.[91] Internal conflict in Cardiff arose out of this, with difficulties within the Trades and Labour Council, and conflict in the ward party of Ely in 1937, and more seriously in Splott in 1938.[92] The Labour councillor due up for re-election in Ely in 1937 was Thomas Llewellyn, an unemployed man, later convicted of corruption. Llewellyn supported the Popular Front and this had brought him close to the Communist Party. One of his fellow Labour councillors in the ward, Tom Muston, felt that Llewellyn's policies were 'more Communistic than Socialistic',[93] and refused to back Llewellyn's re-election in 1937. For this the Trades and Labour Council withdrew the whip from Muston, who in turn received no support from the NEC.

This was the forerunner to the larger dispute the following year in Splott. In 1938 there were two by-elections in quick succession in this ward, early in the year, and the Trades and Labour Council imposed its own candidates. This was much to the disgust of the ward party, which ran its own candidate in the second by-election in opposition to the 'official' Labour nominee. The resulting split vote led to one of the safest Labour wards in Cardiff falling to the anti-Socialists. The Trades Council expelled the Splott officials for the debacle, who in turn, like Muston before them, appealed to the NEC. There was a huge furore over a number of irregularities within the Cardiff Labour ranks and the South Wales Labour Council investigated the affair. Financial irregularities in the administration of the Trades Council headquarters in Charles Street were uncovered. One of the main sources of trouble was a consequence of the Trades Disputes Act of 1927. Some of the Trades Council delegates were affiliated for industrial purposes only and therefore had no right to vote on political matters. The NEC and South Wales Regional Council of Labour therefore 'set out to dismember the Trades and Labour Council to produce the clear distinction between industrial policy and political action which was so dear to Labour orthodoxy'.[94] As a result of this the Cardiff Labour party had a major overhaul, being reformed in July 1939.[95] The inquiry found in favour of the Splott ward members, and the conflict meant the end of the Trades Council, and broke the close association of trade unions, Co-operative movement and Labour party in the city.

Overall the Cardiff Labour party was a moderate and cautious one. Indeed, one commentator has portrayed the inter-war Labour party in Cardiff as lacking in 'political adventurousness', this being 'combined with a deep sense of loyalty to the established movement.'[96] This was befitting a party whose roots were shallow

[90] Evans, 'Cardiff's Labour tradition', p. 84–87.
[91] Tanner, 'The pattern of Labour politics'.
[92] Evans, 'Cardiff's Labour tradition', p. 84–85.
[93] Quoted in Evans, 'Cardiff's Labour tradition', p. 84.
[94] Evans, 'Cardiff's Labour tradition', p. 84.
[95] Tanner, 'The pattern of Labour politics'.
[96] Evans, 'Cardiff's Labour tradition', pp. 86.

and which had rather a narrow social base of support. The city had a Labour tradition, not a socialist one, and had been 'a stronghold of Labourism'. The national desire to break the Cardiff organisation was because there had been a move to the left in the organisation of the Cardiff party in the 1930s. Younger members were involved with the Popular Front, and some of these same people had affinity with the Communist Party.[97] These connections were not at all unusual in the era. The sum total of these difficulties however, inevitably cast the Cardiff Labour party in a bad light, and the troubles within the party added to Labour's difficulties in the elections of the late 1930s.

Labour's appeal in Cardiff lay in its claim to address the ills afflicting the manual working classes. This was a genuine and oft-stated position. More practically Labour's proposed policies were couched in terms of municipal expansion. This involved the extension of council housing, probably the policy area where Labour influence was most apparent, public works for unemployment relief, and direct labour departments, mainly for the construction of council house estates, 'to prevent rings of contractors in league with councillors'.[98] Rarely was the detail of Labour policy given an airing in the local press. In 1932 the Labour candidate in South ward was reported as arguing that

> people ought to send back councillors who would understand their needs, not men who were going to cut down local rates. The real way to cut rates was to insist on taxation of land values, by which rates could be taken off houses altogether.[99]

Overall the policies of Cardiff Labour party were no more extreme than in most of the county boroughs examined in this volume. None of these policies justified the *Western Mail* assaults on 'extremism'.

In conclusion, the first point to stress is that the combined forces of the inter-war Conservative and Liberal parties in Cardiff maintained their strength in the face of the Labour challenge for most of the twenty-year period. Wary of the Labour advance in 1919, the two parties co-operated at the polls throughout the first decade after the First World War, and after 1928 formed an anti-Labour pact which held firm throughout the remaining inter-war years. Both parties claimed to oppose 'spendthrift' Labour schemes for municipal expansion, and few ideological differences existed between the two parties at the municipal level. By contrast, Labour did not achieve a position where power appeared a distinct possibility. The social basis for Labour support was lacking in a city with a large middle class, and a heterogeneous working class. The trade unions before 1914 were far from united, and the Labour movement came late to a commitment to independent Labour representation, and the break with Lib–Labism. The local press did not help Labour either, and internal divisions within Labour were damaging, especially in the late 1930s. At best Labour had achieved political respectability by the 1930s, and progress had been made from the pre-1914 position.[100] A recent commentator

---

[97] Evans, 'Cardiff's Labour tradition', p. 87.
[98] Evans, 'Cardiff's Labour tradition', p. 82.
[99] *Western Mail & South Wales News*, 1 Nov. 1932.
[100] Evans, 'Cardiff's Labour tradition', p. 83.

has suggested that the 'increasing influence that the Welsh Labour Party possessed in Welsh local elections between the wars contributed significantly to the shift from a public "Liberal Wales" to one that was markedly "Labour"'.[101] This insight can be applied to inter-war Cardiff only to a limited degree.

[101] Williams, C., 'Labour and the challenge of local government, 1919–1939', in Tanner, Williams and Hopkin, *The Labour Party in Wales*, p. 138.

A guide to further reading

Newspapers

Western Mail

Secondary sources

Austin Jenkins, J. and Edwards James, R., *The History Of Nonconformity in Cardiff*, (Cardiff and London, 1901).

Davies, J., 'Aristocratic town-makers and the coal metropolis: the marquesses of Bute and Cardiff, 1776 to 1947', in Cannadine, D., (ed.), *Patricians, power and politics in nineteenth century towns*, (Leicester, 1982).

Davies, J., *Cardiff and the Marquesses of Bute*, (Cardiff, 1981).

Daunton, M.J., 'Examines the phenomenal nineteenth-century growth of the harbour facilities in Cardiff', in Williams, S, (ed.), *The Cardiff Book*, Volume 1, (Barry, 1973).

Daunton, M.J., 'Aspects of the Social and Economic Structure of Cardiff, 1870–1914', (Ph.D. thesis, University of Kent at Canterbury, 1974).

Daunton, M.J., *Coal Metropolis: Cardiff 1870–1914*, (Leicester, 1977).

Evans, N., 'Cardiff's Labour Tradition', *Llafur,* vol. 4, no. 2 (1985), pp. 77–90.

Freeman, T.W., *The Conurbations of Great Britain*, (Manchester, 1959).

Hopkin, D., 'The Rise of Labour in Wales 1890–1914', *Llafur*, vol. 6, no. 3, (1994), pp. 120–141.

Jones, R.G., 'Butetown Cardiff: Change in a Dockland Community from the early Nineteenth Century to the Present', (MA thesis, University of Keele, 1980).

Leng, P.J., *The Welsh Dockers*, (Ormskirk, 1981).

Morgan, K.O., *Rebirth of a Nation: Wales 1880–1980*, (Oxford, 1981).

Morgan, P.H., 'Building Use and Social Change in the Inner City: A Case Study of Cardiff, 1850–1950', (Ph.D. thesis, University of Wales, Aberystwyth, 1985).

Rees, W., *Cardiff: A History of the City*, (Cardiff, 1962).

Tanner, D.M., 'The pattern of Labour politics', in Tanner, D.M., Williams, C.M., and Hopkin, D.R., (eds), *The Labour Party in Wales*, (Cardiff, 2000), ch. 5.

Williams, C. 'Labour and the challenge of local government, 1919–1939', in Tanner, Williams and Hopkin, *The Labour Party in Wales*, pp. 137–160.

Williams, S., (ed.) *The Cardiff Book*, Volume 1, (Barry, 1973).

Willson Lloyd, D., *Cardiff 1919: A Commercial and Industrial Centre*, (Cardiff, 1919).

Cardiff wards 1919–1921

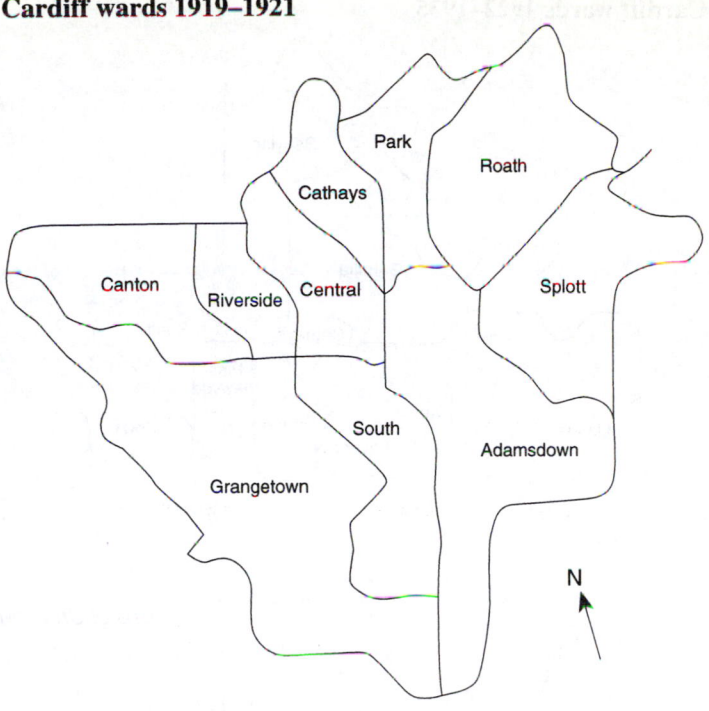

Cardiff wards 1922–1935

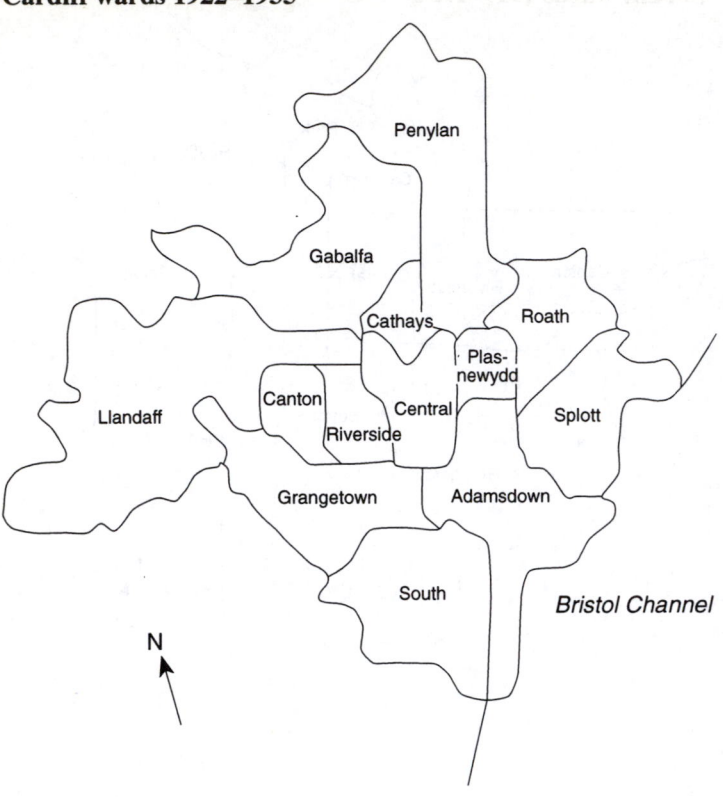

Cardiff wards 1936–1938

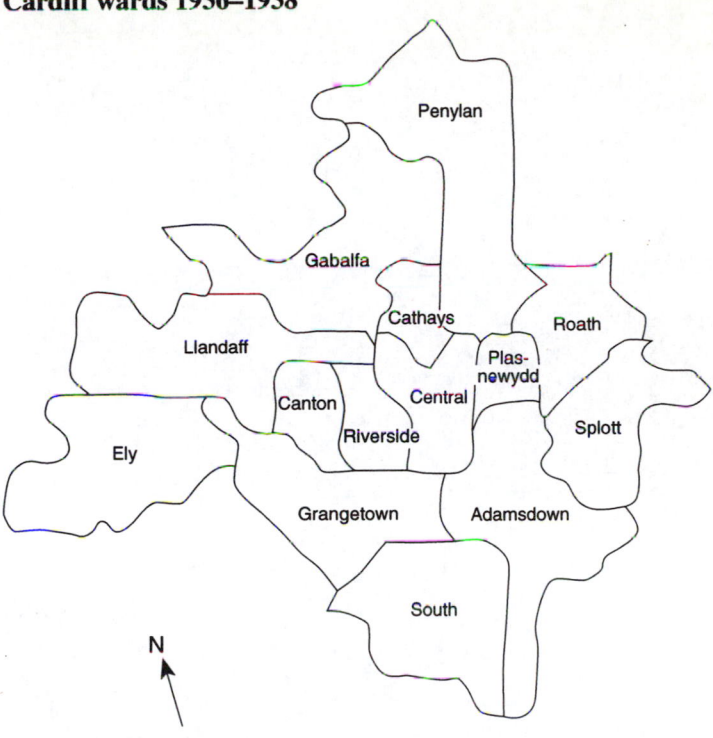

Persons aged fourteen and over classified by industry 1931

	Male	%	Female	%	Total	%
Metal and engineering	9,571	13.2	671	2.4	10,242	10.2
Clothing	1,145	1.6	1,866	6.7	3,011	3.0
Food, drink and tobacco	3,357	4.6	1,914	6.9	5,271	5.3
Building	4,883	6.7	38	0.1	4,921	4.9
Transport	17,418	24.0	346	1.2	17,764	17.7
- Rail	*5,739*	*7.9*	*116*	*0.4*	*5,855*	*5.8*
- Water	*5,495*	*7.6*	*102*	*0.4*	*5,597*	*5.6*
- Docks	*3,285*	*4.5*	*23*	*0.1*	*3,308*	*3.3*
Commerce and finance	15,340	21.1	6,724	24.3	22,064	22.0
Public admin. and defence	6,296	8.7	2,373	8.6	8,669	8.6
- Local government	*3,926*	*5.4*	*1,740*	*6.3*	*5,666*	*5.6*
Professions	1,939	2.7	1,811	6.5	3,750	3.7
Personal service	2,879	4.0	9,815	35.4	12,694	12.7
Other	9,794	13.5	2,142	7.7	11,936	11.9
Total (a)	**72,622**		**27,700**		**100,322**	
Total population (b)	107,309		116,280		223,589	
(a) as % of (b)	67.7		23.8		44.9	
Total out of work (c)	14,586		2,600		17,186	
(c) as % of (a)	20.1		9.4		17.1	
Managerial and own account	8,863	15.3	2,354	9.4	11,217	13.5
Operative	49,173	84.7	22,746	90.6	71,919	86.5
Total (excluding out of work)	58,036		25,100		83,136	

Population statistics 1931

Ward	Acres	Population	Persons/acre	Persons/room
Adamsdown	948	17,209	18.2	0.98
Canton	249	17,273	69.4	0.82
Cathays	340	16,566	48.7	0.81
Central	532	13,544	25.5	0.92
Gabalfa	1,461	18,703	12.8	0.90
Grangetown	925	15,403	16.7	0.98
LLandaff	2,731	27,762	10.2	0.91
Penylan	1,760	14,146	8.0	0.67
Plasnewydd	235	15,056	64.1	0.76
Riverside	319	17,602	55.2	0.76
Roath	749	15,792	21.1	0.75
South	553	13,635	24.7	1.01
Splott	1,182	20,898	17.7	1.01
Total	**11,984**	**223,589**	**18.7**	**0.86**

Overall position on the council 1919–38

	Position				Gains				Losses			
	C[a]	Lab	L	Other	C[a]	Lab	L	Other	C[a]	Lab	L	Other
1919	17	5	15	3	0	4	0	3	4	0	3	0
1920	18	6	14	2	1	1	0	0	0	0	1	1
1921	18	6	14	2	0	0	0	0	0	0	0	0
1922[b]	21	5	18	5	0	0	1	1	0	1	0	1
1923	21	6	21	4	1	1	1	0	2	0	1	0
1924	21	6	21	4	0	0	0	0	0	0	0	0
1925	22	6	19	5	1	0	0	1	0	0	2	0
1926	21	8	19	4	1	2	0	0	0	1	1	1
1927	18	13	18	3	0	5	1	0	3	0	1	2
1928[c]	13	18	17	3	0	4	0	0	3	0	1	0
	A-S	Lab			A-S	Lab			A-S	Lab		
1929[d]	31	19			0	1			1	0		
1930	36	16			4	0			0	4		
1931	40	12			4	0			0	4		
1932	40	12			1	1			1	1		
1933	39	13			0	1			1	0		
1934	38	14			0	2			2	0		
1935	36	16			0	1			1	0		
1936[e]	35	20			0	1			1	0		
1937	39	17			1	0			0	1		
1938	41	15			1	0			0	1		

Aldermen 1919–38

1919 Others–10, Lab–0	1929[d] Anti-Socialists–11, Lab–0
1920 Others–10, Lab–0	1930 Anti-Socialists–11, Lab–2
1921 Others–10, Lab–0	1931 Anti-Socialists–11, Lab–2
1922[b] Others–10, Lab–0	1932 Anti-Socialists–11, Lab–2
1923 Others–13, Lab–0	1933 Anti-Socialists–11, Lab–2
1924 Others–13, Lab–0	1934 Anti-Socialists–11, Lab–2
1925 Others–12, Lab–1	1935 Anti-Socialists–11, Lab–2
1926 Others–13, Lab–0	1936[e] Anti-Socialists–10, Lab–3
1927 Others–13, Lab–0	1937 Anti-Socialists–11, Lab–3
1928 Others–13, Lab–0	1938 Anti-Socialists–12, Lab–2

[a] from 1929 anti-socialist pact between C, L, R and others operated.

[b] 1922 – three new aldermanic seats vacant.

[c] 1928 – one seat vacant.

[d] 1929 – two aldermen elected as councillors, so two aldermanic seats vacant.

[e] 1936 – one new aldermanic seat vacant.

Municipal elections: winning party 1919–28

Ward	1919	1920	1921	1922	1923	1924	1925	1926	1927	1928
Adamsdown	Lab	Ind	Coa	**Lab**	**Ind**	Lab	**Lab**	Lab	**Lab**	**Lab**
Canton	Ex-S	Coa	Coa	**L**	C	L	C	C	L	Lab
Cathays	Lab	L	Coa	Lab	L	L	Lab	Lab	Lab	Lab
Central	Ex-s	**C**	C	L	**C**	C	C	C	C	C
Ely (1)	-	-	-	-	-	-	-	-	-	-
Ely (2)	-	-	-	-	-	-	-	-	-	-
Ely (3)	-	-	-	-	-	-	-	-	-	-
Gabalfa (1)	-	-	-	R	**R**	Ind	Ind	R	R	Ind
Gabalfa (2)	-	-	-	R	-	-	-	-	-	-
Gabalfa (3)	-	-	-	R	-	-	-	-	-	-
Grangetown	Lab	Coa	Coa	Lab	Lab	Ind	Lab	Lab	Lab	Lab
Llandaff (1)	-	-	-	C	C	C	C	C	Lab	Lab
Llandaff (2)	-	-	-	C	-	-	-	-	-	-
Llandaff (3)	-	-	-	L	-	-	-	-	-	-
Park	L	C	L	-	-	-	-	-	-	-
Penylan (1)	-	-	-	L	L	**L**	L	**L**	**L**	L
Penylan (2)	-	-	-	L	-	-	-	-	-	-
Penylan (3)	-	-	-	C	-	-	-	-	-	-
Plasnewydd (1)	-	-	-	C	Ind L	L	C	L	L	C
Plasnewydd (2)	-	-	-	L	-	-	-	-	-	-
Plasnewydd (3)	-	-	-	L	-	-	-	-	-	-
Riverside	Ex-s	Coa	**Coa**	C	**C**	**C**	**C**	**C**	**C**	C
Roath	L	Coa	Coa	L	L	C	**L**	C	L	L
South	C	**C**	C	C	C	**C**	C	C	Lab	Lab
Splott	Lab	Lab	Coa	Ind	Lab	C	Ind	Lab	Lab	Lab

Municipal elections: party wins per year 1919–28

	1919	1920	1921	1922	1923	1924	1925	1926	1927	1928
Lab	4	1	0	3	2	1	3	4	6	7
Others	6	9	10	18	11	12	10	9	7	6
Total	10	10	10	21	13	13	13	13	13	13
Turnout %	42.6	55.0	56.4	54.3	47.8	49.3	56.4	55.5	53.6	61.0
Labour %	35.7	34.2	31.4	26.6	32.5	30.4	34.8	50.2	45.1	44.5

Municipal elections: winning party 1929–38

Ward	1929	1930	1931	1932	1933	1934	1935	1936	1937	1938
Adamsdown	Lab	Lab	Lab	Lab	Lab	Lab	Lab	Lab	**Lab**	**Lab**
Canton	A-S	Lab	R	Lab	Lab	Lab	Lab	Lab	Lab	Lab
Cathays	Lab	A-S	R	R	Ind	R	R	R	R	R
Central	A-S	A-S	Ind	Ind	A-S	Ind	C	C	C	**C**
Ely (1)	-	-	-	-	-	-	-	Lab	Lab	**Lab**
Ely (2)	-	-	-	-	-	-	-	Lab	-	-
Ely (3)	-	-	-	-	-	-	-	Lab	-	-
Gabalfa (1)	A-S	A-S	R	R	R	R	R	R	R	**R**
Gabalfa (2)	-	-	-	-	-	-	-	-	-	-
Gabalfa (3)	-	-	-	-	-	-	-	-	-	-
Grangetown	Lab	A-S	R	Lab	Lab	R	**Lab**	R	R	**Lab**
Llandaff (1)	Lab	A-S	Ind	Lab	Ind	Ind	**Lab**	Ind	Ind	Ind
Llandaff (2)	-	-	-	-	-	-	-	-	-	-
Llandaff (3)	-	-	-	-	-	-	-	-	-	-
Park	-	-	-	-	-	-	-	-	-	-
Penylan (1)	A-S	A-S	L	L	A-S	Ind	L	C	L	L
Penylan (2)	-	-	-	-	-	-	-	-	-	-
Penylan (3)	-	-	-	-	-	-	-	-	-	-
Plasnewydd (1)	A-S	A-S	Ind	Ind	A-S	R	L	**L**	R	C
Plasnewydd (2)	-	-	-	-	-	-	-	-	-	-
Plasnewydd (3)	-	-	-	-	-	-	-	-	-	-
Riverside	A-S	A-S	C	Ind	Ind	Ind	C	**Ind**	C	C
Roath	A-S	A-S	L	Ind	A-S	Ind	C	L	L	C
South	A-S	A-S	Ind	C	L	Lab	Lab	Lab	Ind	R
Splott	Lab	Lab	**Lab**	Lab	**Lab**	Lab	**Lab**	**Lab**	Lab	Lab

Municipal elections: party wins per year 1929–38

	1929	1930	1931	1932	1933	1934	1935	1936	1937	1938
Lab	5	3	2	5	4	4	6	7	4	5
Others	8	10	11	8	9	9	7	9	10	9
Total	13	13	13	13	13	13	13	16	14	14
Turnout %	**48.8**	**53.8**	**52.2**	**48.6**	**49.7**	**50.0**	**47.5**	**48.0**	**46.8**	**47.8**
Lab %	**48.5**	**41.3**	**32.7**	**48.2**	**40.2**	**42.9**	**41.9**	**40.0**	**42.7**	**41.4**

Municipal elections: party wins per ward 1919–38

	Other	Lab	Total	Turnout %	Labour % of all votes
Adamsdown	3	17	20	45.9	63.2
Canton	11	9	20	46.5	43.9
Cathays	13	7	20	53.9	43.0
Central	20	0	20	48.9	33.4
Ely	0	5	5	52.9	65.6
Gabalfa	19	0	19	50.9	31.3
Grangetown	8	12	20	54.9	52.3
Llandaff	14	5	19	48.3	41.8
Park	3	0	3	46.7	9.3
Penylan	19	0	19	48.5	18.1
Plasnewydd	19	0	19	53.5	28.4
Riverside	20	0	20	44.5	30.9
Roath	20	0	20	51.2	30.1
South	15	5	20	52.4	43.1
Splott	4	16	20	61.6	56.0
Total	**188**	**76**	**264**	**51.1**	**39.9**

Seats won by Labour as a percentage of all wins 1919–38   28.8

Parliamentary election results

Cardiff Central constituency
(the following wards [1918 boundaries] were included in Central: Canton, Cathays, Central, Riverside)

General election	Winner	Conservative %	Labour %	Liberal %
14 Dec. 1918	C	41.1	22.4	20.1
15 Nov. 1922	C	50.0	29.4	20.6
6 Dec. 1923	C	38.4	32.0	29.6
29 Oct. 1924	C	49.7	33.8	16.5
30 May 1929	Lab	34.9	39.1	26.0
27 Oct. 1931	N Lab	*(N Lab 69.2)*	30.8	-
14 Nov. 1935	N Lab	*(N Lab 51.6)*	36.7	11.7

Cardiff East constituency
(the following wards [1918 boundaries] were included in East: Park, Roath, Splott)

General election	Winner	Conservative %	Labour %	Liberal %
14 Dec. 1918	L	30.7	28.5	40.8
15 Nov. 1922	C	36.8	31.4	31.8
6 Dec. 1923	L	31.5	32.7	35.8
29 Oct. 1924	C	40.3	32.8	26.9
30 May 1929	Lab	29.1	39.0	31.9
27 Oct. 1931	C	38.6	31.8	29.6
14 Nov. 1935	C	53.5	37.8	8.7

Cardiff South constituency
(the following wards [1918 boundaries] were included in South: Adamsdown, Grangetown, South, along with the urban district of Penarth)

General election	Winner	Conservative %	Labour %	Liberal %
14 Dec. 1918	C	48.5	26.3	25.2
15 Nov. 1922	C	36.4	31.4	32.2
6 Dec. 1923	Lab	35.8	37.9	26.3
29 Oct. 1924	C	49.8	40.3	9.9
30 May 1929	Lab	33.1	45.3	21.6
27 Oct. 1931	C	59.8	40.2	-
14 Nov. 1935	C	50.9	49.1	-

Adamsdown ward

Candidate	Party	Votes	%	Electors	Turnout	Gains
1919						
J. Donovan	Lab	1,597	64.2	4,262	58.3	Lab from L
W. Jones*	L	889	35.8			
Total votes		2,486				
1920						
E. Curran	Ind	1,389	52.7	4,490	58.7	-
W. Williams	Lab	1,247	47.3			
Total votes		2,636				
1921						
F.H. Turnbull*	Coa	1,895	61.1	4,666	66.4	-
W. Williams	Lab	1,204	38.9			
Total votes		3,099				
1922						
J. Donovan*	Lab	Unopp.	-	5,978	-	-
1923						
E. Curran*	Ind	Unopp.	-	5,926	-	-
1924						
W. Williams*	Lab	1,619	65.8	5,811	42.3	-
R. Smith	Ind	841	34.2			
Total votes		2,460				
1925						
J. Donovan*	Lab	Unopp.	-	5,795	-	-
1926						
T.J. Mullins	Lab	2,147	64.4	5,695	58.5	Lab from Ind
T.R. Evans	C	1,187	35.6			
Total votes		3,334				
1927						
W.Williams*	Lab	Unopp.	-	5,564	-	-
1928						
J. Donovan*	Lab	Unopp.	-	5,438	-	-

Adamsdown ward *(continued)*

Candidate	Party	Votes	%	Electors	Turnout	Gains
1929						
T.J. Mullins*	Lab	1,810	70.7	6,235	41.1	-
Miss A.A. Swain	A-S	750	29.3			
Total votes		2,560				
1930						
J. Kerrigan*	Lab	1,612	59.4	6,142	44.2	-
C.S. Hallinan	A-S	1,103	40.6			
Total votes		2,715				
1931						
J.P. Collins*	Lab	1,775	90.3	6,171	31.8	-
L. Jefferies	Com	190	9.7			
Total votes		1,965				
1932						
T.J. Mullins*	Lab	1,693	69.9	6,176	39.2	-
C.A. Horwood	Ind	579	23.9			
L. Jefferies	Com	151	6.2			
Total votes		2,423				
1933						
T.J. Kerrigan*	Lab	1,725	85.9	6,185	32.4	-
R.J. Skyrme	Com	205	10.2			
W.A. Stonebridge	A-S	77	3.8			
Total votes		2,007				
1934						
J.P. Collins*	Lab	1,458	54.0	6,063	44.5	-
Mrs M. Lloyd-Evans	R	1,099	40.7			
R. Cosslett	Com	141	5.2			
Total votes		2,698				
1935						
T.J. Mullins*	Lab	1,893	65.2	6,052	48.0	-
Mrs M. Lloyd-Evans	R	1,012	34.8			
Total votes		2,905				

Adamsdown ward *(continued)*

Candidate	Party	Votes	%	Electors	Turnout	Gains
1936						
T.J. Kerrigan*	Lab	1,864	62.9	6,538	45.3	-
R.T. Smith	R	1,098	37.1			
Total votes		2,962				
1937						
J.P. Collins*	Lab	Unopp.	-	6,513	-	-
1938						
T.J. Mullins*	Lab	Unopp.	-	6,516	-	-

Overall Labour vote   **63.2%**   **Overall turnout**   **45.9%**

Canton ward

Candidate	Party	Votes	%	Electors	Turnout	Gains
1919						
T.L. Francis	Ex-S	1,549	38.3	9,760	41.4	Ex-S from L
W. Grey*	L	1,407	34.8			
T.H. Spence	Lab	1,089	26.9			
Total votes		4,045				
1920						
W.B. Francis*	Coa	3,195	65.9	10,356	46.8	-
A.Marsh	Lab	1,653	34.1			
Total votes		4,848				
1921						
C.F. Sanders*	Coa	3,277	56.6	10,428	55.6	-
J.E. Edmunds	Lab	2,516	43.4			
Total votes		5,793				
1922						
W. Grey	L	Unopp.	-	7,312	-	-
1923						
G. Coombs*	C	1,920	73.1	7,336	35.8	-
W.E. Roberts	Lab	706	26.9			
Total votes		2,626				
1924						
C.F. Sanders*	L	2,299	75.8	7,357	41.2	-
Miss A. Wallis	Lab	733	24.2			
Total votes		3,032				
1925						
H.W.J. Powell*	C	1,887	52.5	7,456	48.2	-
A.C. Humphries	Lab	878	24.4			
Mrs M.A. Watts	L	828	23.0			
Total votes		3,593				
1926						
G. Coombs*	C	1,920	58.4	7,490	43.9	-
A.C. Humphries	Lab	1,368	41.6			
Total votes		3,288				

Canton ward (*continued*)

Candidate	Party	Votes	%	Electors	Turnout	Gains
1927						
C.F. Sanders*	L	1,655	45.8	7,450	48.6	-
B.W. Weston	Lab	1,271	35.1			
T.C. Major	C	691	19.1			
Total votes		3,617				
1928						
J. Heginbottom	Lab	1,826	40.7	7,432	60.3	Lab from C
A.J. Dyne	L	1,445	32.2			
W.A. Prichard	C	1,211	27.0			
Total votes		4,482				
1929						
G. Coombs*	A-S	1,833	52.9	8,349	41.5	-
L. Davies	Lab	1,635	47.1			
Total votes		3,468				
1930						
B.F.C. Weston*	Lab	1,788	41.8	8,268	51.7	-
Miss M.M. Sanders	A-S	1,552	36.3			
A.W.J. Morley	A-S	934	21.9			
Total votes		4,274				
1931						
C. Crabtree	R	2,771	62.1	8,195	54.4	R from Lab
J. Heginbottom*	Lab	1,690	37.9			
Total votes		4,461				
1932						
J. Heginbottom	Lab	2,100	56.3	8,104	46.0	Lab from Ind
G. Coombs*	Ind	1,630	43.7			
Total votes		3,730				
1933						
B.F.C. Weston*	Lab	2,351	60.1	8,035	48.7	-
E.R.T. Jones	R	1,560	39.9			
Total votes		3,911				

Canton ward *(continued)*

Candidate	Party	Votes	%	Electors	Turnout	Gains
1934						
A. Weston	Lab	1,811	54.2	8,128	41.1	Lab from L?
Miss M. Sanders	L	1,531	45.8			
Total votes		3,342				
1935						
J. Heginbottom*	Lab	2,193	60.1	7,917	46.1	-
M. Roberts	R	1,453	39.9			
Total votes		3,646				
1936						
A.J. Williams*	Lab	1,961	55.6	8,005	44.0	-
M. Roberts	R	1,565	44.4			
Total votes		3,526				
1937						
A. Weston*	Lab	2,024	64.1	7,925	39.8	-
E.J. Smith	R	1,134	35.9			
Total votes		3,158				
1938						
J. Heginbottom*	Lab	2,206	60.6	7,769	46.9	-
G.P. Franklin	Ind	1,436	39.4			
Total votes		3,642				

Overall Labour vote   **43.9%**   **Overall turnout**   **46.5%**

Cathays ward

Candidate	Party	Votes	%	Electors	Turnout	Gains
1919						
A.E. Gough	Lab	2,066	55.9	8,621	42.8	Lab from L
W.R. Williams*	L	1,627	44.1			
Total votes		3,693				
1920						
W.R. Williams	L	2,993	60.1	9,370	53.2	-
T.R. Morgan	Lab	1,989	39.9			
Total votes		4,982				
1921						
H. Davies*	Coa	3,539	71.2	9,617	51.7	-
B.O. Davies	Lab	1,434	28.8			
Total votes		4,973				
1922						
A.E. Gough*	Lab	1,648	34.8	7,672	61.7	-
C.R. Harrison	C	1,624	34.3			
I.W. Evans	L	1,458	30.8			
Total votes		4,730				
1923						
W.R. Williams*	L	1,970	56.0	7,745	45.4	-
C.R. Harrison	C	1,546	44.0			
Total votes		3,516				
1924						
H. Davies*	L	2,392	65.9	7,962	45.6	-
M. Edwards	Lab	1,240	34.1			
Total votes		3,632				
1925						
A.E. Gough*	Lab	2,547	51.1	8,047	61.9	-
B. Janner	L	2,438	48.9			
Total votes		4,985				

Cathays ward (continued)

Candidate	Party	Votes	%	Electors	Turnout	Gains
1926						
M. Edwards	Lab	2,058	44.6	7,889	58.5	Lab from L
Miss B. Foxley	L	1,558	33.7			
B.W.P. Morgan	C	1,002	21.7			
Total votes		4,618				
1927						
A.J. Williams	Lab	2,165	52.3	7,861	52.7	Lab from L
Miss B. Foxley	L	1,976	47.7			
Total votes		4,141				
1928						
A.E. Gough*	Lab	3,022	61.2	8,013	61.6	-
O.T. Morris	Ind	1,918	38.8			
Total votes		4,940				
1929						
M. Edwards*	Lab	2,442	56.8	8,266	52.0	-
Ald. W.R. Williams	A-S	1,854	43.2			
Total votes		4,296				
1930						
G.B. Smith	A-S	2,604	53.7	8,198	59.2	A-S from Lab
A.J. Williams*	Lab	2,247	46.3			
Total votes		4,851				
1931						
M. Davies*	R	3,510	69.5	8,386	60.2	-
E.A. Robson	Lab	1,539	30.5			
Total votes		5,049				
1932						
A. Powell	R	2,243	50.5	8,479	52.4	R from Lab
M. Edwards*	Lab	2,200	49.5			
Total votes		4,443				
1933						
G.B. Smith*	Ind	2,670	54.2	8,305	59.3	-
M. Edwards	Lab	2,254	45.8			
Total votes		4,924				

Cathays ward *(continued)*

Candidate	Party	Votes	%	Electors	Turnout	Gains
1934						
M. Davies*	R	2,909	60.4	8,474	56.8	-
J. Cox	Lab	1,905	39.6			
Total votes		4,814				
1935						
A. Powell*	R	2,361	53.8	8,548	51.3	-
T.E. Sweet	Lab	2,027	46.2			
Total votes		4,388				
1936						
G. B. Smith*	R	2,563	53.1	8,801	54.8	-
W. Charles	Lab	2,262	46.9			
Total votes		4,825				
1937						
M. Davies*	R	2,601	58.7	8,724	50.8	-
G.O. Pugh	Lab	1,833	41.3			
Total votes		4,434				
1938						
A. Powell*	R	2,066	52.5	8,461	46.5	-
G.O. Pugh	Lab	1,868	47.5			
Total votes		3,934				

Overall Labour vote 　　**43.0%** 　　**Overall turnout** 　　**53.9%**

Central ward

Candidate	Party	Votes	%	Electors	Turnout	Gains
1919						
T.W. Langman	Ex-S	983	68.9	4,250	33.6	Ex-s from C
F.W.Blower*	C	444	31.1			
Total votes		1,427				
1920						
A.J.A. Stone*	C	Unopp.	-		-	-
1921						
O.C. Purnell	C	1,184	51.5	3,742	61.5	-
C.S. Hallinan	Lab	1,117	48.5			
Total votes		2,301				
1922						
A.L.Owen	L	1,697	52.2	5,909	55.0	L from Ex-s
A. Bond	C	1,554	47.8			
Total votes		3,251				
1923						
G.N. Howell	C	Unopp.	-	5,944	-	-
1924						
O.C. Purnell*	C	1,939	63.2	6,072	50.5	-
B. Janner	L	1,130	36.8			
Total votes		3,069				
1925						
J.G. Gaskell	C	1,640	45.1	5,960	61.1	C from L
J.P. Collins	Lab	1,116	30.7			
A.L. Owen*	L	884	24.3			
Total votes		3,640				
1926						
G.N. Howell*	C	1,692	54.5	5,866	52.9	-
J.P. Collins	Lab	1,414	45.5			
Total votes		3,106				

Central ward *(continued)*

Candidate	Party	Votes	%	Electors	Turnout	Gains
1927						
O.C. Purnell*	C	1,702	57.6	5,769	51.2	-
J.P. Collins	Lab	1,252	42.4			
Total votes		2,954				
1928						
J.G. Gaskell*	C	1,682	51.1	5,779	56.9	-
J.P. Collins	Lab	1,608	48.9			
Total votes		3,290				
1929						
R. Bevan	A-S	1,569	51.5	5,912	51.5	-
J.P. Collins	Lab	1,475	48.5			
Total votes		3,044				
1930						
O.C. Purnell*	A-S	1,828	64.2	5,810	49.0	-
T.J. Harris	Lab	1,021	35.8			
Total votes		2,849				
1931						
E. Curran	Ind	1,929	71.7	5,896	45.6	-
T. Harris	Lab	762	28.3			
Total votes		2,691				
1932						-
R. Bevan*	Ind	1,520	58.4	5,863	44.4	-
E.A. Robson	Lab	1,084	41.6			
Total votes		2,604				
1933						
O.C. Purnell*	A-S	1,732	61.4	5,787	48.8	-
T.A. Murphy	Lab	1,091	38.6			
Total votes		2,823				
1934						
W.T. Banbury	Ind	1,567	58.4	5,830	46.0	-
T.A.Murphy	Lab	1,077	40.2			
W.A. Stonebridge	Ind	37	1.4			
Total votes		2,681				

Central ward *(continued)*

Candidate	Party	Votes	%	Electors	Turnout	Gains
1935						
R. Bevan*	C	1,394	56.3	5,692	43.5	-
H.G. Bartlett	Lab	1,081	43.7			
Total votes		2,475				
1936						
F. Jones*	C	1,363	70.9	5,587	34.4	-
R.G. Walters	Lab	559	29.1			
Total votes		1,922				
1937						
W.T.Banbury*	C	1,429	63.8	5,047	44.4	-
C.L. Hauser	Lab	812	36.2			
Total votes		2,241				
1938						
R. Bevan*	C	Unopp.	-		-	-

Overall Labour vote		**33.4%**		**Overall turnout**		**48.9%**

Ely ward
(created from southern portion of Llandaff ward in 1936)

Candidate	Party	Votes	%	Electors	Turnout	Gains
1936						
W.H.J. Muston	Lab	2,798	24.7	7,482	53.6	-
T.E. Sweet	Lab	2,244	19.8			
T. Llewellyn	Lab	2,152	19.0			
Miss E. Ingledew	Ind	1,456	12.9			
Dr W.E. Neale	Ind	1,396	12.3			
D. Brown	Ind	1,274	11.3			
Total votes		11,320				
Total voters		4,009				
1937						
T. Llewellyn*	Lab	2,778	67.6	7,932	51.8	-
Miss E. Ingledew	C	827	20.1			
E.J. Draper	Ind	505	12.3			
Total votes		4,110				
1938						
T.E. Sweet*	Lab	Unopp.	-	8,597	-	-

Overall Labour vote	**65.6%**		**Overall turnout**	**52.9%**

Gabalfa ward
(added by extension of the borough in 1922)

Candidate	Party	Votes	%	Electors	Turnout	Gains
1922						
A.E. Shippobotham	R	1,767	22.9	5,985	45.2	-
C.H. McCale	R	1,722	22.3			
J.H. Hellyer	R	1,662	21.5			
E.O. Millard	Lab	886	11.5			
F. Smith	Lab	845	10.9			
G.S. Ireland	Lab	842	10.9			
Total votes		7,724				
Total voters		2,703				
1923						
J.H. Hellyer*	R	Unopp.	-	6,291	-	-
1924						
C.H. McHale*	Ind	1,950	58.9	6,547	50.6	-
H. Davies	Ex-S	696	21.0			
G.B. Smith	Lab	667	20.1			
Total votes		3,313				
1925						
A.E. Shippobotham*	Ind	2,042	48.2	6,789	62.4	-
G.B. Smith	Lab	1,159	27.3			
Mrs T. Thomas	Ind	1,037	24.5			
Total votes		4,238				
1926						
J.H. Hellyer*	R	2,435	61.3	6,934	57.3	-
F. Saw	Lab	1,538	38.7			
Total votes		3,973				
1927						
C.H. McHale*	R	2,270	67.1	7,225	46.8	-
H.J. Brown	Lab	1,113	32.9			
Total votes		3,383				
1928						
A.E. Shippobotham*	Ind	2,309	55.3	7,463	56.0	-
H.J. Brown	Lab	1,870	44.7			
Total votes		4,179				

Gabalfa ward (*continued*)

Candidate	Party	Votes	%	Electors	Turnout	Gains
1929						
J.H. Hellyer*	A-S	2,610	59.6	8,516	51.4	-
H. Brown	Lab	1,767	40.4			
Total votes		4,377				
1930						
C.H. McHale*	A-S	3,496	65.9	8,679	61.1	-
E. Hopkins	Lab	1,805	34.1			
Total votes		5,301				
1931						
A.E. Shippobotham*	R	2,933	67.1	8,710	50.2	-
L.C. Davies	Lab	1,437	32.9			
Total votes		4,370				
1932						
J.H. Hellyer*	R	2,829	66.2	8,877	48.2	-
W.G. Chapple	Lab	1,447	33.8			
Total votes		4,276				
1933						
C.H. McHale*	R	3,658	90.5	9,002	44.9	-
C.F. Owen	Com	386	9.5			
Total votes		4,044				
1934						
J.H. Morgan	R	1,900	35.7	9,301	57.3	R from Ind
A.E. Shippobotham*	Ind	1,718	32.3			
W.H. Chapple	Lab	1,709	32.1			
Total votes		5,327				
1935						
J.H. Hellyer*	R	3,131	68.9	9,656	47.1	-
R.W. Colbeck	Lab	1,415	31.1			
Total votes		4,546				
1936						
C.H. McHale*	R	3,320	71.9	9,796	47.2	-
G.H. Pugh	Lab	1,300	28.1			
Total votes		4,620				

Gabalfa ward *(continued)*

Candidate	Party	Votes	%	Electors	Turnout	Gains
1937						
J.H. Morgan*	R	2,608	63.7	10,083	40.6	-
W.G. Chapple	Lab	1,488	36.3			
Total votes		4,096				
1938						
J.H. Hellyer*	R	Unopp.	-	10,368	-	-

Overall Labour vote **31.3%** **Overall turnout** **50.9%**

Grangetown ward

Candidate	Party	Votes	%	Electors	Turnout	Gains
1919						
I.G. Duddridge	Lab	1,753	50.8	8,677	39.8	Lab from C
W.R. Smith*	C	1,219	35.3			
A.B. Sessions	L	478	13.9			
Total votes		3,450				
1920						
H.W. Bruton	Coa	2,154	56.8	8,661	43.8	-
J.H. Rogers	Lab	1,638	43.2			
Total votes		3,792				
1921						
S. Jenkins*	Coa	2,344	52.7	9,110	48.9	-
F.W. Harford	Lab	2,107	47.3			
Total votes		4,451				
1922						
I.G. Duddridge*	Lab	1,855	54.1	6,045	56.7	-
C.S. Hallinan	L	1,572	45.9			
Total votes		3,427				
1923						
J. Griffiths	Lab	1,783	57.0	6,245	50.1	Lab from
H.W. Bruton*	Ind C	1,013	32.4			Ind C
W.R. Freeman	I Lab	334	10.7			
Total votes		3,130				
1924						
C.S. Hallinan*	Ind	2,157	66.8	6,249	51.7	-
E.A. Robson	Lab	1,071	33.2			
Total votes		3,228				
1925						
I.G. Duddridge*	Lab	1,959	79.8	6,191	39.6	-
G. Parsons	Ind	495	20.2			
Total votes		2,454				

Grangetown ward *(continued)*

Candidate	Party	Votes	%	Electors	Turnout	Gains
1926						
J. Griffiths*	Lab	2,524	65.6	6,270	61.4	-
F.J. Andrews	C	1,323	34.4			
Total votes		3,847				
1927						
P. Freeman	Lab	2,194	59.0	6,336	58.7	Lab from Ind
C.S. Hallinan*	Ind	1,523	41.0			
Total votes		3,717				
1928						
I.G. Duddridge*	Lab	2,482	63.4	6,310	62.1	-
T.L. Francis	L	1,435	36.6			
Total votes		3,917				
1929						
J. Griffiths*	Lab	2,312	68.6	6,963	48.4	-
D. O'Neill	A-S	1,056	31.4			
Total votes		3,368				
1930						
G.L. Ferrier	A-S	2,349	56.5	6,975	59.6	A-S from Lab
P. Freeman MP*	Lab	1,809	43.5			
Total votes		4,158				
1931						
A.J. Martin	R	2,410	53.8	6,990	64.1	R from Lab
I.G. Duddridge*	Lab	2,073	46.2			
Total votes		4,483				
1932						
J. Griffiths*	Lab	2,910	67.1	6,944	62.5	-
S. Rayer	R	1,427	32.9			
Total votes		4,337				
1933						
A.K. Little	Lab	2,394	100.0	7,041	34.0	Lab from R
Total votes		2,394				

Grangetown ward *(continued)*

Candidate	Party	Votes	%	Electors	Turnout	Gains
1934						
A.J. Martin*	R	2,235	50.8	7,052	62.4	-
I.G. Duddridge	Lab	2,168	49.2			
Total votes		4,403				
1935						
J. Griffiths*	Lab	Unopp.	-	7,043	-	-
1936						
G.L. Ferrier*	R	2,905	64.6	7,119	63.1	-
H. Collins	Lab	1,590	35.4			
Total votes		4,495				
1937						
A.J. Martin*	R	2,457	58.5	7,507	55.9	-
J. Dooley	Lab	1,740	41.5			
Total votes		4,197				
1938						
J. Griffiths*	Lab	Unopp.	-	7,430	-	-

Overall Labour vote   **52.3%**   **Overall turnout**   **54.9%**

Llandaff ward
(added by extension of the borough in 1922; southern portion became Ely ward in 1936)

Candidate	Party	Votes	%	Electors	Turnout	Gains
1922						
A.E. Lougher	C	1,922	24.8	5,109	54.7	-
A.E. Moore	C	1,705	22.0			
W. Brockington	L	1,512	19.5			
I. Thomas	C	1,465	18.9			
R.E. Phillips	Lab	769	9.9			
A.V. Hobbs	Lab	388	5.0			
Total votes		7,761				
Total voters		2,794				
1923						
I. Thomas	C	1,341	44.8	5,832	51.4	C from L
L. Francis	Ind L	886	29.6			
R.E. Phillips	Lab	769	25.7			
Total votes		2,996				
1924						
E.J. Moore	C	2,160	71.4	5,832	51.9	-
R.E. Phillips	Lab	864	28.6			
Total votes		3,024				
1925						
A.E. Lougher*	C	2,037	61.0	6,845	48.8	-
R.E. Phillips	Lab	1,300	39.0			
Total votes		3,337				
1926						
W.S. Courtis*	C	2,026	51.3	7,684	51.4	-
R.E. Phillips	Lab	1,923	48.7			
Total votes		3,949				
1927						
R.E. Phillips	Lab	2,163	51.8	8,644	48.3	Lab from C
E.J. Moore*	C	2,013	48.2			
Total votes		4,176				

Llandaff ward *(continued)*

Candidate	Party	Votes	%	Electors	Turnout	Gains
1928						
E.J. Draper	Lab	2,890	51.3	9,912	56.8	Lab from C
A.E. Lougher*	C	2,742	48.7			
Total votes		5,632				
1929						
W.H.J. Muston	Lab	2,697	52.8	11,567	44.2	Lab from A-S
Miss E. Ingledew	A-S	2,412	47.2			
Total votes		5,109				
1930						
C.G. Moreland	A-S	2,990	51.8	11,890	48.5	A-S from Lab
R.E. Phillips*	Lab	2,779	48.2			
Total votes		5,769				
1931						
G.E.B. Frewer	Ind	3,421	55.7	12,621	48.7	Ind from Lab
E.J. Draper*	Lab	1,982	32.3			
T. Price	Ex-S	742	12.1			
Total votes		6,145				
1932						
W.H.J. Muston*	Lab	3,058	56.0	13,057	41.8	-
T.L. Francis	R	2,403	44.0			
Total votes		5,461				
1933						
C.G. Moreland*	Ind	3,881	56.1	13,302	52.0	-
Mrs K. Saunders	Lab	3,032	43.9			
Total votes		6,913				
1934						
G.E.B. Frewer*	Ind	3,300	50.5	13,701	47.7	-
Mrs K. Saunders	Lab	3,240	49.5			
Total votes		6,540				
1935						
W.H.J. Muston*	Lab	Unopp.	-	14,550	-	-

Llandaff ward *(continued)*

Candidate	Party	Votes	%	Electors	Turnout	Gains
1936						
C.G. Moreland*	Ind	2,644	73.3	7,934	45.4	-
Mrs R. Davies	Lab	961	26.7			
Total votes		3,605				
1937						
G.E.B. Frewer	Ind	2,642	69.1	8,563	44.7	-
Mrs R. Davies	Lab	1,184	30.9			
Total votes		3,826				
1938						
F. Edwards*	Ind	2,641	66.0	8,435	47.4	-
H.T. Beach	Lab	1,359	34.0			
Total votes		4,000				

Overall Labour vote   **41.8%**   **Overall turnout**   **48.3%**

Park ward
(abolished 1922)

Candidate	Party	Votes	%	Electors	Turnout	Gains
1919						
R.G.H Snook*	L	1,087	48.0	9,189	24.7	-
D. Skelly	Al	1,027	45.3			
A.H.Teague	Ind	152	6.7			
Total votes		2,266				
1920						
E.C. Willmott	C	2,484	42.3	10,045	58.5	C from L
W. Charles*	L	2,141	36.4			
D.J. Skelly	Lab	1,249	21.3			
Total votes		5,874				
1921						
W.H. Pethybridge*	L	3,144	59.4	9,497	55.7	-
F.T. Mossford	Ind C	1,690	32.0			
F.C. Potter	Nuwm	455	8.6			
Total votes		5,289				

Overall Labour vote   **9.3%**   **Overall turnout**   **46.7%**

Penylan ward
(added by extension of the borough in 1922)

Candidate	Party	Votes	%	Electors	Turnout	Gains
1922						
W.H. Pethybridge*	L	2,414	34.0	5,242	54.2	-
R.G.H. Snook*	L	1,985	27.9			
T. Harrison	C	1,900	26.7			
M. Edwards	Lab	809	11.4			
Total votes		7,108				
Total voters		2,843				
1923						
W. Charles	L	1,319	50.7	5,476	47.5	L from C
T. Harrison*	C	1,282	49.3			
Total votes		2,601				
1924						
R.G.H. Snook*	L	Unopp.	-	5,593	-	-
1925						
J. Thomas*	L	1,848	53.6	5,811	59.3	-
T. Harrison	C	1,599	46.4			
Total votes		3,447				
1926						
W. Charles*	L	Unopp.	-	6,000	-	-
1927						
R.G.H. Snook*	L	Unopp.	-	6,136	-	-
1928						
G. Williams	L	2,050	49.7	6,304	65.5	-
T.R. Evans	C	1,247	30.2			
R. Stanton	Lab	831	20.1			
Total votes		4,128				
1929						
G.J. Ferguson*	A-S	2,426	75.3	6,901	46.7	-
I.T. Rees	Lab	795	24.7			
Total votes		3,221				

Penylan ward *(continued)*

Candidate	Party	Votes	%	Electors	Turnout	Gains
1930						
R.G. Robinson*	A-S	2,582	79.0	7,089	46.1	-
F.A. Beard	Lab	688	21.0			
Total votes		3,270				
1931						
G. Williams*	L	3,493	83.4	7,196	58.2	-
G.P. Roberts	Lab	695	16.6			
Total votes		4,188				
1932						
G.J. Ferguson*	L	2,618	81.3	7,317	44.0	-
Mrs. E. Lonsdale	Lab	601	18.7			
Total votes		3,219				
1933						
R.G. Robinson*	A-S	2,401	74.5	7,505	43.0	-
H.G. Bartlett	Lab	823	25.5			
Total votes		3,224				
1934						
G. Williams*	Ind	3,050	82.7	7,732	47.7	-
J. Rogers	Lab	640	17.3			
Total votes		3,690				
1935						
G.J. Ferguson*	L	2,589	74.9	8,223	42.1	-
Mrs H. Evans	Lab	869	25.1			
Total votes		3,458				
1936						
R.G. Robinson*	C	2,645	79.5	7,765	42.8	-
Mrs H. Evans	Lab	681	20.5			
Total votes		3,326				
1937						
G. Williams*	L	2,713	80.2	8,179	41.3	-
Mrs H. Evans	Lab	668	19.8			
Total votes		3,381				

Penylan ward (*continued*)

Candidate	Party	Votes	%	Electors	Turnout	Gains
1938						
G.J. Ferguson*	L	2,731	73.1	8,138	45.9	-
T.E.A. Southern	Lab	1,005	26.9			
Total votes		3,736				

Overall Labour vote   **18.1%**   **Overall turnout**   **48.5%**

Plasnewydd ward
(added by extension of the borough in 1922)

Candidate	Party	Votes	%	Electors	Turnout	Gains
1922						
E.C. Willmott*	C	2,749	31.1	6,769	51.3	-
W.G. Howell	L	2,507	28.4			
H. Johns	L	2,281	25.8			
D.J. Skelly	Lab	1,296	14.7			
Total votes		8,833				
Total voters		3,474				
1923						
H. Johns*	Ind L	2,219	63.8	6,831	50.9	-
E. Lewis	Lab	1,260	36.2			
Total votes		3,479				
1924						
W.G. Howell*	L	2,335	71.8	6,691	48.6	-
D.J. Skelly	Lab	916	28.2			
Total votes		3,251				
1925						
C. Hoare	C	1,504	39.8	6,801	55.6	-
E.J. Sawyer	L	1,351	35.8			
A. Bartlett	Lab	923	24.4			
Total votes		3,778				
1926						
H. Johns*	L	2,496	65.3	6,759	56.5	-
A. Bartlett	Lab	1,326	34.7			
Total votes		3,822				
1927						
W.G. Howell*	L	2,277	67.7	6,608	50.9	-
Mrs A. Kerrigan	Lab	1,085	32.3			
Total votes		3,362				
1928						
C. Hoare*	C	1,663	37.9	6,583	66.6	-
E.J. Sawyer	L	1,368	31.2			
I.T. Rees	Lab	1,356	30.9			
Total votes		4,387				

Plasnewydd ward (*continued*)

Candidate	Party	Votes	%	Electors	Turnout	Gains
1929						
H. Johns*	A-S	2,576	64.0	7,310	55.1	-
Mrs A. Kerrigan	Lab	1,451	36.0			
Total votes		4,027				
1930						
W.G. Howell*	A-S	2,374	70.5	7,178	46.9	-
I.T. Rees	Lab	994	29.5			
Total votes		3,368				
1931						
C. Hoare*	Ind	2,753	73.4	7,207	52.0	-
Mrs A. Kerrigan	Lab	997	26.6			
Total votes		3,750				
1932						
H. Johns*	Ind	2,080	54.5	7,221	52.9	
H.G. Bartlett	Lab	1,028	26.9			
R.P. Green	R	710	18.6			
Total votes		3,818				
1933						
W.G. Howell*	A-S	2,177	65.3	7,217	46.2	-
G.H. Pugh	Lab	1,156	34.7			
Total votes		3,333				
1934						
T.H. Lovitt	R	1,274	36.8	7,088	48.8	R from Ind
G.H. Pugh	Lab	1,113	32.2			
C. Hoare*	Ind	1,074	31.0			
Total votes		3,461				
1935						
H. Johns*	L	2,152	62.2	7,103	48.7	-
G.H. Pugh	Lab	1,113	32.1			
Miss C.M. Hughes	PC	197	5.7			
Total votes		3,462				
1936						
W.G. Howell*	L	Unopp.	-	7,898	-	-

Plasnewydd ward *(continued)*

Candidate	Party	Votes	%	Electors	Turnout	Gains
1937						
T.H. Lovitt*	R	1,521	42.3	7,880	45.7	-
C. Hoare	C	1,150	31.9			
J. Dorgan	Lab	929	25.8			
Total votes		3,600				
1938						
D.T. Williams*	C	1,884	41.1	7,984	57.4	-
J.C. Peterson	L	1,631	35.6			
J.C. Harries	Lab	1,070	23.3			
Total votes		4,585				

Overall Labour vote   **28.4%**   **Overall turnout**   **53.5%**

Riverside ward

Candidate	Party	Votes	%	Electors	Turnout	Gains
1919						
R.C. Brittan	Ex-S	1,518	52.5	6,312	45.8	Ex-s from L?
S. Instone	L	698	24.2			
W.A. Plummer	Lab	674	23.3			
Total votes		2,890				
1920						
J. Daniel*	Coa	2,808	69.3	6,429	63.0	-
R. Hughes	Lab	682	16.8			
B. Janner	Ex-S	562	13.9			
Total votes		4,052				
1921						
C.W. Melhuish*	Coa	Unopp.	-	6,524	-	-
1922						
R.C. Brittan*	C	2,198	76.9	6,922	41.3	-
E. Williams	Lab	661	23.1			
Total votes		2,859				
1923						
Sir J. Daniel*	C	Unopp.	-	7,035	-	-
1924						
J. Young*	C	Unopp.	-	7,088	-	-
1925						
W.H. Parker*	C	Unopp.	-	7,240	-	-
1926						
Sir J. Daniel*	C	Unopp.	-	7,106	-	-
1927						
J. Young*	C	Unopp.	-	6,858	-	-
1928						
W.H. Parker*	C	1,980	62.9	6,773	46.4	-
F. Saw	Lab	1,166	37.1			
Total votes		3,146				

Riverside ward *(continued)*

Candidate	Party	Votes	%	Electors	Turnout	Gains
1929						
Ald. C.W. Melhuish	A-S	1,934	63.7	7,285	41.7	-
F. Saw	Lab	1,103	36.3			
Total votes		3,037				
1930						
A.J. Beecher	A-S	1,424	37.1	7,324	52.4	-
W.S. Courtis	A-S	1,337	34.8			
Mrs K. Saunders	Lab	1,079	28.1			
Total votes		3,840				
1931						
W.H. Parker*	C	2,452	71.9	7,345	46.4	-
Mrs K. Saunders	Lab	956	28.1			
Total votes		3,408				
1932						
C.S. Hallinan	Ind	2,002	63.9	7,479	41.9	-
Mrs. K. Saunders	Lab	1,133	36.1			
Total votes		3,135				
1933						
A.J. Beecher*	Ind	2,418	66.7	7,182	50.4	-
E.J. Draper	Lab	1,205	33.3			
Total votes		3,623				
1934						
W.H. Parker*	Ind	1,636	61.5	7,178	37.1	-
E.J. Draper	Lab	1,024	38.5			
Total votes		2,660				
1935						
C.S. Hallinan*	C	1,889	64.1	7,645	38.6	-
E.J. Draper	Lab	1,060	35.9			
Total votes		2,949				
1936						
A.J. Beecher*	Ind	Unopp.	-	7,487	-	-

Riverside ward *(continued)*

Candidate	Party	Votes	%	Electors	Turnout	Gains
1937						
W.H.Parker*	C	1,749	66.7	7,535	34.8	-
R.J. Skyrme	Lab	874	33.3			
Total votes		2,623				
1938						
C.S. Hallinan*	C	1,906	63.3	7,524	40.0	-
R.J.Skyrme	Lab	1,103	36.7			
Total votes		3,009				

Overall Labour vote   **30.9%**   **Overall turnout**   **44.5%**

Roath ward

Candidate	Party	Votes	%	Electors	Turnout	Gains
1919						
G.F. Evans	L	1,446	33.4	7,906	54.8	-
J.W. Pickles	Lab	1,159	26.8			
W.H. Lever	C	889	20.5			
Mrs J.P. Williams	Womeı	835	19.3			
Total votes		4,329				
1920						
A.J. Howells*	Coa	3,540	71.3	8,151	60.9	-
J.W. Pickles	Lab	1,424	28.7			
Total votes		4,964				
1921						
W.H. Lever*	Coa	2,970	65.8	8,401	53.7	-
Mrs E. Turner	Lab	1,543	34.2			
Total votes		4,513				
1922						
G.F. Evans*	L	2,933	78.0	6,555	57.4	-
R. Llewelyn	Lab	828	22.0			
Total votes		3,761				
1923						
A.J. Howell*	L	2,216	67.5	6,704	48.9	-
G.B. Smith	Lab	1,065	32.5			
Total votes		3,281				
1924						
W.H. Lever*	C	2,410	71.9	6,932	48.4	-
J.P. Collins	Lab	942	28.1			
Total votes		3,352				
1925						
G.F. Evans*	L	Unopp.	-	7,077	-	-
1926						
F.T. Mossford*	C	2,126	59.9	7,144	49.7	-
D.J. Skelly	Lab	1,424	40.1			
Total votes		3,550				

Roath ward (*continued*)

Candidate	Party	Votes	%	Electors	Turnout	Gains
1927						
W.R. Wills	L	1,494	39.5	7,056	53.6	L from C
W.H. Lever*	C	1,227	32.5			
A.J. Phillips	Lab	1,060	28.0			
Total votes		3,781				
1928						
G.F. Evans*	L	2,470	50.7	7,057	69.0	-
A.J. Phillips	Lab	1,353	27.8			
H.E. White	C	1,048	21.5			
Total votes		4,871				
1929						
Ald. Sir C. Bird	A-S	2,574	65.2	7,785	50.7	-
A. Phillips	Lab	1,372	34.8			
Total votes		3,946				
1930						
W.R. Wills*	A-S	2,528	61.6	7,748	53.0	-
Dr J.D. Williams	Lab	1,577	38.4			
Total votes		4,105				
1931						
F. Chapman	L	1,552	41.5	7,701	48.6	L from R
F.T. Mossford	C	1,449	38.7			
E.J. Moses	R	741	19.8			
Total votes		3,742				
1932						
H.E. White*	Ind	2,468	65.8	7,769	48.3	-
J. Rogers	Lab	1,284	34.2			
Total votes		3,752				
1933						
W.R. Wills*	A-S	2,396	64.8	7,685	48.1	-
J. Rogers	Lab	1,042	28.2			
J. Ward	ILP	257	7.0			
Total votes		3,695				

Roath ward (*continued*)

Candidate	Party	Votes	%	Electors	Turnout	Gains
1934						
F. Chapman*	Ind	2,514	71.7	7,729	45.3	-
T. Sweet	Lab	991	28.3			
Total votes		3,505				
1935						
H.E. White*	C	2,497	67.5	8,123	45.5	-
J. Rogers	Lab	1,203	32.5			
Total votes		3,700				
1936						
W.R. Wills*	L	2,130	70.9	7,757	38.7	-
J. Rogers	Lab	874	29.1			
Total votes		3,004				
1937						
F. Chapman*	L	2,104	69.1	7,770	39.2	-
J. Rogers	Lab	940	30.9			
Total votes		3,044				
1938						
H.E. White*	C	3,442	67.0	10,264	50.1	-
L. Abse	Lab	1,696	33.0			
Total votes		5,138				

Overall Labour vote		**30.1%**		**Overall turnout**		**51.2%**

South ward

Candidate	Party	Votes	%	Electors	Turnout	Gains
1919						
J.A. Thompson	C	764	71.9	3,694	28.8	-
J. Griffiths	Lab	299	28.1			
Total votes		1,063				
1920						
W.H. Renwick*	C	Unopp.	-		-	-
1921						
J. Trott	C	945	48.2	3,803	51.5	-
G.F. Sanders	Ind L	770	39.3			
C.L. Price	Nuwm	244	12.5			
Total votes		1,959				
1922						
F. Jones	C	1,625	61.5	5,789	45.7	-
F.W. Harford	Lab	1,018	38.5			
Total votes		2,643				
1923						
W.H. Renwick*	C	1,424	64.5	5,854	37.7	-
E. Williams	Lab	783	35.5			
Total votes		2,207				
1924						
H.C. Prickett*	C	Unopp.	-	5,622	-	-
1925						
F. Jones*	C	1,714	60.7	5,727	49.3	-
E.A. Robson	Lab	905	32.0			
J.R.Wilson	Com	205	7.3			
Total votes		2,824				
1926						
J.G.H. Owen	C	1,614	50.2	5,738	56.1	C from Lab
E.A. Robson*	Lab	1,604	49.8			
Total votes		3,218				

South ward (*continued*)

Candidate	Party	Votes	%	Electors	Turnout	Gains
1927						
E.A. Robson	Lab	1,739	54.1	5,663	56.8	Lab from C
H. Prickett*	C	1,478	45.9			
Total votes		3,217				
1928						
J.T. Clatworthy	Lab	1,759	49.4	5,691	62.5	Lab from C
F. Jones*	C	1,743	49.0			
R. Cosslett	Com	57	1.6			
Total votes		3,559				
1929						
F. Jones	A-S	1,760	54.0	6,175	52.8	-
A. Hunt	Lab	1,465	45.0			
R. Cosslett	Com	34	1.0			
Total votes		3,259				
1930						
J.G.H. Owen	A-S	1,953	55.7	6,096	57.5	A-S from Lab
E.A. Robson*	Lab	1,515	43.2			
R. Cosslett	Com	37	1.1			
Total votes		3,505				
1931						
D.T. Williams	Ind	2,128	63.4	6,161	54.5	Ind from Lab
J.T. Clatworthy*	Lab	1,144	34.1			
R. Cosslett	Com	84	2.5			
Total votes		3,356				
1932						
F. Jones*	C	1,658	50.5	6,266	52.4	-
F.W. Harford	Lab	1,582	48.2			
R. Cosslett	Com	41	1.2			
Total votes		3,281				
1933						
T.G. Leyshon	L	1,700	50.7	6,286	53.4	-
E.A. Robson	Lab	1,656	49.3			
Total votes		3,356				

South ward (*continued*)

Candidate	Party	Votes	%	Electors	Turnout	Gains
1934						
E.A. Robson	Lab	1,704	52.1	6,404	51.1	Lab from Ind
D.T. Williams*	Ind	1,567	47.9			
Total votes		3,271				
1935						
M. Cohen	Lab	2,086	50.7	6,529	63.1	Lab from C
F. Jones*	C	2,031	49.3			
Total votes		4,117				
1936						
H.G. Bartlett	Lab	1,364	37.4	6,597	55.3	Lab from L
E.J. Cazenave	Ind	1,207	33.1			
R.G. Shute	R	1,077	29.5			
Total votes		3,648				
1937						
E.J. Cazenave	Ind	1,801	50.8	6,568	54.0	Ind from Lab
E.A. Robson*	Lab	1,743	49.2			
Total votes		3,544				
1938						
R.G. Shute	R	1,809	55.9	6,531	49.6	R from Lab
Mrs H. Evans	Lab	1,430	44.1			
Total votes		3,239				

Overall Labour vote   **43.1%**   **Overall turnout**   **52.4%**

Splott ward

Candidate	Party	Votes	%	Electors	Turnout	Gains
1919						
G.B. Smith	Lab	1,964	48.1	7,207	56.7	Lab from C
T. Williams	L	1,550	37.9			
G.F. Willett*	C	572	14.0			
Total votes		4,086				
1920						
H.Hiles	Lab	2,295	51.2	7,257	61.8	Lab from Coa
F. Dash*	Coa	2,187	48.8			
Total votes		4,482				
1921						
Mrs R. Parker*	Coa	3,411	64.3	7,581	70.0	-
J. Lombard	Lab	1,897	35.7			
Total votes		5,308				
1922						
T. Williams	Ind	3,360	64.1	7,557	69.4	Ind from Lab
G.B. Smith*	Lab	1,882	35.9			
Total votes		5,242				
1923						
H. Hiles*	Lab	2,915	61.9	7,656	61.5	-
J. Gronow	Ind C	1,792	38.1			
Total votes		4,707				
1924						
Mrs R. Parker*	C	2,926	58.4	7,747	64.7	-
A. Lewis	Lab	2,083	41.6			
Total votes		5,009				
1925						
D.J. Jones	Ind	2,805	52.9	7,803	67.9	Ind from L
A. Lewis	Lab	2,497	47.1			
Total votes		5,302				
1926						
H. Hiles*	Lab	3,649	71.5	7,822	65.2	-
A.W. Prichard	C	1,453	28.5			
Total votes		5,102				

Splott ward (continued)

Candidate	Party	Votes	%	Electors	Turnout	Gains
1927						
G. Steele	Lab	3,029	55.1	8,061	68.2	Lab from Ind
Mrs R. Parker*	Ind	2,467	44.9			
Total votes		5,496				
1928						
A. Lewis	Lab	3,104	53.9	8,357	68.9	Lab from L
E.J. Wilmot	L	2,655	46.1			
Total votes		5,759				
1929						
H. Hiles*	Lab	3,520	64.7	9,536	57.0	-
T. Williams	A-S	1,920	35.3			
Total votes		5,440				
1930						
G.Steel*	Lab	3,497	55.3	9,623	65.7	-
Mrs R. Parker	A-S	2,821	44.7			
Total votes		6,318				
1931						
A. Lewis*	Lab	Unopp.	-	9,587	-	-
1932						
H. Hiles*	Lab	4,026	71.5	9,502	59.2	-
J.T. Roberts	R	1,603	28.5			
Total votes		5,629				
1933						
G. Steel*	Lab	Unopp.	-	9,717	-	-
1934						
A. Lewis*	Lab	3,586	62.8	9,877	57.8	-
F.G. Jeans	R	2,124	37.2			
Total votes		5,710				
1935						
Dr J.D. Williams	Lab	Unopp.	-	10,313	-	-

Splott ward *(continued)*

Candidate	Party	Votes	%	Electors	Turnout	Gains
1936						
G. Steel*	Lab	Unopp.	-	9,633	-	-
1937						
A. Lewis*	Lab	3,525	70.2	9,610	52.2	-
R. Hogan	Ind	1,493	29.8			
Total votes		5,018				
1938						
Dr J.D. Williams*	Lab	3,086	68.2	9,835	46.0	-
E. Moses	R	1,439	31.8			
Total votes		4,525				

Overall Labour vote		**56.0%**		**Overall turnout**		**61.6%**

NINE
Carlisle

CARLISLE

Carlisle was the county town of Cumberland and a cathedral city. Accordingly, it was still a centre of some significance in both secular and religious administration as well as being a long established regional market. Pelling observed that, along with Durham and Newcastle, Carlisle was one of 'the three oldest and most important administrative centres of the North of England'.[1] It had also had a military significance in the past due to its proximity to the Scottish border. It still had an important commercial role as the centre of western communications for the north of England and the borders. In the nineteenth century these advantages of location had been put to new use when Carlisle became a centre for both railway communications and the railway industry. The *Carlisle Guide* of 1881 emphasised the importance of the railways to the success and economic health of the borough:

> There are few towns which have more largely shared in the national prosperity resulting from the development of the railway system than Carlisle ... Railways gave the impetus to these strides of prosperity, which have gone on contemporaneously with the prosperity of the system that called them into existence. Carlisle is now the greatest centre of railway communication. East, West, North, South, the iron roads radiate from it. It is placed on two of the three great trunk lines which run from one end of the kingdom to the other, and has a short and easy access to the eastern and western seas.[2]

The railway and communications industry remained the core of the city's twentieth-century economy. The railway had arrived in 1838 and by 1876 seven rail companies operated to the city.[3] The city had also developed as the industrial heart of the county of Cumberland as well as its main market for both agricultural and manufactured goods. Second to the important railway and communications industry in Victorian Carlisle came textiles. Predominantly involving cotton spinning and weaving, the textile industry also included the manufacture of linen and woollens and general finishing. This industry provided employment for 20 per cent of the occupied population of the borough as late as 1871.[4] The industry, having partially recovered from the adverse impact of the American Civil War, was in difficulty again in the late nineteenth century, yet partially recovered during the inter-war years. By 1911 Carlisle had a total of 2,121 workers in textile bleaching, dyeing, printing and finishing and had two thirds of all the textile workers in Cumberland.[5] Other industries that played a prominent part in the

[1] Pelling, H., *Social Geography of British Elections, 1885–1910*, (Aldershot, 1994), p. 316.
[2] Quoted in Towill, S., *Carlisle*, (Chichester, 1991), p. 113.
[3] Turnbull, J. 'The Impact of Inter-War Housing on Carlisle, 1917–1939', (Ph.D. thesis, Lancaster University, 1991), p. 110.
[4] Marshall, J.D. and Walton, J.K., *The Lake Counties from 1830 to the Mid Twentieth Century*, (Manchester, 1981), p. 24.
[5] Marshall and Walton, *The Lake Counties*, p. 24.

Victorian economy and continued to be of importance after the First World War were food processing, light engineering and metal working, the manufacture of agricultural machinery and bicycles, iron and brass founding, as well as brewing, tanning and felt hat manufacture. Apart from the railways, important firms in the local economy and large-scale employers of labour were Carr's (biscuits), employing over 3,000 people in the 1920s, Cowans Sheldon (cranes), Metal Box Company (packaging from 1922), Morton Sundour (fabrics), and John Laing and Sons (building and engineering contractors).[6] It was a blow to the local economy when the headquarters of Laing's moved to London in 1922. Finally Carlisle in the inter-war years continued to be an important regional market, with banking and commerce providing clerical employment. Walton and Marshall point to the 'tendency to diversity' of Carlisle's industries.[7] By the period of this study Carlisle had 'a well balanced industrial structure'.[8]

Demographically the city continued to grow between the wars, though less vigorously than in the Victorian era, with 39,176 people in 1891, rising to 52,225 in 1921 and to 57,304 in 1931. It is significant that the city was not contracting in what was a period of economic difficulty for many county boroughs. The largest sector of employment for both sexes combined in the industry tables of the 1931 census was commerce and finance, with just under 17 per cent of the employed labour force, a total of over 4,500 workers. This illustrated Carlisle's importance as both a regional market and commercial centre. Perhaps of greater social and economic significance in an era when the male breadwinner was assigned greater importance was the percentage of men working in the rail industry. Amounting to nearly 16 per cent of the male workforce, over 2,800 workers worked for the rail companies, and Carlisle was in first place in the county borough rankings for that category. (See Appendix 11). In the broader transport sector there were over 3,500 workers or 13 per cent of the total employed workforce, mostly men. The food industry employed significant numbers of men and women, accounting for over 11 per cent of the employed labour force. With over 20 per cent of all women so employed and under 7 per cent of men, it was of more importance as a source of livelihood for the former. That other traditionally substantial employer of female labour, the textile industry, was still important in Carlisle in 1931. Over 10 per cent of the workforce in the borough were employed in the manufacture of textiles, with just under 7 per cent in the cotton industry. Employing over 1,000 women, King Cotton accounted for over 800 male workers as well. Another big employer of male labour was the building industry, where the huge municipal housing projects were important. Over 1,600 workers were employed in building, predominantly male and amounting to over 9 per cent of the total male workforce. From this industrial base, and with nearly 90 per cent of the employed population classed as 'operatives' in the 1931 industry tables, it is easy to see that Carlisle had a large manual working class.

[6]   Turnbull, 'The Impact of Inter-War Housing on Carlisle', p. 115.
[7]   Marshall and Walton, *The Lake Counties*, p. 227.
[8]   Fogarty, M.P., *Prospects of the Industrial Areas of Great Britain*, (London, 1945), p. 200.

This is not however the whole story in terms of the social structure of the borough. With over 20 per cent of all employed females in personal service, and with over 3.5 per cent of the total population in that category, Carlisle had a significant middle class. The borough was at forty-first position in the female domestic servant rankings, placing it almost exactly at the median point amongst the county boroughs in this indicator of social class. The modest strength of the middle class is reaffirmed by the city having under 3 per cent in the professional category, being thirty-second in the rankings, and being ranked at sixty-second in terms of the proportions defined as self-employed or managers.[9] In addition, nearly a third of the employed work force of Carlisle was female, employed in the traditional areas of textiles, the food industry and the commerce and finance sectors. The level of female employment in Carlisle was higher than average. In 1929 sixty-six women were employed in Carlisle for every 100 males, falling to fifty-two women for every 100 men in 1939. The equivalent national figures were 37.6 females employed in 1929 and 38.8 in 1939.[10]

With its balanced industrial and commercial base, the city performed comparatively well economically in the 1920s and in the turbulent years of the depression, being seen as 'moderately prosperous before 1939',[11] with lower than national average levels of unemployment.[12] The calamitous 1930s saw the areas of the older extractive industries in Cumberland beyond the city worse hit. Carlisle did not appear to suffer from being outside the Special Area Status of the West Cumberland Development Area set up in 1935.[13] In a 1930 report Carlisle, with 16.2 per cent unemployed, compared favourably with the Cumberland coastal belt which had an unemployment rate of over 24 per cent. Three years later, another survey still showed Carlisle's rate of unemployment lower than other industrial areas of Cumberland. Carlisle was below the national average for unemployment for every year up to 1935, but in the four following years was slightly above the national figure.[14] Although the council did not adopt a direct works department, the private builders contracted to construct the huge public housing estates before the mid 1930s soaked up much local unemployment. There were also some large public works which were undertaken in Carlisle in 1928. These included a water extension scheme costing £62,600, a sewerage works (£36,000), the widening of Currock Road (£3,375) and the laying of electricity mains for £13,000. The last of these two projects were partly financed from the Unemployment Grants Committee of the Ministry of Transport and the local press reported that all these works had been undertaken for the relief of unemployment.[15] Thus the Independent-controlled council, like many in the era, used public works to reduce unemployment in the borough.

The influences of ethnicity, religion and education require comment as factors affecting Carlisle's local politics. The Mechanics Institute, for example, together

[9] See appendices 3, 4 and 5 in this volume, pp. 685–687.
[10] Turnbull, 'The Impact of Inter-War Housing on Carlisle', p. 114.
[11] Fogarty, *Prospects of the Industrial Areas*, p. 200.
[12] Turnbull, 'The Impact of Inter-War Housing on Carlisle', p. 118.
[13] Fogarty, *Prospects*, p. 200, and Turnbull, 'Housing in Carlisle', p. 113.
[14] Turnbull, 'Housing in Carlisle', p. 113–114.
[15] *Carlisle Journal*, 1 Nov. 1929.

with the early Labour associations and the ILP branch had some bearing on the development of the Labour Party, as might the Methodist presence. The Methodist connection however is difficult to assess. It seems that the Wesleyan branch of the connection was important in the city and this would point towards a conservative stance towards established authority. There was also a strong Presbyterian influence in the borough, due to its proximity to Scotland.[16] It can be suggested that as an important centre of Anglicanism, and with its Wesleyanism, Carlisle had the basis for a strong Tory tradition. MacRaild has also noted the presence of Orangeism as late as the mid 1870s. Earlier in the nineteenth century Irish and Scottish immigration to Carlisle was substantial. MacRaild also estimates that by the 1880s there were between 3,000 and 5,000 Irish in the city.[17] Whether Orangeism, with its support for Unionism and the bolstering of local Conservatism, was still a factor as late as the 1920s, is debatable. No overt references to sectarianism can be detected in the press reporting of the local elections in Carlisle. Conversely, the establishment of a number of powerful textile industrialists in the Victorian age, together with broader Nonconformist influences, provided the context to the strength of Liberalism in the locality.[18] One additional point, the establishment of a female grammar school before 1914 may have had something to do with the relatively prominent showing of women in the municipal elections, and especially the presence of the Women's Citizens Association (WCA). The preponderance of female labour, especially in textiles, may also have reinforced the promotion of women in local politics.

Turning to local politics, in the 1820s the local corporation was Tory controlled, although by the end of the next decade this control was being challenged. The formation of a Carlisle Working Men's Club and a 'well earned reputation for radical militancy in the Chartist period' is evidence of at least some threat to the established local elite.[19] The local landed establishment provided political leadership in the borough. The Lowthers and Howards, earls of Lonsdale and Carlisle respectively, together with the Grahams of Netherley were the most influential from the upper class. Their power was to continue to have some sway in the first thirty years of the twentieth century. However, by the mid nineteenth century, the influence of these grandees was being leavened by the new industrialists, especially the inter-married cotton magnates, the Dixons and the Fergusons. This new elite was more Liberal-orientated than the old and was established in local politics by the 1850s.[20] Towill notes that late Victorian Carlisle was 'strongly Liberal' with industrialists in the forefront of local government.[21] Further Marshall and Walton suggest that by the end of the nineteenth century 'a small number of established notables dominated the town council, together with small tradesman and businessmen'. Carlisle council in 1895 was partly a

---

[16] Pelling, H., *Social Geography of British Elections, 1885–1910*, (Aldershot, 1994), p. 331.
[17] MacRaild, D., *Culture, Conflict and Migration: The Irish in Victorian Cumbria*, (Liverpool, 1998), pp. 30, 101, 142 and 144.
[18] Marshall and Walton, *The Lake Counties*, p. 110.
[19] Marshall and Walton, *The Lake Counties*, p. 10.
[20] Towill, *Carlisle*, p. 102.
[21] Towill, *Carlisle*, p. 117.

'shopocracy' comprising four minor gentry, four professionals, fifteen small businessmen and managers, seven shopkeepers and publicans together with four miscellaneous others.[22] By the early twentieth century, the city owned the usual public utilities as well as having a range of public health and educational responsibilities. In 1910 the council could boast that it had 'for many years pursued a vigorous policy, having carried out many important improvements'.[23] Even before 1914 the borough had commenced municipal house construction. This was to mature to a building programme on a huge scale in the inter-war years.

The ten wards extant between 1919 and 1938 had been established in 1912. In that year there had been a boundary extension adding a further 2,000 acres to the city. The new ward of Stanwix and Etterby was created in the extension and the district of Botcherby added to the city. The city became a county borough from April 1914.[24] With its 4,488 acres in area now fixed, Carlisle's ward boundaries did not change again between the wars. Concerning the overall political culture on the eve of the First World War, a civic pride can be detected together with two strongly established Liberal and Conservative parties of near parity in terms of council strength. Labour had a foothold in the city with an ILP branch together with a small presence on the council, never amounting to more than a handful of councillors. J.E. Hutchinson, for example, had entered the council on Labour's behalf as far back as November 1907.

A clear-cut spatial pattern of political support can be identified from the inter-war municipal election results. Much of the industry was situated in the south and west of the city, as were the main districts of working-class occupation, whereas to the north and east lay predominantly middle-class suburbs on either side of the river Eden. Thus Labour won most of its support in a swathe of wards from Newtown and Belle Vue and Caldewgate in the south-west, through to Denton Holme and Currack (sometimes spelt Currock) in the south, to St Nicholas's and Greystone in the south-east. Caldewgate along with Newtown and Currock were noted in the inter-war years for having the highest levels of unemployed and unskilled workers in the borough. Caldewgate and Denton Holme were also picked out in 1908 by the Board of Trade as wards where a large proportion of the city's workforce lived, and the former was noted as a centre of the cotton industry containing many one-room tenements. Currack was a ward where skilled manual workers lived, along with large numbers of railway workers, while St Nicholas's was another where the presence of railway workers was noted as 'strong', and on another occasion was described as 'predominantly working class'.[25]

The only exception in the south was St Cuthbert's, which was a long narrow ward taking in a large part of the city centre and stretching out to the southern boundary of the borough without including much residential housing. There were some skilled workers living here, but the ward was influenced by a preponderance of plural voters entitled to the vote not by residence but by the fact that they paid

[22] Marshall and Walton, *The Lake Counties*, p. 128 and p. 279.
[23] *The Municipal Yearbook*, (London, 1910), p. 49.
[24] *The Municipal Yearbook*, (London, 1914), p. 51.
[25] Turnbull, 'The Impact of Inter-War Housing on Carlisle', pp. 128 and 330; Towill, *Carlisle*, p. 103; *Carlisle Journal*, 4 Nov. 1919 and 5 Nov. 1935; *Cumberland News*, 4 Nov. 1922 and 2 Nov. 1926.

rates on business or commercial premises in the ward.[26]   Labour never once won a seat in St Cuthbert's between the wars. Aside from this Labour's opponents had equally solid support in three other wards in the northern and eastern suburbs, Stanwix, Rickergate and Aglionby. These were the three most affluent wards, where owner-occupation was most concentrated and where professionals, managers and owners of businesses were domiciled.[27] The persons per room figures of the 1931 census confirm the overall spatial pattern of Carlisle. The three northern suburban wards had very low occupancy rates between 0.70 and 0.73 persons per room, well below the average for the borough of 0.95. The southern wards, by contrast, were all above the average, ranging from 0.97 to 1.17 persons per room.

The extensive development of housing in Carlisle between the wars also tended to reinforce this pattern of political support. In proportional terms Carlisle built more council houses per head of population than any other county borough between the wars. Somewhere between 4,500 and 5,000 houses were built, equivalent to one house for every thirteen people in the borough.[28] All the major corporation estates were built on the outskirts of the southern belt of mainly Labour-supporting wards, whereas most of the private housing developments took place in the northern suburbs. The main council estates were Raffles (in Newtown ward, with 1,518 houses), Currack (Currack ward, 1,234 houses), Botcherby (Greystone, 544 houses), Petteril Bank (St Nicholas's, 404 houses), Longsworthy (St Cuthbert's, 300 houses), and Wigtown Road (Caldewgate, 289 houses). On the other hand, the main private developments were in the north, most notably in Stanwix ward, including the Knowefield estate (244 houses), Etterby Lea (112) and Croft Road (74).[29] Not all council-house dwellers were automatically Labour voters, of course, nor were all owner-occupiers uniformly anti-Labour. Nevertheless the overall effect of these housing developments was likely to reaffirm the pre-existing political predisposition of the wards.

Looking at the main protagonists in municipal politics now, co-operation between Conservatives and Liberals is the first thing to be emphasised. From the very first post-war election the Tories and Liberals acted together at the November elections against the Labour party. As the local paper reported, 'the Liberals and Conservatives did not oppose each other and ... in wards where either party was opposed by Labour, the Liberal and Conservative candidates had the support, generally speaking, of the members of both the principle parties of State'. In the following year 'throughout the city there was an alliance of the Liberal and Conservative parties against the Labour Party'.[30] This was not however the usual

---

[26] Turnbull, 'The Impact of Inter-War Housing on Carlisle', pp. 174 and 176.

[27] Turnbull, 'The Impact of Inter-War Housing on Carlisle', pp. 379–380.

[28] See appendix 16, p. 692, where the construction of 4,473 houses is recorded. It should be noted though that these figures were not for the entire inter-war period, some months in 1938 and 1939 not being available; Turnbull, 'The Impact of Inter-War Housing on Carlisle', pp. 125 and 288, puts forward a slightly higher total of 4,803 council houses; Lakeman, W., The Local Government of the City and County Borough of Carlisle, (Carlisle, 1958), p. 32, has a somewhat higher figure again of 5,065.

[29] Turnbull, 'The Impact of Inter-War Housing on Carlisle', pp. 122, 288, 404 and 491–3.

[30] Carlisle Journal, 4 Nov. 1919, 2 Nov. 1920.

scenario of many other county boroughs where a resurgent local Conservative party combined with a weak Liberal party. In Carlisle this was a case, at least in the 1920s, of a co-operation of equals. Thus after the 1919 elections the two parties were each represented by sixteen members.[31] By 1921 co-operation was transformed into an alliance of 'Independents' standing against Labour. With few exceptions this was to be the pattern for the next twenty years. A further help to the alliance was the fact that the two parties had no big differences in ideology, and largely agreed on practical issues of policy. They did so even on the most important issue in the borough, the provision of housing. Overall, the Tories and the Liberals had an agreed position on both the need for parsimony and value for money in the raising and expenditure of the rates.

The reality behind the illusion did change somewhat, however, as the Liberal element of the alliance faded. Disillusion set in among some old Liberal voters with the largely conservative thrust of policy. The Liberals began to be seen as the junior, and not very different, partners of the Tories. Others have identified this trend nationally, arguing that municipal Liberalism was destroyed after 1929 as a result of alliances with Tories.[32] This would have been all the more likely if the last vestiges of radicalism within Liberalism had been destroyed by the confines of alliance. In Carlisle the term 'Independent Alliance' was commonly used, although the name Progressive Alliance was utilised for one year in 1933. Little significance can be read into this change. As one of the representatives of the alliance said 'I have been on the council for the past 26 years, and for the past 20 years I cannot remember a contest conducted by Conservatives and Liberals as such. Everyone has been Independents on the Council, and they have also been Progressive'.[33] By the time of the 1934 contests the Independent political label was back in force. In the 1935 elections, a candidate gave a good exposition of the Independent position:

> Why do we ask the electors to support the Independent candidate in this ward? I think I am putting it fairly when I say that the Independents believe that municipal government is largely a question of good business management, combined with foresight and sympathy. The guiding principle of the Independent Party is good government of the city without fear or favour to any section of the community, but with a special desire to try and help those who are in poorest circumstances. They believe in action rather than talk; they think Party politics should be put on one side in City Council work. Finally, they claim they have taken a leading part in making the city of Carlisle a symbol of good and efficient government amongst the municipalities of the United Kingdom.[34]

Independents also attacked Labour for being a party machine, which often fixed and agreed policies before council meetings. This, it was alleged, was intrinsically

---

[31] *Carlisle Journal*, 4 Nov. 1919.
[32] Cook, C., 'Liberals, Labour and local elections' in Peele, G. and Cook, C., (eds), *The Politics of Re-Appraisal, 1918–1939*, (London, 1975), p. 171.
[33] *Carlisle Journal*, 3 Nov. 1933.
[34] *Carlisle Journal*, 1 Nov. 1935.

anti-democratic. One Independent, who announced that he was proud to call himself a Liberal, denounced Labour rule in which

> cut and dried schemes would be placed before the Council and voted upon without discussion or consideration by the various representatives of the different sections of the community ... They might as well have no City Council as be ruled by a majority who decided before they went to the council what they intended to do. That was not democracy or representative government.[35]

Labour's response to the apolitical stance of the Independents was dismissive. Thus a defeated Labour candidate in 1934 pointed out rather sarcastically that 'though the election was fought on a non-political basis, the Conservative agent was present'.[36] Similar sentiments were expressed in a speech made by George Middleton, the then Labour MP for Carlisle speaking in support of one of the Labour candidates at the 1927 elections. He stated:

> the one reason why they had fought the municipal elections under their political flag was that they saw things in an altogether different light from their opponents. They had heard until they were almost tired the cry during the election that local affairs should not be the subject of party politics, but should be considered by men and women assembled to do business in a purely business capacity. The last people in the world he would trust with the management of his affairs were some of the people who claimed to be business men. What was the use of sending men to the City Council who were independent? The word 'Independent' was all camouflage. They were all anti-Socialists, and if that was not politics he did not know what it was.[37]

Turning the attention now to the main opposition group in Carlisle, it has been claimed that Carlisle had the earliest local Labour party in England.[38] This claim is clearly of dubious value, given the problems of definition. It does suggest, however, the possibility of a relatively early labour organisation in the borough. By the 1890s, Carlisle did indeed have an established ILP branch. Carlisle Trades Council was one of the few bodies of its kind to be represented at the founding conference of the ILP in Bradford in January 1893, and Carlisle had one of the fifteen members of the first National Administrative Council of the organisation in the person of J.C. Kennedy.[39] More important to the labour movement in Edwardian Carlisle were the railwaymen and their unions. David Howell indicates that the railwaymen, a uniformed and respectable section of the Victorian and Edwardian working class, 'were crucial in the development of labour political

---

[35] *Carlisle Journal*, 5 Nov. 1929.
[36] *Carlisle Journal*, 2 Nov. 1934.
[37] *Cumberland News*, 29 Oct. 1927.
[38] Towill, *Carlisle*, p. 116–117, gives the date of foundation as 1889.
[39] Marshall and Walton, *The Lake Counties*, p. 137; Howell, D., *British Workers and the Independent Labour Party 1888–1906*, (Manchester, 1983), pp. 291–296.

organisations', especially in small towns and country districts.[40] Out of the sectional and craft unions of the Victorian railway era, the National Union of Railwaymen (NUR) was formed in March 1913. The NUR was very much an industrial union, and a relatively militant union in its early years.[41] As Philip Bagwell points out, although 'it would be a mistake to over-emphasise the importance of the spread of syndicalism as an influence in the consolidation of railway trade unionism, it would be just as much as mistake not to take it into account as a doctrine fervently held by a minority of active and influential members'.[42] Certainly in the years before the First World War, radicalism and solidarity were exhibited by the Carlisle railwaymen. The infamous case of the Aisgill rail disaster on the Settle to Carlisle line in September 1913 was a source of great anger to the Carlisle railwaymen. Samuel Caudle, a Carlisle driver and a respected member of the city's railway community, was held partly responsible for the Aisgill accident and convicted of manslaughter. Many railwaymen believed Caudle was taking the blame for both procedural failings and the prioritising of profits before safety by the Midland Railway Company. The ugly mood of the Carlisle railwaymen and the wider industrial context was reported to the Home Secretary by R.D. Denman, the Liberal MP for Carlisle. For a variety of mitigating factors, some political, Caudle was speedily pardoned, but the potential militancy of Carlisle railwaymen had been well demonstrated.[43]

The data presented below on the occupations of prospective Labour councillors in Carlisle show that over 40 per cent of them worked on the railways. Railwaymen plainly played a major role in the activities of the local Labour party and thus in the politics of the municipality. The desire of the local Labour party for both direct labour and municipalisation in the late 1920s and 1930s can perhaps be viewed as evidence of the lingering of a more militant tradition amongst the railwaymen, but countervailing political attitudes can also be adduced. These flowed from the continuing loyalty of the railwaymen to the company. In the inter-war years it has often been pointed out that a job on the railways was still 'a job for life'. Additionally 'the Company' was still pivotal to many railwaymen's lives, 'and loyalty was assiduously promoted by managers and supervisors'.[44] Additionally Howell has noted that 'the railway interest' in the Commons 'was dominated by reactionary Tories'.[45] Paternalism and deference played a part in the railway industry, and not all railwaymen were necessarily Labour supporters. Similar relationships and attitudes have also been noted amongst workers in the cotton industry, who also accounted for nearly 7 per cent of the labour force in Carlisle. Given the scale of municipal re-housing and the break up of mill communities, however, the survival of mill-owner paternalism in Carlisle seems

[40]   Howell, D., *Respectable Radicals: Studies in the Politics of Railway Trade Unionism*, (Aldershot, 1999), p. 2.
[41]   Bagwell, P.S. *The Railwaymen: The History of the National Union of Railwaymen*, (London, 1963), p. 333.
[42]   Bagwell, *The Railwaymen*, p. 327.
[43]   For a superb analysis of the Aisgill disaster, see Howell, *Respectable Radicals*, pp. 136–157.
[44]   Howell, *Respectable Radicals*, p. 3.
[45]   Howell, *Respectable Radicals*, p. 150.

less likely than continuing railway company influence. There was certainly a basis for a degree of working-class Conservatism in the borough, but overall the weight of evidence points to the majority of railwaymen and their leaders as being crucial supporters of the Labour party. In a number of years the railwaymen's voting preferences emerged as an important factor in the annual municipal elections.

Tracing the fortunes of the Labour party over the inter-war period, by the time of the first post-war election in 1919 Carlisle had an established local Labour party with a base of four councillors. The November elections in that year were held in the aftermath of the September national railway strike in defence of the recently-won eight-hour day. This was the 'definitive' strike in the industry and a victory for the union, and Carlisle was reported to have experienced an 'Unprecedented stoppage'.[46] The euphoria that followed the success of the strike undoubtedly contributed to Labour's success in the 1919 elections. It was reported that 'the greatest interest was taken' in St Nicholas's and Currock wards, 'where the railway workers are very strong', and it was pointed out that in St Nicholas's Joseph Henderson, who was a prominent member of the NUR and had acted as the secretary to the strike committee, gained the seat for Labour with the highest number of votes won by any candidate.[47] Labour made a net gain of two seats overall, bringing its representation on the council up to six out of the total of forty, soon to be increased by the addition of its first alderman.

As in most other boroughs, Labour then made heavy weather of maintaining the position it had won in 1919, and by 1923 it had fallen back to only five members on the council. The tide turned in 1924 and continued in the following two years, with a total of six gains. The importance of the strong railwaymen's vote for Labour was again highlighted in St Nicholas's in 1926, where 'hundreds of railwaymen' cast their vote for a railway storekeeper.[48] However, Labour made net losses of three seats in 1927 and 1928, in contradiction to the trend in most other boroughs. In 1927 Labour ascribed their losses to the 'wet weather', but as polling day in 1928 was described as 'fine' this excuse could not be repeated. The main reason for these losses appears to have been a belated reaction against Labour by railwaymen due to the consequences of the General Strike and the subsequent passing of the Trade Disputes and Trade Union Act of 1927. It should be remembered that victimisation of strikers was especially severe on the railways, and six months after the strike ended 45,000 members of the NUR were still out of work, over 10 per cent of its membership.[49] Given the sacrifices they had made, some railwaymen became disillusioned by the actions of the NUR leadership in the strike. The political general-secretary of the union and erstwhile Labour member of the Cabinet, J.H. Thomas, was widely perceived by the left as the chief 'traitor' to the miners' cause. Ordinary union members as well 'felt simply that the solidarity of May 1926 had been betrayed by their own leaders.'[50] At the end of 1926 Thomas retrospectively revealed that 'never once ... did I waver in my views,

[46] Bagwell, *The Railwaymen*, p. 387.
[47] *Carlisle Journal*, 4 Nov. 1919.
[48] *Cumberland Evening News*, 2 Nov. 1926.
[49] Morris, M., *The General Strike*, (Harmondsworth, 1976), pp. 99–100.
[50] Howell, *Respectable Radicals*, p. 238.

my certainty that disaster lay in adopting ... a general strike'.[51] Yet he had said nothing against the strike at the crucial pre-strike meeting on 30 April, nor had he considered resigning his position when the NUR supported the strike. At the TUC post-mortem on the strike in January 1927 the industrial general secretary of the NUR, C.T. Cramp, was prominent in declaring 'I do not believe in a general strike ... I have never believed in a general strike'.[52] Such revelations after the event must have caused resentment amongst rank and file railwaymen, many of whom had experienced serious personal hardship and distress for months after the strike. In Carlisle, where railwaymen were so significant, this resentment was turned against Labour, not immediately in November 1926 when the spirit of solidarity was high, but at the next elections in 1927 and 1928 following the dispiriting public pronouncements of their leaders.

By 1929 the impact of the General Strike had receded, and Carlisle shared in the general upsurge in Labour support, with two gains in that year. Two more followed in 1930, which were rather less predictable. It should be remembered that Labour in Carlisle had had a bad year three years previously in 1927, whereas in many other boroughs Labour lost seats in 1930 that it had won in good results three years before. Labour in Carlisle was then saved from the possibility of setback in the following disaster year of 1931. The local parties declared a moratorium on elections in order to reduce public expenditure in the context of the 'national' emergency.[53] Thus Labour lost no seats in Carlisle in a year where elsewhere Labour councillors felt the backlash of reaction to the failure and collapse of the 1929–31 Labour government. In the following four years Labour made gains again, and in 1934 came close to power. After the elections of that year Labour and Independents had fifteen councillors each, but the Independents had a majority by virtue of their holding all ten aldermanic positions. By securing all five aldermanic vacancies on 9 November Labour could draw level with its opponents as long as it won the subsequent by-elections to replace the elevated Labour councillors. They achieved the first part of this plan as illness prevented one of the Independent councillors from attending the crucial aldermanic election meeting.[54] In the event Labour failed to win all the resulting by-elections and Independent control was maintained. Labour had elevated its three councillors for Caldewgate to be aldermen, all of whom had won a degree of personal loyalty from the electors of the ward. Their three replacements proved less popular with the voters, and all three lost. The by-election in Currack ward was also lost, and only in St Nicholas's was a new Labour councillor returned.[55] In the following year Labour reached its inter-war peak of seventeen councillors, but it fell away badly in 1936, losing three seats. Labour also lost one of its five aldermen subsequently, and performed modestly in the last two elections before the war, only regaining one seat in 1938. As in many other boroughs, there was no presentiment in the late 1930s of the dramatic Labour victory of 1945.

[51] Bagwell, *The Railwaymen*, pp. 481–482.
[52] Quoted in Branson, N., *Britain in the Nineteen Twenties*, (1978), p. 202.
[53] *Carlisle Journal*, 3 Nov. 1931.
[54] *Carlisle Journal*, 2 and 10 Nov. 1934.
[55] Turnbull, 'The Impact of Inter-War Housing on Carlisle', p. 415.

The social origins of the municipal representatives of the two main groupings on the council can be established quite clearly. The occupations of all candidates in ten separate years have been collated.[56] There were in total 155 candidates in these elections, of whom there were ninety-two standing as Independents (or in some cases Liberals or Tories in 1920 or 1921). Amongst the Independents, nineteen were small businessmen, eighteen shopkeepers, ten professionals, nine manufacturers, seven retired, six were classified as housewives or unmarried women and five were auctioneers. There were also three categorised as 'gentlemen', three brokers, three secretaries, and nine miscellaneous others, including only one who could be defined as working-class, a railway worker. The ranks of the Independents were plainly dominated by a petit-bourgeois ethos, confirming another local study which concluded that the Independent councillors were drawn mainly from the 'small businessman' category.[57] By contrast there were sixty Labour candidates, amongst whom there were twenty-six railway workers, six clerical workers, six semi and unskilled manual workers and a further four skilled manual workers, three trade union and Co-operative officials, three shopworkers, three housewives or unmarried women, and six others. For Labour, the overwhelming predominance of railway workers is noteworthy, with the main sub occupation here being nine locomotive drivers, shunters and enginemen and five railway clerks. There were also three WCA candidates, all of whom were defined as married women.

In parliamentary elections Labour appeared to be rather more successful in Carlisle than it was in the municipal sphere. Between 1885 and 1910 the constituency had been a Liberal stronghold, never once being lost to the Tories, although the contests were usually fairly close.[58] This emphasised the traditional strength of both the main parties. After the First World War, a coalition Liberal held the seat in 1918, but George Middleton won the seat for Labour in 1922 and again in 1923 and 1929, having been deposed by a Tory in 1924. Carlisle fell to the Conservatives again in 1931, and remained in their hands in 1935. It is significant though that on the three occasions Middleton won there was a three-way split of the vote, with both Liberals and Tories standing against Labour. In fact Middleton never gained much more than 40 per cent of the poll in his three victories, whereas when he lost in a straight fight with the Tory in 1924 he received over 45 per cent of the votes, and again in the disaster year of 1931 he gained almost 43 per cent. The vagaries of the first-past-the-post electoral system were being demonstrated here. When two well-supported Liberals and Tories opposed Labour, effectively they split roughly 60 per cent of the votes between them, allowing the Labour candidate through to win with the other 40 per cent. This contrasted with the municipal elections, where Labour was invariably up against a single opponent, making it far more difficult for Labour to win seats. This puts Labour's apparently better performance at the parliamentary level in rather a different light. It should also be noted that the decline of Carlisle

[56] Calculated from declarations of candidates in *Cumberland News* for 1919, 1921, 1922, 1923 and 1928, and in *Carlisle Journal* for 1920, 1924, 1926, 1932 and 1934.

[57] Turnbull, 'The Impact of Inter-War Housing on Carlisle', p. 390.

[58] Pelling, *Social Geography*, p. 331.

Liberalism in the 1930s was also manifested in the parliamentary results. The Liberal candidate was still a serious contender with over 26 per cent of the poll in 1929, but on the next occasion a Liberal stood in 1935 she lost her deposit, winning only 10 per cent of the poll.

Returning to the municipal sphere, the political issues that dominated elections in Carlisle need to be examined closely. Inevitably the question of housing loomed large here. The council was proud of its inter-war public housing policy, claiming that the 'city's record in providing houses per head of population was the best in the country',[59] a claim substantiated by the figures quoted earlier. Before the First World War, the council had built forty dwellings at Barwise Nook in the Willow Holme district of Newtown ward.[60] Powerful trade unions were apparently 'largely responsible' for persuading the council to build this low-rent working-class housing.[61] The housing problem was further identified in a 1917 housing census commissioned by the corporation, which 'showed that there was a substantial housing shortage in the city, exacerbated by the unsatisfactory quality and condition of many existing dwellings.'[62] From the very outset at the 1919 local elections, therefore, housing was one of the main issues raised by all political parties. To an extent though there was a consensus on the need for council housing. Thus in the 1919 election, the Independent candidate in St Nicholas's ward was all in favour of the housing programme and wanted 'really good houses being provided for our people to live in, they being essential to good health'. It was pointed out at a Labour meeting in St Cuthbert's ward in the same year that 'all the candidates had declared themselves in favour of the housing scheme', and the Labour candidate reiterated his support, hoping that 'men would be sent to the Council who would convert dreams into realities and remove the city's slums.'[63] Overall the Independents displayed a relatively progressive attitude to the social ills of poor housing and shortfalls in the private housing market. They overcame their usual reluctance to spend the ratepayers money, and instead professed that 'efficiency' and 'sound management' could deliver 'value for money' large council estates. It should be noted that under the various Housing Acts, the great council estate building projects of Carlisle were funded partly from central taxation as well as the local rates.

The concepts of efficiency and economy, however, did engender battles with Labour over the means to be employed to achieve the ends. Many of the debates at election time focused on this, with Labour advocating direct works and the council's inauguration of a direct labour department. In March 1926 the town clerk wrote to the Minister of Health requesting information on direct labour schemes in other north-eastern boroughs as Carlisle wished to consider the feasibility of such a method of building council houses. The idea was quickly dropped, however.[64] Labour managed to resuscitate the possibility in the otherwise quiet elections of 1929, but an Independent stated that 'the arguments of the Socialist party had been

59 Turnbull, 'The Impact of Inter-War Housing on Carlisle', p. 125.
60 Lakeman, *The Local Government ... of Carlisle*, p. 31.
61 Turnbull, 'The Impact of Inter-War Housing on Carlisle', p. 202.
62 Turnbull, 'The Impact of Inter-War Housing on Carlisle', p. 123.
63 *Cumberland News*, 1 Nov. 1919.
64 Turnbull, 'The Impact of Inter-War Housing on Carlisle', p. 317.

absolutely exploded' on the question of direct labour.[65] Labour raised it again in 1932, this time as part of a public works programme of relief for the unemployed.[66] All this was to no avail, and private builders constructed the whole of the municipal projects in inter-war Carlisle. Six firms were responsible for the council estates, with two of them, J and R Bell and John Laing, accounting for 93 per cent of the total.[67] Questions of quality and location were also contested by Labour, but in the 1920s, when the majority of the municipal housing was constructed, Labour was anyway too weak to seriously challenge the overall drive of the housing programme. The problem for Labour was that the credit for the housing programme went to the Independents as the ruling group, and Labour's opportunity to exploit any grievances to electoral effect was limited. Labour sometimes tried to claim the credit for themselves, but how much voters believed this is open to question. Thus in the 1927 elections a Labour candidate 'contended that everything that had been done in providing Council houses in Carlisle had been done through the driving force – the members of the Labour party'.[68] An Independent rebuffed these kinds of charges in 1934, stating that

> the Socialist Party claimed credit for many if not all, of the latter-day improvements which have been brought about for local government affairs. Nothing could be further from the truth than to assume from the speeches made in open Council that the Socialist Party "run the show" ... Now if the Socialists have never had a majority and if the present state of affairs must be the result of the majority vote, how can the Socialist Party claim the credit for the present state of affairs?[69]

It is clear that the construction of council housing helped to secure electoral support for the Independents. They were proud of their record and naturally exploited it. Thus in 1935 an Independent speaker trumpeted their past achievements and future plans, both in terms of housing and other public amenities:

> When one remembers that Carlisle has spent over a million and a quarter pounds on housing, and nearly another million in providing the city with baths, electricity, gas, water, etc., one begins to realise what a responsibility it is to govern and to run a big city in modern times. What of future developments, so far as Carlisle is concerned? We have in prospect schemes almost as large – a housing scheme now in operation which will each year produce about 400 new working-class houses, an expenditure of more than £100,000 on improved sewering and sewage disposal, a new Police and Fire Station likely to cost about £60,000, enlargement of the Grammar School and the Girls' High School,

---

65 *Carlisle Journal*, 5 Nov. 1929.
66 *Carlisle Journal*, 25 Oct. 1932.
67 Turnbull, 'The Impact of Inter-War Housing on Carlisle', p. 317.
68 *Cumberland News*, 29 Oct. 1927.
69 *Carlisle Journal*, 30 Oct. 1934.

improvement and enlargement of the elementary schools, a new Library, and a reconstructed hospital at Fusehill – a programme which shows that the City of Carlisle and its officials are far from resting on their oars.[70]

There were occasions when some Independent councillors argued against the council's municipal house building, especially those who were involved in the privately-rented housing market. A detailed study of housing policy in Carlisle confirms, though, that a consensus emerged within the council over housing and that councillors 'no longer protested at the principle' of the corporation 'providing houses for the working class'. The differences were not of substance but 'generally related to the number of houses to be built, their size, facilities and rents.'[71] Thus in 1936 a Labour candidate wondered whether the flat-building programme would be within the means of working-class people and 'pleaded for more housing provision'.[72] There were also sporadic claims that some councillors were lining their pockets through the council's housing programme. Thus in December 1933 two Labour councillors accused Independents of owning some of the worst slum property in Carlisle, and of making substantial profits from the slum clearance schemes.[73]

Labour also made an issue of municipalisation, best exemplified perhaps in a speech made in 1927 at the municipal hustings by George Middleton. Middleton began by defending municipal control of the gas works and electricity generation plants from the Independent charge of being 'Socialist institutions'. Arguing that the Independents had misunderstood the nature of Socialism and that these municipal works belonged to the people of Carlisle, and indeed, that this was 'Socialism in practice', Middleton went further:

> The Labour party took up the view that if they had a publicly-owned service or undertaking or trading concern it was far better to have it administered and worked by people who believed in public ownership than by people who believed in private enterprise. All those people who claimed their suffrage as anti-Labour candidates were supporters of private enterprise and were opposed to any extension of municipal services. And if the truth could be wrung from those people, they were opposed to the present municipal services, and if they could by any means sneak some of these services back into private ownership they would do it. The Labour party believed they should extend the municipal services.[74]

He continued by advocating the municipal take-over of the bus service. To applause, Middleton then attacked the power of the clearing banks, advocating the public control of finance and the setting up of municipal banks. This was one of

[70] *Carlisle Journal*, 1 Nov. 1935.
[71] Turnbull, 'The Impact of Inter-War Housing on Carlisle', pp. 287– 288.
[72] *Carlisle Journal*, 3 Nov. 1936.
[73] Turnbull, 'The Impact of Inter-War Housing on Carlisle', pp. 288–290.
[74] *Cumberland News*, 29 Oct. 1927.

the fullest elaborations of the policy, but it was echoed in other speeches throughout the inter-war period. The call for municipalisation should be put into context. It was a fairly common theme of Labour in the inter-war years, and in that respect Carlisle was by no means unusual.

The scourge of unemployment and the vagaries of the Means Test also emerged as election issues, the former on a regular basis from the late 1920s, the latter especially in the 1932 election. It was not only Labour which addressed the issue of unemployment at election time. Thus an Independent in 1932 argued that unemployment was the one of the four major issues of that year's elections, the others being the means test, housing and education. With reference to unemployment, 'he would support any scheme to relieve it, preferably revenue-producing schemes, or some other that would be a benefit to all ratepayers.' These schemes had to be 'economically managed' and done by private contractors after proper tendering.[75] In the same year Labour's candidates campaigned strongly over unemployment and the Means Test. They hit hard at general injustices in the treatment of the unemployed, and especially the system of granting transitional benefit. Nationally it was claimed that the proportion of claimants absolutely refused benefit was around 20 per cent, while another 30 per cent were only being allowed reduced benefit. The remaining 50 per cent permitted full benefit were 'expected to live decent lives on 15s.3d. per week for a man, and 23s.3d. per week for a man and wife'.[76] Labour's strong performance in the period 1932–35 in many northern boroughs no doubt was due in part to dissatisfaction amongst working-class voters over the treatment of the unemployed.

The final question of some significance in inter-war Carlisle was the role of women in municipal politics. Over the twenty-year period in Carlisle, women stood for the council on thirty occasions, six times for the Labour party, and twenty-four times for all other organisations. This represented 5 per cent of Labour's candidatures, and a comparatively high 12 per cent of all others. It was also unusual that other parties put forward far more women proportionally than Labour.[77] Women were actually elected fourteen times in the November polls, and in addition Mrs Musgrave won in a bye-election in Rickergate in the mid-1920s. On only two occasions did a woman win as a Labour candidate, however, Elizabeth Welsh taking Currack ward in 1934 and again in 1937. The appearance of the WCA should also be noted, Mrs Buchanan winning Rickergate in 1919, and Mrs Reay unsuccessfully contesting Rickergate in 1919 and 1920.

The WCA had been pioneered by Eleanor Rathbone in 1913, who had believed that 'when women eventually won the vote they would require encouragement and education to make use of their new influence'.[78] The WCA was initially concerned with raising the consciousness of women who had not participated so far in feminist organisations. In 1917 it became a national body and in the following year its branches began to be established across the land. The WCA was a largely

---

[75] *Carlisle Journal*, 25 Oct. 1932.

[76] *Carlisle Journal*, 4 Nov. 1932.

[77] See table 10.1 on p. 656 of this volume for the comparative figures for nineteen county boroughs.

[78] Pugh, M., *Women and the Women's Movement in Britain 1914–1959*, (London, 1992), p. 50.

middle-class and non-party body, and it 'enjoyed a lot of common ground and common personnel with existing feminist groups'. In 1924 it merged with the National Union of Societies for Equal Citizenship (NUSEC), a similar organisation comprised mainly of 'educated middle class feminists'.[79] By 1919 the WCA had a clear political agenda to secure the election of women to local government and raise the general consciousness of women's rights and issues. In Carlisle, with Ella Buchanan as 'chairman' (sic) and Lilian Reay as secretary, the movement was particularly dynamic.

A meeting to support Mrs Reay's candidature in 1920, attended by 'about twenty ladies and three of four men', was addressed by a WCA member, Lady Chance. She thought it was 'plucky' of Mrs Reay to stand as she 'had so much prejudice to face', and outlined the reasons why voters should return women to the council:

> First of all, because the world is made up of men and women, and the help of women was needed in its government as well as that of men. Men and women looked at things from different points of view, and they wanted both represented. Every year bills were brought before Parliament affecting the homes, morals, and welfare of children, and municipal bodies had to carry them out when they became law, and the experience and assistance of women were needed in carrying out those laws. ... The subjects for which they especially wanted women on the City Council were education, infant welfare, health and housing, and she would like to see them on the Watch Committee. (Cheers). ... In the days of the suffrage fight they used to be told that women's sphere was the home, which was true; but many women had time for other things besides the home, and in some ways they sometimes had more time to give to public work then men, who had their businesses to attend to. If the home was woman's province they wanted experts to advise on questions affecting children and the home.[80]

The WCA also put questions on policy to other prospective councillors and MPs and subsequently advised women voters on the best candidates to support. The demands of the WCA and the basis of its feminism can be seen by the policies put to the candidates for Carlisle in the general election on 1924. These were all policies drawn up by NUSEC, and both Labour and Tory candidates apparently agreed to support them:

> 1. Equal franchise. 2. Equal guardianship of children. 3. Widows' pensions. 4. Equal pay and opportunities for children. 5. Employment of married women. 6. Equal provision of training or relief for women with dependents. 7. Equal moral standard. 8. Legislation for children of unmarried parents. 9. Separation and Maintenance Order Bill. 10. Women Police. 11. Nationality of

[79] Pugh, *Women and the Women's Movement*, p. 51.
[80] *Carlisle Journal*, 2 Nov. 1920.

married women. 12. Separate taxation of the incomes of married persons. 13. League of Nations.[81]

Some historians have portrayed pre-1914 'equality feminism' being replaced after the First World War by a 'new feminism', of which the WCA and NUSEC could be seen to be leading exponents. This 'new feminism' emphasised the special characteristics and needs of women, and some commentators have characterised it as failing to confront, and indeed contributing to, 'a reconstruction of gender that circumscribed the roles, activities and possibilities of women'.[82] Others have suggested that 'new feminism' engendered 'a new confidence by women in their rightful place in society',[83] while others again have argued that both these perspectives simplify a much more elaborate and subtle range of opinion.[84] It can be seen from the above passage that Lady Chance was firm in her espousal of women's rights and issues. Although promoting the notion of women in public life, she still saw women's role as centred in the domestic sphere, and their main function in public life to advise on those areas of policy that impinged on home and family. The middle-class ethos of the WCA was revealed as well by her assertion that men had their 'businesses' to attend to while women had more time for public work, a sentiment that working-class women in the 1920s were unlikely to have agreed with. The points put to candidates in 1924 reflect a similar emphasis on 'women's issues'. Arguably this evidence suggests a limited agenda both in terms of the class attitudes of the 'new feminism' and its views on gender roles. On the other hand, the arguments in support of women participating in the municipal life of Carlisle, and the detailed policy issues raised, were both elaborate and astute. They do suggest a confidence about women's place in society.

There was one further 'feminist' foray in Aglionby in 1930, by Miss Barnes for the National Council of Women (NCW). Carlisle had a branch of this organisation which had its origins back in the 1880s. The NCW served as an umbrella for an extensive range of charitable and religious organisations for women and by 1914 had 1,450 affiliated societies. After 1918 it was also a mainly middle-class body, with a rather vague social and political outlook.[85] Miss Barnes was seeking to expand women's representation in a ward which always had one female councillor between the wars. After Ella Buchanan had won for the WCA in 1919 she was returned subsequently as an Independent. This made good sense as the non-party nature of the WCA fitted in very well with the supposedly non-political nature of the Independent alliance. Mrs Buchanan was succeeded in turn in Aglionby by Mrs Isa Graham, but Miss Barnes was less fortunate, losing with 30 per cent of the poll in 1930.

---

[81] *Carlisle Journal*, 28 Oct. 1924.

[82] Kingsley Kent, S., 'Gender reconstruction after the First World War' in Smith, H. (ed.), *British Feminism in the Twentieth Century*, (Aldershot, 1990), p. 80.

[83] Davies, S., *Liverpool Labour: Social and Political Influences on the Development of the Labour Party in Liverpool*, (Keele, 1996), p. 180; see also Harrison, B., *Prudent Revolutionaries: Portraits of British Feminists Between the Wars*, (Oxford, 1987), p. 104.

[84] Alberti, J., *Beyond Suffrage: Feminists in Peace and War, 1914–28*, (London, 1989), p. 165.

[85] Pugh, *Women and the Women's Movement*, p. 69.

To conclude, Carlisle was a town dominated by the railways, which had a large working class and also a significant middle class. In the more industrial south of the borough resided most of the working class, while the north of the city consisted mostly of affluent suburbs. Relying primarily on the votes of the electors in the northern suburbs, an Independent alliance remained in power throughout the inter-war years. This alliance cloaked the continued strength of the Conservative and Liberal parties in the 1920s, and Conservative dominance in the 1930s. It was based on a perceived threat from the rise of Labour after the First World War, which by the 1930s was very real. The Labour party was heavily influenced by the activities and support of the numerous railway workers and their unions, and by the mid 1930s was close to winning power. Only the vagaries of the aldermanic system and a decline in support in the late 1930s prevented Labour from winning control of the council. The survival of the Independent alliance was also helped by its adherence to a policy of public expenditure to deal with social needs, in particular through a large-scale council-house building programme. However much this was couched in terms of economy and efficiency, and financed in part by central government funds, it was an impressive achievement which undoubtedly won working-class votes. Finally, the predominantly male world of the railwaymen was not one where women were especially active, and women's influence on the Labour party in Carlisle was correspondingly small. By contrast, middle-class women through organisations like the WCA, and also within the non-party embrace of the Independent alliance, did find a political role, even if their place was circumscribed to an extent by the idea of separate spheres for men and women.

A guide to further reading

Newspapers

Carlisle Journal
Cumberland Evening News
Cumberland News

Secondary sources

Lakeman, W., *The Local Government of the City and County Borough of Carlisle*, (Carlisle, 1958).
Marshall, J.D. and Walton, J.K., *The Lake Counties from 1830 to the mid Twentieth Century*, (Manchester, 1981).
Towill, S., *Carlisle*, (Chichester, 1991).
Turnbull, J., 'The Impact of Inter-War Housing on Carlisle, 1917–1939', (Ph.D. thesis, Lancaster University, 1991).

Carlisle wards 1919–1938

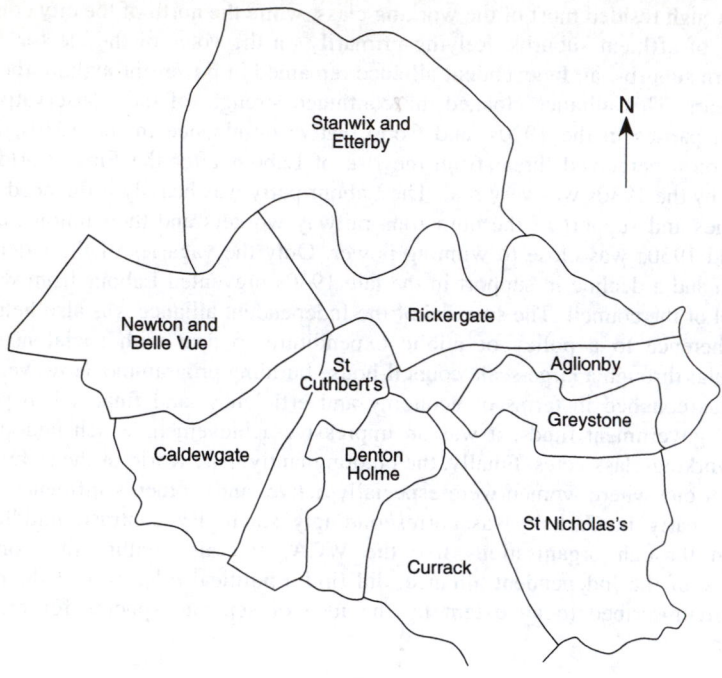

N

Persons aged fourteen and over classified by industry 1931

	Male	%	Female	%	Total	%
Metal and engineering	1,535	8.6	396	4.2	1,931	7.1
Textiles	1,394	7.8	1,510	16.2	2,904	10.7
- Cotton	*844*	*4.7*	*1,021*	*10.9*	*1,865*	*6.9*
Clothing	394	2.2	575	6.2	969	3.6
Food, drink and tobacco	1,244	7.0	1,976	21.2	3,220	11.9
- Food	*1,186*	*6.7*	*1,969*	*21.1*	*3,155*	*11.6*
Building	1,629	9.1	28	0.3	1,657	6.1
Transport	3,486	19.6	45	0.5	3,531	13.0
- Rail	*2,825*	*15.9*	*25*	*0.3*	*2,850*	*10.5*
Commerce and finance	3,161	17.8	1,438	15.4	4,599	16.9
Public admin. and defence	1,461	8.2	468	5.0	1,929	7.1
- Local government	*836*	*4.7*	*385*	*4.1*	*1,221*	*4.5*
Personal service	725	4.1	1,955	20.9	2,680	9.9
Other	2,777	15.6	944	10.1	3,721	13.7
Total (a)	**17,806**		**9,335**		**27,141**	
Total population (b)	26,570		30,734		57,304	
(a) as % of (b)	67.0		30.4		47.4	
Total out of work (c)	2,289		685		2,974	
(c) as % of (a)	12.9		7.3		11.0	
Managerial and own account	1,909	12.3	672	7.8	2,581	10.7
Operative	13,608	87.7	7,978	92.2	21,586	89.3
Total (excluding out of work)	15,517		8,650		24,167	

Population statistics 1931

Ward	Acres	Population	Persons/acre	Persons/room
Aglionby	274	4,715	17.2	0.72
Caldewgate	466	4,712	10.1	1.13
Currack	451	7,947	17.6	0.99
Denton Holme	261	5,190	19.9	1.06
Greystone	259	6,828	26.4	0.97
Newtown and Belle Vue	567	8,845	15.6	1.17
Rickergate	583	4,219	7.2	0.73
St Cuthbert's	265	6,280	23.7	0.97
St Nicholas's	556	5,040	9.1	1.02
Stanwix and Etterby	806	3,528	4.4	0.70
Total	**4,488**	**57,304**	**12.8**	**0.95**

Overall position on the council 1919–38

	Position		Gains		Losses	
	Other[a]	Lab	Other[a]	Lab	Other[a]	Lab
1919	34	6	2	3	4	1
1920	32	8	2	2	2	2
1921	33	7	1	0	0	1
1922	34	6	1	1	1	1
1923	35	5	1	0	0	1
1924	34	6	0	1	1	0
1925	31	9	0	3	3	0
1926	29	11	0	2	2	0
1927	30	10	1	0	0	1
1928	32	8	2	0	0	2
1929	29	11	0	2	2	0
1930	28	12	0	2	2	0
1931	28	12	0	0	0	0
1932	27	13	0	1	1	0
1933	26	14	0	1	1	0
1934	25	15	2	2	2	2
1935	23	17	0	1	1	0
1936[b]	26	13	3	0	0	3
1937	27	13	0	0	0	0
1938	27	13	0	1	1	0

Aldermen 1919–38

1919	Other–10	1929	Other–10
1920	Other–9, Lab–1	1930	Other–9, Lab–1
1921	Other–9, Lab–1	1931	Other–9, Lab–1
1922	Other–9, Lab–1	1932	Other–10
1923	Other–9, Lab–1	1933	Other–10
1924	Other–9, Lab–1	1934	Other–10
1925	Other–10	1935	Other–5, Lab–5
1926	Other–10	1936[b]	Other–5, Lab–4
1927	Other–10	1937	Other–6, Lab–4
1928	Other–10	1938	Other–6, Lab–4

[a] Liberal–Tory alliance operated from 1919, becoming known as Independent alliance by early 1920s; known as Progressives in 1933 only.
[b] 1936 – One aldermanic vacancy.

Municipal elections: winning party 1919–28

Ward	1919	1920	1921	1922	1923	1924	1925	1926	1927	1928
Aglionby	WCA	**Ind**	**Ind**	**Ind**	**Ind**	**Ind**	**Ind**	**Ind**	Ind	**Ind**
Caldewgate	C	Lab	Ind	Lab	Lab	Lab	**Lab**	Lab	Lab	**Lab**
Currack	Lab	L	Ind	**Ind**	Ind	**Ind**	Lab	Lab	Ind	Ind
Denton Holme	**Lab**	C	Ind	**Ind**	Ind	**Ind**	Lab	Lab	Ind	Ind
Greystone	L	C	**Ind**	**Ind**	Ind	**Ind**	Lab	Ind	Ind	**Lab**
Newtown	**Lab**	C	Ind	Ind	Ind	**Ind**	Ind	Ind	Ind	Ind
Rickergate	L	Ind	**Ind**	**Ind**	Ind	**Ind**	**Ind**	**Ind**	Ind	**Ind**
St Cuthbert's	Ind	L	Ind	**Ind**	Ind	**Ind**	Ind	Ind	Ind	**Ind**
St Nicholas's	Lab	Lab	Ind	Lab	Lab	Ind	Lab	Lab	Ind	**Lab**
Stanwix	**L**	C	Ind	**Ind**	**Ind**	**Ind**	**Ind**	Ind	**Ind**	**Ind**

Municipal elections: party wins per year 1919–28

	1919	1920	1921	1922	1923	1924	1925	1926	1927	1928
C	1	4	-	-	-	-	-	-	-	-
Lab	4	2	0	2	2	1	5	4	1	3
L	3	2	-	-	-	-	-	-	-	-
Other	2	2	-	-	-	-	-	-	-	-
Independent	-	-	10	8	8	9	5	6	9	7
Total	10	10	10	10	10	10	10	10	10	10
Turnout %	58.3	64.5	71.1	74.0	72.5	74.5	76.0	77.6	75.7	75.6
Labour %	39.0	38.4	43.3	53.9	41.3	50.8	52.7	50.4	40.7	48.0

Municipal elections: winning party 1929–38

Ward	1929	1930	1931	1932	1933	1934	1935	1936	1937	1938
Aglionby	Ind	Ind	**Ind**	**Ind**	Prog	Ind	**Ind**	**Ind**	**Ind**	**Ind**
Caldewgate	**Lab**	Lab	**Lab**	Lab	Lab	Lab	Ind	Ind	**Ind**	Lab
Currack	**Lab**	Ind	**Ind**	Lab	Lab	Lab	Lab	Ind	Lab	**Lab**
Denton Holme	Lab	Ind	**Ind**	Lab	Prog	Ind	Lab	Ind	Ind	**Lab**
Greystone	Lab	Lab	**Lab**	Lab	Lab	Ind	**Lab**	Lab	Ind	**Lab**
Newtown	Lab	**Ind**	**Ind**	Lab	Lab	Lab	Lab	Ind	Lab	**Lab**
Rickergate	Ind	**Ind**	**Ind**	**Ind**	Prog	**Ind**	**Ind**	**Ind**	**Ind**	**Ind**
St Cuthbert's	Ind	**Ind**	**Ind**	Ind	Prog	Ind	Ind	Ind	**Ind**	**Ind**
St Nicholas's	**Lab**	**Lab**	**Lab**	**Lab**	Lab	Lab	Lab	Ind	Lab	Ind
Stanwix	Ind	**Ind**	**Ind**	**Ind**	Prog	Ind	**Ind**	**Ind**	**Ind**	**Ind**

Municipal elections: party wins per year 1929–38

	1929	1930	1931	1932	1933	1934	1935	1936	1937	1938
C	-	-	-	-	-	-	-	-	-	-
Lab	6	3	3	6	5	4	5	1	3	5
L	-	-	-	-	-	-	-	-	-	-
Other	-	-	-	-	-	-	-	-	-	-
Independent	4	7	7	4	5	6	5	9	7	5
Total	10	10	10	10	10	10	10	10	10	10
Turnout %	**58.7**	**64.2**	-	**61.0**	**65.4**	**71.0**	**70.8**	**65.2**	**68.4**	**59.8**
Lab %	**41.3**	**41.6**	-	**53.2**	**44.3**	**46.0**	**52.5**	**42.9**	**57.5**	**42.0**

Municipal elections: party wins per ward 1919–38

	Other	Lab	Total	Turnout %	Labour % of all votes
Aglionby	20	0	20	56.2	12.5
Caldewgate	5	15	20	67.6	52.4
Currack	10	10	20	72.0	51.5
Denton Holme	13	7	20	72.4	46.4
Greystone	10	10	20	69.9	51.1
Newtown	12	8	20	68.5	50.3
Rickergate	20	0	20	55.8	14.5
St Cuthbert's	20	0	20	63.0	36.7
St Nicholas's	5	15	20	72.7	53.4
Stanwix	20	0	20	64.9	22.7
Total	**135**	**65**	**200**	**68.3**	**46.0**

Seats won by Labour as a percentage of all wins 1919–38   **32.5**

Parliamentary election results

Carlisle constituency

(all wards within the borough [1918 boundaries] were included in the constituency)

General election	Winner	Conservative %	Labour %	Liberal %
14 Dec. 1918	Co L	-	33.2	66.8 *(Co L)*
15 Nov. 1922	Lab	31.3	37.6	31.1 *(NL)*
6 Dec. 1923	Lab	39.3	40.5	20.2
29 Oct. 1924	C	54.5	45.5	-
30 May 1929	Lab	32.8	40.4	26.8
27 Oct. 1931	C	57.3	42.7	-
14 Nov. 1935	C	48.7	41.0	10.3

Aglionby ward

Candidate	Party	Votes	%	Electors	Turnout	Gains
1919						
Mrs E.S. Buchanan	WCA	624	58.1	2,044	52.5	WCA from L
F.J. Doidge*	L	450	41.9			
Total votes		1,074				
1920						
F.W. Tassell*	Ind	Unopp.	-		-	-
1921						
J. Fitzsimmons*	Ind	Unopp.	-		-	-
1922						
Mrs E.S. Buchanan*	Ind	Unopp.	-		-	-
1923						
F.W. Tassell*	Ind	Unopp.	-		-	-
1924						
J. Fitzsimmons*	Ind	Unopp.	-		-	-
1925						
Mrs E.S. Buchanan*	Ind	Unopp.	-		-	-
1926						
F.W. Tassell*	Ind	Unopp.	-		-	-
1927						
J. Armstrong	Ind	1,133	78.2	2,262	64.1	-
W. Johnstone	Lab	316	21.8			
Total votes		1,449				
1928						
Mrs E. S. Buchanan*	Ind	Unopp.	-		-	-
1929						
F.W. Tassell*	Ind	1,070	84.7	2,325	54.4	-
T. Rutherford	Lab	194	15.3			
Total votes		1,264				

Aglionby ward *(continued)*

Candidate	Party	Votes	%	Electors	Turnout	Gains
1930						
Dr. G. Sheehan	Ind	854	70.8	2,217	54.4	-
Miss M.E. Barnes	NCW	352	29.2			
Total votes		1,206				
1931						
Mrs I. Graham*	Ind	Unopp.	-		-	-
1932						
J.H. Minns*	Ind	Unopp.	-		-	-
1933						
Dr G. Sheehan*	Prog	902	80.6	2,036	55.0	-
A.C. Nelson	Lab	217	19.4			
Total votes		1,119				
1934						
Mrs I. Graham*	Ind	960	84.4	*2,015*	56.5	-
S. Armstrong	Lab	178	15.6			
Total votes		1,138				
1935						
J.H. Minns*	Ind	Unopp.	-		-	-
1936						
Dr G. Sheehan*	Ind	Unopp.	-		-	-
1937						
Mrs I. Graham*	Ind	Unopp.	-	1,951	-	-
1938						
J.H. Minns*	Ind	Unopp.	-		-	-

Overall Labour vote		**12.5%**		**Overall turnout**	**56.2%**

Caldewgate ward

Candidate	Party	Votes	%	Electors	Turnout	Gains
1919						
R. Burns*	C	788	65.2	2,024	59.7	-
Mrs McNaughton	Lab	420	34.8			
Total votes		1,208				
1920						
J.R. Potts	Lab	671	51.8	2,008	64.5	Lab from L
T. Thompson	L	625	48.2			
Total votes		1,296				
1921						
T.H.Jenkins	Ind	709	50.9	2,038	68.4	-
C.H. Lowthian	Lab	684	49.1			
Total votes		1,393				
1922						
H. Atkinson	Lab	716	53.9	1,970	67.4	Lab from Ind
G. Lavery	Ind	612	46.1			
Total votes		1,328				
1923						
J.R. Potts*	Lab	782	50.6	2,049	75.4	-
J. Farragher	Ind	762	49.4			
Total votes		1,544				
1924						
T. Dobinson	Lab	930	55.5	2,100	79.9	Lab from Ind
T.H. Jenkins*	Ind	747	44.5			
Total votes		1,677				
1925						
H. Atkinson*	Lab	Unopp.	-		-	-
1926						
J.R. Potts*	Lab	863	56.8	*2,053*	74.0	-
F.J. Tinn	Ind	657	43.2			
Total votes		1,520				

Caldewgate ward *(continued)*

Candidate	Party	Votes	%	Electors	Turnout	Gains
1927						
T. Dobinson*	Lab	881	57.6	2,030	75.4	-
Mrs W.T. Burns	Ind	649	42.4			
Total votes		1,530				
1928						
H. Atkinson*	Lab	Unopp.	-		-	-
1929						
J.R. Potts*	Lab	Unopp.	-		-	
1930						
T. Dobinson*	Lab	762	70.8	2,063	52.2	-
Mrs J. Mann	Ind	315	29.2			
Total votes		1,077				
1931						
H. Atkinson*	Lab	Unopp.	-		-	-
1932						
J.R. Potts*	Lab	676	53.1	2,016	63.1	-
J.K. Vasey	Ind	547	43.0			
G. Sarginson	Nuwm	49	3.9			
Total votes		1,272				
1933						
T. Dobinson*	Lab	776	54.3	2,053	69.6	-
J.H. Hayton	Prog	653	45.7			
Total votes		1,429				
1934						
H. Atkinson*	Lab	790	53.5	*2,053*	72.0	-
J.H. Hayton	Ind	688	46.5			
Total votes		1,478				
1935						
J. Thomlinson*	Ind	783	53.9	2,053	70.7	-
F. Glaister	Lab	669	46.1			
Total votes		1,452				

Caldewgate ward *(continued)*

Candidate	Party	Votes	%	Electors	Turnout	Gains
1936						
J.H. Hayton*	Ind	781	51.7	2,325	65.0	-
A.C.R. Punnett	Lab	730	48.3			
Total votes		1,511				
1937						
R.C. Chance*	Ind	Unopp.	-	2,440	-	-
1938						
A.C.R. Punnett	Lab	835	51.3	2,737	59.5	Lab from Ind
J. Thomlinson*	Ind	793	48.7			
Total votes		1,628				

Overall Labour vote   **52.4%**   **Overall turnout**   **67.6%**

Currack ward

Candidate	Party	Votes	%	Electors	Turnout	Gains
1919						
G.Mathers	Lab	688	61.1	1,974	57.0	Lab from L
C.H. Bonsfield	L	438	38.9			
Total votes		1,126				
1920						
R.G. Muckley	L	888	62.0	1,982	72.3	-
H.G. Potts	Lab	544	38.0			
Total votes		1,432				
1921						
T. Rutherford	Ind	819	57.8	2,043	69.4	-
W. Robinson	Lab	599	42.2			
Total votes		1,418				
1922						
T.L. Gill*	Ind	Unopp.	-		-	-
1923						
R.G. Muckley*	Ind	988	62.6	2,000	78.9	-
J. Wynne	Lab	590	37.4			
Total votes		1,578				
1924						
J.W. Nicholson*	Ind	Unopp.	-		-	-
1925						
J. Kelsall	Lab	1,034	51.8	2,553	78.2	Lab from Ind
T.L. Gill*	Ind	962	48.2			
Total votes		1,996				
1926						
W.H. Cant	Lab	1,216	51.9	*2,943*	79.6	Lab from Ind
R.G. Muckley*	Ind	1,128	48.1			
Total votes		2,344				
1927						
R.A. Clarke	Ind	1,414	54.9	3,333	77.3	-
J. Slack	Lab	1,163	45.1			
Total votes		2,577				

Currack ward *(continued)*

Candidate	Party	Votes	%	Electors	Turnout	Gains
1928						
W.H. Reid	Ind	1,287	50.5	3,365	75.7	Ind from Lab
Rev D.G. Morgan	Lab	1,259	49.5			
Total votes		2,546				
1929						
W.H. Cant*	Lab	Unopp.	-		-	-
1930						
R.A. Clarke*	Ind	1,446	57.1	3,634	69.7	-
T. Dalton	Lab	1,088	42.9			
Total votes		2,534				
1931						
W.H. Reid*	Ind	Unopp.	-		-	-
1932						
W.H. Cant*	Lab	1,702	65.1	3,767	69.4	-
E.J. Williams	Ind	912	34.9			
Total votes		2,614				
1933						
A.C. Powell	Lab	1,531	56.3	3,847	70.7	Lab from Ind
Mrs Scott-Nicholson	Prog	1,190	43.7			
Total votes		2,721				
1934						
Miss M.E. Welsh	Lab	1,525	52.2	*4,073*	71.7	Lab from Ind
W.H. Reid*	Ind	1,396	47.8			
Total votes		2,921				
1935						
T.D. Lancaster	Lab	1,733	54.2	*4,299*	74.4	Lab from Ind
W.H. Reid*	Ind	1,465	45.8			
Total votes		3,198				
1936						
D.C. Halton	Ind	1,545	51.4	4,525	66.5	Ind from Lab
I. Burrow	Lab	1,463	48.6			
Total votes		3,008				

Currack ward (*continued*)

Candidate	Party	Votes	%	Electors	Turnout	Gains
1937						
Miss M.E. Welsh*	Lab	2,083	62.4	4,792	69.6	-
J.D. Allen	Ind	1,254	37.6			
Total votes		3,337				
1938						
T.D. Lancaster*	Lab	Unopp.	-		-	-

Overall Labour vote   **51.5%**   **Overall turnout**   **72.0%**

Denton Holme ward

Candidate	Party	Votes	%	Electors	Turnout	Gains
1919						
E.Lowthian*	Lab	Unopp.	-		-	-
1920						
N.H. Grant	C	895	58.5	2,313	66.2	C from Lab
W.S. Parker*	Lab	636	41.5			
Total votes		1,531				
1921						
G. Rigg*	Ind	929	52.4	2,415	73.4	-
J. Coulthard	Lab	831	46.9			
J.H.C. Wilson	Ind	13	0.7			
Total votes		1,773				
1922						
I. Graham*	Ind	Unopp.	-		-	-
1923						
N.H. Grant*	Ind	1,033	56.1	2,509	73.4	-
J. Coulthard	Lab	808	43.9			
Total votes		1,841				
1924						
M. Thompson*	Ind	Unopp.	-		-	-
1925						
A.J. Watt	Lab	1,030	55.6	2,501	74.0	Lab from Ind
T. Rutherford	Ind	821	44.4			
Total votes		1,851				
1926						
J. Clarke	Lab	983	50.6	*2,456*	79.2	Lab from Ind
N.H. Grant*	Ind	961	49.4			
Total votes		1,944				
1927						
M. Thompson*	Ind	1,085	57.3	2,411	78.6	-
C. Kidd	Lab	809	42.7			
Total votes		1,894				

Denton Holme ward (continued)

Candidate	Party	Votes	%	Electors	Turnout	Gains
1928						
C.W. Hill	Ind	965	52.6	2,411	76.1	Ind from Lab
A.J. Watt*	Lab	869	47.4			
Total votes		1,834				
1929						
J. Coulthard*	Lab	870	55.3	2,567	61.3	-
F.J. Tinn	Ind	703	44.7			
Total votes		1,573				
1930						
M. Thompson*	Ind	972	58.4	2,063	80.6	-
B.B. Murray	Lab	691	41.6			
Total votes		1,663				
1931						
C.W. Hill*	Ind	Unopp.	-		-	-
1932						
J. Coulthard*	Lab	1,005	61.0	2,469	66.7	-
J.V. Fitzsimmons	Ind	643	39.0			
Total votes		1,648				
1933						
J.K. Vasey	Prog	913	51.5	2,473	71.7	-
F. Bolton	Lab	860	48.5			
Total votes		1,773				
1934						
H. Greenop	Ind	1,035	51.3	2,502	80.7	Ind from Lab
F. Bolton*	Lab	983	48.7			
Total votes		2,018				
1935						
J. Coulthard*	Lab	1,166	57.6	2,531	80.0	-
H.J. Rigg	Ind	858	42.4			
Total votes		2,024				

Denton Holme ward *(continued)*

Candidate	Party	Votes	%	Electors	Turnout	Gains
1936						
J.K. Vasey*	Ind	1,048	72.6	2,559	56.4	-
I. Norman	Com	396	27.4			
Total votes		1,444				
1937						
H. Greenop*	Ind	948	54.9	2,480	69.7	-
W.J. Hunter	Lab	780	45.1			
Total votes		1,728				
1938						
J. Coulthard*	Lab	Unopp.	-		-	-

Overall Labour vote **46.4%** **Overall turnout** **72.4%**

Greystone ward

Candidate	Party	Votes	%	Electors	Turnout	Gains
1919						
A. Creighton*	L	772	62.0	2,345	53.1	-
A. Burns	Lab	473	38.0			
Total votes		1,245				
1920						
T.V. Rutherford*	C	702	52.0	2,363	57.1	-
M.Y. Borland	Lab	648	48.0			
Total votes		1,350				
1921						
H.K. Campbell*	Ind	Unopp.	-	2,362	-	-
1922						
A. Creighton*	Ind	Unopp.	-		-	-
1923						
I. Gill	Ind	1,018	55.7	2,457	74.4	-
M.Y. Borland	Lab	811	44.3			
Total votes		1,829				
1924						
H.K. Campbell*	Ind	Unopp.	-		-	-
1925						
M.Y. Borland	Lab	1,020	53.8	2,540	74.6	Lab from Ind
G. Douglas*	Ind	875	46.2			
Total votes		1,895				
1926						
R.S. Harrison	Ind	1,049	50.6	2,524	82.2	
Mrs F. Elliott	Lab	1,026	49.4			
Total votes		2,075				
1927						
D. Thomson	Ind	1,090	52.6	2,508	82.6	Ind from Lab
S.W. Evans*	Lab	982	47.4			
Total votes		2,072				

Greystone ward *(continued)*

Candidate	Party	Votes	%	Electors	Turnout	Gains
1928						
M.Y. Borland*	Lab	Unopp.	-		-	-
1929						
E. Grierson	Lab	1,024	50.1	2,768	73.8	Lab from Ind
R.S. Harrison*	Ind	1,018	49.9			
Total votes		2,042				
1930						
W. Goody	Lab	923	50.2	2,988	61.5	Lab from Ind
G. Douglas	Ind	915	49.8			
Total votes		1,838				
1931						
B.B. Murray	Lab	Unopp.	-		-	-
1932						
E. Grierson*	Lab	1,397	66.1	3,308	63.9	-
G. Douglas	Ind	716	33.9			
Total votes		2,113				
1933						
W. Goody*	Lab	1,346	58.3	3,532	65.3	-
R.S. Duthie	Prog	961	41.7			
Total votes		2,307				
1934						
A.C.G. Thomson	Ind	1,338	50.5	*3,534*	75.0	Ind from Lab
B.B. Murray*	Lab	1,313	49.5			
Total votes		2,651				
1935						
E. Grierson*	Lab	Unopp.	-		-	-
1936						
W. Goody*	Lab	1,324	52.8	3,538	70.9	-
E.J. Williams	Ind	1,185	47.2			
Total votes		2,509				

Greystone ward *(continued)*

Candidate	Party	Votes	%	Electors	Turnout	Gains
1937						
A.C.G. Thomson*	Ind	1,384	51.5	3,650	73.6	-
B.B. Murray	Lab	1,304	48.5			
Total votes		2,688				
1938						
E. Grierson*	Lab	Unopp.	-		-	-

Overall Labour vote		**51.1%**		**Overall turnout**		**69.9%**

Newtown and Belle Vue ward

Candidate	Party	Votes	%	Electors	Turnout	Gains
1919						
C. Kidd	Lab	Unopp.	-		-	Lab from L
1920						
R. Cummings*	C	527	54.7	1,424	67.7	-
J. Coulthard	Lab	437	45.3			
Total votes		964				
1921						
R.C. Chance*	Ind	608	58.9	1,430	72.2	-
H. Atkinson	Lab	424	41.1			
Total votes		1,032				
1922						
J. Tomlinson	Ind	575	51.5	1,430	78.1	Ind from Lab
C. Kidd*	Lab	542	48.5			
Total votes		1,117				
1923						
L. Yates	Ind	682	58.9	1,440	80.3	-
C. Kidd	Lab	475	41.1			
Total votes		1,157				
1924						
R.C. Chance*	Ind	Unopp.	-		-	-
1925						
J. Tomlinson*	Ind	779	56.5	1,712	80.5	-
J. Clark	Lab	600	43.5			
Total votes		1,379				
1926						
R. Carr	Ind	764	51.3	*1,874*	79.5	-
F. Woodhall	Lab	726	48.7			
Total votes		1,490				
1927						
R.C. Chance*	Ind	997	57.4	2,035	85.3	-
F.E. Woodhall	Lab	739	42.6			
Total votes		1,736				

Newtown and Belle Vue ward *(continued)*

Candidate	Party	Votes	%	Electors	Turnout	Gains
1928						
J. Tomlinson*	Ind	928	53.3	2,318	75.1	-
S.W.Evans	Lab	813	46.7			
Total votes		1,741				
1929						
F.E. Woodhall	Lab	933	55.4	2,820	59.8	Lab from Ind
G. Dudson	Ind	752	44.6			
Total votes		1,685				
1930						
R.C. Chance*	Ind	Unopp.	-		-	-
1931						
J. Tomlinson*	Ind	Unopp.	-		-	-
1932						
A.H. Partridge	Lab	1,195	51.8	4,046	57.0	Lab from Ind
L. North*	Ind	1,112	48.2			
Total votes		2,307				
1933						
F.A. Finn	Lab	1,406	51.1	4,111	67.0	-
L. North	Prog	1,347	48.9			
Total votes		2,753				
1934						
H.P. Taylor	Lab	1,548	51.6	*4,164*	72.1	Lab from Ind
J. Thomlinson*	Ind	1,454	48.4			
Total votes		3,002				
1935						
A.H. Partridge*	Lab	1,559	55.9	4,216	66.2	-
F. Williamson	Ind	1,232	44.1			
Total votes		2,791				
1936						
A. Smith	Ind	1,464	52.5	4,395	63.5	Ind from Lab
F.A. Finn*	Lab	1,325	47.5			
Total votes		2,789				

Newtown and Belle Vue ward *(continued)*

Candidate	Party	Votes	%	Electors	Turnout	Gains
1937						
H.P. Taylor*	Lab	1,737	62.1	4,543	61.6	-
C. Clarke	Ind	1,062	37.9			
Total votes		2,799				
1938						
A.H. Partridge*	Lab	Unopp.	-		-	-

Overall Labour vote   **50.3%**   **Overall turnout**   **68.5%**

Rickergate ward

Candidate	Party	Votes	%	Electors	Turnout	Gains
1919						
J. Nichol*	L	388	34.0	2,047	55.7	-
D. Maclaren	Ind	330	28.9			
P. Kerr	Lab	221	19.4			
Mrs L.A. Reay	WCA	202	17.7			
Total votes		1,141				
1920						
D. MacLaren	Ind	783	71.2	2,086	52.7	-
Mrs L.A. Reay	WCA	317	28.8			
Total votes		1,100				
1921						
J.H. Minns*	Ind	Unopp.	-		-	-
1922						
R. Dalton	Ind	Unopp.	-		-	-
1923						
D. MacLaren*	Ind	1,034	74.3	2,267	61.4	-
T.W. Winthrop	Lab	358	25.7			
Total votes		1,392				
1924						
J.H. Minns*	Ind	Unopp.	-		-	-
1925						
R. Dalton*	Ind	Unopp.	-		-	-
1926						
J.C. Studholme*	Ind	Unopp.	-		-	-
1927						
Mrs E. Hallaway	Ind	706	49.5	2,285	62.4	-
Miss Musgrave*	Ind	503	35.3			
J. Wynne	Lab	216	15.2			
Total votes		1,425				
1928						
J.G. Dalton*	Ind	Unopp.	-		-	-

Rickergate ward *(continued)*

Candidate	Party	Votes	%	Electors	Turnout	Gains
1929						
J.C. Studholme*	Ind	777	76.4	2,180	46.7	-
D. Scanlon	Lab	240	23.6			
Total votes		1,017				
1930						
Mrs E. Hallaway*	Ind	Unopp.	-		-	-
1931						
J.G. Dalton*	Ind	Unopp.	-		-	-
1932						
J.C. Studholme*	Ind	Unopp.	-		-	-
1933						
Mrs E. Hallaway*	Prog	898	82.8	1,963	55.3	-
J. McCabe	C	187	17.2			
Total votes		1,085				
1934						
J.G. Dalton*	Ind	Unopp.	-		-	-
1935						
J.C. Studholme*	Ind	Unopp.	-		-	-
1936						
Mrs E. Hallaway*	Ind	Unopp.	-		-	-
1937						
C.K. Coulthard*	Ind	Unopp.	-	1,721	-	-
1938						
E.J. Williams*	Ind	Unopp.	-		-	-

Overall Labour vote		**14.5%**		**Overall turnout**		**55.8%**

St Cuthbert's ward

Candidate	Party	Votes	%	Electors	Turnout	Gains
1919						
T.G. Charlton	Ind	651	46.0	2,301	61.5	Ind from Lab
G. Riddle*	Lab	627	44.3			
R.W. Neale	Ind	137	9.7			
Total votes		1,415				
1920						
W. Vasey	L	1,019	62.0	2,273	72.3	L from Lab
G. Riddle*	Lab	624	38.0			
Total votes		1,643				
1921						
T. Rogerson*	Ind	901	59.3	2,270	67.0	-
J. Miller	Lab	619	40.7			
Total votes		1,520				
1922						
T.G. Charlton*	Ind	Unopp.	-		-	-
1923						
T. Holmes	Ind	1,086	66.1	2,488	66.0	-
J.W. Smith	Lab	556	33.9			
Total votes		1,642				
1924						
E. Grey*	Ind	Unopp.	-		-	-
1925						
T.G. Charlton*	Ind	1,024	56.2	2,567	71.0	-
S.W. Evans	Lab	799	43.8			
Total votes		1,823				
1926						
J.W. Osborne	Ind	1,032	59.3	2,545	68.3	-
R. Bolton	Lab	707	40.7			
Total votes		1,739				

St Cuthbert's ward (continued)

Candidate	Party	Votes	%	Electors	Turnout	Gains
1927						
E. Grey*	Ind	1,164	64.1	2,524	71.9	-
R. Bolton	Lab	651	35.9			
Total votes		1,815				
1928						
T.G. Charlton*	Ind	Unopp.	-		-	-
1929						
J.W. Osborne*	Ind	901	58.3	2,842	54.4	-
W. Johnstone	Lab	645	41.7			
Total votes		1,546				
1930						
E.Gray*	Ind	Unopp.	-		-	-
1931						
G.L.S. Lightfoot	Ind	Unopp.	-		-	-
1932						
J.W. Osborne*	Ind	806	62.6	2,820	45.6	-
J. Scott	ILP	481	37.4			
Total votes		1,287				
1933						
E. Gray*	Prog	1,179	71.8	2,795	58.7	-
R. Bolton	Lab	463	28.2			
Total votes		1,642				
1934						
G.L.S. Lightfoot*	Ind	1,177	60.5	2,789	69.8	-
J. Baxter	Lab	770	39.5			
Total votes		1,947				
1935						
J.W. Osborne*	Ind	894	54.6	2,783	58.8	-
J. Baxter	Lab	743	45.4			
Total votes		1,637				

St Cuthbert's ward (continued)

Candidate	Party	Votes	%	Electors	Turnout	Gains
1936						
W.L.Harris*	Ind	1,037	63.3	2,778	59.0	-
F.G. Cheeseman	Lab	602	36.7			
Total votes		1,639				
1937						
G.L.S. Lightfoot*	Ind	Unopp.	-	2,744	-	-
1938						
J.W. Osborne*	Ind	Unopp.	-		-	-

Overall Labour vote   **36.7%**   **Overall turnout**   **63.0%**

St Nicholas's ward

Candidate	Party	Votes	%	Electors	Turnout	Gains
1919						
J. Henderson	Lab	956	65.4	2,136	68.4	Lab from C
J. Fitzsimmons*	C	505	34.6			
Total votes		1,461				
1920						
W. Beckwith	Lab	698	53.0	2,116	62.2	Lab from L
J.C. Studholme	L	618	47.0			
Total votes.		1,316				
1921						
J. Gray	Ind	813	52.9	2,126	72.3	Ind from Lab
J.L. Robertson	Lab	725	47.1			
Total votes		1,538				
1922						
J. Henderson*	Lab	959	57.6	*2,152*	77.4	-
T. Brown	Ind	707	42.4			
Total votes		1,666				
1923						
W. Beckwith*	Lab	823	50.8	2,178	74.4	-
Mrs A. Creighton	Ind	798	49.2			
Total votes		1,621				
1924						
J. Gray*	Ind	957	53.5	2,554	70.0	-
J.W. Smith	Lab	832	46.5			
Total votes		1,789				
1925						
J. Henderson*	Lab	1,166	65.6	2,236	79.5	-
Miss Musgrave	Ind	612	34.4			
Total votes		1,778				
1926						
J.W. Smith	Lab	974	54.5	*2,217*	80.6	-
D. Barrett	Ind	813	45.5			
Total votes		1,787				

St Nicholas's ward (continued)

Candidate	Party	Votes	%	Electors	Turnout	Gains
1927						
D. Barrett	Ind	950	51.4	2,199	84.1	-
Mrs Elliott	Lab	899	48.6			
Total votes		1,849				
1928						
J. Henderson*	Lab	Unopp.	-		-	-
1929						
J.W. Smith*	Lab	Unopp.	-		-	-
1930						
G.H. Smith	Lab	Unopp.	-		-	Lab from Ind
1931						
A.J.Watt*	Lab	Unopp.	-		-	-
1932						
J.W. Smith*	Lab	Unopp.	-		-	-
1933						
T. Dalton*	Lab	955	55.8	2,356	72.6	-
D. Barrett	Prog	755	44.2			
Total votes		1,710				
1934						
A.J. Watt*	Lab	964	58.2	2,387	69.4	-
W.G. Laidler	Ind	693	41.8			
Total votes		1,657				
1935						
F. Bolton*	Lab	935	50.2	2,418	77.0	-
C. Hoggarth	Ind	927	49.8			
Total votes		1,862				
1936						
W.J. Foster	Ind	949	52.1	2,448	74.4	Ind from Lab
A.C. Powell	Lab	873	47.9			
Total votes		1,822				

St Nicholas's ward *(continued)*

Candidate	Party	Votes	%	Electors	Turnout	Gains
1937						
A.J. Watt*	Lab	1,138	67.3	2,425	69.7	-
W.J.E. Leary	Ind	552	32.7			
Total votes		1,690				
1938						
Mrs M. Fraser	Ind	929	59.1	2,613	60.1	Ind from
R. Graham	Lab	508	32.3			Peop
F. Bolton*	Peop	134	8.5			
Total votes		1,571				

Overall Labour vote   **53.4%**   **Overall turnout**   **72.7%**

CARLISLE

Stanwix and Etterby ward

Candidate	Party	Votes	%	Electors	Turnout	Gains
1919						
J. Wright*	L	Unopp.	-		-	-
1920						
D.L. Thorpe*	C	720	81.6	1,284	68.7	-
Mrs A.D.M. Fyfe	Lab	162	18.4			
Total votes		882				
1921						
H.W. Sewell*	Ind	697	69.5	1,286	78.0	-
W.D. Telfer	Lab	306	30.5			
Total votes		1,003				
1922						
J. Dodd	Ind	Unopp.	-		-	-
1923						
Mrs E. Sewell*	Ind	Unopp.	-		-	-
1924						
H.W. Sewell*	Ind	Unopp.	-		-	-
1925						
J. Dodd*	Ind	Unopp.	-		-	-
1926						
Mrs E. Sewell	Ind	Unopp.	-		-	-
1927						
J. Martindale	Ind	Unopp.	-	1,610	-	-
1928						
J. Dodd*	Ind	Unopp.	-		-	-
1929						
J.W. Storey*	Ind	684	72.8	1,638	57.3	-
A.J. Watt	Lab	255	27.2			
Total votes		939				

Stanwix and Etterby ward *(continued)*

Candidate	Party	Votes	%	Electors	Turnout	Gains
1930						
J. Martindale*	Ind	Unopp.	-		-	-
1931						
R.S. Harrison	Ind	Unopp.	-		-	-
1932						
J.W. Storey*	Ind	Unopp.	-		-	-
1933						
J. Martindale*	Prog	781	78.1	1,668	60.0	-
H.P. Taylor	Lab	219	21.9			
Total votes		1,000				
1934						
R.S. Harrison*	Ind	968	83.7	*1,795*	64.4	-
W. Warwick	Lab	188	16.3			
Total votes		1,156				
1935						
J.W. Storey*	Ind	Unopp.	-		-	-
1936						
Mrs Scott-Nicholson	Ind	Unopp.	-		-	-
1937						
R.S. Harrison*	Ind	Unopp.	-	2,176	-	-
1938						
J.W. Storey*	Ind	Unopp.	-		-	-

Overall Labour vote **22.7%** **Overall turnout** **64.9%**

CONCLUSION
The aggregate and comparative analysis

Conclusion – the aggregate and comparative analysis

It is intended that as each volume of this publication is completed, the electoral data for the individual boroughs will be themselves consolidated to give an aggregate analysis of electoral trends over the inter-war period. As the series develops, therefore, a more and more representative picture of the overall trends will emerge. At the same time, the boroughs will also be compared to one another statistically in terms of turnout and various measures of Labour party support. As further boroughs are covered in later volumes, it will also be possible to categorise them in various ways and analyse them comparatively. Thus regional trends, or trends in larger cities, or in textile towns, for instance, will be revealed. It is also intended that more qualitative comparative analysis of the different boroughs will be undertaken, taking up various contentious and important issues relating to inter-war politics such as the rise of Labour, the decline of Liberalism, the consolidation of Toryism, gender and politics, and so on. In this way these volumes should throw light on many aspects of the politics of the period.

These intentions can now be better fulfilled with two volumes completed. Nineteen of the eighty-three county boroughs have been analysed so far, almost a quarter of the total. These constitute a large enough sample of the whole to be representative in statistical terms. It is also the case that by covering the boroughs alphabetically, a suitably random selection has been made. It can be stated with some confidence that the aggregate trends revealed by the figures for the nineteen boroughs will hold true for the eighty-three boroughs as a whole.

The aggregate analysis

Consolidated figures for the nineteen Volume One and Volume Two boroughs, consisting of various measures of voter support and involvement in municipal elections, are presented below. These provide a view of the overall inter-war trends in the county boroughs, but it is important to be aware of the limitations to the data collected in the series as a whole. First, these figures relate to county boroughs in England and Wales only, excluding Scotland and Ireland (pre- and post-partition). Second, the county boroughs themselves mainly comprised the larger urban centres, all but three of them having a population over 50,000 in 1931. However, there were a number of other local authorities, mostly fast-growing urban district councils in the south-east such as Willesden, Tottenham and Dagenham, and one or two others such as Rhondda and Stretford, which also had populations of over 50,000. As already stated in the introduction to this volume, these authorities held their elections in the spring, and therefore cannot be directly compared with the county boroughs. The biggest urban centre of all, London, was largely represented in its own metropolitan boroughs, with only three county boroughs in the London area, West and East Ham and Croydon, persisting in their own right after the 1899 legislation. Elections were held every three years in the London boroughs, with all councillors coming up for election at the same time.

Additionally, there was only one alderman to every six councillors in these authorities, and for both these reasons the metropolitan boroughs were also not directly comparable to the county boroughs. Third, a significant proportion of the parliamentary electorate (varying somewhere between 10 and 20 per cent over the whole inter-war period) was excluded from municipal elections due to differences in the franchise.[1] In sum then, the county borough elections reflected the voters' preferences of the municipal electorate of most of the larger provincial urban centres of England and Wales. They cannot be taken to be fully representative of the whole voting-age population of Great Britain. In terms of political allegiance, relatively strong Labour-supporting areas at this time such as London, south-west Scotland, and most of the semi-rural coal-mining districts such as South Wales and the North-East, are not included. On the other hand, the predominantly Conservative agrarian rural areas are also missing. It may also be the case that the franchise exclusions favoured Labour's opponents in municipal elections, although this is by no means certain.[2]

A further qualification needs to be considered. In parliamentary elections between the wars most constituencies were usually contested. Only the 1918 and 1931 general elections were exceptions to this rule, for contingent reasons. The effect of unopposed coalition candidates and Sinn Fein candidates in Ireland in 1918 resulted in 107 out of the total of 707 seats being uncontested. The national coalition of 1931 resulted in sixty-seven no-contests out of 615 seats. Fewer than 10 per cent of constituencies were uncontested in all other cases, and in 1929 only three seats in the whole of England, Wales and Scotland were not contested.[3] By contrast, far more elections tended to be uncontested at the municipal level. This was especially the case in the smaller, or more rural, authorities, and also in the London boroughs. At the municipal level, the county boroughs on the whole had the lowest level of no-contests. Even so, as the evidence for Burton or Canterbury in this volume plainly shows, many seats could still be uncontested. The majority of no-contests in this period took place in seats where Labour had little chance of success, and therefore did not put up candidates against its opponents. This tended to make Labour's performance seem better than it really was. Many non-Labour votes, that would have been cast in great numbers in these seats if contests had taken place, were excluded. The decision in these volumes to calculate the Labour vote as a percentage of all votes cast, rather than as a percentage of votes cast only in the seats Labour contested, partially compensates for this. The greater the number of wards Labour conceded without a contest, then the less its total vote tended to be as a proportion of all votes. This was because non-Labour votes would build up in those seats where parties other than Labour confronted each other. This measure thus gives a more realistic impression of Labour's support. Nevertheless, no-contests still produce a distorting effect on the electoral data that

[1] On the franchise and aldermanic systems, see the notes at the end of this volume, pp. 676–677.

[2] Evidence for Liverpool may support this possibility. See Davies, S., *Liverpool Labour: Social and Political Influences on the development of the Labour Party in Liverpool, 1900–1939*, (Keele, 1996), pp. 119–126.

[3] See Craig, F.W.S., *British Electoral Facts 1832–1987*, (Dartmouth, 5th edn, 1989), pp. 21–33.

cannot be precisely quantified. Summary figures for uncontested seats in the nineteen Volume One and Volume Two boroughs are shown below at the end of this chapter in Table 10.3.[4]

Taking all these factors together, one other point needs to be made. However imperfect the aggregate figures of county borough elections may be, the data still constitutes a valuable indicator of trends over time. The distortions can be regarded for the most part as constant factors, affecting the data more or less equally from year to year. The eighty-three county boroughs can be seen in themselves as a large and constant sample, providing a unique view of changes in political support over the twenty-year period. Keeping all these qualifications in mind, therefore, the aggregate figures for the nineteen boroughs in the first two volumes of this series are summarised at the end of this chapter in Tables 10.1, 10.2 and 10.3. It should be noted that the decision to measure party support only in terms of the Labour Party has been taken on entirely pragmatic grounds. Labour was the only party that consistently stood under its proper name throughout the country in municipal politics at this time. In some boroughs the other main parties were sometimes in alliance, and also adopted different names at times. Only Labour, therefore, can be clearly identified for these purposes.

Analysing the trends shown in the three tables, Labour started in the November 1919 municipal elections by winning 37.8 per cent of the votes cast in these nineteen boroughs. This was a dramatic increase from its pre-war position, and a far better performance than it had managed in the 'coupon' general election of December 1918. The heightened social tension and industrial conflict that came in 1919 may have been an underlying factor in Labour's rise this year. Labour may also have been helped by its new constitution, including the famous Clause IV commitment to greater public ownership, and its new and more effective organisational structure. Labour's good performance was also reflected in the fact that it won 37.5 per cent of all seats decided that year. Labour success was achieved on a low turnout of only 43.8 per cent, a feature that was to be repeated on a number of occasions between the wars. This contrasts very much with the post-1945 conventional political wisdom, which has maintained that low turnout has usually hurt Labour most. It should also be noted that Labour did not contest 28.6 per cent of all the seats available, but only 11.6 per cent of all seats were actually no-contests. This meant that Labour's share of the overall vote would have been lowered, as many non-Labour votes were cast in contests where they had no candidate. As a result of the 1919 net gains, sixty-three in total, Labour held 17.4 per cent of all the seats on the nineteen councils after the elections. This total included aldermanic seats as well, of which Labour held only 5 per cent. Labour in fact held 21.5 per cent of the elected councillors.

After this good start, Labour fell back sharply in 1920 on a much higher turnout of 52.6 per cent. Its share of the vote fell to its lowest point between the wars, although the fall from the previous year did not appear so dramatic. This was to some extent due to the contrast being with the artificially-lowered 1919 figure

---

[4]   The figures for no-contests in this volume tend to conflict with the view put elsewhere that there were 'relatively few uncontested elections' in the 1920s; see Cook, C., *The Age of Alignment: Electoral Politics in Britain, 1922–1929*, (London, 1975), pp. 49, 66.

described above. This time far fewer seats where Labour did not stand were contested by other parties, so large numbers of non-Labour votes were not piled up in them. In terms of seats won, the decline was much clearer, Labour winning less than one in five of the seats available, and making only eight net gains. The early 1920s down to 1925 remained disappointing for Labour. Its vote share recovered, but this was in part an artificial boost caused by the increased number of uncontested seats where Labour put up no candidate. This was a result mainly of decreasing Liberal candidatures, and Liberal and Tory pacts or mergers in municipal politics. Labour's share of seats won revealed the real picture, fluctuating in the 18 to 23 per cent range. Overall in the nineteen boroughs between 1920 and 1924, there were fourteen net Labour losses. In 1922, defending the big gains of three years previously, Labour suffered net losses of thirty-nine seats in these boroughs. In 1924, the county borough elections took place three days after the general election in which the 'Zinoviev letter' had played its part. Labour's losses in parliament and the downfall of the first Labour government were faithfully reflected at the municipal level. Labour won only 15.5 per cent of all the seats contested in the nineteen boroughs, its worst performance between the wars. Turnout remained fairly constant through this period at 51 to 55 per cent. In terms of seats held on the councils, Labour had doubled its share of aldermen from 5 per cent to 10.2 per cent between 1919 and 1924, but its share of councillors had actually fallen over the same period from 21.5 per cent to 19.6 per cent. This left its share of all seats on the councils in 1924 at 17.3 per cent, virtually the same level as 1919.

There were signs of Labour recovery in 1925, and Labour support showed a marked shift upwards from 1926, peaking in 1929. The great industrial defeat experienced by the labour movement in the General Strike of May 1926 was accompanied by a swing to the Labour Party at the municipal elections six months later. Further success in 1927 and 1928 presaged the election of the second Labour government in the general election of May 1929. The party's vote share in the nineteen boroughs climbed to the 40 per cent range in this period, hitting 47.1 per cent in 1929, its inter-war peak. Labour made substantial net gains of 131 seats between 1925 and 1929. In 1929 Labour won 43.5 per cent of all seats available, its best inter-war performance, and by that year it held almost one-third of all the seats on the nineteen councils, a reflection of increases both in its share of councillors and aldermen. Between 1924 and 1929 its aldermen had increased from 10.2 per cent to 15.6 per cent of the total, and its councillors from 19.6 per cent to 37.5 per cent, the latter figure again being an inter-war high. In three of the nineteen boroughs, Barnsley, Barrow and Birkenhead, Labour won control of the council for the first time between 1926 and 1928, and in Bradford Labour was on the brink of taking control. The negative correlation between Labour's performance and turnout was also manifested in this period, turnout declining back near to its 1919 level at 43.7 per cent in 1929.

The electoral trends in these nineteen boroughs were reversed sharply by the impact of the second Labour government. Its increasing problems, especially over unemployment policy, led to its disastrous collapse in 1931 and the formation of Ramsay MacDonald's 'national' coalition. These developments took place in the context of the onset of the Depression from 1929. Labour candidates at municipal elections were the recipients of a severe backlash by the voters as a result of these developments. This was manifested quite plainly in November 1930, significantly before the political crisis developed in mid-1931, reflecting general dissatisfaction by the voters with government policies. Unsurprisingly the strong trend against Labour was continued in the 1931 elections, which were held only five days after Labour had suffered calamitous defeat in the general election. Turnout increased in these two years, reaching 51.4 per cent in 1931. Labour's vote share fell from 47.1 per cent to 38.0 per cent between 1929 and 1930, and fell again to 34.5 per cent in 1931, almost as low as its 1920 trough. Labour's share of all wins fell dramatically to 15.2 per cent in 1931, its lowest level between the wars, and a net loss of eighty-one seats was recorded over these two miserable years for the party. For the first time since 1924 Labour's share of seats held on the nineteen councils began to decline again. However, this decline was masked somewhat by the fact that Labour had sharply increased its share of aldermen after the successes of 1929. In boroughs where Labour had achieved a majority of councillors its opponents had no choice in the matter, but in addition in some boroughs where Labour had not won a majority of councillors its opponents conceded it extra aldermen to reflect its much improved position. Thus Labour's share of aldermen increased from 15.6 per cent in 1929 to 24.2 per cent by 1930, while its share of councillors fell in the same year from 37.5 per cent to 33.3 per cent, leaving its overall position only marginally worse. By 1931 the full effects of two disastrous years were manifested, with Labour's share of all seats falling to 24.7 per cent. Labour lost control of the council in Barnsley and Birkenhead in 1930 and 1931 respectively, had lost its parity in Bradford by 1931, and lost its overall majority in Barrow by 1932. It ought to be stressed that Labour's slump was disguised to an extent by the all-party electoral pacts that were instituted on grounds of economy in many boroughs between 1930 and 1932. Thus 40.2 per cent of all seats were uncontested in 1931, the highest rate of non-contests between the wars. In boroughs such as Bolton and Bath, Labour was spared even greater losses by this stroke of good fortune.

The rest of the 1930s saw a general trend towards lower turnout, the 45–47 per cent range becoming the norm. This may well have been the beginning of a much longer-term decline for voter participation in municipal elections that has continued in the post-1945 period.[5] Two distinct periods in Labour performance from 1932 to 1938 can be distinguished. First, in the years from 1932 to 1934, Labour made a rapid recovery from the 1930–31 disasters. Its strong performance in 1932 was all the more remarkable given that only twelve months previously it had been so demoralised by its heavy parliamentary and municipal defeats. Labour's share of the vote increased by twelve points in 1932 to 46.5 per cent, taking it back near to the high point of 1929. The party won 38.8 per cent of all seats up for election in 1932 as well. However, Labour actually suffered a net loss of two seats in the year, precisely because it was defending seats won in the bonanza of three years previously. For the same reason, and also because of aldermanic losses that had followed its 1930–31 decline, its share of seats held

---

[5] For an interesting early attempt to evaluate trends in turnout, see Rhodes, E.C., 'Voting at municipal elections', *Political Quarterly*, vol. 9, pt. 2, (1938), pp. 271–280.

actually fell marginally between 1931 and 1932. Labour's strong recovery persisted into 1933 and 1934 however, eighty-eight net gains being made in the nineteen boroughs in the two years. The party won 34.8 per cent and 35.8 per cent of all seats up for election in these two years respectively, and its consistent performance in this period reinstated it as a serious challenger to Conservative dominance. This was reflected as well in the fact that by 1934 Labour held 32.3 per cent of all seats on the nineteen councils, and by 1935 32.9 per cent, the highest proportion between the wars. Five of the nineteen councils were held by Labour in that year. Control was restored in Barnsley and Birkenhead, an overall majority for Labour was secured again in Barrow, and in 1934 Bootle and Burnley were both won for the first time.

The period from 1935 to 1938 ,however, saw a further reversal of the trend. The year 1935 itself was something of a turning point, with partial signs of a downturn for Labour in the municipal elections being a harbinger of what was to happen in the general election held less than two weeks later. Labour was expected to do far better in the parliamentary poll than it actually did, an expectation based on its by-election successes in previous months, and its good showing in the 1933 and 1934 municipal elections. Labour's rise had peaked in those years though, and the party's support was declining by the November elections. Five net losses were recorded in the nineteen boroughs in 1935, and Labour's share of the vote fell from 44.1 per cent to 42.5 per cent. Labour still won 36.1 per cent of all the seats up for election, though, and it had also increased its share of aldermen after the 1933–34 successes. Labour's fall was more pronounced in the years leading up to the Second World War, with the party suffering a net loss of sixty-five seats between 1935 and 1938. Its share of the vote fell steadily each year to 39.6 per cent by 1938. By 1938 it held only 29.4 per cent of all seats in the nineteen councils, fewer than it had held in 1928. Labour lost control of Birkenhead and Burnley, and its hold on Bootle was only sustained by taking a disproportionate share of aldermanic seats. It had, however, taken control of Bristol, but this was after a revision of ward boundaries and an all-party agreement to allocate aldermen proportionally in 1936 which had helped Labour significantly in that borough. By 1938 Labour was experiencing a net loss of three seats in Bristol as the national trend against Labour began to outweigh the local changes in its favour. In general terms the aldermanic system was benefiting Labour in this period, with its share of aldermen being greater than its share of councillors for the first time in 1937 and 1938. This again masked to some extent the decline in Labour's fortunes in the years leading up to war-time cessation of elections.

The reasons for Labour's decline in this period are hard to pinpoint. The downward trend in turnout suggests that a generalised apathy towards municipal politics may have been developing amongst voters. The buffeting of the British economy by global factors had perhaps by this time been seen by some voters as demonstrating the limited effect local government could have on the resulting mass unemployment and poverty. Conversely, in those areas where the economy was relatively healthy, a degree of complacency amongst voters may have set in, as suggested in the case of Birmingham. The mounting international crisis which was to lead to war may perhaps have diverted attention from seemingly trivial local affairs. There was also a general tendency, noted in a number of the boroughs covered in these two volumes, for Labour to present a more moderate and cautious face in the 1930s. A certain blandness crept in to its municipal policies by contrast with its peak years of dynamism and radical intent from 1926 to 1929. Arguably some of its distinctive electoral appeal was lost in this period.

It should also be stressed that the decline of Liberalism as an electoral force after 1929 was a factor. This post-1929 effect was not as pronounced at the municipal as at the parliamentary level, as in many boroughs Tories and Liberals had already formed electoral alliances against Labour in the 1920s, making three-way contests far less common in municipal elections than in Westminster polls. Most of the boroughs covered in these two volumes have shown this tendency. By the late 1930s though, the full impact of the decline of Liberalism was perhaps working its way through in municipal politics. It may also be the case that improvements in Conservative organisation and propaganda at a local level swung support. The evidence for Bury and Burton in this volume certainly seems to sustain this argument. As other recent research has emphasised, the Tory party, described by some as 'the most successful political organization in the modern world', had to remake itself in the inter-war years. Faced with democracy, the rise of Labour, and a more secular and class-conscious society, Tory electoral hegemony was by no means assured. As David Jarvis has said, 'Conservatives were actively engaged throughout this period in trying to understand the nature of their new audience and reconstructing the social alliances from which their electoral strength derived'.[6] Perhaps they had best achieved this by the late 1930s, when the base of their electoral support seemed as secure and as stable as at any point between the wars. The intervention of war was to disturb this stability though. Whatever the causes of Labour's late 1930s decline, the point that has been made in respect of a number of the boroughs in these volumes needs to be repeated here. There was no sign in the years leading up to the war of the massive increases that Labour would make in 1945. On the contrary, Labour's future prospects looked bleak before war halted the electoral process.

The comparative analysis

The comparative data on turnout and Labour performance for the nineteen boroughs covered in this volume are shown below in Tables 10.4 to 10.7. Some meaningful comments can be made based on these figures. First, the turnout figures in Table 10.4 suggest that interest in municipal elections was considerably higher over these years than it has been in the post-1945 period. With the exceptions of Birmingham, Brighton and Canterbury where turnout overall was below 40 per cent, and Bury where it was in the low 40s, the other fifteen boroughs averaged above 46 per cent in all cases over the whole inter-war period. Turnout was especially high in Barnsley, Barrow, Blackburn, Burnley and Carlisle

[6] Jarvis, D., 'The shaping of Conservative electoral hegemony, 1918–39', in Lawrence, J. and Taylor, M., *Party, State and Society: Electoral Behaviour in Britain since 1820*, (Aldershot, 1997), p. 146.

at almost 70 per cent.[7] There does seem to be a regional effect here, with the northern industrial boroughs tending to have much higher turnout than the southern and Midlands boroughs. Variations in turnout may also have been influenced by differences in size of place, with the largest boroughs such as Birmingham and Bristol having lower turnout, although Bradford with an overall turnout of 57.7 per cent would seem to contradict this. At this stage there are still not enough cases here to test such hypotheses fully.[8] Nor is it possible yet to establish whether there was any connection between turnout and Labour performance, although the evidence here so far is interesting, if inconclusive. Labour was strong in Barrow, Barnsley and Burnley with high turnout, and weak in Birmingham and Bury with low turnout. On the other hand, Labour was relatively successful in Birkenhead and Bootle with fairly low turnout. Further data in future volumes will make it possible to establish whether any consistent patterns existed.[9]

Turning to the comparison of Labour's performance in the nineteen boroughs, the problem of uncontested seats alluded to above clouds the issue somewhat, but nevertheless a reasonably clear picture can be discerned. Labour's success has been evaluated in three ways in Tables 10.4–10.7: in terms of its share of all votes, of its share of all contests won, and of its share of seats (both of councillors and aldermen) held on the councils near the beginning (1919), middle (1929) and end (1938) of the period. By the criteria of share of votes and wins, Labour's strongest boroughs were Barnsley and Barrow, with around half or more of all votes and all contests being won there, and a majority of all seats being held in 1929 and 1938. A second group can be identified, comprised of Birkenhead, Bootle, Bradford, Bristol, and Burnley, where Labour won somewhere between 37 and 47 per cent of all votes and contests, and attained a majority of seats in at least one of the years 1929 and 1938. Blackburn, Bolton, Cardiff and Carlisle made up a third category, where Labour picked up 30–40 per cent or higher of all votes, won around 30 per cent of all contests, but held only 20–30 per cent of all seats and never took control of the council in the inter-war years. A fourth type of borough included Birmingham, Brighton and Burton, where Labour gained a respectable percentage of all votes cast (40 per cent in Birmingham, 33 in Brighton, 31 in Burton), but less than a quarter of all wins, and held less than 30 per cent of all seats even at the high point of 1929. A fifth category was comprised of Bath, Bournemouth and Bury where Labour was very weak on all three criteria, the party having 30 per cent or less of all votes, less than 20 per cent of all wins, and holding 20 per cent or less of all the seats on the council at all three specified dates. Finally Blackpool and Canterbury can be identified as exceptionally barren territory for the party, with very low percentages of votes, wins and seats being gained by Labour.

Various reasons for these widespread differences in Labour's performance have been advanced in the chapters on each borough in this volume, and readers are

---

[7]   The exceptionally low turnout in Birmingham has been commented on already on pp. 229–230 in this volume.

[8]   For consideration of the electoral effects of size of place in parliamentary elections, see Bealey, F. and Dyer, M., 'Size of place and the Labour vote in Britain, 1918–1966', *Western Political Quarterly*, vol. 20, (1967), pp. 84–113

[9]   On variations in turnout, see Rhodes, 'Voting in municipal elections'.

referred to the individual essays for the full details. Some brief comments are appropriate here. The varying socio-economic character of the boroughs was clearly an important influence. Labour's strongest boroughs of Barnsley and Barrow were both overwhelmingly industrial, and in both cases dominated by one industry (mining and shipbuilding respectively). Well-organised, cohesive, and predominantly male workforces in these boroughs produced solid labour movements and relatively strong Labour parties. Conversely, the lack of industry in Bath, Blackpool, Bournemouth and Canterbury produced predominantly middle-class boroughs, and thus the domination of middle-class political organisations. Somewhere between these extremes, boroughs like Birkenhead, Bristol and Cardiff had a significant working class, (although not confined to one dominant industry) but it also had a substantial middle class. Municipal politics in the borough to some degree reflected the interests of both these groups, with Labour beginning to threaten the dominant position of Tory and Liberal parties in the inter-war years.

However, this rather deterministic type of analysis can only be taken so far, and is easiest to sustain for the extreme cases. On the evidence for the nineteen boroughs analysed so far, in most cases there was a far more complex interaction between socio-economic structures and other factors which underlay political practice. For instance, the significance of cultural and political traditions has been stressed to different degrees in this volume. In Bootle religious sectarianism was an important influence, weakening Labour's position in the early 1920s, but then later providing a mainly Catholic base of support on which it could build a real challenge to Conservatism. In Bath, on the other hand, Nonconformist traditions of a popular and radical nature ensured a slightly stronger Labour presence than might have been expected in such a borough. Again, the Nonconformist roots of Birmingham's 'civic gospel' was clearly important in explaining the powerful tradition of Liberal Unionism in the city. Most complex of all was the experience of the cotton-textile towns dealt with in these volumes. A tradition of working-class Toryism was plainly still of importance in Blackburn, Bolton and most of all Bury, which held back the rise of the Labour party in what were predominantly industrial and working-class boroughs. This tradition was based on a number of social, cultural and ideological components, including employer-worker relations (at work and elsewhere) and employer paternalism, gender relations in the cotton industry, economic self-interest, religious beliefs, cultural attitudes to questions such as temperance, and nationalistic and jingoistic sentiments. Yet on the other hand, the weaving town of Burnley, due to its later industrial development and specific industrial configuration, its geographical site close to the Pennines and the West Riding of Yorkshire, and its distinctive religious and cultural traditions, was a centre of radicalism where Labour was able to gain much more support in this period.[10] One might also point to the complexity of the case of Burton, where the domination of one industry, brewing, resulted in a very strong Tory tradition and a near co-option of the Labour party into the ruling group on the council.

---

[10] For a more detailed comparative analysis of these four boroughs, see Davies, S. and Morley, B., 'The politics of place: a comparative analysis of electoral politics in four Lancashire cotton textile towns, 1918–1939', *Manchester Region History Review*, no. 14, (2000).

It is also the case that more contingent and short-term factors could be of importance in municipal politics. Each borough's particular experience of the 1930s Depression was significant, for instance. It is arguable that Birmingham's relatively healthy economy and low unemployment had something to do with the growing strength of the ruling Unionist party there in the 1930s. Blackpool's survival as a major tourist resort through the inter-war period may have encouraged the self-satisfaction of its voters, and thus their solid support for its traditional ruling groups. Conversely, unemployment in Barnsley in particular appears to have been a political issue which Labour used very effectively to its own advantage. Another contingent issue was the impact of the General Strike in 1926. While a noticeable surge in Labour support in the nineteen boroughs overall was seen in the November 1926 elections, it was especially obvious in Birkenhead and Bootle, and unsurprisingly most of all in Barnsley, where a massive turnout of 80 per cent reflected the heightened political interest of that year. The impact of the More Looms Dispute in the weaving industry in 1932 also seemed to have been electorally significant in Burnley, poisoning class relations in the town and encouraging a turn to Labour. Another example of the importance of short-term contingencies was the effect of the second Labour government of 1929–31 and its disastrous collapse. There was a general slump in Labour support in all nineteen boroughs as a whole in the elections of 1930 and 1931. In Bolton, however, the existence of an electoral moratorium on the grounds of economy in both years saved Labour from experiencing the dramatic loss of seats that it otherwise could have expected. This significantly boosted Labour's strength on the council in Bolton in the 1930s, while in other boroughs Labour took three years up to 1934 just to recoup the losses of 1930–31. A similar moratorium benefited Labour in Bath over the same period. Finally, human agency and political organisation made a difference in the outcome of elections. Tory organisation and campaigning in Bury and Burton, for instance, helped cement Tory dominance in these boroughs, while equivalent Labour activity helped boost Labour electoral performance in Bristol and Burnley.

In addition, there were elements of the system of municipal politics itself which influenced Labour's political performance in the different boroughs. The limitations of the municipal franchise at this time, excluding some residents while giving plural votes to others, may have been a factor working against Labour in all boroughs. When more boroughs have been covered in these volumes a more systematic analysis can be applied to give a definitive answer to that question. There were certainly differential effects as well. The case of Blackpool is one obvious example in this volume. Large numbers of temporary workers in the holiday trade were excluded from the municipal franchise there, either because they did not meet the six-month (later three-month) residency test, or because they lived in furnished lodgings and therefore did not pay rates. Labour almost certainly suffered politically for this, perhaps helping to explain its extremely poor performance in the borough. Similar comments can be made about the vagaries of the system of ward boundaries in municipal politics at this time. Birkenhead and Bury are two good examples of where gerrymandering the boundaries could be used to political advantage. There is little doubt that Labour was disadvantaged by the ward reorganisations that took place in 1934 and 1936 respectively in these boroughs. On the other hand, the revision of ward boundaries in Bristol in 1936 plainly was to Labour's advantage, and helps to explain Labour's marked upsurge in strength on the council in the late 1930s.

Most clear of all is the significance of the aldermanic system. A quarter of all the seats in the various boroughs were decided by the elected councillors, rather than by the voters. The evidence from these volumes shows that the aldermanic seats could be crucial in determining political power. A clear pattern can be identified in the nineteen boroughs covered here. In all cases, Labour was initially under-represented on the aldermanic bench. Where Labour remained relatively weak, usually the dominant parties eventually conceded one or two aldermanic vacancies to it (in Bath, Bournemouth, Brighton, Bury, and Cardiff, for instance), as this posed no threat to overall political control. In other boroughs where Labour won a greater degree of support, but still did not endanger the traditional ruling party, rough parity of representation on the aldermanic bench might eventually be conceded (in Birmingham, Blackburn, Bolton and Carlisle). However, where Labour grew strong enough to gain a majority of the elected councillors, and therefore fill aldermanic vacancies to its own advantage, then the aldermanic system became a major and permanent political issue. This was the case in Barnsley (from as early as 1921–22), Barrow (from 1928–29), Birkenhead (from 1926–27), Bootle (from 1933–34), Bradford (from 1929–30), Bristol (from 1936–37) and Burnley (from 1935–36). In these boroughs, control of the council by the late 1930s was largely determined by the coincidence of the timing of the three-year cycle of aldermanic elections in relation to the annual round of council elections. In Barnsley, Barrow, Bootle and Burnley Labour control was secured by taking all or most of the aldermanic vacancies while its position on the council enabled it to do so in the late 1930s. Conversely, Labour's opponents in Birkenhead seized the opportunity after the 1931 council elections to oust half its aldermen. Labour recouped some of these losses in the mid 1930s, but not enough to put itself back into power on a secure footing. In Bradford as well, Labour's opponents swept away most of its aldermen in 1936–37 to put it back in the wilderness. Bristol was the only borough where a formal all-party agreement to elect aldermen on the basis of proportionality was enacted (in 1936), which guaranteed that the aldermanic system could no longer be used to party advantage.

One final point of a general nature needs to be made. It is striking that in all the boroughs considered so far, the political struggle at the municipal level resolved itself quite rapidly after 1918 into more or less a straight fight between Labour and anti-Labour forces. This was equally true for boroughs where Labour's opponents retained their distinctive party labels for municipal purposes (as in Bath, Birkenhead, Birmingham, Blackburn, Blackpool, Bolton, Bootle, Bradford, Burnley and Bury), adopted a common label such as Citizen, Independent or Anti-Socialist (as in Barnsley, Barrow, Bristol, Burton, Cardiff or Carlisle), or eschewed political labels altogether and presented themselves in a supposedly apolitical guise (as in Bournemouth, Brighton, Canterbury). This was also the case despite the fact that at the level of parliamentary politics, Liberals and Tories usually retained their separate identities and continued to fight each other politically at least up to 1929.

There are two important implications that flow from this. One is related to the decline of Liberalism between the wars. In one of the few studies to consider this decline at the municipal level, Chris Cook has seen the fall in the number of Liberal candidates and the shift to municipal alliances primarily as a symptom of the weakness of Liberalism.[11] Arguably it could also be seen as a contributory cause of the decline of the Liberal party. The apparently widespread and early tendency for Liberals to sink their differences with Tories and present an anti-Labour front as far as municipal elections were concerned must have weakened their distinctive political identity in the minds of voters. Cause and effect may be hard to disentangle here, but the evidence of these volumes tends to support the view that these anti-labour fronts 'forced the radical working-class Liberal vote into the Labour camp'.[12] Bristol provides possibly the strongest evidence of this process after 1918. The only clear variant to this may be found in Birkenhead, where it seems possible that one group of local voters at least, namely shipbuilders, transferred their allegiance to Labour in municipal elections, but for pragmatic reasons still retained their loyalty to Liberalism in general elections.

The other implication of this tendency is related to the rise of Labour. There has been a long and contentious argument amongst historians as to whether or not the growth of the Labour party before 1918 can be attributed primarily to increasing class consciousness.[13] For the years after 1918 covered in these volumes, the significance of class in municipal politics stands out. The anti-Labour alliances were only the formal manifestation of the often fiercely-expressed language of class that dominated the discourse of municipal politics in these boroughs. This applies as much to boroughs where Labour was relatively strong, such as Barnsley or Birkenhead, as it does where Labour was at its weakest, in Blackpool. Another apposite case is Bootle, where the language of sectarian politics was dominant at first, but was quite soon subsumed into a Labour–anti-Labour discourse, even if sectarian undertones remained. It should also be stressed that the anti-socialist sentiments of candidates were usually reflected in the local press, which tended to be stridently partisan in its coverage and continually stress the 'dangers of socialism'. On the starkly different political terrain of Blackpool, Bootle and Cardiff, Labour was denounced in strikingly similar language as a 'Bolshevist' threat.[14] Perhaps the only exception to this was Burton, where earlier conflict between Labour and anti-Labour forces was replaced later by a degree of consensus as Labour was co-opted into an informal sharing of power in the borough.

---

[11] Cook, *The Age of Alignment*, pp. 49–70.

[12] Cook, *The Age of Alignment*, p. 56.

[13] At the danger of simplifying two very complex approaches, see, for example, arguing for the significance of class consciousness in the rise of Labour, McKibbin, R., *The Evolution of the Labour Party 1910–1924*, (Oxford, 1974); and tending to downplay it, Tanner, D., *Political Change and the Labour Party 1900–1918*, (Cambridge, 1990).

[14] See pp. 414 and 549 in volume one of this series.

Concluding comments on the comparative method

The remarks made in this conclusion of a comparative nature are only brief and selective, and more detailed and rigorous analysis will be applied at later stages of the production of these volumes. One of the problems of attempting comparative analysis is that at the early stages of the process there is little to compare the initial evidence with. A leading exponent of the method has commented, 'comparison which begins by regarding one particular case as the norm against which comparisons are made with other cases is flawed from the outset', and again, 'the first requirement of a proper comparative history is to be equally interested in all the cases under consideration'. Until an extensive amount of what he calls 'comparative descriptive work' has been carried out, it is hard to make comparative conclusions.[15] These recommendations must be borne in mind both by the authors and the readers of the first two volumes in an eight-volume series. It remains to be seen how much the evidence of future volumes in this series will modify both the aggregate patterns and the comparative suggestions that have been put forward here. Their implications will also need to be considered carefully, both within the series and elsewhere, and not only by the authors of these volumes alone. To repeat the warning made in the introduction to these volumes, election results need to be fully contextualised and analysed for their true significance to be realised. On their own, they have clear limitations, and no straightforward conclusions can be derived from them. Much detailed and subtle work will be required to put the flesh on the bare bones of an analysis that has been given here. It is hoped, though, that a start has been made in these pages.

---

[15] Breuilly, J., *Labour and Liberalism in Nineteenth-Century Europe: Essays in Comparative History*, (Manchester, 1992), pp. 1–2, 14.

Table 10.1 Overall turnout, Labour % of votes, Labour % of wins, Labour % of council seats held, Labour % of councillors and Labour % of aldermen in all nineteen Volume One and Volume Two county boroughs, 1919–38

	Turnout %	Labour % of all votes	Labour % of all wins	Labour % of all seats held	Labour % of councillors	Labour % of aldermen
1919	43.8	37.8	37.5	17.4	21.5	5.0
1920	52.6	34.2	18.1	19.3	23.7	6.2
1921	53.2	36.8	18.5	20.7	24.9	7.7
1922	54.9	37.8	19.8	16.8	19.0	10.0
1923	51.9	38.5	23.0	17.6	20.2	9.8
1924	54.6	37.7	15.5	17.3	19.6	10.2
1925	55.4	39.2	25.7	18.5	21.4	9.9
1926	52.4	45.4	36.6	22.4	26.4	10.2
1927	52.5	43.3	30.2	26.6	31.4	12.5
1928	53.7	44.1	36.9	29.7	35.3	13.2
1929	43.7	47.1	43.5	32.1	37.5	15.6
1930	47.0	38.0	21.7	31.0	33.3	24.1
1931	51.4	34.5	15.2	24.7	25.3	23.1
1932	46.8	46.5	38.8	24.4	25.2	22.0
1933	46.7	45.5	34.8	26.9	30.0	17.5
1934	46.0	44.1	35.8	32.3	35.7	22.1
1935	47.2	42.5	36.1	32.9	35.2	26.1
1936	45.6	41.5	30.8	32.3	33.5	28.6
1937	46.9	41.0	29.2	30.5	30.0	32.2
1938	45.7	39.6	26.4	28.7	27.5	32.4
1919–38	**49.3**	**40.9**	**28.8**	**25.3**	**27.9**	**17.1**

Table 10.2   Labour net gains or losses in all nineteen Volume One and
Volume Two county boroughs 1919–38

1919	63		1929	16
1920	8		1930	-24
1921	8		1931	-57
1922	-39		1932	-2
1923	11		1933	35
1924	-2		1934	53
1925	15		1935	-5
1926	34		1936	-22
1927	35		1937	-17
1928	31		1938	-21
1919–28	**164**		**1929–38**	**-44**

1919–38   120

Table 10.3 Uncontested seats in all nineteen Volume One and Volume Two
county boroughs 1919–1938

	Labour un-contested wins	Other un-contested wins	All seats	% of all seats un-contested	Contested seats with no Labour candidate	% of all seats with no Labour candidate
1919	6	24	259	11.6	50	28.6
1920	10	37	259	18.1	23	23.2
1921	4	45	270	18.1	44	33.0
1922	11	67	273	28.6	36	37.7
1923	10	83	265	35.1	30	42.6
1924	7	75	265	30.9	18	35.1
1925	8	60	265	25.7	30	34.0
1926	2	57	265	22.3	23	30.2
1927	4	57	265	23.0	17	27.9
1928	14	63	268	28.7	22	31.7
1929	11	39	271	18.5	20	21.8
1930	16	64	272	29.4	16	29.4
1931	16	95	276	40.2	11	38.4
1932	16	70	273	31.5	19	32.6
1933	5	76	282	28.7	27	36.5
1934	14	64	288	27.1	24	30.6
1935	31	72	285	36.1	10	28.8
1936	19	80	305	32.5	17	31.8
1937	23	84	325	32.9	27	34.2
1938	24	72	288	33.3	19	31.6
1919–38	**251**	**1284**	**5519**	**27.8**	**483**	**32.0**

Table 10.4 Overall turnout, Labour % of all votes and Labour % of all wins in
each of the nineteen Volume One and Volume Two
county boroughs 1919–38 *(rankings in brackets)*

Borough	Turnout %	Labour % of all votes	Labour % of all wins
Barnsley	*(2)* 69.6	*(2)* 49.1	*(2)* 49.5
Barrow	*(3)* 69.2	*(1)* 49.9	*(1)* 55.0
Bath	*(10)* 53.2	*(14)* 31.5	*(14)* 18.2
Birkenhead	*(13)* 50.3	*(8)* 41.6	*(3)* 42.2
Birmingham	*(19)* 37.9	*(9)* 40.8	*(12)* 23.3
Blackburn	*(1)* 69.7	*(7)* 43.6	*(8)* 33.0
Blackpool	*(9)* 55.5	*(19)* 6.9	*(19)* 0.8
Bolton	*(6)* 58.0	*(12)* 34.7	*(10)* 29.2
Bootle	*(11)* 52.0	*(11)* 38.8	*(4)* 38.9
Bournemouth	*(14)* 48.1	*(16)* 26.6	*(16)* 17.1
Bradford	*(7)* 57.7	*(6)* 44.5	*(6)* 37.1
Brighton	*(18)* 38.3	*(13)* 33.3	*(13)* 22.7
Bristol	*(15)* 46.5	*(3)* 47.0	*(5)* 38.1
Burnley	*(5)* 67.9	*(4)* 46.7	*(7)* 37.1
Burton	*(8)* 57.0	*(15)* 30.8	*(15)* 17.5
Bury	*(16)* 42.5	*(17)* 24.9	*(17)* 13.7
Canterbury	*(17)* 39.1	*(18)* 14.1	*(18)* 1.7
Cardiff	*(12)* 51.1	*(10)* 39.9	*(11)* 28.8
Carlisle	*(4)* 68.3	*(5)* 46.0	*(9)* 32.5
All	**49.3**	**40.9**	**28.8**

Table 10.5   Labour % of all council seats held in each of the nineteen
Volume One and Volume Two county boroughs in
1919, 1929 and 1938 *(rankings in brackets)*

Borough	Labour % of all council seats held 1919	Labour % of all council seats held 1929	Labour % of all council seats held 1938
Barnsley	*(1)* 37.5	*(3)* 52.8	*(1)* 65.0
Barrow	*(3)* 31.3	*(1)* 68.8	*(2)* 62.5
Bath	*(=13)* 12.5	*(15)* 14.3	*(15)* 14.3
Birkenhead	*(4)* 26.8	*(2)* 55.9	*(6)* 41.9
Birmingham	*(6)* 20.2	*(11)* 29.8	*(14)* 16.2
Blackburn	*(9)* 17.9	*(6)* 39.3	*(7)* 33.9
Blackpool	*(18)* 1.9	*(=18)* 0.0	*(19)* 1.8
Bolton	*(15)* 9.4	*(9)* 34.7	*(12)* 21.9
Bootle	*(5)* 22.7	*(5)* 45.8	*(3)* 52.1
Bournemouth	*(17)* 4.5	*(16)* 13.6	*(13)* 16.7
Bradford	*(2)* 35.7	*(4)* 49.4	*(10)* 25.3
Brighton	*(7)* 19.6	*(13)* 23.7	*(11)* 23.7
Bristol	*(10)* 16.3	*(8)* 37.0	*(4)* 50.0
Burnley	*(8)* 18.8	*(10)* 31.3	*(5)* 47.9
Burton	*(11)* 15.6	*(17)* 9.4	*(16)* 9.4
Bury	*(16)* 5.0	*(14)* 15.0	*(17)* 9.1
Canterbury	*(19)* 0.0	*(=18)* 0.0	*(18)* 4.2
Cardiff	*(=13)* 12.5	*(7)* 38.0	*(9)* 26.8
Carlisle	*(12)* 15.0	*(12)* 27.5	*(8)* 32.5
All	**17.4**	**32.1**	**28.7**

Table 10.6 Labour % of all councillors in each of the nineteen
Volume One and Volume Two county boroughs in
1919, 1929 and 1938 *(rankings in brackets)*

Borough	Labour % of all councillors 1919	Labour % of all councillors 1929	Labour % of all councillors 1938
Barnsley	*(1)* 44.4	*(6)* 51.9	*(2)* 53.3
Barrow	*(2)* 41.7	*(1)* 66.7	*(1)* 58.0
Bath	*(=13)* 16.7	*(=15)* 16.7	*(14)* 16.7
Birkenhead	*(4)* 31.0	*(2)* 59.1	*(5)* 39.6
Birmingham	*(8)* 24.4	*(12)* 35.2	*(15)* 13.7
Blackburn	*(9)* 23.8	*(=4)* 52.4	*(4)* 42.9
Blackpool	*(18)* 2.6	*(=18)* 0.0	*(19)* 2.4
Bolton	*(15)* 12.5	*(9)* 40.8	*(12)* 19.4
Bootle	*(5)* 30.3	*(3)* 55.6	*(7)* 36.1
Bournemouth	*(17)* 6.1	*(14)* 18.2	*(13)* 17.8
Bradford	*(3)* 38.1	*(=4)* 52.4	*(11)* 25.4
Brighton	*(6)* 26.2	*(13)* 29.8	*(10)* 26.3
Bristol	*(12)* 18.8	*(8)* 46.4	*(3)* 50.0
Burnley	*(7)* 25.0	*(10)* 38.9	*(6)* 38.9
Burton	*(10)* 20.8	*(17)* 12.5	*(16)* 12.5
Bury	*(16)* 6.7	*(=15)* 16.7	*(17)* 6.1
Canterbury	*(19)* 0.0	*(=18)* 0.0	*(18)* 5.6
Cardiff	*(=13)* 16.7	*(7)* 48.7	*(8)* 31.0
Carlisle	*(11)* 20.0	*(11)* 36.7	*(9)* 30.0
All	**21.5**	**37.5**	**27.5**

Table 10.7   Labour % of all aldermen in each of the nineteen
Volume One and Volume Two county boroughs in
1919, 1929 and 1938 *(rankings in brackets)*

Borough	Labour % of all aldermen 1919	Labour % of all aldermen 1929	Labour % of all aldermen 1938
Barnsley	*(2)* 16.7	*(2)* 55.6	*(=1)* 100.0
Barrow	*(=6)* 0.0	*(1)* 75.0	*(=3)* 75.0
Bath	*(=6)* 0.0	*(11)* 7.1	*(=15)* 7.1
Birkenhead	*(3)* 14.3	*(3)* 46.7	*(=5)* 50.0
Birmingham	*(5)* 6.9	*(7)* 13.3	*(10)* 23.5
Blackburn	*(=6)* 0.0	*(=13)* 0.0	*(=15)* 7.1
Blackpool	*(=6)* 0.0	*(=13)* 0.0	*(=17)* 0.0
Bolton	*(=6)* 0.0	*(=5)* 16.7	*(8)* 29.2
Bootle	*(=6)* 0.0	*(=5)* 16.7	*(=1)* 100.0
Bournemouth	*(=6)* 0.0	*(=13)* 0.0	*(14)* 13.3
Bradford	*(1)* 28.6	*(4)* 40.0	*(9)* 25.0
Brighton	*(=6)* 0.0	*(12)* 5.3	*(12)* 15.8
Bristol	*(4)* 8.7	*(9)* 8.7	*(=5)* 50.0
Burnley	*(=6)* 0.0	*(10)* 8.3	*(=3)* 75.0
Burton	*(=6)* 0.0	*(=13)* 0.0	*(=17)* 0.0
Bury	*(=6)* 0.0	*(8)* 10.0	*(11)* 18.2
Canterbury	*(=6)* 0.0	*(=13)* 0.0	*(=17)* 0.0
Cardiff	*(=6)* 0.0	*(=13)* 0.0	*(13)* 14.3
Carlisle	*(=6)* 0.0	*(=13)* 0.0	*(7)* 40.0
All	**5.0**	**15.6**	**32.4**

NOTES

NOTES

Notes on maps, tables and appendices

MAPS

Ward boundary maps

Ward boundaries have been identified from various sources. The contemporary 2½ inch Ordnance Survey maps showed ward boundaries, but their large scale makes them difficult to use, especially in the case of large towns. Other locally-produced maps were sometimes located in local record offices, and newspapers sometimes showed, or listed, changes in boundaries. Where no maps showing boundaries could be found, as a last resort, all streets listed in contemporary electoral registers by ward were identified on maps in order to establish boundaries. All maps were first hand-drawn by the authors, and some were then converted to digital form by Phil Cubbin, of the Human Geography section of Liverpool John Moores University, to give working copies. The final versions used in this volume were drawn at Ashgate, with the assistance of Ian Wileman.

TABLES

Persons aged 14 and over classified by industry 1931

These tables have been constructed from the industrial tables of the 1931 census reports. It should be noted that the numbers included separately for each category as 'out of work' in the census tables have been aggregated with the employed in the tables included here. All industrial categories that amounted to 5 per cent or more of the total (working and 'out of work') population enumerated, for either men or women, have been included in these tables. Very exceptionally, where the numbers classified in a locally notable industry (which other sources have highlighted) did not quite amount to 5 per cent, these categories may also be included.

Population statistics 1931

These tables have been constructed from the county tables of the 1931 census reports.

Overall position on the council; and aldermen

In these tables, the position on the council and on the aldermanic bench is that which pertained in the immediate aftermath of the elections held on the first day in November. The position could often change very soon after the elections, especially when the aldermanic elections took place at the first council meeting after the election, and also sometimes because councillors changed parties in the light of the results. It is impossible to reflect these changes in a consistent fashion for all boroughs. The first council meeting after the election took place after intervals varying from one borough to another. Vacancies created by the election of new aldermen then had to be filled in by-elections, which were again held after varying intervals, and in which new gains or losses might be made to further confuse the situation. The position immediately after the election is therefore the only acceptable one, as it at least has the merit of being directly comparable across the board.

It should also be noted that the position on the council, and the balance of aldermen, were not always recorded accurately, or even at all, in press reports and directories. The figures given in these volumes have been constructed in many cases from a detailed analysis of the effects of the election results on each individual councillor and alderman.

Gains and losses for parties are only those which took place as a direct result of the elections themselves. Changes which had taken place in between the three-year cycle of elections, due to retirements, deaths, elections to the aldermanic bench, or councillors changing parties, were sometimes recorded in the press as gains, but this was often very misleading as the change might have occurred months or even years before. The gains recorded here reflect the real changes in party strength at the annual elections.

Municipal elections: winning party

In these summary tables of results, no-contests are marked in bold and underlined.

Municipal elections: party wins per year; and per ward

In these tables, it has only been possible to assess Labour Party performance, as Labour was the only party to consistently appear under its own name across the country. Tory and Liberal alliances, and the use of indeterminate labels such as 'Independent' or 'Citizens', make it impossible to assess the other two major parties' support on a comparable basis across the country.

The 'Labour per cent' figure is calculated from the total number of votes won by Labour candidates (in any one year, or ward), as a proportion of all votes cast (in any one year, or ward). This calculation gives a more realistic picture of actual Labour support than if all votes cast only in wards contested by Labour are counted. If this latter method were employed, then in boroughs where Labour was very weak and thus contested very few seats, it could misleadingly appear to do quite well.

In the case of double-member seats, in each individual contest all votes won by Labour candidates have been calculated as a proportion of all votes cast, and then scaled down as a proportion of all electors voting. This ensures that where only one candidate is put up by Labour, this 'weaker' position than if it had fielded two candidates is reflected, on the same principle as applied for single-member seats. The scaling down to take account of all electors voting, as opposed to all votes cast, also ensures that voters' preferences are not double-counted in the aggregated figures for all boroughs.

Parliamentary election results

These tables have been constructed from the full lists of results contained in Craig, F.W.S., *British Parliamentary Election Results, 1918–1949*, (2nd edn, Aldershot, 1989). The details of the wards which were contained within constituencies have been taken from Craig, F.W.S., *Boundaries of Parliamentary Constituencies 1885–1971*, (Chichester, 1972).

Municipal elections (full ward-by-ward results)

Candidates

All female candidates are given the title used in press reports or directories (Miss or Mrs). In some cases women candidates were denoted by the use of their Christian names, with no titles given. For reasons of space, this practice cannot be employed in these tables, and these women have been denoted by the title of Ms, of modern usage. Other titles, especially military titles, have had to be omitted, again for reasons of space. Sitting candidates are indicated by an asterix after their name.

Party

Party labels have been recorded as far as possible as they appeared in the press etc., except where local usage may be misleading. In Birmingham, for instance, Unionist, rather than Conservative, was customarily used for 'Conservative and Unionist' candidates, for good historical reasons. For consistency across these volumes they have been recorded in these tables as Conservatives. Note, though, that the local usage is employed in the text of the essay on Birmingham. Again, some of the more virulently anti-Labour newspapers, such as the *Yorkshire Post*, would only record Labour candidates as Socialists, but the correct party label of Labour has been employed in these tables.

Co-operative Party candidates in some boroughs were treated by the press as if they were Labour candidates. However, in all cases, including the **overall position on the council** tables, they have been treated in these volumes as follows: where candidates were simply labelled Co-operative, they have been treated as Co-operative candidates, separate from Labour (most of these cases occurred in 1919 and the early 1920s, when they were still separate parties); where candidates were labelled 'Labour and Co-operative' or 'Co-operative and Labour', they have been treated as Labour candidates (whether or not formal merger had occurred, these clearly must have had the official endorsement of the local Labour Party).

Votes

The figures for votes given in the tables of results have been derived from a number of sources, including press reports from both regional and local newspapers, or directories of various kinds. As a general rule, where occasionally conflicting figures were given in different sources, directories have usually been preferred to the press, on the assumption that the speed required for newspaper reports was likely to cause more errors or misprints. Similarly, results printed in the newspaper of the particular borough concerned have usually been preferred to those given in national or regional press coverage. This was on the assumption that locally-based reporters picking up the results at the counts were likely to get the right figures. National and regional papers would have got the results for most of the smaller boroughs through agency reports, and transcription errors must have occurred at times. However, these decisions were also dependent on a judgement of the overall quality and reliability of particular newspapers.

In single-member seats, the 'total votes' figure is simply the sum of all votes cast. In double-member seats, an additional figure of 'total voters' has been given. This is the number of voters who actually voted in the poll, which in most cases was given in the press. In a small number of cases where it was not given, estimated figures have been calculated, which have been denoted by printing in italics. These 'total voters' figures have been used in the calculation of the turnout figures (see below), as they reflect the actual turnout of voters. 'Total voter' estimates could be calculated by simply halving the 'total votes', assuming that each individual voter used both his or her available votes. This, however, would result in a significant underestimate of turnout in cases where major parties do not put up two candidates, and where therefore large numbers of voters may not have used both their votes. The estimates in these volumes have been constructed on a different basis to try and take account of this problem, as follows.

A sample of 100 cases in Birkenhead, Bolton and Bootle where 'total voters' figures were given in the press were collated, and then classified into various categories according to the number of candidates put up by parties (e.g. 2 Labour, 2 Tory; 2 Labour, 1 Tory; 2 Labour, 2 Tory, 1 Liberal; etc.) For each category, the number of actual voters was compared with the halved 'total votes' figure, and consistent patterns emerged. Five main categories emerged, in each of which the degree of underestimation of 'total voters' produced by the halving of 'total votes' varied very little, as shown here:

Group A *(10 cases)*
2 C, 2 L, 2 Lab
Highest underestimation - 6.1 %
Lowest underestimation - 3.2 %
Mean underestimation (rounded) - 5 %

Group B *(12 cases)*
2 Lab, 1 C; 2 C, 1 Lab, etc.
Highest underestimation - 21.5 %
Lowest underestimation - 17.2 %
Mean underestimation - 19 %

Group C *(44 cases)*
2 C, 2 Lab; 2 C, 2 L, etc.
Highest underestimation - 7.3 %
Lowest underestimation - 1.0 %
Mean underestimation - 3 %

Group D *(10 cases)*
2 C, 1 Lab, 1 L; 2 Lab, 1 C, 1 L, etc.
Highest underestimation - 23.4 %
Lowest underestimation - 17.3 %
Mean underestimation - 20 %

Group E *(24 cases)*
2 C, 2 Lab, 1 L; 2 C, 2 L, 1 Lab, etc.
Highest underestimation - 14.1 %
Lowest underestimation - 4.6 %
Mean underestimation - 10 %

In each group, the mean underestimation was taken to be representative. In all cases where no 'total voters' figures were available, therefore, the 'total votes' figures were first halved, and then raised by the proportion appropriate for each group. There were too few cases where other minor parties intervened for any patterns to be gauged, so these have been treated as if they were one of the major parties.

The resultant estimates cannot be taken as being entirely accurate, of course, but they will produce turnout figures which will reflect the real situation better than any other alternative.

Per cent

The per cent figures for candidates are the votes cast for each candidate as a proportion of the total votes cast. This applies to both single- and double-member seats.

Electors

As in the case of the figures for votes noted above, the figures for electors in these tables have been derived from a variety of sources, and the same principles of selection have been applied where discrepancies between different sources have been identified. In some cases, turnout figures were provided, from which it was possible to calculate electorate figures once the total number of votes cast was known.

Where it has been impossible to locate electorates, then estimates have been made based on the trend between the last and the next figures known. Thus if one year is missing, and the difference between the previous and the following year is an increase of 100 voters, then it has been assumed that the electorate for the missing year had increased by fifty votes. For missing 1919 or 1938 figures, the succeeding or preceding trends have been used. So if the electorate increased by fifty voters between 1936 and 1937, then it has been assumed that the missing 1938 figure had seen another fifty-voter increase. In all cases, such estimates are shown in italics in the tables of results.

In cases where seats were uncontested, if figures for electors are available, they have been quoted. If no figures are available, no estimates have been made, as they cannot be used for any useful purpose such as calculating turnout. Blanks appear on the tables in these latter cases.

Turnout

The turnout figures have been calculated as the total votes cast as a proportion of the total electorate in single-member seats. In double-member seats they are the 'total voters' figures as a proportion of the electorate, as explained above under *Votes*.

Gains

As explained under **overall position of the council**, gains are only those that took place as a direct result of the November elections. Any earlier changes within the three-year cycle of elections which resulted in gains to parties are discounted.

APPENDICES

Appendix 1

Population of all eighty-three county boroughs 1931

This appendix has been constructed from table XXII of the general report for the 1931 census, which lists all towns with populations over 50,000. The figures quoted here were estimates taking account of seasonal movements, rather than the enumerated populations. It should be noted therefore that these figures vary very slightly from the population figures quoted in the tables for the individual boroughs, which are based on enumerated population. They are used in this appendix because they are more likely to accurately reflect the real size of the boroughs. The enumerated figures have had to be used for the individual boroughs, however, as the individual ward figures were based on the enumerated population. As will be seen, the variations are small, and do not affect the overall ranking of boroughs.

Appendix 2

Persons per room in all eighty-three county boroughs 1931

This appendix has been constructed from the data given in the county tables of the 1931 census for the various county boroughs. To an extent this table can be taken as a general indicator of social class: the more working-class the borough, the higher the person per room figure tended to be. However, differences in types of housing, by borough and by region, obviously complicates this apparently simple relationship.

Appendix 3

Female domestic servants as a percentage of total population in all eighty-three county boroughs 1931

This appendix has been constructed from the data given in the industrial tables of the 1931 census for the various county boroughs. Domestic servants (or 'personal service' in the original tables, and including 'hotels and catering') have been expressed as a percentage of the total population, rather than of the female workforce. The proportion of the female population which was officially defined as working varied greatly from one borough to another, so the proportionate weight of domestic servants could be distorted accordingly. The figures shown here best indicate the significance of domestic service in the boroughs as a whole. As such, they are another indicator of social class: the more middle-class a borough, the higher the proportion of domestic servants tended to be. Again, though, other factors enter into the situation which complicate the picture, a proviso that needs to be made in all these appendixes.

Appendix 4

Percentage of workforce in own account and managerial categories in all eighty-three county boroughs 1931

This appendix has been constructed from the data given in the industrial tables of the 1931 census for the various county boroughs. The total workforce that was recorded as working at the time of the census was divided into three categories: 'working on own account' (taken to mean 'self-employed' in modern parlance), 'managerial' and 'operative'. Those who were recorded as 'out of work' were excluded from these categories. The percentage of the working population defined as 'managerial' and 'working on own account' expressed in this appendix can again be taken as an indicator of social class; the higher the proportion, the more middle-class the borough tended to be. However, special care needs to be taken in interpreting these figures, as varying rates of unemployment may have had a distorting effect. Where unemployment was high, it may have been that a higher proportion of 'operatives' were affected (although there is no absolute proof of this). If so, then these figures would tend to overestimate the 'middle-class' nature of those boroughs where unemployment was especially high.

Appendix 5

Percentage of workforce in professional category in all eighty-three county boroughs 1931

This appendix has been constructed from the data given in the industrial tables of the 1931 census for the various county boroughs. It may again be taken as a general indicator of social class: the higher the proportion of professionals, the more middle-class a borough tended to be. However, the size of a borough was another factor that cut across this possible relationship. In general, larger boroughs tended to have a greater concentration of professionals.

Appendix 6

Percentage of workforce recorded as out of work in 1931 industry tables in all eighty-three county boroughs

This appendix has been constructed from the data given in the industrial tables of the 1931 census for the various county boroughs. All those who stated they were out of work to the enumerator were put in this category. They were all placed in industrial categories as well, on the basis of what job they had previously or usually held, as an addition to those recorded as working.

These figures may have been in one sense a more accurate record of unemployment, as they reflect the attitudes of people themselves as to whether they were 'out of work' or not. The official unemployment figures, of course, recorded only those insured workers who were entitled to benefit. In the case of women particularly, and especially after the Anomalies Act of 1930–31 which excluded many married women and part-time women workers from claiming benefit, many may have been cut out of the official statistics, despite regarding themselves as unemployed.

Appendixes 7 and 8

Percentage of workforce (male and female) in textiles category, top fifteen county boroughs 1931

Percentage of female workforce in textiles category, top fifteen county boroughs 1931

These appendices have been constructed from the data given in the industrial tables of the 1931 census for the various county boroughs. Workers in all types of textiles have been included. The figures have been expressed both in terms of all workers, and women workers only. Both say something about the industrial structure of a borough. The former shows the overall significance of textile production and employment in the local economy. The latter emphasises how significant employment in the textile industries was for women in certain boroughs and regions.

Appendix 9

Percentage of male workforce in mining category, top fifteen county boroughs 1931

This appendix has been constructed from the data given in the industrial tables of the 1931 census for the various county boroughs. All men have been included from the category 'mining and quarrying, and treatment of non-metalliferous mine and quarry products'. The figures have been expressed in terms of male workers only, as in all cases there were so few women in this category that they made no difference to the overall ranking of boroughs.

Appendix 10

Percentage of male workforce in docks and water transport categories, top fifteen county boroughs 1931

This appendix has been constructed from the data given in the industrial tables of the 1931 census for the various county boroughs. All men from the two subcategories of 'water transport' and 'docks, lighthouses, canals, etc.' were included. Again, women were so few in this category that they would make no difference to the overall standings.

Appendix 11

Percentage of male workforce in rail category, top fifteen county boroughs 1931

This appendix has been constructed from the data given in the industrial tables of the 1931 census for the various county boroughs. All men in the 'railways' sub-category have been included. Again, there were very few women in this category.

Appendix 12

Percentage of workforce (male and female) in metalworking categories, top fourteen county boroughs 1931

This appendix has been constructed from the data given in the industrial tables of the 1931 census for the various county boroughs. These figures include all workers (male and female) in the following six subcategories (as numbered in the census): 1. smelting, converting, refining and rolling of iron and steel; 2. extracting and refining of other metals and alloys; 3. founding and other secondary processes in metal working; 8. cutlery, and small tools (not machine tools); 9. other metal industries (not precious metals, jewellery or plate); 10. precious metals, jewellery, plate.

Appendix 13

Percentage of male workforce in shipbuilding categories, top ten county boroughs 1931

This appendix has been constructed from the data given in the industrial tables of the 1931 census for the various county boroughs. These figures include all male workers in the subcategory 'ship building and repairing and marine engineering'. Women workers were again very rare in this category.

Appendix 14

Percentage of male workforce in engineering category, top sixteen county boroughs 1931

This appendix has been constructed from the data given in the industrial tables of the 1931 census for the various county boroughs. These figures include all male workers in the subcategory 'engineering (not marine or electrical)'. Women workers were again very rare in this category.

Appendix 15

Percentage of workforce (male and female) in vehicle construction category, top six county boroughs 1931

This appendix has been constructed from the data given in the industrial tables of the 1931 census for the various county boroughs. These figures include all workers (male and female) in the subcategory 'construction and repair of vehicles'. These vehicles included motor transport, rail transport and aeroplanes, and also horse-drawn vehicles etc.

Appendix 16

Houses constructed by county boroughs to 31 Mar. 1939

This appendix has been constructed from data given in *The Municipal Yearbook*, (1939), pp. 250–278; (1938), pp. 325–340; (1937), pp. 287–308; (1936), pp. 946–965. Superficially these figures show the generosity of boroughs in providing council housing, but factors entered into this which complicated the picture. Varying levels of provision of housing by employers were especially significant. As an example, the very low level of provision in Barrow was clearly related to the fact that the dominant local employer, Vickers, provided large numbers of houses for its workers (see above, p. 64).

General notes

Aldermen

In the county boroughs, there were most commonly three councillors for each ward, and one alderman to every three councillors on the council. Where there were double-member wards, for every six councillors per ward there were two aldermen. Overall then aldermen made up a quarter of the total membership of the council. In exceptional circumstances these rules were broken if a ward with a very small electorate was added to a county borough, in which case the new ward might only be allocated one or two councillors, and no alderman would be added to the council.

Aldermen sat for a term of office of six years. In most cases they were elected on a three-year cycle, with half the aldermanic seats coming up for election three years after the other half. They were usually elected from the ranks of the elected councillors, although of course retiring aldermen could also be re-nominated. It was also possible to nominate people from outside the council, but this was very rarely done. Only councillors, and not the sitting aldermen, were entitled to vote on aldermanic vacancies. If aldermen were voted out of office they left the council immediately. The councillors who succeeded them took their place on the aldermanic bench, and their council seats became vacant and had to be filled in by-elections.

When aldermen retired after their six years of service, the elections to replace them took place at the first full council meeting after the annual council elections on 1 November. This was usually at the end of the following week. When an alderman died in office, or retired prematurely, then the vacancy created could be filled at the next meeting of the council, and a by-election would again ensue.

There were no rules as to whether the numbers of aldermen should be proportional to the number of seats a party held on the council, and each borough decided its own conventions. In some, aldermanic vacancies were filled on the basis of seniority of service on the council, regardless of party, and retiring aldermen were often re-elected without opposition. In others, the principle of proportionality prevailed. In most cases where the balance of power on the council changed hands or was seriously challenged during the inter-war period, party advantage became the determinant of the outcome of aldermanic elections. The party holding the largest number of council seats took all or most of the aldermanic vacancies, thus bolstering its control or enabling it to take control.[1]

---

[1] For further discussion of the aldermanic system in the inter-war period, see Davies, S., *Liverpool Labour: Social and Political Influences on the Development of the Labour Party in Liverpool, 1900–1939*, (Keele, 1996), pp. 110–119, 156–163.

Municipal franchise

The municipal franchise differed significantly from the parliamentary franchise in the inter-war years. The essential principle of the municipal franchise was that only those who paid rates, and their spouses, were entitled to vote. Ratepayers were those who owned property, or occupied unfurnished property. In addition, they had to prove that they had been resident in the property for the six months previous to registration (this period was reduced to three months in 1926). Registration took place twice a year, with the autumn register being the one in force at the annual November elections. Female spouses of ratepayers aged thirty or over gained the municipal vote in the 1918 Representation of the People Act, and this age threshold was reduced to twenty-one in the 1928 Act.

This meant that significant numbers were excluded from the municipal franchise, most notably those who had moved within six months (later three months), non-spouse family members of voting age living in the house of ratepayers (most commonly sons and daughters, and aged relatives), and occupiers of lodging houses and other furnished premises. These exclusions were of significant proportions. At all levels of local government in England and Wales in 1938, there were 21.4 million municipal voters, compared with 28.2 million parliamentary voters, an exclusion rate of 24 per cent.[2]

It should also be noted that the owners or occupiers of business premises were entitled to a vote in the ward where those premises were situated. There were 360,000 of these plural voters in the whole of England and Wales in 1938, amounting to 1.7 per cent of the municipal electorate. However, the business vote could be much more significant in city centre wards, where most business premises were usually situated. No figures are available for municipal wards, but in some parliamentary constituencies the figures were very high. For instance, plural voters in Manchester Exchange amounted to 34 per cent of the parliamentary electorate, 26 per cent in Liverpool Exchange, 18 per cent in Sheffield Central, and an extraordinary 84 per cent in City of London. Obviously city-centre wards, being much smaller, would have had even higher proportions of business voters than these constituency-level figures.[3]

[2]   For these and other figures quoted on the franchise, see *Registrar General's Statistical Review of England and Wales, (1938)*, pt. II, Civil Tables, pp. 61–93.
[3]   For further discussion of the inter-war municipal franchise, see Davies, *Liverpool Labour*, pp. 119–129, 156–163.

Housing and inter-war housing Acts

This note serves as a background to the various Acts that impacted on the housing policies of the county boroughs in the inter-war years. Various Victorian Acts had established the principle of state intervention and local authority responsibility in eradicating slums. The 1890 Housing of the Working Class Act gave local authorities further powers to demolish unsanitary houses and construct council houses using the local rates. The First World War saw the enactment of rent controls as an emergency measure. In July 1919, the Housing and Town Planning Act (the 'Addison' Act, after the Coalition-Liberal Dr Christopher Addison, the Minister of Health) was the first of a series of Acts to encourage large-scale state intervention, in conjunction with the local authorities, to increase the supply of working-class housing. The local authorities, already responsible for slum clearance, 'could be given the job of providing the working-class houses which were urgently needed, for it was assumed that temporarily private enterprise would be neither willing nor able to do so'.[4] The first Addison Act gave open-ended subsidies to local authorities to cover the cost of municipal housing schemes. The county boroughs were obligated to survey the housing needs within their boundaries and produce housing development plans. A second Act provided a subsidy of £260 per house for houses to be built for sale or rent by private enterprise. In 1922, because of central government economy measures, grants from the centre under Addison stopped. By then the Addison scheme had aided the construction of over 200,000 houses.[5] The Housing Act of 1923 (the 'Chamberlain' Act, after Neville Chamberlain, then Tory Health Minister) replaced Addison. The 1923 Act offered a £6 subsidy for twenty years, the houses to be built by the local authorities or private enterprise. Around 500,000 houses were built, largely by private enterprise. By 1929 the subsidy was withdrawn and the Act 'was regarded as a failure in terms of council-house building'.[6] The 1924 Housing Act (or 'Wheatley' Act, after John Wheatley, the first Labour Minister of Health) increased the state subsidy to £9 a year for forty years on houses built to let at a controlled rent. Under this scheme over 500,000 council houses were built before the Act was terminated in 1932. Following Wheatley, the 1930 Housing Act, (or 'Greenwood' Act, after Arthur Greenwood, Minister of Health in the second Labour government) aided further slum clearance with graduated subsidies. The level of subsidy was based on the number of families rehoused and the cost to the authority of the housing clearance. The county boroughs were required to develop five-year plans for slum clearance. The financial crisis of 1931 largely suspended the Act. Next, the 1933 Housing Act aimed at clearing 266,000 unsanitary houses and constructing 285,000 new houses, with the target of rehousing 1.25 million people.[7] Finally the 1935 Housing Act (or 'Hilton Young' Act, after E. Hilton Young, Minister of Health), endeavoured to ensure that local authorities made plans to deal with overcrowding. Marian Bowley calculated that

---

4   Bowley, M., *Housing and the State 1919–1944*, (London, 1947), p. 15.
5   Cook, C. and Stevenson, J., *The Longman Handbook of Modern British History, 1714–1980*, (London, 1985), p. 113.
6   Cook and Stevenson, *Handbook*, p. 114.
7   Cook and Stevenson, *Handbook*, p. 114.

the cost of the schemes between 1923 and 1933, were in 1935–36 a 'modest' £1.9 million to the ratepayer. This was equivalent to 0.9% of the total rate expenditure.[8]

It is worth emphasising that individual county boroughs could react differently to the Acts. This was so whether or not these authorities acted in the spirit of the legislation, let alone in terms of their legal obligations. The differential rate of house construction by the county boroughs could also be the result of history, the existence of differing types and quality of housing stock and particular social needs. Relative economic decline, or otherwise, in the locality, could also be a factor in the extent of local council house building. There was obviously also the question of political will to act on central government's legislation. Obviously this was informed by the political complexion and resources of the council itself. Also the Acts themselves could work unfairly against some districts. Thus Bowley makes the point that under the 1923 Housing Act, 'better-off districts would tend to benefit from the subsidy more than the poorer districts'.[9]

The local press

The local press in the county boroughs has been examined in the writing of each chapter. It is perhaps the major source of the data and comment included in these volumes. The local press served as an instrument of record of the local election results. It also served as a major source for the debates concerning the major issues and social problems which came within the remit of the power of the local council. The press, of course, was more often than not owned by propertied and conservative interests that supported the status quo. Such local newspapers directly or indirectly favoured one or other of the established pre-1918 political parties. In some county boroughs the local press could assume a lofty position of neutrality and even-handedness, openly approving the non-politicisation of municipal affairs. In some boroughs this led to an ostensibly apolitical stance where the allegedly non-partisan 'independents' would be backed by the proprietors of the publication. Rarely were local newspapers supportive of the local Labour party or their policies. Indeed the local press was in the main antipathetic to Labour. This often emerged in open hostility to its aspiring councillors and policies, but sometimes in the more subtle use of pejorative language when discussing Labour in electoral coverage. Thus the local press has had to be used with extreme care as a source of political comment and analysis. As a journal of straightforward record of the bare results, however, the local press could, more often than not, be relied upon to be accurate.

The press reported throughout the year on various events in the political life of the borough. It has been impossible in a publication of this scale to analyse this year-round coverage for every county borough. In most cases the reports around the period of electioneering in October and November of each year have been the main sources. Three types of report which tend to appear in all boroughs on a regular basis were especially useful. First there were reports of nomination day,

---

[8] Bowley, *Housing*, p. 47.
[9] Bowley, *Housing*, p. 39.

when the deadline for nominating candidates was reached. These provided valuable information on candidates, including sometimes their occupations. Speeches made by the candidates were also recorded in many cases, giving their stance on the issues and major problems facing the borough. Second, reports on the declaration of the results, which often took place at the local Town Hall or some other important municipal building. Speeches were made by most of the candidates, successful and unsuccessful, to their waiting supporters, and very often the main election issues were aired at these points. Further meetings were often held later the same night by the individual parties, and these were often reported in some detail. Third, the advertisements placed by aspiring candidates in the local press prior to the November elections were an important source. Here the candidates often outlined their policies, the issues they supported or opposed, their past record of local service and sometimes their political affiliation where the official labelling was unclear.

The issues raised in these three types of reports largely reflected the political debate which had exercised both the council and electorate over the major part of the year. Only where important issues were alluded to (such as boundary changes, for instance) which had been debated at length at other times of the year, were press reports followed up outside the election period. Obviously important events and issues raised in secondary sources were also traced where appropriate.

APPENDICES

*(On sources and other details, see **notes**, pp. 665–680)*

APPENDICES

Appendix 1 Population of all eighty-three county boroughs 1931

1	Birmingham	1,004,300	43 Burnley	98,280
2	Liverpool	856,020	44 Reading	97,970
3	Manchester	766,800	45 Halifax	97,960
4	Sheffield	512,600	46 Wallasey	97,650
5	Leeds	482,900	47 Northampton	92,390
6	Bristol	399,400	48 Grimsby	91,520
7	Hull	314,100	49 Rochdale	90,770
8	Bradford	298,200	50 Newport	89,750
9	West Ham	294,200	51 Ipswich	88,000
10	Newcastle	283,900	52 York	85,600
11	Stoke	276,500	53 Wigan	85,520
12	Nottingham	269,400	54 Smethwick	84,620
13	Portsmouth	249,300	55 West Bromwich	81,230
14	Leicester	240,000	56 Oxford	80,870
15	Croydon	233,900	57 Warrington	79,510
16	Salford	223,300	58 Southport	78,260
17	Cardiff	223,200	59 Bootle	76,810
18	Plymouth	208,200	60 Darlington	72,680
19	Sunderland	186,800	61 Barnsley	71,600
20	Bolton	177,800	62 Merthyr	71,420
21	Southampton	175,600	63 Rotherham	69,600
22	Coventry	167,140	64 Bath	68,760
23	Swansea	164,800	65 West Hartlepool	68,680
24	Birkenhead	148,300	66 Barrow	66,180
25	Brighton	145,300	67 Lincoln	66,050
26	Derby	142,400	68 Exeter	65,940
27	East Ham	142,400	69 Tynemouth	64,880
28	Oldham	140,300	70 Doncaster	63,590
29	Middlesbrough	138,830	71 Hastings	63,130
30	Wolverhampton	133,000	72 Dudley	59,430
31	Norwich	126,500	73 Wakefield	58,990
32	Stockport	125,700	74 Carlisle	57,270
33	Gateshead	123,000	75 Great Yarmouth	57,170
34	Blackburn	122,700	76 Eastbourne	56,730
35	Preston	119,000	77 Bury	56,280
36	Southend	119,000	78 Dewsbury	53,960
37	South Shields	114,400	79 Gloucester	53,280
38	Huddersfield	113,600	80 Worcester	50,720
39	Bournemouth	111,190	81 Burton	49,590
40	St Helens	107,100	82 Chester	41,650
41	Walsall	103,300	83 Canterbury	24,660
42	Blackpool	99,590	**All**	**13,312,920**

Appendix 2 Persons per room in all eighty-three county boroughs 1931

1	Gateshead	1.23	43	Burnley	0.85
2	Sunderland	1.22	44	Chester	0.85
3	South Shields	1.18	45	Coventry	0.85
4	West Ham	1.14	46	Preston	0.85
5	Newcastle	1.13	47	Rochdale	0.85
6	St Helens	1.13	48	Bury	0.84
7	Tynemouth	1.08	49	York	0.84
8	Stoke	1.04	50	Birmingham	0.83
9	Middlesbrough	1.03	51	Blackburn	0.82
10	Dewsbury	1.02	52	Smethwick	0.82
11	West Bromwich	1.01	53	Stockport	0.82
12	Dudley	1.00	54	Bristol	0.81
13	West Hartlepool	1.00	55	Grimsby	0.81
14	Wigan	1.00	56	Southampton	0.80
15	Warrington	0.98	57	Brighton	0.79
16	Barnsley	0.97	58	Nottingham	0.78
17	Plymouth	0.96	59	Worcester	0.77
18	Bootle	0.95	60	Burton	0.76
19	Carlisle	0.95	61	Portsmouth	0.76
20	Salford	0.94	62	Croydon	0.75
21	East Ham	0.93	63	Derby	0.75
22	Liverpool	0.93	64	Doncaster	0.75
23	Darlington	0.91	65	Gloucester	0.75
24	Huddersfield	0.91	66	Reading	0.75
25	Rotherham	0.91	67	Lincoln	0.74
26	Wakefield	0.91	68	Exeter	0.73
27	Walsall	0.91	69	Canterbury	0.72
28	Halifax	0.90	70	Oxford	0.72
29	Swansea	0.90	71	Southend	0.72
30	Barrow	0.89	72	Norwich	0.71
31	Birkenhead	0.89	73	Wallasey	0.71
32	Hull	0.89	74	Hastings	0.70
33	Oldham	0.89	75	Northampton	0.70
34	Bradford	0.88	76	Bath	0.69
35	Merthyr	0.88	77	Eastbourne	0.69
36	Leeds	0.87	78	Ipswich	0.69
37	Manchester	0.87	79	Leicester	0.69
38	Newport	0.87	80	Southport	0.68
39	Sheffield	0.87	81	Blackpool	0.67
40	Wolverhampton	0.87	82	Great Yarmouth	0.65
41	Cardiff	0.86	83	Bournemouth	0.64
42	Bolton	0.85		**All**	**0.86**

Appendix 3   Female domestic servants as a percentage of total population in all eighty-three county boroughs 1931

1 Eastbourne	12.3		43 Barrow	3.3
2 Bournemouth	12.1		44 Sheffield	3.3
3 Blackpool	9.9		45 Wolverhampton	3.3
4 Hastings	9.8		46 Middlesbrough	3.3
5 Southport	9.3		47 South Shields	3.2
6 Brighton	8.6		48 Leeds	3.1
7 Bath	8.3		49 Manchester	3.1
8 Oxford	7.1		50 Nottingham	3.1
9 Southend	6.9		51 Huddersfield	3.1
10 Canterbury	6.3		52 Rotherham	3.0
11 Chester	6.1		53 Dewsbury	3.0
12 Exeter	5.7		54 Stockport	3.0
13 Wallasey	5.3		55 Northampton	2.9
14 Croydon	5.2		56 Salford	2.9
15 Great Yarmouth	5.0		57 Birmingham	2.9
16 Birkenhead	4.7		58 Wakefield	2.9
17 Cardiff	4.4		59 Gateshead	2.9
18 Worcester	4.3		60 Derby	2.7
19 Darlington	4.3		61 Barnsley	2.7
20 Lincoln	4.3		62 Halifax	2.6
21 Ipswich	4.2		63 East Ham	2.6
22 Southampton	4.2		64 Leicester	2.5
23 Portsmouth	4.2		65 Bradford	2.5
24 Reading	4.2		66 West Ham	2.4
25 York	4.2		67 Preston	2.4
26 Newport	4.2		68 Walsall	2.4
27 Gloucester	4.1		69 Coventry	2.2
28 Newcastle	4.1		70 Wigan	2.2
29 Grimsby	4.1		71 Smethwick	2.1
30 Bristol	4.0		72 St Helens	2.1
31 Tynemouth	3.9		73 Merthyr	2.1
32 Plymouth	3.8		74 Bury	2.1
33 Doncaster	3.8		75 Bolton	2.1
34 Sunderland	3.7		76 Dudley	2.0
35 West Hartlepool	3.7		77 Burnley	2.0
36 Hull	3.6		78 Rochdale	2.0
37 Liverpool	3.5		79 Blackburn	2.0
38 Swansea	3.5		80 Oldham	1.8
39 Norwich	3.5		81 Warrington	1.8
40 Bootle	3.4		82 Stoke	1.8
41 Carlisle	3.4		83 West Bromwich	1.8
42 Burton	3.3		**All**	**3.6**

Appendix 4 Percentage of workforce in own account and managerial categories in all eighty-three county boroughs 1931 (excluding 'out of work')

1	Blackpool	29.4	43	Hull	11.6
2	Southport	23.3	44	Merthyr	11.6
3	Southend	21.4	45	Sheffield	11.6
4	Bournemouth	21.0	46	Preston	11.6
5	Hastings	20.9	47	Sunderland	11.5
6	Eastbourne	18.5	48	Wolverhampton	11.5
7	Great Yarmouth	18.1	49	Darlington	11.4
8	Brighton	17.8	50	Walsall	11.3
9	Wallasey	17.5	51	Burnley	11.3
10	Bath	16.8	52	Wigan	11.2
11	Canterbury	16.6	53	Bolton	11.2
12	Exeter	14.4	54	Dewsbury	11.1
13	Blackburn	14.0	55	Newcastle	11.1
14	Croydon	13.9	56	Liverpool	11.1
15	Chester	13.8	57	Leicester	11.0
16	Swansea	13.7	58	Bury	11.0
17	Grimsby	13.6	59	Birmingham	10.9
18	Cardiff	13.5	60	Plymouth	10.8
19	Gloucester	13.3	61	York	10.7
20	Tynemouth	13.2	62	Carlisle	10.7
21	Ipswich	12.9	63	Dudley	10.5
22	Stockport	12.8	64	Middlesbrough	10.5
23	Worcester	12.8	65	Rochdale	10.5
24	Birkenhead	12.7	66	Wakefield	10.3
25	Halifax	12.6	67	Burton	10.2
26	Newport	12.4	68	Barrow	9.8
27	Oxford	12.3	69	Oldham	9.7
28	Bristol	12.3	70	Coventry	9.7
29	Bradford	12.3	71	Salford	9.6
30	Norwich	12.2	72	Barnsley	9.6
31	Leeds	12.2	73	Rotherham	9.4
32	Southampton	12.1	74	Derby	9.2
33	Lincoln	12.1	75	Gateshead	9.1
34	Reading	12.0	76	Smethwick	9.0
35	West Hartlepool	12.0	77	West Bromwich	8.7
36	Northampton	12.0	78	Stoke	8.4
37	Doncaster	11.9	79	Bootle	8.3
38	Huddersfield	11.9	80	East Ham	8.3
39	Portsmouth	11.8	81	Warrington	7.9
40	Nottingham	11.8	82	St Helens	7.8
41	South Shields	11.8	83	West Ham	7.2
42	Manchester	11.7		**All**	**11.9**

Appendix 5 Percentage of workforce in professional category in all eighty-three county boroughs 1931

	M	F	All		M	F	All
1 Oxford	10.8	13.8	11.8	43 Nottingham	1.8	3.2	2.3
2 Hastings	4.8	13.1	8.1	44 Sheffield	1.6	4.0	2.3
3 Eastbourne	5.1	11.4	7.8	45 Wakefield	1.6	4.0	2.2
4 Bournemouth	4.9	9.5	6.8	46 Derby	1.4	4.3	2.2
5 Bath	4.4	10.1	6.5	47 Hull	1.5	4.2	2.2
6 Exeter	4.4	9.9	6.1	48 Preston	2.0	2.6	2.2
7 Southport	4.5	7.2	5.5	49 Leicester	1.9	2.6	2.2
8 Southend	4.3	7.4	5.3	50 Stockport	2.0	2.4	2.2
9 Canterbury	3.8	8.6	5.2	51 Halifax	1.9	2.6	2.2
10 Croydon	4.1	7.3	5.1	52 Burton	1.4	4.0	2.0
11 Brighton	3.8	7.1	4.9	53 West Ham	1.4	3.6	2.0
12 Chester	3.4	7.8	4.7	54 Huddersfield	2.0	2.1	2.0
13 Reading	3.1	7.7	4.5	55 Bradford	1.7	2.4	2.0
14 Wallasey	3.2	6.8	4.3	56 Barnsley	1.5	3.7	2.0
15 Cardiff	2.7	6.5	3.7	57 W. Hartlepool	1.3	4.3	2.0
16 Bristol	2.5	6.2	3.7	58 Tynemouth	1.4	3.5	1.9
17 Blackpool	3.3	3.8	3.5	59 Bury	2.0	1.8	1.9
18 Gloucester	2.4	5.9	3.4	60 Middlesbro'	1.1	4.7	1.9
19 York	2.5	5.6	3.4	61 Rotherham	1.1	5.3	1.9
20 Newcastle	2.3	5.8	3.3	62 Gateshead	1.4	3.1	1.9
21 Norwich	2.3	5.1	3.3	63 Salford	1.5	2.5	1.9
22 Lincoln	2.2	6.4	3.3	64 Wigan	1.4	2.6	1.8
23 Southampton	2.0	6.9	3.3	65 Bolton	1.8	1.9	1.8
24 Ipswich	2.0	6.2	3.2	66 South Shields	1.2	3.7	1.8
25 Northampton	2.4	4.9	3.2	67 Grimsby	1.3	3.3	1.8
26 Birkenhead	2.0	5.7	3.1	68 Blackburn	2.0	1.4	1.7
27 Swansea	2.1	6.6	3.1	69 Bootle	1.2	2.8	1.7
28 Newport	2.1	6.3	3.0	70 Merthyr	1.1	5.3	1.7
29 Gt Yarmouth	2.2	4.5	3.0	71 St Helens	0.9	4.7	1.7
30 Worcester	2.2	4.2	2.9	72 Dudley	1.2	2.8	1.7
31 Plymouth	1.7	6.6	2.9	73 Barrow	0.9	4.7	1.7
32 Carlisle	2.2	4.1	2.9	74 Coventry	1.0	3.2	1.6
33 Liverpool	2.0	4.7	2.8	75 Dewsbury	1.4	2.0	1.6
34 Portsmouth	1.7	5.6	2.7	76 Walsall	1.1	2.5	1.5
35 Darlington	1.6	5.9	2.7	77 Burnley	1.6	1.2	1.4
36 Manchester	2.1	3.4	2.6	78 Oldham	1.4	1.4	1.4
37 Leeds	2.2	3.1	2.5	79 Smethwick	1.1	1.9	1.3
38 Sunderland	1.6	4.9	2.4	80 Stoke	1.1	1.7	1.3
39 Doncaster	1.6	5.0	2.4	81 Rochdale	1.2	1.0	1.1
40 East Ham	2.0	3.3	2.4	82 W. Bromwich	0.7	2.2	1.1
41 Wolverh'ton	1.5	4.6	2.4	83 Warrington	0.8	1.3	0.9
42 Birmingham	1.8	3.5	2.4	**All**	**2.0**	**4.2**	**2.7**

Appendix 6   Percentage of workforce recorded as out of work in 1931
industry tables in all eighty-threee county boroughs

1	Blackburn	32.7	43 Stockport	13.1
2	Merthyr	32.4	44 Warrington	12.9
3	South Shields	30.6	45 Derby	12.7
4	Sunderland	30.3	46 Coventry	12.6
5	West Hartlepool	29.0	47 West Ham	12.6
6	Middlesbrough	24.2	48 Leeds	12.6
7	Burnley	24.1	49 Smethwick	12.3
8	Tynemouth	23.7	50 Birmingham	12.2
9	Gateshead	23.6	51 Southampton	12.1
10	Oldham	22.8	52 Burton	12.1
11	Newcastle	22.4	53 Grimsby	11.4
12	Bootle	21.3	54 Wallasey	11.3
13	Birkenhead	21.1	55 Carlisle	11.0
14	Swansea	20.8	56 Halifax	11.0
15	Liverpool	19.6	57 Nottingham	10.9
16	Wigan	18.9	58 Bristol	10.9
17	Preston	18.6	59 Ipswich	10.8
18	Barnsley	17.9	60 Worcester	10.4
19	Sheffield	17.3	61 York	10.4
20	Walsall	17.3	62 Chester	10.3
21	Cardiff	17.1	63 Plymouth	10.3
22	Bury	16.9	64 Norwich	9.9
23	Rochdale	16.6	65 Wakefield	9.8
24	Barrow	16.6	66 Doncaster	9.7
25	Dudley	16.5	67 Huddersfield	9.2
26	Newport	16.4	68 Leicester	8.8
27	Wolverhampton	16.4	69 Southport	8.6
28	St Helens	16.1	70 East Ham	8.6
29	Stoke	16.1	71 Portsmouth	8.5
30	Darlington	15.9	72 Brighton	8.1
31	Lincoln	15.8	73 Bath	8.1
32	Salford	15.3	74 Northampton	8.1
33	Dewsbury	15.3	75 Reading	7.1
34	Manchester	15.1	76 Hastings	7.1
35	Bolton	15.1	77 Southend	7.0
36	Rotherham	14.8	78 Canterbury	7.0
37	Great Yarmouth	14.7	79 Exeter	6.9
38	Blackpool	14.7	80 Croydon	6.2
39	West Bromwich	13.9	81 Eastbourne	5.8
40	Hull	13.6	82 Bournemouth	5.6
41	Gloucester	13.4	83 Oxford	4.7
42	Bradford	13.1	**All**	**14.7**

Appendix 7   Percentage of workforce (male and female) in textiles category, top fifteen county boroughs 1931

1	Burnley	50.4	9	Preston	32.5
2	Rochdale	49.0	10	Halifax	32.4
3	Blackburn	48.3	11	Stockport	24.8
4	Oldham	46.7	12	Leicester	24.4
5	Bolton	43.0	13	Nottingham	19.5
6	Bradford	38.8	14	Salford	12.0
7	Bury	36.7	15	Manchester	9.3
8	Huddersfield	33.0			

Appendix 8   Percentage of female workforce in textiles category, top fifteen county boroughs 1931

1	Burnley	73.4	9	Halifax	51.7
2	Blackburn	72.1	10	Huddersfield	48.5
3	Rochdale	67.9	11	Leicester	43.3
4	Oldham	67.8	12	Stockport	38.6
5	Bolton	63.9	13	Nottingham	34.2
6	Preston	57.1	14	Salford	18.2
7	Bradford	55.0	15	Manchester	14.6
8	Bury	54.0			

Appendix 9   Percentage of male workforce in mining category, top sixteen
county boroughs 1931

1 Merthyr	53.7	9 Dewsbury	14.3
2 Barnsley	44.1	10 Gateshead	12.0
3 Wigan	37.9	11 Sunderland	11.6
4 St Helens	28.5	12 Doncaster	11.3
5 Stoke	23.5	13 Burnley[a]	9.6
6 Rotherham	19.7	14 Nottingham	9.0
7 South Shields	18.6	15 Walsall	8.6
8 Wakefield	17.5	16 Swansea	7.5

[a] Note that Burnley was excluded from this table in error in volume one.

Appendix 10   Percentage of male workforce in docks and water transport
categories, top fifteen county boroughs 1931

1 Bootle	28.7	9 Cardiff	12.1
2 Southampton	19.2	10 West Ham	10.9
3 Liverpool	16.6	11 East Ham	10.5
4 South Shields	16.5	12 Grimsby	10.1
5 Birkenhead	14.8	13 Middlesbrough	8.7
6 Hull	13.8	14 Swansea	8.0
7 Newport	12.5	15 West Hartlepool	7.3
8 Tynemouth	12.2		

Appendix 11   Percentage of male workforce in rail category, top fifteen
county boroughs 1931

1 Carlisle	15.9	9 Chester	8.1
2 York	12.4	10 Burton	8.0
3 Doncaster	11.3	11 Cardiff	7.9
4 Gloucester	10.0	12 Wakefield	7.5
5 Derby	9.2	13 Gateshead	7.4
6 Newport	9.2	14 Darlington	7.3
7 Worcester	8.6	15 Hull	6.3
8 Exeter	8.5		

Appendix 12 Percentage of workforce (male and female) in metalworking categories, top fourteen county boroughs 1931

	M	F	All		M	F	All
1 W. Bromwich	40.6	31.4	38.0	8 Walsall	29.6	17.8	26.0
2 Sheffield	40.2	25.5	36.2	9 Birmingham	21.4	21.0	21.2
3 Middlesbro'	39.6	2.5	31.7	10 Wolverh'ton	21.5	17.2	20.2
4 Rotherham	36.9	7.6	31.4	11 Swansea	24.1	5.3	20.1
5 Smethwick	32.0	27.5	30.6	12 Newport	19.5	1.3	15.3
6 Warrington	37.8	10.2	29.9	13 Merthyr	13.9	1.6	12.2
7 Dudley	32.2	21.1	29.0	14 Darlington	15.5	1.0	11.8

Appendix 13 Percentage of male workforce in shipbuilding categories, top ten county boroughs 1931

1 Barrow	50.9	6 Plymouth	16.7
2 Sunderland	26.9	7 Portsmouth	16.2
3 Tynemouth	20.0	8 Birkenhead	15.7
4 West Hartlepool	18.1	9 Newcastle	13.4
5 South Shields	18.0	10 Southampton	12.6

Appendix 14 Percentage of male workforce in engineering category, top sixteen county boroughs 1931

1 Lincoln	27.9	9 Newcastle	10.5
2 Darlington	22.4	10 Coventry	10.2
3 Oldham	19.4	11 Bolton	10.0
4 Ipswich	16.3	12 Halifax	9.6
5 Derby	13.5	13 Blackburn	9.1
6 Gateshead	12.5	14 Bury	8.8
7 Rochdale	12.4	15 Leicester	8.0
8 Doncaster	11.8	16 Leeds	7.9

Appendix 15 Percentage of workforce (male and female) in vehicle construction category, top six county boroughs 1931

	M	F	All		M	F	All
1 Coventry	38.5	15.2	32.1	4 Wolverh'ton	15.2	4.5	12.0
2 Oxford	18.8	3.4	13.7	5 Birmingham	12.6	7.9	11.0
3 Smethwick	13.7	8.9	12.2	6 Derby	14.0	2.4	10.7

Appendix 16 Houses constructed by county boroughs to 31 Mar. 1939[a]

Borough	Houses	Pop./house	Borough	Houses	Pop./house
1 Carlisle	4,473	12.80	41 Birkenhead	4,365	33.97
2 Dudley	4,598	12.93	42 Middlesbro'	4,047	34.30
3 Wakefield	4,523	13.04	43 Swansea	4,798	34.35
4 Walsall	7,321	14.11	44 Bradford	8,644	34.50
5 Rotherham	4,711	14.77	45 Cardiff	6,204	35.98
6 W. Bromwich	5,485	14.81	46 Sunderland	5,184	36.03
7 Nottingham	17,265	15.60	47 Oxford[d]	2,195	36.84
8 Wolverh'ton	8,113	16.39	48 Southampton	4,719	37.21
9 Norwich	7,019	18.02	49 Brighton	3,884	37.41
10 York	4,744	18.04	50 Wigan	2,261	37.82
11 Smethwick	4,463	18.96	51 South Shields[c]	3,013	37.97
12 Doncaster	3,271	19.44	52 Gateshead	3,034	40.54
13 Manchester	37,668	20.36	53 Halifax	2,402	40.78
14 Birmingham	49,167	20.43	54 Preston	2,755	43.19
15 Barnsley	3,473	20.62	55 Gt Yarmouth	1,307	43.74
16 Derby	6,786	20.98	56 Burnley	2,140	45.93
17 Sheffield	24,147	21.23	57 Burton	1,060	46.78
18 Northampton	4,301	21.48	58 Plymouth	4,431	46.99
19 Bury	2,456	22.92	59 Bath	1,298	52.97
20 Warrington	3,391	23.45	60 Eastbourne[b]	1,019	55.67
21 Worcester	2,138	23.72	61 Stockport	2,250	55.87
22 Tynemouth	2,703	24.00	62 W. Hartlepool	1,201	57.19
23 Newcastle[b]	11,815	24.03	63 Oldham	2,345	59.83
24 Rochdale	3,660	24.80	64 Blackburn	1,953	62.83
25 Liverpool	34,495	24.82	65 Croydon[b]	3,585	65.24
26 Leeds	18,602	25.96	66 Blackpool	1,448	68.78
27 Chester	1,543	26.99	67 Newport	1,294	69.36
28 Leicester	8,878	27.03	68 Wallasey	1,397	69.90
29 Lincoln	2,408	27.43	69 Darlington	907	80.13
30 Dewsbury	1,958	27.56	70 Southport	924	84.70
31 Bristol	13,677	29.20	71 Salford	2,615	85.39
32 Bootle	2,628	29.23	72 Hastings	730	86.48
33 Exeter	2,178	30.28	73 Portsmouth	2,736	91.12
34 Hull	10,367	30.30	74 Barrow	724	91.41
35 St Helens	3,496	30.64	75 Southend	920	129.35
36 Canterbury	786	31.37	76 Grimsby[b]	664	137.83
37 Huddersfield[b]	3,589	31.65	77 Bournemouth	732	151.90
38 Coventry	5,238	31.91	78 West Ham[d]	1,792	164.17
39 Reading	3,068	31.93	79 East Ham	690	206.38
40 Bolton	5,369	33.12	80 Gloucester	154	345.97
			All	**443,792**	**29.02**

[a] excluding 6 months to 30 Sep. 1938, in all cases; [b] excluding 1937–38 figures;
[c] excluding 1936–38 figures; [d] excluding 1935–38 figures.
No figures given for Ipswich, Merthyr Tydfil or Stoke.

The eighty-three boroughs of England and Wales, 1931

SCOTLAND

Newcastle-on-Tyne
Tynemouth
South Shields
Gateshead
Sunderland
Carlisle
W. Hartlepool
Darlington
Middlesbrough

Barrow-in Furness
York

Burnley Bradford
Blackpool Preston Halifax Leeds
Blackburn Dewsbury
Huddersfield Wakefield
Southport Wigan Bolton Rochdale
Bootle Bury Oldham Barnsley Doncaster Grimsby
Salford Manchester
Liverpool St. Helens Stockport Rotherham
Wallasey Warrington Sheffield
Birkenhead Lincoln
Chester

Stoke on Trent Derby Nottingham
Burton upon Trent

Leicester Norwich Great Yarmouth
Wolverhampton
Dudley Walsall
W. Bromwich Birmingham
Smethwick Coventry
Worcester Northampton Ipswich

Merthyr Tydfil Gloucester Oxford
WALES
Swansea E. Ham
Newport W. Ham Southend-on-Sea
Cardiff Reading Croydon Canterbury
Bristol
Bath

Brighton
Southampton Portsmouth Hastings
Bournemouth Eastbourne

Exeter

Plymouth

Index